LIVES

OF THE

LORD CHANCELLORS OF ENGLAND.

Eng by W. Wellstood & Co. 46 Beekman St. N.Y.

THURLOW

LIVES

OF

THE LORD CHANCELLORS

AND

KEEPERS OF THE GREAT SEAL

OF

ENGLAND,

FROM THE EARLIEST TIMES TILL THE REIGN OF QUEEN VICTORIA.

BY

LORD CAMPBELL.

SEVENTH EDITION.

ILLUSTRATED.

VOL. VII.

WILDSIDE PRESS

CONTENTS

OF

THE SEVENTH VOLUME.

CHAP.	PAGE
CLV.—Life of Lord Chancellor Thurlow from his birth till he was appointed Solicitor General, ...	1
CLVI.—Continuation of the Life of Lord Thurlow till he was made Lord Chancellor, ...	26
CLVII.—Continuation of the Life of Lord Thurlow till the resignation of Lord North and the formation of the second Rockingham administration, ...	47
CLVIII.—Continuation of the Life of Lord Thurlow till he was deprived of the Great Seal on the formation of the Coalition Ministry, ...	67
CLIX.—Continuation of the Life of Lord Thurlow till the King's illness in 1788, ...	80
CLX —Continuation of the Life of Lord Thurlow till he was finally dismissed from the office of Chancellor, . .	104
CLXI.—Conclusion of the Life of Lord Thurlow, . . .	133
CLXII.—Life of Lord Loughborough from his birth till his call to the Scotch bar, ...	203
CLXIII.—Continuation of the Life of Lord Loughborough till he finally left Scotland, ...	217
CLXIV.—Continuation of the Life of Lord Loughborough till he became a Patriot, ...	248
CLXV —Continuation of the Life of Lord Loughborough till he was made Solicitor General, ...	265
CLXVI.—Continuation of the Life of Lord Loughborough till the commencement of hostilities with America, . .	283
CLXVII —Continuation of the Life of Lord Loughborough till he was made Chief Justice of the Court of Common Pleas, ...	310
CLXVIII.—Continuation of the Life of Lord Loughborough till he was appointed First Commissioner of the Great Seal under the Coalition Ministry, ...	332

CONTENTS.

CHAP.	PAGE
CLXIX.—Continuation of the Life of Lord Loughborough till the King's illness in 1788,	361
CLXX.—Continuation of the Life of Lord Loughborough during the discussions respecting the Regency,	376
CLXXI.—Continuation of the Life of Lord Loughborough till he was made Lord Chancellor,	404
CLXXII.—Continuation of the Life of Lord Loughborough till the conclusion of Hastings's trial,	419
CLXXIII.—Continuation of the Life of Lord Loughborough till the commencement of the intrigues which ended in his resignation and the dissolution of Mr. Pitt's administration,	457
CLXXIV.—Continuation of the Life of Lord Loughborough till he resigned the Great Seal,	476
CLXXV.—Conclusion of the Life of Lord Loughborough,	517

LIVES

OF THE

LORD CHANCELLORS OF ENGLAND.

CHAPTER CLV.

LIFE OF LORD CHANCELLOR THURLOW FROM HIS BIRTH TILL HE WAS APPOINTED SOLICITOR GENERAL.

I NOW arrive at a remarkable era in my history of the Chancellors. I had to begin with some who "come like shadows, so depart," and who can only be dimly discovered by a few glimmering rays of antique light.

"Ibant obscuri solâ sub nocte per umbram
Perque domos Ditis vacuas et inania regna."

The long procession which followed, I have been obliged to examine through the spectacles of books.—With these eyes have I closely beheld the lineaments of Edward, Lord Thurlow; with these ears have I distinctly heard the deep tones of his voice.

"Largior hic campos æther et lumine vestit
Purpureo, solemque suum, sua sidera norunt."

Thurlow had resigned the Great Seal while I was still a child residing in my native land; but when I had been entered a few days a student at Lincoln's Inn, it was rumored that, after a long absence from parliament, he was to attend in the House of Lords, to express his opinion upon the very important question, "whether a divorce bill should be passed on the petition of the wife, in a case where her husband had been guilty of incest with her sister?"—there never hitherto having been an instance of a divorce bill in England except on the petition of the husband for the adultery of the wife.

When I was admitted below the bar, Lord Chancellor Eldon was sitting on the woolsack, but he excited comparatively little interest, and all eyes were impatiently looking round for him who had occupied it under Lord North, under Lord Rockingham, under Lord Shelburne, and under Mr. Pitt. At last there walked in, supported by a staff, a figure bent with age, dressed in an old-fashioned grey coat, with breeches and gaiters of the same stuff—a brown scratch wig—tremendous white bushy eyebrows—eyes still sparkling with intelligence—dreadful " crows' feet " round them—very deep lines in his countenance—and shriveled complexion of a sallow hue,—all indicating much greater senility than was to be expected from the date of his birth as laid down in the " Peerage."

The debate was begun by his Royal Highness the Duke of Clarence, afterwards William IV., who moved the rejection of the bill, on the ground that marriage had never been dissolved in this country, and never ought to be dissolved, unless for the adultery of the wife,—which alone for ever frustrated the purposes for which marriage had been instituted.

Lord Thurlow then rose, and the fall of a feather might have been heard in the House while he spoke. At this distance of time I retain the most lively recollection of his appearance, his manner, and his reasoning. " I have been excited by this bill," said he, " to examine the whole subject of divorce, as it has stood in all periods of time, and under all circumstances. Not only among civilized heathen nations, but by the Levitical law, and by the Gospel, a woman may be put away for adultery, and the remedy is not confined to the husband. The ecclesiastical courts in this country having only power to grant a divorce *à mensâ et thoro*, the tie of marriage can only be dissolved by the legislature; and when an application is made to us for that purpose, we ought to be governed by the circumstances of each particular case, and ask ourselves, whether the parties can properly continue to cohabit together as husband and wife ? Common law and statute law are silent upon the subject, and this is the rule laid down by reason, by morality, and by religion. Why do you grant to the husband a divorce for the adultery of the wife?—because he ought not to forgive her and separation is inevitable. Where the wife can not forgive, and separation is inevitable by reason of the crime of the husband, the wife is entitled to the like remedy. Your only objection is—mistrust of yourselves, and a doubt lest, on a future application by a wife, you should not conduct yourselves with sound discretion. Is such mistrust—is such doubt—a sufficient reason to justify a House of Parliament in refusing to put an end to a contract, all the objects of which, by the crime of one party, are for ever defeated? By the clearest evidence, Mr. Addison, since the marriage, has been guilty of incest with the sister of Mrs. Addison. Reconciliation is impossible. She can not forgive him and return to his house, without herself being guilty of incest. Do such of your Lordships as oppose the bill for the sake of morality propose or wish that she should? Had this criminal intercourse with the sister taken place before the marriage, the Ecclesiastical Court would have set aside the marriage as incestuous and void from the beginning; and is Mrs. Addison to be in a worse situation, because the incest was committed after the marriage, and under her own roof? You allow that she can never live with him again as her husband, and is she,—innocent, and a model of virtue,— to be condemned for his crime to spend the rest of her days in the unheard of situation of being neither virgin, wife, nor widow? Another sufficient ground for passing the bill is, that there are children of this marriage, who, without the interference of the legislature, would be exclusively under the control of the father. Now, your Lordships must all agree that such a father as Mr. Addison has proved himself to be, is unfit to be intrusted with the education of an innocent and virtuous daughter. The illustrious Prince says truly, that there is no exact precedent for such a bill; but, my Lords, let us look less to the exact terms of precedents than to the reason on which they are founded. The adultery of the husband, while it is condemned, may be forgiven, and therefore is no sufficient reason for dissolving the marriage; but the incestuous adultery of the husband is equally fatal to the matrimonial union as the adultery of the wife, and should entitle the injured party to the same redress."

I can not now undertake to say whether there were any *cheers*, but I well remember that Henry Cowper, the time-honored Clerk of the House of Lords, who had sat there for half a century, came down to the bar in a fit of enthusiasm and called out in a loud voice, "CAPITAL! CAPITAL! CAPITAL!" Lord Chancellor Eldon declared that he had made up his mind to oppose the measure, but that he was converted; and ex-Chancellor Lord Rosslyn confessed that the consideration which had escaped him,—of the impossibility of a reconciliation,— now induced him to vote for the bill. Having passed both Houses, it received the royal assent, and has since been followed as a precedent in two or three other cases of similar atrocity.[1]

Virgilium vidi tantùm. I never again had an opportunity of making any personal observation of Thurlow; but this glimpse of him renders his appearance familiar to me, and I can always imagine that I see before me, and that I listen to the voice of, this great imitator of GARAGANTUA.

I was struck with awe and admiration at witnessing the scene I have feebly attempted to describe; and I found that any of Thurlow's surviving contemporaries, with whom I afterwards chanced to converse, entertained the highest opinion of what they denominated his "gigantic powers of mind." I must confess, however, that my recent study of his career and his character has considerably lowered him in my estimation; and I have come to the conclusion that, although he certainly had a very vigorous understanding, and no inconsiderable acquirements—the fruit of irregular application,—he imposed by his assuming manner upon the age in which he lived,—and that he affords a striking illustration of the French maxim, "*on vaut ce qu'on veut valoir.*"

This personage—celebrated as a prodigy by historians and poets in the reign of George III., but whom posterity may regard as a very ordinary moral—was born in the year 1732, at Bracon-Ash, in the county of Norfolk. His father, Thomas Thurlow, was a clergyman, and held successively the livings of Little Ashfield in Suffolk, and of Stratton St. Mary's in Norfolk. The Chancellor himself

---

[1] 35 Parl Hist. 1429, Macqueen's Practice of the House of Lords, 594. At the first public masquerade which I attended in London, which was soon after this, there was a character which professed to be LORD CHANCELLOR THURLOW,—dressed in the Chancellor's robes, band, and full-bottomed wig. I am sorry to say that, to the amusement of the audience, he not only made loud speeches, but swore many profane oaths.

never attempted to trace his line distinctly further back than his grandfather, who was likewise a country parson,—although there was an eminent "*conveyancer*" whom he sometimes claimed as the founder of the family. He had a just contempt for the vanity of new men pretending that they are of ancient blood; and some one attempting to flatter him by trying to make out that he was descended from THURLOE, Cromwell's secretary, who was a Suffolk man,—"Sir," said he, "there were two Thurlows in that part of the country, who flourished about the same time: Thurloe the secretary, and Thurlow the carrier. I am descended from the last."[1] Nor could he boast of hereditary wealth, for his father's livings were very small, and there were several other children to be reared from the scanty profits of them. Yet, perhaps, his situation by birth was as favorable as any other for future eminence. Being the son of a clergyman, he escaped the discredit of being "sprung from the dregs of the people," and he had as good an education as if he had been heir to a dukedom. For his position in society, and for his daily bread, he was to depend entirely on his own exertions.[2] His father used to tell his sons betimes, that he could do nothing for them after he had launched them in a profession. The old gentleman would then say (aside) to a friend, " I have no fear about Ned ; *he* will fight his way in the world."

Of Ned's early years, a few anecdotes have been handed down to us. It being known that on account of his lively parts he was destined to be a lawyer, the Reverend W. Leach, whom he was in the habit of visiting while a very young boy, said to him one day, " I shall live to see you Lord Chancellor,"—and, forty years after, obtained from him a stall at Norwich, and a living in Suffolk.

He received his earliest instructions under the paternal roof, and was four years at a school at Scarning under a Mr.

---

[1] In the "Peerages" there is a long pedigree given, tracing him up to a family of Thurlow, of considerable antiquity in the northern part of the county of Norfolk, in which, although I doubt not it is very authentic, the "Carrier" does not appear, and with which, therefore, I do not trouble the reader.

[2] I belong to a club of " Sons of the Clergy of the Church of Scotland," of which the late Dr Ballie, Serjeant Spankie, and Wilkie, the painter, were members. The last was our great ornament. I well remember a speech of his from the chair, in which he said,—" born in the *manse*, we have all *a patent of nobility*."

Brett.[1] Here, according to the fashion of the age, the boys wore wigs, and Ned Thurlow (whether as an emblem of his future greatness I know not), having a "*full-bottom*," used to put it into his pocket when he went to play.

One of the amusements then encouraged at this and most other schools in England—now abolished for its cruelty—was "cock-throwing." By the kindness of a son of a school-fellow of Thurlow,[2] I am enabled to lay before the reader a copy of verses written by him on one of these "Gallicides." Notwithstanding inaccuracies with which he is chargeable, he must be allowed to display in this performance the vigor of mind which afterwards distinguished him;—and it is impossible not to admire his patriotic *fling* at the French, with whom we were then at war, and his well-deserved compliment to the hero of Culloden.

"GALLICIDUM.

"NYMPHAM dum pulchram comitabar forte Belindam,
—Gratia quam sequitur, quamque Cupido coliti;
Qualis ubi in propriam migrat Cytherea Cyprum,
Propitioque agros numine Diva beat,
Cum vinum pateris profusum altaria libat,
Ignibus atque piis mollia thura jacent—
Introii campum, quem ostendit semita planum,
Quo flores teneri et gramina læta virent,
Confusam mirans turbam, puerosque, senseque,
Ignotum vulgus cerno, virosque duces.
Jam magis atque magis populi crebrescere murmur,
Et vox audita est plurima rauca sonans.
Ut si quando Aquilo gelido bacchatus ab Arcto
(Subversis sylvis saltibus atque vagis)
Procumbit ponto, fumantesque asperat undas
Horrisonque mari littora curva ferit.
At clamore novo et magnâ perterrita turbâ
Nympha mihi effugiens hæc sua jussa dedit:
'I turbâ mediâ periuptâ, ex ordine narra
Cur spatium hoc campi tanta caterva premit.'
Dixit; et imperiis parens, caveam ipse petivi,
Quam spatio lato deseruit populus.
Jam pede constrictus frustra volitare laborat
Gallus, frustra alis æthera summa petit.
Adstitit ac heros, cui vim natura paravit,
Cuique artem ludi suppeditavit amor.

---

[1] That very eminent Judge and elegant scholar, Mr Baron Alderson, was educated at the same school, and remembers their great boast when he entered, that *they had produced a Lord Chancellor*.
[2] Charles Frederick Barnwell, Esq, of Woburn Place.

Non alius plures maculavit sanguine fustes,
  Gallorumve dedit corpora plura neci
Hic baculum attollens, mirâ quod fecerat arte,
  Atque manu versans, talia voce refert
'O fustis, nostros nunquam frustrata vocatus,
  Hunc gallum mitte ad littora dira Stygis.'
Nec plura effatus telum contorsit, in auras
  It clamor feriens sidera summa poli
Jupiter ut quondam, mundi miseratus adusti
  (Solis enim flammas sensit uterque polus,
Terraque subsidens Phaetonti dira precata
  Neptunusque suis torridus æquoribus),
Fulmen in aurigam dextrâ libravit ab aure,
  Excussitque rotis atque animâ pariter:
Sic periens cecidit, violento gallus ab ictu
  Nec crura eversum dilacerata ferunt.
Sic Galli intereant omnes ! sic Anglia semper
  Prostrato repetat lætior hoste domum !
Gentes audaces cum ducat Cumbrius heros,
  Quo virtus jubet, et gloria celsa vocat,
Magnanimus populus victricia signa sequatur,
  Et lætus repetat victor ovansque domum !" [1]

---

[1] The following is a translation of these verses by the very eminent *alumnus* of Scarning School, my valued friend, the Honorable Mr. Baron Alderson.—

"COCK-THROWING AT SHROVE-TIDE.

"WITH fair Belinda as I walk'd one day,
Round whom young Love and all the Graces stray,
—She fair as Venus who to Cyprus yields
Her wished-for presence, blessing all its fields,
Where ruddy wines in rich libations flow,
And fires of incense in her temples glow—
We reach'd by devious paths an open ground,
With grass and varied flowers enamel'd round.
There roam'd a crowd at once of men and boys,
All shouting out amain—an awful noise,
Loud as when Aquilo his legions pours,
Or Notus drowns the earth with pelting showers;
Whilst dark and darker still rush down the floods,
Prone in confusion fall the crashing woods;
Old ocean foams beneath th' astounding roar,
And billowy mountains roll and beat the shore,
Alarm'd, the nymph at once in terror fled,
But ere she vanished, thus to me she said.
'Go, sir, at once, and, if you can, find out,
What all this crowd and tumult is about'
She spake—and I obeyed,—I sought the throng,
And reach'd the open central space —Ere long
Tied by the leg, a captive cock I spied
Who oft to use (in vain) his pinions tried;
Whilst near him stood, in Nature's strength, a **clown**,
Taught, by long use, the art of knocking down;
None e'er like him incarnadin'd with stains
So many clubs, or spoil'd so many mains.

At Scarning, Thurlow seems to have been a great Pickle, as well as to have shown some talent, for he was next sent to the grammar school at Canterbury; and Southey, in his Life of Cowper, on the authority of Sir Egerton Brydges, accounts for this movement by narrating that Dr. Downe, his father's friend, having a great spite against Mr. Talbot, head master of that school, with whom he had had a violent quarrel, recommended strongly that young Edward Thurlow should be sent to it,—his secret motive being that the hated pedagogue might have under his care "a daring, refractory, clever boy, who would be sure to torment him."[1] At Canterbury, Thurlow remained some years. We are not told what pranks he played there, and I conjecture that this was his period of steady application,—when he acquired the greatest share of that classical learning for which he was afterwards distinguished.[2]

He was next sent to Caius College, Cambridge.[3] Here

> He seiz'd a stick with wondrous skill prepar'd,
> And thus address'd it as his hand he bar'd —
> 'My trusty club, which never fail'd me yet,
> Fly swift, and let that cock his wages get.'
> He spake and threw,—'Tis done!' exclaim'd the clown:
> Shouted the crowd amaz'd,—' He's down! he's down!'
> As when old Jove his thunderbolts uprear'd,
> ('Twas time) when Sol's ungovern'd son appear'd
> Through heaven and panting earth his car to wheel,
> Till Neptune's self, half-boil'd began to squeal,
> Right on the lad's doom'd head the lightnings beat,
> And he at once lost both his life and seat.
> So fell the cock beneath the heavy blow,
> His legs and spurs far scatter'd to and fro.
> Thus may thy cocks, false recreant Gallia, fall,
> And thou, Old England, then be cock of all.
> Whilst Cumbria's hero, still to conquest leads,
> And British soldiers emulate his deeds.
> O may he soon recross the subject main,
> And seek—in triumph seek—his home again!"

[1] Southey's Life of Cowper, 23.

[2] Thurlow always spoke kindly of Talbot, but considered himself so barbarously used by Brett, that he fostered an inextinguishable hatred of him. While Attorney General, going into a bookseller's shop at Norwich, Brett followed him, and most obsequiously accosted him Thurlow taking no notice of him, Brett said, "Mr Thurlow, do you not recollect me?"—*Mr. Attorney General* "I am not bound to recollect every scoundrel who chooses to recollect me"

[3] By the kindness of the Rev Dr Chapman, the present Master of the College, I have been favored with the following copy of his matriculation. Extract from the Matriculation Book of Gonville and Caius College, Cam-

he affected the character of idleness. He was suspected of sitting up at night to read;—and sometimes in the morning, when pretending to be wandering about in the fields, he "sported the oak,"[1]—shutting himself up to prepare for a College examination,—but he eschewed the chapel and the lecture room, and loved to be seen lounging at the gates of his college,—or loitering in coffee-houses, then frequented by the undergraduates,—or figuring in a nocturnal symposium,—or acting as leader of the University men in the wars between "*town*" and "*gown*." His frequent breaches of academic discipline made him familiar with impositions, confinements within the college, privations of sizings, and threats of rustication. He rather prided himself in such punishments, and, instead of producing reformation, they led to fresh offenses. He is reported to have often taken upon himself the blame of acts in which he had no hand, for the pleasure of arguing the case, and showing his ingenuity in justifying what he was supposed to have done. Equally celebrated was he for waywardness in getting into scrapes and for cleverness in getting out of them. The statutes of the University enjoin that all undergraduates shall wear habits *nigro aut subfusco colore*, and specially prohibit collars or cuffs of a different color from the coat. Thurlow had been a frequent offender against this rule. On one occasion, meeting a fellow when in the prohibited dress, he boldly denied that he had transgressed. "What!" cried the Don, "am I not to believe my own eyes?" "Not always;" and, casting off his coat on the grass-plat, he proved that the gay cuffs and collar were affixed to the vest, and ingeniously turned over the coat. On another occasion, the master having thus rebuked him—"Sir, I never come to the window without seeing you idling in the court,"—the unabashed undergraduate answered, "Sir, I never come into the court without seeing you idling at the window."[2]

bridge, 5th October, 1748 —" Edwardus, filius Reverendi Thomæ Thurlow Vicarii de Tharston, in Com Norf natus apud Braken in eodem Com educatus per biennium in Ædius paternis apud Taccleston, sub Mag^{ro} Browne, dien per quadrien, in Scholâ Publicâ apud Scarning, sub Mag^{ro} Brett, postremo in Scholâ publicâ Cantuariensi sub Mag^{ro} Talbot, annos natus 17, admissus est Oct 5, Pens Minor sub tutelâ Mag^{ri} Smith, et solvit pro ingress, 3s 4d."

[1] Locked the outer door of his rooms

[2] have received another version of the story, which some may prefer.— *Master of Caius:* "Mr. Thurlow, I never look out of this window but I see

At last he was summoned before the dean of his college—a worthy man, but weak and formal—for non-attendance at chapel, and had an imposition set him—to translate a paper of the "Spectator" into Greek. He duly performed the task, taking considerably pains with it; but instead of bringing his translation (as he well knew duty required) to the *imposer*, he intimated to him that he had delivered it to the college tutor, who had the reputation of being a good Grecian. This Mr. Dean construed into an unpardonable insult, and he ordered the delinquent, as in cases of the gravest complexion, to be summoned before the Master and Fellows of the College. The charge being made and proved, Thurlow was asked what he had to say in defense or extenuation of his conduct? "Please your worships," said he, "no one respects Mr. Dean more than I do; and, out of tenderness to him, I carried my exercise to one who could inform him whether I had obeyed his orders." This plain insinuation that the Dean was little acquainted with the Greek tongue was the more galling as being known to be well-founded, and was considered by him an enormous aggravation of the original injury. He denounced it as a flying in the face of all authority, and foretold that the discipline of the College was at an end if they did not now proceed with the utmost severity. In conclusion, he declared that "*rustication* would only be laughed at by the offender, and that *expulsion* was the only adequate punishment."

There was no denying that the offense was a serious one, but considerable sympathy was felt for the young gentleman, who, although his future greatness was little dreamed of, was known to possess social good qualities, and to evince excellent abilities when he chose to exert them. In mitigation, they likewise remembered the dash of absurdity about Mr. Dean which had often made him the butt of the combination room. In particular, Smith, the tutor (afterwards head of the house), put in a good word for the culprit, and, to avoid setting a brand upon him which might ruin him for life, proposed that he

you passing under it." *Thurlow:* "And I never pass under this window, Sir, but I see you looking out of it."

should be permitted to remove his name from the college books, and that no other proceedings should be taken against him. Notwithstanding the stout resistance of the Dean, this suggestion was adopted. Thurlow gratefully acquiesced, and thus left Cambridge without a degree.[1]

Notwithstanding his irregularities, there can be no doubt that he derived great benefit from his residence there. He had occasional fits of severe application; and, always having a contempt for frivolity, when he seemed to be idle he was enlarging his stock of knowledge, and sharpening his intellect by conversing with men of strong sense and solid acquirements.

Among the strange vicissitudes of life, it did so happen that the refractory disciple, thus discarded from the bosom of Alma Mater, reached the highest civil dignity in the state; and it is pleasant to relate, that, when presiding on the woolsack, he recollected the friendly interference of Dr. Smith, and caused him to be appointed chancellor of the diocese of Lincoln.

It is even said that he afterwards handsomely made atonement to " Mr. Dean." The story goes, that he had had an earlier quarrel with this functionary, who had interrupted him, rather sharply, with the question, " Pray, sir, do you know to whom you are speaking?" bidding him to recollect that he was in the presence of no less a person than the DEAN OF THE COLLEGE. This hint was not lost upon Thurlow, who then, and ever after, began

---

[1] In a communication respecting Lord Chancellor Thurlow, with which I have been honored by Dr Chapman, the learned Master of Caius, after stating that the traditions respecting him at Cambridge had become very faint, he says,—" I have always understood that, having set at defiance all College authority, it became necessary to send him away. I have searched our records, and can find no recorded charge against him, or any sentence passed upon him so I conclude his friends were advised to take him from College He was admitted Oct 5, 1748, and elected a scholar on Dr Perse's foundation, Oct. 12, 1748; this he held till Ladyday, 1751, when his last stipend was paid him. I conclude, therefore, that his name was taken off our books about that time, as it does not appear in our list of scholars at Mich 1751 "

A learned friend of mine, now in a judicial station, writes to me—" When I visited Brighton in my first Cambridge vacation, Thurlow asked me of what College I was 'Of Caius,' I replied, and 'I keep the same rooms in which your Lordship is said to have kept' 'I hope *you will keep them*,' was the reply. I did not then know how the ex-Chancellor had lost them."

and interlarded every sentence he addressed to him with the vocative, " MR. DEAN;" this banter being doubly galling to the assertor of the title, as he could not consistently appear to be offended by it. When the flippant youth, who had been so nearly expelled from his college, had a little while held the Great Seal, the individual who had proposed and pressed his expulsion obeying a summons to wait upon him, the Chancellor's first salutation to him was, " Mr. Dean, how d'ye do? I am very happy to see you, Mr. Dean." " My Lord," he observed, somewhat sullenly, " I am no longer, Mr. Dean." " That is as you please; and it shall not be my fault if the title does not still belong to you, for I have a deanery at my disposal, which is very much at your service, Mr. Dean."[1]

This generosity was very honorable to Thurlow, for (as he well knew) on his being made Chancellor his College met to deliberate whether they should not congratulate him (according to custom) on his elevation,—when Dr. Smith, the Master, objected, saying, " that it would be an insult, under the circumstances attending his Lordship's removal from College,"—and the proposal fell to the ground.

His early destination for the bar remaining unaltered, he had been entered of the Inner Temple while an undergraduate at Cambridge;[2] and as soon as he quitted the University he took chambers, and began to keep terms by eating a certain number of dinners in the hall—this, since the disuse of " moots" and " readings," being the only *curriculum* of legal education in England.

The voluntary discipline of a special pleader's office was not yet established, although TOM WARREN, the great founder of the special-pleading race, to whom I can trace

---

[1] This anecdote which has often appeared in print, is probably considerably embellished, but so much I know, from undoubted private authority,—that the Dean's name was Goodrich; that he accepted a College living in Dorsetshire; that at the first visitation of the Bishop of Salisbury after Thurlow was Chancellor, Mr Goodrich said to the Bishop, " I am sure I shall have some preferment from him, as I was the only fellow who dared to punish him." and that the Bishop having mentioned this to the Chancellor, the old Caius man exclaimed, " It is true! he is right, and a living he shall have !"

[2] He is thus described. *Edwardus Thurlow generosus filius et hæres apparens Thomæ Thurlow, de Stratton St. Mary, in csmitatu Norfolk, Clerici.*

up my pedigree, was then beginning to flourish.[1] The
usual custom was, to place the aspirant for the bar as a
pupil in the office of a solicitor, where he was supposed
to learn how actions were commenced and conducted,
with the practice of the different courts of law and equity.
For young Thurlow was selected the office of Mr. Chapman, a very eminent solicitor, who carried on business in
Lincoln's Inn. Here he met, as a brother pupil, the celebrated William Cowper, author of "The Task." The
poet contracted a great friendship for him, and introduced
him to his cousin, Lady Hesketh, who lived in Southampton Row, then a fashionable quarter of the town.
This gay house was much more agreeable to the taste of
the brother-pupils than the smoky chambers of the attorney, smelling of musty parchment; and here they frivo-

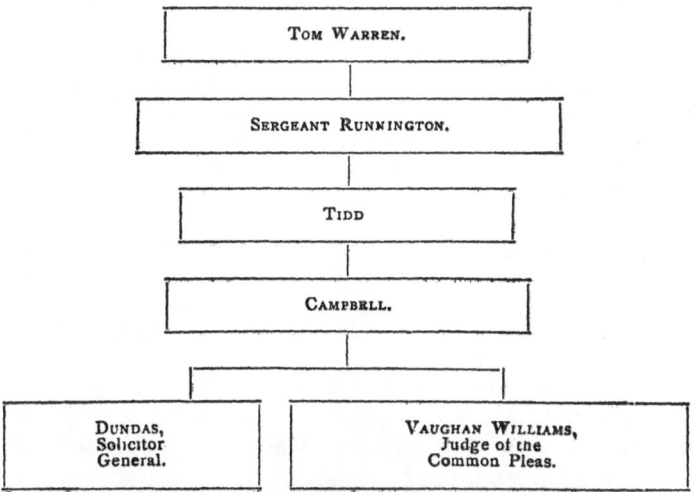

I delight to think that my special-pleading father, now turned of eighty, is
still alive, and in the full enjoyment of his faculties. He live to see four sons
sitting together in the House of Lords—Lord Lyndhurst, Lord Denman,
Lord Cottenham, and Lord Campbell. To the unspeakable advantage of
having been three years his pupil, I chiefly ascribe my success at the bar. I
have great pride in recording that when, at the end of my first year, he discovered it would not be quite convenient for me to give him a second fee of
one hundred guineas, he not only refused to take a second, but insisted on
returning me the first. Of all the lawyers I have ever known, he has the
finest analytical head and if he had devoted himself to science, I am sure
that he would have earned great fame as a discoverer. His disposition and
his manners have made him universally beloved.—A.D. 1847.

lously passed a great part of their time. Cowper, in a private letter written many years after, gives this account of their studies:—" I did actually live three years with Mr. Chapman, that is to say, I slept three years in his house; but I lived, that is to say, I spent my days, in Southampton Row, as you very well remember. There was I and the future Lord Chancellor constantly employed, from morning till night, in giggling, and making others giggle, instead of studying the law."

Thurlow, while denominated "a student of law," affected the character of an idler.[1] He was fond of society; without being addicted to habitual intemperance, he occasionally indulged in deep potations; and, although his manners were somewhat rough and bearish, as he had great powers of entertainment, his company was much courted by the loungers of the Inns of Court. Thus a good deal of his time was stolen from study, and he could not lay in such stores of learning as Selden and Hale, in the preceding century, who, for years together, read sixteen hours a day. But he by no means neglected preparation for his profession to the extreme degree which he pretended. He had an admirable head for the law, with a quick perception and a retentive memory; so that he made greater progress than some plodders who were at work all day long and a great part of every night. He attended the remarkable trials and arguments which came on in Westminster Hall, and picked up a good deal of legal knowledge while he seemed only to be abusing the counsel and laughing at the judges. He would still shut himself up for whole mornings, barring his outer door,— when he not only would seize upon a classic, and get up the literature of the day, but make a serious attack on

---

[1] This affectation, which I believe has gone out of fashion like "hair powder" and "shorts," survived to my time. I knew an exceedingly clever young man, who, having taken a high degree at Cambridge, in reality studied the law very assiduously, but who pretended to be idle, or to read only books of amusement Reversing the practice of the hero of the PLEADER'S GUIDE, —who, if "Hawke" or "Buzzard," or any attorney was approaching, conveyed the object of his affections into the coal-hole, and pretended to be reading the "*Doctrina Placitandi*,"—my friend, who was in the habit of poring over "Coke upon Littleton," had a contrivance by which, on a knock coming to the door, this black-letter tome disappeared, and there was substituted for it a novel, the name of which I may not mention. If he had lived, he would have conquered all such follies, but he was destined to an early grave.

Littleton and Plowden. He did go almost every evening to Nando's coffee-house, near Temple Bar, and swaggered and talked loud there about politics and scandal, new plays and favorite actresses; but—if he had not taken too much of the punch which Mrs. Humphries, the landlady, was celebrated for compounding, and her fair daughter served—on returning to his chambers he would read diligently, before going to rest, till his candles turned dim in the morning light. His contemporary, Craddock, who was admitted to his entire intimacy, and from whom he concealed nothing, writes, "It was generally supposed that Thurlow in early life was idle; but I always found him close at study in a morning, when I have called at the Temple; and he frequently went no further in an evening than to Nando's, and then only in his *déshabillé*."[1] It is quite clear, from his successful combats with the members of the "Literary Club," and with the first lawyers in Westminster Hall, that he had effectually, though irregularly, devoted himself to literature and law. Let me, then, anxiously caution the student against being misled by the delusive hope which the supposed idleness of Thurlow has engendered,—that a man may become a great lawyer, and rise with credit to the highest offices, without application. Thurlow never would have been Chancellor if he had not studied his profession; and he would have been a much greater Chancellor, and would have left a much higher name to posterity, if he had studied it more steadily.

On the 22nd of November, 1754, the benchers of his Society, who were supposed to direct his studies, and to examine into his proficiency, having ascertained that he had kept twelve terms by eating the requisite number of

---

[1] Craddock's Memoirs, vol 1 79 I presume the *déshabillé* meant that he entered the coffee-house without wearing a cut velvet suit and a sword, as lawyers still did when they went into fine company. Having reached extreme old age, he told his youngest nephew (from whom I received the statement) that "when young he read much at night; and that once, while at College, having been unable to complete a particular line in a Latin poem he was composing, it rested so on his mind that he dreamed of it, completed it in his sleep, wrote it out next morning, and received many compliments on its classical and felicitous turn"—This may remind the reader of the monk, who, being appointed to write the epitaph of Bede, and being much puzzled for an epithet, fell asleep, and in his dream was supplied by an angel with the following line —

" Hacce jacent fossâ BEDÆ *venerabilis* ossa."

dinners in the Hall each term,—called him to the bar, vouching his sufficiency to advocate the causes of his fellow-citizens in all courts, civil and criminal. He took his seat in the back rows of the Court of King's Bench, of which Sir Dudley Ryder was then Chief Justice, and he went the Western Circuit, of which Henley and Pratt were the leaders. But for several years he met with little success, either in town or country. He had no family interest or connection to assist him; his reputation for idleness repelled business from his chambers, and he was too proud to *hug* the attorneys or to try to get forward by unworthy means.

When he had been a few years at the bar, he fell into pecuniary straits. His father had expected that fees would immediately flow in upon him, and proposed to withdraw, instead of increasing, the very moderate allowance which was his sole support. It is even said that the future Chancellor, although he practiced a laudable economy, was actually reduced to the following stratagem to procure a horse to carry him round the circuit: He went to a horse-dealer, and said to him that he wished to purchase a good roadster—price being no object to him—but that he must have a fair trial of the animal's paces before he concluded the bargain. The trial being conceded, he rode off to Winchester, and having been well-carried all the way round, but still without any professional luck, he returned the horse to his owner, saying that "the animal, notwithstanding some good points, did not altogether suit him."

At last, fortune smiled upon him. By some chance he had a brief in the case of *Luke Robinson* v. *the Earl of Winchelsea*, tried before Lord Mansfield, at Guildhall. The leader on the opposite side was Sir Fletcher Norton, then the tyrant of the bar, who began by treating the unknown junior with his usual arrogance. This Thurlow resented with great spirit. They got into an altercation, in which Thurlow had with him the sympathies of the bar and the bystanders, and, with a happy mixture of argument and sarcasm, he completely put down his antagonist. The attorneys who had smarted much under Norton's despotic rule were exceedingly delighted, and resolved to patronize the man who had shown so much courage and capacity.[1]

[1] I was myself present when, under very similar circumstances, Topping

Briefs in cases of a peculiar character did come in, and he was now known and talked of in the profession as one supposed to be possessed of great resources, and likely one day to make a figure; but still he had few constant clients, and little regular business. He had not credit for possessing much technical knowledge of the law, and he did not always exhibit that subordination which the leader expects in a junior counsel, and which, indeed, the interest of the client demands. In short, he disdained to "play second fiddle" to those whom he considered inferior performers. There was no chance of his getting forward in the routine progress of professional advancement, and his friends were still under much apprehension of his ultimate failure.

It has often been said that he made his fortune by his great speech at the bar of the House of Lords in the Douglas cause. But this story is utterly demolished by the slightest attention to dates. The hearing of that celebrated appeal, in which he certainly gave the finest display of his forensic powers, did not come on till January, 1769; and before then he had long had a silk gown, he led his circuit, he was engaged in every important case which came on in Westminster Hall, and he had been returned to the House of Commons as member for Tamworth. However, his retainer as one of the counsel for the appellant in the Douglas cause truly had a very material and very favorable influence upon his destiny. The occurrence is said to have happened by the purest accident. According to legal tradition, soon after the decision of the Court of Session in Scotland, that the alleged son of Lady Jane Douglas was a suppositious child purchased at Paris, the question, which excited great interest all over Europe, was discussed one evening at Nando's coffee-house—from its excellent punch, and the ministrations of a younger daughter of the landlady, still Thurlow's favorite haunt. At this time, and, indeed,

once pushed himself into great business at Guildhall, by putting down Gibbs, then Attorney General—quoting the indignant description by Cassius of the tyranny of Cæsar.

> "Why, man, he doth bestride the narrow world
> Like a Colossus, and we petty men
> Walk under his huge legs and peep about
> To find ourselves dishonorable graves.
> The fault—is not in our stars,
> But in ourselves, that we are underlings."

when I myself first began the study of the law, the modern club system was unknown; and (as in the time of Swift and Addison) men went in the evenings, for society, to coffee-houses, in which they expected to encounter a particular set of acquaintance, but which were open to all who chose to enter and offer to join in the conversation, at the risk of meeting with cold looks and mortifying rebuffs. Thurlow, like his contemporary, Dr. Johnson, took great pains in gladiatorial discussion, knowing that he excelled in it, and he was pleased and excited when he found a large body of good listeners. On the evening in question, a friend of his at the English bar strongly applauded the judgment against the supposed heir of the house of Douglas. For this reason, probably, Thurlow took the contrary side. Like most other lawyers, he had read the evidence attentively, and in a succinct but masterly statement, he gave an abstract of it to prove that the claimant was, indeed, the genuine issue of Lady Jane and her husband,—dexterously repelling the objections to the claim, and contending that there were admitted facts which were inconsistent with the theory of the child being the son of the French rope-dancer. Having finished his argument and his punch, he withdrew to his chambers, pleased with the victory which he had obtained over his antagonist, who was no match for him in dialectics, and who had ventured to express an opinion upon the question without having sufficiently studied it. Thurlow, after reading a little brief for a motion in the King's Bench, which his clerk had received in his absence, went to bed thinking no more of the Douglas cause, and ready, according to the vicissitudes of talk, to support the spuriousness of the claimant with equal zeal. But it so happened that two Scotch law agents, who had come up from Edinburgh to enter the appeal, having heard of the fame of Nando's, and having been told that some of the great leaders of the English bar were to be seen there, had at a side table been quiet listeners during the disputation, and were amazingly struck with the knowledge of the case and the acuteness which Thurlow had exhibited. The moment he was gone, they went to the landlady, and inquired who he was. They had never heard his name before; but, finding that he was a barrister, they resolved to retain him as junior to prepare the appellant's case, and to prompt those who were to lead it at the bar of the House of Lords. A difficulty had occurred about the preparation of the case; for there was a wise determination that, from the magnitude of the stake, the nature of the question, and the consideration that it was to be decided by English law Lords, the *plaidoyer* should be drawn by English counsel, and the heads of the bar who were retained, from their numerous avocations—had refused to submit to this preliminary drudgery.

Next morning a retainer, in *Douglas* v. *The Duke of Hamilton*, was left at Thurlow's chambers, with an immense pile of papers, having a fee indorsed upon them ten times as large as he had ever before received. At a conference with the agents (who took no notice of Nando's), an explanation was given of what was expected of him,—the Scotchmen hinting that his fame had reached the " Parliament House at Edinburgh." He readily undertook the task, and did it the most ample justice, showing that he could command, upon occasion, not only striking elocution, but patient industry. He repeatedly perused and weighed every deposition, every document, and every pleading that had ever been brought forward during the suit ; and he drew a most masterly case, which mainly led to the success of the appeal, and which I earnestly recommend to the law student as a model of lucid arrangement and forcible reasoning.

While so employed, he made acquaintance with several of the relations and connections of the Douglas family, who took the deepest interest in the result ; and among others, with the old Duchess of Queensberry, the well-known friend of Gay, Pope, Swift, and the other wits of the reign of Queen Anne. When she had got over the bluntness of his manners (which were certainly not those of the *vieille cour*), she was mightily taken with him, and declared that since the banishment of Atterbury and the death of Bolingbroke, she had met with no Englishman whose conversation was so charming. She added, that, being a genuine Tory, she had considerable influence with Lord Bute, the new favorite, and even with the young Sovereign himself, who had a just respect for hereditary right, lamenting the fate of the family whom his own had somewhat irregularly supplanted. On this hint Thurlow spoke, and, with the boldness that belonged to his character, said that "a silk gown would be very acceptable to him." Her Grace was as much surprised as if he had expressed a wish to wear a silk petticoat—but upon an explanation that the wished-for favor was the appointment to the dignity of King's Counsel, in the gift of the government, she promised that it should be conferred upon him.

She was as good as her word. Lord Bute made no sort of difficulty when told that the number of King's Counsel might be indefinitely increased, bringing only a charge of forty pounds a year on the public, with an allowance of stationery.[1]

Lord Northington, in whose department strictly the job was, boggled a little, for he knew nothing of Thurlow, except remembering him a noisy, briefless junior on the Western circuit; and, upon inquiry, he found that neither from his standing nor his business had he any fair pretension to be called within the bar; but the Duchess of Queensberry contrived that George III., although he then had never seen the man to whom he was afterwards so much attached, should intimate to the Chancellor that this young lawyer's promotion would be personally agreeable to his Majesty himself, and all the Chancellor's objections instantly vanished. In December, 1761, Thurlow boldly doffed his stuff gown for the silk, renouncing his privilege to draw law papers, or to appear as junior counsel for any plaintiff.

In the following term he was elected a Bencher of the Inner Temple, but it was some time doubtful whether he would reap any other fruits from his new rank. Rival barristers complained much, that in the seventh year of his call, being known for nothing except his impertinence to Sir Fletcher Norton, he should be put over the heads of some who might have been his father; while the general consolation was, " that the silk gown could never answer to him, and that he had cut his own throat." He himself had no misgivings, and there were a few of more discernment who then predicted that he would eventually rise to the high-office in his profession.[2]

[1] With this went a certain number of bags to carry briefs; and when I entered the profession no man at the bar could carry a bag who had not received one from a King's Counsel. All these perquisites were swept away by the Reform Ministry of 1830
[2] See vol v p. 254 of Southey's edition of Cowper's Works.

In truth, his success was certain. With the respectable share he possessed of real talents and of valuable acquirements, together with his physical advantages of dark complexion, strongly marked features, piercing eyes, bushy eyebrows, and sonorous voice, all worked to the best effect by an immeasurable share of *self-confidence*—he could not fail. This last quality was the chief cause of his greatness.

Of him, Lady Mary Wortley Montagu seems to have been speaking propetically, if, according to her evident meaning, you substitute "self-confidence" for "impudence,"—which properly belongs only to a shameless impostor. "A moderate merit," writes she, "with a large share of *impudence*, is more probable to be advanced than the greatest qualifications without it. The first necessary qualification is *impudence*, and (as Demosthenes said of action in oratory) the second is *impudence*, and the third still *impudence*. No modest man ever did, or ever will, make his fortune. Your friends, Lord Halifax, Robert Walpole, and all other remarkable instances of quick advancement, have been remarkably *impudent*. The ministry is like a play at court; there's a little door to get in, and a great crowd without—shoving and thrusting who shall be foremost; people who knock others with their elbows, disregard a little kick on the shins, and still thrust heartily forwards, are sure of a good place. Your modest man stands behind in the crowd, is shoved about by everybody, his clothes torn, almost squeezed to death —and sees a thousand get in before him, that don't make so good a figure as himself."

When Thurlow appeared in court with his silk robe and full-bottom wig—lowering frowns and contemptuous smiles successively passing across his visage as the arguments or the judgment proceeded—the solicitors could not behold him without some secret awe, and without believing that he was possessed of some mysterious powers which he could bring into activity in their service. When he had an opportunity of opening his mouth, he spoke in a sort of oracular or judicial tone, as if he had an undoubted right to pronounce the verdict or judgment in favor of his client. He appeared to think that his opponent was guilty of great presumption in controverting any of his positions; and, unless his cause was desperately bad (when he would spontaneously give it up), he tried to convey the notion that the judges, if they showed any disposition to decide against him, were chargeable with gross ignorance, or were actuated by some corrupt motive. By such arts he was soon in first-rate business, and all of a sudden—from extreme poverty—in the receipt of a very large income. I do not find that he was counsel in any celebrated cases before he was Solicitor General; but Burrow and the other contemporary reporters show that, during the eight following years, he argued many of the most important questions of law which came on for decision in Westminister Hall.

Hitherto he had taken little part in politics, and he seemed in a state of perfect indifference between the two parties, associating with the members of both indiscriminately—in conversation, sometimes speaking for and sometimes against the taxing of the colonies, and some times censuring and sometimes defending the prosecution of Wilkes. Now beginning to feel the stings of ambition, and resolved upon political advancement, it was necessary to choose a side. During Lord Chatham's second ministry, the Whigs had gone down in the world most lamentably, and they seemed to have lost for ever their illustrious chief. Toryism was decidedly favored at Court, and had the ascendency in both Houses of Parliament. Thurlow declared himself a Tory, and, on the interest of the party he had joined, in the new parliament which met in May, 1768, he was returned for Tamworth, since illustrated by a still more distinguished representative. To this party he most zealously and unscrupulously adhered till he was deprived of the Great Seal by the younger Pitt; but I am afraid that, in his heart, he cared little about Tory principles, and that he professed and acted upon them so long only to please the King and to aggrandise himself.

It might have been expected, from his impetuous aud sanguine temper, that he would have been eager to gain parliamentary distinction as soon as he had taken his seat; but he had not yet selected his leader from the different sections into which the Tories were then subdivided, and he was cautious not to commit himself till it should be seen who gained the ascendency.

Meanwhile the Douglas appeal, after eight years' preparation, came on to be heard at the bar of the House of Lords, and attracted a greater share of public attention than any political debate in either House. Thurlow led for the appellant, and, having for years devoted himself to the case, by his admirable pleading he showed what excellence he might have reached, and what solid fame he might have acquired, if his industry had been equal to his talent.

This was a very brilliant passage of his life, for he was not only rapturously applauded as an advocate, but he gained immense *éclat* for his courage and gentleman-like deportment in an affair of honor to which the cause gave rise. As counsel for Mr. Douglas, the appellant, he felt it his duty to animadvert with much severity on the conduct of Mr. Andrew Stewart, a gentleman of education and well-esteemed in the world, who had been concerned as an agent in getting up the evidence and conducting the suit for the Duke of Hamilton. As soon as Thurlow had finished his first day's argument, Stewart sent him a challenge, requiring a hostile meeting next morning. Thurlow wrote back for answer, "that the desired meeting Mr. Stewart should have, but not till the hearing of the appeal was concluded." I believe he had said nothing against the challenger but what was justified by his instructions and the circumstances of the case—so that, according to professional etiquette, he might have applied for protection to the House of Lords, who would have treated the challenge as a contempt of their authority and a breach of privilege. When the hearing was over, the meeting actually did take place.

"On Sunday morning, January 14, the parties met with swords and pistols, in Hyde Park, one of them having for his second his brother, Colonel S———, and the other having for his, Mr. L———, member for a city in Kent. Having discharged pistols, at ten yards' distance, without effect, they drew their swords, but the seconds interposed and put an end to the affair."[1]

Mr. Stewart afterwards declared "that Mr. Thurlow advanced and stood up to him like an elephant."[2]

[1] Scott's Magazine for 1769, vol. xxxi. p. 107. Edinburgh Evening Courant, 23rd Jan. 1769
[2] A gentleman still alive, who remembers the duel well, says that, "Thurlow, on his way to the field of battle, stopped to eat an enormous breakfast at

I do not find that the honorable and learned member for Tamworth spoke in the House till the tremendous crisis in January, 1770, upon the reappearance of Lord Chatham in full vigor, the dismissal of Lord Camden, the melancholy fate of Charles Yorke, and the formation of a new government to prosecute Wilkes and to tax the colonies. In the debate on the resolution moved by Mr. Dowdeswell, arising out of Luttrell being seated for Middlesex, because Wilkes was alleged to be disqualified by his expulsion, "that by the law of the land, and the law and usage of parliament, no person eligible of common right can be incapacitated by a resolution of the House, but by an act of parliament only," Mr. Wedderburn supported it against Lord North, saying, "The noble Lord asks 'will the House of Commons censure and disgrace itself?' Let me ask in my turn, will the House of Commons compose the minds of the people? Will they recover the good opinion and confidence of those whom some gentlemen have been pleased to call the *rabble*, the *baseborn*, the *scum of the earth?*"—Then, covered with maiden blushes, thus spoke the honorable and learned member for Tamworth:—

"Sir, as the argument now seems to be carried on by questions, I shall ask in my turn, how came the House of Commons to determine who should sit among them formerly if they can not determine who shall sit among them now? How came they to determine that the Attorney General, the Solicitor General, and the Masters in Chancery, could not sit here, because they might possibly be called upon to attend the House of Lords? and how came this determination to be acquiesced in till those persons were readmitted by a subsequent vote?" [1]

This is a very fair specimen of Thurlow's manner; for he never hesitated to resort to reasoning which he must have known to be sophistical, or to make a convenient assertion,—trusting largely to the ignorance of his audi-

---

a tavern near Hyde Park Corner "—(*1st edit*) This was the Right Honorable Thomas Grenville, now deceased —(*3rd edit*)

[1] 16 Parl Hist 804. A few days before the House had heard the maiden speech of a very different man, the Honorable C J Fox (16 Parl Hist 726) This was a very memorable session in our party history. During the course of it came out Dr Johnson's " False Alarm," and Edmund Burke's " Causes of the present Discontents," in the worst and best styles of the respective authors.

ence. There was no analogy between determining whether by the usage of parliament a particular office was a disqualification to sit in the House of Commons, and enacting a new disqualification by a vote. Moreover, in point of fact, there never had been any votes, such as he supposed, for or against the general right of the Attorney and Solicitor General and the Masters in Chancery to sit in the House. But he spoke in such a loud voice, and with such an air of authority, that no one ventured to contradict him, and he was considered a great acquisition by the Government.

The office of Solicitor General immediately after became vacant by the resignation of Dunning, and Thurlow was joyously appointed to it.[1]

[1] In a Life of Sir W. Blackstone prefixed to his "Reports," it is said that he upon this occasion declined the office of Solicitor General (vol. 1. xvii), but the offer was very faint—merely in compliance with an expectation which had been held out to him when he entered parliament, and it was accompanied with a promise of the first puisne judgeship which should become vacant. The "Doctor," as he was then called, was infinitely superior as a jurist to Thurlow, and was covered with literary glory by the recent publication of his "COMMENTARIES," which rescued our profession from the imputation of barbarism. and, while it contained a systematic digest of English law, was justly praised by Charles Fox for its style as a specimen of genuine Anglicism. But the Doctor, being returned for Westbury at the same time as Thurlow for Tamworth, entirely failed in the House of Commons Being called forth to defend the Government on the Middlesex election, he wrecked his reputation as a constitutional lawyer and George Grenville, leading the book, proved that he had contended for a different doctrine in debate from that which he had laid down in his Commentaries. Having published a pamphlet in his own defense, he got into a controversy with Junius, in which he was signally worsted,* and his retreat from political life was now earnestly desired both by himself and his patrons. Thurlow was their man !

The Duke of Grafton's MS Journal, after stating that Lord North behaved ill to his Solicitor General, thus proceeds —" Mr. Dunning was too highminded to submit to any indignity Not long after, he resigned his office, and was succeeded by Thurlow, a bold and able lawyer, and a speaker of the first rate, as well in parliament as at the bar His principles leaned to high prerogative, and I fear his counsels brought no advantage to the King or the nation."

* See Junius to Sir W. Blackstone, 29th July, 1769, and the four following letters.

CHAPTER CLVI.

CONTINUATION OF THE LIFE OF LORD THURLOW TILL HE WAS MADE LORD CHANCELLOR.

THE new Solicitor General escaped knighthood, now considered a disgrace.[1] He was immediately obliged to present himself before his constituents at Tamworth, but he was re-elected without opposition, and he continued to represent this place till he was transferred to the Upper House.

He did not, by any means, disappoint expectation as a parliamentary partisan. While a representative of the people, he ever readily and zealously followed the instructions of the Government, as if he had been arguing in a court of law from his brief. He often displayed, in the debate, vigorous reasoning and manly eloquence,—and, when beaten, he could always cover his retreat with a broad assertion, a cutting sarcasm, or a threatening look.

The first occasion on which he distinguished himself, after becoming a law officer of the Crown, was in the debate on the motion for leave to bring in a bill to take away the power of filing *Ex Officio* Informations. This was opposed, in a very able and temperate speech, by Sir William De Grey, the Attorney General, who showed, by clear authorities, that the power by law belonged to his office, and argued that there could be nothing unconstitutional in his being allowed, upon his responsibility, to bring a man to trial for sedition before a jury, who would decide upon the truth of the charge. Sergeant Glynn and others followed on the opposite side, contending that the power was liable to abuse; that it had been abused; and that a jury was no protection, on account of the fashionable doctrine now acted upon by Lord Mansfield and other judges, that " the jury had nothing to do with the question of libel or no libel; the criminality or inno-

[1] George III., to keep up the respectability of the order, soon after insisted on the law officers of the Crown, as well as the Judges, submitting to it, and the same rule has since been observed, unless in the case of the sons of peers, who are "honorable" by birth.

cence of the writing charged to be libelous being a pure question of law for the determination of the Court." Thus answered Mr. Solicitor, in that rude, bantering, turbulent, impressive style of oratory which characterized all his parliamentary harangues, and which gained him such a reputation with his contemporaries:—

"Sir, however much a representative may be bound to express the voice of his constituents, I can not greatly approve of that patriotism which prompts any member to adopt every popular rumor, and to assert the rumor as a fact, on his own authority. We ought to make a discreet selection, to distinguish between truth and falsehood, and not to swallow every vulgar prejudice. Therefore, I can not applaud those oblique reflections which, in imitation of pamphleteers and newsmongers, some honorable members seem so fond of casting on this House. Such strokes may serve as stilts to raise the authors up to the notice of the mob, but will not, I am persuaded, add to their character in this assembly. The artifice is too gross to deceive. There is no lawyer, nor any other sensible person, within these walls who will not allow all the prosecutions lately carried on by the Attorney General were extremely proper, if not necessary. Why, then should we, when no real danger, no late encroachment presses, sally forth, like a band of Quixotes, to attack this windmill of a giant, this imaginary magician, who keeps none of our rights, none of our privileges, under the power of his enchantments? Not a single wight, not a single damsel, has he injured. All who pretend to dread him, walk at large, ay, more at large, I suspect, than they ought. Our booksellers and printers have no reason to complain of being held in trammels. They are allowed every reasonable indulgence, and they carry it to its utmost limits. Shall we give licentiousness an ample range? For my own part, I can not help considering the project as a crazy conceit, solely intended for gaining a little popularity; for men, however helpless, will 'spread the thin oar and catch the driving gale,'—the popular breeze, whose murmur is so soothing to certain ears. But the wisdom and gravity of this House must perceive that the power at present lodged in the Attorney General is necessary, as well for speedily punishing as preventing daring libels. If no other process is left but the common one of bringing the affair before a grand jury, the delinquent may in the mean while escape. No offender can be brought to justice. What is the consequence? The licentiousness of the press will increase. Crimes will multiply. Nothing will be published but libels and lampoons. The press will teem with scurrility and falsehood. The minds of the people will be misled and perverted by scandalous misrepresentations. The many-headed beast will swallow the poison, and the land will consequently be one scene of anarchy and confusion." He next applied himself to a recent conviction of a bookseller for the unauthorized act of a servant, and according to the report (which is scarcely credible) he worked himself up to say,—" In civil cases, the master is confessedly answerable for the faults of his servants. How comes he in criminal cases not to be subject to the same rule? The culprit was justly condemned, and will be justly punished." [1] He then comes to handle the rights of juries in cases of libel after they had been solemnly vindicated (be it remembered) by Lord Camden, who had recently resigned the office of Chancellor, having held it for several years with general applause:—" Sir, the other charge is equally groundles and absurd. The construction of libels belongs by law and precedent to the judge and not to the jury, because it is a point of law which they are not competent to decide. If any other rule prevailed,—if the matter were left to the jury.—there would be nothing fixed and permanent in the law. It would not only vary in different counties and cities, according to their different interests and passions, but also in the minds of the same individuals, as they should happen at different times to be agitated by different humors and caprices. God forbid that the laws of England should ever be reduced to this uncertainty! All our dictionaries of decisions, all our reports, and Coke upon Littleton itself, would then be useless. Our young students, instead of coming to learn the law in the Temple and in Westminster Hall, would be obliged to seek it in the wisdom of petty juries, country assizes, and untutored mechanics.

---

[1] This case is expressly provided for by a bill I had the honor to intioduce into parliament, commonly called " Lord Campbell's Libel Act," 6 & 7 Vic. c. 96, s 7, saving the master from criminal responsibility for the unauthorized act of the servan*

Adieu to precision, adieu to consistency, adieu to decorum! All would be perplexity, contradiction, and confusion. The law would be like Joseph's coat, become nothing but a ridiculous patchwork of many shreds and many colors,—a mere sick man's dream, without coherence, without meaning—a wild chaos of jarring and heterogeneous principles, which would deviate further and further from harmony. Yet the prevention of this state is the crime with which our judges are charged! *O tempora! O mores!* to what are we at last come?" [1]

It does seem astounding to us that such a speech should be delivered, and tolerated, and applauded by the Ministers of the Crown after the Revolution, and in the latter end of the eighteenth century. It ought to be recorded, as showing the progress of public opinion and the improvements of the constitution in recent times. The matter in dispute—the Attorney General's power to file criminal informations for libel—is very immaterial. He might safely be permitted, in all cases as public prosecutor, to put parties accused on their trial, and the institution of grand juries will be preserved in this country for its collateral benefits rather than as a safeguard to innocence against unjust accusation. There is no longer any disposition in Attorney Generals to persecute the press: and if there were, no difficulty is ever experienced in inducing grand juries to find bills of indictment in any cases, however frivolous. Looking to the manner in which indictments for perjury and for conspiracy are used as instruments of revenge, vexation, and extortion, it would be a greater improvement upon our juridical institutions to enact that no such indictments shall be preferred without the sanction of a responsible public officer, than that the power of filing criminal informations should be entirely abolished.[2] But the observations by which Thurlow defended it were most insulting to public liberty,

[1] 16 Parl. Hist. 1144.
[2] During my seven years Attorney Generalship I filed only one criminal information—against Feargus O'Connor for libels in the "Northern Star," inciting the people to insurrection and plunder. There could not have been the smallest difficulty in having had an indictment found by the grand jury of the county of York, but I wished to take upon myself the whole responsibility of the prosecution. Cobbett (I think with some justice) complained that the Attorney General, instead of boldly prosecuting him by his own authority, had recourse to the subterfuge of an indictment, and by this, among other topics, obtained an acquittal.

and, if now offered by a law officer of the Crown under what is called a Tory or Conservative government, would insure his being disclaimed by his leader over night, and dismissed from his office next morning.

But Mr. Solicitor Thurlow was so much applauded and encouraged, that on Sergeant Glynn's motion soon after, for an inquiry into the administration of criminal justice, he considerably exceeded his former doings; for he not only proposed a severe censure upon the mover, but plainly intimated an opinion that trial by jury should be abolished in all cases of libel, and that the liberty of the press should be in the exclusive guardianship of a judge appointed by the Crown :--

"If," said he, " we allow every pitiful patriot thus to insult us with ridiculous accusations without making him to pay forfeit for his temerity, we shall be eternally pestered with the humming and buzzing of these stingless wasps. Though they can not wound or poison, they will tease and vex. They will divert our attention from the important affairs of state to their own mean antipathies and passions, and prejudices. I hope we shall now handle them so roughly as to make this the last of such audacious attempts. They are already ridiculous and contemptible. To crown their disgrace, let us inflict upon them some exemplary punishment. In deciding the question of libel, so many circumstances are at once to be kept in view, so many ponderous interests are to be weighed, so many comparisons to be made, and so many judgments formed, that the mind of an ordinary man is distracted, and confounded, and rendered incapable of coming to any satisfactory conclusion. None but a judge who has from his infancy been accustomed to determine intricate cases, is equal to such a difficult task. *If we even suppose the jury sufficiently enlightened to unravel those knotty points, yet there remains an insuperable objection. In state libels their passions are frequently so much engaged, that they may be justly considered as parties concerned against the Crown. No justice can therefore be expected from them in these cases.* In order to preserve the balance of our constitution, let us leave to the judge, as the most indifferent person, the right of determining the malice or innocence of the intention of the libeler. Much dust has been raised about civil and criminal actions; but to what purpose?

Is not reparation to be made to the public for any injury sustained by the public, as much as to an individual? Is the welfare of the nation in general of less consequence than that of a single person? Where then is the propriety of making such a bustle about the malice or innocence of the intention? The injury done is the only proper measure of the punishment to be be inflicted, as well as of the damage to be assessed.[1]

This tirade against trial by jury, and confounding of civil injuries to individuals with crimes against the state, proved so agreeable to the higher powers, that at the end of a month Thurlow was promoted to the office of Attorney General, in the room of De Grey, laid asleep on "the cushion of the Common Pleas;" and the Government was thereby supposed to be greatly strengthened.

When he made these speeches he was exceedingly exasperated against juries, by reason of the verdict in the case of *Rex* v. *Miller*. This was a criminal information for printing and publishing Junius's celebrated letter to the King. It was contrived that the Solicitor General, by reason of his supposed superior vigor, should conduct the trial on the part of the Crown. Notwithstanding his doctrine that the jury had nothing to do with the question whether the letter was a libel or not, he was at great pains in addressing them to impress them with an opinion of its criminality. *More suo* he thus discoursed of the liberty of the press:—"Undoubtedly the man who has indulged the liberty of robbing upon the highway, has a very considerable portion of it allotted to him. But where is the liberty of the man who is robbed? When the law is silent, reputation is invaded, tyranny is established, and an opportunity is given to venal writers to vent their malice for money against the best characters in the country. Do not, under pretense of protecting the liberty of those who do wrong, encourage them in the destruction of all laws human and divine." He then goes over the whole letter, sentence by sentence, denouncing its atrocity, and exclaiming, "For God's sake, is that no libel?" Yet he concludes by telling them, very peremptorily, that they have only to consider whether the defendant printed and published the letter, and by cautioning them not to imitate the conduct of the

[1] 16 Parl Hist. 1290.

infamous author, who had become the accuser of his King, and, attacking all mankind, had not the courage to show his face or to tell his name. The clearest evidence was given that the defendant had printed and published the letter; but after a reply from Mr. Solicitor, more furious than his opening, the jury thought fit to find a verdict of NOT GUILTY—to the unspeakable delight of the assembled crowds, who rent the air with their acclamations.[1]—What added to his mortification was, that another prosecution against Woodfall for printing and publishing the same letter was conducted by Sir William De Grey, the Attorney General himself, who, displaying much more moderation and mildness, prevailed upon the jury to find a verdict of "Guilty of printing and publishing,"—although they added the word "only," on which account a new trial was granted.[2]

Thurlow's first appearance in the House of Commons as Attorney General on the memorable occasion when Crosby, the Lord Mayor, and Oliver, an alderman of London, were brought to the bar, having discharged a printer, arrested by order of the House for publishing debates, and having committed to custody the officer of the House who executed the arrest. Alderman Oliver, instead of making any apology, said, "he owned and gloried in the fact laid to his charge; he knew that whatever punishment was intended, nothing he could say would avert it; as for himself he was perfectly unconcerned; and, as he expected little from their justice, he defied their power." A motion being then made to send him to the Tower, which was resisted by Sir George Saville and Sergeant Glynn, Mr. Attorney Thurlow, resorting to the *genus dicendi interrogans*, of which he was particularly fond, exclaimed,—

"Shall it be said, Sir, that this House is dishonored in maintaining its confirmed privileges? Is not the generosity, is not the pride, of the House alarmed by so degrading a competition? Have not the members of this House as conscientious a veneration for oaths as the Mayor of London? Or are they afraid to punish his licentiousness, when he is not afraid to insult their authority? All that's man, all that's Briton in me, is firing in my bosom while I ask these simple questions! Well may

[1] 28 St. Tr. 870-896.   [2] Ib. 895-922.

our enemies say that we have sacrificed the dearest ties that bound us to our constituents, if we now suffer the whole body of the English Commons to be trod upon by the instruments of a despicable faction. Have we so long defended our privileges against the tyranny of kings, to fall at last before the turbulence of a seditious city magistrate? Or has the constitution given us sufficient title to guard against the encroachments of the Crown, without means of crushing the ambition of an alderman?"

Mr. Attorney received a very severe chastisement from Dunning, who used language consistent with the just preservation of parliamentary privileges,—and to be forever had in remembrance as a caution against the abuse of it:—

"The people will naturally inquire how we, their representatives, have executed our trust, and will as naturally execrate our names

> 'If once we vilely turn that very power
> Which we derive from popular esteem
> To sap the bulwarks of the public freedom.'

Sir, the people have already opposed us by their magistrates, and they will oppose us further by their juries;—though were we, in fact, as much respected as we are already despised,—as much esteemed as we are universally detested,—the establishment of tyranny in ourselves, who are appointed for no purpose but to repel it in others, would expose us to the abhorrence of every good Englishman. Let us, therefore, stop where we are; let us not justify oppression by oppression, nor forget our posterity if we are regardless of our country. Let even the abject principle of self, which actuates, I fear, too many of my auditors, for once operate in the cause of virtue."

Alderman Oliver was sent to the Tower by a majority of 170 to 28, and Crosby, the Lord Mayor, by a majority of 202 to 39;[1] but, by this struggle, the right of publishing parliamentary debates was substantially established, and it is therefore to be reckoned a remarkable æra in our constitutional history.[2]

[1] 17 Parl. Hist. 58-163.
[2] The right never has been questioned since. There is still a foolish standing order of both Houses against publishing debates, but this is a mere dead

In the following session the Minister was much puzzled in meeting General Burgoyne's motion to censure the proceedings of Lord Clive in the East Indies, by which a new empire was added to the Crown of England. The considerate were aware that this extraordinary man deserved to have statues erected to him, but there was a public clamor against him which the Government was afraid to face. It was, therefore, left an open question. "Lord North himself spoke for the inquiry, but faintly and reluctantly,"[1] while the Solicitor General was required to oppose it, and the Attorney General to support it. The latter, who had no notion of ever fighting with muffled gloves, fell foul of his colleague, and of Indian conquest and Indian peculation:—

"The evils complained of," said he, "have been slurred over, or ingeniously palliated, by my honorable and learned friend. How can we better begin the work of Indian reform, which all admit to be necessary, than by resolving that the acquisitions here described are illegal? and how unjust, nugatory, and ridiculous would it be to come to such a determination without taking a retrospective view, and enforcing future regulations by present vigor! I admit that what is done in the heat and hurry of conquest, in the moment of revolution, is not to be examined too critically by the rules of school philosophy and the morality of the closet. But, Sir, these misdeeds are of a very different complexion—cool, deliberate transactions—treaties—negotiations—wars or no wars—the event the same in all—one general scene of rapine and plunder—nabobs dethroned—nabobs elected—pretended conventions with these children of power—these ephemeral sovereigns—not for the advantage of the Company, but for the profit of individuals. Did John, Duke of Marlborough, make treaties with foreign powers, stipulating that himself, Prince Eugene, and the Grand Pen-

---

letter, and the minister who would try to enforce it would be like Canute on his throne forbidding the flowing tide. Indeed, there are very few members who would now speak, if their speeches were not to be reported; and, after a division, proceedings are suspended till the reporters' gallery is re-opened — The effectual protection of the press and the public would require an enactment that no one should be liable to an action or indictment for publishing a fair and *bonâ fide* report of the proceedings of either House. I introduced a clause to this effect in my Libel Bill; but though it was warmly supported by Lord Denman, it was opposed by Lord Brougham, and I could not carry it.

[1] Gibbon to Mr. Holroyd, 11th May, 1773 Miscell Works, 1 469.

sionary should be paid so and so? To what purpose produce cases, if they are not cases in point? The oppressions of Bengal have been as severe in times of peace as in time of war. Can this be right? And if wrong, why not inquire into it? And why inquire into it, if, when your inquiry is finished, it is to produce nothing? No mode of conduct can be so weak as that which only points out crimes, but takes no measure to punish them."

Thus ran on for a long time the powerful but turbid stream of his eloquence, and, notwithstanding a touching address from Lord Clive himself,—to the great embarrassment of the Government, the resolutions were all carried by a large majority.[1]

In the beginning of 1744, Thurlow had his first encounter with Horne Tooke—in which he was foiled. The parson was brought to the bar of the House on a charge of being the author of a libelous letter in the "Morning Advertiser," addressed to Sir Fletcher Norton, the Speaker; but he did not choose to plead guilty, and, there being no evidence to prove the authorship, Mr. Attorney boisterously supported an inquisitorial motion, that certain journeyman printers from the Morning Advertiser office should be examined to know from whom they received the manuscript. He thus concluded:—

"With respect to any cruel intention against Mr. Horne, I disclaim, for one, so foul an idea. It is well known that in my official character I want no author. The printer of a libel is enough for me, and I ever think it injudicious to look beyond the printer. I am not Mr. Horne's prosecutor, and personally, I am not his enemy. Further than the cause of justice is concerned, his acquittal or conviction is to me a matter of utter indifference. If he be innocent, I shall be glad to see him discharged; but if he be guilty, I should be sorry to see a man escape with impunity who has so daringly libeled the British Commons legally assembled in parliament."

Although Mr. Burke had declared that "the motion—begot by folly, and nursed by despotism—was without a precedent in the annals of infamy," it was carried by a large majority:[2] but the printers, being called in, professed the most profound ignorance on the subject, and this time the parson walked off triumphantly.[3]

[1] 17 Parl. Hist. 850-882   [2] 132 to 44   [3] 17 Parl. l 1st 1003-1050.

As the Grenville Act was passing, Thurlow opposed it, and truly foretold that the time would come when the decisions of the committees under it would be deemed as corrupt as those of the House in a body—the distinction in practice being only that the ballot gave a petitioner or sitting member belonging to the Opposition the chance of having in the committee a majority of his own partisans;[1] whereas when the whole House sat as judges, he was almost sure to be "cast," and a decision against the ministerial candidate indicated an approaching change in the administration.

Soon afterwards, Thurlow attacked and threw out the bill for the extension of copyright, then confined to the brief period of fourteen years. He denounced the booksellers as "a set of impudent, monopolizing men, who had raised a fund of £3,000 to file bills in Chancery against any person who should endeavor to get a livelihood as well as themselves, and pretending to have an exclusive right to publish all works, from Homer's Iliad to Hawkesworth's Voyages—a mere composition of trash, for which they had the audacity to demand three guineas!"[2]

But the grand subject of parliamentary discussion now was the dispute with America. As may be supposed, Thurlow took a most zealous part, and uttered very violent language, against the colonists. He scorned the very notion of concession or conciliation; he considered "sedition" and "treason" (like *tobacco* and *potatoes*) the peculiar plants of the American soil. The natives of those regions he thought were born to be taxed; and when his friend Johnson's pamphlet, "Taxation no Tyranny," was published, he lamented that the passage was struck out which had been originally introduced as an answer to the objection that we had not previously taxed them: "We do not put a calf into the plow — we wait till he is an ox."[3]

His first explosion was in the debate upon the Coercion Bill for regulating the government of Massachusetts Bay.

---

[1] 17 Parl. Hist. 1072. I much fear that Sir R Peel's Act on this subject will be found equally inoperative; for, though there is an attempt made by it to exclude chance, and deliberately to trim the balance, unequal weight is always thrown into one scale,—and the degree to which the equipoise is destroyed becomes immaterial   [2] 17 Parl Hist. 1086-1104.

[3] *Johnson:* "They struck it out either critically as too ludicrous or politically as too exasperating —*Boswell,* ii. 327.

Charles Fox having severely attacked it, saying that there was not an American but who must reject or resist the right of taxing them, and that the bill was a clear violation of charters, Mr. Attorney answered :—

"Sir, this Bill is adopted to give magistracy the requisite authority for the execution of the laws ; being a measure of precaution, it carries with it no severity, unless the pleasure of disobeying is cheaply purchased by punishment. To say that we have a right to tax America, and never to exercise that right, is ridiculous ; and a man must abuse his own understanding very much to whom that right can appear doubtful. We are told that we should ask them to tax themselves; but to procure a tax by requisition is a most ridiculous absurdity, the sovereignty being admitted to remain in this country. Their charter is subject to our legislative power, and whoever looks into it will see that no privileges were meant to be given them inconsistent with our right to legislate for them, and to tax them when we think they ought to be taxed."

Burke took him severely to task for these expressions: but so low was the Whig minority at this time, that, on the division, they could only muster 64 to 239.[1]

In the debate which took place on the address to the Crown, shortly before hostilities commenced, Dunning having strongly objected to the term "Rebels," applied by Lord North to the Americans, Thurlow thundered out a dreadful denunciation against them, enumerating their alleged breaches of allegiance, and exclaiming, "Now, sir, if this is not rebellion, I desire the honorable and learned gentleman to tell us what is rebellion." He maintained that they were "rebels;" that they ought to be treated as such ; and that vigorous measures of coercion, before they had marshaled their armies, could alone save us from the ruin which would overtake us if their plan of independence were carried into effect.[2] This controversy was renewed in the debate upon the bill for cutting off

[1] 17 Parl. Hist. 1313.
[2] 18 Parl. Hist. 225. Lord North soon afterwards, at a City dinner, having announced the receipt of intelligence of an advantage gained over the "Rebels," and being taken to task by Charles Fox and Colonel Barrè, who were present, for applying such language to "our fellow-subjects in America," exclaimed, with inimitable talent for good-humored raillery which distinguished him, " Well, then, to please you, I will call them *the gentlemen in opposition on the other side of the water.*"— This has been told me as a traditionary anecdote not hitherto in print.

the trade of the New England colonies, when, Dunning contending that the Americans were only defending their just rights, Thurlow declared " he had deliberately given a written opinion upon papers laid before him, that there was *a rebellion* in Massachusetts Bay ; " but, the House being in committee, Sir Fletcher Norton, the Speaker, properly observed that " rebellion " was not a term known to the law, and that the only legal question was, whether there had been " a levying of war," amounting to *high treason ?* [1]

Of all the orators on the Government side in the debates which ushered in the fatal strife, Thurlow was always the most violent and exasperating ; and he seems to have been actuated by the belief that it was desirable to goad the colonists into open resistance, as they might then be effectually crushed. It is amusing to find him declaring that he did not speak, on such occasions, as a lawyer ; " that he always did, and always would, leave the lawyer in Westminster Hall, and be in that House only a member of parliament ; " [2] by which, judging from his practice, he seemed to consider that he had the privilege, which had been practiced by other Attorney Generals, and by Chancellors, too, in debate, to lay down for law what best suited his purpose at the moment. Of this he soon after gave a practical example, by declaring that there was no illegality in sending Hanoverian troops, without the authority of parliament, to garrison Gibraltar and Minorca, these places being no part of " this kingdom," so that the King might lawfully assemble a large army of foreigners in Guernsey, or Jersey, or the Isle of Man ; whereas, it seems quite clear, that by " this kingdom," in the Bill of Rights, must be understood " the British dominions." [3]

When the American Prohibitory Bill was discussed, he animadverted with scorn upon Mr. Burke's plan of conciliation. He added that, as Attorney General, he had a right, by *scire facias*, to set aside every charter in America as forfeited although he allowed that, in our present situation, such process would be justly the object of ridicule. [4]

---

[1] 18 Parl Hist 300. [2] 18 Parl Hist 609.
[3] Ib 772, 776, 1332. He at last seems to have been ashamed of his bad law—saying, " it was id'e to insist on the legality or illegality of the measure " [4] 19 Parl Hist 939.

Having introduced a bill to suspend the Habeas Corpus Act, with a view to American traitors, he defended it from the objection that it might be put in force at home, by observing that "treason and rebellion were the native growth of America." However, by way of threatening and taunting the members of Opposition, he admitted there might be some individuals in England who, by giving information and encouragement to the Americans, might be considered guilty of treason by "adhering to the King's enemies;" but it was proper that they should be narrowly watched, and that the Government should be armed with powers to counteract their projects.[1]

When the debate arose on Sir Fletcher Norton's famous speech to the King, on the occasion of presenting a bill to augment the Civil List,[2] Thurlow, in trying to do what would be agreeable at Court, sustained a signal defeat. Mr. Rigby having animadverted upon the speech as disrespectful to the Crown, and not conveying the real sentiments of the representatives of the people, the Speaker appealed to the House, and threw himself upon their judgment. Mr. Fox moved a resolution, "that the Speaker on this occasion did express, with just and proper energy, the zeal of this House for the support of the honor and dignity of the Crown in circumstances of great public charge." Sir Fletcher Norton declared that he imagined he was acting in the faithful discharge of the trust committed to him; but if the House thought otherwise, he could not, and would not, remain longer in the chair. Nevertheless, Mr. Attorney General Thurlow furiously opposed the motion, and contended that "the speech neither contained the sentiments of the House, *nor was it strictly supported by fact.*" But Fox gave him a severe castigation, and, pointing out the circumstance that the House had already unanimously thanked the Speaker for this speech, observed that the House would never consent to their own degradation and disgrace in

[1] 19 Parl Hist 9, 19, 37, 39.
[2] "In a time of public distress, full of difficulty and danger, their constituents labored under burdens almost too heavy to be borne, your faithful Commons postponed all other business, and with as much dispatch as the nature of their proceedings would admit, have not only granted to your Majesty a large present supply, but also a very great additional revenue,— great beyond example,—great beyond your Majesty's highest expense But all this, Sir, they have done in a well-grounded confidence that you will apply wisely what they have granted liberally," &c

the person of their Speaker, nor would submit to condemn on a Friday what they had highly praised on the Wednesday preceding. To Thurlow's extreme mortification, the motion was carried without a division, almost unanimously; and was followed by a fresh vote of thanks to Mr. Speaker "for his said speech to his Majesty."[1]

Early in the following session of parliament, Mr. Attorney was placed in a very ludicrous situation, which, on account of his extreme arrogance—making him dreaded both by friends and foes—seems to have caused not only general merriment, but general satisfaction Mr. Fox having moved that there be laid before the House certain papers, relating to what had been done under the Act for cutting off the Trade of the American Colonies, Thurlow rose and inveighed most bitterly against the motion, asserting that it could only proceed from a desire to countenance the "rebels," and contending that it could not be granted with any regard to the dignity of the Crown or the safety of the state. While he was still on his legs, proceeding in this strain, news was brought that in the other House, the very same motion having been made by the Duke of Grafton, the Government had acceded to it, and it had been carried unanimously. The fact was soon known by all present—and Lord North, after showing momentary symptoms of being disconcerted, joined in the titter. Thurlow pausing, the Secretary to the Treasury whispered in his ear the intelligence of what had happened "elsewhere," and the suppressed mirth broke out into a universal peal of laughter,—from the phenomenon that, once in his life, Thurlow appeared to be abashed. It was but for an instant. Quickly recovering himself, and looking sternly round at the Treasury bench, he exclaimed, "I quit the defense of administration. Let Ministers do as they please in this or any other House. As a member of parliament I never will give my vote for making public what, according to all the rules of policy, propriety, and decency, ought to be kept secret."—"*However,*" says the Parliamentary History, "*this did not stifle the laugh, which continued for some time.*"[2] Lord North was frightened, and, standing more in awe of his Attorney General than of his colleagues in the other House, he thought it best still to oppose

[1] 19 Parl. Hist. 230.   [2] Vol. xix 518.

the motion, and it was rejected by a majority of 178 to 80.[1]

We have no detailed account of any other speech of Thurlow respecting America while he remained a member of the House of Commons, but we know that his tone remained unaltered, and that when disasters began to multiply he imputed them all to the Ministers who had repealed the Stamp Act, and to the Opposition leaders, who paralyzed the energies of the country by their spurious patriotism—insisting that, as the "rebels" had recourse to arms, warlike measures of more vigor could alone be expected to decide the controversy.[2]

Before closing my account of his career as a representative of the people, I ought in justice to him to mention that he declared he would not oppose Sir George Savile's bill for the relief of Roman Catholics, and that he went so far as to say "that he highly disapproved the law which debarred a parent from the noblest of all affections, —adopting the system of education which seemed best calculated for the happiness of his beloved offspring; while he would require some consideration before he could agree to Popish priests being allowed freely to exercise the functions of their religion."[3]

Let us now attend to his forensic efforts while he was at the head of the bar,—which, I think, are more creditable to him. In *Campbell* v *Hall*, the Grenada case, upon the four-and-a-half per cent, duties, he delivered a most admirable argument in support of the power of the Crown to legislate for conquered countries; taking a luminous view of the different systems of laws to which our colonies are subject, according to the manner in which they were settled or acquired.[4]

In the Duchess of Kingston's case,—having proved that

[1] Vol. xix. 532.   [2] Ib. 587.   [3] Ib 1140.
[4] 20 St. Tr. 312. On this and similar occasions he was ably assisted by his "devils," Hargrave and Kenyon, who answered cases for him, got up special arguments, and enabled him to devote much of his time to parliament and to jovial society. Kenyon was amply rewarded for his services, being made Attorney General, Master of the Rolls, and Chief Justice of the King's Bench But poor Hargrave died neglected. He was, to be sure, with all his learning, hardly producible in any official office, and latterly his mind was diseased—insomuch that when he was brought to Lincoln's Inn to vote as a Bencher in the choice of a Preacher, and his vote was objected to, Jekyll said, that "instead of being deprived of his vote he ought to have *two* votes, for he was *one beside himself*."

the collusive sentence which she had obtained in the Ecclesiastical Court, annulling her first marriage, though binding upon her, was not binding on the House of Lords when trying her for bigamy, he thus sarcastically concluded:

"The sentence has deprived her of all conjugal claims upon Mr. Hervey; and we acknowledge it to be conclusive upon her, while we insist that it is merely void against all the rest of the world. She is therefore, according to us, a wife only for the purpose of being punished as a felon. These disappointments, these inconvenient consequences of guilt, are the bars which God and the order of nature have set against it; but they have not been found sufficient: it demands the interposition of public authority, with severe checks, to restrain it. Why is she thus hampered with the sentence she fabricated? Because she fabricated it; because justice will not permit her to allege her own fraud for her own benefit, nor hear her complain of a wrong done by herself. She displays to your Lordships not an anxiety to clear her injured innocence, but a dread of inquiry. Was this her solicitude to bring the question here? In such a Court, before so venerable an audience, we are to hear nothing pleaded against a charge of infamy but a frivolous objection to enter upon the trial."

The plea being overruled, Thurlow proceeded to state the facts of the case against her. His proemium is in a better taste than he often displays:—

" My Lords, it seems to be matter of just surprise that, before the commencement of the last century, no secular punishment had been provided for a crime of this malignant complexion and pernicious example. Perhaps the innocence of simpler ages, or the more prevailing influence of religion, or the severity of ecclesiastical censures, together with those calamities which naturally and necessarily follow such an enormity, might formerly have been found sufficient to restrain it. From the moment these causes ceased to produce that effect, imagination can scarcely figure a crime that calls more loudly for the interposition of penal legislation; a crime which, besides the gross and open scandal given by it to religion, implies more cruel disappointment to the just and honorable expectation of the person betrayed by it; which tends more to corrupt the purity of domestic life, and to loosen those sacred connections and close relations designed by Providence to bind the moral world together; or which may create more civil disorder, especially in a country where the title to great honors and high office is hereditary. My Lords, the misfortunes of individuals, the corruption of private life, the confusion of domestic relations, the disorder of civil succession, and the offenses done to religion, are suggested as aggravations not of the particular case now under trial, but as miseries likely to arise from the example of the crime in general; and are laid before your Lordships only to call your attention to the course and order of the trial, and that there may be no misconception to mitigate the atrocity of such a violation of law, or to heighten the dangers with which it threatens the peace of families and the public welfare. The present case, to state it justly and fairly, is stript of much of its aggravation. The advanced age of the parties, and their previous habits of life, would reduce many of these general articles of criminality and mischief to idle topics of empty declamation. No part of the present complaint turns upon any ruin brought on the blameless character of injured innocence; or to any disappointment occasioned to just and honorable pretensions, or to any corruption supposed to be introduced where modesty before prevailed. Nor should I expect much serious attention from your Lordships if I should urge, as aggravations of the lady's guilt, the danger of entailing an uncertain condition upon a helpless offspring, or the apprehension of a disputed succession to the illustrious house of Pierrepont. But your Lordships will likewise bear in mind, that every mitigation which might have induced you to pity an unfortunate passion in younger bosoms is entirely cut off here. If it be true that the sacred rights of matrimony have been violated, I am afraid it must also appear that dry lucre was the whole inducement—cold fraud the only means to perpetrate the crime. In truth, the evidence (if I am rightly instructed) will clearly and expressly represent it as a matter of perfect indifference to the prisoner which husband she adhered to, so that the profit to be drawn from this marriage, or from that, was tolerably equal. The crime, if less revolting in some particulars, becomes only more odious in others. The facts which I will now, with all simplicity, detail, form a case which it would be quite impossible to aggravate, and which it will be extremely difficult to extenuate."

He then gave an interesting narrative of the two marriages, of the sham sentence of nullity, excusing the Ecclesiastical Court by the quotation—

> "For oft though wisdom wake, suspicion sleeps
> At wisdom's gate, and to simplicity
> Resigns her charge; while goodness thinks no ill
> Where no ill seems ———."

After the verdict of *Guilty*, Thurlow, in a strain of rather coarse banter, argued that the Duchess was liable either to be hanged or to be branded with a hot iron, although he must have been aware that she was entitled by her privilege of peerage, for her first felony to go scot free.[1]

His next encounter in a court of justice was with a much more formidable antagonist. On news arriving of the battle of Lexington, a meeting to "sympathize with the Americans" was held in the City; and Parson Horne, who superintended it, drew up a minute of its proceedings, which he published in the newspapers—stating that a subscription was to be raised "to be applied to the relief of the widows, orphans, and aged parents of our beloved American fellow subjects, who faithful to the character of Englishmen, preferring death to slavery, were for that reason only inhumanly murdered by the King's troops at Lexington, in the province of Massachusetts." For this an *ex officio* information had been filed against him, which came on for trial at Guildhall, before Lord Mansfield and a special jury. Mr. Horne was his own counsel, and entered the court resolved to proceed to the utmost lengths in assailing both the Judge and the prosecutor; but he was new to his situation, and did not display much of the cleverness for which he was justly celebrated—while Thurlow fought on his own dunghill, and throughout the

[1] 20 St Tr. 355–651 By 4 & 5 Vict. c 22, passed after the trial of Lord Cardigan, it is enacted, that when an indictment is found against a Peer he shall have no privilege, except "to be tried by his Peers, and that upon conviction he shall be liable to the same punishment as the rest of her Majesty's subjects."—No invidious distinction of the peerage now exists, except the action of *Scan. Mag.* I intended to include the abolition of this in my Libel Bill, but I found the manner of doing it very difficult, for the action rests on statutes which merely forbid the telling of lies, and the spreading of false reports of great men—which it would appear rather absurd to repeal.

whole day had the advantage over him.¹ The most
amusing scene during the trial was when the defendant
insisted on calling the Attorney General as his witness;
but Lord Mansfield held that none of the questions proposed to be put to him were relevant. The jury, with
little hesitation, brought in a verdict of *Guilty.*

Thurlow, in a manner which astonishes a modern Attorney General, eagerly pressed that the defendant, who
was an ordained clergyman of the Church of England,
who was a scholar and a gentleman, should be set in the
pillory. Speaking in aggravation of punishment,—after
observing that any fine would be paid by a seditious subscription, and that imprisonment would be "a slight inconvenience to one of sedentary habits," he thus proceeded:—

"Pillory, my Lords, is the most appropriate punishment for this species of offense, and has been so these two
hundred years—not only while such prosecutions were
rank in the Star Chamber, but since the Star Chamber
was abolished, in the best times since the Revolution.
Tutchin was set in the pillory by Chief Justice Holt.
That libeler, to be sure, complained of being subjected
to the punishment which he said ought to have been reserved for fraudulent bakers. He conceived that the
falsifying of weights and measures was a more mechanical
employment than the forging of lies, and that it was less
gentleman-like to rob men of their money than of their
good name. But this is a peculiarity which belongs to
the little vanity which inspires an author, and it made no
impression upon Sir John Holt, whose name will live
with honor as long as the English constitution. Government can not exist unless, when offenses of this magnitude
are presented to a court of justice, the full measure of
punishment is inflicted upon them. Let us preserve the
restraint against licentiousness provided by the wisdom
of past ages. I should have been very sorry to have

---

¹ If a defendant under such circumstances has the requisite qualifications
for defending himself, he has a far better chance of acquittal being his own
counsel, than with the most eloquent man at the bar to speak for him; but
the self-defense is generally so unskillful that it is sure to end in conviction.
I only recollect two instances to the contrary—Mr Perry obtained a signal
triumph over Sir Vicary Gibbs, and Mr Cobbett over Sir Thomas Denman.
But the latter defendant only succeeded from the experience he had acquired
from several failures In his first contest with Sir James Scarlett he was
very feeble and awkward, and he fell an easy prey to his powerful antagonist.

brought this man before you, in a case attended with so many aggravations, if your Lordships were not to show your sense of his infamy by sentencing him to an infamous punishment."

The sentence, however, was only a fine of £200, and a year's imprisonment; and even Dr. Johnson, inquiring about it, said, "I hope they did not put the dog in the pillory; he has too much literature for that."[1] During this imprisonment the defendant wrote his letter to Mr. Dunning on the "English Particle," which he enlarged into his "Επεα πτεροεντα, or the Diversions of Purley."—Notwithstanding Thurlow's vigorous push to set him in the pillory (as we shall see), they were subsequently reconciled; and the ex-Chancellor, visiting the ex-Libeller in his retreat at Wimbledon, discussed with him questions of philology.

Towards the close of the American War, Mr. Attorney General Thurlow filled a great space in the public eye, and was considered the chief prop of the Government. It is certainly difficult for us to understand his high parliamentary reputation. I have already noticed all his reported speeches of the slightest consequence while he remained a member of the House of Commons, and none of them contain anything like logical reasoning or statesmanlike views, or even good declamation. The defectiveness of the printed reports can not explain the disappointment we feel, for we have most admirable specimens of contemporary speakers—not only of Burke, who carefully edited his own orations, but of Lord Chatham, Dunning, and Lord North,—and even his colleague, the Solicitor General, appears in the "Parliamentary History" to much greater advantage. He must surely have displayed qualities which we can not justly appreciate, to have been so favorably introduced into the graphic sketch of the House of Commons at this period, from personal observation, by the author of THE DECLINE AND FALL OF THE ROMAN EMPIRE: "The cause of government was ably vindicated by Lord North, a statesman of spotless integrity, a consummate master of debate, who could wield with equal dexterity the arms of reason and of ridicule. He was seated on the Treasury bench between his Attor-

[1] Bos III. 382. Johnson added, "Were I to make a new edition of my Dictionary I would adopt several of Mr Horne's etymologies."

ney and Solicitor General, the two pillars of the law and state, *magis pares quam similes;* and the minister might indulge in a short slumber, whilst he was upholden on either hand by the majestic sense of Thurlow, and the skillful eloquence of Wedderburn."[1] Whatever others might think of him, he gave high satisfaction to his employers. Above all, the King was excessively delighted with his strong and uncompromising language respecting the Americans, and long placed a greater personal confidence in him than he had done in Lord Bute, or than he ever did in any other minister—perhaps with the exception of Lord Eldon.

The Government being hard pressed in debate, though strong in numbers in the House of Lords, and the general inefficiency of Lord Bathurst producing serious inconvenience to the public service, it was resolved to accept the offer he had made to resign his office of Chancellor,—and there was not a moment's hesitation about his successor.

CHAPTER CLVII.

CONTINUATION OF THE LIFE OF LORD THURLOW TILL THE RESIGNATION OF LORD NORTH, AND THE FORMATION OF THE SECOND ROCKINGHAM ADMINISTRATION.

THE transfer of the Great Seal took place at a council held at St. James's, on the 3rd of June, 1778, when Thurlow was sworn in Lord Chancellor, and a member of the Privy Council; and on the first day of the following Trinity Term, after a procession from his house in Great Ormond Street to Westminster Hall, he was installed in the Court of Chancery with all the usual solemnities.[2] At the same time, he was raised to the

[1] Gib Mem 1. 146.
[2] "3rd June, 1778 Memorandum.—The Right Honorable Henry, Earl Bathurst, Lord High Chancellor of Great Britain, delivered the Great Seal to his Majesty in Council. His Majesty, on the said 3rd day of June, delivered it to Edward Thurlow, Esq , with the title of Lord Chancellor of Great Britain, who was thereupon, by his Majesty's command, sworn of the Privy Council, and likewise Lord High Chancellor of Great Britain, and took his place at the board accordingly, and on Friday, the 19th of June, went in state from his house in Great Ormond Street to Westminster Hall, accompanied by the Judges, Serjeants, &c , where, in their presence, he took

peerage by the title of BARON THURLOW, of Ashfield, in the county of Suffolk.

A striking homage was now paid to his success by Cowper the poet, who, though sincere and disinterested, exaggerated his merits and was blind to his imperfections, from a tender recollection of their intimacy when brother pupils and idlers in the office of Mr. Chapman, in Lincoln's Inn :—

> " Round Thurlow's head in early youth,
> And in his sportive days,
> Fair Science pour'd the light of truth,
> And Genius shed his ray.
>
> " 'See,' with united wonder, cried
> Th' experienc'd and the sage,
> 'Ambition in a boy supplied
> With all the skill of age !
>
> " 'Discernment, eloquence, and grace,
> Proclaim him born to sway
> The balance in the highest place,
> And bear the palm away.'
>
> " The praise bestow'd was just and wise;
> He sprang impetuous forth
> Secure of conquest, where the prize
> Attends superior worth.
>
> " So the best courser on the plain
> Ere yet he starts is known,
> And does but at the goal obtain
> What all had deemed his own."

The new Chancellor did not disappoint public expectation, and, as long as he enjoyed the *prestige* of office, he contrived to persuade mankind that he was a great judge, a great orator, and a great statesman,—although I am afraid that in all these capacities he was considerably overrated, and that he owed his temporary reputation very much to his high pretensions and his awe-inspiring manners.

He was tolerably well qualified to preside in the Court of Chancery, from his natural shrewdness, from the knowledge of law which he had acquired by fits and starts, and from his having been for some years in full practice as an equity counsel. But he had never devoted himself to jurisprudence systematically; he was almost entirely un-

the oaths of allegiance and supremacy, and the oath of the Lord Chancellor of Great Britain, the Master of the Rolls holding the book, and the Deputy Clerk of the Crown reading the said oaths Which being done, the Solicitor General moved that it might be recorded, and it was ordered accordingly."— *Cr Off. Min Book*, No 2, 1 25

acquainted with the Roman civil law, as well as with the modern codes of the continental nations; and, unlike Lord Nottingham, Lord Hardwicke, and the Chancellors whose memories we venerate, upon his elevation to the bench he despised the notion of entering on a laborious course of study to refresh and extend his juridical acquirements. Much engrossed by politics, and spending a large portion of his time in convivial society or in idle gossip with his old coffee-house friends, he was contented if he could only get through the business of his court without complaints being made against him by the suitors, or any very loud murmurs from the public. Permanent fame he disregarded or despised. He was above all taint or suspicion of corruption, and in his general rudeness he was very impartial: but he was not patient and painstaking; he sometimes dealt recklessly with the rights which he had to determine; and he did little in settling controverted questions, or establishing general principles. Having been at the head of the law of this country nearly thirteen years, he never issued an order to correct any of the abuses of his own court, and he never brought forward in parliament any measure to improve the administration of justice.

He is said to have called in Hargrave, the very learned editor of Coke upon Littleton, to assist him in preparing his judgments, and some of them show labor and research; but he generally seems to have decided off-hand, without much anxiety about former authorities.

Frequently he employed Mr. Justice Buller, a singularly acute special pleader and nisi prius lawyer, to sit for him in the Court of Chancery. On resuming his seat, he would highly eulogize the decisions of "one whom he, in common with all the word, felt bound to respect and admire." But being privately asked "how Buller had acquired his knowledge of Equity?" "Equity!" said he, "he knows no more of it than a horse; but he disposes somehow of the cases, and I seldom hear more of them."

So fiercely did he spring on a luckless counsel or solicitor, that he generally went by the name of the "Tiger;" and sometimes they would, out of compliment, call him the "Lion,"—adding that Hargrave was his "*provider.*"

His habit of profane swearing he could not always control, even when on the bench; and those who were sitting under him, near the Mace and the Purse, occasionally heard a muttering of strange oaths. Yet some supposed that, in reality, he had a great deal of good humor under an ostentatiously rough exterior, and of this he would occasionally give symptoms. It is related that once, at the adjournment of the court for the long vacation, he was withdrawing without taking the usual leave of the Bar, when a young barrister exclaimed in a stage whisper —"He might at least have said d——n you!" The Chancellor, hearing the remark, returned and politely made his bow.[1]

Thurlow is handed down to us, as a Judge, by Brown, Vesey, Jr., and Dickens. It may be partly their fault, but he certainly appears in their Reports to little advantage. His judgments are not only immeasurably inferior to those of such a consummate master of juridical reasoning as Sir William Grant, but are not by any means equal to those of Pepper Arden, for whom Thurlow was accustomed to testify such ineffable contempt.

I will bring before the reader a few of his decisions which appear to me to be the most important and interesting. In *Bishop of London* v. *Fytche*,[2] the question arose, "whether bonds given by an incumbent to the patron of a living for resigning on request, are lawful?" In the Court of Chancery, Thurlow gave a strong opinion in favor of their legality, insisting that they not only were not simoniacal, but that they were not contrary to public policy, and that, being properly controlled by a court of equity, they might be very salutary. He expressed a contrary opinion, however, when the question came before the House of Lords. The Judges, being consulted, were divided upon it, and, the Bishops voting with him, there was a reversal, by a majority of 19 to 18 ; so that general resignation bonds have since been unlawful.[3]

In *Cason* v. *Dale*, Lord Chancellor Thurlow held, upon the "Statute of Frauds," which requires that a will of lands shall be subscribed by the witnesses in the *presence* of the testator, that a will was well executed where a lady who made it, having signed it in an attorney's office, got

---
[1] Hawkin's Memoirs, ii 312.   [2] 1 Brown, 96
[3] Brown's Parl Cas ii 211. See *Fletcher* v *Lord Sondes*, 3 Bingham, 594; 7 & 8 George IV c 25, s 1, 9 Ib c 25 s 94

into her carriage, and the carriage was accidentally backed by the coachman opposite to the window of the office, so that, if she had been inclined, she might have let down the glass of the carriage, and seen the witnesses subscribe the will.[1]

In *Jones* v. *Morgan*,[2] in which the industry of Mr. Hargrave may be pretty clearly traced, the Chancellor obtained great glory by overturning a decision of Lord Hardwicke, and holding that the same construction is to be given to limitations in wills of trusts and legal estates. He likewise delivered a very elaborate judgment in *Pultney* v. *Earl of Darlington*[3] (which could hardly have been composed by Hargrave, for he was counsel in the cause), establishing the doctrine now recognized that where either land is directed to be converted into money, or money to be laid out in land—from the moment the direction might have been executed, the property receives the impression either of personalty or realty, with all the incidents of either estate. This case being brought before the House of Lords by appeal, the decree was affirmed.

Thurlow's decision in *Ackroyd* v. *Smithson*[4] was the foundation of Lord Eldon's fortune at the bar, and may be said to have made him Lord Chancellor. A testator ordered his real and personal property to be sold, and the fund to be divided among certain legatees. Two of them died in his lifetime. The question was, what was to become of their shares? Sir Thomas Sewell, M R., held, against the argument of Mr. Scott, who, after being above a year briefless, had a guinea brief for the heir at law, that the whole should be distributed among the surviving legatees. Upon an appeal brought by other parties, Mr. Scott had another guinea brief to consent, on the part of the heir at law, to an affirmance; but, having a strong opinion that he was right, he argued the case so zealously and ably, that Thurlow was much struck with the manner of the unknown counsel, and, after high compliments to him, reversed the decree,—deciding that the shares of the

---

[1] Brown, 39, Dickens, 586. But it is necessary that the testator should be in such a position as that, by possibility, he may have seen the witnesses sign the will if so disposed, *Doe* v. *Manifold*, 1 Maule & Selw 294, although if he might see them from any one part of a room in which he was, and there be no evidence in what part of the room he was placed, it will be presumed that he was where he might have seen the witnesses *Winchelsea* v *Wauchope*, 3 Russ. 444.   [2] 1 Brown, 206.   [3] Ibid 223   [4] Ibid 503.

deceased legatees were lapsed legacies, and that so much of them as arose out of the real estate should go to the heir at law.

In *Newman* v. *Wallis*,[1] our Chancellor most unaccountably held, with great positiveness, that where a plaintiff claims an estate as an heir at law, and prays a discovery, it is not a good plea *that he is not heir at law;* but in the subsequent case of *Hall* v. *Noyes*,[2] he was driven to retract this opinion, and it is now fully settled that such a plea is good, although a defendant can not, by a plea denying the principal fact, evade a discovery of the collateral facts connected with it.

In the *Countess of Strathmore* v. *Bowes*,[3] where the lady had settled all her property to her separate use, meaning to marry one man, and then, by a stratagem, was induced to marry another, who was ignorant of the settlement, Thurlow established the settlement against the husband, observing, in his characteristic manner:—

"As to the morality of the transaction, I shall say nothing. They seem to have been pretty well matched. Marriage in general seems to have been Lady Strathmore's object; she was disposed to marry anybody, so that at the same time she might keep her fortune to herself. But the question is, has there been a fraud upon the husband? It is impossible for a man marrying in the manner Bowes did, to come into Equity and talk of fraud."

Ex parte O'Reilly[4] was the first of a long string of opera-house cases, which have perplexed Chancellors ever since. The Italian Opera House, in the Haymarket, having been burnt down, a patent for thirty-one years had been granted to the petitioner to enable him to build a new theater upon the site of Leicester House, in Leicester Square; and the question was, whether the Great Seal should be put to this patent? The grant was opposed by the patentees of all the other theaters, and by incumbrancers and others who had an interest in them. After a hearing of four days, Thurlow said:—

"All parties seem to agree that an opera house is a proper establishment in this country, but you will not expect me to determine which of these plans is the best. My office is to see that the King is not deceived, and

[1] 2 Brown, 143   [2] 3 Ib. 489.   [3] 1 Vesey, Jr. 22.   [4] Ib. 112.

that he does not part with any authority which he ought to retain. Many considerations require that public establishments of this nature should be in the hands of the King. In the time of James I., as in the time of Queen Elizabeth, masques and such diversions were under the direction of the Crown—executed partly by the Lord Chamberlain, but more immediately by the Master of the Revels. On the same notion the patent was granted by Charles II. to Killigrew and Davenant, and by Queen Anne to Collier and Sir Richard Steele. But this patent is bad, as it contains covenants with the Lord Chamberlain, and it does not sufficiently connect the grant with the property. It is calculated to create innumerable law suits. I should soon be obliged to direct the Master to take the management of the opera house into his own hands—a task for which, I may venture to say, all the Masters, notwithstanding their great learning and experience as officers of this Court, are as unfit as myself. Dismissing the petition, I shall make a fit representation on the subject to his Majesty, who, I am sure, will do justice to the parties and to the public."

Thurlow generally disdained to resort to the practice, now very common, and found highly beneficial, of delivering written judgments; but I find one judgment, which the Reporter says, " his Lordship having read, gave it to me,"—and I do very much suspect that it is the composition of his " devil," for the style of it is very quiet and moderate, and it enters a good deal into the civil law. The case is *Scott* v *Tyler*, in which the important question arose, whether a condition annexed to a legacy, "that the legatee shall not marry without the consent of her mother," be void, as being in restraint of marriage, so that the legacy shall be considered absolute ?—

"To support the affirmative," he said, "innumerable decisions of this court were quoted; but the cases are so short, and the dicta so general as to afford me no distinct view of the principle upon which the rule is laid down, or, consequently, of the extent of the rule, or of the nature of the exceptions to which its own principle makes it liable." Having given the history of the decisions on the subject in this country, and stated how it is reviewed by the canon law, he proceeds:—" *By* the civil law the provision of a child was considered a debt of nature, the payment of which the prætor would enforce; insomuch, that a will was regarded as *inofficious* by which the child was disinherited without just cause. By the positive institutions of that law, it was also declared, *Si quis cælibatus, vel viduitatis conditionem hæredi, legatoriove injunxerit ; hæres, legatoriusve è conditione liberi sunto ; neque eo minus delatam hæreditatem, legatumve, ex hac lege, consequantur.* In ampliation of this law, it seems to have been well settled in all times, that if, instead of creating a condition absolutely enjoining celibacy, or widowhood, the matter be referred to the advice or discretion of another, particularly an interested person, it is deemed a fraud on the law, and treated accordingly; that is, the condition so imposed is holden for void. On the other hand, the ancient rule of the civil law has suffered much limitation in descending to us. The case of widowhood is altogether excepted by the NOVELS; and injunctions to keep that state are made lawful conditions. So is every condition which does not directly or indirectly import an absolute injunction to celibacy. Therefore, an injunction to ask consent, or not to marry a widow, is not unlawful. A condition to marry or not to marry Titius or Mœvia is good, for this reason, that it implies no general restraint; besides, in the first case, it seems to have in view a bounty to Titus or Mœvia. In like manner the injunction which prescribes due ceremonies, and the place of marriage, is a lawful condition, and is not understood as operating the general prohibition of marriage. Still more is a condition good which only limits the time to twenty-one or any other reasonable age, provided this be not evasively used as a covered purpose to restrain marriage generally."

After proceeding in this tone at great length—without abusing anybody, or uttering anything approaching to imprecation—he dryly decides, that the young lady, having married at eighteen without her mother's consent, was not entitled to the legacy. Perhaps, in the delivery, a few strong expletives were interpolated, to avoid the suspicion that the real author was the meek and placid Hargrave.[1]

[1] 2 Dickens, 712 —My conjecture on this subject has been substantially verified by discovering that Hargrave was counsel for the winning party in *Scott v. Tyler*, and that at the Chancellor's request he furnished him with a

In Thurlow's time there were heavy complaints of delays in Chancery. These, no doubt, arose in some measure from the peculiar nature of equity suits, which, often being between a mutiplicity of parties, and depending on complicated inquiries, are not capable of being rapidly settled like a single issue of fact in an action at law—but there seems reason to think that arrears accumulated for the want of industry and exertion on the part of the Judge. He was rather pleased to be called away to Cabinets and to the House of Lords, and he would not make that sacrifice of time out of court to the consideration of pending cases without which no Judge can do justice to himself or the suitors. He went on uncomfortably with his Master of the Rolls, except for the short time that Sir Lloyd Kenyon held that office; he was at variance with Sir Thomas Sewell; and he contemptuously refused to co-operate with Pepper Arden, whose appointment he had strenuously opposed,—saying to Mr. Pitt, "I care not whom the devil you appoint, so that he does not throw his own damned wallet on my shoulders, instead of lightening my burden."

To finish the sketch of Thurlow as a Judge, it may be convenient to state here that he gave considerable satisfaction in disposing of writs of error and appeals in the House of Lords. In all English cases, he summoned the Judges, and was guided by their opinion. The Scotch cases sometimes puzzled him, as he was neither a great feudalist nor civilian, but his own practice in Scotch appeals when at the bar, had rendered him tolerably familiar with the procedure of the Court of Session: after the able arguments at the bar, he could generally guess at the conclusion with considerable confidence ; and he had always in reserve the comfortable resource of affirming without giving any reasons.

The most important case which the House decided by his advice was *Bruce* v. *Bruce*—in which, Major Bruce, a son of the famous Abyssinian traveler, having been born in Scotland, and having died in India, in the service of the East India Company, the question arose by what law the succession to his personal property, which was partly in India and partly in England, was to be governed? The

opy of his carefully composed argument.—*Judicial Exercitations*, p. 179. *Note to 3rd edition.*)

Court of Session decided that the law of England should prevail as the *lex loci rei sitæ*. Lord Thurlow was of opinion that the judgment was right—but only on the ground that the intestate had died *domiciled* in India. When he agreed with the decision of the court below, he had hitherto simply declared that the judgment was affirmed On this occasion, however, he spoke as follows:

"As I have no doubt that the decree ought to be affirmed, I would not have troubled your Lordships by delivering my reasons, had I not been pressed with some anxiety from the bar, that if there was to be an affirmance, the grounds of the determination should be stated,—to prevent its being understood that the whole doctrine laid down by the Judges of the Court of Session had the sanction of this House. The true ground upon which the cause turns is the Indian domicile. The deceased was born in Scotland , but a person's origin is only one circumstance to be regarded in considering by what law the succession to his personal property is to be regulated. A person being at a place is, *primâ facie*, evidence that he is domiciled at that place. It may be rebutted, no doubt. A person may be traveling , on a visit; he may be there for a time, on account of health or business. A soldier may be ordered to Flanders, and an ambassador may be sent to Madrid, where they may remain many months; England is still their domicile or home. But if a British man settles as a merchant abroad, and carries on business there, enjoying the privileges of the place, and dies there, his original domicile is gone ; although, had he survived, he might possibly have returned to end his days in his native country. Let it be granted that Major Bruce meant to return to Scotland ; he then meant to change his domicile, but he died before actually changing it. All the discussion we have had respecting the *lex loci rei sitæ* is immaterial. Personal property, in point of law, has no locality; and, in case of the decease of the owner, must go wherever, in point of fact, situate, according to the law of the country where he had his domicile. To say that the *lex loci rei sitæ* is to govern the succession to personal as it does to real property, the *domicilium* of the deceased being without contradiction in another country, is a gross misapplication of the rules of the civil law and *jus gentium:* though the law of Scotland, on this point, is constantly asserted to be founded upon them." [1]

Thurlow took his seat in the House of Lords, rather irregularly, on the 14th of July, 1778,—to which day parliament had been prorogued at the conclusion of the preceding session. The Houses now met, not for the dispatch of business, but only to be again prorogued: and, without a speech from the throne stating the causes of the summons, I doubt whether any business whatever can properly be done. Perhaps Thurlow ought to have merely occupied the woolsack as Speaker—but the Journal of this day contains the following entry.—

"The Lord Viscount Weymouth signified to the House that his Majesty had been pleased to create Edward Thurlow, Esq, Lord High Chancellor of Great Britain, a Baron, by the style and title of Baron Thurlow, of Ashfield, in the county of Suffolk: whereupon his Lordship, taking in his hand the purse with the Great Seal, retired to the lower end of the House, and, having there put on his robes, was introduced between the Lord Osborne and Lord Amherst, also in their robes; the Yeoman Usher of the Black Rod, Clarencieux, King at Arms (who in the absence of Garter officiated on this occasion), in his coat of arms, carrying his Lordship's patent (which he delivered to him at the steps before the throne), and the Earl of Clarendon (who officiated in the ceremony in the absence of the Lord Great Chamberlain of England) preceding. His Lordship (after three obeisances) laid down his letters patent upon the chair of state, and from thence took and delivered them to the clerk, who read the same at the table," &c. The entry goes on to state the writ of summons, the taking of the oaths, &c., and that his Lordship "was afterwards placed on the lower end of the Baron's bench, and from thence went to the upper end of the Earl's bench, and sat there as Lord Chancellor, and then his Lordship returned to the woolsack. Clarencieux, King at Arms, delivered in at the table his Lordship's pedigree, pursuant to the standing order."

The prorogation then took place. At the opening of

---

[1] Robertson's *Law of Personal Succession*, 121 A still more important case from Scotland, before Lord Thurlow, on the conflict of laws was *Hog* v. *Lashley*, (ib 126), but as he simply affirmed, without saying a word upon

the session of parliament, on the 26th of November following, the Lord Chancellor, on his knee, delivered to George III. the royal speech, announcing that France had gone to war, and was assisting the revolted colonies in America.[1] He abstained from taking part in the debate which followed upon the address; but on Lord Rockingham's motion, a few days after, respecting the proclamation issued by the English commissioners in America, he made his maiden speech as a Peer, and showed that he had not changed his disposition with his rank. He at once poured red-hot shot into the whole of the Opposition. He began with Hinchcliffe, Bishop of Peterborough, who had inveighed against the employment of savages in carrying on the war in America,—had objected to an item in the army extraordinaries, "scalping-knives and crucifixes for the Indians,"—had declared that, if such were the Christianity we were to teach them, it would be better that they should never hear of the name of Christ,—and was understood to lament the "fruitless desolation" which such measures produced. *Lord Chancellor:* "The Right Reverend Prelate talks of 'fruitless desolation.'—an expression which carries no meaning, and is neither sense nor grammar. It is not supported by any figure of speech, or by any logic, or even by any vulgarism that I ever heard of. 'Fruitless desolation,' my Lords, is rank nonsense. I was not aware before that 'desolation' might be 'fruitful.' To negative what is not to be found in nature, and what the imagination can not conceive, is a species of oratory not wholly incongruous, but so nonsensical that it admits of no answer." He next addressed himself to an observation of the Duke of Grafton, who had said that Ministers carried their measures by corruption: "This," he said, "was well calculated for the temporary purpose of debate, as it required no proof, and admitted of no refutation; and this was all that was intended by it; but he hoped that it would have a contrary effect, and that an impartial nation would honor and respect those against whom nothing could be brought except such indiscriminate and ill-founded charges." He then attacked the Duke of Rich-

any of the important questions which it involved, I must reluctantly pass it over without further notice.
[1] 19 Parl. Hist. 1277.

mond and Lord Shelburne with equal acrimony, and concluded by declaring that, "having in vain appealed to the reason and good sense of America, the only course was to endeavor to influence by their fears those who could not be wrought upon by the nobler principles of affection, generosity, or gratitude."—The Bishop of Peterborough, explaining, said the expression he had used was "fruitless evils," not "fruitless desolation;" although he contended that a desolation, from which no good consequences were ever promised or expected, might well be termed a "fruitless desolation."—The *Lord Chancellor:* "I beg pardon of the Right Reverend Prelate, if I have mistaken his words. But, my Lords, I am equally at a loss to know what sort of 'evils' are 'fruitful'—except of evil. Are some evils productive of good? Let the Right Reverend Prelate more distinctly classify his evils; for at present I am at a loss to distinguish between evils that are fruitless and evils that are fruitful." He had an explanation almost equally uncourteous with Lord Shelburne; but he received a calm and dignified rebuke from Lord Camden who asserted the import of the proclamation in question to be—"We have tried our strength; we find ourselves incapable of conquest, and as we can't subdue we are determined to destroy." As yet the Opposition in the Lords could only muster 37 to 71.[1]

Thurlow spoke several times on the bill for allowing Keppel to be tried by a naval court-martial on shore,—allowing it to pass pretty quietly after a few sarcasms on the Admiral and his supporters.[2] He then caused considerable dissatisfaction in the House, by at first refusing to put a motion, which had been regularly made, for the erection of a bar between the woolsack and the steps of the throne,—on the ground that the object of it was to accommodate members of the House of Commons,—which was contrary to the standing order for the exclusion of strangers;—but he was forced to put it, and to negative it by the ministerial majority.[3] On other occasions, about this time, his manner gave offense to several Peers, and by way of apology he declared "that he never presumed to rise and control the sense of the House, but in instances in which the form of their proceedings was about to be departed from."[4]

[1] 20 Parl. Hist. 1–46   [2] Ib. 94, 95, 102, 105, 110   [3] Ib. 470, 473   [4] Ib.588.

He was becoming highly unpopular; and as his demeanor on the woolsack was very much like that of Lord Chancellor Jeffreys, if a proper course had been pursued to check him, he might have been put down as effectually; but, luckily for him, instead of being reprimanded for his arrogant manners, he was taunted with his mean birth,— an opportunity was offered to him, which he daringly and dexterously improved, of exalting himself, and the suppressed rebellion ended in his establishing a permanent tyranny over the whole body of the Peerage. We have a very lively account of this scene from an eye-witness:—

"At times," says Mr. Butler in his Reminiscences, "Lord Thurlow was superlatively great. It was the good fortune of the reminiscent to hear his celebrated reply to the Duke of Grafton during the inquiry into Lord Sandwich's administration of Greenwich Hospital. His Grace's action and delivery; when he addressed the House, were singularly dignified and graceful; but his matter was not equal to his manner. He reproached Lord Thurlow with his plebeian extraction and his recent admission into the Peerage; particular circumstances caused Lord Thurlow's reply to make a deep impression on the reminiscent. His Lordship had spoken too often, and began to be heard with a civil but visible impatience.[1] Under these circumstances he was attacked in the manner we have mentioned. He rose from the woolsack, and advanced slowly to the place from which the Chancellor generally addresses the House;[2] then, fixing on the Duke the look of Jove when he grasped the thunder, 'I am amazed,' he said in a loud tone of voice, 'at the attack the noble Duke has made on me. Yes, my Lords,' considerably raising his voice, 'I am amazed at his Grace's speech. The noble Duke can not look before him, behind him, or on either side of him, without seeing some noble Peer who owes his seat in this House to successful exertions in the profession to which I belong. Does he not feel that it is as honorable to owe it to these, as to being the accident of an accident? To all these noble Lords the language of the noble Duke is as applicable and as insulting as it is to myself. But I don't fear to

---

[1] I conjecture that he had given umbrage by his dictatorial tone much more than by the frequency of his speeches.
[2] The top of the Duke's bench.

meet it single and alone. No one venerates the Peerage more than I do,—but my Lords, I must say that the Peerage solicited me, not I the Peerage. Nay, more, I can say, and will say, that as a Peer of Parliament, as Speaker of this right honorable House, as Keeper of the Great Seal, as guardian of his Majesty's conscience, as Lord High Chancellor of England, nay, even in that character alone in which the noble Duke would think it an affront to be considered—as a MAN—I am at this moment as respectable—I beg leave to add, I am at this moment as much respected—as the proudest Peer I now look down upon." The effect of this speech, both within the walls of Parliament and out of them, was prodigious. It gave Lord Thurlow an ascendency in the House which no Chancellor had ever possessed; it invested him in public opinion with a character of independence and honor; and this, though he was ever on the unpopular side in politics, made him always popular with the people."[2]

I myself have seen striking instances in a public assembly of the cowardice of brave men, who forget that before an effort of moral courage arrogance quails. From this time every Peer shrunk from the risk of any encounter with Thurlow, and he ruled the House with a rod of iron—saying and doing what he pleased, and treating his colleagues with very little more courtesy than his opponents. He was soon described as

"That rugged Thurlow, who, with silent scowl,
In surly mood at friend and foe would growl."

The Parliamentary History says, that on the next measure which was brought forward "the Lord Chancellor spoke with peculiar feeling, force, and argument;" but I can not help suspecting that his speech was an example of grave irony, and that in his heart he was *laughing*, and wished the discerning to *know that he was laughing*, at the suspicious claims to high blood of some of

---

[1] According to the account given to me many years ago, by another gentleman of great accuracy, likewise present, Thurlow said, "I shall go into no labored defense of the course I have pursued, and shall continue to pursue, but shall content myself with simply putting it to your Lordships—'Who holds his seat in this House by the more honorable tenure—the man who is summoned to the peerage by his Sovereign as the reward of a life passed in serving his country, or he who inherits a seat in this House which was bestowed as the wages of the prostitution of his great grandmother?'"

[2] Reminsc. i 142.

those who despised the descendant of the "Carrier." This was Bishop Barrington's bill "for the more effectual discouragement of the crime of adultery." A Howard—the Earl of Carlisle—having ably opposed it on the ground that adultery, though a deadly sin, was not a subject for criminal legislation, he was answered, with great seeming warmth, by Lord Thurlow, who had not only been noted for youthful profligacy, but, now the first magistrate under the Crown, and Keeper (as he boasted) of the King's conscience, was openly living with a mistress, by whom he had a family of children. He said:— "The matter immediately before the House was, whether or no they would take into consideration a method for more effectually preventing the crime of adultery? If they rejected the bill, they pronounced in form that they were not disposed to put any restraint at all upon this abominable practice. The plain question was, 'Do you, or do you not, think it worth your while to interpose by some method for the prevention of a crime that not only subverts domestic tranquillity, but has a tendency, by contaminating the blood of illustrious families, to affect the welfare of the nation in its dearest interests?' The bill was for the '*protection*' of every husband and father in the kingdom; *but it concerned their Lordships more than any other order in the state.* He begged the House to recollect that the purity of the blood of their descendants was, and must necessarily be, an essential consideration in the breasts of all Peers. Every attempt to preserve the descent of Peers unstained merited their immediate attention: for his part, he declared he saw *the importance of the bill to the Peerage* so clearly, that if he had the blood of forty generations of nobility flowing in his veins, he could not be more anxious to procure for it that assent which it deserved from their Lordships."[1] No puritan could have more vehemently supported the ordinance passed in the time of the Commonwealth, by which fornication was made felony, and on a second conviction was to be punished with death. "A knavish speech sleeps in a foolish ear," and this *persiflage* of the Lord Chancellor was taken in good earnest by a large majority of their Lordships: but the bill which they passed was thrown

[1] 20 Parl. Hist. 594.

out by the Commons—where the professed "protection" was considered less necessary.¹

Some alarm being excited by the discontents of Ireland, which soon after led to the assertion of independence by an armed force, Lord Shelburne brought forward certain propositions for repealing the laws which restricted the intercourse between the two islands, so that both might have a common interest in prosecuting commerce. Thurlow strongly opposed what he called "a dangerous innovation," and, his colleagues showing some symptoms of giving way, he declared "that though he did not wish in general to take the lead, nor pretend to determine, on matters of state, which were foreign to his studies and habits of life, on the present occasion he would act for himself, and meet the motion with a direct negative." This course was adopted, and he had a majority of 61 to 32.²

At the opening of the session in Nov. 1779, after the continuing disasters of the war, the Marquis of Rockingham, with good reason, and, at all events, regularly and constitutionally, having moved an amendment to the address, praying for a change of councils and councillors, it was thus opposed by the Lord Chancellor:—

"Allowing all the suggestions of the noble Marquis to be as true as they are unfounded, would it be just—would it be fair, either in point of form or fact, to condemn, without hearing or inquiring what the parties accused have to say in defense or extenuation? I do not rise as an advocate for any man, or description of men—much less for the persons supposed to compose the present Administration;—but I stand up for the honor of the House. If Ministers have acted improperly, injudiciously, corruptly, or wickedly, the very presumption that they have done so, entitles them to claim a trial. I will suppose they are culprits. That is enough for my argument; they are entitled to the benefit of the laws. The higher the charge,—the heavier the punishment,—the more caution is required in bringing home guilt to the accused.

---

¹ 20 Parl Hist 601. Its absurdities were forcibly pointed out by Charles Fox, who in allusion to Thurlow's indecent sarcasm on the ' Peeresses," pointed out the extreme hardship to which the female sex were exposed in not being allowed to sit in parliament, and having no representatives there.

² Ibid. 675.

But to come by a side-wind—without notice—without evidence, and at once to condemn,—is a mode of proceeding which I can not sanction. It is an outrage on the constitution; it is contrary to candor—to law—to truth, and to every requisite of substantial justice."

Lord Camden made a forcible reply to this "novel logic," but the amendment was negatived by a majority of 82 to 41.[1]

The Chancellor most resolutely set his face against all the economical and constitutional reforms which Burke, Dunning, and the Whigs were now able to carry through the Lower House, where, upon such subjects, they had a majority. But their bills soon received the *coup de grâce* on reaching the House of Lords. The bill to disqualify Government contractors from sitting in the House of Commons, although it had passed there almost unanimously, he threw out, by a majority of 92 to 51, saying that "the fact that the bill had in its favor the general wishes of the people, was worth just so much as it would pass for in their Lordship's estimation."[2]

There being a motion in the House of Lords against the employment of the military to put down Lord George Gordon's riots, the Chancellor, in a speech not confined to assertion and vituperation, but containing an unusual display of reasoning, legal learning, and historical research, proved, in a very able and satisfactory manner, that citizens with arms in their hands still enjoy the rights, and are liable to the duties, of citizens, and are bound, like other citizens, to assist in preserving or restoring the public tranquillity. He likewise gained considerable credit with the judicious for his continued support of Sir George Savile's bill to relax the penal laws against Roman Catholics; although so little progress had the Peers yet made in the school of religious liberty, that, to please them, he said, "he was by no means prepared to carry toleration so far as Mr. Locke;"—and while Roman Catholics were to be permitted to teach music and dancing, he introduced a clause to prohibit them from keeping boarding-schools, so that they might never have Protestant children under their management.[3]

Soon after, a private affair of honor, wholly unconnected with any parliamentary proceeding, was brought before

[1] 20 Parl. Hist 1023–1092.   [2] Ibid. 433   [3] 22 Ibid 759, 764.

the House, by the Chancellor, as a breach of privilege. The Earl of Pomfret, erroneously supposing that a gamekeeper, whom he had discharged, had been countenanced by the Duke of Grafton, wrote some very intemperate letters to his Grace, and insisted on fighting him either with sword or pistol. Thurlow, on the rumor of what had happened, moved that they should attend, in their places, in the House: and, both parties being heard, it was resolved, that the behavior of the Duke of Grafton had been highly laudable and meritorious; and Lord Pomfret, being made to kneel at the bar, was informed that he had been guilty of "a high contempt of the House." Afterwards, the Lord Chancellor, with three-cocked hat on head, administered to him a thundering reprimand.[1] Nowadays, I conceive, the House would refuse to take cognizance of such a quarrel. The supposed breach of privilege would be the same if the challenger were a commoner, although this circumstance would render the interference more preposterous.

In the beginning of the year 1781, Lord Thurlow spoke several times, and at great length, on the rupture which then took place with Holland. The question being one of public law upon the construction of treaties, he strangely said that "his pursuits and habits by no means fitted him for such an undertaking,—so that he could only treat the subject with the portion of common sense and experience Providence had endued him with, and familiarize it so as to bring it on a level with his own poor understanding." Perhaps he maliciously insinuated that, to make himself intelligible to his audience, it was necessary he should adapt his discourse to the meanest understandings[2] But the truth is, that he himself had read very little of the law of nations; that he was very little acquainted with the rights of peace and war; and that his boasted superiority was in pretension, not in knowledge.[3]

He succeeded better in justifying the military execu-

[1] 22 Parl. Hist 855, 866
[2] A remarkably acute friend of mine, formerly at the bar,—the Judges having retired for a few minutes in the midst of his argument, in which, from their interruptions and objections, he did not seem likely to be successful,—went out of the court too, and on his return stated that he had been drinking a pot of porter Being asked whether he was not afraid that this beverage might dull his intellect, "That is exactly my object," said he,—"to bring me down, if possible, to the level of their Lordships." [3] 22 Parl Hist 1007-1078.

tion of Colonel Haynes, a British officer taken fighting for the Americans;[1] and in crushing an attempt to censure Lord George Germaine's elevation to the Peerage, by the title of Viscount Sackville,—when he first refused to put the question, and afterwards denounced as unjust, the general orders issued by the late King against that officer after his court-martial.[2]

But Lord North's Administration was now in the agonies of dissolution; and Thurlow began to coquet a little with the Opposition.[3] Lord Cornwallis had capitulated,—America was lost,—hostilities had commenced with France, Spain, and Holland,—Gibraltar was besieged,—the fleets of the enemy insulted our shores,—Ireland was on the verge of rebellion,—Russia, and the northern powers, under pretense of an armed neutrality, were combined against our naval rights, and were respectively planning the seizure of a portion of our dominions,—and the utter overthrow of the British empire was anticipated. Notwithstanding the King's firm adherence to the present system, a change of ministers was considered inevitable. The Whigs were becoming stronger in the House of Commons on every division; they had been lately strengthened by the accession of the brilliant talents of Pitt the younger, and of Sheridan; and, what was of even still greater importance, the nation, though disposed to make a gallant struggle against the Continental States, which basely sought to take advantage of our misfortunes, was heartily sick of the colonial war, and was willing to acknowledge American independence. Thurlow's official career being supposed to be drawing rapidly to a close, the lawyers began to speculate which Whig lawyer would be his successor, and how the surly ex-Chancellor would amuse and comfort himself in retirement? That he, who more zealously and uncompromisingly than any other member of the Tory government, had supported all its most obnoxious acts, and more scornfully resisted all the popular measures of the Opposition, should retain the Great Seal, never entered the imagination of any human being except Thurlow himself and the King. Which of the two first conceived

[1] 22 Parl. Hist 976.   [2] Ib. 1000–1021.
[3] See his speeches on the Government Almanac Bill (22 Parl. Hist. 542), and on the Address of Thanks (Ib. 672).

the bright thought must for ever remain unknown. When the ministerial vessel did go to pieces, Thurlow was the *tabula in naufragio*—the plank to which his Majesty eagerly clung.

CHAPTER CLVIII.

CONTINUATION OF THE LIFE OF LORD THURLOW TILL HE WAS DEPRIVED OF THE GREAT SEAL ON THE FORMATION OF THE COALITION MINISTRY.

I AM more and more at a loss to account for Lord Rockingham, Lord Shelburne, and Mr. Fox agreeing to sit in the Cabinet with the man who had so violently denounced their opinions on very important questions of foreign and domestic policy which were still pending. The great "Coalition" between the two antagonist parties, which soon after so much shocked mankind, in reality did not involve any such incongruity as this adoption of the most odious member of the late Government, without any renunciation of his principles. To do *him* justice, it should ever be remembered that, instead of saying "*Peccavi*," he continued to glory in all that he had hitherto done and said while proclaiming the Rockinghams and the Shelburnes as enemies to their country. The proposed measures on which the new Administration was founded, were four:—1. An offer to America of unconditional independence as the basis of a negotiation for peace. 2. Economical reform as proposed in Mr. Burke's bill. 3. Repression of the undue influence of the Crown in the House of Commons, by disqualifying contractors to sit there, and by preventing revenue officers from voting at parliamentary elections. 4. The pacification of Ireland by a renunciation of the authority of the British parliament to legislate for that country. The subsequent fusion of Whigs and Tories was plausibly (I think not effectually) defended by the observation that, when it took place, all the questions on which Lord North and Mr. Fox had differed so widely were settled, and that there was nothing to prevent their practical co-operation for the future. But the four great measures which I have specified were still to be brought forward by the Government, and Thurlow had often declared, and was still ready to declare, that they were all unconstitutional and pernicious. The King, upon a proper representation, could not have insisted (as he is said to have done) on the retention of Thurlow as the condition of his giving his consent to the introduction of Mr. Fox into the Cabinet; for although he might have executed his threat of abdicating, and retiring to Hanover, he could not at that hour have remained on the throne of England, indulging personal partialities and antipathies in the choice of his ministers.

Mr. Adolphus, in his History of George III., says, "Mr. Fox, some time before the overthrow of the late Cabinet, acknowledged that his adherents detested Lord Thurlow's sentiments on the constitution; but added, they did not mean to proscribe him."[1] Fox, however, was then speaking of the Lord Advocate of Scotland, not of Lord Thurlow; and he declared that "they would proscribe no man of any principles in the present dreadful moment, but *the five or six men who had been the confidential advisers of his Majesty in all the measures that had brought about the present calamities.*"

I can only account for the wishes of the King prevailing by supposing the existence of jealousies, rivalries, and bickerings among the Whigs themselves as to the disposal of the Great Seal. It is certainly much to be deplored if the apprehensions of the Rockinghams, that the Shelburnes would be too much aggrandized by the appointment of Dunning, deprived him of the fair reward of his exertions, and the public of the benefits of his services. From the time that he accepted the Duchy of Lancaster and a Peerage, he sunk into insignificance. He had a seat in the Cabinet, but that seldom gives much weight without important official functions and a great department to administer.

How Thurlow comported himself when he met his new colleagues at cabinets to concert their proceedings in parliament, we are left to conjecture. It must now have been very convenient for him to practice the habit he is said to have acquired of going to sleep, or pretending to go to sleep, after dinner, during the discussions on which

[1] Vol iii 349

the safety of the state depended. We know that when the measures of Government were brought forward in parliament he opposed them without any reserve.

During the short existence of the Rockingham Administration, the Lord Chancellor might truly be considered the leader of "his Majesty's Opposition" in the House of Lords. He knew the *secret* which the King was at no pains to conceal, and which was loudly proclaimed by all the "King's friends," that the Administration did not possess his Majesty's confidence.[1] His object, therefore, was to take every opportunity of disparaging it, and, above all, of sowing dissension between the different sections of the liberal party of which it was composed.

They lost a little popularity by the defeat of the motion for a reform in the representation of the people in parliament, made by their partisan, Mr W Pitt, then a young lawyer going the Western Circuit. This measure was supported by the Shelburne Whigs, but discouraged by the Rockinghams, who, while they were economical reformers, professed deep reluctance to touch the constitution of the House of Commons.

To evince the sincerity of their professions while in opposition, and to recover their character, Ministers reintroduced, and both their sections eagerly supported the two bills which Thurlow had formerly thrown out in the Lords, for the disqualification of contractors as representatives, and of revenue officers as electors. The bills passed the Commons with acclamation, but when they came before the Upper House, although the existence of the Government was declared to depend upon them, he attacked them with unabated violence. The second reading of the "Contractors' Bill" having taken place without discussion, the Lord Chancellor left the woolsack, and observed, that "he had expected that, before the bill reached that stage, some noble Lord would have had the goodness to explain to the House the principles on which it rested, and the necessity for introducing it at this particular juncture. The bill trenching on the ancient con-

---

[1] "The King declared that, in the whole course of his reign, this was the only Administration which had not possessed his confidence."—*Adolph.* III. 373 This statement is said to be from "private information," and his Majesty often praised the accuracy of this historian The avowal is supposed to have been made by his Majesty after the Administration was dissolved; but from its formation, the fact had been notorious to all the world

stitution of this realm, he considered it highly exceptionable in itself; and it was still more exceptionable in its form, from the very singular, imperfect, careless, and inexplicable style and phrase in which it was worded. He would not, by applying strong epithets to the bill, give it a worse character than it really deserved; but, after having perused it with all the attention he was capable of, he could find no milder words in the English language to describe the impression his perusal of it had left upon his mind, than terming it *an attempt to deceive and betray the people.*[1] Having denied that there ever had been any instances of members of parliament being corrupted by Ministers through the means of contracts, he asked, "If no such instance had ever occurred in the worst of times, why pay so bad a compliment to succeeding Ministers as to presume that they will be so much more depraved, so much more abandoned, so lost to all sense of shame, as to be guilty of what their predecessors would have shunned with abhorrence? Why have his Majesty's present Ministers so little confidence in themselves? Why do they believe that they are more corrupt than those they have succeeded?" A noble Lord said, "No Ministers could be more corrupt than the last."—*Lord Chancellor*: "Then, my Lords, I am relieved from further arguing the question; for if there was perfect purity in such matters (as I know there was) with the last Ministers, supposing them to have been corruptly inclined (as I know they were not), the bill is confessedly unnecessary, and it is a mischievous remedy for an imaginary and impossible evil. It holds out nothing like a reform either in point of economy or influence. I must likewise, in the discharge of my duty, remind your Lordships that two years ago you rejected this very measure when it was proposed in a less exceptionable form. You are bound to act consistently.

[1] This reminds me of a Westminster Hall anecdote of Mr Clarke leader of the Midland Circuit—a very worthy lawyer of the old school His client long refusing to agree to refer to arbitration a cause which judge, jury, and counsel wished to get rid of, he at last said to him, "You d——d infernal fool, if you do not immediately follow my Lord's recommendation I shall be obliged to use *strong language* to you."—Once, in a council of the benchers of Lincoln's Inn, he very conscientiously opposed our calling a Jew to the Bar. I tried to point out the hardship to be imposed upon the young gentleman, who had been allowed to keep his terms, and whose prospects in life would thus be suddenly blasted "Hardship!" said the zealous churchman—"no hardship at all! Let him become a Christian, and be d——d to him!!!"

If you should now, to please the Minister, suddenly wheel round, how are you to surmount the abusive attacks and scurrilous insinuations of anonymous libelers? Such illiberal assassins and scribbling garreteers may now have some color for their attacks upon our dignity. It behoves your Lordships to act so that you may be able to laugh libelers to scorn, and to defy their malice." He actually divided the House, but this was not yet the time to break up the Administration, and he had on his side only 45 against 67—a larger minority, however, than had been ever mustered in the Upper House against any measure of Lord North's Government.

Thurlow continued a most vexatious opposition to the bill in the committee—where, going through it clause by clause, he denounced it as " a jumble of contradictions." It was there defended by the two new law lords, Lord Ashburton and Lord Grantley. They both gallantly fleshed their maiden swords in various rencounters with the " blatant beast," who tried to tread them down.

On some of the divisions in the committee the Ministerial majority was reduced to two votes. The bill was carried. But henceforth the " King's friends " in both Houses openly declared themselves against the existing Government.[1]

The Chancellor got up a similar opposition to the other Government bill for disqualifying revenue officers from voting at parliamentary elections, although Lord Rockingham, in what may be considered a dying speech, deprecated opposition to it, and stated the striking fact that there were no less than seventy boroughs in England in which the return of members depended chiefly on revenue officers appointed and removable by the Government. On the last division on this bill, the Chancellor had the mortification to announce that the *Contents* were 34, and the *Not-contents* (of whom he was one) were 18.[2]

Notwithstanding that Mr. Burke and several other leading members of the Government were hostile to a sweeping measure of parliamentary reform, they concurred with their colleagues in the desire to punish corruption at elections, and the whole party in the House of Commons strongly supported the bill for transferring the franchise of Cricklade to the adjoining " hundreds " on account of

[1] 22 Parl Hist 1356-1382   [2] 23 Parl Hist 95-101.

the universal bribery proved upon the burgesses. But when the bill came up to the Lords, it likewise was vehemently opposed by the Chancellor. The Duke of Richmond thereupon charged the noble and learned Lord on the woolsack with "opposing indiscriminately every measure of regulation or improvement which was laid before the House." The Lord Chancellor complained of the asperity with which he had been treated by the noble Duke, and said, " he thought it rather a peculiar hardship that his manner—that of a plain man, who studied nothing but to convey his sentiments clearly and intelligibly—should be imputed to him as if arising from a habit of indiscriminate opposition or of intentional rudeness."

Lords Mansfield, Camden, Loughborough, Ashburton, and Grantley, having taken part in the discussion, " Lord Fortescue bewailed the degraded dignity of the House, lowered and tarnished by a profusion of lawyers: it was no longer a house of peers, but a mere court of law, where all the solid, honorable principles of truth and justice were shamefully sacrificed to the low pettifogging chicanery and quibbles of Westminster Hall. That once venerable and august assembly now resembled a meeting of attorneys in a Cornish court acting as barristers; the learned Lord on the woolsack seemed fraught with nothing but contradictions and law subtleties and distinctions, and all that." The Chancellor was not to be deterred from his obstructive course by such observations, but, notwithstanding all his efforts, the bill was carried [1]

Again, when a motion was made by the organ of the Government in the House of Lords for an address of congratulation to the Throne on the great victory obtained by Rodney over De Gresse in the West Indies, which was stated to be "conducive to an honorable and advantageous peace," Thurlow objected to these words, as containing *a political opinion on the expediency of peace*; and, for the sake of unanimity, they were omitted."[2]

The Marquis of Rockingham expired on the 1st of July On the 3rd of the same month stood an order of the day for the second reading of Mr. Burke's famous bill to reform the Civil List expenditure—a measure which was highly distasteful to the Court. No arrangement had yet been announced for the appointment of a new Pre-

[1] 22 Parl. Hist. 1383-1395, Adolphus, III. 363 [2] 23 Parl. Hist. 72.

mier. The Chancellor was eager to give a blow to that section of the administration which was most hated by himself and his master—the personal adherents of the deceased minister. Therefore, at the sitting of the House, in an abrupt manner he left the woolsack to make a motion for the purpose of throwing out the bill. After calling their Lordships' attention to its importance, he said—" At this late stage of the session, and with so thin an attendance, it would ill become you hastily to adopt a string of propositions, in themselves very complicated, and in many respects contradictory. But, my Lords, I am surprised to find that the Right Honorable Gentleman who prepared this bill, and who, some years ago, introduced one on somewhat similar principles, has now left out several important offices and places which he formerly represented as peculiarly standing in need of his speculative remedy. One of these offices is occupied by a noble Duke (Richmond) who can not be anxious to receive its emoluments. He certainly would not suffer any corruption to be practiced in any department in which he presides. Whether the ORDNANCE be left out in compliment to his Grace's virtues and talents, I will not pretend to decide; but I am sure that the 'Ordnance' and the 'Mint,' and the 'Duchy of Lancaster,' held by the Right Honorable Gentleman's colleagues, are very properly left out, and I could only wish that he had dealt in the same way with other offices which he has included,—some of them the most ancient and illustrious in the state,—so that to annihilate them was, in fact, an attempt to destroy the constitution." He then started a technical objection, —that there being for the protection of their privileges a standing order, passed in the year 1702, which provided that "no money bill should be allowed to pass containing extraneous enactments," this bill granted a supply to his Majesty of £300,000, and was a money bill, while it abolished or regulated half of the offices under the Crown. "Therefore," said he, "with all my aversion to the evils which the bill seeks to remedy, I can not give it my support. There appears to me to be objectionable and absurd matter almost in every clause of it, and I adjure your Lordships to adjourn the consideration of it—more especially as, if you agree, in compliance with the menaces of another branch of the legislature, to send it to a committee, you will sacrifice your standing order, and surrender your dignity." He concluded by moving that the order for the second reading of the bill should be discharged.

Lord Shelburne pretty clearly indicated his expectation (although Thurlow seems not yet to have been aware of the fact) that he was himself to be the minister, and he felt that, without an entire loss of public credit, he could not abandon the bill. He declared "tha he joined with the House, and the whole public must join, in deploring the heavy loss the country had experienced in the death of the late Marquis of Rockingham. That great man, however, had by his example obliged whoever should be the minister to do his duty to the public, and had left this bill behind him as a pledge of his wisdom, his integrity, and his zeal to further the strictest economy in every branch of the public expenditure." The noble Earl then professed himself favorable to parliamentary reform, and to all measures of improvement, but did not say a word in defense of the author of the bill—which might be the reason that Burke, a few days after, when his Lordship had actually seized the helm, compared him to Cataline and to Borgia. Thurlow still called for a division on his motion against the bill, but was left in a minority of 9 to 44.[1]

Lord Shelburne being declared First Lord of the Treasury, Mr. Fox, Lord John Cavendish, Mr. Burke, the Duke of Portland, and other Rockingham Whigs, resigned. I can not say that they made a dignified or becoming exit. In the explanations which followed, their leader said he had intended to withdraw before the death of the Marquis of Rockingham; but all the world believed the true reason to be, that Lord Shelburne was appointed to succeed him. It had long been quite clear that Thurlow ought never to have been admitted into Lord Rockingham's Cabinet; and that Lord Rockingham ought to have adopted the course afterwards pursued by Mr. Pitt, by asking his Majesty to elect between his First Lord of the Treasury and his Chancellor. At this crisis the retiring ministers should have objected to the retention of Thurlow—not to the promotion of Lord Shel-

[1] 28 Parl Hist 13 ¿—147.

burne. They presented to the nation the spectacle, ever disliked, of a squabble for places, and an unfair attempt to control the discretion of the Sovereign.

Lord Shelburne was strengthened by the accession of young Pitt, who, for the office of Chancellor of the Exchequer, renounced the profession of the law, the highest honors of which, had he continued in it, he must rapidly have attained. Thurlow joyously consented to continue Chancellor, and, the new Administration being less disagreeable to the Court than that of Lord Rockingham, he was much mollified, and gave it his support. Indeed, during Lord Shelburne's ministry, which speedily came to a violent end by the "Coalition," the Chancellor is not recorded to have opposed one Government measure, and in the grand debate on the Preliminaries of Peace, he gallantly supported his colleagues.

On this occasion he followed Lord Loughborough, who, having become a Foxite, had in a long and elaborate speech attacked the terms of the treaty, and particularly, in reference to the article agreeing to the cession of the Floridas, denied the power of the Crown, without an act of parliament, to alienate a portion of the British empire, and to transfer the allegiance of British subjects to a foreign state. Thurlow's answer is supposed to have settled that great constitutional question; but I own it seems to me very unsatisfactory, for, as usual, he deals in sarcasm and assertion, not in reasoning or authority, and he does not define or limit the power he contends for—so as to exclude from its exercise the cession of the Isle of Wight, or the garrison of Portsmouth:—

"My Lords," said he, "I can not claim your attention on the ground of eloquence and wit. These belong peculiarly to the noble and learned Lord who has so long and ably endeavored to fascinate your Lordships, and whose skill and address in managing the passions of his auditors are not to be equaled,—and, by a man of plain meaning and sober understanding like myself, whose only wish is to discriminate between truth and fiction, not to be coveted. The noble and learned Lord has thought proper to allege that the royal prerogative does not warrant the alienation, in a treaty of peace, of territories which were under the allegiance of the Crown of

England. If this doctrine be true, I must acknowledge myself strangely ignorant of the constitution of my country. Till the present day of novelty and miracle, I never heard of such a doctrine. I apprehend, however, that the noble and learned Lord has thrown down the gauntlet on this occasion more from knight-errantry than patriotism, and that he was more inclined to show the House what powers of declamation he possesses in support of hypothetical propositions, than anxious gravely to examine a power wisely lodged in the Crown, the utility, much less the existence, of which has never hitherto been questioned. One would have thought that when a great, experienced, and justly eminent lawyer hazarded an opinion respecting a most important point of the constitution of this country, he would deem it fit to produce proofs from our legal and historical records, or at least that he would attempt to show that the common opinion and consent of Englishmen went with him; but instead of this the noble and learned Lord resorts to the lucubrations and fancies of foreign writers, and gravely refers your Lordships to Swiss authors for an explanation of the prerogatives of the British Crown. For my own part, I at once reject the authority of all foreigners on such a subject. However full of ingenuity Mr. Vattell or Mr Puffendorf may be on the law of nations, which can not be fixed by any solid and permanent rule, I deny their authority, I explode their evidence, when they are brought in to explain to me what may or may not be done by the Sovereign I serve. Speaking from my own judgment, the records of parliament, the annals of the country, I do not think the cession of the Floridas at all a questionable matter. Let the noble and learned Lord bring forward the subject regularly, and I will establish a doctrine clearly contrary to the extraordinary notion now sported by him, or confess my ignorance. I will not combat the noble and learned Lord with vague declamation and oratorical flourishes,—these I contentedly leave to him with the plaudits they are calculated, perhaps intended, to gain,—but with undecorated sense and simple argument. In my opinion, it is safer to stick to the process by which we arrive at the conclusion that two and two make four, than to suffer your understandings to be warped by the fashionable logic which delights in words, and which strives rather to confound what is plain than to unravel what is intricate."[1]

He might just as well, after the manner of Lord Peter, in one sentence have affirmed with an oath that it was so, and uttered an imprecation on all who differed from him.[2] But this ebullition was thought by their Lordships a very ample answer to the objection, and even Lord Loughborough's friends felt that he had made a false point, and that he was completely put down. We must bear in mind Thurlow's voice and manner, and that "he looked wiser than any man ever was."[3]

The ill-advised coalition had now actually taken place between Mr. Fox and Lord North, which produced a censure on the Peace, in the House of Commons, and the resignation of Lord Shelburne.

Till very recently, it had been uniformly stated, and universally believed, that in the formation of a new government, the King still desired to have Thurlow as Chancellor, and that his Lordship was nothing loth to comply with the royal wish, but that Mr. Fox and the Whigs, recollecting the part he had acted under Lord Rockingham, objected, in the most peremptory manner, to such an arrangement; that this dispute caused the delay which gave rise to the motions in the House of Commons during the "interregnum;" and that his Majesty was at last induced to yield to a compromise, by which the Great Seal was put into commission[4] But in a late valuable biographical work it is stated, that "the following particulars were related by Lord Eldon to his brother-in-law, Mr. John Surtees: Mr. Fox, much to Lord Thurlow's surprise, called at his house, and was shown into his drawing-room. Lord Thurlow, immediately that Mr. Fox's visit was an-

[1] 23 Parl. Hist 430
[2] "Look ye, gentlemen," cries Peter in a rage, "to convince you what a couple of blind, positive, ignorant, willful puppies you are, I will use but this plain argument; but, by G—, it is true, good, natural mutton as any in Leadenhall marke.; and G— confound you both eternally if you offer to believe otherwise" After this "thundering proof," his Lordship was allowed to "have a great deal of reason"
[3] Saying of Mr Fox.—In the discussion of the Ashburton treaty, by which the Madawaska settlement, a part of Canada allowed to belong to England, was ceded to the United States, I tried to revive the question, "Whether an act of parliament was not necessary to give it validity?" but I was told that the sufficiency of the prerogative to effect the transfer had been established by "the unanswerable arguments of Thurlow."
[4] Sir F Wraxall's Mem. ii. 315

nounced, determined to receive him (observing, when he narrated the matter, that he did not wish Mr. Fox should suppose him afraid to meet any one), and an interview took place. Lord Thurlow, on being informed by Mr. Fox that he and his party wished the co-operation of his Lordship as Chancellor in the administration they wished to form, said, ' *Mr. Fox, no man can deny that either you or Mr. Pitt are beyond any two men that can be named, fit from character and talents to be at the head of any administration, but as Mr. Pitt is very acceptable to the King, and is in an extraordinary degree popular in the country, I have connected myself with him.*' On Lord Thurlow's refusal, the Great Seal was put in commission." [1] I do not impute the slightest intention willfully to misrepresent either to Mr. John Surtees or to Lord Eldon, but the story is wholly incredible, and there must have been a lapse of memory in one of them, or Thurlow must have intended to mystify. The refusal is more impossible than the offer, and the difficulty can not be solved by an anticipation of a speedy change, for Thurlow would have considered that he might have an opportunity of accelerating this by entering the Cabinet; that acceptance must be agreeable to the King; and that betraying one prime minister was the best prelude to service under another. But, to end the controversy, we have only to look to Mr. Fox's declarations in the House of Commons at this very time respecting him whom it was supposed he was pressing to become his colleague. Mr. Coke, of Norfolk, having moved an address, praying " that his Majesty would graciously take into his consideration the distressed state of the empire, and, in compliance with the wishes of the House, would form an administration entitled to the confidence of the people,"—Mr. Fox observed, " If any wish to see who it is that for the last five weeks has governed the kingdom, and ill-advised his Majesty, let them go to the other House; they will there find the great adviser in his true character. Let them mark the man; they will see difficulty, delay, sullenness, and all the distinguishing features of what has been falsely called *an interregnum*, but in reality been a specimen of the most open and undisguised rule ever known in this country." Governor Johnstone took up the defense of the Chancellor, whom

[1] Twiss's Life of Eldon, i 141.

he described as "a great pillar of state, to whom the country might look up with confidence as a protector of its constitution against those mad projects of reform which threatened its annihilation; therefore, dark insinuations against such a character ought not to be listened to: If the noble and learned Lord acted in the manner insinuated, and had been the cause of keeping the country so long without an administration, either by giving ill-advice to his Majesty, or by any other means, he was a great criminal, but before withdrawing his friendship from one whom he had so long esteemed, he expected to have the fact proved, and he would not consent to presume its truth on mere surmise or assertion. If the right honorable gentleman, actuated by a sense of duty, was for a coalition, let him coalesce with the noble and learned Lord whom he once praised but now calumniated." *Mr. Fox*: "I have still as high personal respect for the noble and learned Lord alluded to as ever; I have merely spoken of his public conduct, which I believe has been the source of great calamities to the country. I acknowledge his abilities, but I contend that they render their possessor an object to be dreaded, as he has in the same proportion the power of doing mischief."[1]

It is quite certain that Thurlow's presence in Lord Rockingham's Cabinet was a principal reason for Fox's resignation on the death of that nobleman; that he found it utterly impossible to act with him; and that he would now indignantly have scorned the notion of again being associated with him. His reluctant assent, at a subsequent period during the King's illness, to ratify the conditional disposition of the Great Seal in favor of Thurlow, only shows more strongly that he never would spontaneously have proposed such a course.

The new Ministry being formed under the nominal headship of the Duke of Portland, with Mr. Fox and Lord North as its efficient members, the Great Seal was taken from Thurlow and put into commission, Lord Loughborough being the First Lord Commissioner.[2]

[1] 23 Parl Hist 658–723.
[2] "7th May, 1783 —Alexander, Lord Loughborough, Chief Justice of the Common Pleas, Sir William Henry Ashurst, Knt, a Judge of the King's Bench, Sir Beaumont Hotham, a Baron of the Exchequer, being by letters-patent, dated 9th April, 1783, appointed Commissioners of the Great Seal of Great Britain, upon the 7th day of May following, being the first day of

CHAPTER CLIX.

CONTINUATION OF THE LIFE OF LORD THURLOW TILL THE KING'S ILLNESS IN 1788.

BUT Thurlow, deprived of the Great Seal, remained "Keeper of the King's conscience," and they both went into hot opposition. If it be ever excusable in a king of England to cabal against his ministers, George III. may well be defended for the course he now took; for they had been forced upon him by a factious intrigue, and public opinion was decidedly in his favor. Thurlow was frequently closeted with him, and they watched for a favorable opportunity to be revenged of the coalitionists. Mr. Pitt, on the resignation of Lord Shelburne, had declined an offer to form a new government, of which he was to be the head—wisely thinking it better to wait till the "coalition" should become more unpopular. For this reason he was for the present looked upon at Court rather coldly, and, though polished and courteous in his manners, yet, on account of his lofty spirit and unbending independence, he never was personally so much beloved by George III. as Thurlow, who, rough and savage to the rest of mankind, was always noted for pliancy and assentation in the presence of royalty.

From April to December, the Term of the Coalition Ministry, Thurlow was constantly considering the most effectual means for effecting its overthrow. Had he been in the Cabinet, he would have had a still better opportunity of thwarting its measures, and his opposition would have had double weight. However, his prudence and sagacity were of essential service in tempering the impatience of the King, and when the proper time arrived he struck the fatal blow with signal vigor and dexterity. It was by secret advice more than by open efforts in parliament that he struggled for his restoration to office, and till Mr. Fox's India Bill arrived in the House of Lords, that assembly was allowed to remain nearly in a passive state.

The ex-Chancellor nevertheless availed himself unscru-

Easter Term, came into the Court of Chancery at Westminster Hall, and in open Court took the oaths, &c.; the senior Master in Chancery holding the book," &c.—*Cr. Off. Min.* No. 2, 30

pulously of any little opportunity that occurred of disparging the Government and embarrassing its proceedings.

On the second reading of the bill framed and introduced by the late Government for abolishing the right of appeal from the Irish Courts of law to the British House of Lords, and acknowledging the supremacy of the Parliament of Ireland, Lord Thurlow, to make his opponents unpopular in one island or the other, or in both,- instead of allowing it quietly to pass, according to the wish of prudent men, said,—" I desire to have a distinct statement of the grounds on which the measure is adopted by the present Ministers. For what purpose is it to be carried? To what end is it to be applied? With what other measures is it to be followed up? There can be no embarrassment to Ministers in answering such questions. The noble Duke [Portland] tells us he looks round for confidence, and claims it from the tenor of his past life. I am in great doubt, my Lords, respecting the meaning of this word '*confidence*.' Does it mean that his Grace has no other plan in view? that his Cabinet have no plan for the government of Ireland? and that they have taken this bill up without inquiry, without consideration, without caring whether it goes far enough or too far? Or does it mean that they have a fine system to develop, but that we must trust to their good character till the day arrives for making it known? Let me have the English of the word '*confidence*.' Unless it means '*no plan*,' no claim can be laid to it by this untried Administration." *Lord Loughborough:* " My Lords, I consider this conversation (for we have had no debate on the merits of the bill) extremely irregular, if not disorderly. No objection being made to the bill, Ministers are called upon to divulge their future system of policy, and to declare what may be their opinions and conduct on various matters not before the House. This is an opposition hardly consistent with fairness, and hardly such as any ministers could expect to encounter. The present Ministers have been so short a time in place, that to require them already to proclaim all their plans, does seem very strange: but above all is it strange, that they should be asked the grounds and objects of this bill. The persons who can best give that information are the Ministers with whom it originated " *Lord Thurlow:* " I deny, my Lords, that I am disorderly in taking the present opportunity of desiring to know the principles on which the present bill is to be passed into a law. If it is adopted without principle, if it is taken up merely on the authority of the predecessors of the present Ministers, then it may well be said to resemble a schoolboy's task, and the former Ministers are to be consideaed as the '*prepositors*' of the noble Lords opposite,—who are mere school-boys, and ought not to hold the reins of government half an hour. But I have too much respect for their understanding, and too much regard for their reputation, to entertain such an opinion. They must have taken up this bill as part of a plan for the government of Ireland. If they will not give us the least intimation of it, let them at least tell us whether they have any plan at all." [1]

During this short interval of opposition, Thurlow, to the surprise and amusement of the public, professed himself a REFORMER; and that he might cast odium upon the Government for throwing out an absurd bill, which professed to correct abuses in public offices, he warmly supported it. Said he, "I feel for the fair fame of the present Administration, and, as a well-wisher to the men of honor and honesty who belong to it, I advise them not to rest satisfied with the pledge of the noble Duke [Portland] that he will do what he can for economy. They are right not to mind the loss of mere popularity. He who rests on the empty clamor of a newspaper is an object only of contempt. But I advise the noble Duke to avoid the condemnation of wise, temperate, and thinking men, who never judge rashly or hastily. All such men must cry out against the resolution to stifle such a bill as this without due investigation. The reform is loudly called for, and we must have it immediately. The nation will not be content with the noble Duke's promise that he will begin the reform as soon as possible. The legislature must interpose. It is not in the power of the best ministers to check abuses in their offices by their own authority. We may have ministers bankrupt in fortune and in name, and therefore the present bill is indispensable." He actually divided the House upon it—but it was rejected by a majority of 40 to 24.[2]

He soon had a better battle-horse. On the 9th of December appeared at the bar of the House of Lords,

[1] 23 Parl. Hist 730-757.   [2] Ibid 1106-1114.

attended by an immense number of coalition members of the House of Commons, Mr. Secretary Fox, who, delivering a parchment roll to Lord Mansfield as Speaker, said: " The Commons have passed a bill *for the better government of the territorial possessions and dependencies of this kingdom in the East Indies*, to which they pray the concurrence of your Lordships." The bill, as a matter of course, being read a first time,—on the motion "that it be read a second time on Monday next," Thurlow launched forth against it to a willing audience, Lord Temple having very intelligibly conveyed the information to their Lordships that the bill was highly disagreeable to his Majesty, and that the rejection of it would enable his Majesty to get rid of ministers whom his Majesty so much disliked. *Lord Thurlow* · " There is much indecency in proposing so early a day for the consideration of such an important measure—a measure perhaps the most important which was ever agitated in parliament. In the first place, it is a most atrocious violation of private property. If it be necessary, the necessity must be fully and fairly proved by evidence brought to your bar; not by the report of a committee of the other House, to which I would give as much faith as to the adventures of Robinson Crusoe. Whatever necessity for interference may be proved, still I contend that the present bill neither goes to the correction of any existing abuse, to the prevention of any evil in future, nor to the relief of the Company's pressing wants. In fact, my Lords, it is a most direct and daring attack upon the constitution of this country, and a subversion of the first principles of government."

Lord Loughborough tried to defend the bill by reason of the insolvent state of the Company's affairs at home, and the deplorable state of their settlements abroad: " What scenes of desolation and distress do we behold! A prince has been driven from his palace,—his treasures have been seized, and he is now a fugitive wandering among the jungles of the Ganges. Fertile provinces have been laid waste—wars have been entered into without provocation and without advantage—and a peace with the Mahrattas will only lead to a fresh war with Tippoo Saib. A country so misgoverned must be wrested from the hands of its present weak or wicked rulers."

Lord Thurlow.—" The noble and learned Lord has not

yet vouchsafed to give any solution to my difficulties. I ask the noble and learned Lord whether he can reconcile the principles of this bill to the principles of the British Constitution, even supposing the necessity for the interference of Parliament to be apparent? The noble and learned Lord presiding in two of our supreme Courts, I might have expected to find him the champion of British justice.¹ It is not fitting that such a character should meddle in the dirty pool of politics. The present bill means evidently to create a power which is unknown to the constitution—an *imperium in imperio;* but as I abhor tyranny in all its shapes, I shall strenuously oppose this most monstrous attempt to set up a power in the kingdom which may be used in opposition to the Crown, and to destroy the liberties of the people. I wish to see the Crown great and respectable; but if the present bill should pass, it will be no longer worthy of a man of honor to wear. The King, by giving the royal assent to it, will, in fact, take the Crown from his own head, and place it on the head of Mr. Fox."²

From the manner in which these observations were received by the House, it was clear that the victory was won. The only consideration was as to the manner in which the bill should be rejected. Without any division, an order was made for hearing counsel and evidence at the bar in support of the Petition of the East India Company against the bill; and Thurlow, notwithstanding the vigorous efforts of Lord Loughborough, being supported by Lord Mansfield and Lord Camden, was able to dictate the mode in which the examinations should be conducted,—so that the final catastrophe was evidently at hand. In the debate on the second reading. Thurlow would not vouchsafe even to deal out any more vituperation or denunciation. He contented himself with calling out, "Question! question! Divide! divide!" The bill was rejected by a majority of 95 to 76.³

Next night, at twelve o'clock, a messenger delivered to the two Secretaries of State, Mr. Fox and Lord North, his Majesty's orders "that they should surrender up the seals of their offices by their under-secretaries, as a per-

---

¹ Lord Loughborough was at this time Chief Justice of the Common Pleas and First Commissioner of the Great Seal.
² 24 Parl Hist 122. ³ Ibid. 226.

sonal interview on the occasion would be disagreeable to him." The seals were immediately given to Earl Temple, who, as Secretary of State, sent letters of dismission the day following to the rest of the Cabinet Council. At the same time Mr. William Pitt, at the age of twenty-four, was declared Prime Minister, and the government was formed which many predicted could not last more than a few weeks, but which proved the strongest and the most durable of any during the long reign of George III.

Thurlow was, of course, to be restored to his office of Lord Chancellor, and he promised very cordially to support the new chief, though laughing at him in private on account of his zeal for reform, and his professions of public virtue. We shall see that, from their very different characters and principles, their mutual jealousies and dislikes were ere long manifested to all the world.

Thurlow's conduct during the Coalition Ministry, though generally blamed with much severity, appears to me the most unexceptionable part of his whole career. He is censured for giving secret advice to the Sovereign when he was not in office; but we must not carry our constitutional notions to a pedantic length. I think George III. was fully justified in wishing to get rid of Mr. Fox and Lord North as soon as possible; and I can not condemn an experienced statesman, who was in opposition, for giving him hints as to the most expedient course to be pursued for gaining that object. Even if he repeated Lord Temple's declaration, that "his Majesty disliked the Indian Bill," I do not see that he was guilty of any very heinous offense. The name of the Sovereign can not be regularly mentioned in parliament to influence debate, but it is absurd to suppose that he can never have any wish except that of his ministers for the time being, and that he alone, of all persons in his dominions, is to be without any private opinion. Although his private opinion on a public measure is not binding, either in or out of parliament, there are rare occasions where it may not improperly be made known, and George III. may deserve some credit for then acting as the Coryphæus of his subjects. No one in the present age believes that the framers of this famous India Bill had the intention imputed to them of erecting a power independent of the Crown; but its policy was doubtful. The join. sway of the Court of Directors and the Board of Control being substituted for the arbitrary rule of the "Seven Kings," our Eastern empire has been governed with wisdom, with success, and with glory.

The Lords Commissioners having some business to wind up in the Court of Chancery, the transfer of the Great Seal did not take place till the 23rd of December. On that day they surrendered it at a council held at the Queen's House, and it was restored to Thurlow, with the title of Lord Chancellor.[1]

It must have been amusing, during the ceremony, to observe the countenances of the two principal performers, who, having been friendly associates, had become bitter rivals—who had been years violently struggling, and who for years continued violently to struggle, for the same bauble. But how little could they penetrate into futurity! The wary Wedderburn, thus obliged to part with the object of his affections, afterwards met with a cruel disappointment, when, on the King's illness, he thought it was within his clutch; and the reckless Thurlow, at that time willing to sacrifice his benefactor and his party, that he might retain it,—subsequently securely in possession of it,—in consequence of his own waywardness and intemperance, saw it transferred to his opponent—who now despondingly believed that his chance of reaching the summit of his ambition was gone for ever.

During the storms which raged in the House of Commons for the remainder of the session, there was a perfect calm in the House of Lords. Here the new Ministry had from the beginning a complete ascendency; while in the House of Commons there were great, though decreasing, majorities against them, led on by Mr. Fox and Lord North.

It was only thought necessary to rouse the Peers into action. The Commons having passed certain resolutions which it was contended amounted to a repeal of an act

---

[1] "23rd Dec 1783 The Lords Commissioners for the custody of the Great Seal of Great Britain having delivered the said Great Seal to the King, at the Queen's House, on Wednesday, the 23id of December, 1783, his Majesty the same day delivered it to Edward, Lord Thurlow, with the title of Lord High Chancellor of Gieat Britain," &c. The entry goes on in the usual form to state his sitting in Lincoln's Inn Hall next day, and his taking the oaths in Westminster Hall the first day of the following Hilary Term, the Master of the Rolls holding the book, &c.—*Cr. Off. Min* No. 2, p 32.

of parliament, and to a denial of the King's right to choose his own Ministers, Lord Effingham brought forward counter resolutions in the Upper House, denying the right of one branch of the legislature to suspend the execution of the laws, and affirming the King's prerogative in the appointment of his ministers. These were opposed by Lord Loughborough, who insisted that the resolutions of the Commons were constitutional, as that House had a control over the supplies, and a right to advise the Crown upon the exercise of the prerogative. He said:—" There is a maxim that 'the King can do no wrong;' but the law admits the possibility of the King being deceived, and there is no doubt that princes are more likely to be imposed upon than other men. According to this principle, the Commons, even before the Revolution, were in the habit, as often as they deemed it expedient, of addressing the King, humbly praying him to change his councils and his counciliors. I doubt not the abilities of many of the present Administration—for some of whom I have the greatest esteem. Yet I think it very ill-advised that they should remain in office after the majorities which have appeared against them. They might see the perilous consequences of a breach between the two Houses of Parliament which they are now precipitating. An attempt is made to establish an executive power independent of parliament, and to create a precedent which may be fatal to the dignity and to the authority of both Houses." The Lord Chancellor, leaving the woolsack, reprobated the resolutions lately come to by the Commons as " the wild efforts of childish ambition." " Is their discretion," continued he, " to be substituted for law? I know how irksome it is to be obliged, from conscience and a love of justice, to oppose the desires of such a powerful body; this is not reposing on a bed of roses; but if I had been placed in the situation of the present Lords of the Treasury when served with the illegal mandate, I trust I should have had firmness to spurn at it with contempt and disdain." He warmly eulogized Mr. Pitt, and particularly dwelt on his disinterestedness in recently refusing the lucrative sinecure of the Clerk of the Pells, "which," said he, " I was shabby enough to advise him to accept, and certainly should, under his circumstances, have been shabby enough myself to have accepted." He recommended the resolutions now moved as "a corrective of the wildness of that mad ambition which, by talking in a nonsensical tone of the dignity and honor of parliament, persuaded men, of whom better things might be expected, to adopt measures extravagant, absurd, and mischievous."[1]

The tide of popular favor running stronger and stronger against the Coalitionists, although Mr. Pitt continued in a minority in the House of Commons, and an address had been carried there praying for a change of ministers,—it was determined to dissolve parliament, and to appeal to the people. While preparations were making to carry this measure into effect, the metropolis was thrown into consternation by the news that the Great Seal was stolen from the custody of the Lord Chancellor; and many, who attached a superstitious reverence to this bauble, imagined that for want of it all the functions of the executive government must be suspended. A charge was brought against the Whigs that, to prevent the threatened dissolution, they had burglariously broken into the Lord Chancellor's house in the night time, and feloniously stolen and carried off the CLAVIS REGNI.

The truth was, that, very early in the morning of the 24th of March, some thieves did break into Lord Thurlow's house in Great Ormond Street, which then bordered on the country. Coming from the fields, they had jumped over his garden wall, and, forcing two bars from the kitchen window, went up a stair to a room adjoining the study. Here they found the Great Seal inclosed in the two bags so often described in the Close Roll,—one of leather, the other of silk,—two silver-hilted swords belonging to the Chancellor's officers,—and a small sum of money. With the whole of this booty they absconded. They effected their escape without having been heard by any of the family; and, though a reward was offered for their discovery, they never could be traced. It will hardly be believed that Lord Loughborough, under whose legal advice the Whig party at this period acted, could be so bad a lawyer as to recommend this burglary as a maneuver to embarrass the Government, although King James II. had thought that he had effectually defeated the enterprise of

[1] 24 Parl. Hist. 513.

the Prince of Orange by throwing the Great Seal into the river Thames.

When the Chancellor awoke and found what had happened, he immediately went to Mr. Pitt in Downing Stret, and the two waited upon his Majesty at Buckingham House to communicate the intelligence to him. A council was thereupon called, at which the following order was made:—

"At the Court of St. James's, the 24th of March, 1784, present, the King's most Excellent Majesty in Council,— Whereas in the course of the last night the House of the Right Honorable the Lord High Chancellor of Great Britain was broken open, and the Great Seal of Great Britain stolen from thence; it is this day ordered by his Majesty in Council, that his chief engraver of seals do immediately prepare a Great Seal of Great Britain with the following alterations:—

"That on the side where his Majesty is represented on horseback, the number of the present year 1784 be inserted in figures on the plain surface of the seal behind his Majesty; and the herbage under the horse's hind legs omitted.

"That on the reverse, where his Majesty is sitting in state, the palm branch and the cornucopia be omitted on the side of the arms at the top; and over the above arms the number of the present year 1784 in figures to be inserted, and at the bottom also the present year MDCCLXXXIIII. in Roman figures.

"And that he do present the same to his Majesty at this board to-morrow for his royal approbation. And the Right Honorable Lord Sidney, one of his Majesty's principal Secretaries of State, is to cause a warrant to be prepared for his royal signature to the said engraver upon this occasion."

Such expedition was used, that by noon the following day the new Great Seal was finished in a rough fashion, and the following order was made:—

"At the Court at the Queen's House, the 25th of March, 1784, present, the King's most Excellent Majesty in Council,—A new Great Seal of Great Britain having been prepared by his Majesty's chief engraver of seals in pursuance of a warrant to him for that purpose under his royal signature, and the same having been this day presented to his Majesty in Council and approved, his Majesty was thereupon graciously pleased to deliver the said new Seal to the Right Honorable Edward Lord Thurlow, Lord High Chancellor of Great Britain, and to direct that the same shall be made use of for sealing all things whatsoever which pass the Great Seal."[1]

From the Council at St. James's his Majesty immediately proceeded to the House of Lords, and, the Commons being summoned (the Lord Chancellor standing on his right hand, holding the new Great Seal in the old purse), thus pronounced the doom of the Coalitionists:—

"My Lords and Gentlemen, on a full consideration of the present situation of affairs and of the extraordinary circumstances which have produced it, I am induced to put an end to this session of parliament; and I feel it a duty, which I owe to the constitution and to the country in such a situation, to recur as speedily as possible to the sense of my people by calling a new parliament."

In allusion to this theft of the Great Seal, the Rolliad, after describing the different classes of nobility in the House of Lords,—in the following lines "proceeds to take notice of the admirable person who so worthily presided in that august assembly:"—

[1] Shortly afterwards, this make-shift was replaced by a new Great Seal of exquisite workmanship, which the artist took a whole year to complete, and which was used during the remainder of the reign of George III, as appears from the following entries —

"At the Court of St James's, the 2nd of April, 1784, present the King's most Excellent Majesty in Council,—It is this day ordered by his Majesty in Council, that his Majesty's chief engraver of seals do forthwith prepare the draft of a new Great Seal of Great Britain, and present the same to his Majesty at this board for his royal approbation"

"At the Court at St. James's, the 14th of May, 1784, present, the King's most Excellent Majesty in Council,—His Majesty in Council having been this day pleased to approve the draft of a new Great Seal of Great Britain, doth hereby order that his chief engraver of seals do forthwith engrave the said Seal according to the said draft, and lay the same before his Majesty at this board for his royal approbation, and that the Rt Hon Lord Sidney, one of his Majesty's principal Secretaries of State, do cause a warrant to be prepared for his Majesty's royal signature to the said engraver upon this occasion"

"At the Court of St James's, the 15th of April, 1785, present, the King's most excellent Majesty in Council,—This day, the old Great Seal being delivered up to his Majesty by the Right Hon Edward, Lord Thurlow, Lord High Chancellor of Great Britain, the same was defaced in his Majesty's presence, and his Majesty was thereupon pleased to deliver to his Lordship a new Great Seal."

> "The rugged Thurlow, who, with sullen scowl,
> In surly mood, at friend and foe will growl,
> Of proud prerogative, the stern support,
> Defends the entrance of great George's Court
> 'Gainst factious Whigs, *lest they who stole the Seal*
> The sacred diadem itself should steal
> So have I seen near village butcher's stall
> (If things so great may be compar'd with small)
> A mastiff guarding on a market day
> With snarling vigilance his master's tray "[1]

When the appeal to the people was made, the Coalitionists were swept away like chaff before the wind; and a House of Commons was returned, ready to do whatever Mr. Pitt should desire them, except to reform the abuses in the representation of the people—a measure which he still urged earnestly, and I believe sincerely.

From the meeting of the new parliament till the question of the Regency arose, Thurlow enjoyed perfect ease, tranquillity, and security. No administration in England ever was in such a triumphant position as that of Mr. Pitt, when, after the opposition it had encountered, the nation, applauding the choice of the Crown, declared in its favor, and the Coalition leaders, with their immense talents, family interest, and former popularity, found difficulty to obtain seats in the House of Commons.

While Mr. Fox, Mr. Burke, and Mr. Sheridan kept up some smart debates upon the Westminster scrutiny and other subjects, the House of Lords usually met only to adjourn.[2] However, there was a little show of resistance there to Mr. Pitt's India Bill, Lord Stormont objecting to its proceeding in the absence of the law Lords; but the Lord Chancellor caused much merriment by showing "that of the six there was only one absent from being entangled in the discharge of professional duty;" and the general opinion was, that the opportunity should not be lost of getting quietly on with the second reading. There was only one division on the bill—when (to prove the little interest which the subject now excited) the numbers

---

[1] Many other *jeux d'esprit* were made upon this occasion, some of which I have heard from men who are now grave judges and dignitaries in the Church, but I may not set down. The most popular was a supposed dialogue between the Chancellor and a lady of his family, beginning—
  " When Thurlow was told warm in bed
    That the Great Seal was stolen, how he cursed and he swore "
[2] Now was uttered the sarcasm on their Lordships, which may still be re-

were 11 to 4.[1] The Chancellor likewise condescended to defend against a sharp attack of Lord Loughborough on Mr. Pitt's famous bill for commuting the tax on tea[2] for one on widows,—ably demonstrating the advantages of low duties and free trade.[3] Nevertheless, before the conclusion of this session, he showed symptoms of that waywardness of temper, or rather dislike of Mr. Pitt, which broke out from time to time, and at last caused his removal from office.

Mr. Dundas, as the organ of the Government, had brought in a bill, which Mr. Pitt supported in an able speech, and which passed the Commons without the slightest opposition, for restoring the estates in Scotland, forfeited in the rebellion of 1745, to the heirs of the former owners who had been attainted. But when it stood in the orders of the day for a second reading in the House of Lords, the Lord Chancellor left the woolsack, and, instead of opening it, as was expected, and moving that it be read a second time, to the great amazement of all his hearers, spoke as follows:—

"My Lords, I desire to know what there is to render it necessary that a bill of such magnitude should pass so suddenly at the very close of the session? I speak of this bill as a private man, for I know nothing of it as a minister. I do lament that I never heard of it till it had been read a first time in the other House. Since then, considering my various avocations, noble Lords will easily believe that I have not had time to consider it with sufficient attention. I must confess, my Lords, I think it would have been more regular if the bill had originated in this House, or with the King himself. In that case I might have been favored with some prior intimation of the grounds on which, it seems, his Majesty has been advised to relax the severity of the laws against treason, framed for the public tranquillity. Bills of remission and lenity have almost invariably been introduced by a message from the Crown to this House. I will not attempt to argue at length against the bill, for all arguments would

peated —"SCENE BELOW THE BAR." *1st Mob*. "How *sleepy* the Lords are!" *2nd Mob* "No wonder, *they rise so early.*"
[1] 24 Parl. Hist. 1290–1310
[2] "While Billy list'ning to their tuneful plea,
In silence sipp'd his *Commutation* tea"—*Rolliad.*
[3] 24 Parl. Hist. 1374.

be vain if the Government be resolved to carry it." He contended, however, that "by a settled maxim of the British constitution, nothing was an adequate punishment for treason, a crime leading to the subversion of government, but the total eradication of the traitor, his name, and family, from the society he had injured. *Fuit hæc sapientia quondam.* This was the wisdom of former times. This was the rule of conduct laid down and invariably acted upon. But if a more enlightened age thinks otherwise, I hope equal liberality is to be shown to the heirs of those attainted in former rebellions." He likewise objected strongly to a clause in the bill, for applying part of the accumulated fund arising from the rents of these estates, to the completion of the Forth and Clyde Canal, which he denounced as a job, and thus concluded: "I am far from imputing any improper motive to those from whom the measure comes. I know them well, and know their honor to be equal to their great abilities; but it is incumbent on me, sitting on the woolsack, to look with an unbiassed mind to every measure that comes before the House, from whatever quarter, and scrupulously to form my judgment upon it according to the principles of justice and equity. Possibly I may stand single in my sentiments respecting this bill; but I think it my duty to deliver them."

He did not venture to divide; or very likely the Lord Chancellor would have been in the novel situation of having no one to appoint teller on his own side. The bill passed without further opposition.[1] The probability is, that the supposed affront arose from the measure being thought so unobjectionable, that the Chancellor, to save trouble, was not consulted about it,—or it might have been discussed at a cabinet when he was asleep. His belief that the King was so devotedly attached to him made him careless about pleasing or displeasing the Minister, and encouraged him to take liberties with the House and with all public men.[2]

[1] 24 Parl. Hist 1363-1375.
[2] We may know what his opponents at this time thought might be plausibly imputed to him from the *jeu d'esprit* in the Rolliad, entitled " THE POLITICAL RECEIPT BOOK for the year 1784:—"

"*How to make a Chancellor.*

"Take a man with great abilities, with a heart as black as his countenance. Let him possess a rough inflexibility, without the least tincture of

In the session of 1785, notwithstanding his former opposition to the same policy, Thurlow now strenuously supported the propositions for a commercial union with Ireland, which do so much honor to the memory of Mr. Pitt, and not only show that he was disposed to govern that country with justice and liberality, but that, being the first disciple of Adam Smith, who had been in power, he thoroughly understood, and was resolved to carry into effect, the principles of free trade. The Chancellor treated with infinite contempt the witnesses who appeared at the bar to prove the ruin which would overtake the manufactures of England if the manufactures of Ireland, where labor was so cheap, might come into competition with them. He spared Peel, the head of the cotton-spinners; but he said, that "while the great Wedgewood was a distinguished *potter*, he was a very bad *politician*." [1]

When parliament met, in the beginning of 1786, in spite of the general tranquillity and the returning prosperity of the nation, an attack was made by Lord Loughborough upon Ministers, respecting their Irish and their Indian policy; but Lord Thurlow defended both very vigorously, and the address was carried without a division.[2] The Opposition Lords do not seem to have offered any resistance to the measures of Government during the remainder of the session. The impeachment of Mr. Hastings was the only subject which now interested the public mind; and this, calling forth unexampled displays of eloquence from Burke and Sheridan, had not yet reached the Upper House.

The session of 1787, though still without any ministerial crisis, was not quite so sluggish. The French commercial treaty concluded with M. de Vergennes, founded on the best principles of international policy, and calculated to draw together, by mutual benefits, two nations, between whom, from prohibitory duties and rankling jealousies, there had for centuries only been a succession of wars and truces, being factiously attacked by Lord Loughborough and other Opposition Peers, was vio-

generosity or affection, and be as manly as oaths and ill manners can make him. He should be a man who will act politically with all parties, hating and deriding every one of the individuals who compose them "—*Rolliad*, 22nd ed. p 430 [1] 25 Parl. Hist. 820-855
[2] Ib 995 This debate is memorable for being the first in which a legislative Union with Ireland was ever publicly proposed.

lently defended by the Lord Chancellor. He, as usual, abstained from any expenditure of argument, of which, whether in judging or debating, he was ever penurious; but he asserted, and adjudged, that the treaty was an excellent treaty, and he pronounced all the objections to it to be frivolous and vexatious. He gained a considerable, but undeserved, triumph over Lord Shelburne (now become Marquis of Lansdowne), who had the temerity to interrupt him. Commenting on certain observations respecting the "Family Compact" between France and Spain, and the erection of new fortifications at Cherbourg, Thurlow said, " I maintain, my Lords, that the Family Compact is a treaty which no nation on earth has a right to tell France or Spain they may not make. If Spaniards in France are to be treated as Frenchmen, and Frenchmen in Spain are to be treated as Spaniards, and there is an alliance offensive and defensive between them, why should we murmur? We are told that a remonstrance should be made against the fortifications now carrying on at Cherbourg. Where is the minister who would venture to make such a remonstrance? [*Marquis of Lansdowne:* 'I would.'] By what part of the law of nations have we a right to remonstrate? [*Marquis of Lansdowne:* 'We have no right.'] Then the noble Marquis would do what he confesses he has no right to do; so that he and his application would be laughed at as absurd and ridiculous."[1]

The House, however, soon after, for once, rebelled against their tyrant. The Duke of Queensberry, and the Earl of Abercorn, while representative Peers of Scotland, being created British Peers, Lord Stormont moved a resolution, which he founded on a just construction of the Articles of Union, that they ceased to sit as representatives of the Scotch Peerage; and Dr. Watson, Bishop of Llandaff, ably supported the motion. *Lord Chancellor :* " Your Lordships are not to listen to supposed or real convenience, to this or that set of men,—nor to consider what an act of parliament ought to be, but what it is. Here you have the Treaty of Union, which contains no such disqualification; and I say you are bound to abide

[1] 26 Parl. Hist 586 We could not have remonstrated on this occasion as we formerly did about the fortifications of Dunkirk,—which, by treaty, were to be demolished, but all warlike preparations may be made the subject of representation and remonstrance—although the law of nations does not forbid a state to arm its citizens, and to make all its territory one garrison.

by the letter of it. I must take the liberty of reprehending the noble Viscount for using the arguments with which he introduced his motion, and the Right Reverend Prelate would have done well to have read the Articles of the Union before he ventured to let loose his opinions on the subject. I insist upon it, my Lords, that giving an English title to a Scotch Peer can not take away or diminish any one function previously belonging to him, and that he is as fully capacitated to be a representative Peer of Scotland as before." Nevertheless, Lord Loughborough, taking the opposite side, and making out a strong case, as well by the words of the statute as by precedent, the motion, to the great mortification of the Chancellor, and the general surprise of the bystanders, was carried by a majority of 52 to 38 [1]

The Chancellor soon recovered his ascendency, and, acting on his usual illiberal principles, threw out "a Bill for the Relief of Insolvent Debtors," which, till he spoke, was in great favor with the House. It had been read a second time without opposition ; but on the motion for going into a committee upon it, Lord Thurlow, denying that he was so malignant an enemy to the happiness of mankind as to feel a satisfaction in the distress of any portion of his fellow-creatures, pointed out what he called the manifest injustice of breaking in upon that power of "coercion of payment" with which the law had armed the creditor for the security of his property. "If there is to be," said he, " such a thing as imprisonment for debt, it ought to continue unchecked and unrestrained, unless in cases of flagrant oppression and unnecessary cruelty. The general idea, that humanity requires the intervention of the legislature between the debtor and the creditor, is a false notion—founded in error and dangerous in practice. A much greater evil than the loss of liberty is the dissipation and corruption that prevail in our prisons; to these your Lordships had better direct your attention, than to defrauding the creditor of the chance of recovering his property, by letting loose his debtor, and taking from him the very hope of payment." So blinded was he by prejudice as not to see that the "dissipation and corruption" of

[1] 26 Parl Hist 596–608.

which he complains were produced by the very power of imprisoning which he defended. It is important that such distorted sentiments should be recorded, for the use of those who are to write the history of human errors. How delightful to think that, imprisonment for debt being abolished, the site of the Fleet prison, the scene of misery and vice, the description of which, in the pages of Fielding and Smollett, harrows up our souls, is now to be converted into a center railway station for the metropolis,—so that those who are henceforth to congregate there, instead of being immured for life in darkness and filth, and forced to resort to ebriety as a temporary relief from despair, may in a few hours be conveyed, for the purposes of useful industry or of innocent recreation, through pure air and over verdant fields, to the remotest extremities of the kingdom![1] While the perfectibility of our nature must be acknowledged to be a delusion contrary alike to religion and philosophy, the vast improvements which have been made in our social system should stimulate and encourage our efforts to diminish the sum of crime and of suffering, and to raise the standard of intellectual cultivation and of material comfort among mankind.

The public attention now began to be entirely engrossed by the prosecution of Warren Hastings. The opinion of a subsequent generation has been, that this great man, who, in a time of national depression, and amidst appalling dangers, preserved and extended our Indian empire,—although he had committed faults, and even crimes,—upon the whole deserved well of his country, and ought to have been honored and rewarded. The Opposition, however, misled by exaggerated accounts of his misconduct, eager to recover the popularity which they had lost by the Coalition, and surrendering themselves into the hands of the vengeful Francis and the enthusiastic Burke, because his accusers, and were insensibly involved in the impeachment,—which, notwithstanding the unexampled *éclat* attending it, conferred upon them as a party no lasting credit or solid advantage. The suspicion is, that Pitt, a little alarmed by the high favor shown to Hastings at Court, and not displeased to

---

[1] Written in 1845, when a bill for this purpose was pending. The scheme was afterwards abandoned as too costly.—*4th Edition.*

see his own adversaries waste their strength in exposing the misgovernment of distant regions, instead of attacking his ministerial measures at home,—although he took a just view of the merits of the cause,—with professions of strict impartiality threw the weight of his influence into the scale of the prosecutors. But Thurlow—partly, let us hope, from a belief of the groundlessness of the charges (although he was not supposed to have had leisure or inclination to examine them)—partly to please the King and Queen, who took Mr. and Mrs. Hastings under their special protection[1]—partly from a desire to find a rival to Pitt, whom he ever regarded with secret enmity—warmly and openly embraced the opposite side; enlarged without qualification on the distinguished virtues and great services of the accused, and supporting him on every occasion "with indecorous violence."[2] Pitt having professed scruples when the King hinted a wish that Hastings, a few months after his return, should be called to the Upper House, Thurlow treated these scruples with contempt, and said, "there was nothing to prevent the holder of the Great Seal from taking the royal pleasure about a patent of peerage." So encouraged, Hastings actually chose his barony. Having fulfilled the resolution he had formed when an orphan boy at a village school—to recover the estate which had been for many centuries in his family,—he now took his title from it, and declared that he would be "Lord Daylesford of Daylesford, in the county of Worcester." But Pitt put an end to all these speculations, after voting for him on the charge respecting the Rohilla war—one of the best established—by voting against him on the charge respecting the treatment of Cheyte Sing—one of the most unfounded—although, when it was to be brought forward by Mr. Fox, a Treasury circular had been sent to all the ministerial members, asking them to attend, and vote against it. Great was

---

[1] In the libels of the day, this reception was ascribed less to to the King's sense of the services of the husband than to the presents made by his wife to the Queen.—Thus in the famous Eclogue of "THE LYARS," we have Bank's stanza to show the power of gold

"Say what mineral, brought from distant climes,
Which screens delinquents and absolves their crimes,
Whose dazzling rays confound the space between
A tainted strumpet and a spotless Queen."

[2] Macaulay's Ess. III 429.

the astonishment of the friends of Mr. Hastings, and of the whole House; but it is said that, a few hours before the debate began, Pitt received intelligence of the intrigue respecting the peerage, and of Thurlow's declaration that, under the King's authority, he would put the Great Seal to the patent without consulting any other minister. The turn was so sudden that even the Attorney General divided against the premier; but the impeachment was carried by a majority of 119 to 79. The other articles were voted without difficulty, and on the 14th day of May, 1787, Mr. Burke appeared at the bar of the House of Lords, attended by many members, and, " in the name of the House of Commons and all the Commons of England, impeached Warren Hastings, Esq., of high crimes and misdemeanors." Thurlow was at no pains to conceal his disapprobation of the proceeding, and resolved to do every thing in his power to defeat it.

Mr. Hastings being arrested by the Sergeant-at-arms of the House of Commons, and handed over to the custody of the Gentleman Usher of the Black Rod, as the officer of the House of Lords,—the Duke of Norfolk proposed that he should be held to bail for £50,000, but the Lord Chancellor not improperly procured the sum to be reduced to £20,000, with two sureties in £10,000 each.[1]

The trial did not begin till the 13th of February in the following year. The charge not being capital, no Lord High Steward was appointed; and Lord Thurlow, during the time he held the Great Seal, presided over it as Chancellor, or Speaker of the House of Lords, although at the conclusion of it, having been deprived of office, he was the lowest in dignity.

"There have been spectacles," says Mr. Macaulay, " more dazling to the eye, more gorgeous with jewelry and cloth of gold, more attractive to grown-up children, than that which was now exhibited at Westminster; but, perhaps, there never was a spectacle so well calculated to strike a highly cultivated, a reflecting, an imaginative mind. Still the various kinds of interest which belong to the near and to the distant, to the present and to the past, were collected on one spot and in one hour. All the talents, and all the accomplishments, which are developed by liberty and civilization, were now displayed with every

[1] 26 Parl. Hist 1217.

advantage that could be derived both from co-operation and from contrast. Every step in the proceedings carried the mind either backward through many troubled centuries to the days when the foundations of our constitution were laid ; or far away over boundless seas and deserts to dusky nations, living under strange stars, worshiping strange gods, and writing strange characters from right to left. The High Court of Parliament was to sit, according to forms handed down from the days of the Plantagenets, on an Englishman accused of exercising tyranny over the lord of the holy city of Benares, and over the ladies of the princely House of Oude."

I could only wish, that in the gorgeous description of the ceremonial which follows—amidst the nobles, judges, orators, statesmen, beauties, artists, and men of letters, who are presented to us, we had been favored with a view of the rugged Thurlow frowning on the woolsack, shaking his awful locks,—terrible to behold.

After the proclamation was made in Westminster Hall by the crier, that Warren Hastings, Esq., late Governor of Bengal, was now at his trial for high crimes and misdemeanors, with which he was charged by the Commons of Great Britain, and that all persons who had aught to allege against him were now to stand forth—a general silence followed, and the Chancellor thus addressed the accused :—

" Warren Hastings, you are brought into this Court to answer to the charges preferred against you by the Knights Burgesses, and Commons of Great Britain—charges now standing only as allegations, by them to be legally proved or by you to be disproved. Bring forth your answers and defense with that seriousness, respect, and truth, due to accusers so respectable. Time has been allowed you for preparation, proportioned to the intricacies in which the transactions are involved, and to the remote distances whence your documents may have been searched and required. You will still be allowed bail, for the better forwarding your defense, and what ever you can require will still be yours, of time, witnesses, and all things else you may hold necessary. This is not granted you as any indulgence : it is entirely your due : it is the privilege which every British subject has a right to claim, and which may be claimed by every one who is brought before this high tribunal."

"This speech" (says Madame D'Arblay), "uttered in a calm, equal, solemn manner, and in a voice mellow and penetrating, with eyes keen and black, yet softened into some degree of tenderness, whilst fastened full upon the prisoner,—this speech, its occasion, its portent, and its object, had an effect upon every hearer of producing the most respectful attention in the cause of Mr. Hastings."[1]

As the trial proceeded, the first contest which arose was at the conclusion of Mr. Burke's great opening oration,—"whether each charge should be treated and concluded by speeches and evidence separately, or the Commons should be required to open all the charges, and give all their evidence in support of them, before the accused was called upon to begin his defense?" Mr. Fox strongly recommended the former mode of proceeding, for the sake of convenience and justice, and in pursuance of parliamentary precedent—particularly the trial of Lord Strafford.

Lord Chancellor. "Mr. Burke, whose imagination is of unparalleled fertility, in stating the case against the defendant, has mentioned circumstances of such accumulated horror, and of such deep criminality, that every thing contained in the written articles of accusation before your Lordships sinks in the comparison to utter insignificance, and the Right Hon. manager has unequivocally declared that he has not assumed the privilege of an advocate to exaggerate. After this I shall hold him to the proof of all he has asserted. Acts of such atrocity, my Lords, were imputed to the defendant, that many very respectable persons who were present have not yet recovered, and probably never will recover, the shock they sustained at listening to the relation of them. But in proportion as I am ready to punish Mr. Hastings with severity when lawfully convicted, I must see that he has a full and fair opportunity of vindicating his innocence. This he can only have by hearing all that is to be said or

---

[1] It will be recollected that Miss Burney, then in the service of Queen Charlotte, partook of all the feelings of the Court in favor of Mr. Hastings. Describing the scene in Westminster Hall, she goes on to say—"Mr Windham, then looking still at the spectacle, which indeed is the most splendid I ever saw, arrested his eyes upon the Chancellor. 'He looks very well from hence,' cried he, 'and how well he acquits himself on these solemn occasions! With what dignity, what loftiness, what high propriety he comports himself!' This praise to the Chancellor, who is a known friend to Mr Hastings, though I believe he would be the last to favor him unjustly now he is on trial, was a pleasant sound to my ear."

proved against him under all the charges, before he is called upon for his defense. With respect to the usage of parliament, of which we have been told so much, as contradistinguished from the common law, I utterly disclaim all knowledge of it. It has no existence. In times of barbarism, indeed, when to impeach a man was to ruin him by the strong hand of power, the usage of parliament was quoted in order to justify the most arbitrary proceedings. In these enlightened days I hope that no man will be tried but by the law of the land, which is admirably calculated to protect innocence and to punish guilt. The trial of Lord Strafford was, from beginning to end, marked by violence and injustice. A licentious and unprincipled fellow, Pym, attacked that Lord with all the virulence and malignity of faction. The real crime of that great statesman was, that he had quitted his party—as if it were not meritorious to serve the state instead of a faction—as if it were a crime to quit a gang of highwaymen. The Commons may impeach, but your Lordships try the cause; and the same rules of procedure and of evidence which obtain in the Courts below, I am sure will be rigidly followed by your Lordships."

Lord Loughborough strongly supported the opposite side, but was beaten by a majority of 88 to 33,—which very distinctly intimated what, at a distant period, would be the final result of the prosecution. [1]

Before the King's illness threw the country into confusion, the only other matter of public interest in which Thurlow took part was "African Slavery." A great change of sentiment had taken place since the times when the ASSIENTO treaty was negotiated, securing to us, with the joy and applause of all parties in the state, in addition to our own slave trade, the privilege of supplying with slaves the colonies of other nations. From the immortal efforts of Granville Sharpe, Clarkson, and Wilberforce, the traffic in human flesh now began to be viewed by many with abhorrence; and even some zealous defenders of whatever is established occasionally doubted whether the practice of acquiring by force or by fraud the possession of human beings, removing them for ever from their native shore, and, after the indescribable horrors of their passage across the ocean, condemning the

[1] 27 Parl Hist. 55-65.

survivors and their progeny to interminable toil for the profit of strangers, under the stimulus of whipping and torture,—was quite consistent with the dictates of humanity, and with the religion of Jesus, who had taught us to consider and to treat all mankind as brethren, and "to do unto others as we would that they should do unto us." In the session of 1788 the subject was brought before the House of Commons, and Mr. Pitt, with the fervor and sincerity of youth, supported the views of those who were resolved to free the country from the disgraceful stain.

As a preliminary measure, a bill was passed to mitigate the atrocities of the "Middle Passage," by enacting that slave ships should not carry beyond a certain number of slaves in proportion to their tonnage,—evidence having been given at the bar, that in those ships no slave had a space to lie in more than five feet six inches in length by sixteen inches in breadth; that not only the decks were covered with bodies thus stowed, but that between the decks and the ceiling there were often platforms or broad shelves similarly covered; that the slaves were chained two and two together by their hands and feet, and were fastened by ring bolts to the deck; that the "dancing" boasted of to prove their cheerfulness, consisted in compelling them to jump a certain time daily on the deck in irons for their health; that the mortality among them was appalling; and that sometimes, when not watched, large numbers of them, from despair, leaped overboard and were drowned.[1] When the bill came up to the House of Lords, the Chancellor opposed it in his peculiar manner, by saying, "that as it stood it was *nonsense*, and that he concluded some amendment would be proposed to correct the *nonsense* of one part of it with the *nonsense* of the other." He afterwards boldly spoke out, saying—"It appears that the French have offered premiums to encourage the African trade, and that they have succeeded. The natural presumption therefore is, that we ought to do the same. For my part, my Lords, I have no scruple to say that if the 'five days' fit of philanthropy' which has just sprung up, and which has slept for twenty years together, were allowed to sleep one sum-

[1] There are several cases in the Law Reports on the question, "whether the underwriters were liable for the death of slaves from suicide?"

mer longer, it would appear to me rather more wise than thus to take up a subject piecemeal, which it has been publicly declared ought not to be agitated at all till next session of parliament. Perhaps, by such imprudence, the slaves themselves may be prompted, by their own authority, to proceed at once to 'a total and immediate abolition of the trade.' One witness has come to your Lordships' bar with a face of woe—his eyes full of tears, and his countenance fraught with horror, and said, ' My Lords, I am ruined if you pass this bill! I have risked £30,000 on the trade this year! It is all I have been able to gain by my industry, and if I lose it I must go to the hospital!' I desire of you to think of such things, my Lords, in your humane frenzy, and to show some humanity to the whites as well as to the negroes." But Mr. Pitt would not allow the Government to be disgraced by the rejection of the bill. It passed the Lords, with some amendments for granting compensation; and these being objected to by the Commons, on the score of privilege, another bill to the same effect passed both Houses and received the royal assent.[1]

CHAPTER CLX.

CONTINUATION OF THE LIFE OF LORD THURLOW TILL HE WAS FINALLY DISMISSED FROM THE OFFICE OF CHANCELLOR.

IN the midst of profound tranquillity at home and abroad, the nation was suddenly thrown into a state of the greatest consternation and alarm by the avowal of his Majesty's complete incapacity to exercise any of the functions of his high office. It is now known that he had labored under a similar illness, for a few weeks, in the year 1765, which was the cause of the regency bill then passed; but the fact was successfully concealed from the public.[2] The symptoms now returned

[1] 27 Parl. Hist 638–649.
[2] "It had been stated by Smollett, in his history of the commencement of this reign, but only a few copies containing the statement were sold, they were eagerly bought up by the Government, and the faint whisper which they caused died away."—*Adolphus*, 1 177

upon him, at first rather gradually, causing unexampled embarrassment to his Ministers. Near the close of the preceding session of parliament, his Majesty was occasionally in a very excited state, and when he returned from his visit to Cheltenham there appeared still greater cause for apprehension. Parliament stood prorogued to the 25th of September.

When that day approached, the King had still intervals of clear understanding, and exhibited demonstrations of accurate perception and an undiminished power of reasoning. A council was held, which went off very quietly,—when an order was made for a further prorogation, and his Majesty signed a warrant for a commission to pass the Great Seal for that purpose, and parliament was, with the usual solemnities, prorogued by the Lord Chancellor till the 20th of November, *then to meet for the dispatch of business.*

At a levee held at St. James's before that day arrived, his Majesty's conversation and demeanor clearly indicated to all who were present the nature of his malady. It was immediately after necessary to put him under restraint; his life for some days was considered to be in imminent danger,—and when this paroxysm subsided, he was still totally and constantly deprived of the use of reason. The royal sufferer was removed first to Windsor, and afterwards to Kew,—where he was put under the care of Dr. Willis, and other physicians supposed to be best acquainted with the treatment of alienation of mind.

Mr. Pitt, whether right or wrong in the opinion he formed, resolved at once, in a direct and straightforward manner, to delay as long as possible the transfer of the power of the Crown to the Prince of Wales, now leagued with the Whigs, and looked upon with distrust by the nation on account of his profligate habits;—to limit materially the exercise of the royal prerogative in the Prince's hands;—to intrust the custody of the King's person, and the patronage of the royal household, to the Queen;—and, for these purposes, to contend that the two Houses of Parliament had the right to appoint a Regent, and to define and restrain the authority under which he was to act. The Prime Minister, assuming for certain that he himself would be dismissed on the accession of the Regent, and wishing to diminish the influence of his successor, had to struggle boldly for a crippled regency, —on the ostensible ground that the rights of the Sovereign supposed to be on the throne might otherwise be endangered.

But the Chancellor was in sad perplexity. Although, only a few weeks before, he thought that he held the Great Seal for life, the dreadful thought now arose that it would be snatched from him by his rival, who had lately seemed for ever destined to the punishment of listening to the drowsy sergeants in the Court of Common Pleas. But Thurlow began to consider with himself whether, having been Chancellor under Lord Rockingham as well as under Lord North, he might not be Chancellor under Mr. Fox as well as under Mr. Pitt. Mr. Fox had not yet returned from his Italian tour, and the Prince's affairs were under the direction of Sheridan and other Whig leaders, who were impatient to see the Prince installed as Regent, who highly disrelished the threatened restrictions, who perceived how useful Thurlow might be if gained over in furthering these objects, who dexterously guessed at his longings and cogitations, and who formed a just estimate of his regard for honor and consistency.

The intrigue with Thurlow is supposed to have been first suggested by Captain Payne, the comptroller of the Prince's household. In a letter to Sheridan, he said: "I think the Chancellor might take a good opportunity to break with his colleagues if they propose restriction. The law authority would have great weight with us, as well as preventing even a design of moving the city." In consequence, a negotiation with the Chancellor was opened, to which the Prince himself was a party. The legal dignitary seemed very placable, and not much disinclined to the doctrine that "the Prince ought to be declared unrestricted Regent," although he took special care, at first, to deal only in general verbal assurances, without entering into any specific engagement.[1] In this state of affairs,

[1] "He studiously sought intercourse with the Prince of Wales, that he might have an opportunity of conveying to him his sentiments on his Royal Highness's situation He recommended to him to lie upon his oars,—to show no impatience to assume the powers of royalty He pointed out to him that if the King's illness were of any considerable duration, the regency must necessarily devolve upon him "—*Nich Recoll* 71.

Captain Payne, again addressing Sheridan, said: "I inclose you the copy of a letter the Prince has just written to the Chancellor, and sent by express, which will give you the outline of the conversation with the Prince, as well as the situation of the King's health. I think it an advisable measure, as it is a sword that cuts both ways, without being unfit to be shown to whom he pleases, but which I think he will understand best himself."

Thurlow, before he would proceed further, required a distinct promise that under the Regency, he should retain the Great Seal. This at first caused much difficulty, for Lord Loughborough had been acting with the Whigs ever since the formation of the Coalition Ministry; a five years' opposition had made them forget all former differences, and it was well understood that he was to gain the grand object of his ambition if they ever came into power. Sheridan, however, advised that, without consulting him, Thurlow, who spurned at the Presidency of the Council, should be bought at his own price, and the bargain was nearly concluded that Thurlow, in consideration of being appointed Chancellor under the Prince when Regent, should support the right of the Prince to succeed to the Regency without restriction.

This was the state of affairs when Fox arrived from Italy. Recollecting what had happened during the Rockingham administration, he had an absolute horror of Thurlow, and heard of the promise given to him with the most bitter regret. However, as things had gone so far, he wrote the following letter to Sheridan, showing his distrust as well as his acquiescence:—

" Dear Sheridan,

" I have swallowed the pill—a most bitter one it was—and have written to Lord Loughborough, whose answer, of course, must be *consent*. What is to be done next? Should the Prince himself, you, or I, or Warren, be the person to speak to the Chancellor? The objection to the last is, that he must probably wait for an opportunity, and that no time is to be lost. Pray tell me what is to be done. I am convinced, after all, that the negotiation will not succeed, and am not sure that I am sorry for it. I do not remember ever feeling so uneasy about any political thing I ever did in my life."

On hearing of this intrigue, so fatal to his hopes, Lord

Loughborough wrote the following letter to Sheridan, by which he tried to counteract it, without disclosing the deep resentment which he felt:—

"My dear S.,

"I was afraid to continue the conversation on the circumstance of the inspection committed to the Chancellor, lest the reflections that arise upon it might have made too strong an impression on some of our neighbors last night. It does, indeed, appear to me full of mischief, and of that sort most likely to affect the apprehensions of our friends (Lord John, for instance), and to increase their reluctance to take any active part.

"The Chancellor's object evidently is to make his way by himself, and he has managed hitherto as one very well practiced in that game. His conversations both with you and Mr. Fox were encouraging, but at the same time checked all explanations on his part, under a pretense of delicacy towards his colleagues. When he let them go to Salthill, and contrived to dine at Windsor, he certainly took a step that most men would have felt not very delicate in its appearance, and, unless there was some private understanding between him and them, not altogether fair, especially if you add to it in the sort of conversation he held with regard to them. I can not help thinking that the difficulties of managing the patient have been invented or improved to lead to the proposal of his inspection (without the Prince being conscious of it), for by that situation he gains an easy and frequent access to him, and an opportunity of possessing the confidence of the Queen. I believe this the more from the account of the tenderness he showed at his first interview, for I am sure it is not his character to feel any. With a little instruction from Lord Hawkesbury, the sort of management that was carried on by means of the Princess Dowager in the early part of the reign may easily be practiced. In short, I think he will try to find the key of the back stairs—and, with that in his pocket, take any situation that preserves his access, and enables him to hold a line between different parties. In the present moment, however, he has taken a position that puts the command of the House of Lords in his hands.

"I wish Mr. Fox and you would give these considerations what weight you think they deserve, and try if any means can be taken to remedy this mischief, if it appears in the same light to you."

This surely must be an exaggerated picture of Thurlow's craft and duplicity;—otherwise, since the time of Richard III., these qualities have not been exhibited in such extraordinary relief by any character in English history. The Chancellor is here represented as interfering with the proper management of the illustrious patient for his own sinister ends,—when admitted to the presence of his afflicted Sovereign, although untouched by the melancholy spectacle, and only anxious about the personal advantages he might derive from it, hypocritically throwing himself into an agony of tears,—plotting alike against his present colleagues, and the party whom he pretended to be about to join,—and appearing by turns to be devoted to his old royal Master—to the Queen—to the Prince—to the Tories, and to the Whigs—ready to betray them all.[1] However much this letter might strengthen the suspicions, entertained by the Prince's friends, of Thurlow's sincerity, it did not induce them to break off the treaty with him, and if he supported them in the impending discussions in parliament, the Great Seal was to be his.

The King being confined at Windsor, the Queen and the Prince, in opposite interests, had both taken up their residence here, and here Mr. Pitt and the Ministers from time to time held their councils. These arrangements were highly convenient to Thurlow, for, by going through

[1] It must be admitted that Lord Loughborough is powerfully corroborated by the very picturesque account we have of "the weeping scene," from Miss Burney, who, then in attendance on the Queen, actually witnessed it :—" It was decreed that the King should be seen both by the Chancellor and Mr Pitt. The Chancellor went into his presence with a tremor such as before he had been only accustomed to inspire, and when he came out he was so extremely affected by the state in which he saw his royal master and patron, that the tears ran down his cheeks, and his feet had difficulty to support him Mr. Pitt was more composed, but expressed his grief with so much respect and attachment, that it added new weight to the universal admiration with which he is here beheld."—*Madame D'Arblay's Diary*, part vii. 338.

The Chancellor seems to have possessed powers of acting grief not inferior to those of the player in *Hamlet*, who—

"But in a fiction, in a dream of passion,
Could form his soul so to his own conceit,
That from her working all his visage wann'd,
Tears in his eyes, distraction in his aspect,
A broken voice, and his whole function suiting
With forms to his conceit."

cloisters and dark corridors to different sets of apartments in the Castle, he could hold a private conference with either party without letting it be known that he communicated with the other. Mr. Pitt was at first duped by such artifices, but suddenly came to the full knowledge of his colleague's perfidy. The exact circumstances of the discovery are variously related, although all accounts agree in stating that it took place at a meeting of the Ministers in Windsor Castle, and that it arose from a mistake which the Chancellor made respecting his hat. Some say that he entered the room, having under his arm the Prince's hat, which he had in the hurry carried off from the Prince's closet instead of his own;—others, that he walked into the room without a hat, and that soon after one of the Prince's pages brought him his own hat, saying that his Lordship had left it behind when he took leave of his Royal Highness;—and others, that entering without his hat, and being reminded of it, he immediately said he supposed he must have left it in another part of the castle, where he had been paying a visit—whereupon the looks of those present immediately made him conscious of the disclosure he had made.[1] But I have received the following account of the discovery from a quarter entitled to the most implicit credit:—
"When a council was to be held at Windsor to determine the course which Ministers should pursue, Thurlow had been there some time before any of his colleagues arrived. He was to be brought back to London by one of them, and the moment of departure being come, the Chancellor's hat was nowhere to be found. After a fruitless search in the apartment where the council had been held, a page came with the hat in his hand, saying aloud, and with great *naiveté*, ' My Lord, I found it in the closet of his Royal Highness the Prince of Wales!' The other Ministers were still in the Hall, and Thurlow's confusion corroborated the inference which they drew."[2]

Mr. Pitt, though now fully aware of his designs, could not immediately throw him off, and still seemed to the public cordially to co-operate with him,—but thenceforth withdrew all confidence from him, and intrusted to Lord

[1] Moore's Life of Sheridan, II. 31; Law Mag. VII. 73, 74.
[2] The Right Honorable Thomas Grenville, who, having at played skittles with Lord Chatham, is since dead, at the age of 90.

Camden the conduct in the House of Lords of all the measures for the establishment of the Regency.

The first debate upon the subject was when, after the examination of the physicians, proving the King's incapacity personally to exercise the functions of government, Lord Camden moved for a committee to search for precedents. Lord Loughborough, on whose legal and constitutional advice the Whigs acted, now reprobated the doctrine broached in the other House, " that the Prince of Wales, the heir apparent to the throne, had no more right to take upon himself the government, during the continuance of the unhappy malady which incapacitated his Majesty, than any other individual subject." He contended strenuously that the regency was not elective; that the two Houses could not interfere with the appointment of the person to exercise the functions of royalty, except upon a total subversion of the government as at the Revolution, or upon the failure of the royal line by the King dying without an heir; that as the two Houses at present confessedly could not pass a turnpike act, much less could they pass an act which might produce a change of the dynasty to fill the throne; and that the heir apparent had a right, during the interruption of the personal exercise of the royal authority, to assume the reins of government—not rashly or violently, but on the authentic notification to him by the two Houses of his Majesty's unfortunate incapacity.

Thurlow was sorely perplexed as to the course he should pursue. Although Dr. Willis gave hopes of the King's speedy recovery, the general opinion at this time was that his malady was incurable—in which case the Prince of Wales must ere long be Regent, with all the patronage of the Crown. He probably was inclined to assert the Prince's right in still more peremptory terms, and to outbid his rival for the Prince's favor. But he could not do so without openly breaking with Mr. Pitt, who had the entire confidence of the Queen, and was sure to be more powerful than ever if his Majesty should indeed be restored. He therefore contented himself, for the present, with appearing to oppose—but opposing very gently—Lord Loughborough's argument, saying that the doctrine of the Prince's right was new, that the discussion was premature; that the question ought not to be in any degree preoccupied ; that such a debate would only afford a subject for a frivolous paragraph in a newspaper, that their Lordships had begun at the wrong end, trying to draw the conclusion before they had settled the premises ; that no objection could possibly be made to the motion of the President of the Council for a committee to inquire ; and that, it being impossible to separate the natural and political character and capacity of the King, while the crown remained firmly fixed on his Majesty's head, the appointment of a Regent must prove a consummation beyond expression difficult." [1] The motion was carried without a division, and for a little while longer Thurlow contrived to keep on decent terms with both parties, giving each hopes of his support, and enjoying the chance of the favor of both. But this double-dealing led him daily into greater perplexities; he saw the danger in a protracted struggle of being himself disgraced, which ever side might prosper; and it is said that he had exclusive information from Dr. Willis of some symptoms in his Majesty's health, which justified a more probable hope of his recovery than had been hitherto entertained.

Accordingly the next time the subject was brought forward in the House of Lords, the Duke of York having made a very sensible speech, renouncing, in the name of his brother, any claim not derived from the will of the people, and lamenting the dreadful calamity which had fallen upon the royal family and upon the nation,—the Lord Chancellor left the woolsack seemingly in a state of great emotion, and delivered a most pathetic address to the House. His voice, broken at first, recovered its clearness,—but this was from the relief afforded to him by a flood of tears. He declared his fixed and unalterable resolution to stand by a Sovereign who, through a reign of twenty-seven years, had proved his sacred regard to the principles which seated his family on the British throne. He at last worked himself up to this celebrated climax:—" A noble Viscount (Stormont) has, in an eloquent and energetic manner, expressed his feelings on the present melancholy situation of his Majesty,—feelings rendered more poignant from the noble Viscount's having been in habits of personally receiving marks of indul-

[1] 27 Parl Hist. 672

gence and kindness from his suffering Sovereign. My own sorrow, my Lords, is aggravated by the same cause. My debt of gratitude is indeed ample for the many favors which have been graciously conferred upon me by his Majesty; AND WHEN I FORGET MY SOVEREIGN, MAY MY GOD FORGET ME?"[1] "GOD FORGET YOU!" muttered Wilkes, who happened then to be seated on the steps of the throne,—eyeing him askance with his inhuman squint and demoniac grin,—"GOD FORGET YOU! HE'LL SEE YOU D——D FIRST."

When the resolution to which the Commons had agreed was moved, "That it is the right and duty of the Lords Spiritual and Temporal, and Commons of Great Britain, now assembled, and lawfully, fully, and freely representing all the estates of the people of this realm, to provide the means of supplying the defect of the personal exercise of the royal authority, arising from his Majesty's indisposition, in such manner as the exigency of the case may appear to them to require,"—and Lord Rawdon (afterwards Marquis of Hastings) having moved an amendment, "That an humble address be presented to his Royal Highness the Prince of Wales, praying his Royal Highness to take upon himself, as sole Regent, the administration of the executive government in the King's name during his Majesty's indisposition," Thurlow, without any reserve, supported the resolution, and inveighed against the amendment. Knowing well that it had been framed very carefully by Lord Loughborough, who had spoken ably in defense of it, he said,—

"I am glad to think that the words of this amendment can not have been supplied by the noble and learned Lord, the Chief Justice of the Common Pleas, for they are not only irreconcilable with the arguments of that great magistrate, but they convey no distinct or precise meaning whatever. I wish that some one, who professes to understand them, had explained their meaning, and given us something like a reason to show their propriety. I beg to know, what is the meaning of the term 'REGENT?' Where shall I see it defined? in what law book, or in what statute? I have heard of 'Grand Justiciars,' of '*Custodes Regni*,' of 'Lieutenants for the King,' of 'Guardians,' of 'Protectors,' of 'Lords Justices:' but I

[1] 27 Parl Hist. 680, Ann Reg 1789, p 125.

know nothing of the office or functions of a 'REGENT.' To what end, then, would it be to ask the Prince to take upon himself an office, the boundaries of which are wholly unascertained? The amendment, to be sure, states that what the Prince, as sole Regent, is to be prayed to take upon himself, is 'the administration of the executive government.' Here, again, the expression is dark and equivocal. What is meant by the 'executive government?' Does it mean the whole royal authority? Does it mean the power of legislation? Does it mean all the Sovereign's functions, without restriction or limitation of any kind? If this had been fully expressed, would any noble Lord have contended that it did not amount to the actual dethroning of his Majesty, and wresting the scepter out of his hand? No man entertains a higher respect for the Prince than I do; I wish him as well as those who affect to be more mindful of his interests; but I deny that, as heir apparent, he has any inherent right to the regency. It is our duty to preserve the Crown safe on the head of the Sovereign, so that when, in the due course of nature, it shall descend to the Prince of Wales, he may receive it solid and entire, such as it was when worn by his Sire."

On a division, the amendment was negatived by a majority of 99 to 66.[1]

Next, a proceeding took place which I will not venture to condemn, but which was certainly very anomalous, and, I conceive, unnecessary; for if the two Houses had the right claimed by them to elect a regent, why should they not have passed an Ordinance for that purpose by their own mere authority, without the false assertion that it was by a regular act of legislation to which the King was a party?[2] There is nothing better settled by our law, than that the Great Seal can only be used to express the will of the Sovereign on the throne; and infinite precautions are resorted to for the purpose of preventing the use of it without his personal intervention.[3] To counter-

[1] 27 Parl. Hist 852–891.
[2] The joint resolution of the two Houses, ordering the commission, required that the authority for putting the Great Seal to it should be thus falsely stated " By the King himself, with the advice of the Lords, Spiritual and Temporal, and Commons assembled, according to the prorogation aforesaid."
[3] See ante, Vol. 1. Introduction.

feit the Great Seal is high treason,—and to affix the true Great Seal to any instrument without the King's authority is not subjected to the like penalty, only because the offense is supposed to be impossible. But, while George III. was under the care of Dr. Willis, Edward, Lord Thurlow, affixed the Great Seal of Great Britain to a commission, authorizing certain prelates and peers to open the parliament in the King's name, and to declare the causes of parliament being summoned.

On account of a severe fit of illness, the Chancellor was not himself present at the ceremony of opening the parliament under the authority of the "*Phantom*," and the Lords Commissioners' speech was delivered by ex-Chancellor Earl Bathurst.[1]

At this time, although Thurlow had ceased to have any communication with Carlton House, and Mr. Pitt looked upon him with much suspicion, he enjoyed the highest confidence and favor with the Queen, and she implicitly followed his advice in all her proceedings respecting the formation of the Regency,—that she might have the custody of the King's person, and the nomination to all the offices in the household. The Prince of Wales having remonstrated with her upon the danger to the monarchy from so materially reducing the power and influence of the Crown, she employed Thurlow to prepare an answer in her name. The following note conveyed her thanks to him for his exertions on that occasion:—

" My Lord,

" I am this instant returned from the King, which is the reason of your servant being detained so long. I return you many thanks for the trouble you have taken in forming so useful an answer for me to the Prince of Wales, which I intend sending to-morrow morning. I am extremely sorry to hear of your indisposition, and I hope you will believe me when I say that nobody does more

---

[1] 27 Parl. Hist. 1163. One of the most ludicrous difficulties in which the House of Commons was now involved arose from the sudden death of Speaker Cornwall, and the election of Mr. W. Grenville to succeed him. Regularly, the new Speaker should have been approved by the King, and should have prayed for a continuance of the rights and privileges of the Commons Burke said, "They had just set up 'a phantom' to represent the Great Seal, and now their Speaker was to bow before it, and to claim their rights and privileges from a creature of their own creation." However, they altogether waived the ceremony.—*27 Parl Hist 1161*

sincerely interest themselves in your recovery and welfare than myself.

"CHARLOTTE.

"Kew, January the 31st, 1789 "[1]

When the Commons sent up the Regency Bill (to which it was intended to give the royal assent by the " Phantom ")—Thurlow strenuously supported all the restrictions put upon the power of the Regent, and the clause vesting in the Queen the nomination of all the officers of the household. Upon the last point he was particularly eloquent and touching :—

"My opinion, my Lords," said he, " is, that all which belongs to the household must, at the same time with the care of the King's person, be put under her Majesty's control and management. To preserve the King's dignity, all his royal attendants must be kept about him. If you deprive the King of his accustomed splendor, you may as well treat him as a parish pauper, put him on board wages, or send him to one of those receptacles that take in unfortunate people at a small charge. This would be the only way to prevent the royal household going to the Queen—but then you are losing your time in contriving means of restoring his Majesty to the throne, on his recovery, for you never can expect a cure. Remember, my Lords, that the Queen is to have the care of her royal patient, not as a wretched outcast, an obscure individual, without friends, without a name, without reputation, without honor,—but as a King to whom his people look up with loyalty, with affection, and with anxious wishes that he may soon be enabled to re-ascend his throne, and again spread blessings over the land he governs. As far as my voice can go, and I shall lift it up loudly and sincerely " [here he rolled out his sentences majestically, and shook his awe-inspiring eyebrows], " I claim for the King all the dignity that ought to attend a royal person, who is entitled to every comfort that can be administered to him in the hour of his calamity. And who shall dare to refuse my demand ? It would, it ought, and it must mortify the Queen if the King were turned over to her in an unfeeling and irreverent fashion—destitute of every mark

[1] The original, in a very distinct, pretty hand, lies before me. Queen Charlotte not only gained a familiar acquaintance with our language, but became in all respects a good Englishwoman.

and remnant of royal state. Is there a man who hears me, who possesses the sensibility common to every human breast, who does not sympathize with her Majesty?" [Here he began to be much affected.] "I protest to God I do not believe there is a noble Lord in the House who wishes to reduce to such a forlorn condition a King laboring under a misfortune, equal to any misfortune that ever happened since misfortune was known in the world. To hesitate about giving the household to the Queen, would show a total extinction of pity for that royal sufferer, whose calamity entitles him to the most unlimited compassion, and even to increased respect:

"' Deserted in his utmost need
By those his former bounty fed'"[1]

Here the orator burst into tears, and he resumed his seat on the woolsack as if still unable to give vent by language to his tenderness.[2]

These exhibitions were probably pretty justly appreciated in the House of Lords, where the actor was known, and they must have caused a little internal tittering, although no noble Lord would venture openly to treat them with ridicule. But they made a prodigious impression on the public. His Majesty was now very popular, particularly contrasted with the Heir Apparent, and his calamity did excite deep sympathy in the great bulk of the nation. There was a general apprehension that, if the Prince's friends once got into power, the good old King would soon be treated as irrecoverable. Thurlow was therefore hailed as a champion of the rights of the Sovereign, and he was supposed to be disinterestedly standing up for his afflicted Master, designedly and nobly sacrificing all prospect of power for the rest of his days. Men compared him to the Earl of Kent in "Lear," and, thinking they had found in real life an exemplification of the

[1] 27 Parl. Hist 1081, 1082, 1085
[2] Thurlow alluded to Burke s speech in the House of Commons. "It had been asked, would they strip the King of every mark of royalty and transfer all the dignities of the Crown to another person? No, heaven forbid! where the person wearing the crown could lend a grace to those dignities, and derived a luster from the splendor of his household But did they recollect that they were talking of a sick King, of a monarch smitten by the hand of Omnipotence, and that the Almighty had hurled him from the throne and plunged him into a condition which drew down upon him the pity of the meanest peasant in his kingdom?"—Burke was called to order for these words, and certainly they are not in the best taste.

devoted attachment which the poet had imagined, were delighted to see the friendship which had long subsisted between the Sovereign and his Chancellor, though obscured in the alienated mind of the afflicted George, still burning in the honest bosom of the faithful Thurlow.[1] Some, however, ironically exclaimed,—

> . . . . " He can not flatter, he!
> An honest mind and plain—he must speak truth!
> —These kind of knaves I know, which in this plainness
> Harbor more craft and more corrupter ends
> Than twenty silly ducking observants,
> That stretch their duties nicely."

A few days after this last lachrymose scene, Burke said openly in the House of Commons—"The Lords had perhaps not yet recovered from that extraordinary burst of the pathetic which had been exhibited before them the other evening; they had not yet dried their eyes or been restored to their former placidity, and were unqualified to attend to new business. The tears shed in that House on the occasion to which he alluded were not the tears of patriots for dying laws, but of Lords for their expiring places. The iron tears which flowed down Pluto's cheek rather resembled the dismal bubbling of the Styx, than the gentle murmuring streams of Aganippe."[2]

On another occasion, Burke descended so low as to draw a caricature likeness of the Chancellor for the amusement of the House of Commons. Commenting on the scheme by which the phantom of royalty was to be raised by touching the Great Seal, he said—"What is to be one when the Crown is in a deliquium? It was intended, he had heard, to set up a man with black brows and a large wig, a kind of scarecrow to the two Houses, who was to give a fictitious assent in the royal name, and this to be binding on the people."[3] He added,—"I have given my allegiance already to the House of Hanover. I worship the gods of our glorious Constitution, but I will not worship PRIAPUS."

Alas! the Whigs were disappointed, and the laugh was

---

[1] Thus wrote his old companion Cowper, who might have known him better. " In *his* counsels, under the blessing of Providence, the remedy is, I believe, to be found, if a remedy there be *His* integrity, firmness, and sagacity, are the only human means that seem adequate to the great emergence." [2] Burke's Speeches, III 382 [3] Ibid 361.

finally with the object of their vituperation. When the Regency Bill, with its restrictive clauses, had been read a second time in the House of Lords, and had made some progress in the committee, rumors were publicly spread that the King's malady was abating; and on the 10th of February, as soon as prayers were over, the Lord Chancellor left the woolsack, and said,—" The intelligence from Kew was that day so favorable, every noble Lord would agree with him in acknowledging that it would be indecent to proceed further with the bill when it might become wholly unnecessary. Amidst the general joy which the expectation of his Majesty's speedy return must occasion, he would therefore move the adjournment of the committee." This was agreed to, and the House rose.

On a subsequent day the Chancellor declared that he had lately been as much as an hour and a quarter with the King, and that very day a full hour—when he had found his mind to be clear and distinct, and that he appeared perfectly capable of conversing on any subject that might be proposed to him. The committee was several times adjourned, and at last, on the 10th of March, there was produced a commission to which the Great Seal had been regularly put, under a warrant signed by the King himself, authorizing the same commissioners named in the sham commission "to open and declare certain further causes for holding this parliament." Then the Commons being summoned, and the commision read, the Chancellor, one of the commissioners, said, "His Majesty, being, by the blessing of Providence, recovered from the severe indisposition with which he has been afflicted, and being enabled to attend to the public affairs of this kingdom, has commanded us to convey to you his warmest acknowledgments for the additional proofs which you have given of your affectionate attachment to his person, and of your zealous concern for the honor and interest of his crown, and the security and good government of his dominions."

Thurlow retained the Great Seal, but his character was seriously injured. Although he impressed on the Queen, and on the King, when recovered, a conviction of his zeal to comply with their wishes, his colleagues, as well as his opponents, were fully aware of his insincerity, and by degrees the full extent of his double-dealing during the King's illness became known to the whole nation.

From this time he fostered a deep enmity to Mr. Pitt, which he was at no pains to conceal. Considering himself the personal "friend," and most cherished minister, of the King,—boasting that the House of Lords was entirely under his control,—and unconscious of his reputation with the public,—he greatly overestimated his political importance, and was disposed to set himself up as the rival of the man who, by splendid eloquence and spotless character, now ruled the House of Commons, and who, with the exception of the Whigs (lamentably reduced in numbers), was respected and supported by the whole nation.

The Prime Minister had no desire to quarrel with the Chancellor, but was resolved to keep him in due subordination. For the present, therefore, he contented himself with submitting a good-humored representation to the King, which praised the Chancellor's abilities and services, but, hinting at his waywardness, stated how desirable it was that there should be entire cordiality among the members of the Cabinet. "The King wrote to Thurlow on the subject, and received such an answer as led him confidently to hope that Mr. Pitt would have no reason to complain again on this subject." [1]

For two or three years the Government went on pretty

---

[1] Tomline's Life of Pitt, ii. 513 It would appear from the "Rolliad," that even before the King's illness the public believed that Thurlow went on very uncomfortably with the Cabinet, and that there was a great desire to turn him out. In the "JOURNAL of the Right Hon HENRY DUNDAS," we have the following entry —" March 9th, 1788 Got Thurlow to dine with us at Wimbledon—gave him my best Burgundy and blasphemy, to put him into good humor After a brace of bottles, ventured to drop a hint of business—Thurlow damned me, and asked Pitt for a sentiment [toast]. Pitt looked foolish—Grenville wise." After an account of the other members of the Cabinet, he proceeds with the Chancellor: "Thurlow very queer. He swore the bill [India Declaratory Bill, then pending in parliament] is absurd, and our correspondence with those cursed directors damned stupid However, will vote and speak with us.—Pitt quite sick of him—says 'he growls at everything, proposes nothing, and supports everything' N B—Must look out for a new Chancellor—Scott might do, but cants too much about his independence and his conscience—what the devil has he to do with independence and conscience?—besides, he has a snivelling trick of retracting when he is caught in a lie—hate such puling fellows GEORGE HARDINGE not much better—must try him though—will order him to speak on Wednesday" Rolliad, 22nd ed. p. 516. George Hardinge had not answered, for he died a Welsh judge.

smoothly: Thurlow, although discontented and sulky. abstained from any public attack on the Government— but watching for an opportunity of showing his sense of the supposed ingratitude of the young man he pretended to have patronized and promoted.

Their first open quarrel was on the appointment, as Master of the Rolls, of an individual against whom Thurlow was known to have a mortal spite. When Mr. Pitt first proposed this, the object of his favor handsomely wished to decline it, saying that "he was sure it would be disagreeable to Lord Thurlow." The Prime Minister replied, "Pepper, you shall be Master of the Rolls; and as to Thurlow, I may just as well quarrel on that as on any other subject with him." The Chancellor, on hearing of the appointment, said, "My time will be spent in reversing that fellow's decrees. I look upon my Court and that of the Rolls to be somewhat like a stage-coach, which, besides the skill of the coachman, requires the assistance of an able postilion to lead the horses, and pick out the best part of the roads. Now if I get an ignorant, furze-bush-headed postilion, he may overset the coach, and tumble us both into the ditch."

The Chancellor was now sulky and silent. In the first session after the King's recovery he did not once interfere for the Government, unless in repressing an irregular conversation commenced by Lord Stormont, about the treaty with Prussia;[1] and he testified his contempt for the part taken by his colleagues in the other House by throwing out, on the first reading, Mr. Beaufoy's bill, which Mr. Pitt had sanctioned in the Commons, for celebrating the centenary of the Revolution.[2]

But (wonderful to relate) he allowed to pass through the House without opposition a bill, remarkable as the first that passed to mitigate the atrocious severity of our criminal code—enacting that women convicted of high

[1] 28 Parl. Hist 138.
[2] The motion, (so unusual, and so affronting to the House of Commons) for throwing out the bill in this stage being made by the Bishop of Bangor, was warmly supported by the Lord Chancellor, and carried by a majority of 13 to 6 —*28 Parl Hist 296* The deliverance of the nation from slavery and popery was celebrated in Scotland, without an act of parliament, by the authority of the Church, when Dr Robertson delivered the sermon in the hearing of Lord Brougham, then a boy—of which his Lordship has given us such an interesting account in the Life of his distinguished kinsman (*Men of Letters, 270*)

or petty treason, instead of being burnt to death, as they had hitherto been, should be hanged.[1]

During the whole of the following session, he never opened his mouth, except upon Lord Hawkesbury's complaint of having been obstructed by the military when coming down to attend the service of the House. The Lord Chancellor took up this matter very warmly, insisting that, for such an insult, no apology could be accepted, and that their Lordships must, in justice to themselves, institute inquiries for the purpose of discovering and punishing the delinquents.[2]

Since the formation of the present Government, Thurlow had hitherto been considered its organ in the House of Lords; but Mr. Pitt declared, that he was never quite certain what part in debate the Chancellor would take, and, less quiet times being in prospect, he was very unhappy lest some important measure, on which depended his reputation and his stability, might be defeated, after being carried triumphantly through the House of Commons.[3] He therefore resolved, at the meeting of the new parliament in Nov. 1790, to have in the House of Lords a new leader, in whom he could place confidence. The person proposed for this post was Mr. William Grenville, who had been Speaker of the House of Commons, and, not giving satisfaction in that office, had been taken into the Cabinet, and was giving striking proofs of his talents as a statesman.[4] The King, unwittingly thinking that the arrangement would be agreeable to the Chancellor, by saving him trouble, at once consented to it, without consulting him; and Lord Grenville took his seat on the ministerial bench. Thurlow was deeply mortified, but, having no plausible cause of quarrel, he for the present concealed his chagrin. Still he persuaded himself that he held the first place in the King's favor, and he hoped that he might, ere long, be able to avenge himself for such a slight. "His coolness and reserve

---

[1] See 4 Adolph, 484.   [2] 28 Parl. Hist. 874.
[3] The Marquis of Stafford and other common friends, had repeatedly remonstrated with Thurlow, respecting his demeanor to Pitt, but entirely without effect.—*Tomline's Life of Pitt,* ii 513
[4] I have heard the late Lord Holland several times say, that considerable abilities are not well adapted to the chair of the House of Commons, for all the Speakers in his time had been pronounced "excellent," except LORD GRENVILLE, and he failed, although the only clever man among them

towards Mr. Pitt increased, although there was no difference of opinion between them on any political question."[1]

For a season the Chancellor concealed his resentment, and he even had such control over his feelings as to support Lord Grenville on the new leader's first appearance in that character in the House. A discussion arose respecting a very doubtful measure of Mr. Pitt, which he was soon obliged to abandon—the armament against Russia, on the taking of Ockzakow and Ismael. Lord Grenville moved the address of thanks, in answer to a message from the Crown announcing that, in consequence of his Majesty not having succeeded in bringing about a satisfactory adjustment of the differences between the Sublime Porte and the Empress Catherine, he deemed it necessary to increase his forces by sea and land. Earl Fitzwilliam having moved an amendment censuring the conduct of the Government, Lord Loughborough made a speech, memorable as containing one of the earliest expressions of opinion in parliament on the French Revolution, which he still regarded with hope and with favor. Having inveighed bitterly against the general policy of Ministers, who seemed disposed wantonly to interfere with the concerns of foreign states all over the world, and particularly condemned the threatened rupture with Russia, he highly eulogized the magnanimous declaration of the National Assembly of France, that "they would for ever avoid wars on speculative and theoretical points,"—which ought to have suggested to us a wiser and more elevated system than that which we were pursuing. He said, "The revolution in France presents to us the means of reducing our establishments, of easing the people, and of securing to the nation, for a length of years, the blessings of peace. But, instead of this, we ransack the most obscure corners of the earth for enemies, and wish to rush into hostilities against a great empire, which is our natural ally, and the present enlightened sovereign of which feels for this country sentiments of unmixed respect and good will."

The Lord Chancellor, stimulated probably by personal rivalry and dislike, left the woolsack, and answered this speech in a very contemptuous tone. He abstained

[1] Tomline's Life of Pitt, ii 513.

from any general defense of Ministers, but he insisted that the objections to the proposed address were wholly frivolous, as the Crown was entitled to confidence on such an emergency, and no noble Lord, by agreeing to the address, was pledged to the wisdom of any measure which the responsible advisers of the Crown might consequently recommend. In putting a construction on their treatie with Russia and Prussia, he affected a modesty which I do not understand, saying that "on subjects of state he begged to be understood as speaking with deference to statesmen." However, somewhat to countenance the notion that he considered himself a mere lawyer, and no statesman, he argued that their Lordships should not look merely to the letter of their contract with foreign nations but should put *an equitable interpretation upon it ;* giving as an illustration, that, although we only engaged to defend Prussia when attacked,—if we saw Russia surrounding Poland in a manner dangerous to the interests of Prussia, we were bound to interfere for the benefit of our ally. Lord Loughborough's compliments to the French Revolution he treated with the utmost scorn, asserting "the National Assembly had never assumed a bold or manly aspect, and that its proceedings were, in his mind a tissue of political fopperies, as distant from true wisdom as from morality and honor."[1]

There being now a new parliament, the important constitutional question arose, whether Hastings's impeachment was abated by the dissolution of the House of Commons which had commenced it? All impartial lawyers were of opinion that it was now to be considered as pending *in statu quo;* and, after a committee appointed to search for precedents had made their report to this effect Lord Porchester moved, "That a message be sent to the Commons, to acquaint them that this House will proceed upon the trial of Warren Hastings, Esquire."

This was strongly opposed by the Lord Chancellor, who contended that the prosecution was at an end with the prosecutors; that Mr. Hastings's recognizance had expired, so that, he being neither in prison nor under bail, he was not subject to their jurisdiction; and that all precedents were in his favor, as well as all reasoning. As to the report of the committee, he had read it with attention

[1] 29 Parl. Hist. 45.

and it seemed to him to be little short of demonstration, that, by the usage and law of that House, an impeachment was universally understood to abate at a dissolution. Lord Loughborough, however, clearly proved that the impeachment, being " in the name of all the Commons of England," was still to be carried on in their name by their present representatives; that the House of Lords is a permanent judicial tribunal, deciding in one parliament appeals and writs of error brought before it in a preceding parliament; that the assumption of the defendant's recognizance being at an end was a mere begging of the question; that the precedents, when rightly understood, were inconsistent with the notion of abatement; and that to sanction the doctrine contended for, would be to put it in the power of the executive government at any time, by a dissolution of parliament, to screen a delinquent minister from deserved punishment. Lord Grenville, and most of the Government Peers, divided against the Chancellor, and he was beaten by a majority of 66 to 18.[1]

But he succeeded this session in defeating Mr. Fox's Libel Bill, under pretense that there was not time to consider the subject, although, to the high credit of Mr. Pitt, who had supported the bill in the Commons, Lord Grenville anxiously declared that ' he should be extremely sorry if it were to go forth to the world that the Administration were against it, or unfriendly to the rights of juries."

Thurlow's official career was now drawing to a close. On the 31st of January, 1792, he, for the last time, delivered into the hands of the King the speech to be read on the opening of parliament. It is exceedingly difficult to understand the wayward conduct during this session which led to his dismission. I have in vain tried to obtain a satisfactory explanation of it by studying contemporary memoirs, and consulting some venerable politicians whose memory goes back to that era. He had formed no connection with the Whigs;—he was more than ever estranged from their society, and opposed to their principles,—and he could not have had the remotest intention of going over to them. I can only conjecture that, as Mr. Pitt's reputation had been a little tarnished by the failure of the Russian armament, and he had not yet been strengthened by the accession of the Duke of Portland, Burke, and the

[1] 29 Parl. Hist. 514–545. [2] Ib. 726–741.

alarmist Whigs, which soon followed,—Thurlow, still reckoning in a most overweening manner on his personal favor with the King, sincerely thought that he could displace the present Premier, whom he regarded as little better than a Whig, and that he could establish a real Tory government, either under himself, or some other leader, who would oppose the Libel Bill, and all such dangerous innovations, and rule the country on true old Church-and-King maxims.

The Chancellor of the Exchequer having announced a plan for bringing tobacco under the excise laws, and for facilitating summary proceedings against those who defrauded the revenue, endeavors were made to exasperate the public mind against him; and these the Lord Chancellor thought fit to abet in charging the jury in a proceeding relative to the coinage, called "*a trial of the Pix.*" "So sacred is the trial by jury," said he, "that I trust the people of England will consider it their indefeasible right; and that under no pretense, either of revenue or of any other object, will this great safeguard of their property and their liberties be intrenched upon: for an infringement of this right, the longest life of the most exalted minister could never atone." Handbills were next day posted all over London, giving this extract from his speech, headed "BRITONS! ATTEND TO THE VOICE OF YOUR CHANCELLOR." [1]

The occasion he selected for commencing hostilities in parliament was the introduction into the House of Lords of Mr. Pitt's celebrated bill "to establish a Sinking Fund for the Redemption of the National Debt." This measure, which has proved a failure, and which almost all financiers now condemn, was considered by its reputed author, his friends, and the bulk of the nation, as the greatest effort of his genius, and a lasting monument of his fame.[2] He staked upon it the stability of his administration. It passed the Commons with applause. But in the Lords, "to the astonishment of every one, it was violently reprobated by the Lord Chancellor"[3] His colleagues must have been even more startled than the rest of mankind, for he had not offered the slightest objec-

[1] Adolphus, v. 234.
[2] The scheme was in fact Dr Price's, and was the worst of three which he suggested. [3] Tomline's Life of Pitt, ii. 513.

tion when the measure was considered in the Cabinet, and, when he left the woolsack to throw it out, he had not hinted to any of them an intention to say a word against it. In truth he had not discovered its fallacy, and he made no attempt to show that, by the creation of additional stock and additional taxation to supply the sinking fund, the aggregate amount of the national debt would be increased, with diminished means of bearing the burden of it. He almost entirely confined himself to a rather futile objection, that an unconstitutional attempt was made to bind future parliaments. No one believed that future parliaments could be bound to provide for the sinking fund, if they should think that the money to be raised had better be left to "*fructify* in the pockets of the people;" but the inability to insure a perpetual adherence to the plan could be no solid argument against attempting it; for, if sound and beneficial, there was every reason to expect that it would become more and more popular. But Thurlow believed that he had gained a complete triumph by thundering out most impressively and awfully, "that the bill exhibited a degree of presumption and arrogance, in dictating to future parliaments, which he trusted the House would never countenance. None but a novice, a sycophant, a mere reptile of a minister, would allow this act to prevent him from doing what, in his own judgment, circumstances would require at the time; and a change in the situation of the country may render that which is proper at one time inapplicable at another." He thus concluded,—"In short, the scheme is nugatory and impracticable—the inaptness of the project is equal to the vanity of the attempt." Such observations were probably better adapted to his audience than others more profound, and he had nearly succeeded in defeating the bill—which must have been followed by the retirement of Mr. Pitt. On the division, it was carried only by a majority of six.[1]

Next morning Mr. Pitt wrote a letter to the King, the tenor of which we may pretty well guess at from the following letter, which he at the same time sent to the Lord Chancellor:—

[1] This very important debate is not even noticed in the Parliamentary History, and the only account we have of it is in a very wretched book, Tomline's "Life of Pitt." See vol ii 513, Gifford's Life of Pitt, iii. 187.

"Downing Street, Wednesday, May 16, 1792.

"My Lord,

"I think it right to take the earliest opportunity of acquainting your Lordship, that being convinced of the impossibility of his Majesty's service being any longer carried on to advantage while your Lordship and myself both remain in our present situations, I have felt it my my duty to submit that opinion to his Majesty; humbly requesting his Majesty's determination thereupon.

"I have the honor to be, &c.   "W. PITT."

The coming storm had been foreseen by several, and the result had been distinctly foretold by that sagacious statesman, Lord North, who, a short time before, had said to a person peculiarly intimate with Lord Thurlow, "Your friend thinks that his personal influence with the King authorizes him to treat Mr. Pitt with *humcur*. Take my word for it, whenever Mr. Pitt says to the King, 'Sir, the Great Seal must be in other hands,' the King will take the Great Seal from Lord Thurlow, and never think any more about him."

And so it turned out. The King at once yielded to Mr. Pitt's wishes, and caused an intimation to be conveyed to Lord Thurlow that "his Majesty had no longer any occasion for his services."

We are not informed of the channel through which the dismissal was announced to the Chancellor, but the act was a dreadful surprise to him, and the manner of it deeply wounded his pride. "I have no doubt," writes the same person to whom Lord North had uttered his prophecy, "that the conduct of the King was wholly unexpected by Lord Thurlow: it mortified him most severely. I recollect his saying to me, 'No man has a right to treat another in the way in which the King has treated me: we can not meet again in the same room.'"[1]

However, as Mr. Pitt was not then provided with any

[1] Nich Recoll 347   The author adds,—"It is well known that, for some years before Lord Thurlow was a second time deprived of the Great Seal, he and Mr Pitt had not lived on pleasant terms   I never could discover the cause of this   I recollect Lord Thurlow's having once said to me,—' When Mr Pitt first became Prime Minister, it was a very unpleasant thing to do business with him, but it afterwards became as pleasant to do business with him as with Lord North   Lord Thurlow strongly disapproved of Mr Pitt's conduct on the impachment of Mr. Hastings; how far that contributed to excite ill-humor in him I can not say."

successor, as great inconvenience would have arisen from putting the Great Seal into commission during the sitting of parliament, and as it was desirable that the present holder of it should continue in office a short time to give judgment in causes which had been argued before him, an arrangement was made that he should not surrender it till the day of the prorogation.

Mean while, he tried to set the King against Mr. Pitt and the Government from which he was retiring, by his violent and somewhat artful opposition to a bill which they had introduced "for encouraging the growth of timber in the New Forest." This provided for the inclosure of some crown land to be planted with trees for the use of the navy, or suspended or mitigated the forestal rights of the Crown over a large district in Hampshire,—these rights being of no practical value to the sovereign, and very injurious to the subject. The bill passed the Lower House with the praise of all parties. But when it stood for a second reading in the Lords, "the Lord Chancellor objected to what he called the *supposed* principle of the bill, for he would not admit that it was founded on any *real* principle, as tending, under false pretenses, to deprive the Crown of that landed property to which it was entitled by the constitutional law of the country. He maintained that it was of consequence that the King should have an interest in the land of the kingdom. He allowed the imperfection of the forest laws, but he insisted that the defects of this bill were infinitely more pernicious. In conclusion, he attacked the framers of the bill, his colleagues in office, in the most pointed and most unjustifiable manner. He openly charged them *with having imposed upon their Sovereign*, and did not scruple to assert that if the members of that House, who were the hereditary councillors of the Crown, did not interfere in opposition to those who had advised this measure, *all was over*." [1] Nevertheless the bill passed, and the resistance to it being explained to his Majesty to be merely an ebullition of spleen from him who had so long piqued himself on the appellation of "the King's friend," no alarm was excited in the royal bosom, and the resolution to dismiss him remained unaltered.

[1] Gifford's Life of Mr. Pitt, iii. 187; Moore's Life of Sheridan, ii. 273.

Seeing his fate inevitable, instead of quietly submitting to it he complained loudly of the ingratitude and faithlessness of princes. But, even without regarding the double part which Thurlow had acted respecting the regency, all must agree that George III. could not properly have hesitated in taking part with Mr. Pitt in this controversy. The wanton desertion of those who had claims upon him by their services could not justly be imputed to this monarch during any part of his reign.

Before the conclusion of the session important debates took place on two measures, which the Government very cordially and creditably supported, and both of these were opposed by the Chancellor. Resolutions came up from the Commons for the abolition of the slave trade, and Lord Grenville having contended "that, for the sake of preserving the national character from disgrace, it ought to be abolished, not only as a traffic founded on inhumanity and injustice, but a traffic unnecessary and impolitic," Lord Thurlow said, "As to the iniquity and atrocity which had been so largely imputed to the slave trade, he could not understand why its criminality had not been discovered by our ancestors, and should become so conspicuous in the year 1792." Then, forgetting his former contempt for colonial legislation, which he had testified during the contest with America, he suggested that the importation of slaves from Africa into the West India islands was a subject of internal commercial regulation, which the planters themselves best understood, and which should be left to their decision. This being considered an open question,—on the division which took place, he carried a majority of 63 to 36 against the Government.[1]

But, luckily, he failed in his dying effort as Chancellor again to defeat the bill to ascertain the rights of juries on trials for libel, and to protect the liberty of the press. He first contrived to get it postponed till near the end of the session ; in every stage he inveighed violently against it ; he obtained a declaration of opinion from the Judges, that "libel, or no libel ?" was a pure question of law for the Court; and, thoroughly beaten by Lord Camden, he proposed a clause which would have rendered the bill nugatory, and to which he pretended that the venerable

[1] 29 Parl Hist. 1341-1355.

patriot could not object,—when he received a memorable answer, which seems actually to have made him ashamed, as he offered no further opposition to the bill. However, when it had passed, he embodied his objections to it in a strong protest, which remains as a monument of his illiberality and his obstinacy.¹

Three days after this protest was signed, he ceased to be Chancellor. The 15th of June, 1792, must have been a sad day for the haughty spirit of Thurlow.

Now came the prorogation, the event to which his dismissal was respited. The King being placed on the throne, and the Commons attending at the bar of the House of Lords, the Speaker, in his Address, before presenting the Supply Bill for the royal assent, eulogized in warm terms the measures of the session—particularly that for establishing a sinking fund to pay off the national debt, and that for ascertaining the rights of juries and protecting the liberty of the press. Nay, in the very speech which the King himself delivered from the throne, and which Thurlow, on bended knees, put into the King's hand, his Majesty was made to say, " I have observed, with the utmost satisfaction, that you have made provision for the reduction of the present national debt, and established a permanent system for preventing the dangerous accumulation of debt in future,"--although it was the scheme which the "keeper of the royal conscience" had so violently opposed, and for opposing which he had received notice to quit his office. The last time he ever spoke in public as Chancellor was in proroguing the parliament, by his Majesty's command, till the 30th day of August then next.²

As soon as this ceremony had been performed, he drove to St. James's Palace, where a council was held, and he surrendered the Great Seal to his Majesty,—having the mortification to see Sir James Eyre, Chief Baron of the Exchequer, Sir William Ashurst, a Judge of the King's Bench, and Sir John Wilson, a Judge of the Common Pleas, in attendance to receive it as Lords Commissioners. Resignation of office into the hands of the Sovereign by a Ministry retiring in a body, though not a joyous scene, is attended with some consolations. They probably feel, in common, that they have fought a good fight; they

¹ Ante, vol. vi p 401. ² 29 Parl Hist 1555

know that the same fate has overtaken all; and their misfortune is not only softened by mutual sympathy, but by the prospect of going together into opposition, and of returning together into place. Poor Thurlow was now a solitary outcast; he had brought his disgrace upon himself by his own waywardness and intemperance; he had no question to agitate before the public; he had no political party to associate with; he had lost the pleasures of office, without the excitement of opposition; and hope even was gone, for there was no conceivable turn of parties that could ever again bring power within his reach. When he drove home from St. James's to Great Ormond Street, without the Great Seal, which had been his beloved companion so many years, he must have been a good deal dejected. The only boon bestowed upon him was a remainder of his peerage to the sons of his two brothers,[1]—and no ray of kingly favor ever after shone upon him for the rest of his days.

He soon comported himself, however, with apparent firmness, and he showed a friendly and generous disposition by the advice he now gave to Sir John Scott, the Attorney General, who, having been advanced by him, wished to share his fall. "Stick by Pitt," said the retiring Chancellor; "he has tripped up my heels, and I would have tripped up his if I could. I confess I never thought the King would have parted with me so easily. My course is run, and for the future I shall remain neutral. But you must on no account resign; I will not listen for a moment to such an idea. We should be looked on as a couple of fools! Your promotion is certain, and it shall not be baulked by any such whimsical proceeding." It is creditable to both, that, in the party vicissitudes which followed, their intimacy and cordiality remained unabated.

[1] On the 12th of June, 1792, he was created Baron Thurlow, of Thurlow, in the county of Suffolk, with remainder, on failure of his own heirs male, to the heirs male of his brother, the Bishop, and John Thurlow, Esq.

CHAPTER CLXI.

CONCLUSION OF THE LIFE OF LORD THURLOW.

OUR ex-Chancellor was at this time only sixty years of age, with an unbroken constitution. Considering his abilities and reputation, he might, as an independent member of the legislature, have had great weight and he might have continued to fill a considerable space in the public eye—being of some service to his country, and laying the foundation of some additional claim to the respect of posterity. But with his office he seemed to have lost all his energy. When he again entered the House of Lords, he was like a dethroned sovereign, and he could not bear his diminished consequence. Seen without his robes, without his great wig, sitting obscurely on a back bench instead of frowning over the assembly from the woolsack,—the Peers were astonished to discover that he was an ordinary mortal, and were inclined to revenge themselves for his former arrogance by treating him with neglect. Finding his altered position so painful, he rarely took any part in the business of the House, and he might almost be considered as having retired from public life. He had a very favorable opportunity of improving our institutions, and correcting the abuses in the law which he had observed in his long experience; but he would as soon have thought of bringing in bills to alter the planetary system, or to soften the severity of the climate,—for he either believed what was established was perfect, or that the evils experienced in the administration of justice were necessary and ought to be borne without murmuring. Almost the only subject which excited him was the attempt to abolish the slave trade,—" a dangerous sentimentality," which he continued to resist and to reprobate.

He now spent the greatest part of his time at a villa he had purchased near Dulwich. The taste which, in early life, he had contracted for classical literature, proved during some months a resource to him. But reading without any definite object he found tiresome, and he is said to have suffered much from the *tedium vitæ*. His principal relief was in getting young lawyers to come to him in the evening to tell him what had been going on in the Court of Chancery in the morning; and he was in the habit of censuring very freely the decisions of his successors.[1]

For a few years he pretty regularly attended the hearing of appeals and writs of error in the House of Lords, but refused to come any longer.[2] Having no pension or retired allowance, he did not consider that the public had any claim upon his time;[3] he could not well endure to appear as a subordinate where he had so long dictated; and as there was no reasonable prospect of his return to office, he was indifferent about keeping up his law by acting as a judge. In January, 1793, his mortification was increased by seeing the Great Seal in the possession of his rival Wedderburn, on the secession of a large section of the Whig party from Mr. Fox—an event to which Thurlow's own retirement had materially contributed.

An attempt was made to bring him back to the Cabinet as President of the Council,—which is referred to in the following letter from the Earl of Carlisle to the new Chancellor:

"My d^r L^d,

"I forgot to mention to you that on Thursday I found the P. extremely hot upon a project that I think right to advertise you of, though perhaps, by this time, it may be no longer in his thoughts. He was prodigiously bent upon making L^d. Thurlow President, and seemed very desirous to know your ideas upon this subject. He is immediately to go to the K. upon it; in short, he has settled the business with his usual ease and quickness. You will be able to judge whether this springs from himself, or whether it

---

[1] Mr. Leach, afterwards Sir John, and Master of the Rolls was his chief reporter. It is curious that Mr. James Allen Park, afterwards a Judge, acted in the same capacity to Lord Mansfield whenre tried from the Court of King's Bench

[2] I have been favored with the perusal of a large collection of letters which he wrote when ex-Chancellor to Sir Ilay Campbell, the Lord President of the Court of Session, respecting Scotch cases before the House, showing a very creditable anxiety to obtain information and to arrive at a just decision, but they are of too technical a nature to be generally interesting.

[3] Although there was then no parliamentary retired allowance for ex-Chanchancellors, they were better off than at present Thurlow was a Teller of the Exchequer, and had given sinecures to all his relations, for one of which his nephew now receives a commutation of £9,000 a year.

rises from another source: you know he has been living with your predecessor If *he* (L^d. T.) can digest what indeed he brought upon himself, he is a match for an ostrich; but that his affair. To talk of business of almost equal importance, I think your cook did very well yesterday.

'Ever yours, my d^r. L^d most aff^y,

"C."[1]

But the Prince had thought no more of this scheme, or it had been disliked by the parties interested: for Thurlow never tasted office more, although he had very little relish for a private station. When he showed himself in the House, he was observed to look sulky and discontented. He was even at a loss where to seat himself, for he hated equally the Government and the Opposition. He took no part in the important debates which arose on the French Revolution, or on the origin of the war with the French Republic. In the session of 1793 he contented himself with opposing a bill to increase the sum for which a debtor might be arrested from £10 to £20,[2] and expressing an opinion that there is no appeal in criminal cases from the Courts in Scotland to the House of Lords.[3] In the beginning of the following year he resisted the attempt that was made to obtain a reversal of the atrocious sentence of transportation passed by the Court of Justiciary, at Edinburgh, on Muir, for advocating parliamentary reform.[4]

Out of office he continued a warm partisan of Mr. Hastings, although he could hardly have expected that the aged and vituperated ex-Governor General could now be set up as a rival to Mr. Pitt.

Thurlow's zeal in defeating the impeachment was heightened by his antipathy to Burke, with whom he continued from time to time to have "passages of arms." A committee of the House of Commons, appointed to inquire

[1] Rosslyn MSS; indorsed, in handwriting of Lord Loughborough "E. of Carlisle, 1793."
[2] 30 Parl Hist 650.   [3] Ibid. 928
[4] 20 Parl Hist 1302, 1304 The trials which took place in Scotland about that time can not now be read without amazement and horror,—mixed with praises to heaven that we live in better times In the year 1834, being a candidate to represent the city of Edinburgh in parliament, I was reproached for not being sufficiently liberal in my opinions I said truly, that, although Attorney General to the Crown, I had uttered sentiments for which, forty years before, I should have been sent to Botany Bay. "The Martyr's Monument," on the Calton Hill, erected to the memory of Muir and his companions, is a striking proof of the servitude of a former generation, and of the freedom of the present.

into the causes of the length of the trial, having presented an elaborate Report drawn by the chief manner, which reflected with severity upon the manner in which the Lords had conducted the proceedings, and particularly their practice of deciding all questions upon the admissibility of evidence according to the rules of the common law as declared by the Judges,[1] the ex Chancellor loudly complained of it as a libel on the House of Lords, denominating it "a scurrilous pamphlet, published by one Debrett in Piccadilly,"—which had that day been put into his hands, reflecting highly upon the Judges and many members of that House. He said "it was indecent and disgraceful, and such as ought not to pass unpunished, as it vilified and misrepresented the conduct of judges and magistrates intrusted with the administration of criminal justice,—an offense of a very heinous nature,—tending with the ignorant and the wicked to lessen the respect due to the law itself."

We have a fuller account of Burke's retaliation next day in the House of Commons. After stating the attack made on "the pamphlet published by one Debrett in Piccadilly," he said,—"I think it impossible, combining all the circumstances, not to suppose that this speech does reflect upon a Report which, by order of the committee on which I served, I had the honor to present to this House. For anything improper in that Report, I and the other members of the committee are responsible to this House, and to this House only. I am of opinion, with the eminent person by whom that Report is censured, that it is necessary at this time very particularly to preserve the authority of the Judges. But the Report does not accuse the Judges of ignorance or corruption. Whatever it says, it does not say calumniously. This kind of language belongs to those whose eloquence entitles them to a free use of epithets. It is necessary to preserve the respect due to the House of Lords; it is full as necessary to preserve the respect due to the House of Commons, upon which (whatever may be thought of us by some persons) the weight and force of all authorities within this kingdom essentially depend. The Report states grave cause of complaint, to the prejudice of those whom we represent. Our positions we support by reason and precedent, and no senti-

[1] 31 Parl. Hist. 288.

ment which we have expressed am I disposed to retract or to soften. Whenever an occasion shall be regularly given for discussing the merits of the Report, I shall be ready in its defense to meet the proudest name for ability, learning, or reputation which this kingdom can send forth."[1]

Thurlow remained quiet till the trial was at last to close; and the arraignment having taken place before one generation, the judgment was to be pronounced by another. One hundred and sixty Peers had walked in the procession the first day, and only twenty-nine voted on the question of *guilty or not guilty*. "The Great Seal was borne before Loughborough, who, when the trial commenced, was a fierce opponent of Mr. Pitt's government; while Thurlow, who presided in the court when it first sat, estranged from his own allies, sat scowling among the junior Barons."[2]

But when the debates upon the merits began among the Lords themselves, in their own chamber, the ex-Chancellor's pugnacity returned in full vigor, and he valiantly assailed his successor, who, formerly and still closely connected by party ties with Mr. Burke, contended that all the charges except three were fully established. Thurlow treated all these arguments with contempt, and insisted that even the charges on which six Peers said "*Guilty*," were either entirely frivolous, or unsupported by a shred of evidence. He had, on this occasion, not only the majority of the House, but the voice of the public on his side, there having been for some time a strong reaction against the accusation; and he must have enjoyed a great triumph in being present while Lord Loughborough was compelled to announce the acquittal, and to behold the triumphant Hastings, still standing at the bar, overwhelmed with congratulations.[3]

The vulgar, who do not penetrate the workings of the human heart, were astonished now to discover that Thurlow, who had been a furious ultra-Troy, was beginning to incline to the liberal side in politics. He was taken into favor by the Prince of Wales; he formed an intimacy with Lord Moira, a leader of the Carlton House

[1] 31 Parl. Hist. 605–609.   [2] Macaulay's Essays, III. 456
[3] Trial of Warren Hastings, published by Debrett, 1797; Mill's History of India, vol v. c 2.

party, and he was even disposed to cultivate the acquaintance of Mr. Fox. "Idem sentire de republicâ" was the cement of Roman friendships; and in England there is nothing so effectual to reconcile old political, and even personal, enmities as a common hatred of the Minister for the time being. Low as the Whigs now were in point of numbers, from the dread of Jacobinism,[1]—Thurlow showed strong symptoms of a wish to coalesce with them. He assisted Lord Lauderdale in opposing the suspension of the *Habeas Corpus* Act, although, during the American war, he scorned all who had any scruple about such unconstitutional measures,—and he divided against the Government in a minority of 11 to 119.[2]

To strengthen his connection with Carlton House,—when the bill was passing to grant the Prince an annuity on his inauspicious marriage, Thurlow expressed deep regret that a larger allowance was not proposed for his Royal Highness. He anticipated much good conduct both from the Prince and the Princess, and he prophesied "that, when the new order of things was observed, the generosity of the nation would be roused by the change, and they would readily come forward and relieve the Prince from the necessity of longer continuing in retirement and obscurity." The Duke of Clarence highly complimented the noble and learned Lord on the regard and attachment he had manifested for the Prince and the Royal Family.[3]

Thurlow now became a "flaming patriot." We have arrived at a period of English history which, by exaggeration, has been called "the Reign of Terror," and upon which I shall often have to animadvert in writing the lives of Loughborough, Erskine, and Eldon. Under the apprehension of revolutionary principles,—without any intention of permanently encroaching upon the constitution, but with the hope of adding to the strength of the administration by spreading alarm over the nation,—after the failure of the ill-advised trials in which an

---

[1] I heard old George Bing say, at the dinner given him to celebrate the 50th anniversary of his having sat for Middlesex, alluding to those times,—"It has been asserted that the Whigs would all have been held in *one* hackney coach. This is a calumny; we should have filled *two*."

[2] 31 Parl. Hist. 586.   [3] 32 Parl. Hist. 124-139.

attempt was made to take the lives of Mr. Horne Tooke and others, for following the example lately set by the Prime Minister in struggling for parliamentary reform,—bills were brought in of a very stringent character, to restrain the holding of public meetings, to extend the law of high treason, and to subject persons found guilty of seditious libels to transportation beyond the seas.

These having been strenuously resisted by Fox, Grey, and Erskine in the House of Commons—when they reached the House of Lords they found a bold opponent in ex-Chancellor Thurlow. He asked, "Was it fitting that a man should be subject to such penalties for saying it was an abuse that twenty acres of land below Old Sarum Hill, without any inhabitants. should send two representatives to parliament? All were to be punished who attempted to create a dislike to the established constitution; and of the established constitution this renowned rotten borough is a part. He was decidedly of opinion that the old constitutional laws of the country were quite sufficient to put down offenses against the state. New statutes and severe penalties he thought little calculated to attain the object proposed. A jury would be inclined to acquit a mischievous libeler rather than expose him to be transported seven years to Botany Bay. Cruel laws never conduced to the safety of a prince or the preservation of an established government."[1] On another occasion he said, "He would have the existing law improved against libelous and seditious meetings,—which he had no doubt might thus be put an end to. The speeches quoted were insolent and impertinent, but were they so dangerous as to call for the proposed enactments? It was the glory of the English constitution that it imposed no previous restraint on the people, in the exercise of the important privilege of meeting to discuss grievances and petition parliament for their redress. That privilege stood precisely on the same ground with the freedom of the press. Its use was free and unrestrained, but its abuse was open to punishment. Montesquieu, in his 'Spirit of Laws,' said that 'the existence of political freedom in England depends on the unrestrained right of printing.' If the people feel the pressure of grievances, and may not complain of them, we are slaves indeed. To

[1] 32 Parl. Hist 255.

declare, therefore, that 'the people have nothing to do with the laws but to obey them,' was as fallacious as it was odious.¹ There was no ground for saying, that if people met to discuss public questions, they meant to overcome the legislature; they might wish to awaken in the people a due attention to a subject involving their dearest and most invaluable rights. During the fervor of the Middlesex election, some had gone so far as to declare that no resolution or act of the House of Commons was of any validity while Mr. Wilkes was excluded. Subsequently other doctrines had been broached equally extravagant and alarming, but he had never heard that bills such as the present were necessary to restrain them. This bill about public meetings was likewise liable to the gravest objection, from the wording of its clauses, and either betrayed great negligence in those who framed it, or afforded suspicion of its originating in an awkward motive. The bill gave magistrates the power of taking all persons into custody 'who should hold any discourse for the purpose of inciting or stirring up the people to hatred and contempt of the person of his Majesty, *or the government and constitution of this realm, as by law established.*' If these words were allowed to stand in the bill, there was at once an end of all discussion with a view to parliamentary reform. The inequality between Yorkshire and Old Sarum—each returning its two members—could not be mentioned without derision and ridicule,—which an ignorant magistrate would construe into an incitement of the people to hatred and contempt of our representative system, and consequently of 'the government and constitution as by law established.' The worthy magistrate would dissolve the meeting, and take all present into custody. A prosecution might be brought for excess of authority, but the prosecutor would come into court with a rope about his neck. To such an extent did the bill go as to enact, by one clause, that 'if an assembly met for public discussion, should continue together peaceably to the number of twelve, one hour after proclamation to depart, all present were guilty of felony,' and the magistrate

¹ Sentiment of the Bishop of Rochester, which we are told Thurlow violently reprobated when it was uttered, although this does not appear from the Parliamentary History The Bishop was now allowed to explain the expression so as to render it unexceptionable.

was ordered to put them to death, or at least was saved harmless if they lost their lives in resisting him. The bill was founded on what was called the growth of French principles in this kingdom To produce such outrages as had disgraced France, nothing could more directly tend than violent measures like the present. He could not give his assent to a bill wantonly circumscribing that liberty which England had so long enjoyed, and under the auspicious influence of which she had so long flourished." Upon a division, the minority mustered 18 against 107.¹

Having failed in these endeavors, the ex-Chancellor followed the example of the Whig leaders—without forming any express coalition with them—in seceding from parliament ; and during the two following sessions his name does not once occur in the parliamentary debates.

However, in the autumn of 1797, there was suddenly a prospect (which, while it lasted, gave him great delight) of his being restored to his old office of Lord Chancellor. Mr. Pitt's administration had fallen into very considerable discredit, from the conquests of the French Republic on the Continent, from the disturbed state of Ireland, from the mutiny in the fleet, and from the unexampled commercial embarrassment which had led to the suspension of cash payments at the Bank. But Mr. Fox, hated by the King, was at present by no means popular with the nation. In these circumstances a project was set on foot, under the auspices of the Prince of Wales, to form a new administration, from which Mr. Pitt and Mr. Fox should both be excluded, and of which the Earl of Moira was to be the head, with Thurlow as his Lord Chancellor, and Sir William Pulteney as his Chancellor of the Excheqner. The King, although never disheartened in the midst of

---

[1] 32 Parl. Hist. 505–556. The Earl of Malmesbury gives the following account of this debate in a letter to the Duke of York. "The debate in the House of Lords began at five, and did not end till a quarter past three The speakers against the bill (and usually in opposition) were those your Royal Highness mentioned in your last letter. Lord Thurlow was artfully and cautiously factious ; Lord Moira (I am very sorry to say) loudly and violently so ; and I think I never heard a speech with so much unfair and unprovoked invective against ministers It was evident to me, from the manner of these new partisans of the opposition, and from the part they had allotted to themselves on this occasion, that they have it in their expectations that the present ministry will not last ; that Fox and his party will not be chosen to succeed them , and that *they* shall be the persons to fill the offices"—*Correspondence of Lord Malmesbury,* iii 256.

difficulties, began to look at his minister with some distrust, and was not unfriendly to the change. But no confidence was placed in the sufficiency of the proposed new chief,—Mr. Sheridan absolutely refused to belong to an administration excluding Mr. Fox,—and the plan, without making more progress, proved abortive.[1]

The disappointed ex-Chancellor then carried on a negotiation on behalf of the Princess of Wales for a separation from the Prince; and he appears to have been very strongly impressed with a sense of her wrongs. I select two of his letters on this subject to Lord Chancellor Loughborough, which, I think, place the writer in a very amiable point of view:—

"My dear Lord,

"It seems to me that a correct statement of the difficulty which occurred to the Princess of Wales, namely, that *their tempers do not suit each other*, &c., will stand nearly thus—that the expression accords less with the actual state of her mind than his Royal Highness has been led to suppose. She disclaims all resentment of anything which has passed, and entertains the most cordial disposition to conform in all possible respects to the Prince's pleasure; but she finds, to her sorrow, that she has the misfortune of being altogether unacceptable to his Royal Highness. Under these circumstances, she is not surprised at meeting with mortifications, besides the constant and corroding reflection that, however innocently, she is the source of uneasiness to him. So far, therefore, as the consideration turns upon her personal happiness, she would expect more of that in a separate establishment. But she does not forget that she has the honor of being placed in the Royal Family of Great Britain; and consequently that she is not at liberty to choose her own condition, or to do more towards it than to wait his Majesty's commands, which she is ready to receive with perfect deference and gratitude.

"For the rest, considering the Prince's circumstances, she regards the establishment offered by his Royal Highness as liberal and generous: but the article in it which

---

[1] A rumor being spread that Mr Sheridan had agreed to accept office under this projected administration, Lord Moira wrote a letter, which was published in the newspapers, to contradict it. See Moore s Life of Sheridan, ii 273, 302

she values infinitely above all pecuniary considerations, is the being allowed to exercise a mother's tenderness in the care of her infant child.

"I have the honor to be,
"My dear Lord,
"Your most faithful and obedient Servant,
"THURLOW.

"Thursday, Dec. 14, 1797."[1]

"My dear Lord,

"The Princess agrees that her sentiments are expressed in my last to your Lordship correctly as she delivered them. But she repeated another topic which she had mentioned before, and which, perhaps, I ought to have inserted,—her hope that when the Prince should notice the reserve in which she proposed to live, clear of every appearance which the wildest jealousy could misinterpret cabal, he would find himself more friendly disposed towards her.

"I read her that passage in your letter where the Princes and you *think it best for her to remain in a state of absolute inaction, and to write no more on the subject, nor answer without advice.* She expressed great sensibility of their goodness and yours in favoring her with your advice, in which she acquiesces implicitly.

"Perhaps the zeal she excites for her private happiness warps one's judgment on the public part; but if I were not checked with the authority of contrary opinions, I should, after much reflection, pronounce with confidence that justice, humanity, and policy combine to demand this separation. If the thing were not absolutely dishonest in itself, which it surely is, can it be thought more honorable or reputable for the Princes and the Royal Family to detain her in that wretched state which the public regards with horror, than to place her in a state of tranquillity? That she is separated, in every offensive sense of the word, divorced, is notorious in a degree to which the avowal can add nothing. Those who have opportunity and curiosity to hunt such anecdotes report, and it is generally believed, that the whole art of tormenting is exhausted upon her, with every advantage which the relations of husband and father can give it. Surely it would be desirable to remove the sensations which

[1] Rosslyn, MSS.

spring from this source; and is there serious hope of that but in a separation? Those who look up to the King's authority and the countenance of the Royal Family for her protection, will find it secured by this arrangement, There are, moreover, those who fear something worse from an irritable mind goaded by despair.

"These are my private thoughts, of which, so far as relates to myself, I should make no secret; but the delicacy of the subject imposes reserve; and particularly that which you know is my fixed sentiment, that no move can be made in the business but by royal authority.

"I have the honor to be,
"My dear Lord,
"Your most faithful and obedient Servant,
"THURLOW.

"Sunday, 17 Dec. 1797"[1]

These humane efforts were fruitless; and the controversy continued to bring scandal on the Royal Family and the nation for a quarter of a century.

Thurlow seeing Pitt, whom he so much disliked, again in the possession of undisputed power, not only abstained from taking part in the debates of the House of Lords, but ceased to feel any interest whatever in politics, and declared that he had finally abandoned parliamentary strife. He never went to the King's court, but he kept up an intercourse of civility with Carlton House. On rare occasions, he showed himself among the Peers, and expressed an opinion on subjects not connected with faction. In the year 1898, he delivered a very sensible and dispassionate speech against a bill for increasing the assessed taxes,—not in his old style, declaring "its principle to be iniquitous, and its clauses nonsensical and contradictory," but calmly examining the different ways and proportions in which individuals should be made to contribute to the necessities of the State—so as to lead to the conclusion that he had been devoting a portion of his leisure to the study of finance and political economy.[2]

The following year he interposed with good effect to support the equality and dignity of the peerage—advantageously reminding those who heard him of his lofty stand against the Duke of Grafton, soon after his first

[1] Rosslyn MSS.   [2] 33 Parl. Hist. 1290.

entrance into the House. The Duke of Clarence (afterwards William IV.) having delivered a long speech in defense of the slave trade, Lord Grenville, rising after him, said, " between him and his Royal Highness there could be no personal debate, because between them there was no equality." Lord Romney having spoken to order, and Lord Grenville having repeated his words, Lord Thurlow rolled out these sentences with all his ancient energy, graced with a suavity which was new to him ; " I wish it to be clearly understood 'whether it is the constitution of this House that we are unequal in our right to speak here ?'. I am one of the lowest in point of rank. I contend not for superiority of talent, or for any pretension whatever above any of your Lordships. But, my Lords, I claim to be exactly equal not only to the illustrious personage who has just spoken, but to the Prince of Wales himself, if he were present in this House as a Peer of parliament. I know of no difference between Peers of parliament, considered in their parliamentary character, and I maintain that the lowest, in point of precedence, while we are debating here, is equal to the highest. If rank or talent created an inequality in our right to speak in this House, the illustrious Prince who has lately addressed you would have a far higher right to be heard than I pretend to ; but, in speaking my sentiments to your Lordships, I claim for my humble self a perfect equality with every Prince of the blood, and with those of the highest intellectual position in this assembly." He afterwards closed the debate by a violent attack on the bill, unnecessarily ridiculing what a bishop had said who had tried to prove the morality of the Africans by " their women wearing petticoats,"—an article of dress which another Right Reverend Prelate asserted had been laid aside by the opera dancers. Thurlow then went on boldly to maintain " that there was no prohibition against slavery in the Christian religion ; and that as we did not pretend to destroy the *status*, there was no propriety in putting down the ancient commerce by which slaves were to be supplied where they were wanted. The bill was altogether miserable and contemptible. A society had sprung up to civilize the Africans ; that is to say, they would send a missionary to preach in a barn at Sierra Leone to a set of negroes who did not understand one word of his language." However, we ought never to despair of truth gradually and finally prevailing among any set of men, however prejudiced: the Lords were improving, and there being now an equality of votes on each side (36 to 36), the bill was only lost by the maxim of this House, "*semper presumitur pro negante*"—which sometimes makes their decisions depend upon the manner in which the question is worded.[1]

Lord Thurlow did not again appear in public till the 20th of May, 1801, the occasion on which I myself saw and heard him, and of which I have imperfectly attempted to give some account at the commencement of this Memoir."[2]

He had then the consolation of seeing Mr. Pitt obliged to retire into a private station, and the woolsack occupied by one much less obnoxious to him than his ancient rival: Mr. Addington was Prime Minister, and Lord Eldon was Chancellor. Thurlow's spirits so far rallied, that he spoke several times with animation and efficiency. He opposed a bill to indemnify the late Administration for what they had done during the suspension of the *Habeas Corpus* Act. He said, "Instead of *a bill of indemnity*, it ought to be entitled *a bill to suppress actions for personal injuries.* He could not see on what ground of policy a man should be imprisoned for eight years without being brought to trial. It was impossible for him to withhold his compassion from persons lingering in prison for a series of years, who had again and again waited investigation of their conduct; nor could he resist the inclination to deem such men innocent until tried and convicted."[3]

His next effort was in favor of an old enemy whom, when Attorney General, he had prosecuted and sent to jail, and struggled to place in the pillory, but with whom he was now living on terms of personal intimacy.

The following extract from the Diary of a distinguished political character, some years deceased,[4] gives an interesting account of their first meeting after the convicted person had been marched off to Newgate:—

---

[1] 34 Parl. Hist 1092–1141. As every Peer votes upon a division, and no one has a casting vote, some rule becomes necessary to govern the decision in case of an equality of voters. The one adopted is supposed to stop any proceeding not sanctioned by a majority

[2] Ante, p 2.   [3] 35 Parl Hist 1539.   [4] Mr Creevy.

"Lady Oxford, who then (1801) had a house at Ealing, had by Lord Thurlow's desire (I believe), but at all events with his acquiescence, invited Horne Tooke to dinner to meet him: Lord Thurlow never having seen him since he had prosecuted him when Attorney General for a libel in 1778, and when the greatest bitterness was shown on both sides—so that this dinner was a meeting of great curiosity to us who were invited to it. Sheridan and Mrs. Sheridan were there, the late Lord Camelford, Sir Francis Burdett, Charles Warren, with several others, and myself. Tooke evidently came forward for a display, and as I had met him repeatedly, and considered his powers of conversation as surpassing those of any person I had ever seen (in point of skill and dexterity, and, if at all necessary, in *lying*), so I took for granted old, grumbling Thurlow would be obliged to lower his top-sail to him—but it seemed as if the very *look* and *voice* of Thurlow scared him out of his senses from the first moment—and certainly nothing could be much more formidable. So Tooke tried to recruit himself by wine, and, though not generally a drinker, was very drunk: but all would not do; he was perpetually trying to distinguish himself, and Thurlow as constantly laughing at him."

Horne Tooke, after he had escaped the greater peril to which he had been exposed by another Attorney General of being hanged, beheaded, and quartered as a traitor, had taken up his abode at Wimbledon, and thither Thurlow used to ride from Dulwich, that he might pass a morning with him in talking over the trial of *Rex* v. *Horne* before Lord Mansfield, and in discussing some of the questions started in the $Ε\pi εα\ \pi τεροεντα$.[1] The ex-Chancellor would likewise occasionally dine with the ex-Parson, and joyously meet the motley company there assembled,—Hardy, the shoemaker, sitting on one side of him, and Sir Francis Burdett on the other.

Horne Tooke, though unsuccessful as a candidate against Mr. Fox at Westminster, had recently been returned to parliament for Old Sarum by Lord Camelford; and a question having arisen whether, as a priest in orders, he was

[1] I have been informed by my late valued friend, Mr Philip Courtenay, who, when a boy, used to be much with Horne Tooke at Wimbledon, that two or three years after this, a new edition of the "Diversions of Purley" passing through the press, Thurlow asked and obtained a sight of the proof sheets—saying, "he was afraid he should not live till the book was published."

disqualified to sit in the House of Commons, a bill passed that House to *declare* and enact that, in all future parliaments, no person who had been ordained a priest should be allowed to serve as a representative of the people. When this bill stood for second reading in the House of Lords, Lord Thurlow violently opposed it. He began with the doctrine he had been used to propound in Wilkes's case, respecting the Middlesex election, expressing his astonishment "that the Commons, who indubitably were the only judges of the question of '*who ought to sit in their House*,' should, on this occasion, voluntarily consent to forego the exercise of functions peculiarly their own, and send up a bill to their Lordships upon the subject of eligibility to a seat among them, calling thereby upon another branch of the legislature to regulate their rights and privileges." He then expressed a desire to know who could be the author of such a bill, and took an opportunity of showing unabated ill-will to Mr. Pitt, by an invidious eulogy on his successor:—"At the head of the government," he said, " was now placed a man of great respectability, of known integrity, of unassuming manners, *not seeking to engross all the power of the state into his own hands*,—who had discharged the arduous duties of his office much to his own credit, and to the entire satisfaction of the public; it was impossible that such a man should be so prodigal of his reputation as to propose such an absurd measure. The eligibility of a priest who had been ordained should be decided by a committee under the Granville Act. Where was the propriety of introducing a bill to *declare* that a particular class of persons are ineligible by the common law to sit in parliament? It seemed very hard that a person once ordained, who, from conscientious motives, ceased to exercise any clerical function, should be told that he must not enter any other profession because his priestly character was indelible. But why should this indelible character disqualify a priest to sit in the one House more than in the other? The right reverend bench opposite were very short sighted if they supported this bill, for it would speedily lead to the revival of the act for their expulsion from parliament." He concluded by expressing his high value for the franchise of being eligible to represent the people in the legislature, which he considered as wantonly violated by this bill. However, he met with no support,—the present Lord Chancellor, the late Lord Chancellor (became Earl of Rosslyn), and the Bishop of Rochester, standing up for the indelibility of orders, and considering this to be a permanent disqualification to represent the people in parliament;—so that he did not venture on a division, and he allowed the bill to pass without further opposition.[1]

Lord Thurlow's last recorded appearance in the House of Lords was in the debate on the Peace of Amiens, when, still displaying his love for Addington, or rather his unappeasable enmity to Pitt,—in answer to Lord Grenville, who had complained that former treaties with France had not been renewed, he said that "all subsisting treaties being at an end by hostilities, *the abrogation of these treaties was to be imputed to the Government, which had plunged the country into the war*, and that the revival of treaties depended on the will of the contracting parties." This defense, however, was disclaimed by Lord Chancellor Eldon, who denied the position that all former treaties not expressly renewed were to be considered abrogated, and declared that if the consequence of the omission were such as had been supposed, an address should be voted to his Majesty to dismiss his present Ministers from his councils for ever.[2]

Disgusted by such a repudiation of his help, or conscious of decaying powers, and seeing his influence for ever lost, he bade an eternal adieu to the assembly of which he had for many years been the most conspicuous member, and in which he found himself reduced to insignificance. He now permanently retreated into private life, spending his time at his villa, with occasional excursions to Brighthelmstone, to Bognor, to Scarborough, and to Bath.

Although no longer taking any share in parliamentary or party warfare, he continued to be consulted, till within a few months of his death, respecting the unhappy dif

---

[1] 35 Parl Hist. 1541.
[2] 36 Parl. Hist 596. The distinction is between treaties, which, from their nature, are meant to be permanent and perpetual, such as for cession boundary, or exchange of territory; and such as from their nature are extinguished by hostilities, such as for commercial intercourse See Vattel, b xi. c. xii. s. 153: Martens, s. 58, Wheaton, part iii c. xi; Kent's Commentaries, 1 177, *Sutton* v *Sutton*, 1 Russell & Mylne, p 663.

ferences which prevailed in the Royal Family. On occasion of the first communication of the charges made by Lady Douglas against Caroline, Princess of Wales, the Prince directed that Lord Thurlow's opinion should be taken as to the course to be followed on a matter of such delicacy; and in the Diary of Sir Samuel Romilly we have the following interesting statement of the interviews which then took place between him and the ex-Chancellor. Having mentioned that Colonel M'Mahon brought him Lady Douglas's "Narrative," he thus proceeds:—

"After I had read it, by the desire of the Prince, I called on Lord Thurlow. Colonel M'Mahon accompanied me. Lord Thurlow had been very ill, which had been the cause of our interview being postponed for a week. He was still indisposed, and appeared to be extremely infirm; he was, however, in full possession of his faculties, and expressed himself, in the conversation we had together, with that coarse energy for which he has long been remarkable. He said that he had not been able to read all Lady Douglas's narrative, it was written in so bad a hand, but that he had gone rapidly over it, and collected the principal facts (and, in truth, it appeared, from the observations he made, that no fact of any importance had escaped him); that the first point to be considered was, whether her account were true, and that for himself he did not believe it. He said that there was no *composition* in her narrative (that was the expression he used),—no connection in it—no dates; that some parts of it were grossly improbable. He then said, that when first he knew the Princess, he should have thought her incapable of writing or saying any such things as Lady Douglas imputed to her, but that she might be altered; that, to be sure, it was a strange thing to take a beggar's child, but a few days old, and adopt it as her own; but, however, princesses had sometimes strange whims which nobody could account for; that, in some respects, her situation was deserving of great compassion. Upon the whole, his opinion was, that the evidence the Prince was in possession of would not justify taking any step on his part, and that he had only to wait and see what facts might come to light in future. In the mean time, however, that it would be proper to employ a person to collect evidence respecting the conduct of the Princess."[1]

No other meeting with Thurlow took place, and the "Delicate Investigation" proceeded—the misconduct of both the illustrious parties continuing to outrage the public long after he had left this world.

Brighthelmstone was now his favorite retreat. The Diary I have before quoted, for an account of his reconciliation with Horne Tooke, gives a lively representation of the life he led there in his declining days:—

" Another very curious person whom I saw a great deal of in the autumn of 1805, sometimes at the Pavilion, sometimes at other houses where the Prince dined, and repeatedly at his own house, was Lord Thurlow, to whom the Prince always behaved with the most marked attention and deference.

" Thurlow had declined greatly in energy from his encounter with Horne Tooke, at Lady Oxford's. He used to read and ride out in the morning, and his daughter (Mrs. Brown) and Mr. Sneyd the clergyman were both always occupied in procuring any strangers, or any other persons, who they thought would be agreeable to the old man, to dine with him—the party being thus ten or twelve every day, or more. I had the good fortune to be occasionally there with my wife, which was a civility we owed to some former attentions from her to one of his daughters, in the county of Durham, and however rough he might be with men, he was the politest person in the world to ladies. These two or three hours of his at dinner were occupied in lying in wait for any unfortunate slip or ridiculous observation that might be made by any of his *male* visitors, and whom, when caught, he never left hold of, till I have seen the sweat run down their faces from the scrape they had got into, and the unmerciful exposure he made of them. Having seen this property of his, I took care, of course, to keep clear of him, and have often been extremely amused in seeing the figure those have cut who came with the evident intention of *showing off* before him. Curran, the Irish lawyer, I remember, was a striking instance of this. I dined with him at Thurlow's, one day, and he (Thurlow) just made as great a fool of him as he did formerly of Tooke. He was

[1] Mem. of Sir S. Romilly, II. 125.

always dressed in a full suit of clothes of the old fashion, great cuffs and massy buttons, great wig, long ruffles, &c. His black eyebrows exceeded in size any I have ever seen, and his voice, though by no means devoid of melody, was a kind of rolling, murmuring thunder. He was a man of great reading, particularly classical, and was a very distinguished as well as most daring converser. I never heard of any one but Mr. Hare who had fairly beat him, and that this happened I know from persons who were present. Hare turned the laugh against him more than once at Carlton House and at Woburn.

" Sir Philip Francis, whom I knew intimately, and who certainly was a remarkably quick and clever man, was perpetually vowing vengeance against Thurlow, and always fixing his time (during this autumn of 1805) for making ' an example of the old ruffian,' as he called him, either at the Pavilion, or wherever he met him; but I have seen them meet afterwards, and though Thurlow was always ready for battle, Francis, who on all other occasions was as bold as a lion, would never stir. The grudge he owed to Thurlow was certainly not slightly grounded. When Francis, and General Clavering, and Monson, were sent to India, in 1773, to check Hastings in his career, their conduct by one party in parliament was extolled to the skies, whilst, on the other hand, Lord Thurlow, in the House of Lords, said, ' the greatest misfortune to India and to England was, that the ship which carried these three gentlemen out, had not gone to the bottom of the sea in her passage.'

" Lord Thurlow was induced to dine with George Johnstone, who, being the most ridiculous toady of great men, and aspirer to what he thought genteel manners, said to him, ' I am afraid, my Lord, the port wine is not as good as I could wish,'—upon which, Thurlow growled out, ' I have *tasted better.*'

" On one occasion one of the caterers of company for Lord Thurlow's amusement thought he had secured a great card, when he took Sir —— ——, an F R.S., a solemn conceited pedant of great pretension on very moderate foundation, to call upon him. In mentioning the circumstance afterwards, Lord Thurlow merely observed, ' *A gentleman* did me the honor to call upon me to-day; *indeed, I believe he was a knight !* '

"He was fond of good music, and was, I believe, a critic in it. When he came into the drawing-room after dinner, he generally put his legs up on a sofa, and one of his daughters played on the piano-forte some of Handel's music; and though he might sometimes appear to be dozing, if she played carelessly, or music he did not like, he immediately roused himself, and said, 'What are you doing?'

"As a proof of the 'attention and deference' above mentioned always paid to Lord Thurlow by the Prince, I may add that one day when Thurlow was engaged to dine at the Pavilion during the race week, Sir John Ladd arrived at Brighton, and the Prince invited him to dinner. The Prince was in the room before Thurlow arrived, and mentioned to one of the party his fear that Thurlow would not like the company, and when 'the old Lion' arrived the Prince went in to the anteroom to meet him, and apologized for the party being larger than he had intended, but added, 'that Sir John Ladd was an old friend of his, and he could not avoid asking him to dinner;' to which Thurlow, in his growling voice, answered, 'I have no objection, Sir, to Sir John Ladd in his proper place, which I take to be your Royal Highness's coach-box, and not your table.'

"One day at dinner at his own house, he heard one of the company use the word 'chromatic,' as he thought affectedly. 'What does he say?' growled out Thurlow, and made his poor victim attempt to explain his meaning in a manner that probably cured him of using the word for the rest of his life. He was very particular about the dessert; and on one occasion, when I was present, a dish of peeches being brought to him which he found great fault with, he had the whole dessert, which, *for Brighthelmstone*, was a fine one, thrown out of the window!"[1]

Again, we have the ex-Chancellor, in the autumn of the following year, when he was very near his end, presented to us in a striking manner by Mr. Jerningham, the brother of Lord Stafford:—

"We afterwards dined at —— to meet Lord Thurlow, and his daughter Mrs. Brown. A large party were assembled there. I was never more struck with the ap-

[1] Diary of Mr. Creevy.

pearance of any one than with that of Lord Thurlow. Upon entering the drawing-room, where he was seated on a sofa, we were all involuntarily moved to silence, and there was a stillness which the fall of a pin would have disturbed. He did not move when we came into the room, but slightly inclined his head, which had before hung down on his breast. He was dressed in an old-fashioned gray suit buttoned very loosely about him, and hanging down very low; he had on a brown wig with three rows of curls hanging partly over his shoulders. He was very grave, and spoke little. His voice is rough, and his manner of speaking slow. Lord Thurlow is, I believe, only seventy-five; but from his appearance I should have thought him a hundred years old. His large black heavy eyes, which he fixed at intervals upon you, are overshadowed with perfectly white eyebrows, and his complexion is pallid and cadaverous. Upon literary subjects he ordinarily converses with much seeming pleasure, but having been this morning to the races he was fatigued and said very little. At dinner he drank a good deal, but nothing afterwards. In the course of conversation Mr. Mellis being remarked as a great favorite of the populace, Lord Thurlow said, ' They like him as a brother blackguard;' and then added, 'I am of their opinion: I dislike your pious heroes; I prefer Achilles to Hector, Turnus to Æneas.' Lord Thurlow has a surprising memory, and will not allow the want of it in any one else; but says it is a want of attention, and not of memory, that occasions forgetfulness. Being asked how long it was since he had been to Norfolk, he replied, 'About fifty or sixty years ago.' He went home very very early, calling loudly for his hat, which I remarked as being of black straw, with a very low crown, and the largest rim I ever saw. It is easy to see that in his observing mind the most trifling incidents remain graven. Thus upon Lady J. being asked a second time at the end of dinner whether she would have any wine, Lord Thurlow immediately exclaimed in a gruff voice, ' Lady J. drinks no wine!'

" We went to-day to dine at Lord Thurlow's, and upon being summoned from the drawing-room to dinner, we found him already seated at the head of his table in the same costume as the day before, and looking equally grave and ill. Lord Bute being mentioned, and some one observing that his life was going to be written, Lord Thurlow sharply observed, 'The life of a fly would be as interesting."[1]

Thurlow's career in this world was now near its close. The year 1806 was remarkable for the death of several of the greatest men England ever produced. In January the proud spirit of William Pitt, unable longer to witness longer the discomfiture of his foreign policy, and the triumph of his country's foes, had fled to another state of existence; and his illustrious rival and successor had scarcely begun to exercise the functions of the high office which, after such struggles, he had attained, when he too was summoned away while forming plans for the glory of England and for the liberties of mankind.

A few hours before the death of Charles James Fox,— an event which, from the important part he was then performing excited universal interest and general sympathy,[2]—Thurlow, who had formerly filled so large a spaces in the public eye, breathed his last—almost unobserved and unpitied. Soon after the dinners just referred to, while he still remained at Brighthelmstone, he was suddenly seized with an attack of illness, which carried him off in two days. I have not learned any particulars of his end, but I will hope that it was a good one. I trust that, conscious of the approaching change, having sincerely repented of his violence of temper, of the errors into which he had been led by worldly ambition, and of the irregularities of his private life, he had seen the worthlessness of the objects by which he had been allured; that having gained the frame of mind which his awful situation required, he received the consolations of religion; and that, in charity with mankind, he tenderly bade a long and last adieu to the relations and friends who surrounded him. He expired on the 12th of September, 1806, in the seventy-sixth year of his age.

Although the news of this event cannot be said to have produced any deep sensation in the public mind, the few

---
[1] Law Magazine, vol. vii. 90, "Life of Lord Thurlow"
[2] Even Walter Scott, a bitter political opponent, after a beautiful tribute to the services of Pitt, exclaimed—
"Nor yet suppress the generous sigh
Because his rival slumbers nigh."

survivors who had lived with Thurlow on terms of intimacy spoke and thought of him with respect and tenderness. I have pleasure in recording, to the honor of the Prince of Wales, that he immediately sent for a nephew of the deceased, then a very young man,—kindly made him an offer of assistance in any profession he might choose—spoke of his uncle as one whom he sincerely loved, —a faithful friend and upright councillor;—and, lamenting his loss, was so much moved that he could not refrain from tears.

The ex-Chancellor's remains were sent privately to his house in Great George Street, Westminster, and were conveyed thence, with great funeral pomp, to the Temple Church; Lord Chancellor Eldon, the Chiefs of the three superior Courts, and other legal dignitaries and distinguished men, attending as mourners,—followed by almost the whole profession of the law.

Being still only a student at Lincoln's Inn, I did not witness the solemnity; but I well remember the account, given by those who were present, of its grandeur and impressiveness. The coffin, with the name, age, and dignities of the deceased inscribed upon it, and ornamented with heraldic devices, was deposited in the vault under the south aisle of this noble structure, which still proves to us the taste as well as the wealth of the Knights Templars.[1]

[1] Here I saw Thurlow reposing, whenn, early forty years after, at the conclusion of funeral rites as grand and far more affecting, I assisted in depositing the body of my departed friend, Sir William Follett, by his side *— May I be allowed to pay a passing tribute of respect to the memory of this most eminent, amiable and virtuous man?--If it had pleased Providence to prolong his days, he would have afforded a nobler subject for some future biographer than most of those whose career it has been my task to delineate. When he was prematurely cut off, the highest office of the law was within his reach; and I make no doubt that, by the great distinction he would have acquired as a judge, as a statesman, and as an orator, a deep interest would have been given to all the incidents of his past life, which they want with the vulgar herd of mankind, because he never sat on the bench, nor had titles of nobility conferred upon him One most remarkable circumstance would have been told respecting his rise to be the most popular advocate of his day, to be Attorney General, and to be a powerful debater in the House of Commons—that it was wholly unaccompanied by envy Those who have outstripped their competitors have often a great drawback upon their satisfaction by observing the grudging and ill-will with which, by some, their success is

* Sir R. Peel, the Prime Minister, Lord Lyndhurst, the Chancellor, and many distinguished persons on both sides in politics, were present.

In the choir was soon after placed his bust in marble, with the following inscription by the Reverend Martin Routh, D. D., President of Magdalen College, Oxford:—

> "Baro Thurlow a Thurlow,
> Summus Regni Cancellarius,
> Hic sepultus est
> Vixit Annis LXXV Mensibus X.
> Decessit anno Salutis Humanæ MDCCCVI.
> Idibus Septembris
> Vir altâ mente et magnâ præditus
> Qui
> Nactus præclarissimas occasiones
> Optimè de patriâ merendi
> Jura Ecclesiæ, Regis, Civium
> In periculum vocata
> Firmo et constanti animo
> Tutatus est."

This unqualified praise may be excused in an epitaph; but the biographer, in estimating the character and the conduct of the individual so extolled, is bound to notice his weaknesses, and to warn others against the faults which he committed. Even as a Judge, the capacity in which he appears to most advantage, although he was entirely free from personal corruption or undue influence, and uniformly desirous to decide fairly, he was not sufficiently patient in listening to counsel, and he did not take the

beheld Such were Follett's inoffensive manners and unquestioned superiority, that all rejoiced at every step he attained—as all wept when he was snatched away from the still higher honors which seemed to be awaiting him. It is said—

> " Envy will merit, as its shade, pursue,
> But, like a shadow, proves the substance true."
> " Fame calls up calumny and spite,
> Thus shadow owes its birth to light."

But *envy* may be conquered. I do not agree in the sentiment contained in Pope's letter to Addison " I congratulate you upon having your share in that which all the great men and all the good men that ever lived have had their share of—envy and calumny. 'To be uncensured and to be obscure is the same thing,'"—nor in the aphorism of Mr. Burke " Obloquy is a necessary ingredient in the composition of all true glory,"—nor in the Spanish proverb to be found in Lopez de Vega:

> " Dixo un discreto que era matrimonio
> Polibio, el de la enbidia y el de la fama
> Que se apartava solo con la muerte,"—

thus translated by Lord Holland —

> " Envy was Honor's wife, a wise man said,
> Ne'er to be parted till the man was dead."

There is a superlative degree of excellence which, like that of superior intelligences, men cease to envy, because they feel that to them it is hopelessly unattainable.

requisite pains to extricate the facts or to comprehend
nice legal distinctions in complicated cases which came
before him. Without devoting much time out of court
to the duties of his office, no judge can satisfactorily discharge them, and Thurlow seems to have dispised the
notion of reading law to extend or keep up his stock of
professional knowledge. Only on very rare occasions
would he take the trouble in his library of examining the
authorities cited at the bar, and he used to prepare himself for giving judgment on his way from Great Ormond
Street to the Court of Chancery. "An old free speaking
companion of his, well known at Lincoln's Inn, would say,
'I met the Great Law LION this morning going to Westminster and bowed to him, but he was so busy reading in
the coach what his *provider* had supplied him with, that he
took no notice of me.'"[1] He certainly had an excellent
head for law and with proper pains he might have rivaled the fame of Lord Nottingham and Lord Hardwicke;
but he was contented with the character of a political
Chancellor and, so that he retained power, he was indifferent as to the opinion which might be formed of him by
his contemporaries or by posterity.[2] He often treated the
bar with rudeness, and his demeanor to the other branch
of the profession sometimes awakened recollections of
Jeffreys. A solicitor once had to prove a death before him
and being told upon every statement he made, " Sir, that
is no proof," at last exclaimed, much vexed, " My Lord,
it is very hard that you will not believe me; I knew him
well to his last hour; I saw him dead and in his coffin,
my Lord. My Lord, he was my client." *Lord Chancellor:*
"Good God, sir! Why did you not tell me that before?
I should not have doubted the fact one moment; for I
think nothing can be so likely to kill a man as to have
you for his attorney."[3]

As to legal reform, instead of imitating those who held

[1] Cr. 180

[2] Lord Eldon used to be fond of quoting Thurlow as a great lawyer; but this was partly from personal liking. Thurlow having patronized him at the bar, and was partly *in odium* of Lord Loughborourh, whom he despised as a Judge, and of Lord Mansfield, whom he always wished to depreciate from the time when he bade adieu to the King's Bench, on the ground that only Westminster and Christchurch men were favored there — *Twiss's Life of Eldon.*

[3] This jest, which was probably thought innocuous by the author of it, is said to have ruined the reputation and business of the unfortunate victim.

the Great Seal in the time of the Commonwealth and soon after the Revolution, he not only originated no measures of improvement himself, but he violently and pertinaciously opposed those which were brought forward by others. Mr. Pitt. though thwarted by Thurlow, really seems to have had a desire to reform our jurisprudence as well as our commercial policy, till the breaking out of the French Revolution,—when the terror of Jacobinism put an end to all improvement, and it was unwisely determined to try to cure disaffection by rendering the laws more arbitrary.

Of statesmanship Thurlow several times declared, with much candor and truth, that he knew very little. Unless when he went into open opposition to the Minister under whom he held the Great Seal, he blindly adopted whatever measures were brought forward by the Government, supporting them much less by information and argument than by zeal and violence. Yet he seems to have been considered a very useful partisan—from the protection he could afford to his friends, and the terror he inspired into his enemies. He served Lord North with unwearying good faith, and I really do not think he can justly be accused of treachery to Lord Rockingham, as, while in the Cabinet with that nobleman, he avowedly led the opposition from the woolsack. His double-dealing during the King's illness has affixed a permanent blot upon his character; but his subsequent hostility to Mr. Pitt, though very intemperate and wrong-headed, cannot be denominated perfidious, as it was openly manifested in parliament, instead of working in secret intrigues. His career, after he was deprived of office, must be allowed to have been obscure and inglorious,—his late-born zeal for liberty appearing to have sprung from personal dislike of the Minister—not from any altered view he had taken of constitutional rights,—and having died away with the chance of his own restoration to office.

His judicial patronage was upon the whole well exercised, notwithstanding his occasional indulgence in personal antipathies, as in the case of Pepper Arden.[1] When created Lord Chancellor, he would not remove any of the

[1] Thurlow's preference of Buller to Pepper Arden is thus referred to by Peter Pindar.—
"And *bonâ fide*, not of rapture fuller,
Thurlow, the Seal and loyal conscience keeper

officers appointed by his predecessors, or any Commissioners of Bankrupt,[1] except one, who offended him by applying for the interest of his mistress.[2] The public owed to him the services of Lord Kenyon, and other eminent Judges; and he first discovered, and put in the line of promotion, the greatest lawyer of our times— John Scott, afterwards the Earl of Eldon.

In his ecclesiastical appointments he is said to have been less scrupulous, and to have been chiefly influenced by personal favor or political convenience. Yet, forming a high opinion of Horsley, merely from accidentally reading his Letters to Priestley, he gave him a stall at Gloucester, saying that "those who supported the Church should be supported by it;" and afterwards recommended him to the episcopal bench. When Potter, who dedicated to him a translation of Æschylus, had published his

See his prime favorite, Mr. Justice Buller,
High thron'd in Chancery, grieve the poor Sir Pepper."

I have steadily refrained from printing or even showing complimentary letters addressed to me as an author, but I must make an exception in favor of the following from the late Lord Alvanley, a most accomplished nobleman, and long the charm of intellectual society in London :—

"Bath, Dec. 23rd, 1846.
"My dear Lord,
"I trust you will allow a man who, during the last year, has been suffering under a most excruciating disorder, to thank you for the relief and pleasure which he has received in the perusal of your admirable work, 'The Lives of the Chancellors,' a book which, both here and abroad, has already taken its station among the great classical authors of biography in this or any other age, and which has most justly done so, for in it are blended with peculiar felicity and good taste, the grave and vigorous style fitted to deep research, and the lighter one adapted to anecdote and traits of character, and where without reference to party or country, praise has justly and without flattery, been bestowed on the great and good, and blame where blame was due, has been tempered by a proper consideration of the times in which the various characters lived, and extenuating allowance made for the weaknesses of human nature I shall make no apology for writing to you, notwithstanding our slight acquaintance, because, in the first place you have become public property, and must submit to be thanked by those whom you have instructed and amused, and in the next, because I should be ungrateful did I not show you my gratitude for having vindicated my father's character from the slight and oppression which he underwent at the hands of Lord Thurlow—slight and oppression to which, however, time has done justice, through the opinions of wiser lawyers than Lord Thurlow ever was. Thanking you again for this act of justice, and for the gratification which I have had in the study of your work,   "I am
            "Your obedient servant,   "ALVANLEY."

[1] It had been usual for a new Lord Chancellor to have what was called " a scratch,"—sweeping away the greater part of the seventy, and substituting his own favorites
[2] He thus imitated the conduct of George II. with respect to Lady Suffolk.

translations of Sophocles and Euripides, Thurlow procured for him a stall at Norwich, observing that "he did not like to promote him earlier, for fear of making him indolent." He first put other eminent divines in the line of high promotion.[1]

On one occasion, a considerable living fell vacant in the Chancellor's gift, which was solicited by Queen Charlotte, and promised to her *protégé*. The curate, who had served in the parish some years, hearing who was likely to succeed, modestly applied for the Chancellor's intercession, that, on account of his large family, he might be continued in the curacy. The expectant rector calling to return thanks, Thurlow introduced the case of the curate, which he represented with great strength and pathos; but the answer was, "I should be much pleased to oblige your Lordship, but unfortunately I have promised it to a friend." *Thurlow:* "Sir, I can not make this gentleman your curate, it is true; but I can make him the rector, and by G—d he shall have the living as he can not have the curacy." He instantly called in his secretary, and ordered the presentation to be made out in favor of the curate,—who was inducted, and enjoyed the living many years.[2]

The following anecdote is sent to me by a venerable dignitary of the Church: "A poor curate, with some difficulty (it was supposed he fee'd the porter), obtained admission into Lord Thurlow's house, and waited for him till he returned from the Chancery Court. When Lord Thurlow saw him, he broke out in his usual manner, by abruptly and loudly asking him questions. "Who are you? What do you want? How came you here? What interest have you? Who sent you? What *Lord's name* do you come in? What *Lord's name,* I say, do you come in?" "Indeed, my Lord," was the answer, "I came to apply for the living of ——; but I have no interest. I come in no Lord's name but the Lord of Hosts!" "The

---

[1] Having received the copy of an Essay from a Yorkshire parson which pleased him, he thus wrote to him "Sir,—I return many thanks for the Essay you have sent me Give me leave, in my turn, to inquire after your situation, and how far that or your inclination attaches you to Leeds or Yorkshire. I am Sir, your obt serv*, THURLOW —I wish your answer in return of post"

[2] This anecdote I have from a nephew of the Chancellor. How he settled the matter with the Queen I have not heard, but we may suppose that her Majesty highly approved of this *equitable decision.*

Lord of Hosts!" said the Chancellor, "the Lord of Hosts! Well! you are the very first parson that ever applied to me in *that* Lord's name before, and I'll be ―― if you shan't have the living."

Of his oratory I have given the most favorable specimens I could select, using the freedom to correct his inaccuracies of language; for even the printed reports justify Mr. Butler's remark, that "though Lord Thurlow spoke slowly and deliberately, yet his periods were strangely confused, and often ungrammatical."[1] It argues little for the discrimination and taste of those to whom they were addressed, that they were listened to with profound attention, and produced a deep effect, though chiefly made up of "sound and fury;" while Edmund Burke acquired the nickname of the "*Dinnerbell*," by delivering the finest speeches for depth of thought and beauty of diction to be found in our parliamentary records.

Thurlow himself appears always to have had a great contempt for his audience in the House of Peers, and to have reckoned with daring confidence on their ignorance. Of this we have a striking instance in the Memoirs of Bishop Watson, who, having informed us that in a speech made during the King's illness in 1788, respecting the right of the Prince of Wales to be Regent, he himself had quoted a definition of "right" from GROTIUS, thus proceeds: "The Chancellor in his reply boldly asserted that he perfectly well remembered the passage I had quoted from Grotius, and that it solely respected *natural*, but was inapplicable to *civil* rights. Lord Loughborough, the first time I saw him after the debate, assured me that, before he went to sleep that night, he had looked into Grotius, and was astonished to find that the Chancellor, in contradicting me, had presumed on the ignorance of the House, and that my quotation was perfectly correct. What miserable shifts do great men submit to in supporting their parties!"[2]

We have the following very striking representation of his oratory from a skillful rhetorician:—" He rose slowly from his seat; he left the woolsack with deliberation; but he went not to the nearest place like ordinary Chancellors, the sons of mortal men; he drew back by a pace

[1] Reminisc. i. 142. [2] Life of Watson, 221.

or two, and, standing as it were askance, and partly behind the huge bale he had quitted for a season, he began to pour out, first in a growl, and then in a clear and louder roll, the matter which he had to deliver, and which, for the most part, consisted in some positive assertions, some personal vituperation, some sarcasms at classes, some sentences pronounced upon individuals, as if they were standing before him for judgment, some vague mysterious threats of things purposely not expressed, and abundant protestations of conscience and duty, in which they who keep the consciences of Kings are somewhat apt to indulge."[1]

Butler, who had often heard him, ascribes to him a finesse which I should not have discovered from the printed reports of his speeches,—for his apparent ignorance I should judge wholly unaffected. and he seems to me always to aim direct blows against his adversary:—
" He would appear to be ignorant of the subject in debate, and, with affected respect, but visible derision, to seek for information upon it; pointing out, with a kind of dry solemn humor, contradictions and absurdities which he professed his own inability to explain, and calling upon his adversaries for their explanation. It was a kind of masked battery, of the most searching questions and distressing observations; it often discomfited his adversary, and seldom failed to force him into a very embarrassing position of defense; it was the more effective, as, while he was playing it off, his Lordship showed he had command of much more formidable artillery."

Lord Thurlow does not figure in Horace Walpole's list of noble and royal authors—never, as far as I know, having taken the trouble even to publish a pamphlet or a speech. Although he knew nothing of political economy, or of any science,[2] he had made himself thoroughly acquainted with the classics, Latin and Greek. These studies were the delight of his old age. When living in retirement at Dulwich, he found some consolation for the loss of power and of political excitement, in superintending the classical education of his nephews, who lived

---

[1] Lord Brougham's Characters, 1 94.
[2] He is said to have been very fond of music, and to have understood the theory of it perfectly, although the soothing charm usually imputed to it does not seem to have operated upon him.

under his roof, and to whom he was very tenderly attached. For their instruction and amusement he would sometimes himself attempt to translate into English verse favorite passages of the ancient authors they were reading. As a curious specimen of his poetical powers I am enabled to lay before the public the following translation of a Chorus, from the "Hippolytus" of Euripides:[1]

[1] The learned reader will recollect that the guilty love of Phædra for Hippolytus had been disclosed to him by the Nurse, and that the heroine, on account of the repulse she met with, had declared her determination to hang herself —I subjoin the original Chorus:

Ἡλιβάτοις ὑπὸ κευθμῶσι γεννοίμαν,
Ἵνα με πτεροῦσσαν ὄρνιν
Θεὸς ἐν ποταναῖς ἀγέλῃσιν θείη.
Ἀρθείην γὰρ ἐπὶ πόντιον κῦμα
Τᾶς Ἀδριηνᾶς ἀκτᾶς,
Ἠριδανοῦ θ' ὕδωρ.
Ἔνθα πορφύρεον σταλάσσουσιν
Εἰς οἶδμα πατρὸς τριτάλαιναι
Κόραι, Φαέθοντος οἴκτῳ, δακρύων
Τὰς ἠλεκτροφαεῖς αὐγάς.
Ἑσπερίδων δ' ἐπὶ μηλόσπορον ἀκτὰι
Ἀνύσαιμι τᾶν Ἀοιδᾶν,
Ἵν' ὁ ποντομέδων πορφυρέας λίμνης
Ναύταις οὐκ ἔθ' ὁδὸν νέμει, σεμνὸν
Τέρμονα κυρῶν οὐρανοῦ τὸν Ἄτλας ἔχει.
Κρῆναι τ' ἀμβροσίαι χέονται
Ζηνὸς μελάθρων παρὰ κοίταις,
Ἵν' ὀλβιόδωρος ἄξει ζαθέα
Χθὼν εὐδαιμονίαν θεοῖς.
Ὦ λευκόπτερε Κρησία
Πορθμὶς, ἃ διὰ πόντιον
Κῦμ' ἁλίκτυπον ἅλμας
Ἐπόρευσας ἐμὰν ἄνασσαν
Ὀλβίων ἀπ' οἴκων
Κακονυμφοτάταν ὄνασιν.
Ἦ λὰρ ἀπ' ἀμφοτέρων,
Ἢ Κρησίας ἐκ γᾶς δύσορνις

"Oh could I those deep caverns reach,
　Where me, a winged bird, among
　　The feather'd race
　　Some God might place!
And rising could I soar along
The sea-wave of the Adrian beach!
And by the Po my pinions spread,
　Where, in their father's ruddy wave,
Their amber tears his daughter shed
Still weeping o'er a brother's grave!
Or to those gardens make my way,
　Where carol the Hesperian maids,
　　And He, who rules
　　The purple pools,
The sailor's further course impedes,
The awful limits of the sky
Fixing, which Atlas there sustains!
And springs ambrosial near the dome
Of Jove still water those rich plains,
Whence to the Gods their blessings come.

I

" White-wing'd bark of Cretan wood,
　Which across the briny main,
Over the sea-raging flood,
　From her happy home our Queen
Convey'd, a most unhappy bride,
In ill-starr'd wedlock to be tied!

II

" Dire both omens, when her flight
　Left behind the Cretan land ;
And when Athens came in sight,
　Where on the Munychian strand,

Ἔπτατο κλεινὰς Ἀθήνας, Μουνυχίου δ' ἐπ' ἀκταῖς
　ἐκδήσατο
Πλεκτὰς πεισμάτων ἀρχὰς,
Ἐπ' ἀπείρου τε γᾶς ἔβασαν.
Ἀνθ' ὧν οὐχ ὁσίων ἐρώτων δεινᾶ φρένας Ἀφροδίτας
　νοσῳ κατεκλάσθη.
Χαλεπᾷ δ' ὑπέραντλος οὖσα
Συμφορᾷ, τεράμνων
Ἀπὸ νυμφιδίων κρεμαστὸν
Ἄψεται ἀμφὶ βρόχον
Λευκᾷ καθαρμόζουσα δέρᾳ,
Δαίμονα στυγνὸν καταιδεσθεῖσα, τάν τ' εὔδοξον
　αὐθαιρουμενα
Φάμαν, ἀπαλλάσσουσά
Τ' ἀλγεινὸν φρενῶν ἔρωτα.

Eur. Hip. 732.

>   They tie the hawser's twisted end,
>   And on the mainland straight descend.
>
> III.
>
> " For unhallow'd passion rent,
>   Planted deep, her lab'ring breast,
>   Dire disease which Venus sent,
>   And, with sore misfortune prest,
>   The chord suspended from the dome
>   Of her ill-fated bridal room.
>
> IV.
>
> " Round her milk-white neck she'll tie
>   Dreading much the adverse frown
>   Of the Goddess—prizing high
>   Her unspotted chaste renown—
>   And from her heart resolv'd to move,
>   This only way, the pain of Love."

There is likewise extant, in his handwriting, a translation of the whole of the *BATPAXOMYOMAXIA*, or " Battle of the Frogs and the Mice," the merit of which may be judged of by the following extract:—

BLADDER-CHEEK, his Ranish Majesty, having vauntingly begun the dialogue,—

>   " Him CRUMB-CATCH answer'd quick in vocal sounds,
>   ' Why, friend, my birth demand, so known to men,
>   To Gods, and to the fowl who wing the sky?
>   My name is *Crumb-Catch*, and I am the son
>   Of Nibble-Biscuit, my great-hearted sire;
>   Lick-Mill's my mother, King Gnaw-Gammon's child.
>   She bore me in a hole, and brought me up
>   With figs, and nuts, and ev'ry sort of food
>   But how make me thy friend, unlike in kind?
>   Thy living is in waters, but my food
>   Whatever man is us'd to eat   The loaf
>   Thrice-kneaded, in the neat round basket kept
>   Escapes not me, nor wafer, flat and long.
>   Mix'd with much sesame, nor bacon slice,
>   Nor liver, cloth'd in jacket of white lard,
>   Nor cheese, flesh curdled from delicious milk,
>   Nor the good sweetmeats, which the wealthy love,
>   Nor what else cooks prepare to feast mankind,
>   Pressing their dishes with each kind of sauce.
>   .   .   .   .
>   But these two chief I fear in all the earth,
>   The hawk and cat who work me heavy woe;
>   And doleful trap where treach'rous death resides.
>   .   .   .   .
>   BLADDER-CHEEK, smiling to all this, replied:
>   ' Upon the belly's fare thou vauntest high,
>   My guest! We, too, have wonders to behold,
>   Numberless, both by water and by sod;
>   For to the frogs the son of Saturn gave

A lot amphibious, to leap on earth,
And under water hide their body safe.
If thou wouldst these explore, they are at hand.
I'll take thee on my back.'"[1]

[1] Τὸν δ' αὖ Ψιχάρπαξ ἠμείβετο φωνήσεντε.
Τίπτε γένος τοὐμὸν ζητεῖς, φίλε, δῆλον ἅπασιν
Ἀνθρώποις τε, θεοῖς τε, καὶ οὐρανίοις πετεηνοῖς;
Ψιχάρπαξ μὲν ἐγὼ κικλήσκομαι· εἰμὶ δὲ κοῦρος
Τρωξάρταο πατρὸς μεγαλήτορος, ἡ δέ νυ μητὴρ
Λειχομύλη θυγάτηρ Πτερνοτρώκτου βασιλῆος,
Γείνατο δ' ἐν καλύβῃ με, καὶ ἐξεθρέψατο βρωτοῖς,
Σύκοις καὶ καρύοις καὶ ἐδέσμασι παντοδαποῖσι.
Πῶς δὲ φίλον ποιῇ με, τὸν εἰς φύσιν οὐδὲν
   ὁμοῖον;
Σοὶ μὲν γὰρ βίος ἐστὶν ἐν ὕδασιν· αὐτὰρ ἔμοιγε,
Ὅσσα παρ' ἀνθρώποις, τρώγειν ἔθος. Οὐδέ με
   λήθει
Ἄρτος τρισκωπάνιστος ἐπ' εὐκύκλου κανέοιο,
Οὐδὲ πλακοῦς τανύπεπλος ἔχων πολὺ σησαμότυρον,
Οὐ τόμος ἐκ πτέρνης, οὐχ ἤπατα λευκοχίτωνα,
Ου τυρὸς νεόπηκτος ἀπὸ γλυκεροῖο γάλακτος,
Οὐ χρηστὸν μελίτωμα, τὸ καὶ μάκαρες ποθέουσιν,
Οὐδ' ὅσα πρὸς θοίνας μερόπων τεύχουσι μάγειροι
Κοσμοῦντες χύτρας ἀρτύμασι παντοδαποῖσιν.

. . . .

Ἀλλὰ δύω μάλα πάντα, τὰ δείδια πᾶσαι ἐπ' αἶαν,
Κίρκον καὶ λαγέην, οἵ μοι μοι μέγα πένθος ἄγουσι,
Καὶ παγίδα στονόεσσαν, ὅπου δολόεις πέλε πότμος·

Πρὸς τάδε μειδήσας Φυσίγναθος ἀντίον ηὔδα·
Ξεῖνε, λίην αὐχεῖς ἐπὶ γαστέρι· ἔστι καὶ ἡμῖν
Πολλὰ μάλ' ἐν λίμνῃ καὶ ἐπὶ χθονὶ θαύματ' ἰδέσθαι·
Ἀμφίβιον γὰρ ἔδωκε νομὴν βατράχοισι Κρονίων,
Σκιρτῆσαι κατὰ γῆν, καὶ ἐφ' ὕδασι σῶμα καλύψαι,
(Στοιχείοις δυσὶν μεμερισμένα δώματα ναίειν.)
Εἰ δ' ἐθέλεις καὶ ταῦτα δαήμεναι, εὐχερές ἐστι.
Βαῖνέ μοι ἐν νώτοισι.————

Hom. Batr. 24.

The ex-Chancellor would likewise drive away *ennui* by writing Latin verses. The late Rev. F. Howes, when a boy of sixteen, having sent him the following charade,—

> "Formâ sum duplici · sub amico pectore, Lector,
> Dum legis hæcce, tuo, pars *mea prima* latet
> Frigida sit quamvis et candida, parte *secundâ*
> Non est candidior, frigidiorve Cloe
> *Tota* quidem nigra sum , vox est mihi rauca rudisque;
> Fata tamen Veteres me cecinisse ferunt."

In two days his Lordship replied thus:—

> "Quicquid delirat *Cor* vatis inania questi,
> Candidior *nix* est frigidiorque Cloe.
> Nec Priscis tantùm sua *Cornix* ora resolvit,
> Si nobis etiam garrula prodit avis "

Tired of deeper studies, Thurlow became, in his retirement a great reader of novels; and, in one instance, so interested was he in the plot, that he dispatched his groom from Dulwich to London, after ten o'clock at night, for the concluding volume, that he might know the fate of the heroine before trying to go to sleep.

His great ambition from early youth, and through life, was to shine in conversation, and in this department of genius he seems to have met with brilliant success. He had a stupendous memory, a quick sense of the ridiculous, a copious flow of words, and an *emphasis* in talk which occasionally supplied the place of epigram. With these qualifications, if he had not made his fortune in the law, he would have risen to great eminence as a "diner-out." He was rather fond of literary society, and, laying aside all official privilege, he boldly descended into the arena against controversial gladiators. He received this high compliment from Doctor Johnson, while yet at the bar: " Depend upon it, sir, it is when you come close to a man, in conversation, that you discover what his real abilities are: to make a speech in a public assembly is a knack. Now I honor Thurlow, sir; Thurlow is a fine fellow; he fairly puts his mind to yours." After his Lordship had been elevated to be Chancellor, the great Lexicographer said to Boswell, " I would prepare myself for no man in England but Lord Thurlow. When I am to meet him, I should wish to know a day before." Jemmy goes on to say, " How he would have prepared himself, I can not conjecture. Would he have selected certain topics, and considered them in every view, so as to be in readiness to argue them at all points? And what may we suppose those topics to have been? *I once started the curious inquiry to the great man who was the subject of this compliment; he smiled, but did not pursue it."* [1]

Thurlow was not ill-natured in conversation; and Johnson was considered a more terrible opponent. Craddock, who knew both intimately, says, I was always more afraid of Johnson than of Thurlow; for though the latter was sometimes very rough and coarse, yet the decisive stroke of the former left a mortal wound behind it." [2]

According to the fashion still prevailing in his time, he used to have long symposiac *sittings* after dinner, during which his wit was stimulated by the brisk circulation of the bottle. " In the afternoon of life, conviviality, wine, and society unbent his mind. It was with Mr. Rigby, Lord Gower, Lord Weymouth, Mr. Dundas, and a few other select friends, that he threw off his constitutional severity." [3] Though by no means subject to the charge of habitual intemperance, yet from occasional indulgence he sometimes found himself in scenes which, according to our sober notions, were not very fit for a Chancellor. " Returning, by way of frolic," relates Sir Nathaniel Wraxall, "very late at night, on horseback, to Wimbledon from Addiscombe, the seat of Mr. Jenkinson, near Croydon, where the party had dined, Lord Thurlow, the Chancellor, Pitt, and Dundas, found the turnpike-gate, situate between Tooting and Streatham, thrown open. Being elevated above their usual prudence, and having no servant near them, they passed through the gate at a brisk pace, without stopping to pay the toll, regardless of the remonstrances and threats of the turnpike man, who, running after them, and believing them to belong to some highwaymen who had recently committed some depredations on that road, discharged the contents of his blunderbuss at their backs. Happily he did no injury." [4]

Old Baron Maseres, who used to say that he was born on the day when Lord Holt tried Tuchin, the libeler, and whom I well remember walking about, at the age of ninety in the costume of the reign of George I., had been very intimate with Thurlow, and used to relate this anecdote

---

[1] Boswell's Life of Johnson, iv. 192, 350. [2] Cr. 1. 74.
[3] Wrax. Mem. 1. 527. [4] Ibid. 1. 478.

of him:—"When Attorney General, for some reason or another, by way of frolic, he had disguised himself as a sailor, and returning home very late at night through Long Acre, he was seized by a press-gang, and, his oaths rather being at variance with his protestations that he was *a gentleman*, they carried him to their rendezvous at the Tower. Thence he wrote a letter to the First Lord of the Admiralty for his release—which, after many imprecations upon those who had deprived him of his liberty, thus good-humoredly concluded: "I hope your Lordship will not insist on my becoming a *foremast-man*, knowing that I am already serving his Majesty as a *General officer*."

There are a few of Thurlow's pointed sayings handed down to us, but I suspect that even a Boswell could not have supported for him the reputation he enjoyed in his own time. In the Duchess of Kingston's case, two learned Doctors of the Civil Law pouring forth heavily much recondite lore, having gravely argued that the sentence of the Ecclesiastical Court, annulling her first marriage, was decisive in her favor,—the Attorney General was pleased to remark, that " the congress of two civilians from Doctors' Commons always reminded him of the noted observation of Cicero, '*Mirabile videtur quod non rideat Haruspex cum Haruspicem viderit.*'"[1] In the debates on the Regency, a prim Peer, remarkable for his finical delicacy, and formal adherence to etiquette, having cited pompously certain resolutions, which he said had been passed by a party of noblemen and gentlemen of great distinction at the Thatched House Tavern, the Lord Chancellor, in adverting to these, said, "As to what the noble Lord in the red riband told us that he had heard at the *alehouse*——." Such strokes of coarse jocularity tell more certainly in either House than the play of the most refined wit. Even when in administration, he affected to laugh freely at official men and practices. Thus, when on the woolsack, having mentioned some public functionary whose conduct he intimated that he disapproved, he thought fit to add, " But far be it from me to express any blame of any official person, whatever may be my opinion; for that I well knew would be sure to bring down upon me a panegyric on his character and his services!" Lamenting the great difficulty he had in disposing of a high

[1] De Natura Deorum lib. 1. c. 26.

legal situation, he described himself as long hesitating between the intemperance of A. and the corruption of B., but finally preferring the man of bad temper. Afraid lest he should have been supposed to have admitted the existence of pure moral worth, he added,—"Not but that there was a d—d deal of corruption in A's intemperance."—Happening to be at the British Museum viewing the Townley Marbles, when a person came in and announced the death of Mr. Pitt, Thurlow was heard to say, "A d—d good hand at turning a period!" and no more.[1]

The following ancedote was related by Lord Eldon:—
"After dinner, one day, when nobody was present but Lord Kenyon and myself, Lord Thurlow said, 'Taffy, I decided a cause this morning, and I saw from Scott's face that he doubted whether I was right.' Thurlow then stated his view of the case, and Kenyon instantly said, 'Your decision was quite right.' 'What say you to that?' asked the Chancellor. I said, 'I did not presume to form a judgment upon a case in which they both agreed. But I think a fact has not been mentioned which may be material.' I was about to state the fact and my reason. Kenyon, however, broke in upon me, and, with some warmth, stated that I was always so obstinate, there was no dealing with me. 'Nay,' interposed Thurlow, 'that's not fair. You, Taffy, are obstinate, and give no reasons; you, Jack Scott, are obstinate, too; but then you give your reasons, and d—d bad ones they are!'"

Thurlow having heard that Kenyon had said to a party who had threatened to appeal from his decision, by filing a bill in Chancery, "Go into Chancery then: *abi in malam rem!*"—the next time he met the testy Chief Justice, he said, "Taffy, when did you first think the Court of Chancery was such a *mala res?* I remember when you made a very *good thing* of it."

Pepper Arden, whom he hated and persecuted, having been made a Welsh Judge by Pitt, and still continuing to practice at the Chancery bar, was arguing a cause against his boon companion, Graham, and something turning upon the age of a lady, who swore she was only forty-five, he said he was sure she was more, and his antagonist looking dissent, he exclaimed, so as to be heard by all present,

[1] This last saying I have from a person who was present.

"I'll lay you a bottle of wine of it." Thurlow did not swear aloud, but, by an ejaculation and a frown, called the unwary counsel to a sense of the impropriety he had committed. *Pepper Arden.*—" I beg your Lordship's pardon: I really forgot where I was." *Thurlow.*—" I suppose, sir, you thought you were sitting on the bench in your own court administering justice in Wales!"

Considering Thurlow's relish for literary society, we must wonder and regret that he did not continue to cultivate the friendship of the man with whom he had been so intimate when they were fellow pupils in the solicitor's office; but he does not seem by any means properly to have appreciated the fine imagination, the quiet humor, the simple manners, or the affectionate heart, which ought to have attached him to Cowper. While the poet watched with solicitude the career of the lawyer, rejoicing at every step of his advancement, the lawyer was quite indifferent to the successes or the sorrows of the poet. Cowper, though neglected and forgotten by his brother idler of Southampton Row, who now filled the most exalted office in the kingdom, hearing that he was laid up by the gout, lovingly blind to all his faults, thus writes to Mr. Hill:—" These violent attacks of a distemper so often fatal, are very alarming to those who esteem and respect the Chancellor as he deserves. A life of confinement and anxious attention to important objects, where the habit is bilious to such a terrible degree, threatens to be a short one; and I wish he may not be made a topic for men of reflection to moralize upon, affording a conspicuous instance of the transient and fading nature of all human accomplishments and attainments." On Thurlow's elevation to the woolsack, Cowper was strongly advised to remind him of their former intimacy, but he declined to do so for the reasons expressed in the following letter to Mr. Unwin:—" I feel much obliged to you for your kind intimation, and have given the subject of it all my best attention, both before I received your letter and since. The result is, that I am persuaded it will be better not to write. I know the man and his disposition well; he is very liberal in his way of thinking,—generous and discerning. He is well aware of the tricks which are played on such occasions; and, after fifteen years interruption of all intercourse between us, would translate my letter into this language,—' Pray remember the poor.' This would disgust him, because he would think our former intimacy disgraced by such an oblique application. He has not forgotten me : and if he had, there are those about him who can not come into his presence without reminding him of me; and he is also perfectly acquainted with my circumstances. It would, perhaps, give him pleasure to surprise me with a benefit ; and if he means me such a favor, I should disappoint him by asking it."—However, at the continued instigation of his friends, he afterwards sent Thurlow a copy of his published poems, by this time familiar and dear to all men of taste, with the following stiff letter of compliment :—

"Olney Bucks, Feb. 25, 1782.

" My Lord,

" I make no apology for what I account a duty ; I should offend against the cordiality of our former friendship should I send a volume into the world, and forget how much I am bound to pay my particular respects to your Lordship upon that occasion. When we parted, you little thought of hearing from me again, and I as little thought I should live to write to you, still less that I should wait on you in the capacity of an author.

"Among the pieces which I have the honor to send, there is one for which I must entreat your pardon ; I mean that of which your Lordship is the subject.[1] My best excuse is, that it flowed almost spontaneously from the affectionate remembrance of a connection which did me so much honor.

" I have the honor to be, though with very different impressions of some subjects, yet with the same sentiments of affection and esteem as ever, your Lordship's faithful and most obedient humble servant,

" W. COWPER."

Strange to say, for at least two months no notice was taken of this communication, as we learn from a letter to another correspondent from the poet,—who, though piqued by this mortifying neglect, tried to reconcile himself to it by recollecting how much the Chancellor's time was occupied. Afterwards, through the mediation of Hayley, Thurlow, who seems to have much admitted the tinsel of this versifier, was induced to take some notice

[1] Ante, p. 48.

of the author of THE TASK and of JOHN GILPIN,—without either making any provision for him, or soothing him with personal kindness. Yet when Thurlow was out of office, in the year 1783, Cowper writes thus tenderly to Mr. Hill.—" I have an etching of the late Chancellor hanging over the parlor chimney. I often contemplate it, and call to mind the day when I was intimate with the original. It is very like him; but he is disfigured by his hat, which, though fashionable, is awkward; by his great wig, the tie of which is hardly discernible in profile; and by his band and gown, which give him an appearance clumsily sacerdotal. Our friendship is dead and buried."

After Thurlow had been some years restored to office, Cowper, being again urged to apply to him for some promotion, thus wrote to Lady Hesketh:—" I do not wish to remind the Chancellor of his promise. Ask you why, my cousin? Because I suppose it would be impossible. He has no doubt forgotten it entirely, and would be obliged to take my word for the truth of it, which I could not bear. We drank tea together, with Mrs. C———e, and her sister, in King Street, Bloomsbury, and there was the promise made. I said, 'Thurlow, I am nobody, and shall be always nobody, and you will be Chancellor. You shall provide for me when you are.' He smiled, and replied, 'I surely will.'—'These ladies,' said I, 'are witnesses.' He still smiled and said, 'Let them be so, for I will certainly do it.' But, alas! twenty-four years have passed since the day of the date thereof, and to mention it now would be to upbraid him with inattention to the plighted troth. Neither do I suppose that he could easily serve such a creature as I am if he would."

Cowper seem to have persevered in his resolution not to claim performance of the promise. Yet, a few months after, he thus writes to Mr. Hill, showing his disinterested and unabated regard for his surly friend:—" The paper tells me that the Chancellor has relapsed, and I am truly sorry to hear it. The first attack was dangerous, but a second must be more formidable still. It is not probable that I should ever hear from him again if he survives; yet, of what I should have felt for him had our connection never been interrupted, I still feel much-

Everybody will feel the loss of a man of such general importance."[1]

While Cowper was thus neglected, the advances of Hayley, a stranger, met with a more flattering reception. From the low taste for poetry then prevailing in England, he was during a fleeting space, celebrated as a genius, and Thurlow was pleased with being considered one of his patrons. We have, from the very amiable but vapid versifier, a rather amusing account of their meeting:—

"Nov 11.

"It will, I know, afford you pleasure to hear that I am engaged to breakfast with the Chancellor, at eight to-morrow morning. He has sent me a polite and cordial invitation by our friend Carwardine."

"Nov 12.

"Though honors are seldom, I believe, found to be real enjoyments, yet I may truly say that I have had the honor of breakfasting to-day with the Chancellor, and thoroughly enjoyed it. Breakfast, you know, is my favorite social hour; and though I was by no means recovered from an oppressive cold, yet I passed a very pleasant hour, or rather two, with this singular great man. On my entrance, I told him that I was particularly flattered in being admitted at that friendly hour; for that I was such a hermit, and such a humorist, that I had a horror of dining with a great man. As I came away, he said he hoped I would come some day to a private dinner with him where there was no more form than at his breakfast-

[1] Thurlow was probably disinclined to patronize Cowper from the part taken by the poet on the question of the African slave trade He who thought the condition of the blacks much improved when sent from their own country to the West Indies, must have viewed with contempt

"THE NEGRO'S COMPLAINT.
"Forc'd from home and all its pleasures,
  Afric's coast I left forlorn,
To increase a stranger's treasures,
  O'er the raging billows borne.
"Men from England bought and sold me,
  Paid my price in paltry gold;
But, though slave they have enroll'd me,
  Minds are never to be sold"

The Chancellor's neglect of his early friend is thus ironically recorded by Peter Pindar:—

"Yet let *one* action of the day shine forth,
  (And candor loves to dwell upon my tongue),
Thurlow could see a Cowper's modest worth,
  And crown with fair reward his moral song."

table; to which I replied, that if I found his dinner like his breakfast, I would come whenever he pleased."[1]

Hayley, emboldened by this condescension, sent the Chancellor a copy of some of the very worst of his poems, and immediately received the following complimentary answer:—"The Chancellor presents his best respects to Mr. Hayley, and returns him many thanks for his poems. They give a bright relief to the subject. William is much obliged to him, and Mary more; and, if it may be said without offense, liberty itself derives advantage from this dress." Hayley exclaimed, "There's flattery for you from the great? Can any poetical vanity wish for more?"[2]

The intercourse between the two Southampton-Row idlers was afterwards renewed. Thurlow, in his retirement hearing that Cowper was engaged in a blank verse translation of Homer, expressed to a common friend some regret that he should not have preferred rhyme, of which he was so great a master, and in which he had been so successful. The poet thereupon, when he could no longer be suspected of flattering power, thus addressed the ex-Chancellor:—

"I did not expect to find your Lordship on the side of rhyme, remembering well with how much energy and interest I have heard you repeat passages from the 'Paradise Lost,' which you could not have recited as you did unless you had been perfectly sensible of their music. It comforts me, therefore, to know, that if you have an ear for rhyme, you have an ear for blank verse also. It seems to me that I may justly complain of rhyme as an inconvenience in translation, even though I assert in the sequel, that to me it has been easier to rhyme than to write without, because I always suppose a rhyming translator to ramble, and always obliged to do so."

The following answer displays great critical acumen and depth of thought:—

"The scrawl I sent Harry I have forgot too much to resume now. But I think I could not to mean to patronize rhyme. I have fancied that it was introduced to mark the measure in modern languages, because they are less numerous and metrical than the ancient; and the name seems to impart as much. Perhaps there was melody in

[1] Mem of Hayley 1. 370.   [2] Ibid. 1. 369.

ancient song without straining it to musical notes, as the common Greek pronunciation is said to have had the compass of five parts of an octave. But surely that word is only figuratively applied to modern poetry. Euphony seems to be the highest term it will bear. I have fancied also that euphony is an impression derived a good deal from habit, rather than suggested by nature; therefore, in some degree, accidental, and consequently conventional. Else why can't we hear a drama with rhyme, or the French one without it? Suppose the 'Rape of the Lock,' 'Windsor Forest,' 'L'Allegro,' 'Il Penseroso,' and many other little poems which please, stripped of the rhyme, which might easily be done, would they please as well? It would be unfair to treat rondeaus, ballads, and odes in the same manner, because rhyme makes in some sort a part of the conceit. It was this way of thinking which made me suppose that habitual prejudice would miss the rhyme, and that neither Dryden nor Pope would have dared to give their great authors in blank verse.

"It was impossible to obtain the same sense from a dead language and ancient author, which those of his own time and country conceived; words and phrases contract from time and use such strong shades of difference from their original import. In a living language, with the familiarity of a whole life, it is not easy to conceive truly the actual sense of current expressions, much less of older authors. No two languages furnish *equipollent* words; their phrases differ, their syntax and their idioms still more widely. But a translation, strictly so called, requires an exact conformity in all those particulars, and also in numbers; therefore it is impossible. I really think at present, notwithstanding the opinion expressed in your preface, that a translator asks himself a good question,— 'How would my author have expressed the sentence I am turning into English?' for every idea conveyed in the original should be expressed in English as literally and fully as the genius and use and character of the language will admit of. You must not translate literally,—

'Old daddy Phœnix, a God-send for us to maintain.'

"I will end by giving you the strictest translation I can invent of the speech of Achilles to Phœnix, leaving you the double task of bringing it closer, and of polishing it into the style of poetry :—

> 'Ah ! Phœnix, aged father, guest of Jove !
> I relish no such honors, for my hope
> Is to be honored by Jove's fated will,
> Which keeps me close beside these sable ships,
> Long as the breath shall in my bosom stay,
> Or as my precious knees retain their spring.
> Further I say, and cast it in your mind !
> Melt not my spirit down by weeping thus,
> And wailing only for that great man's sake,
> Atrides . neither ought you love that man,
> Lest I should hate the friend I love so well.
> With me united, 'tis your nobler part
> To gall his spirit, who has galled mine
> With me reign equal, half my honors share.
> These will report, stay you here and repose
> On a soft bed, and with the beaming morn
> Consult we, whether to go home or stay.'"

Cowper replied :—

"We are of one mind as to the effect of rhyme or euphony in the lighter kinds of poetry. The piece which your Lordship mentions would certainly be spoiled by the loss of it, and so would all such. The ALMA would lose all of its neatness and smartness, and HUDIBRAS all its humor. But in grave poems of extreme length, I apprehend that the case is different. I agree with your Lordship that a translation perfectly close is impossible, because time has sunk the original strict import of a thousand phrases, and we have no means of recovering it. But if we can not be unimpeachably faithful, that is no reason why we should not be as faithful as we can· and if blank verse affords the fairest chance, then it claims the preference."

Thurlow, probably not convinced, sent the following good-humored rejoinder :—

"I have read your letter on my journey through London, and, as the chaise waits, I shall be short. I did not mean it as a sign of any proscription that you have attempted what neither Dryden nor Pope would have dared, but merely as a proof of their addiction to rhyme, for I am clearly convinced that Homer may be better translated than into rhyme, and that you have succeeded in the places I have looked into. But I have fancied that it might have been still more literal, preserving the ease of genuine English and melody, and some degree of that elevation which Homer derives from simplicity."

The soothed bard closed the correspondence with the following epistle, the last that ever passed between these remarkable men, who had known each other half a century:—

"My Lord,

"I haunt you with letters, but will trouble you now with a short line only, to tell your Lordship how happy I am that any part of my work has pleased you. I have a comfortable consciousness that the whole has been executed with equal industry and attention, and am, my Lord, with many thanks to you for snatching such a busy moment to write to me,

"Your Lordship's obliged and affectionate
"humble Servant,
"WILLIAM COWPER."[1]

Thurlow's generous anxiety to assist Dr. Johnson proves to us that he was capable of appreciating real excellence, and should make us view his own failings with some forbearance. It is well known that the great lexicographer, shortly before his death, felt a strong desire, for the benefit of his health, to travel into Italy, and that, to enable him to do so, his friends wished to obtain for him an augmentation of his pension from Government. The bustling Boswell having applied on the subject to the Chancellor, receiving an answer containing these kind-hearted expressions:—"I am much obliged to you for the suggestion; and I will adopt and press it as far as I can. The best argument, I am sure, and I hope it is not likely to fail, is Dr. Johnson's merit. But it will be necessary, if I should be so unfortunate as to miss seeing you, to converse with Sir Joshua on the sum it will be proper to ask—in short, upon the means of setting him out. It will

---

[1] Cowper, referring to these letters, writes to the Rev. Walter Bagot:— "In answer to your question, 'if I have had a correspondence with the Chancellor?' I reply—Yes! We exchanged three or four letters on the subject of Homer, or, rather, on the subject of my Preface He was doubtful whether or not my preference of blank verse, as affording opportunity for a closer version, was well founded On this subject he wished to be convinced; defended rhyme with much learning and much shrewd reasoning, but at last allowed me the honor of victory, expressing himself in these words. *I am clearly convinced that Homer may be best rendered in blank verse, and you have succeeded in the passages that I have looked into.*"—*Hayley's Life of Cowper*, III. 28.

be a reflection on us all if such a man should perish for want of the means to take care of his health." Mr. Pitt, who, though himself a scholar, and well grounded in political science, it must be confessed, never testified much respect for literary men, refused in the commencement of his administration to do anything that might be construed into a job. "The Chancellor called on Sir Joshua Reynolds, and informed him that the application had not been successful; but, after speaking highly of Dr. Johnson as a man who was an honor to his country, desired Sir Joshua to let him know that, on granting a mortgage of his pension, he should draw on his Lordship for five or six hundred pounds—explaining the meaning of the mortgage to be, that he wished the business to be conducted in such a manner that Dr. Johnson should appear to be under the least possible obligation." The offer was declined, but called forth the following effusion of gratitude most honorable to both parties:—

"My Lord,—After a long and not inattentive observation of mankind, the generosity of your Lordship's offer raises in me not less wonder than gratitude. Bounty so liberally bestowed I should gladly receive, if my condition made it necessary; for to such a mind who would not be proud to owe his obligations? But it has pleased God to restore me to so great a measure of health, that, if I should not appropriate so much of a fortune destined to do good, I should not myself escape from the charge of advancing a false claim. My journey to the Continent, though I once thought it necessary, was never much encouraged by my physicians; and I was very desirous that your Lordship should be told of it by Sir Joshua Reynolds as an event very uncertain: for if I grew much better, I should not be willing; if much worse, not able to migrate. Your Lordship was first solicited without my knowledge; but, when I was told that you were pleased to honor me with your patronage, I did not expect to hear of a refusal; yet as I have had no long time to brood hope, and have not rioted on imaginary opulence, this cold reception has been scarce a disappointment; and from your Lordship's kindness I have received a benefit, which only men like you are able to bestow. I shall now live *mihi carior*, with a higher opinion of my own merit."[1]

[1] Boswell's Life of Johnson, vol. iv. p 372.

Johnson, writing at the same time confidentially to Sir Joshua Reynolds, said, "Many words, I hope, are not necessary to convince you what gratitude is excited in my heart by the Chancellor's liberality, and your kind offices."[1]

Thurlow afterwards made a generous atonement for his rough rejection of the claims of another man of genius. Crabbe, the poet, when he first came to London, being in a very destitute condition, wrote to the Lord Chancellor, inclosing him a short metrical effusion, and received for answer a note, in which his Lordship "regretted that his avocations did not leave him leisure to read verses." The indignant bard addressed to the professed contemner of poetry some strong, but not disrespectful, lines, intimating that in former days the engagement of literature had been considered as a duty appertaining to the illustrious station which his Lordship held. Of this remonstrance no notice whatever was taken for a long time. But Burke and Sir Joshua Reynolds having mentioned in Thurlow's presence the genius and the destitution of the new aspirant, and that he was about to enter the Church, Crabbe, to his great amazement, received a note from the Lord Chancellor, politely inviting him to breakfast the next morning. The reception was more than courteous, the Chancellor exclaiming in a frank and hearty tone—"The first poem you sent me, sir, I ought to have noticed—and I heartily forgive the second." They breakfasted together, and at parting his Lordship put a sealed paper into the poet's hand, saying, "Accept this trifle, sir, in the meantime, and rely on my embracing an early opportunity to serve you more substantially when I hear that you are in orders." Instead of a present of ten or twenty pounds as the *donee* expected, the paper contained a bank note for £100, a supply which relieved him from all present difficulties. The promise of a living, I make no doubt, would have been fulfilled, had not Crabbe soon after become chaplain to the Duke of Rutland, and received preferment from that liberal-minded nobleman.[2]

Thurlow was early in life honorably attached to an accomplished young lady, Miss Gooch—of a respectable family in Norfolk, "but she would not have him, for she

---

[1] Boswell's Life of Johnson, vol. iv. p 372.
[2] Life of Crabbe, 56, 101.

was positively afraid of him." He seems then to have forsworn matrimony.

It is with great reluctance that I proceed; but I should give a very imperfect sketch of the individual and of the manners of the age, if I were to try to conceal that of which he himself was not ashamed, and which in his lifetime was known to all the world, without occasioning much censure. Not only while he was at the bar, but after he became Lord Chancellor, he lived openly with a mistress, and had a family by her, whom he recognized, and, without any disguise, brought out in society as if they had been his legitimate children.—In like manner, as when I touched upon the irregularities of Cardinal Wolsey, I must remind the reader that every man is charitably to be judged by the standard of morality which prevailed in the age in which he lived.[2] Although Mrs. Hervey is sometimes satirically named in the "Rolliad" and other contemporary publications, her *liaison* with the Lord Chancellor seems to have caused little scandal. In spite of it he was a prime favorite, not only with George III. but with Queen Charlotte, both supposed to be very strict in their notions of chastity; and his house was not only frequented by his brother the bishop, but by ecclesiastics of all degrees, who celebrated the orthodoxy of the head of the law—his love of the Established Church, and his hatred of Dissenters.[3] It should likewise be stated

---

[1] Her own words in extreme old age. She was married to Dr. D'Urban, a physician at Shottisham, the father of the venerable Sir Benjamin D'Urban. There was a relationship between the Gooches and the Thurlows—and their intercourse being renewed, old Mrs Gooch used to call Edward Thurlow "child," while he called her "mother." She often related that Thurlow, when Attorney General, having rode over to Shottisham to visit them, as he was taking leave, and mounting his horse, she said to him, "Well, child, I shall live to see you Lord Chancellor." His answer was, "I hope so, mother."

[2] Shortly before this, the Duke of Grafton, when Prime Minister, lived openly with Nancy Parsons, and escorted her to the opera in presence of the Queen What should we say of such an outrage on decency in the reign of Victoria?

[3] When I first knew the profession, it would not have been endured that any one in a judicial situation should have had such a domestic establishment as Thurlow's, but a majority of the Judges had married their mistresses. The understanding then was, that a man elevated to the bench, if he had a mistress, must either marry her or put her away. For many years there has been no necessity for such an alternative.—The improvement in public morals, at the conclusion of the 18th century, may mainly be ascribed to George III and his Queen, who—though, being unable to lay down any violent rule, or to bring about any sudden change, they were obliged to wink

in mitigation, that he was an affectionate parent, and took great pains with the education and breeding of his offspring. A son of his is said to have died at Cambridge when about to reach the highest honors of the university. His three daughters accompanied him in all the tours he made after his retirement from office, and were in good society. Craddock relates that "one evening the Miss Thurlow's being at a Hampstead assembly, in returning, were in some danger from a riot at the door, and that they were rescued by a young officer, who handed them to their carriage. In consequence, the Lord Chancellor calling upon him next morning to thank him, and finding him at breakfast, offered to partake of it."[1] Two of them were well married. The third made a love-match against his will, and though he was reconciled to her, he never would consent to see her husband.

It has been said that Thurlow was a sceptic in religion: but I do not believe that there is any foundation for this assertion, beyond the laxity of his practice, and an occasional irreverence in his expressions on religious subjects, which, however censurable, were not inconsistent with a continuing belief in the divine truths he had been taught by his pious parents. A letter from him to a gentleman who had obtained a prize for a theological essay, and to whom he gave a living, displays great depth of thinking, and may be reconciled to orthodoxy:—

"Oct. 13, 1785.

"Sir,

"I return you many thanks for your Essay, which is well composed, notwithstanding the extent, difficulty, and delicacy of the subject. The mode of future existence is not delineated to the human mind; although the object is presented to their hope, and even recommended to their imagination. Upon this, the humbler, perhaps the safest reflection seems to be, that human sense is capable of no more, while perfect Faith is recommended. Is it not dangerous to insinuate, that sensible conviction

---

at the irregularities of the Lord Chancellor—not only by their bright example, but by their well-directed efforts, greatly discouraged the profligacy which was introduced at the Restoration, and which continued, with little abatement, till their time

[1] "An anecdote introduced to prove that Lord Thurlow could be a courteous nobleman, as well as an affectionate parent"—*Crad.* i. 75.

might lessen the importance of worldly concerns too much? (p. 23.)

"Perhaps, also, the speculation is not free from danger, when improved disquisition, enriched imagination, and livelier affection are distinctly assumed, as the attainments of a state, which is to be so much changed, that it can not be, or at least is not, revealed to the human sense. (p. 12, 15, 17.)

"Perhaps more is put upon the immateriality of the soul than the negative of a thing so unknown as matter, is worth. (p. 7.)

"The observation at the head of the next page seems to dispose of the question more solidly and piously. When the Philosopher despises a Heaven on the other side of the blue mountains, in which the company of a faithful dog makes a principal article of enjoyment, is he sure that his visions are more wise, in proportion as they are less sensible?

"Perhaps the certainty that God is good, affords a surer hope, and not less distinct.

"Yours, &c.,
"THURLOW."

There seems to have been, however, a prevalent opinion among his contemporaries that he was lax in his religious observances. Of this, Burke took rather an unfair advantage during Hastings's trial. Commenting upon the arrest of a Rajah at the hour of his devotions, he said:—
"It has been alleged, in extenuation of the disgrace, that the Rajah was not a Brahmin. Suppose the Lord Chancellor should be found at his devotions (*a laugh*), surely we may suppose the keeper of the King's conscience so employed (*renewed laughter*),—and suppose that, while so employed, he should be violently interrupted and carried off to prison, would it remove or lessen the indignity that he was not a Bishop? No! the Lord Chancellor would think of the prayers he had lost, and his feelings would be equally acute as if he wore lawn sleeves in addition to the robes of his office, and his full-bottom wig." The reporter adds, "None were grave at this sally, save the Chancellor himself, who looked like a statue of JUPITER TONANS, and cared as little for exercises of piety."

Under ostentatiously rough manners, I am inclined to believe that he preserved great kindness of disposition:

and there can be no doubt that, if at last a little hardened from being long hackneyed in the ways of the world, he was naturally tender-hearted. When still a young man, he lost his favorite sister, to whom he had been most affectionately attached. I have great pleasure in laying before the reader a most feeling and beautiful letter, written by him to the physician who had attended her, and who had announced to him her dissolution after a long and painful illness.

"Dear Doctor Manning,

"I return you many thanks for your letter, which I can almost bring myself to call agreeable. The two last letters I received from my brother, convinced me that she was not to be saved by nature or art ; and it quite harrowed me to reflect on the pain she endured. I suppose the frailty of all human things makes it a common accident : but I have brought myself to think it my own singular ill-fortune to be disappointed in everything I have ever set my heart upon. In general, it is my point to withstand any extraordinary affection for any article in life, but I forgot myself in this instance. My sister was singularly agreeable to me, and I was equally assiduous in courting her friendship and cultivating her affection. The wretched end of it is, that I never was so unhappy before.

"But it is foolish to trouble you with any more of this : I can not omit, however, expressing my sensibility of your tenderness and attention to her, and my perfect satisfaction, in your skill and care; a mighty dull and gloomy satisfaction, but it is all the ablest and kindest physicians can expect in so melancholy an hour.

"I am, dear Sir, with great respect,
   - "Your most obliged
      "and obedient Servant,
            " E. THURLOW.
"Inner Temple, Friday."[1]

Lord Thurlow was very kind to his brothers. For one of them he obtained successively the great living of Stanhope, the Mastership of the Temple, the Deanery of Rochester, the Deanery of St. Paul's, the Bishopric of Lincoln, and the Bishopric of Durham. On a son of this brother he conferred a sinecure in the Court of Chancery,

[1] Written about 1768.

for which a compensation is now received of £9,000 a year. He provided, likewise, very amply for his other kinsmen. What more proved the goodness of his disposition was, that, notwithstanding occasional gusts of passion, which they were a little afraid of, he continued to live with them all on terms of great familiarity. Soon after he was made Lord Chancellor, he addressed his clerical brother in the following terms:—" Tom, there is to be a drawing-room on Thursday, when I am obliged to attend; and as I have purchased Lord Bathurst's coach, but have no leisure to give orders about the necessary alterations, do you see and get all ready for me." The Bishop forgot to get the arms altered, and the Earl's coronet reduced to a Baron's. Afraid of a storm, he resorted to the expedient of ordering the door to be opened as soon as the carriage stopped at the house, and held open till the Lord Chancellor was seated, who, having examined the interior, stretched out his hand, and most kindly exclaimed, " Brother, the whole is finished entirely to my satisfaction, and I thank you."[1] The same expedient was resorted to again at his return from St. James's, and by the next levee-day the carriage was altered according to the rules of heraldry.

I have already had occasion to refer more than once to Thurlow's personal appearance, and particularly to his dark complexion and bushy eyebrows. O'Keefe, the famous farce writer, has left us a little portrait of him, shortly before he was removed from office, at a moment when he must have been suffering from bodily pain:— " I saw Lord Thurlow in court; he was thin, and seemed not well in health; he leaned forward with his elbows on his knees, which were spread wide, and his hands clutched in each other. He had on a large three-cocked hat. His voice was good, and he spoke in the usual judge style, easy and familiar." But, generally speaking, although pretending to despise the opinion of others, he was acting a part, and his aspect was more solemn and imposing than almost any other person's in public life—which induced Mr. Fox to say, " it proved him dishonest, since no man could *be* so wise as Thurlow *looked*."

His manner made an awful impression on all who beheld him; and I have seen this successfully mimicked by the

[1] Cr. 1. 75.

late Lord Holland, so as not only to create a belief of profound wisdom, but to inspire some apprehension into the company present of being committed to the Fleet, or of being taken into custody by the Gentleman Usher of the Black Rod. Yet, in private life, he could, on rare occasions, lay aside his terrors,—affecting mildness and politeness. Once when at Bath, he went to the pump-room and sat there booted and spurred. Being informed, by the master of the ceremonies, that it was against rule to appear there with spurs, he said, "The rules of Bath must not be disputed," and not only ordered his spurs immediately to be taken off, but that an apology should be made in his name to the company.' He was remarkably affable and kind to the young. A friend of mine, who knew him when he was living in retirement at Dulwich, says, "A morning call at his house, especially about luncheon time, was a great treat to a schoolboy; and I well remember the *ore-rotundo* 'Give the lad more pie!' addressed to Kitty Thurlow (afterwards Lady Saltoun), who had helped one of us as she would have helped herself."

"Many stories of Thurlow's rudeness," says his friend Craddock, "have been in circulation; but it should be fairly stated that he was ever more cautious of speaking offensively among inferiors than among the great where he sometimes, indeed, seemed to take a peculiar pleasure in giving proofs of his excessive vulgarity. A single instance of this singular humor will be sufficient. On his return from Scarborough, he made visits to some of those splendid mansions with which the county of York so greatly abounds; and a friend of mine had the honor to meet him at one of them, then full of very high company. While walking in the garden, and they were all admiring the elegancies which surrounded them, the noble proprietor, being near the hot-house, turned to the Lord Chancellor, and politely asked him whether he would not walk in and partake of some grapes. 'Grapes!' said Thurlow, 'did not tell you just now I had got the gripes?' The strangers in the company were all petrified with astonishment."

A gentleman of huge bulk and bodily strength, but of slender mental endowments, although a Commissioner of

¹ Cl. i. 78.

Customs, having waited on Lord Chancellor Thurlow to explain a memorial he had composed to prepare him to defend a Government bill in the House of Lords, received this compliment from him : " You may be fit, sir, to *draw* a broad-wheeled wagon, but you are wholly unfit to *draw* a memorial."

A body of Presbyterians made an application to him to assist in repealing certain statutes which disqualified them from holding civil offices. He received the deputation with great civility, and, having heard them out, said, " Gentlemen, I'll be perfectly frank with you. Gentlemen, I am against you, and for the Established Church, by G—. Not that I like the Established Church a bit better than any other church, but because it *is* established. And whenever you can get your d——d religion established, I'll be for that, too. Good morning to you."[1] They retired, smiling, and probably less dissatisfied than if he had tried to reason them into a conviction of the justice of the Test and Corporation Acts.

Although he by no means despised the smiles of royalty, and " principibus placuisse viris " was not a low object of ambition with him, he was a courtier in his own peculiar fashion, and sometimes he used a freedom of speech which from any other man would have been offensive. Lord Eldon used to relate the following anecdote :—" Once, when the mind of George III. was not supposed to be very strong, I took down to Kew some acts for his assent, and I placed on a paper the titles and the effect of them. The King, perhaps suspicious that my coming down might be to judge of his competence for public business, as I was reading over the titles of the different acts, interrupted me, and said, 'You are not acting correctly; you should do one of two things, either bring me down the acts for my perusal, or say as Thurlow once said to me on a like occasion: having read several, he stopped and said, It was all damned nonsense trying to make me understand them, and that I had better consent to them at once.'"

On the occasion of a public procession, the Prince, who had taken offense at something Thurlow had said or done, rudely stepped in before the Chancellor. Thurlow ob-

[1] As related by Dr. Rees the compiler of " The Cyclopedia," who was present.

served, "Sir, you have done quite right: I represent your royal Father: Majesty walks last. Proceed, Sir."

At Brighthelmstone the Prince of Wales, living with a gay set of frivolous young men who displeased the ex-Chancellor much, asked him frequently to dinner, but always met with an excuse. At last, walking in front of the Pavilion in company with them, he met Lord Thurlow, and pressed him much to dine with him, saying, "You must positively name a day." Lord Thurlow, looking at the party who were with the Prince, said, "If I must name a day or time, it shall be when your Royal Highness keeps better company."

On another occasion Lord Thurlow had voluntarily given the Prince some advice, which was far from being palatable. His Royal Highness was so angry, that he sent to him to say that in future Carlton House gates would be shut against him. Lord Thurlow answered,— "I am not surprised; proffered favors always stink." The Prince, conscious of the ungenerous return he had made, acknowledged his error, and they again became friends.

The Prince once sent Sir Thomas Tyrwhitt to the ex-Chancellor, to ask his opinion respecting some difference in the royal family. "You may tell your master," said Thurlow, "I shall not give him my opinion." "My Lord," said Sir Thomas, "I can not take that message to His Royal Highness." "Well, then," said Lord Thurlow, "you may tell him from me, that if he can point out one single instance in which he has followed my advice, I will give him my opinion on this matter."

Traditionary anecdotes, to show the violence of his temper, particularly on the marriage of his favorite daughter without his consent, I pass over as not sufficiently authenticated;[1] but it is certain that, by reason of a quarrel he had with Holland, the architect, who had contracted to build a grand new house for him at Dulwich, he would never enter it, and he continued to live in a small inconvenient lodge close by.[2]

[1] His family accounted for his whimsicalities in his later years by the shock he sustained from the flight of this daughter—to whom he had been so much attached, that he made himself master of the principles of thorough-bass that he might superintend her musical practice

[2] An action brought against him by Holland came on for trial before Lord Kenyon, who, for the dignity of the Chancellor, got it referred to arbitration.

His chateau remaining untenanted, though furnished,—as he was one day coming out of the Queen's drawing-room, a lady stopped him, and asked "when he was going into his new house?" "Madam," said he, "the Queen has just asked that impudent question; and as I would not tell her, I will not tell you."

In Thurlow's time the habit of profane swearing was unhappily so common, that Bishop Horsley and other right reverend prelates are said not to have been entirely exempt from it. But Thurlow indulged in it to a degree that admits of no excuse. Walking with the Prince of Wales, on the Steyne at Brighton, they met Horsley, and, entering into conversation with him, the Bishop said he was to preach a charity sermon next Sunday, and hoped he might have the honor of seeing his Royal Highness among his congregation. The Prince graciously intimated his intention to be present. Then turning to the ex-Chancellor, the Bishop said, "I hope I shall also see your Lordship there." The answer was, "I'll be d——d if you do; I hear you talk nonsense enough in the House of Lords; but there I can and do contradict you,—and I'll be d——d if I go to hear you where I can't."[1] I have been told by an old gentleman, who was standing behind the woolsack at the time, that Sir Ilay Campbell, then Lord Advocate, arguing a Scotch appeal at the bar in a very tedious manner, said, "I will noo, my Lords, proceed to my seevent pownt." "I'll be d——d if you do," cried Thurlow, so as to be heard by all present; "this House is adjourned till Monday next," and off he scampered. Sir James Mansfield, Lord Chief Justice of the Common Pleas, used to relate that while he and several other legal characters were dining with Lord Chancellor Thurlow, his lordship happening to swear at his Swiss valet when retiring from the room, the man returned, just put his head in, and exclaimed, "I von't be d——d for you Milor," which caused the noble host and all his guests to burst out into a roar of laughter.[2] From another valet he received a still more

[1] This anecdote was often told with great glee by the Bishop himself.
[2] I am much afraid that profane swearing was then much practiced by men of all degrees in Westminster Hall I remember when Sir James Mansfield was Chief Justice of the Common Pleas, and the unruly members of the coif who practiced before him led him a most wretched life, it was said that one evening, having fallen asleep on a sofa in a lady's drawing-room, he was heard to call out several times in his dream, "G—d d—— the Sergeants."

cutting retort. Having scolded this meek man for some time without receiving any answer, he concluded by saying, " I wish you were in hell." The terrified valet at last exclaimed, " I wish I was, my Lord ! I wish I was !" But the happiest retort he ever received conveyed to him a salutary hint of the ultimate consequences of his habit of swearing. He was one morning put into a great rage by finding that a cartload of paving stones had been shot before his door for the purpose of repairing the street. Observing an Irish pavior near the heap, he addressed him in a furious tone as the culprit, and ordered him to remove them. *Irish Pavior :* " Where shall I take them to, please your honor?" *Lord Thurlow :* " To h—ll, and be d——d to you!" *Irish Pavior :* " If I were to take them to t'other place, your honor, don't you think they might be more out of your honor's way?" Once he was completely beaten by his own weapon. He thus began an objurgation to Mr. Quarme, the Deputy Usher of the Black Rod, who I very well remember was esteemed a remarkably meek man : " God d——n you, Mr. Quarme, what do you ——" Mr. Quarme, interrupting, exclaimed, " God d——n you, Mr. Quarme ! God d——n you, Mr. Quarme ! ! God d——n *you,* my Lord ! ! ! " This unexpected outbreak was followed by a profound silence ; and Thurlow, feeling some respect for one by whom he had been outsworn, behaved civilly to him ever afterwards.

Sir Thomas Davenport, a great nisi prius leader, had been intimate with Thurlow, and long flattered himself with the hopes of succeeding to some valuable appointment in the law, but, several good things passing by, he lost his patience and temper along with them. At last he addressed his laconic application to his patron :—" THE CHIEF JUSTICESHIP OF CHESTER IS VACANT ; AM I TO HAVE IT ? " and received the following laconic answer :— " NO ! BY GOD ! KENYON SHALL HAVE IT ! "

Having once got into a dispute with a Bishop respecting a living of which the Great Seal had the alternate presentation, the Bishop's secretary called upon him, and said, " My Lord of —— sends his compliments to your Lordship, and believes that the next turn to present to —— belongs to his Lordship." *Chancellor :* " Give my compliments to his Lordship, and tell him that I will see him d——d first, before he shall present." *Secretary :*

"This, my Lord, is a very unpleasant message to deliver to a bishop." *Chancellor :* "You are right, it is so; therefore tell the Bishop that I will be d——d first before he shall present."

His blustering manner was sometimes assumed, to conceal the uneasiness which preyed upon his mind. His brother, the Bishop, pressing him to give a living to a very poor clergyman with a very numerous family, he said "No." Then followed this dialogue: — *Bishop;* "To whom do you intend to give it?" *Chancellor :* "I believe, I shall give it to the fellow after all." *Bishop :* "In that case, why not tell him so?" *Chancellor :* "Why the devil should I?" *Bishop :* "Because it would make him so happy to know that he is to have bread for his children." *Chancellor :* "D——n him! The poor parson with his starved children is already much happier than I am."

With all his faults, it must be remembered to his honor, that, by his own abilities alone, without flattery of the great, or mean compliances with the humors of others, he raised himself from obscurity to the highest dignity in the State;—that no one can ascribe his rise to reputed mediocrity, which is sometimes more acceptable than genius;— and that for a period of forty years he not only preserved an ascendency among distinguished lawyers, statesmen and orators, but that he was regarded with respect and esteem by eminent poets, moralists and divines.

I shall conclude this memoir with sketches of him by some of his contemporaries, which may better enable the reader justly to estimate his merits than any observations of mine. The first is from a volume published in 1777, when he was Attorney General, entitled "Public Characters," in which it is remarked that his name is spelt "Thurloe," like that of Cromwell's secretary: — "His voice is harsh, his manner uncouth, his assertions made generally without any great regard to the unities of time, place or probability. His arguments frequently wild, desultory and incoherent. His deductions, when closely pressed, illogical; and his attacks on his adversaries, and their friends, coarse, vulgar and illiberal, though generally humorous, shrewd, and *pointedly severe.*"

"The Chancellor Thurlow," says Bishop Watson, "was an able and upright Judge; but as the Speaker of the

House of Lords he was domineering and insincere. It was said of him in the Cabinet, he opposed everything, proposed nothing and was ready to support anything. I remember Lord Camden's saying to me one night, when the Chancellor was speaking contrary, as I thought, to his own conviction. "There now, I could not do that: he is supporting what he does not believe a word of."[1] "Few," says Colton, "have combined more talent with more decision than Lord Thurlow. Nature seems to have given him a head of crystal and nerves of brass."

Sir Nathaniel Wraxall, describing the state of parties in the year 1781, says, "Lord Thurlow, who at this time had held the Great Seal between two and three years, though in point of age the youngest member of the Cabinet, enjoyed in many respects greater consideration than almost any other individual composing it.—Lord North had derived the greatest assistance from his eloquence and ability, His removal to the House of Peers would have left an awful blank on the Treasury bench in the midst of the American war, if his place had not, during the two succeeding years, been ably, perhaps fully, supplied by Wedderburn. As Speaker of the Upper House, Lord Thurlow fulfilled all the expectations previously entertained of him. His very person, figure, voice and manner, were formed to lend dignity to the woolsack. Of a dark complexion, and harsh but regular features, with a severe and commanding demeanor, which might be sometimes denominated stern, he impressed his auditors with awe before he opened his lips. Energy, acuteness, and prodigious powers of argument, characterized him in debate. His comprehensive mind enabled him to embrace the question under discussion, whatever it might be, in all its bearings and relations. Nor, if we except Lord Camden, who was already far advanced in life, did the Opposition possess any legal talents in the House of Peers that could justly be put in competition with those of Lord Thurlow. These admirable points were, nevertheless, by no means unaccompanied by corresponding defects. As Lord Chancellor, he was accused of procrastination in suffering the causes brought before him in his court to accumulate without end. Perhaps this charge so frequently made against those

[1] Life of Watson, 221.   [2] "Lacon," 1. 45.

who have held the Great Seal, was not more true as applied to him, than of others who succeeded him in his office. But even in parliament his temper, which was morose, sullen, and untractable, sometimes mastering his reason, prevented him from always exerting the faculties with which Nature had endowed him, or at least clouded and obscured their effect. In the Cabinet, these defects of character, which rendered him often impracticable, were not to be surmounted by any efforts or remonstrances. It can hardly be believed, that at ministerial dinners, where, after the cloth was removed, measures of state were often discussed or agitated, Lord Thurlow would frequently refuse to take any part. He has even more than once left his colleagues to deliberate, while he sullenly stretched himself along the chairs, and fell, or appeared to fall, fast asleep. If I had not received this fact from an eye-witness, and a member of the Cabinet, I should not, indeed, venture to report so improbable a circumstance. Notwithstanding the ruggedness and asperity which he displayed,—qualities that procured him the nickname of *the tiger*,—no man could at times appear more pleasing, affable, and communicative in conversation. I have once or twice seen him on such occasions, which were more highly valued because they were rare or unexpected. Possessed of faculties so transcendent, however mingled with human weakness and infirmity, he must always be considered as one of the most eminent individuals who sat in the councils of George III. at any period of his reign."[1]

In 1796, Bishop Horsley thus dedicated to Thurlow his " Prosodies of the Greek and Latin Languages." "Although I wish at present to be concealed, I can not persuade myself to send this Tract abroad without an acknowledgment, which perhaps may betray me, of how much my mind has been informed, and my own opinions upon this subject have been confirmed, by conversations which many things in this Essay will bring to your recollection. Were I to form a wish for my country, it should be that your Lordship might again be called to take part in her councils, where you would display that wisdom, firmness of principle, and integrity, with which you so

[1] Wraxall's Memoirs, vol. i. 527.

long adorned one of the highest public stations. A better wish, perhaps, for you may be, that you may enjoy many years of learned leisure."

Next comes the portrait of Thurlow by Dr. Parr, which, although the features be exaggerated almost to caricature, certainly presents a very striking likeness:—
" Minas possumus contemnere vocemque fulmineam Thrasonici istius oratoris τοῦ τὰς ὀφρῦς κυανέας ἐπηρκότος, cujus vultum, uti Noviorum istius minoris} ferre posse se negat quadruplatorum genus omne et subscriptorum. Quid enim? truculentus semper incedit, teterque, et terribilis aspectu. De supercilio autem isto quid dicendum est? annon reipublicæ illud quasi pignus quoddam videtur? annon senatus illo, tanquam Atlante cœlum, innititur? Profecto non desunt qui Novium existiment in 'summa feritate esse versutissimum, promtumque ingenio ultra Barbarum.' Quod si demseris illi aut σφοδρότητα quanto in Bruto fuit, aut πικρότητα vere Menippeam, aut προσώπου σκυθρότητα propriam et suam, facile ejus vel prudentiæ vel fidei juris nodos legumque ænigmata ad solvendum permiseris. Fervido quodam et petulanti genere dicendi utitur, eodemque, nec valde nitenti, nec plane horrido. Solutos irridentium cachinnos ita commovet, ut lepores ejus, scurriles et prorsus veteratorios diceres. Omnia loquitur verborum sane bonorum cursu quodam incitatio, itemque voce, qua ne subsellia quidem ipsa desiderant pleniorem et grandiorem. In adversariis autem lacerandis ita causidicorum figuras jaculatur, ita callida et militiosa juris interpretatione utitur, ita furere et bacchari solet, ut sæpe mirere tam alias res agere optimates, ut sit pene insano inter disertos locus. Fuit ei, perinde atque aliis, fortuna pro virtutibus. Didicit autem a Muciano, satis clarum esse apud timentem, quisquis timeatur. Corpore ipse ingens, annimi immodicus, verbis magnificus, et specie inanium magis quam sapientia validus, studia ad se Optimatium illexit, eamque adeptus est auctoritatem, quæ homini novo pro facundia esse posset. Scilicet, quæ bonis Titio, Seioque turpissima forent, Novium nostrum maxime decent, siquidem e subselliis elapsus de Tribunali nunc pronuntiet, et ex præcone actionum factus sit institor eloquentiæ senatoriæ. Quam igitur in civitate gratiam dicendi facultate Q. Varius consecutus est, vastus homo atque fœdus, eandem Novius in-

telligit, illa ipsa facultate, quamcunque habet se esse in Senatu consecutum—

> ' Ellum, confidens, catus :
> Cum faciem videas, videtur esse quantivis preti :
> Tristis seventas inest in voltu, atque in verbis fides.' "[1]

After the effort of perusing this somewhat pedantic production, the reader may be relieved by a few characteristic notices of our hero from the pen of *Dr. Wolcot*, a lively though scurrilous poet, who under the title of PETER PINDAR, amused the latter end of the eighteenth century: in his Ode "to the Royal Academicians," on portrait painting, he gives them this caution:

> " Copy not Nature's form too closely
> Whene'er she treats your *sitter* grossly
> As, for example, let us now suppose
> Thurlow's black scowl and Pepper Arden's nose."

In another satirical ode, he thus refers to Thurlow's rough manners and habit of swearing:

> " How pithy 'twas in Pitt, what good sense,
> Not to give Majesty the least offense !
> Whereas the Chancellor, had he been there,
> Whose tutor, one would say, had been a bear ;
> Thinking a Briton to no form confin'd,
> But born with privilege to speak his mind,
> Had answer'd with a thundering tongue,
> ' I think your Majesty d———n wrong.' "

And he is made to go on to swear still more profanely.

In enumerating those who assisted in the public Thanksgiving at St. Paul's, on the King's recovery, this satirist describes—

> " A great Law Chief, whom God nor demon scares,
> Compell'd to kneel and pray, who *swore* his prayers :
> The devil behind him pleas'd and grinning ;
> Patting the angry lawyer on the shoulder,
> Declaring aught was never *bolder*,
> Admiring such a *novel* mode of sinning."

By reason of Peter Pindar's violent attacks on Thurlow and other peers, there was a proposal to bring him to the bar of the House for a breach of privilege—to which Peter in his " Ode to the Peers" refers :—

> " Yes ! yes ! I hear that you have watch'd my note,
> And wish'd to squeeze my tuneful throat ;
> When Thurlow your designs most wisely scouted,
> Swearing the poet should not *yet* be knouted."

---

[1] Preface to Bellendenus.

The ex-Chancellor's intimacy with the Prince, attracting the attention of the public, was celebrated in an Epistle from Peter Pindar, thus beginning—

> "Thurlow now is the Carlton House Mentor;
> You know him, Nic, bony and big,
> With a voice like the voice of a Stentor,
> His old phiz in a bushel of wig.
> All the pages, and footmen, and maids,
> As his *Wisdom* march'd solemnly in,
> (The impudent vailets and jades!)
> Gather'd round him with wonder and grin."

In conclusion there is this softening stanza:—

> "Yet this in his praise I will say,
> That whether he's sober or mellow,
> Though as blunt as a bear in his way,
> True Genius *admires* the old fellow."

I have now much pleasure in giving a sketch of him by a surviving kinsman, who knew him well, and was tenderly attached to him:—" His countenance was that of a man of the strongest sense, and his eye most penetrating and commanding. His stature was lofty and full of dignity, and his manners and address highly polished. He could assume the sternest character if necessary, or the sweetest smile I ever beheld. This stern exterior was, I have often thought, put on to cover the most kind and feeling heart, and his real nature was but little known but to those who had the happiness of living in his society. I remember hearing Lord Thurlow read from Shakespeare's play of the Merchant of Venice that beautiful scene of the judgment of Portia. 'Then must the Jew be merciful.' *Shylock;* 'On what compulsion must I? tell me that.' *Portia:* 'The quality of mercy is not stained, it droppeth as the gentle dew from Heaven upon the place beneath,' &c.; and perceiving a slight tremulousness in his voice, I looked up and saw the tears in his eyes.—When Lord Thurlow had a severe fit of the gout, he used to be wheeled in a Merlin's chair from his sitting-room to his bed-room at an early hour; it was in the summer season, and when the proper minute came, his valet Buissy, without asking any quetions, told his master it was time to go to bed, and began to wheel the chair with the ex-Chancellor in it towards the bed-room. 'Let me alone,' said the ex-Chancellor. 'My Lord, it is time to go to bed.' 'I won't go yet, come again.' 'No, my

Lord, it is time for your Lordship to go to bed, and you must go.' 'You be d——d, I will not go.' Away went the ex-Chancellor, threatening and swearing at the man, which I could hear like deep thunder for some time. The ex-Chancellor had succumbed, knowing that his good only was considered by his faithful domestic."

I shall conclude with a metrical effusion from the Rolliad, professing to be composed by the Lord Chancellor Thurlow himself, to show his qualification for the office of Poet Laureate, then vacant. I need not remind the reader that, with some just satire upon his swearing propensity, and other failings imputable to him, this *jeu d'esprit* shows the malice of the discomfited Whigs, who were driven to console themselves in almost hopeless opposition by personal attacks on their opponents—not sparing royalty itself:

"IRREGULAR ODE,
"By EDWARD, LORD THURLOW,
"*Lord High Chancellor of Great Britain.*

I.

" Damnation seize ye all!
Who puff, who thrum, who bawl, and squall,
Fir'd with ambitious hopes, in vain,
The wreath that blooms for other brows, to gain.
Is Thurlow yet so little known?—
By —— I swore, while George shall reign,
The Seals, in spite of changes, to retain,
Nor quit the woolsack till he quits the Throne!
And now, the bays for life to wear.
Once more with mightier oaths, by —— I swear!
Bend my black brows that keep the Peers in awe,
Shake my full-bottom wig, and give the nod of law.

II.

" What though more sluggish than a toad,
Squat in the bottom of a well,
I, too, my gracious Sov'reign's worth to tell,
Will rouse my torpid genius to an Ode!
The toad a jewel in his head contains—
Prove we the rich production of my brains!
Nor will I court with humble plea,
Th' Aonian Maids to inspire my wit;
One mortal girl is worth the Nine to me;
The prudes of Pindus I resign to Pitt.
His be the classic art, which I despise;
Thurlow on Nature, and himself, relies.

III

" 'Tis mine *to keep the conscience of the King;*
To me each secret of his heart is shown:
Who then, like me, shall hope to sing
Virtues, to all but me unknown?

Say who, like me, shall win belief
  To tales of his paternal grief,
When civil rage, with slaughter dy'd
  The plains beyond th' Atlantic tide?
Who can, like me, his joy attest,
  Though little joy his looks confest,
When Peace, at Conway's call restor'd,
  Bade kindred nations sheathe the sword?
How pleas'd he gave his people's wishes way,
And turn'd out North, when North refus'd to stay?
How in their sorrows sharing too, unseen,
For Rockingham he mourn'd at Windsor, with the Queen

IV.

" His bounty, too, be mine to praise,
  Myself th' example of my lays,
    A Teller in reversion I ;
  And unimpair'd I vindicate my place,
  The chosen subject of peculiar grace,
Hallow'd from hands of Burke's economy :
  For so his royal word my Sovereign gave ;
And sacred here I found that *word* alone,
  When not his Grandsire's *patent*, and his own,
To Cardiff, and to Sondes, their posts could save.
  Nor should his chastity be here unsung,
    That chastity, above his glory dear ,
    [1] But Hervey, frowning, pulls my ear ;
Such praise. she swears, were satire from my tongue.

V.

" Fir'd at her voice, I grow profane,
  A louder yet, and yet a louder strain !
To Thurlow's lyre more daring notes belong.
  Now tremble every rebel soul,
  While on the foes of George I roll
The deep-ton'd execrations of my song.
  In vain my brother's piety, more meek,
  Would preach my kindling fury to repose ;
  Like Balaam's ass, were he inspired to speak,
'Twere vain ! resolv'd I go to curse my Prince's foes.

VI.

"' Begin ! begin !' fierce Hervey cries ;
  ' See ! the Whigs, how they rise !
    What petitions they present !
    How *tease* and *torment !*
D—mn their bloods, d—mn their hearts, d—mn their eyes.
  Behold yon sober band,
  Each his notes in his hand ;
  The witnesses they, whom I browbeat in vain ;
    Unconfus'd they remain,
    O ! d—mn their bloods again ;

[1] " I originally wrote this line :
        ' But Hervey, frowning as she hears,' &c.
It was altered as it now stands by my d—mn'd Bishop of a brother, for the sake of an allusion to Virgil :
            ———' Cynthius aurem
        Vellit, et admonuit.'

> Give the curses due
> To the factious crew!
> Lo! Wedgewood, too, waves his Pitt-potts[1] on high!
> Lo! he points where the bottoms, yet dry,
> The *visage immaculate* bear,
> Be Wedgewood d—mn'd, and double d—mn'd his ware.
> D—mn Fox, and d—mn North,
> D—mn Portland's mild worth;
> D—mn Devon the good,
> Double d—mn all his name;
> D—mn Fitzwilliam's blood,
> Heir of Rockingham's fame;
> D—mn Sheridan's wit,
> The terror of Pitt;
> D—mn Loughb'rough, my plague—would his bagpipe were split!
> D—mn Derby's long scroll,
> Filled with names to the brims:
> D—mn his limbs, d—mn his soul,
> D—mn his soul, d—mn his limbs!
> With Stormont's curs'd din,
> Hark! Carlisle chimes in!
> D—mn *them,* d—mn all the partners of their sin;
> D—mn them, beyond what mortal tongue can tell;
> Confound, sink, plunge them all to deepest, blackest Hell!'"[2]

I have only further to state that Lord Chancellor Thurlow dying without legitimate issue, his first title of Baron Thurlow of Ashfield became extinct, and that his second of Baron Thurlow of Thurlow, in the county of Suffolk, under a limitation in the patent by which it was created, descended to his nephew, the eldest son of his brother, the Bishop of Durham, the father of the present highly respected head of the family.[3]

I can not conclude this Memoir without expressing deep regret that Thurlow himself had not dedicated a portion of his leisure to the task of writing an account of his own career, and of the times in which he lived. Considering the events which he had witnessed, the scenes in which he had personally mixed, the eminent men with whom he had been familiar, and his powers of observation and of description, what an interesting work he might have left to us! Born in the period of universal tranquillity which

---

[1] "I am told that a scoundrel of a potter, one Mr. Wedgewood, is making 10,000 vile utensils, with a figure of Mr. Pitt in the bottom; round the head is to be a motto—

> We will spit.
> On Mr. Pitt,

and *other such* d—mn'd rhymes, suited to the use of the different vessels."

[2] Rolliad, p 321, 22nd edition.

[3] Grandeur of the Law, p. 142.

followed the Peace of Utrecht,—he could remember the civil war which rendered it for some time doubtful whether the nation was to continue under the constitutional rule of the House of Brunswick,—or the legitimist doctrine of hereditary right was to prevail by the restoration of the Stuarts. He could have told us the hopes and fears which prevailed on the advance of Prince Charles and his Highlanders to Derby, and the varying joy and consternation produced by the news of the victory at Culloden.—He might have contrasted the gloom in the public mind from the disappointments and disasters of the war terminated by the treaty of Aix-la-Chapelle, with the popular exultation and enthusiasm arising from the capture of Quebec, and the other glories of the administration of Chatham.—Himself playing an important part soon after the commencement of the reign of George III., he might have explained to us the new policy of the Court, and made us better acquainted than we shall ever be with the short-lived administrations and factious movements which distracted the realm from the fall of Lord Bute to the premiership of Lord North.—Thence he could have laid bare to us the infatuated councils by which the empire was dismembered, and he might have disclosed his matured sentiments on the errors which were committed, and the line of policy which might have saved the country from the calamities by which it was nearly overwhelmed.— What an account he might have given us of his position in the Rockingham cabinet, and the diversion he had, surrounded with Whigs, in playing off one section of them against another, and preparing the return of Tory domination!—What an agreeable variety might have been presented to us when he was not only in opposition, but out of office, during the Coalition government— remaining still the secret adviser of the sovereign!—Then would have come the defeat of the Coalitionists,—with the mitigation of his triumph in finding himself under a boy statesman who professed a respect for public liberty, and was actually disposed to reform the law and the state.—Next would have appeared their mutual maneuvers for "tripping up the heels" of each other.—But, oh! what "Confession" might our autobiographer have made when he arrived at the Regency!—favoring us with the details of his double negotiations,—and informing us of the process whereby he had tears at his command at the sight or sound of royal suffering,—which is the true version of the story of his being detected by the disappearance of his hat,—and whether he heard from the woolsack the prophecy uttered by Wilkes, sitting on the steps of the throne, as to the catastrophe which was to happen before he could be "forgotten."—We should have known who communicated to him the astounding intelligence that he was dismissed; and we should have seen his towering indignation when he found that the Master who he thought valued him so highly threw him, like a worthless weed, away.—His opinion of his brother Peers, both while he presided over them and when he became the lowest in rank among them, would have been particularly racy.—He would not have felt himself at liberty to publish to the world all he had observed of the Prince of Wales, and other members of the royal family; but, without indiscreet disclosures, he might have given us a view of the Court of England at the end of the eighteenth and beginning of the nineteenth century, which would have been highly instructive.—His private opinion of Hastings would have been curious,—and we should have been still more desirous to learn his real sentiments of the French Revolution, and his anticipations of the victor of Marengo, whom he lived to see elevated to the office of Chief Consul.—After all, the most valuable chapters would have been those wherein he introduced the great literary characters of his age, and narrated the different "rounds" in his intellectual combats with them, compelling Samuel Johnson to declare, that when he was to meet Thurlow he should wish to know a day or two before, that he might prepare for the encounter.—Indulging in a satirical vein, the homage paid to Mrs. Hervey, from the hope of benefiting by her supposed influence in the disposal of his legal and ecclesiastical patronage, might have afforded a topic still more fruitful.—I make no doubt, at the same time, that, if he had done justice to himself, he would have given us fresh reason to admire not only the vigor of his understanding, but the warmth of his affections; and some parts of his character and conduct which appear to us censurable or equivocal might have been cleared up and vindicated.

I am painfully conscious that this Memoir of him,

notwithstanding the pains I have bestowed upon it, is very imperfect ; and my consolation is, that, feeling the awful responsibility cast upon me to guard public and private morality, and to do equal justice to the dead and to the living, I have sincerely striven to obey the precept which biographers ought to reverence as if it were found in holy writ: "Nothing extenuate, nor set down aught in malice,"—I am afraid I may still have to appeal to my own consciousness of impartiality, from the censures of friends and partisans, as I proceed with my undertaking, and when I shall have finished it with the Lives of Loughborough, Erskine, and Eldon.

CHAPTER CLXII.

LIFE OF LORD LOUGHBOROUGH,[1] FROM HIS BIRTH TILL HIS CALL TO THE SCOTCH BAR.

IT is with conflicting feelings that I enter upon the composition of this memoir. I am glad to hail a man of brilliant talents and varied accomplishments, —whose early history carries me back to the institutions, manners, and distinguished literary characters of my native country,—whose subsequent career was connected with the most striking vicissitudes of the eventful times in which he lived,—who, having been a Ruling Elder in the Kirk of Scotland, presided over the Lords Spiritual and Temporal in the Parliament of the United Kingdom,—who, without any Scotsman as an example, in struggling for this elevation showed that it was possible to conquer his native dialect, and the prejudice against his countrymen. —who reminded the Scottish youth that, if they could no longer hope to rival the fame of Belhaven or Fletcher of Saltoun in their own land, and if the decrees of their supreme Court were to be subjected to revision in the British House of Lords, loftier objects of ambition were presented to them than to their forefathers, and that

---

[1] I prefer the historical title of "Lord Loughborough," to that of "Earl of Rosslyn," conferred upon him after his retirement,—as I have written the Lives of "Lord Ellesmere" and of "Lord Bacon," not of "Lord Viscount Brackley" and of "Lord Viscount St. Alban's."

they might enjoy the power, and eclipse the fame, of a Somers or a Hardwicke. But it is painful and humiliating to be obliged to recollect, and to confess, that this harbinger of good fortune—of whom we might have been so proud—was almost entirely devoid of public principle, and in all his movements seems to have been actuated exclusively by a view to his own aggrandizement,—careless about any improvement of the laws and constitution, contented with the present possession of high office,— and reckless of his reputation with posterity:

———"Pudet hæc opprobia nobis
Et dici potuisse et non potuisse refelli."

Nevertheless, it is a consolation to me to think that I can relieve his memory from some portion of the obloquy which has been so unsparingly cast upon it. Surrendering him to severe censure as a politician, I must say that his delinquencies were considerably exaggerated by his contemporaries, and he has been hardly treated by those who, since his decease, have attempted to delineate his character. It will be found that he not only uniformly conformed to the manners and rules supposed to distinguish a "gentleman," but that in his changes of party he was never guilty of private treachery, and never attempted to traduce those whom he had deserted; that before he became a "Wilkite," Lord Bute had withdrawn from public life; that he had formed no engagements with Lord Chatham or Lord Rockingham, of which they could complain when he joined Lord North; that to this leader he remained true till the "Coalition" associated him with the Whigs; and that when he left the liberal party to grasp the Great Seal, he was accompanied by Mr. Burke, the Duke of Portland, Lord Spencer, and Lord Fitzwilliam. For his conduct during "the reign of terror" which followed, I am afraid that the prevaling dread of revolutionary doctrines can form little palliation; but it will be refreshing to behold him, while still in possession of the Great Seal, the patron and protector of the author of the VINDICIÆ GALLICÆ against the narrow-minded persecution of the Benchers of Lincoln's Inn. Although his occupations after his fall were not very dignified, perhaps he was as harmlessly employed in trying at Windsor to cultivate the personal favor of the old King as if he had gone into hot opposition, or had coquetted with all parties in the

House of Lords in the vain hope of recovering his office.[1]

Alexander Wedderburn,[2] afterwards Lord Loughborough, Earl of Rosslyn, and Lord Chancellor of Great Britain, was born in Edinburgh on the 13th of February, in the year 1733.[3] He was the eldest son of Peter Wedderburn, who was owner of a small estate in East Lothian, called Chesterhall, and who exercised the profession of an advocate in Edinburgh with the reputation of a good lawyer, though without making a large professional income. Indeed, at this time the *pabulum* for the Scotch Bar was very scanty, so that an advocate was supposed to be in great practice who made £500 sterling a year; and the appointments of the "Senators of the College of Justice," or "Lords of Session," or "Judges of the Supreme Civil Court in Scotland," were not more considerable.[4] The Wedderburns of Chesterhall, though not very wealthy, were of ancient descent, and had acted a prominent part. They were sprung from the Wedderburns of Wedderburn (or of that ilk), whose chief, Walter de Wedderburn, signed the Ragman Roll, and (I am ashamed to say), along with the chief of the Campbells, did homage

---

[1] The Very Reverend Principal Lee of Edinburgh, who is a great genealogist, as well as a profound scholar and divine, has proved to me that I am related to the subject of this memoir through the Halliburtons, but I can not for this reason retract or alter anything I have said of my Cousin.—*3rd Edition.*

[2] The name was often spelt with a final *e;* but I make no doubt that this is the most accurate, as well as the modern orthography, the place from which the family name is taken being evidently the "burn," or brook, in which the "wethers" were washed—the Scotch mode of pronouncing it to this day being "Wetherburn."

[3] The following is an extract from the register of baptisms for that city.—

"Thursday, 15 February, 1733.

"To Peter Wedderburn, Advocate, and, —— Ogilvy, his Lady, a son, named Alexander.—W.* Mr. John Drummond, younger of Blair, and George Cheap, Esq. Born, 13th

A valuable correspondent who has furnished me with these particulars adds, "All the Scotsman who have ever held the Great Seal of England were natives of Edinburgh.—Loughborough, Erskine, Brougham."

[4] Till 1718, the fees of counsel were regulated by *Acts of Sederunt*, and, absurdly enough, not according to the importance of the cause, but to the rank of the client. The highest fee allowed was two guineas But annual retainers were common. By Act of Sederunt, Jan. 15, 1704, all candidates for the Bar were forbidden to give entertainments on the occasion of their examinations under a penalty of 500 merks.—*Spottiswood's Forms of Process.*

---

*This means *witnesses.*

to Edward I.,—a disgrace which they redeemed at Bannockburn.

In the year 1640, the Chancellor's ancestor, Mr. Alexander Wedderburn, of Chesterhall, was deputed by the Scots, along with the Earl of Dunfermline, and Sir Patrick Hepburn, to settle several important points with the English Parliament, shortly before the commencement of the civil war, and Sir Peter, his great-grandfather, was appointed by Charles II., first a commissioner of the royal revenue in Scotland, and afterwards a judge of the Court of Sessions.[1] Peter, his father, was likewise elevated to the Bench by George II. in July, 1756, under the title of Lord Chesterhall,[2] but had a very short enjoyment of his dignity, dying while his hopeful son was still practising at the Scotch Bar,—although dreaming of conquests in Westminster Hall

I have picked np only one ancedote of young Alexander's infant years. This bears some resemblance to an occurrence which befell Lord Somers about the same age, and was supposed to foretell that Chancellor's future greatness, but the omen of the Scottish boy might have been interpreted as marking him out for outrage and disgrace—from which he was barely to escape with his life. When he was between three and four years old, having provoked a fierce turkey-cock by hallooing to him,—

> "Bubbly Jock your wife is a witch,
> And she is going to be burnt with a barrel of pitch."[3]

the animal flew at the child, laid him flat on the ground, and seemed disposed to peck his eyes out, when he was saved by his nurse, who rushed into the rescue with a broom in her hand. A young lad, then acting in the family as assistant to the gardener, witnessed this scene. Many years afterwards, when passing through London, he was carried into the Court of Chancery to see Lord Loughborough in all his glory; but,—instead of being, as was expected, overwhelmed with admiration and awe,— after he had coolly contemplated the scene for some time,

---

[1] See Bianston and Haig's "Historical Account of the Senators of the College of Justice," pp 394, 521.
[2] My readers are probably aware that these titles are enjoyed merely by courtesy with the office of judge, without conferring any privileges of peerage.
[3] I know not the meaning of this nursery rhyme; but I have myself, when a child, often heard it applied to turkey-cocks,

he exclaimed, "Weel! weel! he may be a great man noo, but I mind fine he was aince sair hadden don by his mother's bubbly jock!"

This lady, celebrated for the care which she took in the rearing of her children as well as of her poultry, was born an Ogilvie, was descended from the Earls of Airlie, and was possessed of a taste for literature—rare among the females of that day. While the "laird" was absorbed in the business of the Parliament House at Edinburgh, or at the farm at Chesterhall, she not only taught little Alec to read, but early inspired him with a love of books, so that he made wonderful progress in his studies, and displayed a precocity in his intellect as well as his acquirements which (as we shall see) excited the admiration of the literati of Scotland.

When about six years old he was sent to a school at Dalkeith, then kept by Mr. James Barclay, a very able and successful teacher. Here he met the famous Harry Dundas, afterwards Lord Viscount Melville, and a friendship was established between them, which, in spite of political differences, lasted for life. I have not ascertained whether they were in the same form, or whether either of them was "Dux," or whether they were often subjected to the discipline of the "tawse,"[1]—in those times considered a necessary instrument for the inculcation of learning; but they are both said to have been remarkable boys, Dundas being distinguished for vigor and rough jocularity, and Wedderburn for dexterity and cunning.[2] While here, they acquired a considerable knowledge of the Greek language, which was, and is, shamefully neglected at most Scotch grammar schools.

In his fourteenth year Wedderburn was removed to the University of Edinburgh. The rebellion of 1745 had suspended the scholastic pursuits of this learned body. Prince Charles being for a considerable time in possession of the city, while the Castle stood out for King George, and the professors, according to their inclinations, actively assisting the opposite side.[3] But after the battle

[1] The Scottish *ferula*.
[2] I have since been informed, that, although at the same school, they could not have been class-fellows, Dundas being several years younger than Wedderburn —*3rd Edition*.
[3] Sacred as well as civil functions gave way to arms; and Dr. Robertson, the historian, then minister of Gladsmuir, carried a musket as a private in

of Culloden lectures were resumed, and the studies of the place proceeded as peaceably as if a highland claymore had never been brandished in the Canongate, nor a cannon-shot boomed from the battlements of the Castle. At this juncture young Wedderburn began his academical career. He was matriculated on the 18th of March, 1746.

Our young collegian had no taste for mathematics, which Maclaurin had at this time rendered rather popular in Scotland; nor did he ever show much of the metaphysical turn for which his countrymen were beginning to be distinguished; but he devoted himself sedulously to classics, political science, and modern belles-lettres. The University could not yet boast of such instructors as Robertson, Blair, Munro, Black, and Dugald Stuart; but a general ardor for study prevailed, and the development of genius, which soon after displayed itself, was quietly advancing. I have not been able to obtain any particulars of young Wedderburn's demeanor in the "Humanity Class," with which he began, or in any of the others during the "philosophy curriculum." The degrees of B.A. and M.A. had then fallen into desuetude at Edinburgh, and there were no public examinations or honors to excite emulation or to reward proficiency. But much more depends on the spirit of the time and of the place than on positive institutions; and there can be no doubt that Wedderburn's mental cultivation and attainments (setting aside a minute skill in "longs and shorts") were superior to those of most young men of his years, who had all the advantages of Westminster or Eton, of Oxford or Cambridge. He was even then in daily intercourse, and on a footing of perfect equality, with several of the most distinguished literary characters whom Scotland has ever produced. Dr. Robertson, deeply engaged in preparing his History of Scotland, delighted to see him at Gladsmuir, and foretold his future eminence. When a child he had been noticed by Adam Smith—who, filling the Moral Philosophy chair at Glasgow, frequently

the Edinburgh Volunteers. Such a proceeding, sanctioned by many precedents in the Old Testament, gives no offense to pious Presbyterians I remember, when a French invasion was expected, my father, the Rev. Dr George Campbell, one of the most venerated of the clergy of the Church of Scotland, while he preached with unction every Sabbath-day, on week-days was drilled in the ranks of the Cupar Volunteers.

corresponded with him.[1] But his greatest friend and admirer was David Hume, now Librarian to the Faculty of Advocates, and after the publication of his philosophical works, employed on his "Apology for the Stuarts." With such men to direct his studies, and to reward him by their praise, we can hardly wonder that our Edinburgh student worked with as much enthusiasm and effect as if he had had before his eyes the glory of a "double first," or of being at once "Senior Wrangler and Senior Medalist."

Being of a *famille de robe*, an order long well known in Scotland as in France (of whom the Dundases, Hopes and Wedderburns were distinguished branches), he was early destined to the Bar, and in his seventeenth year he began his professional training—which did not consist, as in England, in eating a certain number of dinners in the hall of an inn of Court, but required that he should attend courses of lectures on the Roman civil law and the different departments of municipal jurisprudence, and that he should undergo private and public examinations to test his progress and proficiency, before he was authorized to practice as an advocate, or qualified to be appointed a judge. It had been under deliberation whether he should not, according to a custom which had long prevailed in Scotland, be sent to study the civil law at Leyden; but the reputation of this once famous university had been for some time declining, while that of Edinburgh was rising as a school of law, as well as of medicine,—and the advantage of studying under the laborious and accurate Erskine, afterwards the author of the "Institutes," was thought too considerable to be sacrificed.

Wedderburn now laid in the chief stock of law on which he traded for the rest of his days---for he never

[1] Dugald Stewart, in his Life of Adam Smith, says, "In the year 1748 he fixed his residence in Edinburgh, and during that and the following years read lectures on Rhetoric and Belles Lettres, under the patronage of Lord Kaimes About this time, too, he contracted a friendship, which continued without interruption till his death, with Mr. Alexander Wedderburn, now Lord Loughborough" Wedderburn, in 1748, was only fifteen, and as Smith went to Glasgow in 1751, this enduring friendship must have been settled on its foundation,—at the latest when our hero was verging to eighteen. This does strike me as a remarkable proof of his early development. Perhaps no subsequent honor which he attained raises him more in our opinion than the consideration that before his manhood he was respected and cherished by Robertson, Smith, and Hume.

again studied this science systematically; and afterwards he was contented to make himself acquainted with particular questions as they arose *pro re nata*—aiming at the character rather of a dexterous practitioner than of a profound jurist.

He felt within him very early, not only the stings of ambition, but a consciousness of his own powers, and a sanguine anticipation of success if opportunity were afforded to him. It has been supposed, even by such diligent inquirers as Lord Bougham,[1] that Wedderburn had no thought of trying his fortune in England till his famous quarrel with Lockhart in the Parliament House;— whereas it is quite certain that, while still a stripling— "from the time he could look about him, and compare himself with others,"[2] he had become dissatisfied with the prospect of spending his life before Lords Ordinary and in the Inner House, without the hope of earning £1,000 a year at the Bar or on the Bench, and that he had listened with rapture to the almost incredible stories which reached Edinburgh of the immense profits made by Mr. Yorke, before he had practiced four years in Westminster Hall — of the power and riches of English Attorney and Solicitor Generals, and of the glory of the Chancellor, the highest civil dignitary in the kingdom. He recollected that this officer was designated "Lord High Chancellor of GREAT BRITAIN," and there seemed to him no reason why the office should not be filled by a Scotsman as well as by an Englishman. It was true no countryman of his had yet thought of distinction, and no one educated in Scotland had yet tried his luck at the English Bar. Hamilton, an advocate of some eminence, the father of "Single-speech Hamilton," had gone up to reside in London immediately after the Union; but he had entirely confined his practice to Scotch appeals at the bar of the House of Lords. William Murray, born in Scotland, was now Attorney General, with the highest offices of the law within his reach; but he had been "caught" when a boy, and, never revisiting his native country, he had been bred at Westminster and Christ Church.

Old Chesterhall, when consulted about this plan, thought it very visionary, but, to humor the lad, carried him to the country seat of the Earl of Marchmont, to show him

[1] Statesmen in Reign of George III., 1st series, p. 70.   [2] His own words.

to Hume Campbell, who was there on a visit, and who, from having some little business at the English Bar, and from his brother's position, had a considerable reputation in Scotland. Lord Loughborough, when he had become a great man, gave the following account of this inspection: "I took up at once a great contempt for the said Hume Campbell; and whether I had made myself purposely disagreeable, or disliking the whole notion of being so exhibited, only appeared very stupid, I do not know; but the result was, that Hume Campbell voted me a 'hopeless dunce,'—declared that it would be quite extravagant to send me to the English Bar,—urged my father not to think of sending me even to the Scotch Bar, as I was quite unfit for the profession of the law, and advised him to ship me off to sea, or to try to get a commission for me in the army."[1] He added, "I had my revenge; for, very early in business in London, an opportunity of attacking Hume Campbell occurred to me, and I inflicted such a castigation upon him, that I drove him out of the Court of King's Bench, and forced him to seek relief in the Court of Chancery."

On his return to Edinburgh from Marchmont, Wedderburn's resolution to go to the English Bar remained unshaken; and he devoted himself with more ardor to the pursuits which he thought might qualify him for it—particularly striving to acquire a style of sarcastic, cool, cutting invective. He translated Pascal's Letters twice over with his own hand,—while engaged in this task never losing sight of Hume Campbell.

Indulging in day dreams of future greatness, he reached his twentieth year, when, being endowed with a large portion of wariness as well as of enthusiasm, he was somewhat appalled by the known and unknown perils of his scheme. The hatred of the Scots, which disgraced the English nation in the time of Lord Bute, had not burst forth; but he

[1] I am indebted for this and other interesting anecdotes of Wedderburn's career, to the present Lord Justice Clerk Hope who had them from his uncle, the late Earl of Haddington. Lord Loughborough was fond of having young men of rank from his own country about him, and with Lord Haddington, who, from his powers of conversation and shrewd knowledge of the world, was a special favourite, he was often in the habit of dwelling upon his early life, and would speak of the manner in which his own character had contributed to his own rise, very much as a third person intimately acquainted with him might have done.

was conscious, that as yet he could not speak the language of the country where he meditated such achievements, and that beyond the *res angusta domi* there might be obstacles in his way which were wholly insurmountable. He exclaimed,

> " The wide, th' unbounded prospect lies before me,
> But shadows, clouds, and darkness rest upon it."

At last he resolved to take a journey to London, that he might himself view the promised land, and not only judge of its productions, but form some notion as to the practicability of his ever obtaining a share of them.[1]

He communicated his intended journey to his friend David Hume, without fully confessing to him, or to any one else, his *arrière pensée*, and received from the philosopher the following letter of introduction to Dr. Clephane, a Scotch physician, settled in London, whose acquaintance Hume had made when they served together under General St. Clair in the expedition to the Isle of Rhè, and with whom he had continued to keep up a friendly correspondence:—

"Edinburgh, 6th March, 1753.

" DEAR DOCTOR,

" This is delivered to you by my friend Mr. Wedderburn, who makes a jaunt to London, partly with a view to study, partly to entertainment. I thought I could not do him a better office, nor more suitable to both those purposes, than to recommend him to the friendship and acquaintance of a man of learning and conversation. He is young,

> ———' Mais dans les âmes bien nées
> La vertu n'attend pas le nombre des années.'

It will be a great obligation both to him and me, if you give him encouragement to see you frequently; and after that, I doubt not you will think that you owe me an obligation—

> ' Ha in giovenile corpo senile senno.'

But I will say no more of him, lest my letter fall into the same fault which may be remarked in his behavior and conduct in life—the only fault which has been remarked

---

[1] " To clear this doubt, to know the world by sight,
To find if books or swains report it right,
He quits his cell; the pilgrim's staff he bore.
And fix'd the scallop in his hat before."

in them,—that of promising so much that it will be difficult for him to support it. You will allow that he must have been guilty of some error of this kind, when I tell you that the man with whose friendship and company I have thought myself very much favored, and whom I recommend to you as a friend and companion, is just twenty.

"I am, dear Doctor,
"Your affectionate friend and servant,
"D. HUME."

It was the end of March before Wedderburn reached London, and the circuits going on, he was disappointed in finding neither the courts of law nor the Court of Chancery sitting, and that almost all the eminent lawyers were out of town. However, through Dr. Clephane and others, to whom he had letters of introduction, he inquired into the course of legal education in England, the manner in which business was at first acquired at the Bar, and the chances of professional advancement. When presented to Mr. Attorney General Murray, he could not enter on such topics with so great a man; but he contrived to make acquaintance with some junior barristers on their return from the circuit, who initiated him in all the mysteries of the study and practice of the law of England. His courage rose. He was relieved from all apprehension of being obliged to submit to a tedious course of lectures and examinations before he could be called to the English Bar. He was told that zealous friends might do a good deal for a young barrister at his first start: he thought that the whole of the Scotch interest might be exerted in his favor, there being no countryman to divide it with him; and instances were mentioned of the fortune of a young barrister having been made by a single lucky opportunity. In after-life he likewise confessed that he felt increased confidence in comparing himself with some English counselors who were succeeding well; for, though they could quote the classics glibly without any misgiving about a false quantity, he found that he had a much greater store of general information, and that he was infinitely better acquainted with Vinnius and Voet. The chief obstacle he dreaded was his defective knowledge and vicious pronunciation of the vernacular tongue. Although he could write English, as well as Latin, with tolerable purity, in common conversation he was often reduced to great embarrassment from not being sure that he knew how to express himself properly about the most trifling matters; and he could easily perceive that, notwithstanding the politeness of the Englishmen he met, they had great difficulty in commanding their gravity when he spoke in the native accent of the Canongate, and still more when he rashly attempted to imitate them, and came out with the jargon called "High English."

Relying, however, on his own perseverance, energy, and good luck, he wrote a long letter to his father, pointing out that he had a better chance of success in Westminster Hall than in the Parliament House, and praying for an immediate and absolute change of destination. Chesterhall. himself still laboring at the Scotch Bar to little purpose, could not deny the truth of a good deal of Alec's reasoning. but was appalled at the thought of the adventurous youth being swallowed up by a troubled ocean on which no Scotsman had ever embarked before. His prudent resolve at last was to give his consent to the boy entering himself of an Inn of Court, and keeping terms, so that he might be qualified hereafter to be called to the English Bar, if such a step should be deemed expedient, but on the express condition that he should at the same time complete his legal *curriculum* at Edinburgh, pass advocate there, and, in the first instance, seriously and earnestly try his fortune in his own country, where his prospects, though less splendid, would be more secure; at all events, he would thus have two strings to his bow.

Wedderburn piously submitted to this compromise, and acted upon it with entire good faith. He immediately entered himself of the Inner Temple in the following words:—"Alexander Wedderburn, gentleman, son and heir-apparent of Peter Wedderburn, of Edinburgh, Esquire—admitted 8th May, 1753."[1]

He remained in London a few weeks longer, and dined ten times in the Hall, by which Easter and Trinity Terms were kept; and he returned to Edinburgh before the termination of the summer session in the Parliament House. To please his father, he immediately entered upon his "Civil Law Trials."

[1] Books of Inner Temple.

It has often been said that he "passed advocate" or was called to the Scotch Bar, while still under age; but this was impossible. On the 28th of February, 1750, the Lords of Council and Session passed an Act of *sederunt*, ordaining "that hereafter no person shall be admitted a member of the Faculty of Advocates but such as having been effectively tried upon his proficiency, not only in civil law, but also in the municipal law and practice of Scotland, shall be found duly qualified by the examinators appointed by the Faculty for that purpose; as also, the private examinators are hereby *prohibited and discharged to proceed to the examination of any intrant upon the civil law, unless he shall previously produce reasonable evidence to their satisfaction* THAT HE HAS ATTAINED THE AGE OF TWENTY YEARS COMPLETE, which proof of evidence shall by them be reported to the Dean and Faculty, if he shall be found duly qualified by his knowledge in the civil law. And the said Lords further statute and ordain, that no person shall be admitted to the trial of his knowledge of the municipal law and practice aforesaid *until one full year* shall have elapsed after his examination upon the civil law."

Having undergone his civil-law trials very creditably, Wedderburn devoted himself to Craig, M'Kenzie, and Bankton, comparing the Scotch with the English system of jurisprudence, through the medium of Blackstone's Commentaries recently published in London,—and when the proper time had arrived he was fully prepared for a compliance with all the prescribed requisitions prior to putting on the gown. In addition to his trials in the municipal law, he had to write a Latin thesis on a juridical subject, and to defend it against all impugners. Our northern brethren, like ourselves of the English Inns of Court, had relaxed much the strictness of ancient discipline on such occasions. Fifteen public examinators (generally the fifteen junior members of the Bar) were still appointed by the Faculty to impugn every thesis, but they showed no pugnacity, however questionable might be the positions to be impugned.[1]

---

[1] Soon after, even the form of appointing impugners by the Faculty was dropped, and the usage since has been for each impugnee to choose some of his own friends at the Bar to go through the farce of *impugning*. This is pretty much on a footing with the disputation in Lincoln's Inn, beginning

In due time, before the appointed day, appeared on the College gates the following notice and challenge:—

"DISPUTATIO JURIDICA
Ad Tit I. Lib. XIX. Pand.
De Actionibus empti venditi
QUAM,
FAVENTE NUMINE
Ex auctoritate clarissimi ac consultissimi Viri,
D. ROBERTI DUNDAS,
Ab Arniston,
Inclytæ Facultatis juridicæ Decani,
Nec non
Ex ejusdem FACULTATIS consensu et decreto, pro
ADVOCATI munere consequendo,
publicæ disquisitioni subjicit
ALEXANDER WEDDERBURN, *Auct & Resp.*
Ad diem 29 Junii, 1754, hora 12 meridiana, loc. sol."

Then and there did he thus begin:—

"Quintus Scævola, Pontifex maximus, summam vim dicebat esse in iis arbitriis, in quibus adderetur EH FIDE BONA, fideique bonæ nomen existimabat manare latissimè, idque versari in *rebus emptis venditis:* in his magni esse judicis statuere, quid quemque cuique præstare oporteret. Hinc oritur disquisitio de actionibus empti venditi, quæ, ut uterque contrahentium, quod sibi invicem præstari oportet, judicis auctoritate, etiam eb invito, consequatur, comparatæ sunt." He then proceeded to lay down very learnedly the law of vendor and purchaser, fortifying all his positions by references to the *Corpus Juris Civilis*, and stating the points on which doctors differed. Thus:— "Neratius ait, venditorem in re tradenda debere præstare emptori, ut in lite de possessione potior sit; sed Julianus, *l.* 15, *Dig.,* nec videri traditum, si superior in possessione emptor futurus non sit, *l.* ii. § 13, *ff. h. t.* Si tamen emptor incertum quid, veluti jactum retis, emerit, venditor tantum tenetur præstare quantum in se est; si igitur retem jactaverit, etiamsi nihil ceperit, emptore pretium præstare necesse habebit, *l.* ii. § 18, *ff. h. t. in fin.* Si vero jactum retis emerit et jactare retem piscator noluerit, incertum ejus rei æstimandum, Celsus ait, *l.* xii. *ff. h. t.*" There is a tradition that the young impugners started some puzzling objections to him respecting *cast of the net*—putting analogous questions touching the sale of the fees of an advocate during his first session, and whether the

with the statement of the case "John Danvers seized in fee,"—and they stand equally in need of reform.

price would be due—" etiamsi nihil ceperit"—and the degree of diligence with which he would be required to ply in the Parliament House—and how far he would be held bound at the instance of the " emptor" to be civil to the solicitors? But the aspirant answered them triumphantly. He was accordingly in due form presented to the Fifteen as worthy to be made a member of the Faculty, and he was invested with the long robe, wearing a cocked hat over his powdered hair,—for barristers' wigs were not yet known beyond the Tweed.

The following is the entry of his call in the Records of the Faculty of Advocates:—

"Edinburgh, 29th June, 1754.

"Mr. Alexander Wedderburn, son to Mr. Peter Wedderburn, Advocate, was publicly examined upon Tit. I. Lib. XIX. Pand. 'De actionibus empti venditi,' and found qualified."

Under the *Imprimatur* of Sir Gilbert Elliott and Sir David Dalrymple on behalf of the Faculty, he printed and published his thesis with the following dedication:—

"SPECTATISSIMO ET ORNATISSIMO
SCIOLTO CAROLO DOMINO de *Aberdour*
JACOBI Comitis de *Morton*
FILIO DIGNISSIMO;
FELICEM ENNI INDOLEM
OMNIBUS VITÆ CULTIORIS STUDIIS
SUB OPTIMI PATRIS AUSPICIIS
COLENTI;
DISPUTATIONEM HANC JURIDICAM
STUDIORUM PRIMITIAS,
AMICITIÆ A TENERIS ANNIS EXCULTÆ
MONUMENTUM,
D. D. C Q
ALEXANDER WEDDERBURN

CHAPTER CLXIII

CONTINUATION OF THE LIFE OF LORD LOUGHBOROUGH TILL HE FINALLY LEFT SCOTLAND.

FOR three whole years Wedderburn continued regularly and energetically to ply his profession in Scotland, except that each spring he slipped away for a few weeks to London, to eat dinners in the

Inner Temple Hall, so that he might still have the English Bar as a resource. In 1775 he was supposed to gain a great advantage by the elevation of his father to the Bench,—from succeeding to the business of certain family clients, and from the expected favor of the court to the causes patronized by the son of a judge—a feeling much more prevalent in Scotland than in England. Each successive year he was appointed by the Faculty one of the advocates for the poor—one of the fifteen public examiners and impugners—and one of the curators of the Advocates' Library.

The following is the account he gave of his maiden brief:—" Knowing the character of my countrymen at that time, I was at great pains to study and assume a very grave, solemn deportment for a young man, which my marked features, notwithstanding my small stature, would render more imposing. Men then wore in winter small muffs, and I flatter myself that, as I paced to the Parliament House, no man of fifty could look more thoughtful or steady. My first client was a citizen whom I did not know. He called upon me in the course of the cause, and becoming familiar with him, I asked him, ' how he came to employ me?' The answer was, 'Why, I had noticed you in the High street going to Court '—the most punctual of any as the clock struck nine, and you looked so grave and business-like, that I resolved from your appearance to have you for my advocate.'" He spoke with great satisfaction of the success resulting from the deportment he had assumed.

Although he seems early to have excited a very considerable sensation in his own country, I can find no trace of his eloquence in the Court of Session till the very close of his career there,[2] and my southern readers will be astonished to hear, that the great theater for his rhetorical

---

[1] To understand this thoroughly, the habits of Edinburgh in the middle of the last century—the groups assembled for conversation near the Cross, and the practice of shopkeepers to stand at their shop-doors, and to notice all who passed, saluting those whom they knew—should be kept in remembrance. I myself, when a boy, have witnessed a remnant of such habits— whereas now the great shopkeepers read the newspapers in a counting-house, elegantly fitted up, and the lawyers drive to the Parliament House in their coaches.

[2] There is a bare mention of his name once or twice in the Faculty Reports, the last as counsel in Hunter *v.* Aitkin, 6th July, 1757. Morrison's Dictionary of Decisions, p. 3448.

displays was the General Assembly of the Church of Scotland—not as counsel at their bar, but as a Ruling Elder, leading their deliberations on grave questions of heresy and church discipline.

At this time, in the absence of a parliament, the General Assembly was considered a sort of national representative body, and many of the nobility and gentry sat in it as lay members, after being ordained elders—being deputies of presbyteries, royal burghs, and universities. But next to the venerable fathers of the Kirk, the great speakers were young advocates, who contrived to be sent up as elders,—I am afraid, less with a view to further the objects of religion, than to gratify their own vanity, and to show how well qualified they were to manage causes before the Courts of Session and Justiciary.

Wedderburn was of a Presbyterian family; and to be qualified for the General Assembly, immediately after he was called to the Bar, at the age of twenty-one he was privately ordained an elder of the parish in which his father resided in East Lothian. For the General Assemby which was to meet in the month of May following, he was elected representative by the royal burgh of Inverkeithing.

Scotland was at this time in a state of extraordinary ferment from the philosophical writings of David Hume, and a work of Henry Home, just made a judge under the title of Lord Kames, which was supposed to contain doctrines little less pernicious.[1] The zeal of the orthodox was quickened by a proceeding in England which they wished to outdo. About a year before, there had been a presentment by the Grand Jury of the city and liberty of Westminster against Mallet for publishing the works of Lord Bolingbroke. In the north, such offenses were considered more properly within the cognizance of the ecclesiastical courts, and a certain Reverend Dr Anderson, who published many pamphlets on the subject, now resolved to have the two great delinquents at the bar of the supreme sacred tribunal on earth, and to launch against them the terrors kept in store by those vested with the true power of the keys.

I have not been able to find any record of the maiden speech of the Elder for Inverkeithing, or the part which

[1] "Nature and Obligations of Morality."

he took in the proceedings of this Assembly; but the probability is that he seconded the efforts of the more moderate and discreet friends of religion, who succeeded in suppressing the introduction of the names of any particular writers for public discussion, and who acquiesced in a general expression of opinion against prevailing infidelity and immorality.[1]

Anderson, however, was by no means satisfied, and as soon as the Assembly was dissolved, he published another pamphlet, which ran through many editions, attempting to prove, by texts of Scripture, that it was the imperative duty of the Church, for the reformation of the wicked, for the protection of the unwary, and in the due exercise of the power vested in true believers constituting the visible Church, to cut off from its communion and to hand over to the Devil those who had violated their baptismal vow: and that a great national sin would be incurred unless personal proceedings were instituted and sternly carried on against the individuals who were now misleading so many, and who were little better than that Antichrist from whom their fathers, under the pious and unflinching Knox, had delivered the land.

David Hume and Lord Kames became seriously alarmed. The former was then Keeper of the Advocates' Library, and candidate for the chair of Moral Philosophy in the University of Edinburgh. The latter, clothed in ermine, was not yet warm in his seat as a judge. Sentence of the "greater excommunication" would not only

[1] The Assembly passed unanimously the following 'Act against Infidelity and Immorality'.—"The General Assembly Church being filled with the deepest concern on account of the prevalence of Infidelity and Immorality, the principles whereof have been, to the disgrace of our age and nation, so openly avowed in several books published of late in this country, and which are but too well known amongst us; do therefore judge it proper and necessary for them at this time to express the utmost abhorrence of these impious and infidel principles, which are subversive of all religion, natural and revealed, and have such pernicious influence on life and morals. And they do earnestly recommend it to all the Ministers of this Church to exercise the vigilance and to exert the zeal which becomes their character, to preserve those under their charge from the contagion of these abominable tenets, and to stir up in them a solicitous concern to guard against them, and against the influence of those who are infected with them." It has been stated to me that "Wedderburn, for the sake of his friends, who were well-known to be struck at, wished to move the previous question, but found that he was struggling against a stream which would have overwhelmed him—and said he was sure, while their names were not mentioned, they would consider the general censure *brutum fulmen.*"

have exposed them to a vast deal of social annoyance,—causing them to be regarded with horror by the godly, and with ridicule by the profane,—but might have very seriously injured them in ther worldly interests. Their main reliance was on the good sense of Dr. Robertson, and the influence he had established in the Church, but they were likewise solaced by the friendly zeal and enterprising activity of Wedderburn. Having, for some unexplained reason, quarreled with Inverkeithing—to secure himself another seat in the General Assembly, our Elder contrived to make himself Provost of Dufermline, and he acquired a complete ascendency over the council of this burgh. He was unanimously elected their representative for the Assembly summoned to meet in May, 1756,—from which greater things were expected than had been achieved for the true faith since the Reformation. As the time approached, Anderson and his associates varied their plan of operations, and, letting alone for the present Lord Kames, whose book was liable to the charge of heterodoxy rather than of infidelity, they resolved to bend all their efforts against David Hume,—to summon him to the bar,—to examine him *viva voce* respecting his writings and religious opinions, and, if he proved contumacious, to make a great example by inflicting upon him the highest censures of the Church.

Accordingly, on the 28th of May, 1756, an overture or motion was made, that " The General Assembly, judging it their duty to do all in their power to check the growth and progress of infidelity; and considering that as infidel writings have begun of late years to be published in this nation, against which they have hitherto only testified in general, so there is one person, styling himself ' DAVID HUME, Esq.,' who hath arrived at such a degree of boldness, as publicly to avow himself the author of books containing the most rude and open attacks upon the glorious Gospel of Christ, and principles evidently subversive even of natural religion and the foundations of morality, if not establishing direct atheism: therefore the Assembly appoint a Committee to inquire into the writings of this author, to call him before them, and prepare the matter for the next General Assembly."

The speech of the mover was alarmingly well received; and it contained arguments which there was great difficulty in answering without being subjected to the popular reproach of "latitudinarianism," or of 'indifference about religion." Wedderburn (I hope and believe from sincere conviction, and at all events from prudence) would have been very sorry to have been supposed to share the speculative doubts of the individual to be defended; but,—knowing that he was to be supported by men of unsuspected orthodoxy and piety, warmed by the recollection of the kindness for which he might now make some return, and no doubt excited by the favorable opportunity of gaining distinction,—rose to move what amounted to the previous question; very properly not venturing upon a direct negative. The following is a short sketch of his speech on this occasion. In reading it, we are surprised at the sarcasms on which he ventured, and it rather corroborates the opinion of his eloquence given by some venerable fathers of the Church, who were his contemporaries and long survived him:[1]

"I trust, Moderator," said the youthful elder for Dunfermline, "it is wholly unnecessary that I should follow the example of the reverend divine who has preceded me, by making any profession of zeal for the pure Presbyterian Church established in this country. I say with him, 'peace be within her walls! prosperity within her bulwarks!' Our object is the same, and we can only differ as to the means by which that object is, under Providence, to be attained. Now, notwithstanding the headlong fervor I see prevailing in some quarters, and the impatient eagerness to crush Mr. Hume with the censures of the Church, I would humbly advise the venerable Assembly to dismiss the 'overture,' and to trust to reason and Scripture for the refutation of his errors. In the first place, let me very respectfully ask whether all who are now disposed to concur in this vote have read the writings to be condemned? Am I to believe that the holy presbyters, trusted with the care of souls of which they are to give an account, instead of preaching, praying and catechising, have been giving up their days and their nights to Mr. Hume's 'Treatise

[1] The Very Reverend Principal Lee from whom I have received many traditions respecting him, writes, "Wedderburn was not a favorite speaker in the General Assembly He was disliked for his occasional bursts of insolence. Of the lawyers in the Assembly, by far the most pleasing and successful speaker was Mr Andrew Pringle (afterwards Lord Alemore), whose flowing and dignified eloquence attracted universal admiration."

on the Human Understanding,' or to his ' Essays on Miracles,' and on 'Cause and Effect,' writings said to be so poisonous and so pernicious,—in neglect of the spiritual good of others, and possibly to the peril of their own principles? But suppose these wicked books to have been deliberately read by every member of this Assembly, by how many of you have they been understood? And are you to defer coming to a decision till you are all agreed on their meaning? and are all of one mind upon the various abstruse questions which they discuss? Can you all tell us the difference between *coincidence* and *causation?* One Essay, very acrimoniously alluded to by the reverend mover of the overture, is on ' Liberty and Necessity;' but some have declared elsewhere that the views of the essayist thus reprobated are in entire harmony with the doctrines of Calvin and Knox on predestination and the eternal decrees of God—by which the fall of man was preordained before the foundation of the world, and all those who are to perish everlastingly are under the doom of eternal reprobation. Such notions may be unphilosophical, and may be unscriptural, but when are you to come to a unanimous and satisfactory conclusion on the questions broached by your overture? You must have made up your minds upon them before you call in Mr. Hume,—who may be better prepared than it may be convenient for some of you, to prove that they are not at variance with the standards of the true Presbyterian faith. I would, with all possible respect, request you to recollect the procedure in another meeting of intelligence, with which I would venture to compare this venerable Assembly only for eloquence, and a deep theoretical knowledge of divine truth. When these causists, though of more than mortal grasp of thought,

> ————' reason'd high
> Of providence, fore-knowledge, will and fate,
> Fix'd fate, free will, fore-knowledge absolute,
> They found no end, in wandering mazes lost.'

The opinions complained of, however erroneous, are of an abstract and metaphysical nature—not exciting the attention of the multitude—not influencing life or conduct; your spiritual censures should be reserved for a denial of the divine right of presbytery, or practical errors which lead to a violation of the ten commandments. What advantage do you really expect from the course which is proposed? Is there any chance of your convincing Mr. Hume, and of making him cry *peccavi?* Alas! I am afraid he has withstood the reasonings of the subtlest philosophers who have attempted to refute him; and you can hardly expect that a miracle should again be performed—one of your number being specially empowered to speak to him. Upon his proving contumacious, you are resolved to punish, if you can not reform, him; and the awful sentence of the 'Greater Excommunication' is to be pronounced—by which he is to be excluded from the society of all Christians, and to be handed over to the evil one. But this is a sentence which the civil power now refuses to recognize, and which will be attended with no temporal consequences. You may wish, for the good of his soul, to burn him as Calvin did Servetus; but you must be aware that, however desirable such a power may appear to the Church, you can not touch a hair of his head, or even compel him, against his will, to do penance on the stool of repentance.[1] Are you sure that he may not be so hardened as to laugh at your anathemas, and even to rejoice in them as certainly increasing the circulation of his books and the spread of his opinions? If he is grave and sarcastic, may he not claim the right of private judgment, for which your fathers have bled? and if you deny it to him, may he not call upon *you* to obey the mandates of the Roman Catholic Church, and again to keep company with that Lady of Babylon whom you hold in such abomination? But there is one other point, which, being a lawyer, as well as a member of this venerable Assembly, I wish, before I conclude, to bring under your serious consideration—where is your jurisdiction to proceed in this case? I admit your jurisdiction in spiritual matters over all the members of your Church. But you assert that Mr. Hume is not even a Christian. Why are you to summon him before you, more than any Jew or Mohammedan who may happen to be traveling within your bounds? Your 'libel,' as we

[1] This form being often occupied by young ladies who become mothers without being wives, and are rebuked from it in the face of the congregation, is usually called the "*Cutty* stool," but was formerly the place where all delinquents sat when rebuked before the congregation.

lawyers call it, is *ex facie* inept, irrelevant, and null, for it begins by alleging that the defender denies and disbelieves Christianity, and then it seeks to proceed against him and to punish him as a Christian. Your charge must be true or false. If it is false, it is to be rejected as contrary to truth and justice; and if it be true, the party charged is unfortunately one of those who, in the language of the Bible, are '*without*,' and consequently are not proper objects of Christian discipline. For these reasons, I move—'That while all the members of the General Assembly have a just abhorrence of any doctrines or principles tending to infidelity or to the prejudice of our holy religion, yet they drop the overture anent Mr. David Hume, because it would not, in their judgment, minister to edification.'"

Wedderburn was rather roughly handled by several clerical speakers who followed. They abstained from any insinuations against his own sincerity or orthodoxy, but maintained—"that Mr. Hume's writings were a fit subject for the animadversion of the supreme court of the Church, as they were directly subversive of all religion, natural and revealed. It was limiting the power of God to suppose that an erring mortal might not be brought to a right frame of mind through the instrumentality of the punishments and prayers of the Church; and, at any rate, the reformation of the peccant individual was less to be regarded than the safety of others. No views of expediency should interfere with the plain precepts contained both in the Old and New Testament for the correction, by the instrumentality of the Church, of heresy and schism, including most especially a denial of the being of a God, or of the mission of his Son Jesus Christ. It was by no means so clear that excommunication would be treated so lightly by Mr. Hume. He had hitherto seemed desirous of enjoying the worldly advantages of being considered a Christian, after having forfeited all title to the name: his writings henceforth would be shunned by all in any danger of being corrupted by them: and, above all, it was most desirable that a broad line of separation should be drawn between him and all who profess to be Christians; for it was lamentable to think that, at present, ordained clergymen of the Church of Scotland were in the daily habit of associating with him, to the great scandal of all real Christians.¹ The objection on the question of jurisdiction was a quibble, and would go to put an end to such prosecutions in the worst cases ; for in proportion as the crime against religion was great, the power to punish it would be taken away. Let a man utterly deny and revile the Holy Scriptures, and the learned elder for Dunfermline would tell you, ' You have no power to censure him, for he is not a Christian.' Mr. Hume, who had been received at his birth into the Church of Christ, had never been formally excluded from it, and had not only never renounced his baptism, but he continued to profess himself a Christian, and to talk of Christianity as ' *our* most holy religion.' "²

Dr. Robertson (now fully established in the lead of the Church), according to his custom, concluded the debate with admirable tact and discretion ; a great many ministers left the house, to avoid the opprobrium of voting on either side ; and, on a division, the amendment to dismiss the " overture " was carried, by a majority of 50 to 17.

This alarm, joined to the bad success of his History on its first appearance, caused such disgust in the mind of Mr. Hume, that Wedderburn, and his other friends, had great difficulty in dissuading him from putting in execution the plan of for ever renouncing his country, changing his name, and spending the remainder of his days in a remote provincial town in France.

He was soon freed from all apprehension of further disturbance on account of his opinions, by the penal visitations of the Church being directed against other objects.³ A few months after the dissolution of the last General Assembly there was brought out on the stage at Edinburgh

¹ This was chiefly aimed at Dr Robertson.
² " Our most holy religion is founded on *Faith*, not on Reason."—*Essay on Miracles*.
³ He had previously entertained the vain hope that his errors might be forgotten in the controversy then raging between the ancient and modern psalmody. Upon the maxim " that the Devil ought not to have all the good music," an attempt was now made to introduce into the service some of the best airs of a solemn character composed in modern times ; but this was resisted as a dangerous innovation, and the faithful were as equally and as keenly ivided upon it as upon the recent question of the Free Church. Not unfre. ently, when the psalm had been " given out," and the singing was to egin, in contempt to the precentor one half of the congregation would sing the appointed lines to an old tune, and the other to a new. But through the mediation of Dr Blair, the Church escaped this peril, and the threatened disruption did not take place.

the tragedy of DOUGLAS, written by the Reverend John Home, minister of Athelstonford,—which threw all Scotland into a ferment. The great majority of the inhabitants were intoxicated ; for, not content with the just belief that this was a most beautiful poem, and admirably adapted to scenic representation, they asserted that it was by far the finest drama that had ever appeared in the English language; that Shakespeare was to be eclipsed, and that Corneille and Racine were to be rivaled, by a Scottish bard.[1] But great scandal was caused by the behavior of many of the clergy upon this occasion. Not only the author, but several of his reverend brethren having cures in the city and neighborhood, were in the theater on the first representation of the piece; and, at the successive repetitions of it, ministers and elders from distant parts of Scotland did not scruple to attend and applaud. The old presbyterians, like the English puritans, had severely reprobated all theatrical exhibitions, and had strictly forbidden them to the laity as well as to the clergy. Many, therefore, considered the passion for the stage with which the nation seemed suddenly struck as " a delusion of Satan."[2]

At the approach of the next General Assembly, it was resolved that the most energetic measures should be taken to stay the plague. Mr. Home himself would not face the storm, and withdrew from the jurisdiction of the Kirk by resigning the living of Athelstonford. Two or three clergymen, who had been identified as being present as the theater, when brought before the Assembly acknowledged their offense—one of them urging in mitigation that " he had ensconced himself in a corner, and had hid his face with a handkerchief, to avoid scandal." They were let off with a severe reprimand from the Moderator. So far the proceedings were conducted with unanimity; but a very animated debate arose respecting measures for

[1] It is curious that David Hume himself, from his dislike to the literature of the English, joined, or professed to join, in the general enthusiasm,—as he affected to consider "Douglas" superior to "Macbeth," and the "Epigoniad" equal to "Paradise Lost." On the first representation of "Douglas" in London, when the curtain dropped amidst thundering applause, an Aberdeen man in the front row of the shilling gallery, overpowered with delight, shouted out in the racy dialect of his district, " Ou fie, lads ! fat think ye o' yir Willy Shakespeare noo ?"
[2] Scott's Magazine, 1746-7, MS. Journal of Lord Commissioner Adam.

the future. It was proposed that the General Assembly should pass a new and stringent act against all members of the Church, lay or clerical, who should be present at any theatrical exhibition. According to the form of proceeding, the preliminary question put was, "whether there should be an overture anent the stage?"

Wedderburn, again representative for the burgh of Dunfermline, took the negative side, and according to Lord Commissioner Adam, " made the best speech ever delivered by him in his native country."[1] Unfortunately the conclusion of it only is preserved to us :—

" Be contented with the laws which your wise and pious ancestors have handed down to you for the conservation of discipline and morals. Already have you driven from your body its brightest ornament, who might have continued to include the precepts of the Gospel from the pulpit, as well as embodying them in character and action. Is it, indeed, forbidden to show us the kingdom of heaven by a parable? In all the sermons produced by the united genius of the Church of Scotland, I challenge you to produce anything more pure in morality, or more touching in eloquence, than the exclamation of Lady Randolph—

> ———'Sincerity !
> Thou first of virtues ! Let no mortal leave
> Thy onward path, although the earth should gape,
> And from the gulf of hell destruction cry
> To take dissimulation's winding way.' "[2]

It was carried " that there should be an overture," by 120 to 54.[3] An act was then proposed subjecting to ecclesiastical

---

[1] Lord Commissioner Adams's MS Journal.

[2] This famous passage, however, of which the Scotch were so proud, was (probably for that reason) vilipended by Dr. Johnson, who, on its being quoted by old Mr. Sheridan, repeated with great emphasis the well-known description, by Juvenal, of a man of inflexible virtue—" Esto bonus miles, tutor bonus," &c , adding, "and after this comes Johnny Home, with his *earth gaping* and his destruction *crying.* Pooh !" *

[3] Preparatory to the meeting of this Assembly, Wedderburn had printed in the newspapers several songs and epigrams against the persecutors of " Douglas," and Carlyle had published an ironical pamphlet under the title of " Reasons why the tragedy of Douglas should be burned by the hands of the common hangman " It is confessed, however, by the author of the MAN OF FEELING, in his review of those times, that " the parodies and squibs in verse were, in general, not remarkable for their wit or pleasantry." It must be admitted that my ratiocinative and metaphysical countrymen have very

* Boswell's Tour, 376,

censures all members of the Church, male and female, lay and clerical, who should be present at any theatrical exhibition; but this being strongly opposed by Wedderburn, and even by Dr. Robertson, although, under a vow he had made to his father he himself had never entered the door of a play-house, was rejected, and the following act was passed, entitled, in the Acts of the General Assembly, " Recommendation to Presbyteries to take care that none of the ministers of this Church attend the theater :"

" The General Assemby, considering how much the success of the Gospel depends on the regular and inoffen· sive behavior of the ministers of this Church, do earnestly recommend to the several presbyteries to take such wise and effectual measures as may promote the spirit of our holy religion, and preserve the purity and decorum of the ministerial character; and that they take care that none of the ministers of this church do, upon any occasion, attend the theater."

Before another General Assembly met, Wedderburn was transferred to a very different sphere. But we must attend him in some of the other scenes in which he drew public notice before he bade adieu to his native land. He is to be recorded as a distinguished member of the POKER CLUB. This had a political origin, although it soon became purely convivial. When the militia system was first established in England, there was a loud demand that it should be extended to Scotland; but the government was afraid to put arms into the hands of those who were still believed to be partisans of the house of Stuart. An association was formed to *stir up* the national discontent on account of this affront, and the members agreed to meet twice a week, on Tuesdays and Fridays, at a house called the *Divesorium*, in the Netherbow. To aid their deliberations they had a copious supply of excellent claret, which was drawn from the cask at the rate of eighteen-pence the quart. The grievance of the militia was forgotten, but a club was constituted under the name of the " POKER,"—Mr. Johnstone, afterwards Sir William

little notion of anything that approaches to raillery. Hume's Essays, in which he tried to imitate Addison in lightly commenting on manners, are wretchedly bad. They were very properly excluded by him from subsequent editions of his works, and they have been most uncharitably repiinted by his recent biographers.

Pultney, being elected *secretary;* and the famous advocate, Mr. Andrew Crosbie, *assassin.* Besides occasionally indulging in "high jinks," they had regular discussions on literary and scientific subjects, and they were beginning to consider themselves equal to a preceding club in Edinburgh, which had carried on a philosophical correspondence with the celebrated Berkeley, Bishop of Cloyne, upon the existence of matter. Although Wedderburn was not a very regular attendant, when he was present he contributed his full share of epigram, anecdote, criticism, and hilarity. But, alas! this club, while still in the freshness and vigor of youth, was suddenly extinguished by the tax laid on French wines. The members, though learned and witty, being poor, could not afford to have the price of their favorite beverage doubled at a blow; and they abhorred port, the beloved beverage of their southern fellow-subjects.[1] To punish the government, they agreed, on the motion of Mr. Wedderburn, to dissolve the "Poker," and to form another society which should exist without consumption of any exciseable commodity—purely for mental improvement and gratification—defying the Chancellor of the Exchequer and all his works—to be called the "Select." The founder was Allan Ramsay, the painter, the son of the author of the GENTLE SHEPHERD. The first meeting was held in the Advocates' Library, in the month of May, 1754, when on the motion of Mr. Ramsay, Mr. Wedderburn, who had just completed his twenty-first year, was called to the chair. The original minutes of this meeting (by the special favor of the Faculty of Advocates) now lie before me. Mr. Alexander Wedderburn's name comes the fourth; and there are to be found in the list of original members then present—

Mr. DAVID HUME.
Mr. JOHN HOME, Minister of Athelstonford.
Mr. WILLIAM ROBERTSON, Minister of Gladsmuir.

[1] On this occasion were written the well-known lines by John Home:—
"Firm and erect the Caledonian stood,
Old was his mutton, and his claret good;
'Let him drink port,' an English statesman cried;
He drank the poison, and his spirit died."
Mackenzie, in his Life of the author, says, "As to port wine, it is well known that Mr Home held it in abhorrence. In his younger days claret was the only wine drank by gentlemen in Scotland,"

Mr. HUGH BLAIR, Minister of Edinburgh.
Mr. ADAM SMITH, Professor of Glasgow.
Sir DAVID DALRYMPLE, Advocate.
Dr. ALEXANDER MONRO.
Dr. JOHN HOPE.
Mr. ANDREW PRINGLE, Advocate.
Mr. WILLIAM JOHNSTONE, Advocate.

Wedderburn must have obtained a wonderful ascendency, considering his years, to be elected "Præses" at such a meeting. The great object of the members was to improve themselves in public speaking—a department of education which had hitherto been almost entirely neglected in Scotland. The members were at first limited to fifty, and all candidates were afterwards to be balloted for. The admission fee was only five shillings sterling. The meetings were to be every Wednesday evening, from November to August, in the Advocates' Library, between six and nine, when a subject given out by the præses of the preceding meeting was to be debated. "Every member might propose any subject of debate, except such as regard revealed religion, or which might give occasion to vent any principles of Jacobitism—to be received or rejected by a vote of the committee, and, if received, to be entered in a book to be kept for that purpose." The rule about speaking is perhaps the most curious, and it may afford hints for the regulation of other deliberative assemblies: "That every person may speak three times in a debate, and no oftener: the first time fifteen minutes, and ten minutes each of the other times—addressing himself to the member presiding. And if two or more stand up at the same time, the member presiding shall call upon him whom he first perceived rising—always giving preference to him who has not spoke, or not so frequently as the person or persons rising with him; unless any member rises to explain anything said by him and misunderstood; for which purpose he shall be allowed two minutes and no more."

The præses at the second meeting was Mr. Adam Smith, and he named as the next subject of debate, "Whether bounties on the exportation of corn be advantageous?" But when the debate came on he took no part in it himself; and both he and David Hume, though they attended frequently, always remained mute.

Wedderburn was active both in speaking and in managing the affairs of the Society. The following entry shows that he was very presumptuous, and that he was treated with great forbearance:—" 7th Aug., 1754. The committee have refused the following question :— 'Whether the law of Queen Joan of Naples, allowing licensed stews, would be of advantage to a nation,' Mr. Wedderburn, who proposed it, appealed to the Society, *and the determination of the appeal was delayed till next session.*" [1]

I copy some of the questions which were debated:
" Whether the common practice in Scotland, of distributing money to the poor in their own homes, or the receiving the poor into work-houses and hospitals, be most advantageous?" " Whether the establishment of Banks in Scotland has increased wealth?" " Whether the bounty should be continued on the exportation of linen?" " Whether the laws against bribery and corruption ought to be repealed?" " Whether Brutus did well in killing Cæsar?" " May a lawyer of ordinary parts become eminent in his profession?" " Whether the Repenting Stool ought to be taken away?" Whether whisky ought to be laid under such restrictions as to render the use of it less frequent?" " Whether the stage ought to be permitted in a well regulated government?" " Whether the place given to love and gallantry in modern tragedy be not unnatural?" " Whether ought we to prefer ancient or modern manners, with regard to the condition and treatment of women?" " Whether the difference in national character be chiefly owing to the nature of different climates, or to moral and political causes?" " Whether is an epic poem or a tragedy the most difficult and most perfect composition?" " Have the moderns done well in laying aside the use of a chorus in tragedy?" " Whether entails in perpetuity be for the good of families and the improvement of the country?" " Whether a university in a metropolis or in a remote town be more proper for the training of youth?" " Whether an academy for painting set up in Scotland would deserve the encouragement of the public?" " Whether the right of primogeniture ought still to take place?" " Whether courts of law ought to be allowed

[1] This was a gentle mode of deciding against him, whereas he ought to have been reprimanded for proposing the question and preferring the appeal.

to take cognizance of parliamentary privilege?" "Whether presentation by patrons, or election by the parishioners, is the best mode of settling ministers?" "Whether an union with Ireland would be advantageous to Great Britain?" "Whether a Foundling Hospital erected at Edinburgh, and supported by a tax laid upon old bachelors, would tend to the prosperity of Scotland?" "Can a marriage be happy when the wife is of an understanding superior to that of the husband?" "Whether have mankind decreased in stature, strength and virtue, during the last 3,000 years?" "Whether doth a successful author feel most pleasure or pain?" "Whether the institution of slavery be advantageous to the free?" "Whether the practice of the ladies in painting their faces ought not to be prohibited by every wise government?" "Whether an excess of impudence or of modesty is most hurtful to a man in the commerce of the world?" "Whether in love we are happier in the passion we feel or in that we excite?" "Whether quackery is not more useful for obtaining success in the liberal professions than real merit?" "Whether the delays and expense attending judicial proceedings are not both necessary and useful to society?" "Whether divorce by mutual consent should be allowed?" "Ought there to be trial by jury in civil as well as criminal cases?"

The questions, more or less grave and well-chosen, may be curious, as they show the subjects which interested Scotland in the middle of the 18th century—the period of her greatest literary glory, and as the discussions upon them probably afforded many hints for the composition of Hume's "Political Essays," and of 'the "Wealth of Nations."

The Select Society soon became so popular that its members were trebled, and it contained many men of rank, who professed to be themselves philosophers and men of letters, or the patrons of philosophy and literature—such as Lord Kames, Lord Elibank, the Earl of Glasgow, the Duke of Hamilton, the Earl of Lauderdale, and the Earl of Bute. The speakers consisted chiefly of two classes—the ministers, and the lawyers. For lucid order, for sustained sweetness, and for solid information, Robertson was allowed to be decidedly first; while Wedderburn's sallies fixed the attention of the audience, and were sometimes found amusing by their extravagance. "The Select Society," says Lord Kames, "was instituted in 1754, and, though soon more numerous and promiscuous than its title warranted, included most of the men of letters at that time resident in Edinburgh and its vicinity." "The Society," says Dugald Stewart, "subsisted in vigor for six or seven years, and produced debates such as have not often been heard in modern assemblies,—debates where the dignity of the speakers was not lowered by the intrigues of policy and the intemperance of faction; and where the most splendid talents that have ever adorned this country were roused to their best exertions by the liberal and ennobling discussions of literature and philosophy. To this institution, while it lasted, Dr. Robertson contributed his most zealous support, seldom omitting an opportunity of taking a share in its business, and deriving from it an addition to his own fame; which may be easily conceived by those who are acquainted with his subsequent writings, or who have witnessed those powers of argument and illustration which in the Ecclesiastical Courts he afterwards employed so successfully on subjects not so susceptible of the embellishments of eloquence." In the Select Society was likewise trained the defender of Clive—the assailant of Franklin—the future Chancellor of Great Britain.

I am sorry, however, to be obliged to go on to relate that this respectable institution was finally covered with ridicule by an insane scheme which there is strong evidence to prove was entered into with the full concurrence of Robertson, Wedderburn, and its most distinguished members—the scheme being nothing less than at once to change the spoken language of the country.

The famous Charles Townshend, connected with Scotland by having married the Dowager Countess of Dalkeith, had been admitted a member of the Select Society, and had spoken once with great brilliancy; but he never could be prevailed upon a second time to take part in the debate, and he threw out a number of gibes against the dialect in which the members expressed themselves,—doubting whether he could be intelligible to the audience,—hinting that he was often unable to follow their reasoning, or fully to apprehend their rhetorical figures. He jestingly asked them "why they did not learn to speak as

well as to write the English language?" and proposed
that in the meantime an interpreter should be employed.
Eager for the national honor, and blind to the lurking
malice of the *suthron wit*, they really thought it was in
their power all of a sudden to rival Hardwicke, Chester-
field, and Pitt in oratory—by attending to the just power
of the letters of the alphabet, and to pauses and cadences
in their discourse.

The dialect then universally used in Scotland by persons all ages and all degrees, was certainly very barbarous. In early times there was little difference between
the languages spoken in England and in the lowlands
of Scotland. "Barber's Bruce" and the poems of our
James I. bear a considerable resemblance to Chaucer,
and are fully as intelligible to Englishmen of the present
day. But the long succession of wars which followed the
vain attempt of Edward I. to subjugate Scotland, cut off
all intercourse between the two countries, except by
"raids" and "forays," and there was a growing divergence
between their dialects. While Scotland retained a native
court, there subsisted a standard to appeal to, and her
Anglo-Saxon might, perhaps, be considered as classical and
as polished as that of her rival; but after the union of the
crowns, the lowland Scotch became a mere provincial *patois*
—and the want of a proper medium of communication with
the learned world, almost extinguished the literary genius
of the people, which had burst forth with such luster on
the revival of letters. Arbuthnot, Mallet, Thompson, and
Armstrong had first shown that Scotchmen might be
taught to write English; and this accomplishment was
very generally possessed by men of education of the existing generation. But still they conversed and they
thought in the language which they had learned from
their nurses, and which was spoken by the peasantry.
This varied a good deal in different counties, but in all
was uncouth and irregular. In its roots it bore a considerable resemblance to the English of the 18th century,
but was very different in its inflections and idioms; and
these resemblances and differences made the accomplishment of speaking English with purity and confidence
more difficut to a Scotchman than to a Pole. Wedderburn, in his yearly trip to London to keep his terms in the
Inner Temple was more and more struck by the disad

vantage under which he must, in this respect, labor, if he should ever really try his luck at the English bar; and he is said eagerly to have joined in the plan of lingual reform.

It so happened, by a strange coincidence, that at this very time old Sheridan (the father of Richard Brinsley Sheridan) came to Edinburgh to deliver lectures on elocution, and, speaking with a strong Irish brogue, undertook, to teach all the delicacies of English intonation. By such nonsense as this did he delude some Scotchmen of mature years:—

"The next progression of number is when the same note is repeated, but in such a way that one makes a more sensible impression on the ear than the other, by being more forcibly struck, and therefore having a greater degree of loudness,—as *ti-tùm*, or *tùm-ti-tùm-ti;* or when two weak notes precede a more forcible one, as *ta-ta-tùm;* or when they follow one, as *tùm-ti-ti,-tùm-ti-ti.*"

The Select Society, seeing only the desirableness of the object, overlooked entirely the difficulties and impossibilities which opposed it,—such as the want of models of correct pronunciation for the great mass of the inhabitants—the rigidity of the organs of speech of adults—and the succession of persons from the lower orders, and from the remote provinces, who must have the accents as much as the features of their parents. Our grave divines, lawyers, and philosophers thought that the Scottish dialect was to be got rid of by a lecture, as they had known a cutaneous disease to be cured by ointment. They consequently resolved unanimously "That it would be of great advantage to this country, if a proper number of persons from England, duly qualified to instruct gentlemen in the knowledge of the English tongue, the manner of pronouncing it with purity, and the art of public speaking, were settled in Edinburgh; and if, at the same time, a proper number of masters from the same country, duly qualified for teaching children the reading of English, should open schools in Edinburgh for that purpose." With this view they determined that a fund should be raised by contribution, and that the contributors, together with the members of the Select Society, should take the name of "The Society for promoting the reading and speaking of the English language in Scotland."

A large body of directors was named, including Lord Auchinleck, Dr. Robertson, the Earl of Errol, the Earl of Eglinton, the Earl of Galloway, and the Earl of Elgin.

To benefit the nation by their example, they resolved that, from and after a given day, they themselves would all begin to speak English, according to the rules of grammar, and Sheridan's scale of progression—"*ti-tùm* or *tùm-ti-tùm-ti*."

According to all accounts, never, since the confusion of tongues at Babel, was there such an exhibition. Few persevered in the attempt more than twenty-four hours and it was soon discovered that they might as well have petitioned Parliament for a law forbidding red hair, or high cheek-bones, in any part of Scotland!

The ridicule of what they had attempted, even prevented them from going on with educational measures, which might have been practicable and advantageous. "The Society for promoting the reading and speaking of the English Language in Scotland" did publish an advertisement in the "Edinburgh Courant and Caledonian Mercury," "that they had engaged Mr. Leigh, a person well qualified to teach the pronunciation of the English tongue with propriety and grace; but here its labors ended. It immediately fell to pieces, and no such national scheme has since been attempted, although individuals have from time to time exposed themselves to a little laughter, and have materially injured their success in public life, by violently attempting to get rid of their Scotch accent, and to speak "High English." [1]

---

[1] It is said in Ritchie's Life of David Hume, in which there is a lively account of these vagaries, that Dr. Robertson ever after adhered to his resolution to speak English, and was successful in his language, although not in his intonation. But I have been told by my father, who enjoyed the familiarity and friendship of the historian, that, "although he could write English better than any Englishman, in conversation he spoke broad Scotch without any attempt at disguise." This corresponds with the compliment paid to him in England, that "he must not expect to speak as well as to write English better than the English;" as well as with the solution Boswell gives of his silence in society in London, that " he was afraid of falling into Scotticisms "

From my standing and long experience, perhaps I may be forgiven if I earnestly warn my young countrymen against "clipping the Queen's English." A Scotch accent, being often found in company with birth, education, and talent, is not vulgar, and it will in no degree impair the effect of eloquence either in the House of Commons or at the bar of the House of Lords But Scotsmen do no justice to their powers when they hesitate about the pronunciation of a word, and after all, they are sure to make greater blunders than

I have little more to relate of Wedderburn in his own country, except the share which he had in starting the original "EDINBURGH REVIEW." Unfortunately there was no Sydney Smith to give us graphically the history of this publication, as of its more distinguished and prosperous successor, which appeared under the same name just half a century later. Whether the projectors had any private bond of their association, such as—

"———tenui musam meditamur avena."[1]

and whether they tried to find a public motto from some ancient author whom they had never read,—will for ever remain unknown to the world.[2] All that is certain is, that some of the most eminent members of the "Select Society" resolved, in the beginning of 1755, to establish a Review on a new plan, to be published half-yearly, to contain criticism, chiefly upon works printed in Scotland, but with notices of others printed in England and on the Continent; the analyses of the works criticised and the dissertations to be introduced to be of a profounder and bolder character than those which appeared in the monthly publications, to which reviewing in England had been confined. Wedderburn was the editor. Thus was the first number entitled,—

"The
Edinburgh Review,
Numb 1.
[To be published every six months].
Containing an account of all the BOOKS AND PAMPHLETS that have been published in Scotland from the 1st of January to the 1st of July, 1755.

To each Number will be added an APPENDIX, giving an account of the Books published in England and other countries, that are most worthy of notice."

The PREFACE was by Wedderburn, and as this is almost the only literary composition which can be distinctly traced to him, there may be a general desire to peruse it. I own it seems to me to be a very promising specimen of his powers, and it may raise regret that he afterwards abandoned authorship in quest of fame more fleeting, if more flattering:—

they avoid, for purity of accent to a Scotchman who continues domiciled in Scotland is utterly unattainable.

[1] "We cultivate literature upon a little oatmeal."
[2] The historiographer of the present Edinburgh Review says, "We took our present grave motto [Judex damnatur cum nocens absolvitur] from Publius Syrus, of whom none of us had, I am sure, ever read a single line" - *Preface to Sydney Smith's Works*

"The design of this work is to lay before the public, from time to time, a view of the progressive state of learning in this country. The great number of performances of this nature which, for almost a century past, have appeared in every part of Europe where knowledge is held in esteem, sufficiently proves that they have been found useful.

"Upon the first revival of letters in Europe their progress in Scotland was very rapid and very remarkable. The force of Buchanan's numbers, the elegance of his manner, and the undaunted spirit of liberty he breathes, entitle him to be named with the most chosen spirits of Leo X.'s age, and reflect a splendor upon the rise of science in the North. From such a beginning Scotland might well have flattered herself with hopes of attaining a distinguished rank in the literary world. But those happy prospects soon gave place to the melancholy scene of disorder and violence which civil dissensions produced. Letters could not be cultivated where humanity was neglected; the precepts of philosophy suited ill with the rage of party; nor could the arts of peace flourish in a country averse to industry and rent with divisions. Upon the accession of James VI. to the crown of England, the minds of men were entirely occupied with that event. The advancement of their own fortune became an object of attention to very many; whilst the general interest of their country was little regarded. The more unquiet it remained, the more influence would each individual share who had ambitious desires to gratify. Thus, unfortunately private interest was opposed to the public good, and the improvement of Scotland was not at that time an agreeable idea to England, jealous and disgusted with the preference shown by the monarch to particular Scotsmen.

"From this state of languor and retardation in every species of improvement Scotland soon passed through a series of more dreadful evils. The devastation of Charles I.'s reign and the slavery of Cromwell's usurpation were but ill repaired by the tyranny and oppression of Charles II.'s ministers and the arbitrary rule of James VII. Amidst all the gloom of those times there were still some men who kept alive the remains of science, and preserved the flame of genius from being altogether extinguished. At the Revolution, liberty was re-established and property rendered secure; the uncertainty and rigor of the law were corrected and softened; but the violence of parties were scarce abated, nor had industry yet taken place. What the Revolution had begun, the Union rendered more complete. The memory of our ancient state is not so much obliterated but that, by comparing the past with the present, we may clearly see the superior advantages we now enjoy, and readily discern from what source they flow. The communication of trade has awakened industry; the equal administration of laws produced good manners; and the watchful care of the government, seconded by the public spirit of some individuals, has excited, promoted and encouraged a disposition to every species of improvement in the minds of a people naturally active and intelligent. If countries have their ages with respect to moral advancement and decline, North Britain may be considered in a state of early youth, guarded and supported by the more mature strength of her kindred country. If in anything her advances have been such as to mark a more forward state, it is in science. The progress of knowledge depending more upon genius and application than upon any external circumstance, wherever these are not repressed they will exert themselves. The opportunities of education, and the ready means of acquiring knowledge in this country, with even a very moderate share of genius diffused through the nation, ought to make it distinguished for letters. Two considerable obstacles have long obstructed the progress of science. One is the difficulty of a proper expression of ideas in a country where there is either no standard of language, or, at least, one very remote. Some late instances, however, have discovered that this difficulty is not insurmountable; and that a serious endeavor to conquer it may acquire, to one born on the north side of the Tweed, a correct and even an elegant style. Another obstacle arose from the slow advances that the country had made in the art of printing; no literary improvement can be carried far where the means of communication are defective; but this obstacle has been of late entirely removed; and the reputation of the Scotch press is not confined to this country alone.

"It occurred to some gentlemen that at this period, when no very material difficulties remain to be conquered, a periodical view of the gradual advances of science would incite our youth to a more eager struggle to improve their minds, to gain distinction for themselves, and to do honor to their country. With this object the present work was undertaken,—in which it is proposed to *give a full account* of all books published in Scotland within the compass of half a year; and to take some notice of such books published elsewhere as are most read in this country, or seem to have any peculiar title to public attention.

"These are the motives and the plan of the present undertaking: the execution of it the public must judge of. Those who are concerned in carrying it on, hope, if the public should ever judge unfavorably of the execution, they will not condemn the attempt. One may judge of other men's writings with talents much inferior to those of the author; and to criticise is known to be easier than to compose. They are only to exercise over every book that right which the author confers upon the meanest of his readers; they are to judge with candor, but with freedom; opinions they are only to state, not to combat. Falsehood they will upon all occasions endeavor to detect; immoralities they would rather choose to bury in oblivion. Principles of irreligion or disaffection they will always strive to expose; as a zeal for the religion and constitution of their country can never be inconsistent with the greatest candor. It will always be more agreeable to them to find occasion for praise than for censure. But as their inclination leads them powerfully to indulge the one, their duty to the public will sometimes require them to exercise the less pleasing office. The authors expect no praise to themselves for a work in which to be useful is their only aim. In the conducting of it they hope they shall merit no personal blame. The success of the work they have earnestly at heart, as it may be attended with national benefit. To advance this end they will cheerfully accept the assistance of any gentleman who will contribute towards it by transmitting to the publisher his sentiments of any book;—or in general any literary memoirs, criticisms, or observations he would wish to communicate to the world."

Wedderburn contributed to the first number one short article on the "Rudiments of the Greek Tongue by Mr.

James Barclay, schoolmaster at Dalkeith," in which he took occasion to pay a tribute of respect and gratitude to his old preceptor: "A more plain and familiar Greek Grammar was certainly wanting. Mr. Barclay, to whose merit as a schoolmaster we are glad to bear testimony, has thought it his duty to endeavor to supply this want. It is his practice to teach his pupils Greek at a much earlier period than is usual in other places. The success of this method sufficiently appears in the progress several of his scholars have made, who frequently come from his school better Greek scholars than many of those who have been three years at an university." The more prominent articles on Scotch publications were written by Robertson, Blair and Jardine. The Appendix contained a criticism on Dr. Johnson's Dictionary, by Adam Smith, strikingly displaying the profound philosophical knowledge of the formation of language possessed by this philosopher.[1]

The first number of the EDINBURGH REVIEW, was well received, and in January, 1756, it was succeeded by a second, which had likewise an extensive sale. But, says Lord Kames, "the censure they most justly bestowed on some fanatical preachers excited such an outcry, that a regard to the public tranquillity, and their own, determined the Reviewers to discontinue their labors." I am rather at a loss to understand what articles are referred to; for all the discussions on theological subjects are conducted with such decency and propriety, that they could hardly have given offense to the most intolerant. Doubts are expressed in an article supposed, without any certain authority to have been written by Wedderburn, as to the expediency of the University having expelled, and the Presbytery excommunicated, the author of an infidel publication,—but in the following becoming terms, which might have been used by the most pious father of the Church: "We are almost ashamed to say we have read this pamphlet. 'Tis such a low, scurrilous libel, that even the most necessitous printer or bookseller must be at a

---

[1] There was a great mystery observed for a long time respecting the authorship of the different articles, and, indeed, with respect to all the names connected with the publication. For some reasons not explained, David Hume was not a contributor, and was not let into the secret.—*Lord Commissioner Adam's Journal.*

loss to find a decent excuse for publishing it. And, therefore, we hope our readers will excuse our giving any extract of such a thing as it is. We shall only add, that, in our opinion, both the University and Presbytery did wrong in taking so much notice of such a criminal; for it was impossible for them to inflict a more severe sentence than that to which he has brought himself, and from which 'tis not in their power to absolve him, viz., *Universal Contempt.*" From whatever cause, after the second number, the Review was abandoned, and, notwithstanding the extreme modesty of the preface, the authors were probably a good deal disappointed in their hopes of deriving from it both fame and emolument

Wedderburn's successes and reverses equally fostered in him a growing discontent with his own country. When he considered the *éclat* which he had acquired from his oratorical powers, he was impatient to display them on a wider stage. Again, while he was restrained by prudence from exceeding his narrow income, he had a passion for expense and magnificence which he could never hope to gratify from the scanty fees of the Parliament House. He likewise fostered a lofty ambition which would be by no means satisfied by his becoming, like his ancestors, a " Senator of the College of Justice at Edinburgh." Delighted to converse with Robertson, Hume, and Adam Smith, he was shocked by the prospect of spending his life among a people so bigoted and intolerant that they would not endure a publication undertaken to civilize and enlighten them, although it was conducted with perfect respect for religion, and with a laudable tenderness even for existing prejudices.

A melancholy event had dissolved the chief tie which attached him to his native country. On the 11th of August, 1756, his father died suddenly, when little turned of fifty, and with the prospect before him of long life. Next day appeared the following notice of this event in the "Caledonian Mercury," supposed to be a tribute to his memory, in the midst of deep grief, from a pious son :

" Yesterday morning, died here, Peter Wedderburn, Esq., of Chesterhall, one of the Senators of the College of Justice; a man of ability, of integrity and candor; whose disinterested benevolence and manly spirit was adorned rather than obscured by a remarkable degree of modesty. The universal and uncommon regret which his death has occasioned, proves, indeed, that true fame is the certain attendant of genuine worth; but also proves how seldom characters so truly excellent appear in the world. When he had reached a situation that rendered his services more conspicuous, and most extensively useful, he was removed from us by a death which seems untimely, on account of his early years, notwithstanding the public veneration for his virtues."

Wedderburn, however, still wanted courage to take the desperate leap which he had long meditated; and he went on prosecuting his profession in Scotland nearly a year after his father's death. He continued to be appointed a public examiner, an advocate for the poor, and a curator of the Faculty's Library. At the anniversary meeting of the curators, held on the 4th of January, 1757, "Mr. Alexander Wedderburn acquainted the Faculty that he had been authorized by David Hume, Esquire, to intimate to them his resignation of the office of their library keeper, and to assure them that he had, and would always retain, a due sense of the honor done him by the Faculty in conferring that office upon him; and being interrogated whether he had any commission to show from Mr. Hume for that purpose, answered that he had no commission in writing, which was thought not necessary, as Mr. Hume had this very day acquainted divers other members of the Faculty, of that matter. The Faculty were of opinion that Mr. Hume should direct a letter to the dean or vice-dean, signifying the same, under his hand."[1]

A letter was then written by Hume, containing a formal resignation of the office of librarian, which he had obtained with such difficulty, and which had been of such service to him in the composition of his History, but which he had for some time found irksome on account of disputes with some members of the Faculty in which it had involved him. The selection he made of an agent on this occasion shows the confidence he continued to repose in Wedderburn, as yet only in his 24th year.

But I suspect much that our advocate did not stand so high in the estimation of the W. S.'s and S. S. C.'s who had the distribution of briefs; and that, in spite of his

[1] See Buiton's Life of Hume.

solemn step and grave deportment, unless when he pleaded for some "Peter Planestanes," suing *in forma pauperis*, he was generally silent before the Lords Ordinary and the Inner House.

Nevertheless, he might have remained at the Scotch Bar, meditating his great scheme of southern conquest till revolving years rendered the attempt impossible, had it not been for a scene which took place in the Parliament House towards the end of the summer session of this year, and which fixed his destiny. The leader of the Bar at that time was Mr. Lockhart, afterwards Dean of Faculty and Lord Covington, a man of learning, but of a demeanor harsh and overbearing. It had ever been considered the duty of the chiefs of the body of advocates, to be particularly kind and protecting to beginners;[1] but Lockhart treated all who came in contact with him in a manner equally offensive, although he had been engaged in a personal altercation with a gentleman, out of court, who had threatened to inflict personal chastisement upon him; and there were some circumstances in his domestic life supposed to render his reputation vulnerable. At last four junior advocates, of whom Wedderburn was one, entered into a mutual engagement that he among them who first had the opportunity should resent the arrogance of the tyrant, and publicly insult him. It was by mere accident that the opportunity occurred to Wedderburn, who certainly made a good use of it.[2]

In the very end of July or beginning of August, 1757 (the exact day I have not been able to ascertain),[3] Wedderburn was opposed in the Inner House to Lockhart, and was called by him "a presumptuous boy," experienc-

---

[1] One of the most effectual interpositions in favor of a junior was by old John Clerk, afterwards Lord Eldon. A presumptuous youth, to whom he was opposed, and against whom the Court decided in a very peremptory manner, having declared that "he was much *astonished* at such a decision," there was a threat of committing him to the *tolbooth* for his *contempt*, when Clerk caused a universal laugh, in which the reverend sages of the law joined the loudest, by saying, "My Lords, if my young friend had known your Lordships as long as I have done, there is no decision of your Lordships which could have *astonished* him!!!"

[2] *Letter to me from the ex-Lord Justice General* HOPE —He adds, "I do not now recollect the names of all the young men, but the late Sir Wm. Pultney, then Mr. Johnstone, was one of them."

[3] I know that it must have been after the 26th of July, for on that day he was re-appointed by the Faculty one of the Advocates for the poor—and it must have been before the 10th of August, when the summer session ended.

ing from him even more than his wonted rudeness and superciliousness. When the presumptuous boy came to reply, he delivered such a furious personal invective as never was before or since heard at the Scottish Bar. A lively impression still remains of its character; but newspaper-reporting was then unknown in Edinburgh, and oral tradition has preserved only one sentence of that which probably was the meditated part of the harangue :—" The learned gentleman has confined himself on this occasion to vituperation; I do not say that he is capable of *reasoning*, but if *tears* would have answered his purpose I am sure tears would not have been wanting." Lockhart here started up and threatened him with vengeance. *Wedderburn:* " I care little, my Lords, for what may be said or done by a man who has been disgraced in his person and dishonored in his bed." Lord President Craigie, being afterwards asked why he had not sooner interfered, answered, " Because Wedderburn made all the flesh creep on my bones." But at last his Lordship declared in a firm tone, that " this was language unbecoming an advocate and unbecoming a gentleman." Wedderburn, now in a state of such excitement as to have lost all sense of decorum and propriety, exclaimed that "his lordship had said as a judge what he could not justify as a gentleman." The President appealed to his brethren as to what was fit to be done,—who unanimously resolved that Mr. Wedderburn should retract his words and make an humble apology, on pain of deprivation. All of a sudden, Wedderburn seemed to have subdued his passion, and put on an air of deliberate coolness,—when, instead of the expected retractation and apology, he stripped off his gown, and, holding it in his hands before the judges, he said, " My Lords, I neither *retract* nor *apologize*, but I will save you the trouble of *deprivation;* there is my gown, and I will never wear it more;—*virtute me involvo.*" He then coolly laid his gown upon the bar, made a low bow to the judges, and, before they had recovered from their amazement, he left the court, which he never again entered.

That very night he set off to London. I know not whether he had any apprehension of the steps which the judges might have taken to vindicate their dignity, or whether he was ashamed to meet his friends of the Parliament House; but he had formed a resolution, which he faithfully kept, to abandon his native country, and never more to revisit it.'

That I may conclude all that I have to say of him connected with Scotland, I may here notice that on the anniversary meeting of the Faculty, on the 3rd of Jan. 1758. "It being represented that Mr. Alexander Wedderburn, a curator of the library, was now residing in London, and therefore that it would be proper to name some person in his room, the Faculty deferred to appoint a successor to him, until they should understand from himself whether he intended to return soon to this country, and appointed that Mr. Andrew Pringle, His Majesty's solicitor, the now senior curator, should write to Mr. Wedderburn for information on that matter." I suspect that no answer was returned; and that nevertheless a year of grace was allowed him; for, under date Jan. 2, 1759, there is the following entry in the minutes of the Faculty· "Mr. Alexander Wedderburn, one of the curators of the library, being now resident in London, and unable to attend to the duties of this office, Mr. Adam Fergusson is substituted in his room."

My own opinion is, that Wedderburn's exit from the Parliament House was unpremeditated. Many suppose, however, that it was contrived to give greater *éclat* to his change of destination. Lord Commissioner Adam says, "He always intended to quit Scotland, and pursue the profession in England; and he is believed to have taken that opportunity of showing his determination by stripping his gown from his shoulders and laying it on the bar." He himself was conscious that his conduct was wholly unjustifiable as regarded Lockhart, and still more as regarded the Lord President Craigie. "I lived," adds the Lord Commissioner, "in great intimacy with Lord Loughborough for very many years, and he never came upon this part of his life in Scotland. Mr. Lockhart's eldest son, a very sensible man, who was at the English Bar, re-

---

[1] Lockhart was afterwards, at the age of seventy-five, promoted to the Bench, and (as it is said) on the recommendation of Lord Loughborough He was a very useful Judge for some years. It is also said that Lord Loughborough gave a gown to Lord Polkemmet as a compensation for having given him bad advice to try a cause, and appeal it to the House of Lords Baillie v. Tennant, 17th June, 1766—Morrison, 1491. This was more questionable both in principle and in result.

ceived great attention from his lordship; and it always struck me that he had particular pleasure, from his natural kindness of disposition, in making amends for any wrong that had been done to the father."

CHAPTER CLXIV.

CONTINUATION OF THE LIFE OF LORD LOUGHBOROUGH TILL HE BECAME A PATRIOT.

TRAVELING by a heavy stage coach which carried six inside passengers—the swiftest public conveyance then known between the two capitals of Britain—Wedderburn reached his destination early in the morning of the sixth day after his departure from Edinburgh.[1] We are left to conjecture what his feelings were as the clumsy vehicle rattled down the High Street, whose lofty houses he was to behold no more—as he caught the last glimpse of Arthur's Seat, from which he had so often admired the beautiful environs of his "own romantic town"—as he crossed the bridge over the Tweed, and recollected that, however he might fare in his great adventure, there was no retreat for him—as, in the gray light of the last dawn that was to break upon him in his fatiguing journey, he descried from Highgate the towers of Westminster Abbey, near which was the scene of all his hopes and fears. He had given orders for his books to follow him by a Leith trader, and his wardrobe accompanied him in his portmanteau. These constituted the great bulk of his wealth, for his father had left Chesterhall burdened by debt to the full amount of its value, and his scanty earnings at the Scotch Bar had been insufficient to maintain him without the assistance of his family. But he brought with him not only brilliant talents and

---

[1] When I first reached London, I performed the same journey in three nights and two days, Mr Palmer's mail-coaches being then established, but this swift traveling was considered dangerous as well as wonderful,—and I was gravely advised to stop a day at York, "as several passengers who had gone through without stopping, had died of apoplexy from the rapidity of the motion" The whole distance can now be accomplished with ease and safety in twelve hours, and intelligence may be communicated from the one capital to the other in as many seconds.

varied accomplishments, but an unconquerable resolution to justify to his friends and to the world the hazardous step which he was taking. He had screwed his courage to the sticking-place, and he could not fail.

He was set down at the Bull and Mouth Inn, behind St. Paul's, and he remained quartered there for a few days, till he was lucky enough to be able to hire on moderate terms a small set of chambers in the Temple. The City was in the noisy bustle by which it is characterized at all seasons of the year; but beyond Charing Cross he found shutters all closed, and grass beginning to grow in the streets. However, he little regretted the absence of gay company, for he was eager to devote himself day and night to the preparation for his call to the English Bar. Dr. Clephane was in town, and received him kindly; but he now seldom indulged in a visit to the old physician, who, although of a highly cultivated understanding and agreeable manners, had been born in the county of Fife, and spoke in a Scottish dialect peculiarly broad and drawling. Wedderburn's desire to purify his own accent had grown into a passion, and for this purpose there was no exertion or privation to which he was not willing to submit. Scotchmen he long avoided, as if he had been afraid of some contagious disease by shaking hands with them.

To his great delight he found that Sheridan, in whose *tùm-tī-tùm* he still placed entire confidence, was in London, negotiating an engagement on the stage, and superintending the publication of his "Lectures on Elocution." The old gentleman was much flattered by the homage he received from the Scotch advocate, whom he had seen holding such a high position at Edinburgh,— and, in consideration of this rather than of the pecuniary compensation offered to him, agreed to take him as a pupil, and to give up to him the greatest portion of his time. Sheridan came daily to the Temple at an early hour in the morning, and, with a short interval for breakfast, they continued talking, reading, reciting, and declaiming together during the greater part of the day. It being now the depth of the long vacation, they were in little danger of disturbing any student by their loudest tones. In the evenings, when left alone, Wedderburn would open Blackstone and Lord Coke; but such studies excited little interest comparatively in his mind; and when he sunk to sleep, instead of arguing in his dreams a case before Lord Mansfield on a contigent remainder, he conceived himself repeating Antony's speech over the dead body of Cæsar, under the correction of his master,—or actually making an attack on a public delinquent, in the House of Commons, amidst the cheers of his audience. He never had the advantage of being pupil with a conveyancer, special pleader, or equity draughtsman. He would have been pleased to attend a course of lectures on the municipal law of England, but none were delivered.

In the middle of October, Sheridan was obliged to go over to Ireland on some theatrical business, and his place was supplied by Macklin. This great actor and dramatist had not yet distinguished himself by his abuse of the Scottish nation, and he professed himself much taken by the sprightly manners and conversation of Wedderburn, to whom he had been introduced by Smollett. He was too much occupied to devote so much time to him as Sheridan had done; but he was more useful in modeling cadences, and regulating action. Under these two instructors Wedderburn continued to practice alternately, and sometimes under both on the same day, for many months,—till by degrees a great change was worked upon his accent and delivery.

Mr. Croker, in his edition of Boswell, naturally enough observes; "This is an odd coincidence. A Scotchman who wishes to learn a pure English pronunciation employs one preceptor who happens to be an Irishman, and afterwards another, likewise an Irishman; and this Irish-taught Scot becomes (and mainly by his oratory) one of the chief ornaments of the English senate, and the first subject in the British empire." It is very doubtful whether Garrick or Kemble would have succeeded better than the two Hibernians.—We must likewise recollect that they introduced their pupil to their histrionic associates, and that he became a frequenter of the Green Room, where he could advantageously practice some of the rules they had laid down for him. Through these means the effect of Wedderburn's eloquence ceased to be at all impared by pronunciation; and his vicious manner became polished and impressive. But still there never flowed from him a natural stream of eloquence; he always seemed studying how he could give most effect to his expressions, and, unless when he was occasionally impassioned, his manner was precise and affected. When his transformation was at all events gratifying to his vanity, there may be some doubt how far it was the foundation, as is generally supposed, of his good fortune; for his old schoolfellow Harry Dundas, who took no thought about such things, and ever continued to talk as broad Scotch as when they were under the discipline of Mr. Barclay at Dalkeith, was listened to with equal favor in the House of Commons, and enjoyed more power and influence in the State—-having been for many years king of Scotland, and having guided with the younger Pitt the destinies of the empire.[1]

It is said that in the decline of life Wedderburn's Scotticisms and venacular tones returned, showing that all the while his "English" was the effect of constant effort, which could not continue when his attention was relaxed, and his powers were enfeebled.[2]

He had only one additional term to keep, to complete his curriculum of English juridical study; and having eaten five more dinners in the Hall,—on the 25th of November, 1757, he was called to the English Bar. Next day he put on his bombazine gown, his cambric band, and his well-powdered wig, and took the oaths of allegiance, supremacy, and abjuration, in the Court of King's Bench.

[1] The following is Boswell's estimate upon this subject: "Mr. Macklin indeed shared with Mr. Sheridan the honor of instructing Mr. Wedderburn; and though it was too late in life for a Caledonian to acquire the genuine English cadence, yet so successful were Mr. Wedderburn's instructors and his own unabating endeavors, that he got rid of the coarse part of his Scotch accent, retaining only as much of the 'native wood-note wild' as to mark his country, which if any Scotchman should affect to forget, I should heartilly despise him. Notwithstanding the difficulties which are to be encountered by those who have not had the advantage of an English education, he by degrees formed a mode of speaking to which Englishmen do not deny the praise of elegance. Hence his distinguished oratory, which he exerted in his own country as an advocate in the Court of Session and a ruling Elder of the *Kirk*, has had its fame and ample reward in much higher spheres. When I look back on this noble person at Edinburgh, in situations so unworthy of his brilliant powers, and behold Lord Loughborough at London, the change seems almost like one of the metamorphoses in Ovid. and as his two preceptors, by refining his utterance, gave currency to his talents, we may say in the words of that poet, '*Nam vos mutastis.*'"—1 *Boswell*, p. 365.

[2] Lord Brougham's "Statesmen," vol. 1. p. 72.
[3] Books of Inner Temple.

It is difficult to conjecture by what process he expected to get forward in the profession, and he probably trusted a good deal to fortune and accident. The system of periodical publication of law reports had not then begun, and the composition of law books by young men as a proof of proficiency, was not thought of. Quarter Sessions were rarely attended by barristers; and Wedderburn had so little interest in any part of England, that, out of economy, he resolved not to go any circuit. Lord Mansfield, his countryman, to whom he had been introduced, favored only Westminster and Christchurch men, and he had not slightest acquaintance with any other Judge on the Bench. To all English attorneys and solicitors he was wholly unknown, and he by no means possessed the acquaintance with practice and pleading which might induce them in their difficulties to resort to a stranger. He expected some encouragement from the Scotch agents before the House of Lords for retainers in Scotch appeals, and he had an extensive Scotch connection in London, from which briefs might be expected. His sister had married Sir Harry Erskine, an intimate friend of Lord Bute; there was hardly any prosperous Scotchman in London whom he could not influence, and being the only Scotchman at the English Bar, if he could once show that he was likely to rise, he had good hopes from the nationality of his countrymen.

He was regular in his attendance in the Court of King's Bench in the morning, but did not shut himself up in chambers in the evening. He went a good deal into society, and was frequently to be seen at the theater. But in reality he was more actuated by a love of business than by a love of pleasure. Circumstanced as he was,

" To shun delights, and live laborious days."

did not seem to be the discreet course. He was to make friends who were to push him on. His system was to recommend himself rather by being a good listener than a great talker. We have the following picture of his modest demeanor in company at this time in the Autobiography of Richard Cumberland :—

" The play of the 'Wishes,' under the auspices of Lord Bute, was pr vately rehearsed at Lord Melcombe's villa of La Trappe. It was a beautiful summer evening when it was recited on the banks of the Thames by O'Brien, Miss Elliott, Mrs. Haughton, and some few others, under the management of Foote and Murphy, who attended on the occasion. At this rehearsal there was present a youth, unknown to fame, who was understood to be protected by Lord Bute, and came thither in a hackney coach with Mrs. Haughton. This gentleman was of the party at the supper with which the entertainment concluded; he modestly resigned the conversation to those who were more disposed to carry it on, while it was only in the contemplation of an intelligent countenance that we could form any conjecture as to that extraordinary gift of genius which, in course of time, advanced him to the great seal of the kingdom and the earldom of Roslyn."

To strengthen himself Wedderburn now established a club somewhat on the plan of the " Poker." This at first consisted of the most distinguished Scotsmen then residing in London,—Smollett, Armstrong, Pitcairn, William Hunter, John Home (now wearing a brown coat), Sir Gilbert Elliott, Mr. Robert Adam, the architect, and Sir Harry Erskine. They met at the " British Coffee House," in Cockspur Street, ever a favorite Scottish haunt, and then kept by a very clever lady, Mrs. Anderson, sister of Douglas, Bishop of Salisbury. Garrick, and several celebrated Englishmen, were afterwards admitted. They all felt a lively interest in the progress of "brother Wedderburn," and looked out for opportunities to recommend him to a brief. When the occasion required, he was capable of the most intense application, and he could submit to any sacrifice. He was ever cautious to avoid the example of Murphy, and other legal friends, who, by a love of literature and the drama, had been led astray from their professional career. He had little respect for authorship, and he would sooner have been Lord Hardwicke than Shakespeare.

About the means he used to procure employment, he seem to have been by no means over-delicate. His countryman, Strahan, the printer, now rode in a coach, and had much to say with the City attorneys. Wedderburn, without scruple, applied to him for his interest to get briefs in causes at Guildhall,—and with some effect. Strahan having afterwards mentioned this circumstance in the presence of Dr. Johnson and Boswell, the question was discussed, "how far it is allowable for a barrister to canvass for business." Johnson rather defended the practice, saying, "I should not solicit employment as a lawyer,—not because I should think it wrong, but because I should disdain it."

Professional etiquette has been carried to a ridiculous extent,—as in forbidding a barrister on the circuit to dine with an attorney, or to dance with an attorney's daughter —whereas the attorney is often a gentleman as well born, as well educated, and as well mannered as the barrister. But the respectability of our order,—consequently, the public good,—peremptorily requires that all solicitation of business by barristers should be forbidden, and that all indirect means to obtain it should be considered discreditable. There is a useful *surveillance* exercised on the circuits by means of the GRAND COURT, whereby such practices are repressed; and it would be highly beneficial if we had in London a DEAN OF FACULTY, with a council, to lay down and enforce salutary rules of discipline for preventing or punishing irregularities among members of the Bar, that merit may enjoy its fair chance of success.

Wedderburn, notwithstanding all his good and evil arts, never seems to have had a regular set of clients, or a steady flow of business while he remained in a stuff gown. He was employed at intervals, in cases in which a "splash" was to be made,—particularly where actors and authors were the parties. Newspapers began occasionally to notice trials of public interest, although there were no daily reports of "Law proceedings," and Wedderburn's name appeared more frequently in print than that of others who, in truth, were going on much more steadily and successfully. Doctor Robertson, misled by this circumstance, in a visit he made to London in 1759, wrote as follows to his friend, Dr. Jardine :—"Wedderburn makes all the progress we could wish: even the doorkeeper of the House of Peers tells me 'he is a d——d clever fellow, and speaks devilish good English.' This very morning he was retained in a Plantation cause, before the Privy Council, which is a thing altogether extraordinary for so young a man. You can not imagine what odd fellows his rivals are, and how far, and how fast, he is likely to go."

But Wedderburn's fee-book did not present a flattering result; there was little chance of his getting on at the Bar by rising professional reputation, and he concluded that it was only through politics that he could hope for legal preferment. For the first three years of his residence in England, party struggles had entirely ceased,—there was hardly a division in either House of Parliament in a whole session,—and it seemed as if never again would there be any scope for adventure in courtiership or patriotism. To our keen-eyed Scotchman, however, "coming events cast their shadows before." George II., though in good health, had reached a great age. Lord Bute, on very intimate terms with the Princess Dowager of Wales, was supposed to enjoy a great influence over the heir-apparent to the throne, and had instilled into his mind principles of government which, when acted upon, were sure to bring about a complete change in the aspect of public affairs. The embryo minister had been a member of the "Select Society" at Edinburgh, and had taken much notice of our *débutant* from the time when he was called to the English Bar, not only introducing him into fashionable London Society but confidentially conversing with him respecting the plans and prospects of Leicester House.

On the 25th of October, 1760, it was announced that the old King was no more, and a sudden joy was infused into the minds of all those who had looked forward with impatience to a new reign. The multitude believed that there would be no change in the public councils, and that Pitt, who had so raised the national glory, might continue to hold the reins of government as long as Sir Robert Walpole; but the initiated knew that a scheme had been laid to break down the Whig aristocracy, which for half a century had monopolized all the favors of the crown; to encourage the doctrine of divine hereditary right, and to rule on the genuine Church-and-King maxims which had been thought incompatible with the title of the Hanoverian dynasty.

The favorite's dependents enjoyed the satisfaction of seeing him first sworn a privy councillor, then made secretary of state, and, finally, placed at the head of the Treasury, and declared prime minister. Neither upon the present nor any subsequent turn of his fortune was

Wedderburn at all troubled by political qualms,—and with an unclouded mind he only considered what course was most for his own advantage. He belonged to a Whig race, and he would never in his own country join any of the clubs who, on their knees, drank to "the King over the water,"—although a majority of the advocates retained the same Jacobitical opinions which animated them when they so graciously received the medal from the Duchess of Gordon, with the motto "Suum cuique tribuito." He was now willing to think that not only was it improper to exclude one great party in the state from the participation of power and patronage, but that the right of the people to interfere in the affairs of government had been pushed to an inconvenient length from the necessity of guarding against a Popish ruler,—and that when Protestantism was at last secure under a monarch who wished to show himself truly the "Defender of the Faith" by refusing civil privileges to all who did not belong to the established religion of the country, the time was come when popular licentiousness might be repressed, and the people, ever incapable of governing themselves, might be governed by that prerogative which, for their benefit, God had bestowed upon his vicegerent the King. He therefore professed himself a warm partisan of Lord Bute, and by his influence was returned to the House of Commons for the Rothsay and Inverary district of Scotch burghs.[1]

From the very defective account we have of parliamentary proceedings at this period, we are left in almost entire ignorance of Wedderburn's early parliamentary career. We know that he was a steady voter, and a frequent speaker, in support of Lord Bute while that minister remained in office and as long as there was any chance of his return to power.[2] He braved all the fury of the storm which burst out against his nation, and joined in

[1] Journals, 12th Parliament of Great Britain.
[2] The only information I can find of any particular debate in which he took part, is in a letter signed Clio, published in the Morning Post, in the year 1775. "He once entered the lists with Mr Pitt, under Lord Bute's administration, upon the subject of general warrants, by producing one of that Minister's for seizing a ship. Wedderburn asked with great triumph if martial law existed on the river? Pitt, amidst a blaze of indignant eloquence, asked, if the great Statute of Treasons there existed? defended himself with becoming spirit and ran down the Scotchman beyond the possibility of a reply."

the resolution "that the North Briton, No. 45, should be burned by the hands of the common hangman." He had the mortification to see his friend and preceptor Macklin pandering to the bad passions of the English mob by bringing Sir Archy Macsarcasm and Sir Pertinax Macsycophant on the stage, with some touches of character which he was supposed to have taken from Wedderburn himself. It is said that Wedderburn tried to retaliate in the periodical publications of the day, and that he was particularly severe in exposing the irregularities of the profligate Churchill, who, in his " Prophecy of Famine," had with great felicity ridiculed the pride and poverty of the Scotch ;[1] but I have been unable to learn any particulars of this warfare which he carried on, to justify the national motto—" Nemo me impune lacessit."[2]

There seems much probability in the story of his personal quarrel with Churchill, from the savage manner in which he is assailed in the " Rosciad:"

> " Roscius deceased, each high aspiring player
> Push'd all his interest for the vacant chair."

Wedderburn is introduced to us as counsel for Murphy:

> " To mischief trained, e'en from his mother's womb,
> Grown old in fraud, though yet in manhood's bloom,
> Adopting arts by which gay villains rise
> And reach the heights which honest men despise,
> Mute at the bar, and in the senate loud,
> Dull 'mongst the dullest, proudest of the proud,
> A pert prim prater of the Northern race,
> Guilt in his heart, and famine in his face,
> Stood forth ; and thrice he waved his lily hand,
> And thrice he twirl'd his tye—thrice s'roked his band ;—

---

[1] I know few finer efforts of *imagination* than his description of Scotland in the " Prophecy of Famine," beginning—
> " Far as the eye could reach no tree was seen,
> Earth clad in russet, scorn'd the lively green;
> No living thing whate'er, its food, feasts there,
> But the Cameleon who can feast on air ;
> No birds, except as birds of passage, flew,
> No bee was known to hum, no dove to coo."

[2] Generally speaking, the Scotch in London at this time as little resented as provoked the persecution excited against them. The state of the public mind is described in a lively manner by Hume, in a letter to Robertson, dated 14th January, 1765. " The rage and prejudice of parties frighten me; and above all, this rage against the Scots, which is so dishonorable, and, indeed, so infamous to the English nation. We hear that it increases every day, without the least appearance of provocation on our part. It has frequently made me resolve never in my life to set foot on English ground "

'At friendship's call' (thus oft with trait'rous aim,
Men void of faith, usurp faith's sacred name)
'At Friendship's call I come, by Murphy sent,
Who thus by me develops his intent'"

Meanwhile Wedderburn reaped the first reward of his party zeal by obtaining a silk gown—then a high distinction. He immediately communicated the good news to his mother at Edinburgh in the following letter, which shows the great difficulty he had to give the old lady a notion of the nature of his new office :—

"Lincoln's Inn, Feby. 18th, 1763 [1]

"DEAR MAMMA,

"You will not be sorry to hear that I have kissed his Majesty's hand for a preferment which the newspapers had bestowed on me long ago. It is an honor which may be of considerable service to me hereafter, though attended with no present profit. But it is what I wished for extremely, and I feel myself under the highest obligations to the Chancellor for this instance of his protection and goodness to me.

"I can't very well explain to you the nature of my preferment, but it is what most people at the bar are very desirous of, and yet most people run a hazard of losing money by it. I can scarcely expect any advantage from it for some time equal to what I give up,—and, notwithstanding, I am extremely happy, and esteem myself very fortunate in having obtained it.

"I am sure it will give great pleasure to my aunt and you, to know of my having met with any good fortune—and I er'er am,

"Your dutiful and affection son,
"AL. WEDDERBURN."

I now reach a passage of his history which shocks us lawyers excessively, although its enormity may not be so palpable to the "*lay gents*,"—the uninitiated. He had never yet gone any circuit, and no rule can be better established among us than that a barrister is not for the first time to join a circuit, having already acquired a great professional reputation whereby he may at once step into full business, and suddenly disturb vested rights. For

[1] He had some time before transferred himself to Lincoln's Inn, for the convenience of occupying chambers there, and he was at this time elected a Bencher of that Society.   [2] Ross MSS

this reason a barrister may only change his circuit once, and this must be done (if at all) while he is still " clothed in stuff." The penalty for the transgression of such a rule is, that the offender is excluded from the Bar-mess on the circuit ; and, although, he can not be prevented from appearing in Court and pleading a cause for any client who may employ him, no other barrister will hold a brief with him, and he is " sent to Coventry."

The spirit, if not the letter, of this law was now flagrantly broken by Wedderburn. Sir Fletcher Norton, long " the cock of the walk," had just left the Northern Circuit on being made Attorney General, and had given up an immense quantity of business to be struggled for. There were various speculations as to the manner in which it would be distributed among his juniors, who had long been impatient for his death or promotion—when the incredible report was spread, that Mr. Wedderburn with his new silk gown meant to join the Northern Circuit, in the hope of stepping into the lead. This was not believed till he actually made his appearance at York. The horror of the barristers was then much enhanced by the intelligence, that he was attended, as clerk, by the clerk of Sir Fletcher Norton, well acquainted with every attorney north of Trent. He did not boldly set professional etiquette entirely at defiance, but in vain tried to justify himself by contending " that never yet having gone any circuit, he could not be within the regulation against changing circuits—that every man called to the Bar had a free right to choose a circuit—and that no attempt had ever before been made to limit the time within which the choice must be exercised." An extraordinary meeting of the Northern Circuit Bar was immediately called, when it was moved, that no member of it should hold a brief with the interloper. If this had been carried unanimously, he must have packed up his wig and his silk gown and instantly returned to London. He was saved by there being one dissentient, although one only. This was Wallace, afterwards Attorney General—then a hard-headed special pleader—who pretended to take the liberal side of the question, but was suspected of being sordidly actuated by a desire to promote his own interest—anticipating that Wedderburn's reputation must bring him briefs, and that he himself would always be retained as his junior.[1] The new silk gown was accordingly tried in several important causes, but though he could make an excedingly good statement of the facts of the case, he was defective, from inexperience, in the examination of witnesses—on which the verdict often depends, much more than on the figures of rhetoric,—and, notwithstanding the cramming he underwent at consultation, he was evidently distressed when an important point of law unexpectedly arose during the trial. There was too much foundation for Jack Lee's saying, circulated with much complacency—that "what little law Wedderburn took in at York had run through him before he got to Newcastle." In short, this bold maneuver proved a failure, and after one or two years he gave up the circuit, under the pretense that it interfered with his business in London; although Scott, afterwards Lord Eldon, and other Equity practitioners, continued long after to attend the assizes.

In the Court of Chancery, nevertheless, Wedderburn now took root and flourished. Here he was much more at home than in conducting *nisi prius* causes; the forms of proceeding were more analogous to those he had been accustomed to in Scotland, where facts were decided by the judges on written depositions,—and his superior knowledge of the civil law sometimes gave him a formidable advantage over his rivals.

He still continued, occasionally, to frequent the theater, and to mix with authors and actors in the Green Room; and he kept up a close correspondence with his absent literary friends. The following epistle, which is addressed to him by David Hume, gives a very interesting view of French manners, and of the intoxicating effect upon the philosopher of the incense offered up to him by the Parisians:—

"MY DEAR SIR,

"I believe I shall write you a very short letter, and yet have a great deal to say. I have not absolutely leisure

---

[1] Wedderburn himself told Lord Haddington that, finding the opposition made to him on the Northern Circuit, "he challenged two of the senior counsel, and there was an end of it." but I do not find any other account of these challenges From the records of the Grand Court of the Northern Circuit which I have since had an opportunity of inspecting, it appears that Wedderburn, although at first so roughly received, afterwards had ingratiated himself with his brother circuiteers, and joined them in all their revelry.

to look about me; what between business and company, what between receiving and returning civilities, between the commerce of the great and the learned, it is scarce possible for me to think of an absent friend." . . . .

[After enumerating some books he had purchased for Mr. W. and forwarded to London, he proceeds.]

"I reconcile myself daily to this course of life, and nothing leads more to familiarize me to a scene so different from that to which I had so long been accustomed, than the amiable manners and the cordial friendship of the family with whom I live. I find, likewise, the use of the French tongue gradually returns to me, though I am still somewhat awkward in returning a compliment. The scene which passed to-day really pleased without embarrassing me. I attended Lord Hertford to Versailles in order to be presented to the Dauphiness and the young Princes, the only part of the royal family whom we had not yet seen. When I was presented to the Duc de Berry, a child of ten years of age, he said to me, 'Monsieur, vous avez beaucoup de réputation dans ce pays-ci; votre nom m'est très-bien connu; et c'est avec beaucoup de plaisir que je vous vois." Immediately upon which his brother the Comte de Provence, who is two years younger, advanced to me and said, with great presence of mind, 'Monsieur, il y a longtemps que vous etes attendu dans ce pays-ci avec beaucoup d'impatience; je compte avoir bien du plaisir quand je pourrai lire votre belle histoire.' But what is more remarkable, when we were carry'd to make our bows to the Comte d'Artois, who is about five years of age, and to a young Madame of between two and three, the infant Prince likewise advanced to me in order to make his harangue, in which, though it was not very distinct, I heard him mumble the word *Histoire*, and some other terms of panegyric. With him ended the civilities of the royal family of France towards me; and I may say it did not end till their power of speech failed them; for the Princess was too young to be able to articulate a compliment. You may see, by this instance alone, what you could not fail to remark in many other instances, how much greater honor is paid to Letters in France than in England. I do not mean with regard to me alone, whom some factious barbarians, under the appellation of Whigs, are fond to decry; but with regard to every other person. And the effects are visible by the different state of Letters in the two countries.

"I am, dear Wedderburn,
"Your's sincerely,
"DAVID HUME.
"Paris, 23rd Nov., 1763.

"P. S. I daily reconcile myself more to this place, and expect soon to be a Parisian. I have so often changed my places of abode, that I am come to think that, as far as regards happiness, there is no great difference among them. But yet, if there is a preference to be given, this city seems entitled to it."[1]

Notwithstanding Wedderburn's success as an Equity counsel, he looked to politics as his main stay; and, strange to relate—incredible it must long have appeared to his old associates, and particularly to David Hume, who, was talking with such bitter contempt of the Whigs—he now became a flaming patriot. He perceived the imbecility and caducity of the several administrations which followed the downfall of Lord Bute, and, instead of attaching himself to any of them, he thought it better policy to go into hot opposition—to censure the measures which were taken respecting the taxation of America, and to insist that the constitution was violated by the persecution of Wilkes,—all whose abuse of Scotland and Scotsmen he now charitably forgave. Still his policy was only "*reculer pour mieux sauter.*" When George Grenville had quarreled with the Court, Wedderburn at times affected to consider him as his leader, and he occasionally coquetted with Lord Chatham; but he evidently looked all along to a reconciliation with the "King's friends" on the first favorable opportunity; his present patriotism was, by showing his consequence, to raise his price, and he cautiously abstained from entering into any party engagement which might embarrass him, or expose him to the charge of private treachery, when the fit moment for his going over should arrive.[2]

[1] Rossl MSS.
[2] We shall never know the steps by which from being an Ultra-Tory he became a "Whig and something more." Parliamentary reporting had ceased, or rather had been suppressed, at this time, and we know nothing of parliamentary proceedings except from private letters In a letter from Mr. Cooke to Lord Chatham, dated 17th Dec. 1765, giving an account of a de-

As is usually the case, his reputation as a debater rose very much when, instead of speaking or being silent according to the orders of a leader, and if called upon to defend and abuse, he could only urge the topics prescribed to him, he was at liberty to assail the government when and how he chose. The *éclat* he acquired in St. Stephen's operated very beneficially on his Bar practice. Though opposed to such a formidable rival as Thurlow, he had a considerable ascendency in the Court of Chancery: he was employed in almost every Scotch appeal at the bar of the House of Lords, and he was the decided favorite at the Cockpit. He was counsel for the respondent in the famous Douglas cause, which was admirably adapted to his peculiar powers. Accordingly he here outshone all his competitors. Charles Fox often declared that "Wedderburn's speech on this occasion was the very best he ever heard on any subject;" and Horace Walpole, in his Memoirs of the Reign of George III., says, "Mr. Alexander Wedderburn (for the Hamiltons) spoke with greater applause than was almost ever known."[1] But not a scrap of his speech is extant, and we read of it as of a great performance by Garrick on the stage, remembered only by the admiration which it excited. The judgment of the House of Lords, it is well known, was against him—the decree of the Court of Session declaring the claimant to be spurious being reversed—with some strong observations from law lords on the conduct of Andrew Stuart, the agent for the Duke of Hamilton, the respondent. There is preserved to us a letter to this gentleman, from Wedderburn, very creditable to the writer, as it shows more heartiness and disregard of giving offense to those who might injure him, than he usually indulged in:—

"MY DEAR STUART,

'I have read over the newspaper account of the Chancellor's[2] speech in the Douglas cause, which, in my opinion, he has more reason to be offended with than you have. It is the publication of one who had only capacity enough to retain those parts of the speech which I am persuaded the Chancellor would wish to be least remem-

bate on the right to tax America, the writer says,—"Mr. Wedderburn acted like a true Scotchman," which, in the language of that day, meant *most basely;* and it would appear that even then he had hopes of pleasing the Court by subserviency. He was still member for Rothsay.

[1] P. 302.   [2] Lord Camden.

bered.[1] Nothing ever was worse founded than any aspersions upon your conduct in that cause, which in its whole progress was carried on, not only with the strictest probity on your part, but with a candor and delicacy that very few men would have thought themselves bound to observe. I have more than once thought, in the course of the inquiry, that you acted with too nice a sense of honor in a contention with people who made no scruple to take every advantage, though I respected the principle on which it proceeded. It was impossible you could escape abuse (let your conduct be ever so correct) at a time when, for much less interests, all characters are daily traduced, and personal invective is become a standing mode of argument. I am sorry, upon their own account, that it should be adopted by those who having felt what calumny is, should be cautious how they give a sanction to it. Upon your account I feel very little anxiety; because, besides the testimony of your own mind, you have the satisfaction to know that all those who have been eye-witnesses of your conduct, not only justify it, but applaud it; that of the many judicious people who have studied the cause, very few indeed join in the reflections upon you; and that even your adversaries do your conduct that justice in private, which in public they have sacrificed to the interests of their cause. They have succeeded, and the decision must compel your submission; but assent can only flow from conviction —and the opinion I had entertained of the cause is not altered by any reasoning I have heard upon it. My ideas of justice are a little perplexed by the decision; and I consider it as a striking example that no cause is certain or desperate. You will probably be gone from London before I return to it, and I could not help writing to you, as I shall not have an opportunity for some time of meeting you. Adieu, my dear Stuart, and believe me ever

" Yours most sincerely, " A. WEDDERBURN."[2]

[1] This is, no doubt, malice prepense; but I once heard a Puisne Judge say to Lord Chief Justice Tenterden, with great *naiveté*, " What nonsense the newspapers do make you talk!"

[2] There is a curious letter on the subject of the Douglas cause from David Hume to Dr. Blair—to be accounted for from the philosopher's friendship for Wedderburn and Stuart.—

His forensic reputation now repaid what it had borrowed from his parliamentary, and his weight in the House of Commons was much enhanced. He expected some tempting offer from the Court; but none being made, he resolved—keeping himself disentangled from any express party engagements—to go for a season into the hottest opposition.

CHAPTER CLXV.

CONTINUATION OF THE LIFE OF LORD LOUGHBOROUGH TILL HE WAS MADE SOLICITOR GENERAL.

SOON after came on the grand debate in the House of Commons on the resolutions for declaring Mr. Wilkes disqualified to be re-elected a member of the House of Commons in consequence of his expulsion, and for seating Luttrell as member for Middlesex, although he had only 296 votes against 1143. Wedderburn, taking the popular side, seems to have made an admirable speech. The "Parliamentary History" does not even notice his name as having spoken; but, according to Sir Henry Cavendish, he reasoned thus:—

'The question comes to this, was the person for whom the majority of electors voted, legally disqualified? He is, we are told, by a vote of this House. But has such a vote the force of law? that is the point. If it has not, it may control our own proceedings, but it will not have the effect that the votes given for Mr. Wilkes are thrown away. The position laid down is, that a vote of the

"28 March, 1769.
"I was struck with a very sensible indignation at the decision of the Douglas cause, though I foresaw it for some time. It was abominable with regard to poor Andrew Stuart, who had conducted that cause with singular ability and integrity, and was at last exposed to reproach, which unfortunately can never be wiped off. For the cause though not in the least intricate, is so complicated, that it never will be reverenced by the public, who are besides perfectly pleased with the sentence, being swayed by compassion and a few popular topics. To one who understands the cause as I do, nothing could appear more scandalous than the pleadings of the two law lords. Such gross misrepresentation, such impudent assertions, such groundless imputations, never came from that place. But all was good enough for their audience, who, bating their quality, are most of them little better than their brethren the Wilkites in the streets.

House of Commons is law. My learned friend says, that it imports a common-law disqualification. If it does, by the usage of parliament, as part of the common law, you can prove it to me; you can show me precedents, you can quote authorities, or succeed by deductions of reason; but in support of such a monstrous proposition we have had neither precedents, nor authorities, nor arguments."[1]

Earl Temple, in giving Lord Chatham a brief abstract of the debate, says, "Not a shadow of argument in favor of the disqualification! Wedderburn made a most excellent speech with us. It has cost his seat in Parliament, which he has this day vacated in consequence of Sir Lawrence Dundas's reproaches and desire, from what I think too generous a delicacy."[2]

Representing the close borough of Richmond, for which he had been returned by its owner, as a Tory, at the general election in April, 1768,—according to the notions which prevailed, and were almost invariably acted upon in the good old times, he would have incurred great disgrace if he had retained his seat. Next morning he applied for and obtained the Chiltern Hundreds.[3] Now he was looked upon as a martyr, although in reality not more of a Wilkite than Wilkes himself. A dinner was given to him at the Thatched House Tavern by the Opposition leaders, including George Grenville, Edmund Burke, Lord John Cavendish, Tommy Townshend, Lord Clive, Lord George Sackville, Sir George Savile, Alderman Beckford, and Colonel Barré. They drank his health with three times three, under the title of " THE STEWARD OF THE CHILTERN HUNDREDS;" and he made a very inflammatory reply, denouncing in no measured terms the usurpation of the rights of the people by their own representatives, and concluding with this oath of abjuration suitably taken by him on receiving an office from the Crown, for which he had vacated his seat : " I do from my soul denounce, detest and abjure as unconstitutional and illegal, that damnable doctrine and position, that a resolution of the House of Commons can make, alter and suspend, abrogate or annihilate the law of the land." Whereupon he kissed the bottle. Various other toasts were given to testify the attachment of the meet-

[1] Cavendish Deb., 1. 352.   [2] Chatham Correspondence.
[3] A new writ was moved for Richmond, 9th May, 1769. 32 Com. Jour. 452.

ing to the cause which Wedderburn had so nobly
defended; such as—"The rights of electors!" "The
law of the land!" "The immortal memory of Lord
Chief Justice Holt!"—all introduced by speeches eulo-
gizing the new patriot's exertions and his sacrifices.[1] It
is said that Wilkes himself became a little jealous of this
" North Briton;" for, though not much of a Wilkite, he
would not like to have been superseded as the most
notorious public man of the day. Wedderburn did begin
to agitate in good earnest; and, while he was out of
Parliament, went about making harangues, and supporting violent resolutions against the Government, particularly at a public meeting held in the city of York.[2]

The interval, however, was very short; and at the
commencement of the next session he again took his seat
in the House of Commons, having been returned for
Bishops Castle by Lord Clive,[3] who was thanked by
George Grenville and others, for this proof of his regard
for the Constitution.[4]

[1] Lord Temple giving an account of the dinner at the Thatched House
says.—" Everything passed most miraculously well, and the whole meeting
appeared to be like brothers united in one great constitutional cause."—*Chatham Correspondence.*

[2] " Mr. Wedderburn exerted himself as much in the defense of Mr Wilkes
as he ever did in his condemnation; and, at length, to convince such as
might not probably be persuaded that he was in earnest, he made a public
tour throughout the several ridings, towns, and districts in the extensive county
of York, to warn them of the dangers with which they and all the freeholders of
Great Britain were threatened on account of the late unconstitutional corrupt
decisions of the House of Commons in the affair of the Middlesex election.
He did not hesitate to reprobate in all its parts the Court system, and he pursued the same line of conduct uniformly until the death of Mr. Grenville "—
Public Characters, p. 68. " He subsequently supported the Administration
through thick and thin in every measure but on the motion for rescinding the
resolution on the Middlesex election—when he absented himself, or, as some
say, divided against the minister."—*Ib.* 72.

[3] "Westcombe, 10th May, 1769.

" SIR,—I am sorry that any personal or party motives should have deprived
you of that seat in parliament which you filled with so much honor and unbiassed ability; if another seat be acceptable I have one at your service, in
which you will at all times be at liberty to exert your talents upon your own
principles.—I am, with sentiments of the greatest esteem, Sir, your most
obedient humble servant, "CLIVE.

"To Alexr Wedderburn, Esq." *

[4] The following is a copy of George Grenville's letter to Lord Clive, thank-
ing him for offering to return Wedderburn for Bishop's Castle
" MY DEAR LORD, " Bolton Street, May 10, 1769.
" I have just this moment received the honor of your letter while Mr. Wed

* Rossl MSS.

Now came on one of the most tremendous party struggles recorded in our annals. Lord Chatham, whose public career was considered as having been terminated by the loss of his intellects, reappeared with all his pristine vigor, animated by the most furious rage against the disqualification of Wilkes; Lord Camden was deprived of the Great Seal for supporting him; and Charles Yorke was supposed to have laid violent hands upon himself three days after he was prevailed upon to receive it. Wedderburn must have cast a longing glance at the bauble, and, if it had been then offered to him, I am afraid he would not have rejected it, nor shown any remorse for his perfidy. But in the absence of an overture from the Court he deemed it his best course to continue to act with apparent zeal on the popular side.

Accordingly, in the Committee on "the State of the Nation," Mr. Dowdswell having moved a resolution (which he said he was to follow up by some others, to be afterwards stated), "That in matters of elections this House is bound to judge according to the law of the land;" and Lord North, after complaining that the other proposed resolutions were not brought forward at the same time, having moved that the motion be amended by adding these words, " and that the judgment of this House, declaring John Wilkes, Esquire, disqualified to sit in this present Parliament, was agreeable to the said law of the land, and fully authorized by the law and custom of Parliament,"—" Mr. Wedderburn observed, that Lord North, with respect to his motion, acted like an old woman, who being examined as a witness, and asked her name, said, ' she would not tell it till she knew what ques

---

derburn was with me, to whom I have executed your commission. He is extremely sensible of this great mark of your Lordship's esteem and regard and still more so of the honorable manner in which you have made the proposition for re-choosing him into parliament. . . . . If anything could give me a higher opinion of your character and conduct than that which I entertained before, it would be your behavior on this occasion."

Lord Temple, writing a few days after to his cousin, Lord Chatham say "A seat is already found and fixed for Wedderburn; but it is a great secret and more offers than one have been made to him. Beckford and Trecothic proposed to him the freedom of the city in a gold box, and Lord George Cavendish, at the dinner at the Thatched House Tavern, toasted ' The Steward of the Chiltern Hundreds.'"—*Chatham Correspondence.*

A vacancy was created in Bishops Castle by the retirement of his Lordship's cousin, William Clive. 32 Com. Journ. 457.—*Gentlemen's Magazine* vol. xl. p. 47.

tions were to follow;' he said he was glad the noble lord had nothing to object to the question, except that it was unnecessary ; but he hoped that objections of another kind against the amendment were so manifest, as that no gentleman would join him in voting for it." This is the whole report of a speech that lasted above two hours, and we are lucky in having a little inkling of the points which he made; for sometimes we have only such general notices as the following of his most brilliant efforts:—" Mr. Wedderburn was excessively great this evening ; " or, " The Solicitor General Wedderburn, in answer to Mr. Fox, defended the Administration in a fine vein of oratory." Lord North's amendment was carried by a majority of 224 to 180. At the risk of commitment to Newgate for breach of privilege, a list of the minority was printed and circulated, with Wedderburn's name in it, along with those of Barré, Burke, George Granville, Lord George Sackville, and Lord John Cavendish.[1]

On a subsequent day, in the debate on Mr. Dowdswell's motion, " That by the law of the land, and the known law and usage of Parliament, no person eligible by common right can be incapacitated by vote or resolution of this House, but by Act of Parliament only," Wedderburn again spoke immediately after Lord North, attacking him very vehemently, and saying, " When this committee sat last, the conclusion that it came to concerning this question was in every respect strange and unnatural. The resolution now moved for will put all right. The noble lord asks, ' Will the House of Commons censure and disgrace itself?' Let me ask, in my turn, Will the House of Commons compose the minds of the people? will they recover the good opinion and confidence of those whom some gentlemen have been pleased to call the *rabble*, the *base-born*, the *scum of the earth ?* "[2]

The report of his speech in the next debate on this subject I suspect was prepared by himself, and it is certainly calculated to give us a high opinion of his powers. The

[1] 16 Parl. Hist. 797.
[2] This is all that is set down for him in the report, and he is fortunate in being so noticed; for the wearied reporter goes on to say, " Sir W Blackstone opposed the resolution, and was answered by Mr. Edmund Burke. Mr. Charles Fox spoke in answer to Mr. Burke, but the topic has been so exhausted, that their speeches would neither contain anything new, nor exhibit anything in a new light."—*16 Parl. Hist. 803.*

city of London had presented to the King an address, framed in very violent language, complaining of the proceedings of the House of Commons against Mr. Wilkes, and had received in answer a very sharp rebuke from His Majesty. A motion was now made by a supporter of the Government for a copy of the address, with a view to institute proceedings against the citizens of London for a breach of privilege. This was strongly resisted by the Opposition leaders, who severely animadverted on the answer which the King had been advised to return to the address. Lord North having thereupon avowed that he was the adviser of the answer, and responsible for it, and declared that nothing should deter him from inquiry into the conduct of others where, as in this case, inquiry appeared of utility to the public, Mr. Wedderburn is said to have spoken as follows:—

"Sir, if the issue of this debate regarded the responsibility[1] of the minister only, and was not of infinite importance to the kingdom at large, I should be one of the first to approve the candor of the noble lord who spoke last, and to own, that if he does not possess more wisdom than his predecessor, he at least shows more manliness and more probity in publicly acknowledging himself the adviser of the answer to the City remonstrance. But, Sir, it is not the responsibitity of a minister which is now under consideration, but the inexpediency, the injustice, of censuring any part of the people for the exercise of a right which is warranted by the Constitution, which is supported by the dictates of reason, the authority of precedents, and the positive declaration of our laws. Our sole consideration is, simply, whether the people have, or have not, a right to petition; whether they are, or are not, legally authorized to lay their grievances before the throne whenever they imagine themselves opposed; and whether all prosecution for the exercise of that right is not prohibited by the Bill of Rights? Sir, the loudest advocate for the motion before the House will not pretend to deny the right of the people to petition, nor pretend to deny that they are wholly exempted from judicial censure on that account. Among the many blessings arising to the kingdom from the glorious Revolution, the privilege o

[1] Wedderburn had not revised the "proof," for this word is misprinted "ostensibility."

complaining to the throne without the danger of punishment is one of the noblest. The people, in this respect, are the sole judges of the necessity for petitioning: it is as much a part of their prerogative, if I may so express myself, as it is a part of the royal prerogative to assemble parliaments, or to exercise any other power warranted by the Constitution. I must ask, then, with what shadow of propriety, with what color of reason, we arrogate a liberty of examining their proceedings? How do we presume to fly in the face of the law, and confidently assert that they shall be punished for what the law says we shall not examine? If this is our idea of reason, our conception of justice, let us, for the future, be distinguished for inconsistency and violence. Even admitting, Sir, that on the present occasion the people have been mistaken, that they have erred, that they have, in reality, no grievances to complain of, and that the manner of their remonstrance is as disrespectful as the matter of it is unjust; still, Sir, as the law positively pronounces on their right of petitioning, and their consequent exemption from prosecution, we are precluded from every inquiry into their conduct. They may be indiscreet, they may be warm, they may be turbulent: but let not us be rash, violent, and arbitrary. Let us not, while we are so nicely attentive to the errors of others, rush into palpable illegalities ourselves. Our power is great, but the power of the law is much greater. When you have got a copy of the petition, the petitioners may defy you. For this reason I oppose the motion, I can not consent that our love for equity should make us inequitable, that our regard for peace should lead us to spread the flames of discord through the land, or that our solicitude for the safety of the constitution shall vindicate our stabbing that Constitution to the heart. Remember, Sir, that one of the capital blemishes of James II.'s reign was punishing the seven bishops for petitioning. Similar causes must always be productive of similar effects. We are yet safe; it is yet in possibility to retrieve all; whereas if we proceed from violence to violence, if we go on exercising our power against the sense of our conviction, and sacrifice our honesty to gratify the malignity of our resentment, the consequences must be dreadful in the end. The people may be injured for a time, but they will prefer annihilation to chains: universal anarchy must ensue, and, as the poet forcibly expresses,

> '*Darkness be the burier of the dead.*'[1]

On Lord North's motion for a partial repeal of the American Revenue Act of 1767, imposing the tea duty, Wedderburn made a violent harangue against the Colonial policy of the Government.

"If," said he, "this is considered as a measure calculated to pacify America, it is an extremely weak and idle one: it is one step further in that system of contradiction which has obtained with regard to the colonies from 1766 to the present day. After all the time that has elapsed no plan has been adopted, no system thought of; and the session is to pass over with only a further instance of contradiction. I heard with infinite concern the observation of the gallant General (Conway), 'that to tax America is impolitic and unjust, but that it was one of the latent powers vested in the government.' What, Sir, declare that you have a right, and at the same time declare that the exercise of it would be impolitic and unjust!"[2]

Wedderburn was equally truculent in supporting Mr. Burke's motion for an inquiry into the causes of the late disturbances in America. He said,—"It is the continued system of contradiction and absurdity in government that has produced the melancholy situation in which we now stand. But, says the noble lord, 'Look forward and see what we shall next do for America.' This House must interfere and provide for the future government of America, or America is lost for ever. How long are we to wait? When nothing offers itself but despair; when nothing is offered to us but professions, both in the speech from the throne and in the language, or rather in the significant silence, of Ministers, Parliament must trace the evil to its source, and if you find matter for punishment, you must punish."

Lord North, in answer, said,—"This speech might raise the reputation of the learned gentleman as an orator, but would not add to his character for veracity."[3]

When Wedderburn next addressed the House he acquired applause by showing his familiarity with Shakespeare. Indeed, in all my reading and hearing of parliamentary debates, I do not recollect a more felicitous

[1] 16 Parl. Hist. 881.   [2] Cavendish Deb. 498.   [3] 2 Ib. 28.

quotation. George Grenville, leader of the Opposition, having brought forward his famous bill for the trial of controverted elections,' it was opposed by Lord North and the Government,—and De Grey, the Attorney General, made a long speech against its dangerous innovations, thus concluding,—" In short, Sir, although there no doubt have hitherto been irregularities and even abuses while the House retained to itself its constitutional power of deciding election petitions, it is better to endure the evils of which we know the extent, than in a sudden start of disgust and humorsome passion, 'fly to others which we know not of.'"

Wedderburn, rising immediately after, continued Hamlet's soliloquy :—

> And thus the native hue of resolution
> Is sicklied o'er with the pale cast of thought;
> And enterprises of great pith and moment,
> With this regard, their currents turn awry,
> And lose the name of action."

" The opposition to this bill by the Government," he added, " I consider most disgraceful. They do not deny the evils of the existing system to be as great as we have described them, and they offer no other remedy. In resisting it they make no distinct objection to it ; their only resource is blindly to address themselves to our fears. They acknowledge the danger, they admit that we approach the brink of the precipice, and they would rather see us dashed to pieces among rocks or swallowed in the cataract below, than that we should turn into a new path for safety. Wherever reason, justice, honor, point the way, there the most ungenerous among them, like my learned and honorable friend the Attorney General, set up bugbears, and phantoms, and chimeras dire. They would frighten us with dangers, not only 'which we know not of,' but which they themselves can not describe or imagine." The report goes on to say, that " he then turned to Lord North and his friends, and in a strain of irony apologized for their neglect of the business of legislation, as they were devoting themselves day and night to their executive functions, in conducting our foreign and colonial

---

[1] Wedderburn had been directed by the House along with George Grenville, "to prepare and bring in the same" (32 Com. Journ 760), but he had only revised it, and corrected some of the legal phraseology

policy, although it had unhappily turned out, in spite of their statesmanlike efforts, that France had been allowed treacherously to add Corsica to her dominions, and that our transatlantic colonies were on the verge of rebellion."[1] The bill was carried by a majority of 185 to 123, and was long celebrated as an absolute piece of perfection, but afterwards fell almost into as great disrepute as the ancient practice of deciding elections in the House by a ministerial majority.

Wedderburn, before the close of the session, had an opportunity, which he very zealously improved, of attacking the whole system which had been pursued for some years with respect to America. This was upon Mr. Burke's first great attempt to save the empire from dismemberment, by bringing forward the celebrated Resolutions, explaining the causes of the discontents in the colonies, which began to be so alarming, and the measures of conciliation which ought to be resorted to. He rose late in the debate, and we have only an imperfect report of his speech; but it seems to have been very elaborate and effective. Forgetting the changeable propensity which he himself had already exhibited, and not anticipating the sudden wheel which he himself was destined very speedily to exhibit, he daringly began with taunting Lord Clare for having illustrated the ease with which great statesmen might reconcile inconsistencies between opinion and conduct, by warmly supporting the American Stamp Act,—then taking office under a minister who repealed it,—and now again standing up for the right to tax America. He asserted that such had been the folly of late measures respecting America, that they had united all thinking and honest men of all parties in condemning them. He went on to declare, that by these measures the American colonies were no longer part of the British dominions—more than Calais, which was once a British province. He concluded by inveighing against the appointment of a third Secretary of State for the Colonies, insisting that the minister placed at the head of that department was wholly unfit for it, and that the Resolutions ought to be supported, as they must lead to his removal.

The reporter says, that "Lord North followed, and

[1] 16 Parl. Hist. 921.

took up some expressions which Mr. Wedderburn had used in high terms, and returned a flat contradiction to them; his Lordship then came to the ground of answering the several matters of charge against the Ministry article by article, and said as much as could be for them."[1] This was the last of a series of personal conflicts between the minister and the aspiring Opposition lawyer. They probably soon after came to a secret understanding that they were as quickly as possible to be friends; but it was necessary to wait for an opening in the law before this object could be accomplished, and the year 1770 expired without any legal dignitary dying or resigning.

Meanwhile, a new session of Parliament began in November, and Wedderburn still professed to belong to the Opposition; but he confined himself in debate to the discussion of legal questions. A motion being made to take away the power of the Attorney General to file *ex-officio* informations,—that he might still appear to be on the popular side he supported it, although he must have been well aware that the same power belonged to the public prosecutor in his own country with respect to all offenses whatsoever, and that the system had there worked most beneficially. Nevertheless, he found it convenient to say,—

"It can not be denied, that the proposed alteration will be attended with possible and even probable advantages, and the possibility, much more the probability, of advantage is a sufficient ground for change. If our ancestors had been so tenacious of old institutions, what would have become of our liberties? When reason and the principles of the Constitution dictate reformation, must we be deterred by mere names? The unlimited and discretionary power of prosecuting is not to be endured in a free state. A grand jury examines witnesses and rejects the bill, if it seems to be founded on injustice, malice or oppression. The same process holds where an information is granted in the King's Bench. The party accused is there heard, and if he can produce any extenuating circumstances he is never brought to trial. These things are not done in a corner; and judges, from a view to their own character, act with gravity and circumspection. Why is not the Attorney General's power

---

[1] 16 Parl. Hist. 1009.

circumscribed within the same limits? Need I say more to prove that this power ought to be abolished or modified?"[1]

But Wedderburn's Opposition career in the House of Commons was now drawing to a close. The last oration delivered by him, standing on the left hand of the Speaker, was in the debate on Sergeant Glyn's motion respecting the administration of criminal justice and Lord Mansfield's direction to juries on the trials for the publication of Junius' Letters. He thus boldly began:—

"Sir, it is with reluctance I trouble the House at so late an hour of the night. But the importance of the question will plead my excuse. My silence might be branded with the odious imputation of *trimming;* and I would have it understood, that when the Constitution is in danger I always take a decided part, and scorn the mean subterfuge of an invidious neutrality. Sir, it is not that I do not perceive the difficulties with which I am surrounded. I see the narrow path on which I stand, and the rocks and precipices which threaten on either side. If I lean to the inquiry, I shall be termed a child of faction: if I incline to the opposite side, I shall be denounced as a slave to the Court. In this dilemma how shall I act? As every honest man ought. Regardless of consequences, I will follow the dictates of conscience; and if I can not satisfy others, at least satisfy my own mind." He then gives it as his opinion that, according to precedent, juries are confined to the question, whether the alleged libel was published by the defendant, but that by a new law the power of deciding upon the general guilt or innocence of the defendant ought to be conferred upon them. "Sir," said he, "while matters continue on their present footing, while judges think the intention a matter of law cognizable only by them, and juries imagine this to be an encroachment on their jurisdiction, they will be eternally at variance. A constant struggle for superiority will subsist, and justice being placed in the middle between them, will be mangled and torn in pieces. Acted upon by two forces in opposite directions, it will share the fate of criminals whose limbs are tied to the tails of wild horses. Juries thinking law and liberty to be at stake, and judges standing up for their own

[1] 16 St. Tr. 1147, 1188.

authority, and what they consider the cause of order, neither will give up the contest till the land becomes one scene of anarchy and misrule. Indeed, who does not see that this is already the case? The most audacious libelers can not be convicted. Secure in the opposition of juries, they laugh at all the terrors of *ex-officio* informations. The Attorney General with all his power is despised. Like an old worn-out scarecrow in a field, his head is made a roosting-place, or something worse, by these obscene birds. It is time for us to reconcile the practice of the law with the principles of the Constitution. Juries seem to me not only the proper but the sole judges of the intention—of the innocence or malice of a libel, because it is really and essentially a matter of fact and not of law. It depends solely on the opinion which is entertained of the libel by the public. What passed in the Roman Senate for polite raillery, would in this House be deemed a gross affront, and perhaps lead to bloodshed. What Roman virtue called 'Attic eloquence,' modern honor would construe 'rude Billingsgate.' Libel is founded entirely on public opinion. There is no other standard by which it can be measured or ascertained. Who, then, so proper as the people to determine the point? If juries are to be confined to the single fact of publication, instead of leaving them only this shadow of power, would it not be better to annihilate them entirely? What then will become of our envied Constitution? This main prop being removed, the whole fabric will tumble to the ground, and crush us under its disjointed fragments. Sir, in all our legal system, there is nothing that can boast a preference to the institution of juries. The plan is great, noble and comprehensive, and well worthy of its royal founder. Judges may err, judges may be corrupt. Their minds may be warped by interest, passion and prejudice. But a jury is not liable to the same misleading influences. Twelve men of the vicinage, chosen as they are, can have no bias—no motive to show favor or malice to either party. They must find a verdict according to evidence and conscience. Ask a foreigner what are his ideas of English liberty? He will tell you, with uplifted hands and a look of admiration, that it consists in the right which every Englishman has of being tried by his equals. But where is the propriety of any panegyric, if the jury are only to try the most insignificant part of a cause, and leave the rest to the judge, who is not the equal of the accused? Were the proposed scheme adopted, the present ferment would subside, and juries would spontaneously give a check to the licentiousness of the press. I think no restrictions necessary. I am far from adopting the creed of my honorable and learned friend the Attorney General, 'that if we were less learned we should be better men.' I hold, on the contrary, that the diffusion of learning, by the liberty of the press, is necessary to public liberty and public morality. Like all the great and powerful nations that ever existed, we are tending towards effeminacy. What then would become of us without the press? Not to speak of the rational and elegant amusements which it affords, we owe to it all the spirit which remains in the nation. Were an *imprimatur* clapped upon it, and a licenser appointed, we should soon come to the last stage of barbarism. We should be worse than Turks and infidels,— the setting of the sun of science being much more gloomy and dismal than the dark hour which precedes its rise Let us then guard the liberty of the press as watchfully as the dragon did the Hesperian fruit. Next to the privileges of this House and the rights of juries, it is the main prop of the Constitution. Nay, without it, I fear the other two would prove very ineffectual. Though it be sometimes attended with inconveniences, would you abolish it? According to this reasoning, what would become of the greatest blessings of society? None of them come pure and unmixed. Religion itself is apt to degenerate into enthusiasm or superstition. Must we, therefore, exterminate Christianity? God forbid! Why, then, be so severe on the liberty of the press? If it poisons the minds of the people, it likewise administers an antidote. The same wagons, the same flies and stages, that carry down into the country the lies of faction, carry down also the counter-statements of the Ministry. If any one is bit by the tarantula of the Opposition, he is cured by the music of the Court."[1]

---

[1] 16 Parl. Hist. 1294. Lord Chatham in reference to this speech wrote to Calcraft.—" Mr. Wedderburn I hear, did, upon the matter of juries' right to judge, speak openly and like a man. I shall ever truly honor him."—*Chat. Cor.* iv. 46.

There is a tradition that Wedderburn had now (in parliamentary slang) "dropped down to St. Helen's, lying there at single anchor;" or, in other words,—that he sat in the neutral row, below the gangway, on the Opposition side of the House, ready to go over to the Treasury bench. His patriotism had all along been regarded with suspicion. "In vain," wrote Junius to the Duke of Grafton, "would he have looked round him for another character so consummate as yours: Lord Mansfield shrinks from his principles; his ideas of government, perhaps, go further than your own, but his heart disgraces the theory of his understanding: Charles Fox is yet in blossom; *and as for Wedderburn, there is something about him which even treachery can not trust.*" This great Unknown, on another occasion, pretended to have fully appreciated the character of our political *Condottiere:*— " Let us profit by the assistance of such men while they are with us; and place them, if it be possible, in the post of danger, to prevent desertion. The wary Wedderburn, the pompous Suffolk, never threw away the scabbard, nor ever went upon a forlorn hope: they always treated the King's servants as men with whom, some time or another, they might possibly be in friendship."

Wedderburn was now more desirous of taking place under the present Government, on account of the death of George Grenville, with whom he would not enter into any positive engagement, but whose return to power he had considered not improbable. Lord North was not only a favorite with the King, but was gaining the confidence of the House of Commons and of the nation; and those who should continue to stand out against the usurpation of the House of Commons in disqualifying Mr. Wilkes, and against the injustice of England in taxing America, seemed doomed to long years of hopeless exile from the Treasury Bench.

Before making any direct overtures to the Government, he sounded the inclinations of the patron of the borough which he represented, and was greatly comforted by receiving from him the following answer, which must be allowed to be very creditable to the writer:—

"Bath, 18th Nov. 1770.

"DEAR SIR,

"If the receipt of your very obliging and confidential

letter had not roused me, I doubt much whether I could have prevailed upon myself to put pen to paper, though I feel something within that tells me I shall at last overcome a disorder so very distressing to the mind, and so degrading to human nature. Either the air or water of Bath agrees with me better than any place I have yet tried ; yet still, I am afraid a journey abroad must be undertaken before I can attain a perfect recovery of my health.

"Mr. Grenville's death, though long expected, affected me very deeply. Gratitude first bound me to him; afterwards, a more intimate connection gave me an opportunity of admiring his abilities and respecting his worth and integrity. The dissolution of our valuable friend has shipwrecked our hopes and expectations for the present: and my indisposition has not only made me indifferent to what passes in Parliament, but to the world in general. But if I can think for myself in such a situation, I wish to support that independence which will be approved of by my friends and by the public. My sentiments coincide entirely with yours in the present critical situation of affairs.

"Your delicacy towards me serves only to convince me of the propriety of my conduct in leaving you the absolute master of yourself in Parliament, subject to no control whatever but that of your own judgment; and I am happy in this opportunity of giving under my hand, what I have declared on all occasions by word of mouth.

"Your great and uncommon abilities must, sooner or later, conduct you to the first posts in this kingdom, and you may be assured no man on earth wishes more to see your honor and your independency firmly established in this kingdom, than,
"Dear Sir,
"Your affectionate friend and obliged servant,
"CLIVE."[1]

Notwithstanding the general suspicion of Wedderburn's lubricity, so high at this time was his reputation for ability, and so valuable were his services considered to the party he should support, that while Lord North was looking for a favorable opportunity to enlist him in the Government ranks, Lord Chatham thought it worth while to make an

[1] Rossl. MSS.

effort to keep him true to the Liberal side, and with this view (knowing the man) addressed himself to his interest, and tried to do a job for him in the City. Eyre, the recorder, had given mortal offense by refusing to read the famous " Remonstrance " to the King, or to attend at St. James's when it was presented.

The Court of Common Council thereupon passed resolutions—That Mr. Recorder Eyre be no more employed in any City causes; that Sergeant Glyn (who had gained such applause in the Middlesex election) should be retained as their leading counsel; and that the freedom of the City should be presented in a gold box to Mr. Dunning (who when Solicitor General had defended in Parliament the right to petition and remonstrate). Lord Chatham wrote a letter, to be made public, in which, after praising these resolutions, he goes on to suggest that something should likewise be done for the patriotic Scot, who, notwithstanding his country, had made such sacrifices for liberty:—" I could wish Mr. Wedderburn's merit to the cause of the Constitution not to be forgot. I think it is a species of injustice, if, on some proper occasion, it be not intended to show him that his spirited, disinterested conduct is felt as it deserves. I fear some mixture of narrow ideas and local antipathy. To speak plain, nothing is more contrary to the public good than to retain the smallest grain of alienation or suspicion towards a Scotchman, renouncing and thoroughly resisting Scotch influences and despotism."[1]

The freedom of the City was actually voted to Wedderburn, but as the scheme of having him appointed to a city law office failed, and he was evidently cooling towards

[1] Chatham Correspondence.
To show the violence of the prejudice in London at this time against Scotsmen, Mr. Wedderburn used to relate the following anecdote.—" John Home, elated by the success of DOUGLAS, had written another tragedy, called RIVINE, the name of the heroine being taken from a fragment of Ossian. Garrick, afraid that there could be no chance for the combination of a Scotch writer and a Scotch subject, changed the title of the piece to THE FATAL DISCOVERY, and got a young English gentleman from Oxford to father it. Under this disguise it drew crowded houses;—whereupon the real author incautiously discovered himself. It could not now be damned, but after languishing for a few nights it was withdrawn." This is a good pendant to the authentic story of Sir John Owen, clad in buckskin breeches and top-boots, being rapturously applauded in the House of Commons, while he was supposed to be a country gentleman, but being coughed down when in the middle of his speech it was discovered that he was a lawyer.

the popular cause, Lord Chatham thought that he might fix the waverer by personal attentions,—which many would then have preferred to place and power,—and proposed to call upon him,—that they might together concert measures for the public good. This proposal was most embarrassing; it could not be directly declined without a discovery that a very different negotiation was pending; and as this negotiation might break off, it was essential for some time longer to have patriotism for a resource; yet the news of an interview with Lord Chatham, which would have been immediately known over all the clubs in London, might have caused his absolute proscription at St. James's.

The communication with the old patriot was carried on through his bosom friend, Calcraft. To him Wedderburn wrote a very artful letter, expressing his deep sense of the honor to be conferred upon him, and his eager impatience for the proposed meeting; but suggesting some difficulties as to to time and place, and proposing that " on the first fitting opportunity he should wait upon the illustrious statesman who had vouchsafed to notice his exertions for the public good." Lord Chatham wrote back the following letter, to be read by Calcraft to Wedderburn: " If you will be so good as to answer Mr. Wedderburn's letter, as having communicated it to me, and if you please to express in my name the sense I have of his most obliging manner of meeting my earnest wishes to have an opportunity of seeing him and exchanging sentiments, as far as he will give leave, with a person for whose handsome conduct and great abilities I have a very real and high esteem."[1] On various pretenses the interview was postponed, and Lord Chatham and his friends plainly saw that Wedderburn was for ever lost to them. Lord Camden wrote to his great leader, " The opinion is universal that Wedderburn is in the act of negotiating, or open to it." These rumors were much strengthened by the news that De Grey, the Attorney General, was immediately to be made Chief Justice of the Common Pleas, and that Thurlow, Solicitor General, was to become Attorney,—so that the Solicitor Generalship would be vacant. Parliament had been adjourned for the Christmas holidays on the 20th of December to the 25th of January. On this very

[1] Chatham Correspondence.

day the London Gazette announced that "Alexander Wedderburn, Esq., was appointed Solicitor General to his Majesty."

We are not informed of any particulars of the negotiation with Lord North, and it was probably not attended with much difficulty on either side. Great was the public indignation when the result was known; and this must be confessed to be one of the most flagrant cases of *ratting* recorded in our party annals. There not only was no change in the Government, but there was no change of circumstances or of policy,—and a solitary patriot was to cross the floor of the House of Commons that he might support the measures which he had had been so loudly condemning. His own saying was now in everybody's mouth: "Bit by the tarantula of Opposition, he is cured by the music of the Court." Perhaps there was nothing more cutting than Lord Camden's remarks in sending the intelligence to Lord Chatham: " I am not surprised, but grieved."[1]

CHAPTER CLXVI.

CONTINUATION OF THE LIFE OF LORD LOUGHBOROUGH TILL THE COMMENCEMENT OF HOSTILITIES WITH AMERICA.

ALTHOUGH it was said that " Lord Clive was full of indignation at the desertion of Wedderburn,"[2] Mr. Solicitor vacating his seat, was re-elected for Bishops Castle without opposition;[3] but he had before him the disagreeable prospect of walking up to the table between two Treasury members (his Liberal associates now shunning him), and of slinking down on the Treasury bench between Lord North and John Robinson.[4] He dreaded that opposing parties, suspending their general hostility, would, on this occasion, interchange well under-

[1] Chatham Correspondence, iv. 72.   [2] Ibid 80
[3] The new writ was moved 25th Jan 1771.—Com. Journ. vol xxxiii p 62.
[4] This famous *job-master*, then Secretary to the Treasury, was probably active in bringing him over Soon after, Sheridan, alluding to a government agent by whom members were corrupted, and a cry arising, "*Name him ! name him !*" said, " Sir, I *could* name him, as easily as say JACK ROBINSON."

stood looks, occasioned by mutual wonderment at his apostasy. When the time came, he is said virtuously to have blushed, and to have appeared much distressed, till his colleague Thurlow shook him by the hand, and with an oath welcomed him to that side of the House which he ought never to have quitted. He for some time wore an embarrassed air, and when he had anything to say he seemed to have lost all his fluency. It was probably with reference to these exhibitions that Junius remarked, " To sacrifice a respected character, and to renounce the esteem of society, requires more than Mr. Wedderburn's resolution; and though in him it was rather a profession than a desertion of his principles (I speak tenderly of this gentleman, for, when treachery is in question, I think we shou'd make allowance for a Scotchman), yet we have seen him in the House of Commons overwhelmed with confusion, and almost bereft of his faculties."

He was much aided by an attack made upon him, which gave him an opportunity for a dexterous explanation, and enabled him to recover to a considerable degree of his position in the House. Having given notice of motion for a committee to inquire into the riots near the Houses of Parliament, on the commitment of Brass Crosby, the Lord Mayor of London, and Alderman Oliver, to the Tower, Colonel Barré rose and said very irregularly,—

" I thank the honorable and learned gentleman for his intention of moving for a committee to inquire into the causes of these riots. He will be the fittest man to conduct such an inquiry, seeing that he knows more of such matters than any of the King's present servants. I hope he will inquire not only into the causes of the assembling of recent mobs, but of those which have alarmed the public for the last three or four years, as I know that the honorable and learned gentleman has frequently declared in this House and in other places, that 'this wicked Administration has been the cause of all the misfortunes that have befallen the country—that nothing but the removal of this wicked Administration, and the dissolution of this profligate Parliament, could restore the peace and happiness of the kingdom.' I am persuaded that all his powers of eloquence will be directed to those great objects. This inquiry will afford him the finest possible opportunity of discharging the debt which he still owes to his country. As no man is better able, so no man, I am sure, can be better inclined to do it; for I have heard him declare from this bench that the King's chief minister ought to be impeached. The honorable and learned gentleman has kept exceeding *good* company—I do not say *great* company—but what I consider very *honest* company—the freemen of the corporation of London! If I am not mistaken, he did not disdain himself to become a member of that body; and I believe he was pleased to receive the freedom of the city in a gold box. Although since that time the honorable and learned gentleman has formed new connections, he cannot have altogether abandoned the sentiments by which he was formerly actuated. Of all men, therefore, he is the fittest to bring the causes and the occasions of these disturbances to public light."

Mr. Solicitor General Wedderburn.—" I hope the House will permit me to express my obligations to the gallant officer who has thought fit to make my political conduct the subject of his argument. Of that conduct, Sir, I shall always be ready to give an account. It may easily be summed up,—and in a very few words. With regard to the measures which I have supported in this House, and the public part I have taken out of it,—I have not repented of any measure I have ever supported—I have not learned to approve of any measures I ever opposed. I shall be extremely happy to have my future conduct tried by any principles I may at any time hitherto have professed. As to personal connections, I stand up, with great frankness and great truth, to declare that I had a personal connection which I infinitely valued and respected, and by which I held myself sacredly bound till death dissolved it—a connection founded upon friendship, founded upon gratitude, founded upon a conviction of the many virtues, public and private, of him with whom my lot was cast. It is a misfortune, not only to me but to this country, that we are deprived of the services of that excellent man [George Grenville]. In point of personal connections, he left me a solitary, unconnected individual. In following the line of conduct which seems to me most consistent with my public duty, no one can say that I have broken any private engagement into which I have ever entered."[1]

[1] 2 Cavendish's Debates, 474.

This dexterous use of Mr. Grenville's death misled many, and made the more knowing regard with a feeling aproaching to respect the tact of him who could so defend himself by such a fallacy.[1]

When he had got over the disgrace which, even in those days, was for a time incurred by such a sudden change of party, he proved to be a brilliantly effective supporter of the Government. "It was a proud day for the Bar," says Matthias,[2] "when Lord North made Thurlow and Wedderburn Attorney and Solicitor General; for never before that day were such irresistible, overbearing talents and powers displayed by the official defenders of Ministers.

"—— Hos mirabantur Athenæ
Torrentes, pleni et moderantes fræna theatri."

"The minister," observed Horne Tooke,[2] "sat secure between his two brazen pillars, Jachin and Boaz, to guard the Treasury bench."

Said Gibbon, giving an account of his entrance into the House of Commons, "The cause of Government was ably vindicated by Lord North, a statesman of spotless integrity, a consummate master of debate, who could wield with equal dexterity the arms of reason and ridicule. He was seated on the Treasury bench, between his Attorney and Solicitor General, *magis pares quam similes;* and the minister might indulge in a short slumber whilst he was upholden on either hand by the majestic sense of Thurlow, and the skillful eloquence of Wedderburn."[4]

Mr. Adolphus, in contrasting them, says, "Thurlow was nervous, impressive, and majestic, he delivered the resolute dictates of a superior intellect without soliciting applause. From him truth appeared above the aid of art; and the judgment was summoned to yield without an appeal to the intervention of fancy. Wedderburn was acute, perspicuous, elegant, and persuasive; he alternately essayed

---

[1] Calcraft, in a letter to Lord Chatham, referring to this debate, says,—"Wedderburn was fully paid off for his insolence by Barré, who dressed him with dignity, propriety, and great severity."—*Chatham Correspondence,* iv. 138 But Lord Commissioner Adam, in his MS. sketch of Wedderburn, says: "He had to defend himself against a bitter attack for accepting the office of Solicitor General under Lord North. His speech on that occasion produced a most unaccountable impression. When I came into the House of Commons in 1774, he was one of the speakers most in favor with the House." [2] Pursuits of Literature. [3] State Trials. [4] Memoirs, p. 146.

the force of reason and the charms of eloquence; sometimes attacking the judgment with refined argument, at other times appealing to the fancy with the powers of wit and graces of elocution."[1]

I have likewise much pleasure in introducing a very happy parallel between them by Mr. Townsend:—" Both law officers exercised considerable sway in the House, but in a perfectly distinct style and manner; the one the Ajax, the other the Ulysses, of debate. The one, blunt, coarse, and vigorous, hurled hard words and strong epithets at his opponents in a tremendous voice, with a look and tone of defiance; the other, elegant, subtle, and insinuating, arrayed his arguments in all the persuasive guises of rhetoric, and where he could not convince the reason, or move the passions, sought to silence objections with ironical pleasantry and bitter sarcasm. Their rival feats of eloquence may be compared to the trial of strength and dexterity between Cœur de Lion and Saladin, mentioned in the 'Talisman' by Sir Walter Scott. King Richard, with his two-handed sword, cut asunder the iron bar which no arm but his could have severed; the Soldan could exhibit no such miracle of muscular strength, inferior as he was in brawn, and sinew, and muscle; but with his blue scymetar he severed the cushion and veil into two equal parts, displaying at the same time the extreme temper and sharpness of the weapon, and the exquisite dexterity of him who used it."[2]

[1] Vol. ii p. 150
[2] Lives of Twelve Eminent Judges, vol i. p. 185.

Here is an amusing peep behind the curtain, showing how the actors got up their parts "Lord Haddington asked W. once, when he was Chief Justice, how he possibly contrived to get on with Thurlow when he was under him as Solicitor, considering the unwonted quantity of public work they had to do together, both as to America, France, and Spain, owing to the indolence of Lord North and the incapacity of several of his colleagues. 'Nothing was so easy,' said Lord L., 'I knew Thurlow to be a bully, and only a bully, with no moral nerve—but intolerable if not subdued; so I resolved on my course The first paper I had to prepare was one of great importance and difficulty, and I sent it to him that he might consider and revise. When I saw him, he swore fearfully, declared that 'there never was anything so ill done—it could not be used He had no time to correct it; it was too bad to be corrected, I must do it over again.' I said, 'I beg your pardon—I have done my best. I know there are great imperfections in it—I am not satisfied myself, but I can not do it better, I have bestowed my whole mind on it, and if you can not take it, you must prepare the paper yourself' He growled very savagely, but he saw I was quite determined, and so I left it with him. When we next met, he produced my paper without a word of

We have extremely defective reports of Wedderburn's speeches in the House of Commons, from which he gained so much contemporary applause. He seems to have taken some pains in revising them while he was an Opposition orator, but now to have been too much occupied to pay the slightest attention to them, although parliamentary reporting was then at the lowest ebb, Dr. Johnson having long withdrawn from this employment, and no other man of education having taken it up. The following is his account of those on whom, in his time, the reputation of the orator depended: " Of all people, shorthand writers are the farthest from correctness ; there are no men's words they ever hear that again return. They are in general ignorant, as acting mechanically ; by not considering the antecedent, and catching the sound and not the sense, they pervert the meaning of the speaker, and make him appear as ignorant as themselves."[1] Yet he acknowledged that they occasionally showed ability, if not accuracy. Being once asked if he had really delivered a certain speech which the newspapers reputed to him, he replied, " Why, to be sure, there are in that report a few things which I did say, but many things which I am glad I did not say, *and some things which I wish I could have said.*"

One subject entirely engrossed the attention of the House of Commons during the first sesssion of Wedderburn's official life,—the Privilege question, arising out of the attempt to prevent the publication of debates. From the stimulus given to political discussion by the controversy on the Middlesex election, and by the "Letters of Junius," there was an increased curiosity respecting parliamentary proceedings, and the newspapers began to give,

alteration—said he had no time to alter, that it must just do, but it was a perfect disgrace to us both, and he should say so—for he was ashamed of the paper.' ' Indeed, Mr Attorney, you *shall not say so*, and it is better that we understand each other once for all. I·will assist you to the utmost of my power, if you can not use the papers I draw, then of course I may be unfit for my office, and you must do the work, but if you adopt my paper, it is no longer mine—it is yours, and *must* be yours, and yours alone. I will have neither merit nor discredit from it' I said this with the utmost coolness : he swore away, but said,' Well, take it away—it will do as well as anything else; I suppose' I never afterwards had a single difference with him."

[1] Burke's famous sentiment,—" Virtue does not depend on climate or degrees," was at first given to the world—" Virtue does not depend on *climates and trees* "—He has nobly vindicated his reputation by reporting and publishing his own speeches.

though in a rude fashion, while Parliament was sitting, speeches said to have been delivered in either house, with the names of the speakers at full length.[1] The audacious printers were summoned to appear at the bar, and not appearing, a proclamation was put forth offering a reward for their apprehension. Then was the messenger of the House, who had been sent to arrest them, committed to prison by the City magistrates, and a printer arrested was immediately liberated and bound over to prosecute the messenger. Next came the imprisonment, in the Tower, of the committing magistrates, Brass Crosby, the Lord Mayor, and Alderman Oliver,—with innumerable petitions and motions for their discharge. The Solicitor General must necessarily have taken an active part in these proceedings, but he is only mentioned by the "Parliamentary History" as having spoken on the 19th of March, when a question arose as to the right of one Twine Carpenter, a printer's devil, to a reward for having laid hold of a Mr. Wheble, his master, one of the printers named in the proclamation, and conducted him to the Mansion House, where he was set at liberty by Mr. Wilkes,—there being an allegation that this arrest was merely collusive, so that the reward might be claimed, and the authority of the House turned into ridicule

Mr. Solicitor General Wedderburn.—"Sir: Whether the proclamation be legal or not, I shall not now say. A court of law is the proper place to determine that question. As to Mr Twine Carpenter, for whom the honorable gentleman is so warm an advocate, I shall certainly resist giving him any countenance. He is neither more nor less than a familiar of Mr. Wheble, called his 'devil,' by a bargain between this devil and Wheble the devil arrests him. Now, as it manifestly appears that the devil and the printer are in compact, I think the wisest thing we can do is to leave the devil to the printer, and the printer to his devil. Whether printer beats devil, or devil beats printer, is of no consequence. There is the devil to pay; but that is nothing to us. I hope the devil will find no friends in this House, and that, however busy he may have been in the city, and however busy the City

---

[1] Formerly the Reports did not come out till after the prorogation—pretending often to be of the senate of Lilliput, and never venturing on more than the initials of the names of the speakers.

may have been with him, we shall have nothing to do with him, nor give him an opportunity of having any thing to do with us."¹

Lord North moved, as an amendment, that Mr. Wilkes should attend to explain his conduct. This, like the other Government motions on the subject, was carried by an immense majority : but public opinion was so strong against the House, that the Ministers were compelled to drop these proceedings,—a great constitutional victory was gained, and the right to publish parliamentary debates was forever practically established,—in spite of the *brutum fulmen* of a standing order against it.²

About this time Wedderburn gained high credit as an enlightened protector of literary merit. Mr. Thomas Townshend had complained in the House of Commons of the pension granted to Dr. Johnson, saying, " I consider him a man of some talent, but no temper. The principles he upholds I shall ever detest. This man, a Jacobite by principle, has been encouraged, fostered, pensioned, because he is a Jacobite."

Mr. Solicitor General Wedderburn.—" The misinformation of the honorable gentleman, if not corrected, will do injustice to two persons, both absent. From the course of my pursuits, I have not seen Dr. Johnson four times in my life. This, however, I know,—that he was not pensioned because he was a Jacobite, nor on account of his political principles ;—that he was not pensioned from any such illiberal motive. The only motive for granting that pension was Dr. Johnson's distinction in the literary world and his prospect of approaching distress. The person who solicited it for him was totally unacquainted with anything beyond his merit as an author and his poverty. Was not the ' Dictionary of the English Language' reason enough for a mark of public bounty, without supposing that bad principles were to be encouraged, or corrupt services to be purchased ? The Minister to whom the application was made, and the man who made the application, never inquired into his political or religious tenets. If a papist, or a theoretical admirer of a republican form of government, should be a great mathematician or a great poet, doing honor to his country

¹ 17 Parl. Hist. 58–164, Annual Register, 1771.
² Chatham Correspondence, vol. iv p. 115.

and his age, and should fall into destitution, is he to be excluded from the royal bounty? Let not such language be held in this House, or in any society where there is any respect for intellectual greatness." [1]

The Minister applied to was Lord Bute, and the man who made the application was Mr. Wedderburn himself. Boswell says, "Lord Bute told me that Mr. Wedderburn, now Lord Loughborough, was the person who first mentioned the subject to him. Lord Loughborough told me that the pension was granted to Johnson solely as the reward of his literary merit, without any stipulation whatever, or even tacit understanding that he should write for Administration. Lord Bute said to him expressly, 'It is not given for anything you are to do, but for what you have done.'" [2]

For above two years following, England enjoyed profound public tranquillity. The dispute with Spain about the Falkland Islands having been adjusted, there was a cordial understanding with all foreign nations,—the discontents in the American colonies smouldered, although accurate observers perceived that they would soon burst into a flame,—and Wilkes, Brass, Crosby and Aderman Oliver being set at liberty, soon fell into almost entire neglect.[3] During this lull there were brought forward in parliament few questions more stirring than the subscription to the Thirty-nine Articles,—the amendment of the law of charitable bequests,—the protection of literary property,—the establishment of courts of justice in India,—and the renewal of the Grenville Act. On the presentation of a petition to dispense with subscription to the Thirty-nine Articles in the Universities, a long debate arose, whether the petition should be received? Lord North opposed it; but it being considered an open question, the Solicitor General took the opposite side,

[1] 2 Cavendish Deb. 457.
[2] Boswell, pp 353, 354. Yet Dr Johnson did, out of gratitude, write "The False Alarm," and "Taxation no Tyranny," the proof-sheets of which were revised at the Treasury
[3] It would appear from a letter of Wedderburn to his client and friend, Lord Clive, that their liberation even went off tamely —"There are no public news in town. We had a little mobbing last night (on the release of the Lord Mayor from the Tower), but not to any great excess My neighbor the Speaker had his windows mauled exceedingly, but by great good fortune the gentlemen were so busy with his, that they left mine untouched"— *Townsend's Lives*, vol. 1. p 179.

indulging always in a hankering after popularity where he safely could. He urged that the subject was clearly within the cognizance of Parliament, and that they were bound to hear the alleged grievances of the people, although they might not deem it expedient to grant the relief prayed. The objection on the Act of Union he ridiculed, after the alterations since made both in the English and Scotch Church—in the English by the law against occasional conformity—in the Scotch by the restoration of lay patronage. " The Universities," said he, " which are to prepare for all the learned professions, and to rear fit members of parliament, ought not to be confined to those of a particular creed ; and we must reform them, if they will not reform themselves. I can not conceive that the propriety or efficacy of a prescription can depend upon whether the physician has or has not signed the Thirty-nine Articles of the Church of England." The petition was rejected, however, by a majority of 217 to 71.[1]

In the next session, Mr. Solicitor brought forward a bill on a subject which still continues to perplex legislators—" the regulation of charitable trusts." His speech was very able, but proved ineffectual. The reporter of the debate says, " Mr. Edmund Burke answered him with infinite ability and candor. We do not remember that gentleman making a speech in which he stuck so close to the argument, and made so few flights into the regions of fancy and imagination."[2]

Wedderburn, having been counsel at the bar of the House of Lords in the great case of copyright, delivered a most admirable argument, to show that an author, by the common law, has a property in his work after he has

---

[1] 17 Parl Hist 294 Of this debate Gibbon gives the following scoffing account to Lord Sheffield, " Boodle's, Saturday night, February 8, 1772. Though it is very late, and the bell tells me that I have not above ten minutes left, I employ them with pleasure in congratulating you on the late victory of our dear mamma, the Church of England. She had last Thursday 71 rebellious sons, who pretended to set aside her will on account of insanity ; but 217 worthy champions, headed by Lord North, Burke, Hans Stanley, Charles Fox, &c , though they allowed the thirty-nine clauses of her Testament were absurd and unreasonable, supported the validity of it with infinite humor "—*Misc. Works*, vol 1 p. 447 The very rare occurrence happened, on this occasion, of publishing a list of the minority,—in which the world must have been surprised to find the name of the " wary Wedderburn."

[2] 17 Parl Hist 846

published it, so as to be entitled to prevent its being reprinted without his authority;[1] and, being defeated, he very ably supported, against Thurlow, the bill for extending the period of exclusive enjoyment beyond fourteen years, originally fixed by the statute of Anne.[2] India judicature, and the general affairs of the East India Company, being pressed on the attention of Parliament, Wedderburn carried some palliating measures on the part of Government through the House of Commons; but they then excited no interest—men little foreseeing that in ten years more, this was a subject on which administrations would be dissolved, and the nation would be convulsed.[3] The proposal to make the Grenville Act perpetual, raised another open question,—and Lord North and the Attorney General having opposed it, we are told, " The Solicitor General, in a long and masterly speech, expatiated on the foundation of the bill. He was very severe on Mr. Charles Fox, who, he said, had dreadful apprehensions of losing his privileges. But if the young gentleman were not of such an obstinate disposition, he would endeavor to convince him of his error. He spoke much in favor of the decision of elections that had been tried by this act, and concluded by giving his consent to its being perpetual."[4] There was a majority of 250 to 122 for the bill—although Fox continued so eager against it, that he was teller for the minority.

As some have asserted that Wedderburn was "Junius," it may be proper to notice the course he took when a complaint was made against Henry Sampson Woodfall, and John Horne Tooke, for a libel on the Speaker. This had appeared in Woodfall's newspaper, "The Daily Public Advertiser," and he had declared at the bar that he had received it from Horne Tooke,—but there was no evidence to corroborate him. The Solicitor General spoke several times in the course of the proceeding, and certainly did show a considerable leaning in favor of the

[1] 17 Parl. Hist 963. [2] Ib. 1087. [3] Ib. 848
[4] Ibid. 1071 I must own that I think the arguments against the trial of contested elections by a statutable tribunal under the control of the courts of common law very powerful, and that the House of Commons would have done better to have framed committees by resolutions, under their own exclusive authority. They wanted nothing for this purpose but the power of administering an oath,—which in all cases ought to be exercised by them as well as by the House of Lords.

publisher of the mysterious letters which had lately so astounded the public. "I own, Sir, with great readiness," said he, "that as Mr. Woodfall is involved in the guilt of this publication, I shall not, either on principles of law, or principles of humanity, give my vote for Mr. Horne's conviction, if nothing more is produced against him. Mr. Woodfall, Sir, however he may have been distinguished for his private probity, stands before us now in the light of a delinquent, and we can not convict upon his uncorroborated testimony, whatever may be our private opinion, and whatever suspicion may attach to the accused. From the candid behavior of Mr. Woodfall, when he was before the House, he is probably not in a very perilous situation: but it remains to be seen how we shall deal with Mr. Horne; if his friends do not really suspect his innocence, they have no cause to tremble for his situation. I think that Mr. Woodfall's journeymen should be examined. We are not trying Mr. Horne twice for the same offense; we shall only adjourn the trial to ascertain whether he be guilty on the original charge." A motion for examining Mr. Woodfall's journeymen was carried by a majority of 132 to 44.[1] When called in they all professed entire ignorance of the subject,—so that Horne Tooke for this time got off scot free. There was a proposal to send Woodfall to Newgate, but, from the good word of the Solicitor General, he was dismissed with a reprimand.—The notion that Wedderburn himself had been the greatest of libelers, now gained a little ground, notwithstanding the bitter abuse of him and of his country in which Junius pretended to delight: but (as I shall afterwards show) this extravagant suspicion is without proof or probability.

From the want of opportunity and of excitement Wedderburn's reputation for eloquence was declining,— when it was revived by General Burgoyne's resolutions against Lord Clive. Lord North affected to support the prosecution, but did not treat it as a government question and Wedderburn, though he knew that he was to be opposed by Thurlow, made a gallant defense for his friend and patron:—

"The honorable mover," said he, "has entered into a long recapitulation of events which happened sixteen

[1] 17 Parl. Hist. 1028-1050.

years ago, and from them he adduces two matters of
charge : those I desire leave to examine · the one is the
dethroning and putting to death Surajah Dowlah ; and the
other is a general officer's name being fixed to an order of
assassination. Upon the subject of the resolution I shall
observe, that it is a most narrow and illiberal idea to suppose that great and striking events—subversions of
government, wars, and conquests—are to be carried
through upon the direct and absolute principles of school
philosophy and morality ;—such a supposition would be
idle, would be preposterous. I will venture to assert that
a revolution so important never was, and never will be,
so conducted. Throughout the honorable gentleman's
copious narrative of the transaction, I am rather astonished that we should have heard not a word of the
character of Surajah Dowlah,—no allusion to the black
hole at Calcutta,—not a word of that vengeance and retri-
butive justice which must have been prompted by the
most cruel, black, and horrid exercise of tyranny which
stains the annals of human nature. Is this candid ? Is
this the principle to guide inquiry, and to mete out
punishment ? The real fact is this ;—a monster of
tyranny, a murderer and a villain, our mortal enemy, is
to be dethroned. He is dethroned by a conquering
army, and put to death. This transaction—a series of
fighting and victory—was so rapid, that every moment
was filled with great events. From these originated the
vast empire of the East India Company. Without these
the East India Company would have continued pedlars
instead of being transformed into mighty sovereigns.
The honorable gentleman has declaimed much on the
stain upon the British name from the manner in which
this revolution was conducted. I am of a very different
opinion : when our feuds and animosities are forgotten,
the recorded pen of a candid historian will trace in im-
perishable characters the just eulogy, that in a revolution
which acquired to the Company a dominion larger,
wealthier, and more populous than ever Athens possessed,
or Rome herself when she had conquered the Italian
states,—larger than France, and in revenues superior to
most of the powers of Europe,—that in the career of such
conquests very few occurrences happened which reflected
dishonor on individuals,—none that tarnished the British

name. As to General Caillaud's signature standing to an order of assassination, he solemnly declares that the whole was a feint of the Nabob to discover the sentiments of the army, protests that, had he known the use which was made of it, he would not have done it for a thousand worlds: in this he appeals to the testimony of the whole army and navy, and to every officer in the civil service. One of the resolutions is, that all the fortunes then made are, after sixteen years, without distinction, to be refunded. For shame! What! is this to be the national gratitude for exploits which have been the pride of Britain, the envy of Europe, and the admiration of the whole world? Upon such odious insinuations are we to raise an envious hand against those laurels which flourish on the brows of men who have done so much? You would now plunder the men to whose bravery, conduct, and unparalleled activity you owe this vast empire. You would imitate the democratic tyranny of an Athenian mob, envious of every great and noble name,—taking off one for his wealth, imprisoning another for family, and banishing a third for his fame. It is this detestable spirit which would establish real tyranny at home, in complaining of imaginary grievances in distant lands."

The resolutions were all carried, but there was a reaction in the public mind in favor of Clive, after his melancholy end, and posterity has done him justice, by regarding him as one of the greatest of conquerors and of statesmen.[1]

We find, from the following familiar letter to him, that

---

[1] 17 Parl Hist 862. Gibbon, who heard this speech of Wedderburn, seems to have thought justly that it was rather declamatory. "11th May, 1773.—The House of Commons sat late last night. Burgoyne made some spirited motions Wedderburn defended the Nabobs with great eloquence, but little argument The hounds go out again next Friday They are in high spirits, but the more sagacious ones have no idea they shall kill Lord North spoke for the inquiry, but faintly and reluctantly"—*Miscell Works*, vol 1. p 469—Lord Clive was very desirous of having this vindication of his conduct revised and printed by the author, but Wedderburn was wisely contented with the éclat he had acquired from the newspaper reports of it I have known several instances of an orator kicking down the reputation of a successful speech by publishing it—success in speaking often arising from accidental circumstances which do not touch the reader It is better, therefore, that there should be an opening for friends to allay public disappointment by observing,—" What a pity he did not follow the example of Burke, and publish a full and correct edition of his speech, instead of trusting to *vile newspaper reporting*"

Wedderburn, ever most zealously earnest to exalt his actions and to clear his character, was striving to see justice done to him by the great patriarch of literature, who was then supposed to be able to guide the opinions of mankind on all civil affairs.

"MY DEAR LORD,

"Mr. Stuart informs me that he has sent your Lordship a letter he received from the gentleman (Dr. John More) who has the care of the Duke of Hamilton, at Geneva, expressing the desire that Voltaire has to be informed of the affairs of the East Indies, and to celebrate the great actions that have been done there. I took the precaution of desiring Mr. Clive to load his trunk with the most important papers that are printed on that subject; but it has occurred to me that he would deliver them with a better effect if they were introduced by a few lines from your Lordship, or at least a written message to the old gentleman. I don't know whether Mr. King is at Walcot; he would be delighted to have an occasion of addressing his favorite author on this subject. Lady Clive will, I am afraid, scruple at a correspondence with so free a writer; but whatever mischief his works may do for a better state, in this world they are very entertaining; and that justice to yonr fame, which is everywhere your due, will have a good effect in England, coming from the pen of a Frenchman, writing at the foot of the Alps. I have seen no creature but lawyers for a fortnight past, and I know no news. Robert desires I would make his apology to your Lordship for suffering himself to be seduced by me to give me one day at Mitcham, which I am sure you will forgive. Mrs. W. joins me in compliments to Lady Clive and Miss Ducarelle, and I am, my dear Lord,

"Yours most sincerely,
"A. W.

"Lincoln's Inn Fields, 9th July, 1773." [1]

I should be glad, for the relief of the reader, if I could

---

[1] Townsend's Lives, vol i. p. 179. Wedderburn continued on friendly terms with Lord Clive, and there are to be found in the Rosslyn MSS a considerable number of letters from the one to the other, but they turn chiefly on the local politics of the county of Salop, and on private business. I give an extract from a letter of Lord Clive to Mr. Wedderburn of a different complexion, dated Geneva, Dec 19, 1775, showing the enthusiastic impiety of Voltaire, which unhappily was then much admired —"To prevent our being

here present the subject of this memoir as he then was in private life; but I have been able to find little except his struggles for professional and political advancement. On the 1st of December, 1767, he had married Betty Anne, sole child and heir of John Dawson, of Marly in the county of York, Esq, who brought him a considerable fortune, and he lived with her harmoniously and courteously,—but he was childless, and his chief enjoyment seems to have been in ambition. He never abandoned himself to the amusement of the hour; he was not even solicitous to shine in conversation, considering the *éclat* from a *bon mot* in the salon poor compared with that from a brilliant speech in Parliament. Having little pleasure in literature for its own sake, he referred to books only that they might assist him in his speeches, and he mixed with literary men that they might sound his praise. He was now able to gratify his passion for splendor, in which he seems to have taken delight, independently of its tendency to raise his consequence in the world. He told Lord Haddington that the day he was made Solicitor General he ordered a service of plate which cost him £8,000. Lord Clive for his services had not only given him lacs of rupees and returned him to Parliament, but had magnificently made him a present of a splendid villa at Mitcham, in Surrey. Here he used on Saturdays and Sundays to entertain the great and the witty. He likewise had an elegant house in Lincoln's Inn Fields, not far from that occupied by the Duke of Newcastle— a quarter which I recollect still remaining the envied resort of legal magnates. A coach and six was no longer considered indispensable for a law officer of the Crown;[1]

quite melancholy, however, the Château de Ferney has furnished us with a little anecdote. it is almost too trifling for a place in a letter, its only claim is the want of other events more interesting   Monsieur Gibber, one of the Paris literati paid a visit to Ferney.   Voltaire was ill, and not to be seen; he gave orders, however, for his visitors being well entertained.   Monsieur Gibber, after having dined and waited a long time ineffectually, in hopes that Voltaire would appear for a moment, wrote on a card these lines.—

'Je crois voir ici le vrai Dieu du Génie,
L'entendre, lui parler, l'admirer en tout point:
Mais il est comme Dieu dans l'Eucharistie,
On le mange, on le boit, mais on ne le voit point'

'"Que l'on m'amène," cries Voltaire, 'ce cher impie, ce cher incrédule!'"

[1] When Sir Dudley Ryder (who had not been long dead) was Attorney General having a house in Chancery Lane, and a villa at Streatham, he always traveled between them in a coach and six   When I was Attorney

but in horses and equipages he rivaled the nobility, so that, if his debts had been all paid, it is doubtful whether at this time he would have been found richer than when he was set down at the Bull and Mouth by the Edinburgh stage coach. Yet he never allowed such matters at all to interfere with his attention to business, and he could throw his whole soul into any cause in which public distinction was to be acquired.

I now come to his memorable contest with Benjamin Franklin.[1]

"The babe that was unborn might rue
The *speaking* of that day."

It mainly conduced to the civil war which soon followed, and to the dismemberment of the empire,—by exciting overweening arrogance on one side, and rankling revenge on the other. Had Franklin been soothed, instead of being insulted, America might have been saved. As yet, though eager for the redress of the wrongs of his transatlantic brethren, he professed, and I believe he felt, respect and kindness for the mother-country, and a desire that all differences between them might be honorably reconciled. Being agent for the province of Massachusetts, and having got possession, by mysterious and probably unjustifiable means of certain letters written by Mr. Hutchinson, the Lieutenant-Governor, and Mr. Oliver, the Chief Justice of that province, to Mr. Whately, who had been private secretary to George Grenville,—recommending the employment of a military force for the suppression of the discontents there,—he transmitted them to the Speaker of the House of Assembly, and, being publicly read, they were considered evidence of a conspiracy to destroy the liberties of the colonies. A petition to the King was unanimously agreed to, praying for the recall of the Lieutenant Governor and the Chief Justice. This petition was very imprudently referred to a committee of the Privy Council, that its allegations might be openly discussed. The Executive Government ought quietly to have disposed of it, either by refusing its prayer, or by transferring the parties complained against to some other sphere, where their services would be more

General I had the pleasure of traveling, when I chose, on the top of a stage coach or in an omnibus—in which I met a ducal member of the Cabinet.

[1] See Chatham Correspondence, iv 322

available for the public good ; but it was thought that a glorious opportunity had occurred of publicly inveighing against the colonists, and of heaping odium on their champion.

As the day for the hearing approached, public expectation was raised to a higher pitch than it had been by any juridical proceeding in England since the trial of Sacheverell. The scene was the Council-chamber at the Cockpit, Whitehall. Thirty-five privy councillors attended,--with Earl Gower, the Lord President at their head. Accommodations was made near the bar for Burke, Priestley, Jeremy Bentham, and other distinguished strangers, and the adjoining rooms and passages were crowded by an innumerable multitude, who could only catch some distant murmurs of the vituperation, and inquire from time to time what was likely to be the result. We have, from Jeremy Bentham, a curious description of the apartment, and the appearance of him who was beheld of all beholders:—" The president's chair was with the back parallel to and not far distant from the fire ; the chimney piece, projecting a foot or two, formed a recess on each side. Alone, in the recess on the left hand of the president, stood Benjamin Franklin, in such a position as not to be visible from the situation of the president, remaining the whole time like a rock, in the same posture, his head resting on his left hand, and in that attitude abiding the pelting of the pitiless storm." Dunning and Lee stood at the bar as counsel for the petitioners. Wedderburn, as Solicitor General, alone attended for the Crown, or, more properly speaking, as assessor to the Privy Council. " His station was between the seats of two of the members on the side of the right hand of the Lord President." [1]

Dunning and Lee began, but their speeches are entirely lost ; they are said to have spoken feebly, being ashamed (as some insinuated) of the manner in which the letters had been obtained and made public. [2]

Wedderburn did not stand in need of the stimulus of a fierce attack ; but came fully charged with venom, which

---

[1] Jeremy Bentham. When the Attorney and Solicitor General now attend as assessors to the Privy Council, they are placed at a small table at the upper end of the great table at which the members sit

[2] See a letter from Priestly, *Monthly Magazine*, Nov. 1802. 2 Adolph 41

he had long been distilling. We have by no means a full report of his speech, but some of the most striking passages of it have been handed down to us. "The present question," he observed, "is of no less magnitude than whether the Crown shall ever be permitted to employ a faithful and steady servant in the administration of a colony? His Majesty, in appointing Mr. Hutchinson, followed the wishes of his people; no other man could have been named in whom so many favorable circumstances concurred to recommend him. A native of the country, whose ancestors were among its first settlers—a gentleman who had for many years presided in the law courts —of tried integrity—of confessed abilities—and who has long devoted himself to the study of the history and constitution of the country he was to govern. Against him the petitioners do not attempt to allege one single act of misconduct during the four years he has ruled over them. So the Chief Justice, equally remarkable for his learning and his integrity, stands unaccused and unsuspected of any malversation in his office. Yet both are to be punished by a disgraceful removal. Let me examine the only ground which my learned friends have taken in support of the petition. Abstaining from any charge of official misconduct, they have read to your lordships the Assembly's address,— they have read the letters, and they have read the censures passed upon them. But having then contented themselves with praying the dismissal of these meritorious servants of the public, they frankly admit to your lordships that there is no cause to try; there is no charge—there are no accusers—there are no proofs. They simply say, 'the Lieutenant Governor and the Chief Justice should be censured, because they have lost the confidence of those who complain against them.' This is so very extraordinary a proceeding that I know of no precedent, except one, but that, I confess, according to the Roman poet's report, is a case in point:—

'Nunquam, si quid mihi credis, amavi
Hunc hominem Sed quo cecidit sub crimine? Quisnam
Delator? Quibus indicibus? Quo teste probavit?
Nil horum verbosa et grandis epistola venit
A Capreis—bene habet. nil plus interrogo'"

Having examined the letters, and contended that they were harmless, and at all events that they were private, so that they could not possibly be made the foundation of a charge of public misconduct, he said:—"On the part of Mr. Hutchinson and Mr. Oliver, however, I am instructed to assure your lordships that they feel no spark of resentment even against the individuals who have done them this injustice They are convinced that the people, though misled, are innocent. If the conduct of a few ill-designing men should provoke a just indignation, *they* would be the most forward, and I trust the most efficacious, solicitors to avert its effects. They love the soil, the constitution, the people of New England; they look with reverence to this country, and with affection to that. For the sake of the people they wish some faults corrected, anarchy abolished, and civil government re-established. But these salutary ends they wish to promote by the gentlest means. They wish no liberties to be abridged which a people can possibly use to its own advantage. A restraint from self destruction is the only restrain they desire to be imposed upon New England." Wedderburn then, as the *coup-de-grace* to his victim, whom he thought he had almost sufficiently tortured, proceeded to consider the manner in which the letters had been obtained and published. "How they came into the possession of any one but the right owners," he said, "is still a mystery for Dr. Franklin to explain. He was not the rightful owner, and they could not have come into his hands by fair means. Nothing will acquit Dr. Franklin of the charge of obtaining them by fraudulent or corrupt means, for the most malignant of purposes,—unless he stole them from the person who stole them. This argument is irrefragible. I hope, my lords, you will mark and brand the man, for the honor of this country, of Europe, and of mankind. Private correspondence has hitherto been held sacred in times of the greatest party rage, not only in politics, but in religion. The betrayer of it has forfeited all the respect of the good, and of his own associates. Into what companies will the fabricator of this iniquity hereafter go with an unembarrassed face, or with any semblance of the honest intrepidity of virtue? Men will watch him with a jealous eye—they will hide their papers from him, and lock up their escritoires. Having hitherto aspired after fame by his writings, he will henceforth esteem it a libel to be called *a man of letters*—'*homo trium literarum.*'[1]

[1] *Fur*, a thief

But he not only took away these papers from one brother, he kept himself concealed till he nearly occasioned the murder of another. It is impossible to read his account, expressive of the coolest and most deliberate malice, without horror.[1] Amidst these tragical events, of one person nearly murdered—of another answerable for the issue—of a worthy governor hurt in the dearest interests —the fate of America in suspense—here is a man who, with the utmost insensibility of remorse, stands up and avows himself the author of all. I can compare him only to Zanga in Dr. Young's REVENGE—

> ......' Know then, 't was I.
> I forged the letter—I disposed the picture—
> I hated, I despised—and I destroy.'

I ask, my Lords, whether the revengeful temper attributed by poetic fiction only to the bloody-minded African, is not surpassed by the coolness and apathy of the wily New Englander?"

The effect of this invective upon the hearers was greater than almost anything we read of in the history of English eloquence. Says Jeremy Bentham, "Without any prejudice in favor of the orator, I was not more astonished at the brilliancy of his lightning, than astounded by the thunder that accompanied it." We can easily conceive the delight of the assembled Privy Councillors, who had been selected and summoned on this occasion—from their known hatred of the discontented Americans, and their impatient desire to coerce them— but, without very strong testimony, we could not give credit to the stories circulated of their demeanor,—considering that they were sitting as judges, and that at least the *affectation* of impartiality might have been expected

---

[1] This refers to a duel in Hyde Park between a Mr. John Temple, of Boston, accused of having been instrumental in procuring and publishing the letters, and Mr Wm Whately, a brother of the gentleman to whom they were addressed, and from whose effects they were supposed to be purloined. Thereupon, Dr Franklin wrote a letter to a newspaper, in which he said, " I think it incumbent on me to declare (for the prevention of future mischief) that I alone am the person who obtained and transmitted to Boston the letters in question They were not of the nature of *private letters between friends :* they were written by public officers to persons in public stations, on public affairs, and intended to procure public measures , they were therefore handed to other public persons who might be influenced by them , their tendency was to incense the mother country against her colonies, and, by the steps recommended, to widen the breach —which they effected."

from them. "Nevertheless," says Dr. Priestley, "at the sallies of his sarcastic wit, all the members of the Council (the President himself, Lord Gower; not excepted) frequently laughed outright. No person belonging to the Council behaved with decent gravity, except Lord North, who, coming late, took his stand behind a chair opposite me"[1] Some accounts represent that they actually cheered him, as if they had been listening to a spirited party-speech in Parliament. Lord Shelburne, in a letter to Lord Chatham, writes, "The indecency of their behavior exceeded, as is agreed on all hands, that of any committee of election;"[2] and Charles Fox, in the debate on the renewal of the war in 1803, warning the House not to be led away by the delusive eloquence of Pitt, reminded them "how all men tossed up their hats, and clapped their hands in boundless delight, at Mr. Wedderburn's speech against Dr. Franklin, without reckoning the cost it was to entail upon them."[3]

The Committee of the Privy Council instantly voted, "That the petition was false, groundless, vexatious, and scandalous, and calculated only for the seditious purpose of keeping up a spirit of clamor and discontent in the province." The King in Council confirmed the report, and Dr. Franklin was dismissed from the office of Deputy Postmaster General in America. He himself had sat during the whole of the proceedings before the Privy Council, although all eyes were directed upon him, in the position in which Jeremy Bentham has described him,— without moving a muscle. He pretended to despise the vituperation as "the idle air one hears but heeds not"— saying, "It was a matter of indifference to him that a venal lawyer was hired and encouraged to abuse the petitioners and their agent in the grossest terms scurrility could invent—and that a man so mercenary, if well fee'd, would have been equally loud in his praise, or in praise of the Devil." But the speech which Franklin thus pretended to despise, had rankled in his heart. What secret

---
[1] Letter from Dr Priestley, *Monthly Magazine*, Nov 1802
[2] Chatham Correspondence, iv 322 —Lord Shelburne adds, "The scurrilous invective was occasioned, as Dr. Franklin says, by some matter of private animosity, as Mr Wedderburn says—by his attachment to his deceased friend Mr Whately, the publication of whose correspondence contributed to inflame the Assembly to their late resolutions"—*Letter*, dated 3rd Feb 1774
[3] Lord Brougham's Characters, vol 1 74

vow he made he never revealed, but, years afterwards, on the termination of the war by which the independence of America was established, being then Ambassador of the United States at Paris, he signed the articles of peace in the identical dress which he had worn when inveighed against by Wedderburn. "He had stood," says Dr. Priestley, "conspicuously erect during the harangue, and kept his countenance as immovable as if his features had been made of wood But the suit of 'Manchester velvet' which he then wore, was again put on at the treaty of Paris. These clothes had never been worn since or afterwards. I once intimated to Dr. Franklin the suspicion which his wearing those clothes on that occasion, had excited in my mind, when he smiled, without telling me whether it was well or ill founded."

Wedderburn must be severely condemned for thus pandering to the low passions of his countrymen, instead of honestly trying to enlighten them. So objectionable was this proceeding, which he probably prompted, and in which he played the principal part,[1] that Adolphus, the almost indiscriminate apologist of all the measures of George III.'s reign, is driven to confess that "the character of the inquiry, and the dignity of the tribunal to whose investigation it was submitted, were not duly considered. Ministers, taught by experience, ought to have known the degradation which they must inevitably incur when they elevated an individual into the rank of a personal opponent. Dr. Franklin, who had recently completed his sixty-seventh year, who was known and honored in the most eminent philosophical and literary societies in Europe, sat, with his gray unadorned locks, a hearer of one of the severest invectives that ever proceeded from the tongue of man; and an observer of a boisterous and obstreporous merriment and exultation, which added nothing to the dignity of his judges. He had sufficient self-command to suppress all display of

---

[1] "Lord Haddington, who witnessed the scene in the Privy Council, ascribed the onslaught (the impolicy of which every one felt at the time) to some passionate quarrel that had occurred shortly before between W and F. Many years after, Lord Loughborough being asked whether he had not taken up some violent personal dislike to Franklin, admitted it, but he was blindly keen on the American question, and political feeling may account for all the vituperation he bestowed on the Bostonian."—*Lord Commissioner Adam.*

feeling; but the transactions of the day sunk deeply into his mind, and produced an inextinguishable rancor against this country which colored all the acts of his subsequent life, and occasioned extensive and ever-memorable consequences."[1]

Although the present exultation was unbounded, a day of repentance and humiliation was to follow;

> "Turno tempus erit, magno cum optaverit emtum
> Intactum Pallanta, et cum spolia ista diemque
> Oderit."

Meanwhile, to keep up the annoyance and irritation, Wedderburn caused a bill in equity to be filed against Franklin, under pretense of praying an account of the profits which he had made by publishing the letters from Boston, but with the real view of compelling him to discover on oath from whom and by what means he had received them. In his answer he swore "that he neither caused nor was privy to the printing of the letters, and that he had not made nor ever intended to make any profit by them." To the rest of the discovery he put in a demurrer, which, on the argument of the Solicitor General, was overruled by Lord Bathurst; but this petty warfare in the Court of Chancery was interrupted by the glare of conflagrations and the booming of artillery on the western shore of the Atlantic.

It happened that immediately after the judgment of the Privy Council, by which the giddy multitude, comprehending persons in the highest station, thought that the pretensions of the Americans were forever crushed, and that they must be brought into a state of quiet, if not contented, subjugation, news arrived of the combination at Boston against the consumption of taxed tea, of the seizure of several cargoes of this commodity, and of the burning of an English ship of war sent to enforce regulations for the levying of the tea duty.[2] A royal

[1] 11 Adolph 46. See Franklin's Memoirs, i. 185
[2] The Gaspée. It is hardly possible to conceive that the continent of North America could have permanently continued an appendage of our little island, and the actual event is perhaps better even for us, but had it not been for the infatuated resolution to persist in this wretched tax, for the purpose of showing that we possessed a power, which all parties now agreed could not be beneficially exercised—the connection between the two countries might have long continued—till at last they amicably separated It required a long course of wanton irritation to root out the disposition of the vast mass of the

message was immediately sent to both Houses of Parliament, demanding measures of vengeance. The "Boston Port Bill," and the "Bill for the improved Administration of Justice in the Province of Massachusetts Bay," were introduced, and warmly supported by Wedderburn. In answer to the argument that these bills violated charters, he boldly said: "It will be found necessary to disregard their charters if you mean to restore subordination among them; but I hope and firmly wish that even the idea of your authority being known to them will at once prevent the exertion of it. I agree with the honorable gentleman (Colonel Barré) that conciliation is desirable; but while you hold out the olive branch in one hand, you must grasp your sword with the other. Peace will be established on proper principles when there is a power to enforce it; and your authority once established, I would then drop the point of the sword, and stretch out the olive-branch to the vanquished." "The learned gentleman's speech," exclaimed Burke, "demands blood: the sword must convince the Americans, and clear up their clouded apprehensions! The learned gentleman's logical resources surely desert him if he is obliged to call such a coarse argument as an army to his assistance. Not that I mean to cast any personal reflection upon him: I always respect, and sometimes dread, his talents."[1]

On one clause of the Massachusetts Bill, Wedderburn gained a decided advantage over his opponents. This suspended the power of bringing "an appeal of murder"—a proceeding which, according to the common law of England, might be resorted to by the heir of the deceased after an acquittal by a jury on a prosecution in the name of the King,—in which the trial was by BATTLE, and in which, upon a conviction, the Crown had no power to pardon. Such is the force of faction in perverting the understanding and the feelings, that an outcry was now made against the Government, as if a resolution had been formed entirely to abolish trial by jury. "I rise," said Dunning, "to support that great pillar of the constitution, the appeal for murder: I fear there is a wish to establish a precedent for taking it away in England as

colonists in favor of the mother country, and to overcome their reluctance to abandon their regular industrial pursuits.

[1] 17 Parl. Hist. 1207

well as in the colonies. It is called a remnant of barbarism and Gothicism. The whole of our constitution, for aught I know, is Gothic Are you, then, to destroy every part of that Gothic constitution, and set up a Macaroni one in its stead? Under a system of ministerial despotism, every institution is denounced which may tend to support our rights and liberties. I wish, Sir, that gentlemen would be a little more cautious, and consider that the yoke we are framing for the despised colonists may be tied round our own necks." Nay, the grave, the enlightened, the didactic, the philosophical Edmund Burke, said, " There is nothing more true than that man has given up his share of the natural right of defense to the state, in order to be protected by it. But this is a part of a system of jurisprudence which ought to be viewed as a whole. If there is an appeal for rape and robbery, you ought to have one for murder. If this brach of our privileges is lopped off, you may soon lay the axe to the root of the tree in our own country. I allow that judicial combat was part of this appeal—which was superstitious and barbarous to the last degree; yet I can not consent that the subject should be dealt with piecemeal—and that any thing valued by our ancestors should be taken away from one part of his Majesty's subjects while it is retained by another."

Mr. Solicitor General Wedderburn.—" Sir, the taxation of America was once denounced as a grievance by gentlemen opposite; but that seems to have sunk into insignificance in their eyes compared with the grievance of suspending in that country trial by battle in cases of murder. The apprehension lately professed by them of the establishment of tyranny at home by the arbitrary acts of the House of Commons, is absorbed in the danger to our liberties by a similar privation. They allow that the appeal of murder is only an effort of private revenge—that it may lawfully be stopped at any time by the appellant on receipt of a sum of money—and that, if it proceeds, the appellee, or accused, by throwing down his glove, is entitled to have his guilt or innocence determined by a deadly combat between the parties or their champions. Certainly in times not very remote the Judges of the Court of Common Pleas did seat themselves on their tribunal in Tothill Fields to see a Writ of Right so determined. But the public was scandalized—the fight was stopped—and no attempt has been made since the reign of Elizabeth to resume this mode of elucidating truth. I must be allowed to doubt whether it is an essential part of our constitution. What a blow, then, did our constitution sustain when the *ordeal* fell into disuse, and women no longer proved their chastity by walking blindfold over burning plowshares! But I should in vain try to reconcile those gentlemen to the proposed alteration or the law if it were to be permanent, and I can only try to soften their opposition by reminding them that the act is meant only to be temporary; so that, at no distant day, they may hope to see their fellow-subjects in America restored to the right which they enjoy, and which patriots in England so highly prize."

Mr. Fox came to the rescue of his friends. He said that he was for abolishing appeals in all criminal cases, and he allowed that the circumstance of their taking away the power of pardoning from the Crown was an insuperable objection to them—but he said he condemned the partial, pitiful legislation of this clause, and he should vote against it. The clause was withdrawn upon the understanding that there should be a general act upon the subject, according to the suggestion of Mr. Fox[1]—but the law continued unaltered till the year 1819, when, an appellee having thrown down his glove on the floor of the Court of King's Bench, and demanded trial by battle, all such appeals were swept away.[2]

[1] 17 Parl Hist. 1291.
[2] 59 George 3, c. 46. See Ashford *v.* Thornton, 1 Barnewall and Alderson, 405, and the proceedings against the brother of Lord Chancellor Cowper, *ante*, Vol. V.

CHAPTER CLXVII.

CONTINUATION OF THE LIFE OF LORD LOUGHBOROUGH TILL HE WAS MADE CHIEF JUSTICE OF THE COURT OF COMMON PLEAS.

IN the beginning of the following year, notwithstanding the measures of coercion resorted to, the exasperation and the courage of the Americans rose; they prepared for resistance, and civil war was clearly impending. In the grand debate which then took place on Lord North's motion for an address to the King, to assure him of the support of Parliament in putting down the rebellion, Wedderburn answered Burke, and he still made use of very intemperate language. He treated rather lightly the distress which had arisen from the interruption to trade in consequence of the measures of Government in America. "In the present instance," said he, "interests are at stake of much greater magnitude. The power of Parliament is defied; a portion of his Majesty's subjects, although they have not yet formally cast off their allegiance, are actually in open rebellion. An enemy in the bowels of the kingdom is surely to be resisted, although manufactures should be interrupted and commerce should languish. The integrity of the empire is more to be regarded than the accumulation of wealth. The question is not now how we may derive most advantage from our American colonies, but whether we are to keep possession of them. The sufferings of individuals are nothing, compared with the safety of the state."[1] Government then had a majority of 304 to 105.

Wedderburn's reckless advocacy may be conceived from the following account of his speech, when, after the affairs of Lexington and Bunker's Hill, regular hostilities had been carried on, and Mr. Fox moved for inquiry into the causes of the ill success of the British arms:—" The Solicitor General defended administrations throughout, not only what they had already done, but every action of theirs, and every consequence arising from their conduct. He insisted that the war was just and expedient, that the

[1] 18 Parl. Hist. 233.

ministers abounded with wisdom, and the army and navy in military prowess." [1]

When Lord John Cavendish made his motion for "a revisal of all acts of parliament by which his Majesty's subjects in America think themselves aggrieved," Wedderburn still urged that force was the only remedy. "Take the sword," said he, "out of the hands of the governing party in America, and I have not a doubt that the country will return to its allegiance with as much rapidity as it revolted. Is it possible to imagine that the Americans themselves can sincerely wish for a continuance of their present government? From freemen they have become slaves. The Congress does not govern America, but tyrannize over it. The arbitrary power of imprisonment exercised there, is inconsistent with every idea of liberty or law. The freedom of the press is annihilated, nor is even sacredness of private correspondence respected; nay, destruction hangs over the man who even in private conversation ventures to express a sentiment distasteful to those who, for the moment, have usurped supreme power. A due regard for the rights of your fellow-subjects imperatively requires the employment of troops to enable the oppressed Americans safely to avow their opinions, to return without danger to their duty, and to recover the blessings of the British constitution." It would appear, from the commencement of Burke's answer, that, on a recent occasion, for once Wedderburn's nerve had failed him;—" Rejoiced I am, Sir, that the gentleman has regained his voice, if not his talent. He would not, or could not, stand up the other night to my honorable friend who inflicted on him such grievous wounds. He lay like Milton's fallen angel, prostrate 'on the oblivious pool.' Why, sir, would he not still remain silent instead of attempting to answer what, in truth, was unanswerable? But the learned gentleman has now called to his assistance the bayonets of 12,000 Hessians, and, as he thinks it absurd to reason at present with the Americans, he tells us, that by the healing, soothing, merciful ministrations of German mercenaries, their understandings will be enlightened, and they will be enabled to comprehend the subtleties of his logic." The Opposition on this occasion could only muster 47 votes. [1]

[1] 18 Parl. Hist. 1154.   [2] Ib. 1431-1448.

But, alas! arrived the disastrous news of the surrender of General Burgoyne and his army at Saratoga. Still the tone of the Solicitor General was undaunted. In the debate on the Address, at the commencement of the next session of parliament, he scorned the notion of conciliation, saying, "The object of the Government should be to oblige the rebels to lay down their arms, and then to treat of conditions: not a hundredth part of America is in arms; to those armed, however, it is necessary to talk with arms in hand; the honor of Britain requires unconditional submission from insurgent subjects." He inveighed against the bitterness of invective that marked the modern oratory of the House, and wished that gentlemen in opposition would learn to gloss over with more decency their incentives to rebellion. Burke ironically praised " the learned gentlemen's humanity, for first cutting the throats of the Americans, and then wishing to truck up a conditional piece with them." [1]

On a subsequent day Wedderburn spoke in a better spirit, which in ancient Rome might have gained him thanks that he did not despair of the republic: "The calamity, he could not deny, was great; but he could not infer from it that our condition was hopeless. We had often received checks, but the spirit of the nation had always made us rise superior to our distresses; an exertion of that spirit would, on the present occasion, infallibly rescue us from danger. Britons ever showed magnanimity in distress, and certain victory was the consequence.

[1] 19 Parl. Hist 444. Although Wedderburn considered himself bound, in parliament, to be a "thick and thin" defender of Ministers, no one was more sensible of their misconduct In letters written shortly before this to his bosom friend, Mr Eden (afterwards Lord Auckland), he says, "I am persuaded that the suspicion in America of instructions that limit the General, is totally false, but surely the want of authority to direct the conduct of a General, if the indecision of his own judgment makes it necessary to direct him—the giving unlimited power without any confidence—the rewarding misconduct—are errors in system that leave us no right to blame fortune."

. . "The peculation in every profitable branch of the service is represented to be enormous, and, as usual, it is attended with a shocking neglect of every comfort to the troops The hospitals are pest-houses, and the provisions served out are poison, those that are to be bought, are sold at the highest prices of a monopoly It hath long been a subject of deep regret with me that Amherst is suffered to remain at home, and I am persuaded he will be sent out still—six months too late" The misfortunes of the war preyed upon his mind From Bath he writes, " I could do vastly well here if I could get out of the sound of the word 'America,' and if I did not dream of it while I go to sleep The waters cure all other complaints."

He wished, therefore, that gentlemen would not be cast down; before now as great misfortunes had happened to us, from which we reaped substantial advantages. As to the fact of a whole army surrendering, which had been described as unprecedented, the annals of this country had furnished a remarkable instance of it in the glorious reign of Queen Anne, when after the Battle of Almanza, General Stanhope was obliged to capitulate, with the whole of the British forces under his command. This, however, did not damp the ardor of the British nation, but urged them on to greater and more successful exertions."[1]

It would appear that about this time Wedderburn had given personal offense, in debate, to Edmund Burke, who had required and received an apology. There is no allusion to the affair in print, but the following letter is found among the Rosslyn MSS.:

"SIR,

" Mr. Fox has informed me of your obliging desire of seeing me, and giving any farther explanation which might be necessary to complete that you had given in your letter of last night. I am very sensible of your politeness and civility on this occasion. But as the letter itself was perfectly satisfactory, I do not wish you to give yourself any further trouble about the matter; and hope we shall both of us banish it entirely from our thoughts.

"I am, with great esteem and regard,
"Sir,
" Your most obedient and humble servant,
"EDM. BURKE.

"Dec. 4, 1777."

Wedderburn now refused the office of Chief Baron of the Exchequer, because it was not to be accompanied with a peerage, and although attempts were made to soothe him, by other offers, he seems to have been very much dissatisfied with the manner in which he was treated by the Prime Minister. When the offer was first made to him through Mr. Eden, he wrote back:—

" My temper, you know, does not lead me to be overanxious about gain, and my ambition has hitherto been more gratified by serving my friends than myself. You

[1] 19 Parl. Hist. 539.

may possibly recollect that you foretold, when I accepted my office, that I should not advance my own situation by it. I imagined that the proof I then gave, and those I should continue to give, of attachment to the connection I was forming, would defeat your prophecy. It has turned out differently. In two years I found myself unsupported, and soon afterwards the indirect object of a long-concerted attack, which I was left to withstand as I could. Neither the one instance nor the other abated my zeal, and you know perfectly that I never, under any circumstance of even recent disgust, entertained the least idea of a cabal or of separation from Lord North, but have always wished his influence and authority to be extended and maintained. I must confess to you, however, that neglect has damped my zeal exceedingly, and nothing but distress and difficulty are likely to raise it to its former pitch. In this situation I should act very imprudently, however disgusting retreat may at first seem to an eager mind, if I did not take an opportunity of extricating myself from a position where danger is the only pleasure in possession or in prospect."

After some further negotiation, and an additional *solatium* offered to him, he writes to Mr. Eden :—

"If Lord North, having found me sometimes troublesome, has any degree of indisposition towards me, or even if he is indifferent about me, I hold it to be better to thank him, and to decline the civility he offers. In politics, it is almost the rule of the game to get what you can, and begin upon a new score; but it is a game that neither my temper nor a dread of what I should feel to be a just reproach will allow me to play. If I had no aversion to it, you ought, as a friend of Lord North, to apprise him of the disadvantage; merely to get rid of the present embarrassment, with an opening left for a future misunderstanding, is not worth to him half what he offers. I will now suppose that Lord North's sentiments of me are as friendly as his conversation, and that he is really disposed to treat me as a person attached to him, whose interest he ought to promote. The case will then stand thus: A judicial office of a decent rank actually vacant,—an offer made to the Attorney General, and refused,—the same offer proposed to be made to me, but that intention defeated, because the same promise can not accompany the second offer,[1]—my situation, already not advantageous, somewhat the worse for this event, and Lord North proposes to make it up in some other way. In the first place, I have no inclination to accept the vacant office without any prospect of succeeding to one of those that have been usually attended with the only circumstance that in my estimation makes one such place better than another,—a place in the legislature.[2] At my age, it would be too mortifying to renounce that idea, and I presume Lord North does not wish that I should yet disqualify myself. I should certainly feel myself much strengthened by the application of an office (provided it lay on this side of the Tweed) that would enable me to extend my view beyond my profession, without interrupting me in the pursuit of it. If I am not to rely upon Lord North's friendship, let the matter rest as it does, and an end be put to the appearance of connection at any time when it can be done with the least inconvenience to yourself or any other of my friends. Whatever disadvantage there is in quitting the pretensions that office alone gives, I will submit to that disadvantage if it is only to affect myself. If Lord North seriously wishes to attach me to him as a friend (and you must know better than I can how that point stands), I have then nothing to ask, and no terms to make. He will be as much disposed to serve me as I could wish ; and if he thinks this a proper occasion to demonstrate his friendship in any manner, I shall receive it with pleasure as a favor that I may be able to return. I will make no bargain, nor desire any promise, for with a friend I would rather be obliged to his inclination to serve me than to the constraint of an engagement. In either event I have no wish to keep the present vacancy in suspense one moment. It is a very material object that it should be properly supplied. The 'Customs and Excise' will pay for the folly of a Chief Baron,[3] and it is neither expedient nor handsome to leave

---

[1] I presume that a peerage had been offered to Thurlow in respect of his having been long Attorney General, while it was refused to the Solicitor.

[2] He refers to the chiefships of the King's Bench and Common Pleas. The only Chief Baron who has been a Peer is Lord Abinger.

[3] At that time, it seems to have been considered that the only business of the Chief Baron was to try smugglers. When Sir W. Garrow was Attorney General, he claimed this office on the death of Chief Baron Thomson, but Lord Eldon insisted on the patronage as belonging to the Great Seal, and

it open to such solicitations as I hear are used to obtain it."

An accommodation was brought about by the promise of a sinecure, and the highest judicial promotion in the wake of Thurlow. While Wedderburn held his present office, he shone forth chiefly as a a politician, and we do not hear much of his efforts at the Bar. However, he was in the full lead in the Court of Chancery against Thurlow, and, by artful statement of facts, he was supposed to have more influence over the mind of Lord Bathurst than that formidable rival could acquire by a more confident manner and a deeper knowledge of law.[1] He assisted, as counsel for the Crown, in the prosecution of John Horne Tooke for a libel, but he contented himself with examining a witness, to prove that the MS. from which it was printed was in the handwriting of the defendant, and after the conviction, he did not join in praying that the infamous punishment of the pillory might be inflicted.[2] He contrived to avoid being mixed up in the controversy which Thurlow conducted fiercely for so many years, respecting the rights of juries on trials for libel; and at no period of his career, till the breaking out of the French Revolution, did he show himself unfriendly to the liberty of the press. His best forensic argument was on the trial, before the House of Lords, of the Duchess of Kingston, for bigamy, to prove that the sentence she had collusively obtained in the Ecclesiastical Court against the validity of her first marriage, was no bar to the prosecution. This was distinguished by lucid

showed that no Attorney General had been made Chief Baron for hundreds of years.

[1] As an advocate, his merit is very considerable He is patient, attentive, constant to his business, and speaks with judgment, force, and zeal. He discerns very readily the strong and weak parts of his cause, and accordingly dwells on or hastens over them He has practiced constantly in the Court of Chancery, as the court in which his knowledge of the civil law would be of most use to him; and has obtained there a degree of eminence, in which, by reason of the Attorney General's indolence, be at present stands without a competitor He is now warmly supported by the first influence in the kingdom, namely, those who are at the head of that set of men who term themselves 'King's friends,' and it is only because the pretensions and interest of this gentleman and of the Attorney General are equally balanced, that they have both kept their places, and that the present Chancellor has been suffered to keep the Seals so long "—*Extract from a Letter printed in the Public Advertiser, March 3, 1778, and signed "Observer"*

[2] 20 State Trials, 651, 1380. *Ante*, Ch CLVI.

arrangement, cogent reasoning, and a scientific acquaintance with the great principles of juridical procedure,—and it may now be studied both with pleasure and advantage.[1]

Immediately upon the close of the session, in June, 1778, Thurlow received the Great Seal, and Weddurburn succeeded him as Attorney General.[2] This office he held two years, exercising its invidious functions with for-

---

[1] 20 State Trials, 464 The whole of it is too close and connected to admit of any extract being made of it, and it has the merit of great severity of composition—avoiding both proemium and peroration. The follow is a very interesting account of this proceeding, by the Lord Justice Clerk Hope, from the narrative of his uncle, the late Earl of Haddington —" Lord H. always spoke of W.'s oratory in the Duchess of Kingston's case as the *most accomplished* he ever heard The case, as is well known, was got up by the Duchess herself, to show herself off, and attract notoriety after her long absence. Of course, the result was necessarily apparent to every one from the first. The scene was the great fashionable spectacle of the day, and attracted a great concourse. W treated the whole affair exactly as the Duchess intended it to be, a useless and ostentatious exhibition He neglected no part of the legal argument as to the sentence of the Ecclesiastical Court (as the report showed), but made that quite subordinate to the occasion of exalting himself, and eclipsing in the spectacle the Duchess herself In this he completely succeeded. Thurlow was coarse, vehement, and full of zeal; and on the other side, the civilians labored always as if anything could follow out of the affair but the laugh in which it all ended W. played with the whole matter—quizzed the Duchess inimitably, and with infinite wit—jeered Thurlow—bantered Dunning and the civilians, and delighted the fine gentlemen and ladies who attended, and the very result of the solemn farce was what two of the persons acting in it intended,—that all London talked of the Duchess's splendid figure and appearance for her age, and of W.'s wit, eloquence, and superiority of public talent "

[2] It would appear that shortly before this he had met with a great mortification in not being appointed to a sinecure, which he conceived that Lord North had promised him, and which was given to Mr M'Kenzie He writes to Mr Eden " If Lord North doubts my attachment to him after the many proofs he has had of it, your testimony or my declaration would be of little use to demonstrate it. But I am persuaded he is convinced of it, and upon that supposition I can not conceive a reason for his treatment of me, except an opinion that I would take it very patiently. Now, though my attachment to Lord North has been very much marked, yet I flatter myself it hath not discovered itself to be pointed either towards his office or my own, nor am I conscious of any feature in my character that should distinguish me as very liable to submit to ill-usage. I have some curiosity, therefore, to know the *ratio suasoria* for canceling an engagement to me that had been publicly known for years,—in complaisance to Colonel Murray's importunity. If you can tell me any sufficient reason for not only the unkind, but humiliating, neglect Lord North has made me feel upon this occasion, I shall endeavor to put up with it, but if you can find none, I must then beg the favor of you to acquaint him that I have been too much, and too warmly, his friend to sink down quietly into the humble servant of his office " Mr Eden brought about a reconciliation, which was much facilitated by the approaching vacancy in the Attorney Generalship.

bearance and mildness. Notwithstanding the licentious publications which now came forth, such as "Resistance no Rebellion," in answer to "Taxation no Tyranny," he wisely filed no *ex-officio* information for libel; and his Excise and Customs prosecutions in the Exchequer were allowed to be conducted only with a view to punish frauds on the revenue, and to protect the fair trader.

He had to conduct one very important prosecution in the Court of King's Bench, which had been directed by the House of Commons against Mr. Stratton and other members of the Council of Madras for deposing Lord Pigot from the Government of, that presidency. His opening Speech, and his reply, detailing and commenting upon very complicated transactions, were exceedingly able; but the case is now chiefly memorable for having called forth one of the earliest displays of the extraordinary eloquence of Erskine. The defendants being found guilty, Mr. Attorney, in obedience to his instructions, pressed for a sentence of imprisonment; but the Court let them off with a fine of £1,000 a-piece—to the high dissatisfaction of Edmund Burke, who repeatedly animadverted in the House of Commons on the impunity thus held out to outrages in India.[1]

While Attorney-General, Wedderburn had the merit of assisting in the first relaxation of the Roman Catholic penal code in Ireland, and of co-operating on this subject with men opposed to him in general politics, although I am afraid that, in his old age, factious and selfish motives carried him over to the side of intolerance. Thus he now wrote to Edmund Burke:—

"I suspect the passage of the Papist bill[2] will not be so smooth as I wish; and that I shall be obliged to break the silence I meant to observe, and write something upon the test. You can, I know, and I hope without much trouble to yourself, refer me to chapter and verse for all that part of ecclesiastical history that regards our tests. Was not occasional conformity once prevented in Ireland? Has it not since—and when—been connived at or permitted by some law? Is not the sacramental test at present merely used as in England, to qualify for acceptance, without

[1] 21 St. Tr. 1025-1294
[2] To be introduced into the Irish Parliament, having been first submitted to the English law officers.

any obligation to receive it during the possession of an office? And is there not, in fact, an act from session to session to allow further time to qualify? If the answer to my questions take more of your time than my stating them does of mine, I do not mean to transfer from myself to you the trouble of consulting an index; but in subjects of daily observation I trust more to the knowledge of one informed by fact, as well as reading (especially when I know the accuracy of my informer), than I dare trust to my own researches."

Wedderburn had now a weighty task in the House of Commons, where the defense of Government chiefly fell upon his shoulders,—with some occasional assistance from his old schoolfellow, Henry Dundas, become Lord Advocate for Scotland. Wallace, the new Solicitor General, was the rough special pleader who had taken part with him in his *forray* on the Northern Circuit,—whom he had afterwards gratefully appointed his devil, and whom he now contrived to draw up after him as a law officer of the Crown; but who was wholly unfit to speak on any subject except a technical point of law.

The new Attorney General took a prominent part in the debate on the first night of the ensuing session. He urged that the House ought to be unanimous in prosecuting the contest with America, and referred to the conduct of Admiral Blake, who, though he disliked the measures of the Usurper, yet, being in the service of his country, called his crew together before he began an engagement, and told them, "however they might differ in opinion as to the first causes of the war, it was now their duty to see that they were not *fooled by the enemy*."[1] In private, however, he was for conciliation. In a letter to Mr. Eden, written shortly before this time, he says,—

"The more I consider the subject (and I have thought of it constantly since I saw you), the more convinced I am of the necessity of a commission to hold out propositions to the Americans, and that the powers of that commission must be as extensive as it is possible in the nature of our government to make them. I would shut the door against no possible proposition; even the idea of a representation from America, if their minds in any corner of the continent should take that bias, should not be ex-

[1] 19 Parl. Hist. 1360.

cluded; the power of offering places, honors, money, should be included. These things can not be expressed either under the Great Seal or in any act of the legislature; and therefore the more open and general the comsion is, the more it resembles the full powers of a minister, the more convenient I think it would be found in the execution."

But no such commission was issued till the close of the contest, when, under an act of parliament, our plenipotentiaries were authorized to treat with those of the United States of America for a treaty of peace.

In parliament Wedderburn stood forth to defend the principle on which the war with the colonists had been begun, and the manner in which it had been conducted; but I can not afford more space for these discussions, although they must be ever interesting to the whole of the Anglo-Saxon race. The contest for American independence was substantially over, and England had to provide for her own safety against a conspiracy of European states that threatened her destruction. Franklin, now ambassador at Paris, instead of putting in an answer to Wedderburn's bill of discovery in the Court of Chancery, about the Boston letters, had induced the French government to enter into a treaty of alliance with the republic which he represented; and the combined fleets of France and Spain not only threatened our possessions in distant parts of the world, but caused an alarm of immediate invasion at home.

To meet this exigency, the Attorney General, as the organ of the Ministry, brought forward a measure of great vigor in a very extraordinary manner. One night, at twenty minutes past twelve o'clock, as the House of Commons was about to adjourn, he rose in his place, and without any previous notice, moved "for leave to bring in a bill to suspend all exemptions from impressment into the navy, together with the right of those impressed to sue out a writ of habeas corpus for their liberation." This, in truth, was to authorize the Government, by a conscription, to man the navy with any portion of the inhabitants of Great Britain at their discretion. The arbitrary nature of the measure he did not attempt to disguise. He defended it on the score of necessity—urging that when the invasion of the soil of Britain was meditated by perfidious foes, it was proper to remove all legal impediments in the way of calling every man to the aid of the state,—to hold out encouragement to the willing,—and to compel the reluctant to join in defending their native land. He stated, that there were six or eight ships of the line ready for sea at Portsmouth, which were useless for want of sailors, and that they could not be manned if the power of impressment continued clogged with common law and statutable restrictions. "Will you, then," he asked, "continue these impediments—submit to an inferiority at sea—allow your men-of-war to rot in your harbors—and trust the existence of this country to the fate of a battle on shore? So confident does the Government feel in the co-operation of Parliament on this occasion, that I do not scruple to tell you, that the unrestricted impressment which this bill is to authorize is begun, that I make this motion at this late hour, without notice, for the purpose of rendering the measure effectual,—and that I hope, by the suspension of standing orders, it may to-morrow be carried through all its stages." *Sir George Savile.*—"I must oppose the motion which is made in a manner so unprecedented, and I wonder the learned gentleman is not ashamed to avow that his reason is *concealment*—reducing the members of this House to act like midnight conspirators! Here, indeed, is vigor to make up for former supineness. The act is to be retrospective;—ministers by anticipation are actually putting it into execution,—and all the salutary forms of parliament are trampled upon, ' lest the public should be apprised of it.' The learned gentleman is not here defending the errors of others. This must be his own measure. He alone could devise it—he alone could propose it. Would the learned gentleman not let one father, one husband, one brother, or one child escape in this general scene of oppression and injustice?" *Wedderburn.*—" The honorable gentleman may easily point out hardships suffered under the usual system of impressing seamen for the navy, but the suffering of a few must be disregarded for the public safety. In times of national misfortune like the present, much must be sacrificed without scruple, and much must be borne without repining. The inconvenience is temporary,—to save us from irremediable degradation and perpetual bondage. The personal obloquy attempted to be thrown upon myself I shall contentedly submit to, if thereby I can be of service to my country." This appeal silenced all further opposition. At one o'clock the bill was brought in, and read a first and second time. The following day it was sent to the Lords, and on the third day it received the royal assent.[1] The victory of Rodney was the consequence. Notwithstanding the faults of Lord North and his colleagues in commencing the American war, and still more in conducting it, we must in candor allow that they displayed great energy in repelling the aggression of France and Spain, and counteracting the machinations of the Northern Powers,—so that their successors were enabled to conclude a peace, safe, and not inglorious.

It would appear that Wedderburn had other rather wild schemes for relieving the country from its difficulties. Thus he writes to his friend, Mr. Eden:—

"A brother projector of mine, Mr. Hart, will call upon you to-morrow morning. He is possessed of a plan for an accommodation with the Americans, which he proposes to sell upon very reasonable terms. You have got mine gratis, and I wish that you would return it to me, if plans bear a price. Mr. Hart, I suspect, is a little mad, but perhaps he may not make the worse politician for that. You may form the same judgment of me when I tell you that I am convinced the safety of the state depends upon two measures, one of which you deem impracticable, and the other, if practicable, useless. The first is a strong levy of Irish Catholics, under French or Austrian officers. I believe it will not succeed if left to the operation of a cold letter to Lord B.; but the case would be very different if some person of confidence were sent over to him, instructed to say more than will ever be expressed in any letter, public or private, of which a regular copy is to be taken. You know what I think of Col. Smith, but I would detach him upon that service, instead of letting him ride a great horse at Whitehall. The second measure is *Ld. Amherst,* and I am persuaded, if properly tried, can not fail; some courting and some commanding may be necessary, and either of them alone will fail. If neither of these points take place, I would not give the price of Mr. Hart's plan for your places or my own prospects. I am prepared to creep back to my shell at

[1] 20 Parl. Hist. 962–966.

Lincoln's Inn, and I shall not find it less easy to get in than I did to come out of it."

But he was shortly to be rescued from the danger of making such an experiment. His last speech in the House of Commons, as counsel for the Ministry, was in the debate on the Earl of Upper Ossory's motion respecting the alarming state of Ireland. That country, left by the Government wholly without military defense in the new European war which had suddenly sprung up, was raising volunteer corps without the sanction of the Crown; and the great mass of the population, although still speaking the language of loyalty, manifested a clear determination by force to obtain a redress of commercial grievances, and to throw off their dependence on the British Parliament. The Opposition took the opportunity to impute this additional peril to the improvidence and imbecility of the Ministers,—and the object of the resolution now moved was to have a censure passed upon them, which might lead to their dismissal. Burke, Dunning and Fox took part in the discussion with even more than their wonted animation, and Lord North (who, we now well know, at that time sincerely wished to retire) seemed to have lost that gayety of heart which in all past misfortunes had hitherto supported him. But Wedderburn rose at a late hour, and restored some credit to the cause of the Government, by a speech which, though imperfectly reported, we can discover to have been a fine one:—

"The honorable members opposite," said he, "no doubt considering themselves absolute perfection, are impatient to be ministers. I will not say that the noble lord who sits near me and his colleagues are not chargeable with faults. Where is there, indeed, a perfect minister, or a perfect man? The question is not of an abstract nature—but one of comparison. We ought not first to establish in our minds the idea of a perfect minister, and then judge his Majesty's present servants by that standard. It is objected to them that they depend for their existence on the favor of the Crown and their adherents in this House. Truly, then, they hold their offices constitutionally. If they could defy the Crown and the Parliament by a great cabal in the country, or by a combination of great families, I would unhesitatingly vote for their removal. I never wish to see a Ministry that will not respect the Throne, and that is not willing and is not obliged to call to its aid all the virtue and all the abilities of the nation. Should a contest take place, such as is anticipated by the honorable gentleman (Mr. Fox), great as his influence is, I hope the Sovereign will prove more powerful. I disapprove of all parties, whether aristocratic or merely popular, which proceed on an exclusive principle. The honorable gentleman has said that the friends he acts with are the friends of their country—that they are united—and that they are determined never to act with the present Ministers or their friends. This is a frank, and may be a useful, avowal. Whether in or out of office, I for one will most certainly set my face against such a monopoly of power."[1]

After trying to show that the present distracted state of Ireland arose from causes over which England had no control, he concluded by saying, that as no neglect had been proved against Ministers, and if there had, this was not the time to pass a vote of censure upon them, he should give his hearty negative to the motion.[2]—On a division there appeared 100 ayes to only 192 noes—an increasing minority, which raised great alarm among placemen, and made Wedderburn inquire with much solicitude respecting the health and looks, the probable death or resignation, of the Chief Justices.

In those days we have seen an Attorney General would not condescend to accept the office of Chief Baron, which was indifferently paid, and not held in high estimation. Lord Mansfield had now been Chief Justice of the King's Bench above twenty years, and, although he was still in the full possession of his faculties, hints were thrown out, but in vain, that it was time for him to enjoy that ease to which he was so well entitled. There appeared a better chance of obtaining for Wedderburn the inferior dignity of Chief Justice of the Common Pleas. De Grey, who then held it, was old and feeble, and often unfit for his work; but there being as yet no fixed retiring allowance

---

[1] *Nescia mens hominum fati, sortisque futuræ.* Ere long Fox was to coalesce with Lord North, and Wedderburn was to be legal adviser of the Whigs, on whose supposed aristocratic feelings he was now so severe.

[2] 20 Parl. Hist. 1239.

for the judges, he was unwilling to give up its large emoluments—particularly as there was an old prothonotary nearly as infirm as himself, whose place he hoped to sell before dying or resigning. The Great Seal was Wedderburn's ultimate object of ambition; but he had no setttled plan for clutching it at this moment, as Thurlow was cordially united with Lord North. The Attorney General could even hear without much excitement of the Chancellor's dangerous fit of the gout; promotion to an office of such frail tenure not being very desirable under a falling minister.

While this negotiation for the retirement of De Grey lingered, Wedderburn was much alarmed by a motion brought forward by Sir George Savile, for a list of the pensions granted by the Crown during the present reign. The abuses of the Pension List afforded an admirable subject for the popular declamation down to the time when they were rectified, at the beginning of the reign of Queen Victoria,—and such a motion was always formidable to a weak Government.[1] Mr. Attorney, however, gallantly came forward, and contended that the fund out of which the pensions were paid was to be considered the private property of the Sovereign, and that the public had no right to interfere with its distribution, and to require the names of those who, by the royal bounty, partook of it:—

"The Crown," he observed, "having a right to deal out its bounty and charity without account, no reason but curiosity can be assigned for producing the names of pensioners. No constitutional ground can be pretended for the disclosure, as no one holding a pension so granted can sit in this House." [A voice, "There are wives of members of parliament in the list!"] "If it be so, is this age become on a sudden so virtuous, that what is given to a wife is always given to the husband? The gentleman might as well say he wishes to see the list, because one member's aunt is in it, and another's third cousin. We are told, ' *The Irish Pension List is printed;* ' but what good has arisen from this publicity? The relations of many respectable families are to be found in it—the ladies

---

[1] I lost my election for Dudley, in the spring of 1834, chiefly through the unpopularity cast upon Lord Grey's Government by Daniel Whittle Harvey's motion respecting the Pension List

of noble peers. Does the pain thus inflicted on individuals produce any benefit to the nation? Without obvious advantage,—to have the virtuous, the noble, the tender-hearted, the innocent, scornfully pointed at, is an invidious exercise of power:

> ' Invidiam placare paras, virtute relictâ?
> Contemnere, misei——'

Would you sacrifice honorable pride at the shrine of malice and expose all that is delicate and sensible, all that indigent and modest virtue wishes to hide, to the licentious obloquy, to the injurious misrepresentation, to the wanton criticism, to the bitter sneer, of the envious and the disappointed? Finally, it is asserted that there are some unworthy persons in the list. That they may be detected, are you to place in the pillory all the innocent and meritorious objects of royal munificence? Such reformation, or such punishment, will make every feeling mind cry out, with Job, 'If you be wicked, woe unto you: and if you be righteous, yet shall ye not lift up your head!'"[1]

The ministry was saved by a majority of two only,[2] and Wedderburn looked more wistfully than ever to the "cushion of the Common Pleas." The application to De Grey was renewed, and higher terms were offered to him to induce him to retire. While he was deliberating and doubting, news of this intrigue reached Sir Fletcher Norton, the Speaker, and threw him into an agony of rage, for he had long watched the declining strength of the tottering Chief Justice, and had reckoned with absolute certainty on succeeding him. He took an opportunity of venting his spleen when the House was in a committee on Mr. Burke's bill for economical reform. He said that on the death of Sir John Cust he had been induced to accept the chair, at the instance of the Duke of Grafton, then Prime Minister, by a promise that he was by no means to be taken out of the line of his profession, and that the way was to be kept open for his return to Westminster Hall, whenever an opportunity offered. He added, "When my character, my standing, and my

[1] 21 Parl Hist 96. To the reproach of my country I am obliged to add that the only other member who held such language was Harry Dundas,—which induced Colonel Barré to observe that "no Englishman could be got to defend the Pension List—so disgraceful was it."   [2] 188 to 186.

general pretensions are considered, I believe it will not be deemed arrogance or vanity in me to say, that I was then at the head of my profession as a common lawyer. But I hear from undoubted authority, that it is in agitation to remove a certain Chief Justice, giving him a pension, and to appoint the Attorney General in his room. I do not doubt that honorable and learned gentleman's abilities, but my assertion will be borne out, when I affirm that he does not stand fairly between me and my claims to professional advancement. I take the earliest opportunity of requiring a full explanation on the subject from the noble lord at the head of the Government. I declare, upon my honor as a gentleman, that I never meant to solicit your attention to the subject while it was quite personal to myself, but I feel that the fountains of justice should be kept pure and unpolluted, and there is now a danger that they may be corrupted. I am ready to prove that money has been offered in order to bring about this arrangement." Lord North denied that he was bound to the promises of his predecessor, and disclaimed all knowledge of any such negotiation as had been referred to.

Mr. Attorney General.—" I can no longer remain silent. The committee must not be left under the false impression that I am a party to any bartering for a judicial office. Whatever might have happened, I never would have accused the noble lord of a breach of promise to me; for I never will negotiate for emolument out of the line of my profession, nor for preferment in it, with the noble lord or any other minister. I have now served his Majesty ten years in the offices of Solicitor and Attorney General, and I have endeavored to do my duty in them with all the zeal and ability which I possess. I hope I shall not be reckoned guilty of presumption if I hint that, during that time, I have received frequent intimations of the intended bounty of my royal master, but that, duly appreciating the favorable opinion of my services entertained in that exalted quarter, my uniform rule has been to pursue the line of my profession, patiently waiting for its honors, if they should ever be spontaneously offered to me. The right honorable gentleman ought to know that I never treated—that I never negotiated—that I never asked for office. As hitherto, I will not go to it—

it shall come to me. I will not lower the profession to which I belong, I will not disgrace my own character, by seeking sinecure emoluments as a compensation for my loss of practice,[1] and then place myself in the way of those who may have a just title to promotion. I know the great respect due to the character and station of the right honorable gentleman. No doubt, when he honors a committee with his opinion, he reduces himself to the level of an ordinary member; but I have been so much accustomed to see him in that chair, the dignity of which he so well supports, that I can not separate him from his office. I therefore bow with submission to his accents and I seek, with lowly reverence, to combat the weight of his authority. I am fully sensible of the justice of his remark, with respect to my unfitness for the bench, compared with his own great requisites. In proportion as I think highly of his professional abilities, I think humbly of my own. I am as ready to allow his superiority as he is eager to assert it. But when the right honorable gentleman quitted Westminster Hall to slide into the enjoyment of a great sinecure, and to be exalted to the high situation he now holds, he left behind him men who continued to labor with industry and assiduity, in hopes that the line of preferment would be open to them. It is rather hard upon them that the right honorable gentleman should secure a claim to return to the profession—not for the purpose of joining in the toil of it, but merely to enjoy those posts of dignity which others in the routine of business had labored to merit, and in their turn to enjoy. For my own part, I look upon the office of judge to be in its nature so delicate, that it is unfit for solicitation; while, at the same time, I own I have not such an opinion of my own insufficiency as to induce me to reject the appointment if it were voluntarily offered to me by those who have the just right to dispose of it. Whatever honors his Majesty may choose to bestow upon so humble an individual, I will receive them with respect and gratitude—but I never will enter into a negotiation with any minister, or exact a promise from him." Then turning to Lord North, he thus concluded: " If the noble lord had spontaneously

---

[1] Sir Fletcher was Chief Justice in Eyre.

made any promise to me, I can assure him that I never would remind him of it, or accuse him of the breach of it. I never shall be so forgetful of my own character, as to make private differences matter of public complaint. I shall never so far degrade myself, and become lost to all sense of the decorum due to the House, as to call upon them to interfere in a personal controversy. I shall never so far forget my duty to my country, as to make a private difference with a minister the ground of my opposing a beneficial public measure."[1]

The vote was taken on the clause for abolishing the Board of Trade, when it was carried, by a majority of 207 to 199.[2]

The Government was thought to be in imminent peril, and the negotiation with De Grey was renewed with fresh energy, he rising in his terms in proportion to the importunity of those who were bargaining with him. But all these speculations were suddenly interrupted by Lord George Gordon's riots. From the timidity of the magistrates, the mob was triumphant, and there was great

---

[1] The Lord Justice Clerk Hope, having had an account of this scene from the late Earl of Haddington and the late Lord Melville who both witnessed it, writes to me —" They both said the effect was most surprising Wedderburn's exordium, though off-hand, seemed quite theatrical and studied. He was so perfectly cool that he either assumed the air of being, and was believed to be, most indignant and vehement,—or he went on with the most deliberate slowness,—as he thought suited the occasion. He spoke for two hours—never took his eagle eye off Norton, whom he was addressing—made *every word tell*— and every word was killing—he made every look and gesture last long enough to produce full effect. I recollect Lord M. said he could not understand how any one could for such a length of time go on with such sarcasm and invective, with such prolonged slowness, as if he had not words, —though all knew and felt that it was done to make the torture which he inflicted more cruel."

[2] 12 Parl. Hist 234-278. In allusion to this vote Gibbon says in his Autobiography —" Among the honorable connections which I had formed, I may justly be proud of the friendship of Mr. Wedderburn, at that time Attorney General, who now illustrates the title of Lord Loughborough and the office of Chief Justice of the Common Pleas. By his strong recommendation, and the favorable disposition of Lord North, I was appointed one of the Lords Commissioners of Trade and Plantations, and my private income was enlarged by a clear addition of between £700 and £800 a year. The fancy of a hostile orator may paint in the strong colors of ridicule the ' perpetual virtual adjournment and the unbroken vacation of the Board of Trade.' But it must be allowed that our duty was not intolerably severe, and that I enjoyed many days and weeks of repose without being called away from my library to the office. I can never forget the delight with which that diffusive and ingenious orator, Mr. Burke, was heard by all sides of the House, and even by those whose existence he proscribed."—*Miscell. Works*, vol. 1. p. 156.

reason to apprehend that the whole metropolis would be laid in ashes.

George III. and his Attorney General both deservedly acquired high credit for their energy in this crisis. When the King heard that the troops which had been marched in from all quarters were of no avail in restoring order, on account of a scruple that they could not be ordered to fire till an hour after the Riot Act had been read, he called a council, at which he himself presided, and propounded for their consideration the legality of this opinion. There was much hesitation among the councillors—as they remembered the outcry that had been made by reason of some deaths from the interference of the military in Wilkes's riots, and the eagerness with which grand juries had found indictments for murder against those who had acted under the command of their superiors. At last the question was put to the Attorney General, who attended as assessor, and gave a clear, unhesitating, and unqualified answer,—to the effect, that if the mob were committing a felony, as by burning down dwelling-houses, and could not be prevented from doing so by other means, the military, according to the law of England, might and ought to be immediately ordered to fire upon them, the reading of the Riot Act being wholly unnecessary and nugatory under such circumstances. We do not know his exact words on this occasion, but they were probably nearly the same which he used when he expounded the true doctrine upon the subject judicially soon after:—" It has been imagined, because the law allows an hour for the dispersion of a mob to whom the Riot Act has been read by the magistrate, the better to support the civil authority, that during this period of time the magistracy are disarmed, and the King's subjects, whose duty it is at all times to suppress riots, are to remain quiet and passive. No such meaning was within the view of the legislature; nor does the construction of the act warrant any such notion. Magistrates are left in possession of those powers which the law had had given them before: if the mob collectively, or a part of it, or any individual, within and before the expiration of that hour, attempts or begins to perpetrate an outrage amounting to felony, it is the duty of all present, of whatever description they may be, to endeavor, by the most effectual means, to stop the mischief, and to apprehend the offender."¹ The council plucking up courage and unanimously concurring, his Majesty said that "this had been decidedly his own opinion, though he would not previously venture to express it—but that now, as supreme magistrate, he would see it carried into effect."² The requisite orders were issued to the troops, the conflagrations were stopped and tranquillity was speedily restored.

With becoming promptitude the rioters were to be tried under a special commission, and Lord Chief Justice De Grey had notice, that he would be required to preside. But he was so alarmed at the thought of such a task that he instantly sent in his resignation, although the old prothonotary, whose place he so much longed to dispose of, still "languishing did live." Wedderburn immediately claimed the Chief Justiceship as by law "the pillow of the Attorney General."³ Lord North in vain tried to induce him to remain in the House of Commons, where his services were so essential to the Government, pointing out to him his chance of the Great Seal if anything should happen to Thurlow, and the certainty of his becoming at no distant time Chief Justice of England in the room of Lord Mansfield; but the wary Scot would not exchange an excellent certainty for contingent splendor, and very adroitly suggested that he might still have an opportunity of supporting the Administration in Parliament, for although it had not been very usual to make the Chief Justice of the Common Pleas a peer, there was at least one precedent for it in the case of Lord Trevor.

On the 14th day of June, 1780, a new writ was moved

¹ 21 St. Tr. 493.
² According to some accounts, he said there was at all events one magistrate in the kingdom who would do his duty.
³ When I was Attorney General, my most amiable as well as witty friend, the late Chief Justice Tindal used, with imitable good humor, to tell the following story :—' I had a stumbling horse that had come down with me several times to the great peril of my life, and many of my friends strongly advised me to get rid of him, but he was very quiet and a great favorite, so that I continued to ride him,—till one day I met Campbell as I was dismounting at Westminster, who said, ' That is a nice horse you have got, Chief Justice ?' I answered, ' Yes, but he has come down with me several times, and I am advised to part with him.' ' Don't, my dear Chief Justice,' cried Mr. Attorney; ' I'll warrant you he is very sure-footed for all that.' I walked home, and sold the animal next morning "—The allegations of fact on which a good story rests may not be traversed.

in the House of Commons for the election of a burgess to serve for Bishops Castle in the room of Alexander Wedderburn, Esq., appointed Chief Justice of the Court of Common Pleas, and summoned to the Upper House by the title of Lord Loughborough, Baron Loughborough of Loughborough, in the county of Leicester.

CHAPTER CLXVIII.

CONTINUATION OF THE LIFE OF LORD LOUGHBOROUGH, TILL HE WAS APPOINTED FIRST COMMISSIONER OF THE GREAT SEAL UNDER THE COALITION MINISTRY.

WEDDERBURN'S promotion, notwithstanding the decided part he had taken in politics, was generally approved of. He was known not to be as yet very deeply versed in English law, but hopes were entertained that, renouncing party connections, he would devote himself to the duties of his new office, and that he would turn out both a learned and an impartial judge. Edmund Burke, with whom he had had so many conflicts in the House of Commons, generously sent him the following letter of congratulation and advice :—

"Charlotte Street, June 15, 1780.

" MY LORD,

" Before I say any thing on business, permit me to congratulate you on your office and your honors. I hope you will auspicate both by your firmness in the course of real government, and that, instead of bringing the littleness of parliamentary politics into a court of justice, you will bring the squareness, the manliness, and the decision of a judicial place into the House of Parliament into which you are just entering. 'Ut tu fortunam.' If you

[1] At the general election, in 1774, Wedderburn had been returned for Castle Rising (London Gazette, 5 Nov) and also for Oakhampton (Ib. 19 Nov.) On the 23rd Nov, 1774, Alexander Wedderburn, Esq, having elected to serve for the borough of Oakhampton, a new writ was ordered for Castle Rising —(35 Com. Journ 62) On the 3rd of June, 1778, on his becoming Attorney General, a new writ was moved for Oakhampton, and he was then returned for his old borough of Bishop's Castle, which happened then to be vacant by Mr. Strachey having accepted office at the same time—(36 Com. Journ. 1006 ; 5 Collins's Peerage, 440).

do this, no difference of sentiment or of connection shall hinder me from rejoicing in your elevation. If I know any thing of myself, I have taken my part in political connections and political quarrels for the purpose of advancing justice and the dominion of reason, and I hope I shall never prefer the means, or any feelings growing out of the use of those means, to the great and substantial end itself."

He then goes on to state certain resolutions which he urges that the Government should move in the House of Commons respecting Dissenters and Roman Catholics, and adds,—

" Until this step is firmly taken, the House will continue under the impression of fear,—the most unwise, the most unjust, and the most cruel of all counselors." [1]

Lord Loughborough began his judicial career by presiding under the Special Commission issued for the trial of the rioters at St. Margaret's Hill, in Southwalk. He gained immense applause on this occasion by his charge to the Grand Jury,—most men, after recovering from their panic, being very indignant against those who had caused it, and thinking, that since the guilt of the offenders could hardly be overcharged, there need be little scruple as to the means of bringing them to punishment. But, although he could not be accused of showing any political bias, the outrages having proceeded entirely from Protestant fanaticism, reflecting men grieved that he still strove for rhetorical fame, and that he displayed the qualities rather of an eager advocate than of a grave judge. I copy some of the most admired passages of this celebrated harangue:—

"GENTLEMEN OF THE GRAND JURY,

" If you have come here totally strangers to the transactions which have lately passed in this neighborhood, or if it were possible for any of you who were not witnesses of them not to have heard of the devastations that have been committed,—the remnants of the flames which have been lately blazing in so many parts of the metropolis, and which must have presented themselves to you in your way to this place, will have sufficiently declared the occasion for which you are called together. His Majesty's paternal care for the welfare of all his subjects would not

[1] Burke's Correspondence, vol. ii. p. 356.

permit him to suffer offenses so daring and so enormous to remain longer unexamined than was legally necessary to convene a jury to enter upon the inquiry. . . . . I think it an essential part of my duty to lay before you, in one general view, a short account of those dangers from which *this kingdom* has been lately delivered. I use this expression, because it will clearly appear, that the mischief devised was—not the destruction of the lives or fortunes of individuals, or of any description of men—no partial evil—but that the blow which it has pleased Providence to avert was aimed at the credit, the government, and the very being and constitution of this state. . . . . A very short time disclosed, that one of the purposes which this multitude was collected to effectuate was, to overawe the legislature and to obtain the alteration of a law by force and numbers. . . . . How the leaders of the insurrection demeaned themselves—what was the conduct of the crowd to members of both Houses of Parliament, it is not my intention to state. My purpose is to inform—not to prejudice or inflame. For this reason, I feel myself obliged to pass over in silence all such circumstances as can not—and as ought not to—be treated of but in stronger language and in more indignant terms than I choose at present to employ. . . . .

"Upon the 3rd of June there was a seeming quiet—a *very memorable circumstance!* for sudden tumults, when they subside, are over. To revive a tumult evinces something of a settled influence, and something so like design, that it is impossible for the most candid mind not to conceive that there lies at the bottom a preconcerted, settled plan of operation. Sunday, the next day,—a day set apart by the laws of God and man as a day of rest, and as a day not to be violated even by the labors of honest industry,—in broad sunshine, buildings and private houses in Moorfields were attacked and entered, and the furniture deliberately brought out and consumed by bonfires. *And all this was done in the view of patient magistrates!*" . . . . "Fresh insults of the most daring and aggravated nature were offered to Parliament, and every one who was in London at the time must remember that it bore the appearance of a town taken by storm. Every quarter was alarmed; neither age nor sex, nor eminence of station, nor sanctity of character, nor even an humble though honest obscurity, were any protection against the malevolent fury and destructive rage of the lowest and worst of men. But it was not against individuals alone that their operations were now directed. What has ever been, in all countries, the last effort of the most desperate conspirators, was now their object. The jails were attacked, the felons released; men whose lives had been forfeited to the justice of the law were set loose to join their impious hands in the work of destruction. The city was fired in different parts. The flames were kindled in the houses most likely to spread the conflagration to distant quarters. And in the midst of this horror and confusion, in order more effectually to prevent the extinguishing of the flames, an attempt to cut off the New River water was made; and this was followed by an attack on the Bank of England, with the view of ruining public credit." .... "In four days, by the incredible activity of this band of furies, parading the streets of the metropolis with burning torches, seventy-two private houses and four public jails were destroyed—one of them the county jail, built in such a manner as to justify the belief that it was impregnable to an armed force. Religion—the sacred name of religion—of that purest and most peaceable system of Christianity, the Protestant Church—was made the profane *pretext* for assaulting the Government, trampling upon the laws, and violating the most solemn precepts which inculcate the duty of man to God and to his neighbors. I am sure there is no man in Europe so weak, so uncandid, or so unjust to the character of the Reformation, as to believe that any religious motive could, by any perversion of human reason, induce the most fanatical to assault magistrates, to release felons, to destroy the source of public credit, and to lay in ashes the capital of the PROTESTANT FAITH. I have now related to you the rise and progress of that calamity from which, by the blessing of Providence upon his Majesty's efforts for our preservation, this kingdom has been delivered—a situation unparalleled in the history of our country."[1]

Having excited the feelings of the jury by a gross exaggeration of the facts, and an artful insinuation that,

[1] 21 St. Tr. 485.

out of tenderness to the prisoners, he had kept back much that might have been truly stated against them, he proceeds to lay down the law, in a manner not quite unexceptionable; and he decidedly *misdirects*, by saying, "You are only to inquire whether the party accused is charged with such probable circumstances as to justify you in sending him to another jury;" for a grand jury ought not to find a true bill unless a case is made out before them against the accused, which, if unanswered, would justify the petty jury to pronounce a verdict of *guilty*.[1]

Burke, feeling that his advice had been thrown away, observes in the "Annual Register," then under his care,— "This charge having been the topic of much conversation, we submit it to the judgment of our readers. The opinions of men respecting the legal propriety of it have been various: as a piece of oratory it has been admired; but its tendency to influence and direct the jury, and inflame their passions against men who ought all to have been supposed innocent till found guilty by their country, has been generally spoken of in terms of indignation by those who are jealous of the rights of humanity."[2]

"Within a short month after the riots themselves," says Lord Brougham, "six-and-forty persons were put upon their trial for that offense, and nearly the whole of the Chief Justice's address consisted of a solemn and stately lecture upon the enormity of the offense, and a denial of whatever could be alleged in extenuation of the offenders' conduct. It resembled far more the speech of an advocate for the prosecution than the charge of the judge to the grand jury.[3] Again, when we find a composition which all men had united to praise as a finished specimen of oratory falling to rather an ordinary level, there is some difficulty in avoiding the inference that an abatement should also be made from the great eulogies bestowed upon its author's other speeches which have not reached us; and we can hardly be without suspicion that much of their success may have been owing to the power of a

---

[1] See Lord Shaftesbury's case, ante, Vol. IV. Chap. XC.
[2] Ann Reg 1780
[3] In the present time no counsel in opening a prosecution would venture to make such a speech, for it is chargeable not only with inflammatory topics, but with a willful over-statement of the facts of the case.

fine delivery and a clear voice in setting off inferior matter."[1]

I do not find any complaint against Lord Loughborough in the progress of these trials, when he came to sum up particular cases to the petty jury. All the prisoners tried before him on this occasion were men of an inferior condition of life, and were clearly guilty, in point of law, of the felonies for which they were indicted; but as they had been urged on by fanatical zeal and the blind fury of others, Burke compassionated their condition, and wrote to the Chief Justice the following letter, so creditable to his humanity, — in the vain hope of saving them:—

"MY LORD,

"I have been out of town for the greater part of the last week, and am only come hither this morning. During that time I have not seen a single newspaper. On my reading the paper of this day, I find that many executions are ordered for this week, although the stock of criminals to be tried is not exhausted; and therefore a distinct view can not be taken of the whole, nor, of course, that selection used, with regard to the number of criminals and the nature of crimes, which, in all affairs of this nature, is surely very necessary. If you remember, I stated to your Lordship, when I met you at Lord North's, what had struck me on this subject, and I thought it had then his and your approbation. I afterwards mentioned the same thing to the Chancellor, and sent him a memorandum on it just before I left town. I am convinced that long strings of executions, with the newspapers commenting on them, will produce much mischief. I do earnestly beg of your Lordship, whose humanity and prudence I have no doubt of, to turn this business in your mind, and to get the executions suspended until you can think over the matter, with a proper consideration of the whole and of the several cases: for you know what a disgrace it would be to Government that the order of time of trial should settle the fate of the offenders, especially as they are low in condition, and the managers have had the wicked address not to expose themselves. I beg you to excuse my solicitude. I am really uneasy, and forbode no good from this business

[1] Lord Brougham's Statesmen of George III., vol. 1. p. 77.

unless your good judgment and good nature exert themselves from the beginning to the end. I have the honor to be always, with sincere regard and esteem,
"My Lord,
"Your Lordship's most obedient and humble servant,
"EDMUND BURKE.
"Charlotte Street, Monday, July 17, 1780"[1]

A great example was deemed necessary, and the rioters were executed by the score.

Luckily for Lord George Gordon, it was found that he had not done anything in the county of Surrey which could be construed into an overt act of high treason, and therefore his case was not within the cognizance of this Special Commission. Had he been now arraigned, the unexampled eloquence of his counsel would probably only have stimulated the rivalry of the new Chief Justice, and he could hardly have escaped an ignominious death; but his trial was postponed till the public mind was in a calmer state, and it then came on before a milder Chief Justice.[2]

Lord Loughborough continued in the Court of Common Pleas during a period of nearly thirteen years. As a common-law judge he did not stand very high in public estimation, although he displayed some important qualifications for his office, and his conduct was not liable to any serious charge. He was above all suspicion of corruption,—he was courteous, patient, and impartial,—being neither led astray by the influence of others, nor by ill temper, prejudice, favoritism, or caprice. His manner was most dignified, and from his literary stores, and his acquaintance with the world, he threw a grace over the administration of justice which it sometimes sadly wants when the presiding judge has spent the whole of his life in drawing and arguing pleas and demurrers. By the consent of all, Lord Loughborough came up to the notion of a consummate magistrate when the cause turned entirely upon facts. These he perceived with great quickness and accuracy, and in his summing up he arranged them in lucid order, and detailed them with admirable perspicuity as well as elegance,—so as almost with certainty to bring the jury to a right verdict—instead of wearying and perplexing them by reading over the whole

[1] Rossl. MSS.   [2] See post, Life of Erskine.

of the evidence, and interlarding it with twaddling comments. But the discovery was soon made that he was sadly deficient in a knowledge of the common law, and no confidence was reposed in his decisions. He must have been aware of this defect himself, and if he had supplied it (as he might have done) with the energy he had displayed in getting rid of his Scotch accent, he would have rivaled Mansfield; but he did not consider professional ignorance a bar to the accomplishment of his ambitious projects. The Great Seal was his dream by night, and the subject of his daily contemplations, and this was to be gained—not by a reputation for black-letter lore, but by struggling for a high station in the House of Lords, and by watching and improving party vicissitudes. He thought that by a discreet use of the scanty stock of law he had scraped together, and by availing himself freely of the assistance of his brethren, he could decently get through the duties of his present office, and that when not engaged in the actual discharge of them, he could spend his time most profitably as well as most agreeably in preparing himself for parliamentary contests, and in keeping up his political connections.

He was, however, considerably mortified by observing the very small number of suits which came before him,—while the neighboring Court of King's Bench was overflowing,—and he was accused (probably very unjustly) of trying to induce plaintiffs to resort to him by summing up for heavier damages than they could have got elsewhere.[1]

He certainly was very anxious to conceal from the public the deserted state of his tribunal, and for this purpose he would spin out business that he could well have more rapidly disposed of. It is related that once, being indisposed on the first day of his sittings after term at Guildhall, and having a cause paper which with good husbandry might have lasted a week, he got Mr. Justice Buller to sit for him,—who cleared it all off in a few hours,—and, boasting of his exploit, said, in allusion to the unwieldiness and slow motion of the sergeants-at-law—the advo-

---

[1] This was chiefly alleged with regard to "sea batteries," *i. e.* actions by sailors against their captains in the merchants' service for flogging them on a charge of mutiny,—and the suspicion might arise from his attempt to correct such a very questionable system.

cates in that Court—"I have been giving the *heavy blacks* a gallop this morning."

During the first eight years of Lord Loughborough's Chief Justiceship, for want of a "vates sacer," his decisions (unfortunately or fortunately for him) have perished, there being a chasm in the series of Common Pleas Reports from Trinity Term, 19 Geo. 3 (1779), the last by Sir William Blackstone, till Easter Term, 28 Geo. 3 (1788), the first by Henry Blackstone, his son. Those of the five following years make one octavo volume, and among them are to be found some important and well-reasoned judgments. No constitutional question ever came before our Chief Justice, and he had chiefly to decide upon points of practice, and upon the technicalities of real property, which are unintelligible to the non-professional reader. Perhaps the most stirring case which arose in his time was *Steel* v. *Houghton*, where the question was, " whether the poor of the parish have a legal right to glean in a corn-field, after the reapers, in harvest time?" A benevolent association supported the right,—agitating for it, and defraying the expense of the litigation. They had in their favor one of the Judges of of the Court, Mr. Justice Gould, who relied upon certain dicta of Hale and Blackstone, and above all, on the text in Leviticus (xix. 9, 10): "And when ye reap the harvest of your land, thou shalt not wholly reap the corners of thy field; *neither shalt thou gather the gleanings of thy harvest:* and thou shalt not glean thy vineyard, neither shalt thou gather all the grapes of thy vineyard; *thou shalt leave them for the poor and stranger:* I am the Lord your God." A Chief Justice fond of popularity would have gained a great name in the newspapers and with the vulgar, by showing how his Court, when appealed to, could protect the starving gleaner from a wicked combination of tyrannical squires and hard hearted farmers. Lord Loughborough, however, acted a more manly part, and gave due weight to the principles of law and the dictates of reason :—

"There can be no right of this sort," said he, "to be enjoyed in common except there is no cultivation, or where that right is supported by joint labor; but here neither of these criteria will apply. The farmer is the sole cultivator of the land, and the gleaners gather each for himself, without any regard either to joint labor or public advantage. If this custom were part of the common law, it would prevail in every part of the kingdom, and be of general and uniform practice; but in some districts it is wholly unknown, and in others variously modified and enjoyed. The law of Moses, cited as a foundation for this claim, enjoins that a part of the crop shall remain unreaped by the owner of the field; and such political institutions of the Jews can not be obligatory upon us, since even under the Christian dispensation the relief of the poor is not a legal obligation, but a religious duty. The consequence which would arise from this custom being established as a right would be injurious to the poor themselves. Their sustenance can only arise from the surplus of productive industry; whatever is a charge on industry is a very improvident diminution of the fund for that sustenance;—the profits of the farmer being lessened, he would be less able to contribute his share to the rates of the parish, and thus the poor, from the exercise of this supposed right in the autumn, would be liable to to starve in the spring."

Mr. Justice Heath and Mr. Justice Wilson concurred, and gleaning without the consent of the owner of the field was adjudged to be a trespass.[1]

Lord Loughborough's most elaborate common-law judgment was in the case of *Lichbarrow* v. *Mason*, when he presided in the Court of Exchequer Chamber, on a writ of error from the Court of King's Bench. The question was one of infinite importance to commerce—"Whether the right of the unpaid seller of goods to stop them while they are on their way to a purchaser who has become insolvent, is divested by an intermediate sale to a third person through the indorsement of the bill of lading, for a valuable consideration?" He concluded by saying:—" From a review of all the cases it does not appear that there has ever been a decision against the legal right of the consignor to stop the goods *in transitu* before the case which we have here to consider. The rule which we are now to lay down will not disturb, but settle, the notions of the commercial part of this country on a point of very great importance, as it regards the security and good faith of their transactions. For these reasons

[1] 1 Hen Black. 51.

we think the judgment of the Court of King's Bench ought to be reversed." But a writ of error being brought in the House of Lords, this reversal was reversed, and the right of the intermediate purchaser as against the original seller has ever since been established.[1]

The finest "scene" in which he ever took a part was acted shortly before his elevation to the woolsack. While sitting at Nisi Prius at Westminster, before the jury were sworn, he desired (no doubt in consequence of some information he had received out of Court) that he might see the record in a cause about to be called on. The parchment being handed up to him, he perused it; then rising, he threw it indignantly on the table, and said with much solemnity,—

"Do not swear the jury in this cause, but let it be struck out of the paper. I will not try it. The administration of justice is insulted by the proposal that I should try it. To my astonishment I find that the action is brought on a wager as to the mode of playing an illegal, disreputable, and mischievous game called HAZARD; 'whether, allowing seven to be the main and eleven to be a nick to seven, there are more ways than six of nicking seven on the dice?' Courts of justice are constituted to try rights and to redress injuries, not to solve the problems of the gamester. The gentlemen of the jury and I may have heard of HAZARD as a mode of dicing,—by which sharpers live, and young men of fortune and family are ruined; but what do any of us know of 'seven being the main,' or 'eleven being a nick to seven?' Do we come here to be instructed in this lore, and are the unusual crowds (drawn hither, I suppose, by the novelty of the expected entertainment) to take a lesson with us in these unholy mysteries, which they are to practice in the evening in the low gaming-houses in St. James's Street, pithily called by a name which should inspire a salutary terror of entering them? Again, I say, let the cause be struck out of the paper. Move the Court, if you please, that it may be restored, and if my brethren should think that I am wrong in the course I now take, I hope that one of them will officiate for me here, and save me from the degradation of trying 'whether there be more than six ways of nicking seven on the dice, allowing seven to be the main,

[1] 1 Hen. Black. 357.

and eleven to be a nick to seven,'—a question, after all, admitting of no doubt, and capable of mathematical demonstration."[1]

A rule having been obtained, next term, for restoring the cause to the paper, it was argued at great length, and with much gravity, by the learned sergeants:—

Gould, J.—"I think my Lord Chief Justice did perfectly right in refusing to try this cause. The game of hazard stands condemned by the law of England; there are many statutes that make it illegal; and nothing can be more injurious to the morals of the nation than a public discussion of this nature before an audience whose curiosity is whetted to attend the trial of such questions. The refusal to submit it to the jury was both legal and laudable." *Heath, J.*—"All games at dice, except backgammon, are prohibited by law; and I think it would be vilifying and degrading courts of justice if they were to hear, by means of a wager, a discussion of prohibited games." *Lord Loughborough.*—"This was a mere idle wager; and I have no hesitation in saying that I think a court or a jury ought not to be called upon to decide such wagers. I adhere to the opinion which I expressed at the trial." *Rule discharged.*[2]

Lord Loughborough, while a common-law Judge, went the circuit every summer, although the Chiefs of the

---

[1] A report was circulated that Lord Loughborough himself, at this period of his life, was much given to gaming—that he constantly frequented Brookes's and White's, where there was very deep play, and that before delivering this very tirade, he had sat up the whole night at "hazard," having merely shaved and put a wet towel round his head before coming into Westminster Hall. The real truth probably was, that he did frequent these clubs, and occasionally looked on when Charles Fox and other great orators and statesmen with whom he associated were desperately adventuring,—so that he must have pretty well known the rules and the phraseology of "hazard," but there is no reason to believe that he himself was ever tainted with the destructive and almost incurable vice of gaming.

[2] *Brown* v. *Leeson,* 2 Hen. Black. 43. So Lord Mansfield refused to try a wager on the sex of the Chevalier D'Eon, Cowp. 729; and Lord Ellenborough refused to try a wager upon a cock-fight, 3 Camp 140, and Abbott, C J., on a dog-fight, 1 Ryan and Moody, 213 But an action has been held to be maintainable on a wager of "a rump and dozen whether the defendant be older than the plaintiff?" We ought long ago to have adopted the provision of the civil law, whereby "sponsiones ludicrae" could not be enforced in a court of justice I long tried in vain to induce the legislature to agree to this, and to change the absurd custom where an issue of fact is directed by a court of equity, of stating it to the jury in the form of a wager of a sum of money between the parties. But I have at last succeeded by 8 & 9 Vict. c. 109, § 18, § 19, sched 2.

King's Bench and Common Pleas were excused this duty in the spring,—one Judge only being sent on the Norfolk, and one on the Midland, circuit.

Of his first judicial tour, we have the following account, in a letter from himself to a lady, which perhaps will not much add to his reputation for pleasantry :—

"Lancaster, 28th August, 1780.

"I am supposed by the newswriters to be trying folks in the North for their lives and liberties, and hanging and whipping in a very shocking way. Nothing like it, I assure you. From Durham to Lancaster, I have not missed an assembly; and the *hanging* sleeves of the misses, whose grandmothers I used to admire, are the only things I have seen that gives me the least idea of *hanging*. On this Western coast, where in former days the misses never appeared, and there was no fiddling nor dancing, I feel much younger than at Durham and Newcastle, and accordingly, I have been twice detected, in the city of Carlisle, coming out of a house kept by a fine young woman, at broad daylight, after supper. It was not quite known that the Judge had a wife; and the old lady who lodges us at Carlisle, and who is blind, very gravely lamented to me that I could not marry all the young ladies of the family."

From a speech which he made in the House of Lords, he might have been expected to be found very severe in dealing with criminals, so as to be placed in the category of "hanging judges." "I have always held it," said he, "to be more humane, as well for the example of others, as for the enforcement of the object and intention of the Legislature, where the guilt is evident and glaring, rather to let the law take its course, than by a mistaken lenity to multiply offenders, and accumulate sacrifices at the shrine of what is falsely considered the sanguinary spirit of our criminal laws."[1] Yet he is said in practice to have been very mild in the trial of prisoners,—giving them a fair chance of being acquitted,—and not hurt (as judges are apt to be) if the sentence was mitigated by the Crown, after he had reported that there was no room for the exercise of mercy.[2] He is advantageously contrasted with Mr.

---

[1] A. D. 1789 ; 27 Parl. Hist. 1066.
[2] He said in the House of Lords,—"I recollect a case where four prisoners had been capitally convicted before me, and I had not on a most careful re-

Justice Gould, in an anecdote told in the House of Commons, for the purpose of illustrating the evil of discretionary punishments:—

" Not a great many years ago, on the Norfolk Circuit, a larceny was committed by two men in a poultry-yard, but only one of them was apprehended; the other, having escaped to a distant part of the country, had eluded the pursuit. At the next Assizes the apprehended thief was tried and convicted; but Lord Loughborough, before whom he was tried, thinking the offense a very slight one, sentenced him only to a few months' imprisonment. The news of this sentence having reached the accomplice in his retreat, he immediately returned and surrendered himself to take his trial at the next Assizes. The next Assizes came, but, unfortunately for the prisoner, it was a different Judge who presided; and, still more unfortunately, Mr. Justice Gould, who happened to be the Judge, though of a very mild and indulgent disposition, had observed, or thought he had observed, that men who set out with stealing fowls generally end by committing the most atrocious crimes. Building a sort of system on this observation, he had made it a rule to punish this offense with peculiar severity; and he accordingly, to the astonishment of this unhappy man, sentenced him to be transported for seven years to Botany Bay.' While the accomplice was taking his departure for this remote region, without hope of ever again seeing his native country, the term of the principal's imprisonment had expired; and what must have been the notions which that little public

vision of the trial discovered to my own mind any difference in their cases which could warrant me in reporting favorably of any one of them, yet I am happy to think that the Royal mercy was extended to one of them—on the consideration that one might be saved without injury to the effect of the law."

† Buller was said always to hang for sheep-stealing, avowing as a reason that he had several sheep stolen from his own flock. Heath, acting more on principle, used to hang in all capital cases, because he knew of no good secondary punishments. Said he, "If you imprison at home, the criminal is soon thrown upon you again, hardened in guilt. If you transport, you corrupt infant societies, and sow the seeds of atrocious crimes over the habitable globe There is no regenerating of felons in this life, and for their own sake, as well as for the sake of society, I think it is better to hang."—When sitting in the Crown Court at Gloucester, he asked a lying witness from what part of the county he came, and being answered, "From Bitton, my Lord,' he exclaimed, "You do seem to be of the Bitton breed, but I thought I had hanged the whole of that parish long ago."

who witnessed and compared these two examples formed of our system of criminal justice?"

Lord Loughborough, when presiding at the Assizes, was ready to exercise his authority with much rigor when the occasion seemed to require it. He threatened a jury, who persisted in finding a verdict contrary to his direction, with an "attaint;" he committed to prison a juryman who had got drunk; and he laid a fine of £500 upon the inhabitants of Essex for the insufficiency of the county jail.—Still, even on the bench, although his decisions were according to law, he kept up his character as a courtier. The following anecdote, which I have on undoubted authority, illustrates the foolish excess of his insincerity. "At Durham the Chapter was wont to be a very opulent and hospitable body—not too much distinguished by qualities of a higher order than those which might befit a cœnobium of Protestant Benedictines. It happened that at an Assize at Durham, at which Lord Loughborough presided in the Crown Court, the criminal calendar was unusually light, and the noble and learned Chief Justice, in his charge to the Grand Jury, congratulated them on a result which he could not but attribute to the county being blessed with the residence within it of such a body of men as the truly reverend Chapter of Durham!"

Before I conclude his judicial career, prior to his holding the Great Seal, I ought to mention that he had a great and unlucky ambition to shine at Quarter Sessions. In right of his wife he was possessed of an estate in Yorkshire. Here he loved to reside in the vacation, and to act the country gentleman. Being in the commission of the peace *virtute officii*, he took out his *dedimus*, imprisoned poachers, and made orders of bastardy. Not contented with the glory to be acquired at Petty Sessions, he got himself elected chairman of the Quarter Sessions, and there he tried appeals respecting poor rates and orders of removal. On these occasions, it is said, he was almost always wrong, and the Court of King's Bench had a wicked delight in upsetting his decisions. He seems, however, himself to have had a high opinion of his capacity for "justice-business." Thus he writes to Lord Auckland:—"Your letter found me in Yorkshire, employed very eagerly in a manner you would very little expect; I was attending the Quarter Sessions at Pomfret, having not only become a country squire, but an active Justice of Peace. If I could conveniently indulge my present disposition, I should never see the inside of any Court but a Quarter Session, and be very well contented to be *relégué* beyond the Trent."

But we must now behold him in a sphere much more congenial to his talents and acquirements. On the 19th day of June, 1780, he took his seat in the Upper House of Parliament.[1]

Great surprise and disappointment were caused by the line which he at first took there. It was supposed that he had been made a peer expressly for the purpose of strenuously supporting the falling Government against the attacks of Lord Shelburne, Lord Rockingham, and Lord Camden. His assistance was much wanted; for although, upon a division, there was still a large majority of peers for subjugating America, and for lauding all the blunders of Ministers, they were awfully weak in debate, having nothing better to rely upon, after the uncertain advocacy of Thurlow, than such drowsy, commonplace speakers as Lord Stormont and Lord Hillsborough. Wedderburn in the House of Commons had shone in the very first rank of orators. For the last two years he had borne the whole brunt of the Opposition, and had proved that, with a better cause, he would have been a match for Dunning, Burke, or Fox. Become Lord Loughborough, and transferred to the House of Peers, it was thought that as a debater he would be equally active, and apparently more brilliant, like the moon among the lesser lights.

Although he attended regularly in his place, and voted with the Government, he long cautiously abstained from opening his mouth on any subject connected with party

---

[1] "19 June, 1780.—Alexander Wedderburn, Esq. Lord Chief Justice of the Court of Common Pleas, being by letters bearing date, &c. created Lord Loughborough, of Loughborough in the county of Leicester, was (in his robes) introduced between Lord Willoughby de Broke and the Lord Grantham (also in their robes), the Gentleman Usher of the Black Rod and Garter King at Arms preceding. His Lordship on his knee presented his patent to the Lord Chancellor on the Woolsack, who delivered it to the clerk, and the same was read at the table: his writ of summons was also read. Then his Lordship took the oaths, &c, and was afterwards placed on the lower end of the Baron's Bench."—*Lords' Journals.*

politics, and he witnessed the fall of Lord North without making an effort to save him. He plausibly pleaded the sacredness of the judicial character, which he had now to support, and declared that he would never sully his ermine by engaging in parliamentary strife. Those who knew him well, suspected him to be actuated by the consideration that he had nothing more to expect from the present Ministry, Thurlow firmly holding the Great Seal, —and they foretold that he would unscrupulously mix in the fray when he had a prospect of sharing in the plunder. From the time of his being made a peer, till the formation of the Rockingham Cabinet, on Lord North's resignation, in March, 1782, he is stated to have spoken only twice; first, respecting the release of a Russian officer, apprehended for having been engaged in Lord George Gordon's riots;[1] and again on a bill for regulating the administration of justice in the Isle of Man.[2] Even in the debate on our rupture with Holland, and our disputes with the Northern Powers respecting the search of neutral ships, he had remained silent, although, from his acquaintance with international law, he might have been expected to have supported the belligerent rights of Britain—without subjecting himself to the imputation of being a political judge, which he now pretended so much to dread. He boasted that his great object was to keep down arrears in his Court.[3]

The following letters, written by him to Mr. Eden, in the beginning of 1782, give a striking view of the distracted state of affairs shortly before the resignation of Lord North:—

"Speculations are, of course, the consequence of last night's division. Those I have seen, think the Admiralty must change, but you know as well as I do how strongly against probability that station has continued unaltered. You will hardly believe that I am as little informed as I am interested in the subject. The only pursuit that gives me any real satisfaction is to fill the little corner of West-

---

[1] 21 Parl. Hist. 750, 752. [2] 22 Ibid. 561.
[3] This achievement seems to have been accomplished with very slight labor. He thus on one occasion explains his reason for leaving his villa at Mitcham during term time, and taking up his residence in London: "I found I could not manage the little business of Westminster Hall in this term without sometimes looking at a book and meeting in an evening, so that I have betaken myself to town for a month."

minster Hall allotted to me with some credit."[1] . . . . "I arrived in town the night before last, and, as the newspapers will inform you, had yesterday a most gracious reception, but no particular conversation. Lord Hillsborough was very desirous of entering fully into discourse, but it was soon interrupted, and our appointment to meet again has not yet taken place. I saw Lord N. this morning, and had a very frank, but at the same time a very loose and desultory, conversation with him. The Chancellor was at court, but did not seem to have much curiosity about him, nor a much clearer countenance than when I last saw him.[2] It seems to me that there is a great disposition to think lightly of the difficulties of Government on your side of the water,[3] and to suppose that the first wish of every Lord Lieutenant is to be easy at home. It will require many conversations to oppose prejudices so very mischievous. Both the persons I talked to seemed to start from the subject of the 'volunteers,' as if they were afraid to know too much of it. Lord N. told me he had a great deal to say to me, and that we must meet soon, but fixed no time, though I almost tendered myself to go down to Busby with him. I shall be glad to know whether you suppose your letters undergo any examination, for if they do I shall be very much puzzled to correspond with you."[4] . . . . . "On Wednesday last it was given out with great industry, and the rumor was very eagerly adopted, that Lord N. and Lord S. had resigned. The same thing was continued yesterday, but the credit of it sunk towards the evening, especially as Lord N. had given the lie to it by his appearance in the House of Commons It was a story raised, I believe, to favor the division for Opposition on the motion of this evening, which is to the same effect as the last. From all the intelligence I could learn last night, the majority is likely to be better for Government than it was last

---

[1] 22nd February, 1782, on General Conway's motion for putting an end to the American war, when Ministers had a majority of *one*.

[2] Jealousies between these legal dignitaries seem already to have sprung up, and Thurlow looking forward to a ministerial crisis, was already afraid that Wedderburn might be intriguing to succeed him.

[3] Mr Eden was then Chief Secretary in Ireland.

[4] Notwithstanding the liberties used by Sir James Graham at the Post Office, I do not think that in our own times there would be a suspicion of Government surreptitiously prying into letters written to or from the Irish Secretary.

week. Several country gentlemen, alarmed at the consequences of their own votes, have, I hear, been with Lord N. to assure him of their support. Last night at White's where I supped, no man in Opposition would accept a bet offered on each number that the majority would be 10, 20, 30. Lord Coventry offered to take 15, 30, 45—declaring that the country gentlemen were the true rats, and had gone back to their old haunts. Rigby was in very high spirits, and exulting in the confession that the landed interest were the support of Lord N. The true state of things, as far as I can judge, is, that Lord N. on the unfavorable appearance of the House has desired that any arrangement might be without regard to him,—without taking any part in the attempt to make, and at the same time with a declaration that he would do his duty to the last moment. The charge of this arrangement has been committed to the Chancellor, Lord G. and Lord W., and afterwards the Duke of G. and Lord C^a, have all excused themselves, as you would naturally suppose they would,—having each of them retreated from difficulties much less than the present. What other applications have been tried I know not, though I am certain that there have been others. The only part I have had in it is, that I have told Lord N. and Lord Chr. severally, that they begin at the wrong end, and that the first object is to strengthen the weakest post by offering Lord Howe the Admiralty, which he can not be weak enough not to accept. This done, there would be scope and time to proceed with the rest. Neither of them contradicted my idea. But the first gave me to understand that it was not at present in his hands; the second admitted by his manner that it was, but gave me no reason to conjecture what his plan of operations might be. Supposing the division to-night more favorable to Government than it has lately been, my conjecture is that the present negotiations will prove abortive, and that Lord N. will again be obliged, reluctant and unequal as he feels himself to the arduous undertaking, to engage with the public difficulties, and that he will take no warning from what has happened, nor use any exertions to strengthen his Administration. I saw him last Sunday, and have offered him every attention in my power. He is sensible of the kindness expressed for him, indifferent in appearance to any demonstrations of zeal for him as minister, and in as cheerful spirits as ever you knew him to possess. In a state to be plagued to death by the folly, ingratitude and perverseness of the people who come to him, and to be tortured by the shameful and wretched exhibition which the country makes, I am not sure whether all this accumulated distress does not, in some degree, lighten the misery that another cast of mind would expose most men in his situation to feel." . . . . . . " There are men here of great consideration, who think that if we had peace elsewhere, we should be obliged in sound policy to teach some of your gentlemen to treat us with more respect; that it is absurd to suppose Ireland can be independent, and that the option to be exercised on your side is to be dependent on France or on England. According to that idea whatever language we may tolerate or overlook, we must do no act that can admit the high-sounding language of Irish patriots to be constitutional. Without discussing it, this is an opinion (you may depend upon it) that prevails very much in this country; and those who think most loosely on the subject are the present Administration and their friends. Wherefore it is very just that they should be popular on your side of the water, in comparison of those who will have most sway should they be removed." . . . . "Out of respect to the curiosity you must have to hear from hence at this singular period, I write to you by this post, though nothing has happened to make a postcript to my last letter necessary. My information about the persons sent for, and consulting, was not quite accurate: his Majesty sent early in the morning for Lord Storm., who was afterwards sent to the Chancellor; and Lord N. did not go to St. James' till both the others had been there. A great statesman, and your constant correspondent, surmises that there is an attempt to make some arrangement, and that the Chancellor has had authority to negotiate. He further supposes that Lord Gower may be persuaded to lend himself for a little time in the Treasury, till matters can be settled. I don't imagine this is better founded than upon the observations which the whispering about the Woolsack always occasions. The Chancellor talks a very manly language in censure of the vote of Wednesday; but I think it not unlikely that he may follow that with a comment on the neglect which produced that vote. The answer seems well guarded, and not liable to much attack; but on Monday either that or an attack on Lord Sandwich is expected from Fox, as Lord N. has put off his taxes. I went this morning to show the goodwill which, in spite of all the reasons against it that you know, I really feel for him, and saw him for a minute, with as cheerful and as lively a countenance as if he had been at the head of his table. Hatsell says he will give fifty guineas to receive a guinea a-day while Lord N. remains in the Treasury. There were some unlucky incidents in the division, which must have arisen from the bad conduct of the debate on the part of Government. Mr. Wild, with a million of the loan in his pocket, was with much difficulty dragged to the House, but voted against Lord North. Sir Gilbert Elliot's speech did much mischief, for Sir William Dolben had declared himself satisfied with the Minister's declaration, and that he should therefore vote differently from the vote he had given on Friday; for which he was, as you may imagine, exposed to much attack, and pelted, as an example to deter others; after which Sir Gilbert got up, professing himself *unsatisfied*, though a hearty friend in general to Administration. The effect of the comparison between the two was to fix all the wavering well-wishers in the same line with Sir Gilbert. I have no patience with him, for he can not be the dupe of his own reasoning so much as to convince himself that a vote of the House of Commons is an ingredient for making peace. I hope all the mischief we are making here will come too late to breed any disturbance to you in Ireland."[1]

While these struggles were proceeding, Lord Loughborough looked on as a curious spectator, considering that peradventure they might bring him some good; and although he always voted with Lord North, and professed strong attachment to him, he seems not without secret satisfaction to have witnessed his fall.

Meanwhile he was solaced by an auspicious event in domestic life. Having been some time a widower,[2] he announced to his friend Sir Ralph Payne (afterwards

---

[1] These letters are not dated, but evidently refer to the debates and divisions in the House of Commons, from 27 Feb. to 19 March, 1782. See 22 Parl. Hist. 1087–1214; Adolphus, vol iii 325–343
[2] The first Lady Loughborough died 15th Feb. 1781.

Lord Lavington) his resolution again to enter the holy state of matrimony, and received from him the following congratulation:—

"Broadlards, Sept 16, 1782.

"I trust, my dear Lord, that you are too well satisfied of the credit which I give you, in my heart, for every testimony of friendship which you have ever shown to me, to doubt the sense which I entertain of this last instance of it; and that it is as unnecessary to assure you of my gratitude as it is to make any protestations of the sincere pleasure and satisfaction which Lady Payne and I feel at the very kind information which you have communicated to us. You have such sufficient securities, my dear Lord, for your own future happiness, that it would not be more impertinent in me to offer to compose speeches for you in the House of Peers, than to persecute you with my prayers for your enjoyment of all the blessings that the world can afford. But there is one prayer which I can not forbear to offer, which is, that you would realize the happiness of which you have as yet only held out a prospect to Lady Payne and myself, and give us the earliest opportunity that you can of paying our devoirs, where you may imagine us not little desirous of a better acquaintance that can be formed even from your own report. Until you can procure us this pleasure, we shall be forming a thousand conjectures and imaginations, which, with all the pleasure and partiality that will attend them, will be teasing, while attended with the impatience that we feel upon the occasion. Not having the Peerage at my finger's ends, nor Lord Palmerston having it in his library, I am at present at some loss to identify the lady to whom you allude in your letter. I only hope that she is not a sister of Lord Courtenay, who gave the ton last year to the festivities of Fonthill, where, I understand, she was so much the general subject of panegyric among her own sex, that it would be a great pity that she should be now pulled to pieces by any Lady Betty or Lady Ann, as she probably might, for making a monopoly of your Lordship, and where she was so much admired by the men, that poison must probably be the lot of any one who should presume to think of appropriating her. Don't think that this anecdote is the result of any indiscreet investigation consequent to your letter. I assure you that

I heard of it in Dorsetshire before I knew that you had any interest in any lady of that name. . . . . . .

"With respect to Brighthelmstone, I should ill deserve that opinion which I am very solicitous to obtain, were I to utter the least complaint, or entertain the least dissatisfaction at your breach of an engagement which is now so much more honored in the breach than the observance. I only hope that Lady Loughborough will hereafter recollect that a wife ought, in equity, to be as responsible for such debts of her husband as she is capable of discharging, as a husband is in law bound for those of his wife; and that her ladyship and you will, at proper seasons, think it just to liquidate with interest a demand, for the satisfaction of which we are contented to wait some time longer.

"Your affectionately attached
"RALPH PAYNE."[1]

The marriage between Lord Loughborough and Miss Courtenay took place soon after, and proved a very comfortable one, although the bridegroom had not much tenderness in his nature, and placed his happiness chiefly on the stirring events of public life.

On the formation of Lord Rockingham's Administration Lord Loughborough was astonished to see Thurlow still in possession of the Great Seal. From this time there was much coldness, and before long there was open hostility, between these former friends and colleagues. The Chief Justice saw with jealousy and envy the Chancellor's unbounded favor with the King, and perceived that there was no hope for himself, unless the royal will could be thwarted. He therefore lay by for an opportunity of engaging in some plot for storming the Cabinet.

During Lord Rockingham's short administration he assisted the Chancellor in defeating the two Government measures of the Contractors' Bill,[2] and Burke's Economical Reform Bill,[3] and, from factious motives, he opposed the bill for declaring Irish independence,—arguing, with considerable force, the impossibility of the two countries continuing long together on the new footing.

Now he had his first open conflict with Thurlow,— moving, by way of slur upon the Government for omitting

[1] Rossl. MSS.   [2] 22 Parl. Hist. 1379   [3] 23 Ibid 144.

to do so, an address of congratulation to the Crown on Lord Rodney's victory. The Chancellor at first violently opposed it, but was obliged under some modifications to concur in it.[1] Lord Loughborough's position meanwhile was very irksome; for if he supported the Government, he aided men with whom there seemed no chance of his holding office; and if he helped to turn them out, this would only humor the King and make Thurlow more powerful. Suddenly, the face of affairs was changed by Lord Rockingham's death and the premiership of Lord Shelburne. On this occasion he received the following letter from Burke, showing an intimacy between them which by and by facilitated the " Coalition:"—

"MY DEAR LORD,

" I received your very kind and obliging letter from Beechwood, and I thank you for it very sincerely. It was much the more acceptable on account of the place it came from, combined with the remembrance of the worthy master. I met him since in not so pleasant a place, under St. James's Gate, and had a hearty shake of the hand with him. It was very good of you both in such a situation, formed for every kind of calm satisfaction, to throw a thought upon a scene so full of confusion as this, and on my poor part in it, which, contrary to all order, is as troublesome as it is inconsiderable. I remember several years ago a few most pleasant days that I passed with you and Sir John under his noble beech trees, in a manner and with thoughts perfectly remote from my course of life and the train of my ideas. Since then, many winters have snowed upon my head without making it in proportion wiser, and God knows whether I have done good to others in any proportion to the innumerable unspeakable vexations which I have suffered during that whole time. I can not say that these troubles were not mixed with many consolations. But it requires at least my whole stock of philosophy to bear up against the events which have lately happened, and which have indeed gone very near to my heart. I have lost, and the public has lost, a friend. But this was the hand of God manifestly, and according to the course and order of his providence. I had no hand in it. But to think that all the labors of his life and that all the labors of my life should

[1] 23 Parl. Hist. 67, 72, 73.

in the very moment of their success produce nothing better than the delivery of the power of this kingdom into the hands of the Earl of Shelburne—the very thing, I am free to say to you and to everybody, the toils of a life ten times longer, and ten times more important than mine would have been well employed to prevent,—this, I confess, is a sore, a very sore trial. It really looks as if it were a call upon me at least wholly to withdraw from all struggles in the political line. This was the first impression on my mind. I do not know how long it will continue. We are naturally changeable. There is a great deal of difficulty at my time of life and in my circumstances in changing, even to a course that would seem more suitable to decline and disappointment. On the other hand, if we go on, there must be some sort of system. If so, all is to begin again. A great part of our construction is (what I call) sound. But there is a great, and I fear irreparable, breach. With what to build it up, that will bind and coalesce, I do not see.

"Indeed, I do not see anything in a pleasant point of view. I bear up, however, better than my present style would seem to indicate. I do so rather by force of natural spirits than by the aid of reason, though now and then reason whispers some sort of comfort even by suggesting one's own blindness, and that there is a good ground to think, whatever appearances may be, that in some way or other, at some time or other, or in some place or other, the effect of right endeavors must be right. 'Nota est illis operis sui series ; omniumque morum per manus suas venturarum scientiæ in aperto est semper; Nobis ex abdito subit.'·

"Your Lordship sees that, like Hudibras, discomfited and laid in the stocks, I
   'Comfort myself with ends of verse
   And sayings of philosophers.'

"I wish you most heartily a pleasant circuit, moderate litigation, and as little hanging as possible. Alas! it is not worth while to swing out of the world those you have to send away. When shall we have a *grand* Jail Delivery? "I am, with great esteem and regard,
  "My dear Lord,
   "Your most obedient humble servant,
"Whitehall, July 17, 1782. "EDMUND BURKE.

"Here still—but out in law.

"I forgot to tell you that I had a most friendly note from Adam Smith at his departure for Scotland."[1]

Thurlow's hold of the Great Seal seemed at first firmer than ever, for instead of leading the Opposition, he acted cordially with the Chief Minister; but before long a ray of hope dawned upon Loughborough. Fox was so exasperated against Lord Shelburne for overreaching him, that he vowed he would never serve with him again, and declared that he considered Lord North a less obnoxious character; while Lord North was dissatisfied by observing that the King really seemed to have gone over to the Shelburne Ministry, and was estranging himself from those who had stood by him during the whole American contest. If there could be a coalition between the Rockingham Whigs, now called "Foxites," and the party of Lord North, they would greatly outnumber the adherents of Lord Shelburne, the King must surrender, and the Great Seal must be wrested from Thurlow. In a letter written by Lord Loughborough while on the summer circuit of 1783, he shows his growing impatience of Lord Shelburne:—

"The people I have seen, and the places I have passed through, are all hostile to the administration in their general course of politics. One would not, therefore, form any judgment of the disposition of the country from the appearances in this quarter; but I hear from all quarters that there is a most general opinion of the incapacity of the Minister. The shop-tax is universally odious; and following so soon the window-tax, which is much more felt in country towns than in London, both sums are added together when men compute the additional burden, and the amount is very difficult to bear. If there is likely to be anything of a stirring character in Parliament, I shall hasten my return, though I am sure my absence was of very little consequence in the late debates, where the superiority of our friends appears very conspicuous in Mr. Woodfall,—imperfect as his reports now are."[1]

However, Parliament was prorogued without any opportunity of striking a blow; and Lord Loughborough, after the circuit, retired to Buxton, laboring under disease,

[1] Rosslyn MSS.   [2] 19 Parl. Hist. 1260.

and much depressed in spirits. Thence he wrote to a friend :—

"This place has hitherto been of no service to me, and I am heartily tired of the unsuccessful experiments that the physician has made to prevent the waters from disagreeing with my stomach. I am fully persuaded I should enjoy more health and happiness from a moderated retirement than I can ever find in the increase of public business. This idea has been gaining upon my mind for some time; and I am so far from feeling the least anxiety to remove any obstacle that prevents my being irretrievably fixed in a political situation, that, were the way to it perfectly open, I should be very unhappy to enter upon it."

Getting out of this short fit of depression, he was more eager than ever for the promotion he had been deprecating, and, Parliament again meeting, a certain prospect was held out of his ambition being speedily gratified by the famous " Coalition."

There was no regular negotiation between the Tories, and Foxite Whigs, and no formal treaty was signed. Both hating the Minister, they were gradually and insensibly united. The energy of Fox was chiefly effective in consolidating the Coalition; but there is no doubt that the subtlety of Loughborough powerfully contributed, by removing the scruples of Lord North, over whose mind he exercised considerable influence. The grand united attack was to be made on the articles of peace with France and America.

The Lord Chief Justice of the Court of Common Pleas now buckled on his armor, which had almost become rusty, and, throwing aside all his pretended scruples about the sacredness of the judicial character, mixed in the thickest of the fray.

The debate on the " Preliminaries " coming on in the House of Lords, there was a struggle between Lord Loughborough and the Prime Minister which should have the advantage of following the other; but the latter was forced up, and the former is said to have exclaimed,—" The Lord has delivered you into my hand." He immediately followed, and his speech was very masterly. It is reported at considerable length, but the reader will be contented with a few detached extracts from it. Thus he began:—" I could not in fairness rise to offer any opinion in this debate till I had the explanation and the defense of the First Minister of the Crown, for he has the fullest information of all the circumstances under which this treaty has been concluded, and he possibly might have removed my objections to it. But having attentively listened to him, I am sorry to say that my objections are strengthened. I now clearly see that, by the fault of the Government in carrying on these negotiations, the country is disgraced, and, I fear, is undone. I require only one point to be admitted—that the condition of the kingdom was not so desperate as to oblige us to accept any terms of capitulation which our enemies chose to offer. Neither the Prime Minister nor his colleagues have defended their conduct by denying this position; and they have talked of the preliminaries, not as a capitulation, but as a treaty. When two powers at war have opened to each other their desire of making peace, it is obvious that some point must be fixed as the basis of the negotiation—either the actual state of possession, or the state of possession before the commencement of hostilities, or the state of possession at some intermediate period. But each of these has been considered too favorable to be accorded to us, and the only basis of this treaty has been, to correct what was distasteful to France in any former treaties which we have concluded with her." He first attacked the stipulation allowing the repair of the fortifications of Dunkirk, which by the treaty of Utrecht, by the treaty of Aix la Chapelle, and by the treaty of Paris, were to be demolished—thus putting our enemies in the undisturbed possession of a great port in the very mouth of the Thames—which in time of war must be fatal to our commerce, and must expose us to the peril of invasion.[1] He proceeded to the removal of the restriction to fortify St. Pierre and Miquelon in the West Indies, and Pondicherry in the East, with the extension of the right of fishery on the coast of Newfoundland. He then goes to Africa, and contends that British interests had been wantonly sacrificed in every quarter of the globe. He was particularly severe upon the article by which, upon evacuating New

---

[1] It is amusing to observe what a bugbear Dunkirk was to us for a century and how harmless it has been.

York, Long Island, and the positions we retained in America, we should deliver up all houses, goods, and persons found there. "If," said he, "this were the capitulation of a besieged town, it would be scandalous to surrender on such terms. At the lowest ebb of distress, reduced and almost undone, the necessity can hardly be conceived, that should oblige a state to subscribe to an article evidently inserted for no other purpose than to blast forever the hitherto untainted honor of the nation. Francis I., vanquished and captive, wrote to his subjects, 'All is lost except honor,' and the spirit of that sentiment preserved his kingdom and restored his fortune. If we had implored, in this instance, the aid of France and Spain, though our enemies,—the generosity of these two great countries would have interposed in favor of our fellow-subjects whom we have deserted. In every treaty that has terminated a civil war, the articles of mutual forgiveness and restoration have ever been the easiest to settle." After giving the instance of the Catalonians by the treaty of Utrecht, and the Irish Roman Catholics by the treaty of Limerick, he continues: "In ancient or in modern history, there can not be found a parallel to this shameful desertion of men who had sacrificed all to their duty, and who perish by their reliance on our good faith. There is even a horrible refinement in the cruelty of the article; they are told that one year is allowed them to solicit from the lenity of their persecutors that mercy which their friends refused to secure to them—to beg their bread from those by whom they have been stripped of their all, and to kiss the hands that have been reddened by the blood of their parents." He concluded by denying the power of the Crown to cede British territory in our possession without the authority of parliament.[1] Upon a division, Ministers had a majority of 13 in the House of Lords, but there was a majority against them of 17 in the House of Commons,—for censuring the articles of peace; and Lord Shelburne was driven to resign.[2]

Loughborough expected to be Lord Chancellor in three days. But, amid the difficulties opposed by a hostile Court to the formation of a new government, there

[1] This question I have previously discussed in the Life of Lord Thurlow, Vol. VII. p. 75.
[2] 23 Parl. Hist. 421, 435, 571.

was an interregnum of five weeks—at the end of which, the Coalition leaders found it necessary to agree to put the Great Seal into commission, the King being so decidedly averse to have any keeper of his conscience except the pious Thurlow—and our baulked aspirant was obliged to be satisfied, for the present, with a slight foretaste of his future greatness, by being made First Lord Commissioner.[1] His brother Commissioners were Sir William Henry Ashurst, a justice of the Common Pleas, and Sir Beaumont Hotham, a baron of the Exchequer. The Great Seal was delivered to them on the 7th of April, 1783, and two days after, they were sworn in, and took their seats in the Court of Chancery.[2]

CHAPTER CLXIX.

CONTINUATION OF THE LIFE OF LORD LOUGHBOROUGH TILL THE KING'S ILLNESS IN 1788.

LORD LOUGHBOROUGH continued First Lord Commissioner of the Great Seal rather more than eight months,—during which time he forsook the Court of Common Pleas, and devoted himself to the Court of Chancery, but no cases of much interest came

---

[1] The following is the Duke of Portland's announcement to Lord Loughborough of his appointment.—

"My Lord,—You will receive from the Secretary of State an official notice of his Majesty having been graciously pleased to appoint you first Commissioner for the Great Seal, and of his having signified his pleasure that you attend him to-morrow at the levée at St James's for the purpose of receiving it. But I can not refuse myself the satisfaction of communicating to you this event, in which I flatter myself that the part I have taken is a demonstration of my respect and esteem for your Lordship, and a very convincing proof of the sense I entertain of my duty to the public.

"I have the honor to be, with great regard,
"My Lord,
"Your Lordship's most obedient humble servant, "PORTLAND.

"I had the King's commands to offer the Speakership to Lord Mansfield, he was at dinner when I called, and therefore I can not inform your Lordship of his intention in that respect."—*Rossl. MSS*

Although Lord Mansfield was Speaker of the House of Lords while the "Coalition" lasted, Lord Loughborough had all the juridical patronage usually belonging to the office of Chancellor.

[2] Cr. Off. Min. Book, No. 2, fol. 29, 30.

before him,[1] and I shall postpone my view of him as an Equity Judge till he sat there singly as Lord Chancellor. One good act which he did as Lord Commissioner, should be commemorated—he gave a silk gown to Erskine; and it should be stated to his credit, that during his whole career he was always disposed to show respect for men of genius, however widely their political principles might differ from his own.

Notwithstanding his disappointment, he put forth all his strength to support the "Coalition" in the House of Lords. He did not preside there, the woolsack being occupied by Lord Mansfield, as Speaker; but, although he was not formally a member of the Cabinet, he was considered the organ of the Government. Here the storm was at last conjured up which proved fatal to the "Coalition;" but comparative tranquillity for some time prevailed, the "Opposition," headed by his Majesty, confining their efforts to the Lower House.

Meanwhile, Thurlow showed his factious hostility by opposing the bill for establishing the judicial independence of Ireland, which had been introduced by the late Government when he himself held the Great Seal. He particularly complained that no sufficient explanation had been given of the principle of the bill, or of the measures which were to accompany it. Lord Loughborough answered, "that the Ministers, who were the authors of the bill, could not with much decency require to be informed of its grounds and tendencies, and insist on knowing the policy of which it forms a part." Thurlow still growled, but lay by for a better opportunity to avail himself of the dislike of the present Administration, which he knew lurked in the hearts of a large majority of the House.[2]

Next came a motion which Thurlow had ingeniously concocted, although decency prevented him from appearing openly to support it. A personal attack was made upon Lord Loughborough for being a Commissioner of

---

[1] See the decisions of the Lords Commissioners Loughborough, Ashurst, and Hotham, 1 Brown's Chancery Cases, 267-337. They affirmed several decrees of Lord Thurlow reheard before them, and disposed satisfactorily of a good many questions on the law of legacies, and respecting dower and courtesy. All the three generally deliver their opinions; but Loughborough must have ruled the Court, for the other two were very incompetent.

[2] 23 Parl. Hist. 747.

the Great Seal while he held the office of Chief Justice of the Common Pleas. It was put into the hands of the Duke of Richmond, who, affectedly disclaiming the intention of giving pain to any individual, pointed out very invidiously the evil consequences of the present arrangement. He dwelt much upon the importance of preserving the independence of the Judges, and contended that they must be under the influence of the Crown, if, in addition to the judicial offices which they permanently held, they might be raised to another of great power and profit, to be held during pleasure—there being no more effectual mode of working upon their hopes and fears. He likewise complained of the obstruction to public business which must necessarily arise from such unseemly pluralities, and contended, that the practice might (though no doubt without reason) give rise to particular suspicion in the present instance, as the salary of Chief Justice of the Common Pleas, while the office was held by Lord Loughborough, had been increased £1,000 a year by his Majesty.[1] He said he had intended to move, that a committee be appointed " to inquire into the independency of the Judges, and into the best means of securing it;" but he was aware that a naked vote of that kind might be deemed unparliamentary and objectionable, and he should only move a resolution, " That putting the Seals in commission *durante bene placito*, and appointing judges Commissioners, with large salaries and perquisites to be received by them during the existence of a commission, originating in and solely dependent on the will and pleasure of the Crown, tends to invalidate the Act 13 William 3, for securing the independency of the Judges." He was backed up by several court-seeking peers in the guise of patriots—one of them denouncing the commission as " a job for time serving purposes and factious ends, subversive of the system which his Majesty, at the commencement of his reign, in the true spirit of a patriot king, had been so graciously anxious to establish, and only calculated to bolster up that infamous and ruinous coalition of parties by which this country had lately been murdered, cursed, and damned."

Lord Loughborough.—" I never offered myself to the attention of the House under circumstances that required

[1] At this time the Judges' salaries were payable out of the Civil List, and might be increased without an application to the Legislature.

so large a share of your Lordships' favor and indulgence. I am indeed in a situation of great difficulty. Although personality has been studiously disclaimed, I am sure all your Lordships feel that the question is purely and entirely personal, and that your Lordships would certainly have been spared the pain of this discussion if my name had not been found in the commission recently issued for the custody of the Great Seal. Under these circumstances, it is not easy to say anything with propriety, and my wish must be to remain silent. On the other hand, silence might be construed into an acquiescence in the imputation of noble lords, so suddenly and miraculously inspired with a passion to correct abuses, and to limit the power of the Crown."

He then made a long and dexterous statement, showing that the salary of the Chief Justice of the Court of Common Pleas had been permanently raised in a lawful manner, on account of its former inadequacy; that the custom of putting the Great Seal into commission, and making the judges Lords Commissioners, had subsisted since the Revolution, as well as before, without the slightest objection from any the most furious reformer; that exigencies had from time to time occurred, and would continue to occur, when this course must be adopted for the good of the public service; that the hopes and fears of judges could not be excited by such appointments, which were rare, and known to be only temporary; that the "good old Whig," Sir Joseph Jekyll, and other judges celebrated for their integrity and high spirit, had acted as Lords Commissioners of the Great Seal, without complaint or suspicion; that the present state of business both in the Court of Chancery and in the Courts of Common Law proved that no injury had been sustained by the suitors; and that the character of the Judges was as much venerated as ever in this country, notwithstanding the attempts to assail it by some noble lords, the instruments of others who knew better, and did not dare openly to support what they instigated.—Still the Government was afraid to meet the motion with a direct negative. The previous question was put and carried without a division.[1]

When this Government was formed, Wedderburn and

[1] 23 Parl. Hist. 974.

Charles Fox looked rather shyly at each other; but it would appear by the following letter from the Secretary of State to the First Commissioner of the Great Seal, that a strict intimacy soon subsisted between them, as if they had always taken the same views in politics:—

"You will have heard before this, that the Empress has put in effect her resolution with respect to Cuban and Crim Tartary, without any resistance whatever. The French are extremely chagrined at it; but whether their dissatisfaction will have any consequences or not, remains to be seen. I rather think not. I confess I think the event a very important one; and, if it has the effect of introducing a new naval power into the Mediterranean, a very good one for this country.

"I belive I may now venture to say that the definitive Treaty will certainly come signed in the course of a week or ten days at furthest.

"I believe I have told you all that you can have any curiosity about in this part of the world, except that there is a report of Lord Ashburton being dead, which is so likely that I am inclined to believe it.

"I am, very sincerely, my dear Lord,
"Yours ever,
"C. J. Fox.

"Wimbledon, 24th August, 1783."

He was not admitted into the Cabinet, but he seems to have been on the most familiar terms of intimacy with all the members of it. The followng is a very confidential communication to him from the Duke of Portland, respecting the adjustment of a quarrel with the King:—

"My dear Lord,

"The reception I met with in the closet was so gracious that I know not how to describe it; and I am almost ashamed to mention the very full apology that was made for the harsh terms which had been used in the letters I took the liberty of showing you."[1]

At last the resolution was taken to put a violent end to the Coalition Government. The very hour when Mr. Fox presented his India Bill at the bar of the House of Peers, Lord Temple, who had proclaimed out of doors the King's disapprobation of it, and that all who sup-

[1] Rossl. MSS.

ported it were the "King's enemies," protested against it as an *infamous* measure, and expressed a hope that it would speedily meet the fate it deserved from their Lordships, in spite of its having been carried with a high hand in another place. Thurlow now came forward to ride on the whirlwind and direct the storm. Yet Loughborough, unappalled, showed a gallant bearing; and in answer to the opposition to the first reading of the Bill, offered so unusually and irregularly, pointed out the necessity for it, and the benefits it was likely to confer. After describing the bankrupt state of the East India Company's affairs at home, he drew a melancholy picture of the countries under their rule. "What scenes of desolation and distress do we there behold! A prince has been driven from his palace, his treasures have been seized, and he is now a fugitive through the plains of Indostan. Fertile provinces have been laid waste, wars have been unnecessarily waged, and a treaty concluded with the Mahrattas has, in fact, only led us to a new war."

The course adopted by Thurlow and the "King's friends" was, after this ebullition, quietly to allow the bill to be read a second time, to hear counsel and evidence against it at the bar, and, after trying to bring it into public odium, to throw it out on the motion that it be "committed." The speeches of counsel and their examination of witnesses seeming to be interminable, Lord Loughborough made several vain attempts to check them, but found the sense of the House to be against him. He ventured to divide against a very unreasonable application for an adjournment, to enable the petitioners to discover more witnesses,—but he was beaten by a majority of 8. He thenceforth entirely lost heart, and in the final and memorable debate on going into the committee he took no part. His fears were realized, the bill being rejected by a majority of 95 to 76,—and he had before his eyes the certainty of resigning the custody of the Great Seal, that it might be delivered back to Thurlow, with whom he was now on terms of the bitterest enmity.[1]

While Mr. Fox and Lord North were instantly dismissed, with circumstances to mark the Royal indignation, the Lords Commissioners were allowed to retain the

[1] 24 Parl. Hist. 124-196.

Great Seal for a week, that they might give judgment in several cases that had been argued before them; but at the end of that time they were summoned to St. James's, and surrendered it into the hands of the King, who could not conceal his exultation in receiving this trophy of his victory, although he affected to thank them for the diligent discharge of their duty while they had sat in the Court of Chancery.¹

The struggle, however, was not yet quite over. Although the King could do what he liked in the House of Lords, there remained a very large majority of Coalitionists against him in the House of Commons, and there efforts were making to crush the new Administration which he had formed. If these should succeed, Lord Loughborough's ambition must have been fully gratified, for his Majesty's likings and sympathies would no longer have been consulted, and to the expedient of putting the Great Seal into commission the victorious Coalitionists would not again have submitted. So violent had the ex-First Commissioner become, that he was prepared to deny the power of the Crown to dissolve or prorogue Parliament,— having gloomy forebodings as to the issue of the contest. "It is a matter of no slight doubt," he wrote in a letter to a member of the House of Commons, " whether a dissolution or prorogation (the public bills depending) be a legal exercise of prerogative. In a pamphlet of the reign of Charles II., ascribed both to Sir William Jones and to Somers, this question is very ably argued, and many authorities are cited to prove the act to be illegal in the advisers. This topic should be a little canvassed. My fears are not very strong as to a dissolution; but I do not feel the same confidence that you and most people do upon the result of the first week. I expect to fiud more coldness and backwardness in the bulk of your friends to adopt any strong measure—much inclination in many to accommodate—and a general disposition to allow the Ministers to produce their plans. During the interval which these humors will afford, offers will be privately and openly made, which will divide men's opinions, and draw them off from the resolutions with which they set out."

The Lords continued for some time quietly to look on;

¹ Crown Off Min. Book, f 31.

but addresses being carried by the Commons for the dismissal of Mr. Pitt, followed by an order forbidding the Lords of the Treasury to make certain payments, it was thought fit to commence active operations in the Upper House, and the Earl of Effingham there moved a resolution, " That it is not competent to either House of Parliament to suspend the execution of the law." This was warmly opposed by Lord Loughborough, who contended that the Commons had not exceeded their constitutional powers. " The Commons," said he, " have formerly been told that they had nothing to do with intricate and weighty affairs of state, and that their duty was only to grant money, or to deliberate upon what was set before them. But, thank God, the times are altered. Since the glorious Revolution till now, liberty of free debate and a power of animadverting on the conduct of Ministers have not been denied to either House of Parliament. It is a wise maxim in our Constitution, that the King can do no wrong; but it is a presumption of law that the King may be deceived; and, according to experience, princes are more likely to be imposed upon than other men. Upon this principle, where the Sovereign has been deceived in his selection of the most proper and able Ministers, the House of Commons, long before the Revolution, was in the habit of addressing him for their removal. I doubt not the abilities of many of the present Administration—for some of whom I have the greatest esteem—but I think they are very ill-advised in not resigning after such large majorities against them, and still more in pressing a resolution like the present, which has such a strong tendency to produce a breach between the two Houses and to create general confusion. I can tell you, your Lordships will suffer in the coming conflict. The Commons may continue to send up bills praying your concurrence, and the forms of the Constitution may be observed, but your real power will be extinguished. Your present effort is to establish an Executive Government independent of Parliament, and to set at nought the representatives of the people. Success would only insure your own degradation, and make you an appendage to Royalty." But the resolution was carried by a majority of 100 to 53, and was followed by an address to the King, acknowledging his Majesty's undoubted right to choose his own Ministers, and assuring him of the zealous support of the House in the exercise of his just prerogative.

None of the fatal predictions of ruin to the House of Lords were verified; for it was now in the situation, which at very rare intervals it has occupied, of being a rallying point for public opinion against the factious and tyrannical proceedings of the House of Commons. The nation had been exceedingly shocked by the coalition between Mr. Fox and Lord North, and strongly condemned the votes of their representatives by which it was supported. The King, for the first time since his accession, was very popular; and many exclaimed, " Thank God, we have a House of Lords!"

However, Lord Loughborough stoutly encouraged the factious proceedings in the House of Commons, and composed the following paper of instructions for the guidance of his friends there :—

" In stating our resolution, you can not help observing that there can be no distinction between a discretionary power by common law and one given by act of parliament; and that a discretionary power given to Commissioners of the Treasury is given in truth to them as officers of executive government—ministers—not as trustees specially chosen. The necessary effect of the principle stated in our resolution is to deny the right of either House to interfere, by discretion or advice, with any part of the Executive Government in the vast circle of discretionary powers that are now and must always be lodged with it for the public service,—which would leave you nothing but the right (always difficult in exercise) of punishing. Where there is no power to prevent abuse, there will not be much power to punish.—This leads to stating from your Journals a great train of instances of such interference, and marks the necessity for it. You will then come to conclusions more general and declaratory of the rights of Parliament, as well as to the particular ones; and perhaps it will be right to frame them with a view of being communicated to us. In short, I would have a strong though temperate manifesto, explaining and asserting the rights of Parliament against the doctrines laid down in the Chancellor's speech. In doing this, you expose the wickedness and danger of that system which would throw all government into the hands of Ministers, and sink Parliament to its ancient insignificance. The Chancellor said in so many words that the best times were those in which Parliament did not pretend to interfere with the Executive Government. He must mean the reigns of the Tudors, for there have been no such times since."

A few days after, he wrote to a friend, affecting to think that the cause was prospering. " Everybody is so active, that there is no occasion for prompting. Lord N. has kept open house, and his dinners have been very lively. There is not a trace of any desertion. One or two whom there was some reason to doubt have very explicitly cleared themselves. I am persuaded that a dissolution is a resource in view; but if ever the Ministry consider the measure in detail, they will find it impracticable at such a period of the session. The report from St. James's is, that the hope of the Administration rests on an agreement with the India Company, and a bill, framed by consent, so reasonable that all moderate men must consent to it. At the same time I hear that Johnstone,[1] who knows all that transaction, says the Ministry can not continue."

These anticipations were vain; but the pugnacious Chief Justice, during the remainder of the session, took every opportunity of assailing the new Government and he seems sincerely to have thought that it could not stand.

At last came the dissolution, and the hopes of the Whigs were extinguished. Their Peers luckily could not be ejected, but the members who had swelled the majorities in the Lower House against the Peace, and on the subsequent divisions, hardly ventured to show themselves on the hustings; and only a miserable remnant of them ever again saw St. Stephen's Chapel.

From the meeting of the new Parliament till the King's insanity, a period of four years and a half, Lord Loughborough's prospects were very gloomy. Lord North may almost be considered as having retired from public life. Our Chief Justice thus laments the inactivity of his old

[1] Afterwards Sir Wm. Pultney.
[2] See in particular his speech against Mr. Pitt's famous Commutation Tax, 24 Parl. Hist 1376.

political chief on Mr. Pitt's celebrated motion for parliamentary reform :—" Lord North is rather low-spirited, and does not like to be personally attacked, or to take a very active part in any measure. He was very improperly advised to be absent yesterday on Mr. Pitt's motion, which he might have had the credit with all sober men of rejecting by a much greater majority than twenty." [1] By degrees the Tory section of the Coalition almost entirely disappeared, and Loughborough became a regular, zealous, and seemingly attached Foxite, having no scruples about parliamentary reform or any other Whig measure. Strange to say, Mr. Fox, Mr. Burke, and Mr. Sheridan seem to have admitted him to their confidence without the slightest suspicion or misgiving, as if he had always been a consistent politician and they had never differed from him. He was considered the leader of the Whig party in the House of Lords, and he had great influence respecting all their movements.

I can not affirm that his advice led them to take the discreditable course of opposing Mr. Pitt's measure for establishing free trade between England and Ireland; but when it came up to the House of Lords, the pupil of Adam Smith delivered a violent speech for "protection to native industry," contending that if there were an unrestricted intercourse between the two countries—from the cheapness of labor in Ireland, English manufactures would be ruined.[2] He added,—" If there are at this moment any idle and silly conceits engendering in the minds of men, of opening a trade with France, and of taking her wines in return for our hardware, I have no doubt that the good sense and enlightened policy of the nation will overturn any such speculative chimera." [3]

Although Mr. Pitt's popularity increased in spite of the cry of "protection," Lord Loughborough tried to work himself into the vain belief that there was a *reaction* in favor of the Whigs. In a letter written by him from Harrowgate in the autumn of 1785 to a friend in Ireland, after describing the "weak and disgraced state of the Government in both countries," he observes,—" A very

[1] Letter to Mr. Eden, dated "Wednesday, 7th May."
[2] I fear he was now speaking against his better judgment, for he had learned better principles from David Hume and Adam Smith, and from the debates of the Select Society.
[3] 25 Parl. Hist. 864.

zealous partisan of Pitt has spent a week here, and his discourse is the most certain indication I have seen that the rage for Pitt is totally calmed. Nothing but the shame of avowing their own folly prevents his late adherents from declaring openly against him. The amusement of our society has been a theater, in a barn, which we have most regularly attended." The Duke of Portland, under the same delusion, thus addressed Lord Loughborough :—

"I have received accounts from Scotland within these few days of the best possible disposition of the manufacturers in and about Glasgow and Paisley, who have of their own accord, and independently of any suggestion from our political friends, drawn up a sketch of an address, in which they state, in firm but discreet and well managed terms, the incapacity and weakness of the present Ministers, and with the same prudence desire a general remedy, *the particular application of which can not be misunderstood*, and I am assured that if it is suffered to go forward it will be most respectably and generally signed. I know no person to whose judgment I can so well apply for the information necessary to enable our Northern friends to determine their conduct. I shall certainly write to Lord Sheffield, and Eden, and some of our principal friends who reside in the manufacturing counties; but, without compliment (which would be very inconsistent with the sincerity of my regard for you), there is no one who is possessed of such general knowledge of the subject as yourself."[1]

Lord Loughborough, however, was sadly disappointed in the anticipations of popular favor entertained by him and his Whig associates, and he soon became much dejected. The well-founded rumors circulated of violent disputes between the Prime Minister and the Chancellor, afforded no consolation, for they could do no good to *him*, and his only chance of the Great Seal was upon the total rout of an Administration that now seemed more firmly established than any during the present reign.

However, he did not lose his courage. His great object was to cultivate the favor of the Heir Apparent, and the following note shows that he had made some progress in this line :—

[1] Rossl. MSS.

"MY DEAR LORD LOUGHBOROUGH,

"Since I had the pleasure of seeing Lady Erskine this evening, I have been thinking that it might possibly be as convenient and agreeable to you, and perhaps more so to us both, were you to come and eat your mutton chop quietly, tete-a-tete with me, about six o'clock to-morrow. I shall be happy to see you, and to have an hour's conversation with you over a bottle of port.

"I remain, my dear friend, ever most truly yours,
"GEORGE P.

"Carlton House, Sunday night, 12 o'clock,
April 29, 1787."[1]

When M de Vergennes' commercial treaty with France came on to be debated,—thinking this a favorable opportunity for exciting clamor about "native industry," he furiously opposed it, and divided the House against the address to the Crown approving of it,—although he was left in a minority of 24 against 74.[2]

He gained a victory on a question not considered a party one, viz., "Whether Scotch representative peers being created British peers, they should continue to sit as part of the sixteen, or their place should be supplied by a new election?" Upon a very able argument of his against the Chancellor, the House determined, by a majority of 52 to 38, "That the Earl of Abercorn, who had been chosen to be of the sixteen peers by the treaty of Union, to represent the peerage of Scotland in Parliament, being created Viscount Hamilton, by letters patent under the Great Seal of Great Britain, doth thereby cease to act as a representative of the peerage of Scotland."[3]

Yet, when Government put forth its force, all argument was unavailing, and after an admirable speech against a bill for allowing the most mischievous species of gaming that ever was invented—the insurance of lottery tickets —he was defeated by a majority of 38 to 7.[4]

I am much amused, and so will my *legal* readers be, with a view which Lord Loughborough gives of the office of Chancellor in Ireland, and of the state of jurisprudence in that country. Mr. Eden, who had been called to the English Bar, but had soon left it for politics, having adhered to Mr. Pitt's Government, was now engaged in the diplomatic line, in which he afterwards reaped such high

[1] Rossl. MSS.   [2] 26 Parl. Hist. 585, 595.   [3] Ibid 603.   [4] Ib.d 619.

reputation; but his probable promotion here being very slow, the Chief Justice of the Common Pleas thus advised him to turn to better account his favor with the Minister:—

"My project for you may seem very chimerical, but it is not half so unlikely as it once was, that you should be fixed in the *corps diplomatique.* Why should you not return to your old corps and to Ireland? I have never heard of a successor for old Lifford,[1] who was in every respect fitted for the office, which requires much more than a technical knowledge of law. All that is wanting in that respect you would, with your application, acquire in a twelvemonth; *and in half that time I am sure you would possess as much as any man at the Irish Bar.* Take over with you as Secretary some clever man bred in the Register's office here, and I would engage your decrees should be more accurate and more expeditious than they have been for many years in Ireland. The country would have no objection to you, nor you to it,—and I am certain you would find that court in a little time a more pleasant station than any court of Europe."[2]

Lord Loughborough, in the absence of all party excitement, seems now to have taken to study more than at any period since he left Scotland. He gives this account of himself in the beginning of 1788:—

"I have passed a month in the country, entirely alone, but very much employed. You can not imagine how valuable a present you made me in the 'Assizes of Jerusalem,' which I have studied as diligently as ever I did Littleton. The result of it will make its appearance in print in the course of this year—not by my means, however, but through a much better channel. Gibbon had long been in pursuit of the book for a part of his History, and as the language of it was less obscure to me than to him, I have employed myself in furnishing him with an abstract of it.[3] My own researches are now swelled to a very considerable bulk, but they have very little chance of ever making their appearance abroad, as I never can satisfy myself with any form in which they arrange themselves upon paper."[4]

[1] For an account of this Chancellor, see ante, Ch. CXLIV.
[2] 12th Sept. 1787. Auckland MSS.
[3] The book is written in Norman French, the original dialect of English law.
[4] 12th Jan. 1788, Auckland MSS.

Party politics were at this time in a most languid state, and it seemed as if the rest of the King's reign were to slip away in drowsy repose: yet the following year was one of the most stirring in our annals.

It was ushered in by the impeachment of Mr. Hastings. Throughout the whole course of this protracted trial Loughborough and Thurlow were pitted against each other, the former zealously taking part with the prosecutors, and the latter with the accused. The Lords first had to determine a question upon which the result mainly depended,—" Whether each charge was to be conducted and determined separately, or the managers were to finish their case on all the articles of impeachment before Mr. Hastings was to be called upon to enter upon his defense?"

Lord Loughborough contended that the charges should be taken *seriatim*, urging that, from their multifariousness and entirely distinct and separate character, justice could not otherwise be done between the parties. Thurlow, of course, took the other side, and succeeded by a majority of 88 to 33,[1]—which was considered tantamount to a verdict of acquittal, — although this was not formally pronounced till many years after, when Loughborough had become Chancellor, and Thurlow was reduced to the rank of the junior peer.

During this session, in opposing the East India Declaratory Bill introduced by Mr. Pitt, the new Foxite took occasion to deliver a labored panegyric upon his present Chief. Among other things he said, " The bill of my right honorable friend, like his own mind, was manly and open. He was above the meanness of concealment, and scorned the scandalous baseness of a lie. My right honorable friend asserted, and asserted openly, that patronage and power were inseparable; and as the best possible guard against abuse, he placed the patronage of India in the hands of honorable men, with complete responsibility. What did the other bill do? Expression fails me. I can find no adequate term to describe its operation—short of the Old Bailey. It stole the patronage, and put it in the pocket of the Minister. Delusion is now over, and misrepresentation and falsehood stand refuted and detected. My right honorable friend has

[1] 27 Parl. Hist. 56, 63.

reason to be proud of his present position. Out of place, he possesses patronage,—and patronage of the noblest kind—the protection of defenseless millions,—a species of patronage more congenial to his mind than the giving away of satrapies. The unremitting exercise of this patronage is the best answer to the calumny and slander which, in the hour of popular frenzy, industrious clamor had cast upon his name. My right honorable friend will go to the next general election confident of success, appealing to the two India bills,—his of 1783, as commented upon by its enemies, and his rival's of 1784, as now explained by its friends."—However, he could only muster 28 peers to divide against the Government. In reality, the nation had as yet in no degree forgiven the "Coalition," and placed increasing confidence in Mr. Pitt, which would have been proved if a dissolution of Parliament had then taken place.

But when there was no murmur of party strife, and Mr. Fox, abandoning objects of ambition, solaced himself in the soft climate and classic scenes of Italy, the monarchical power in the Constitution was suddenly in abeyance, and the two Houses of Parliament were called upon to supply the deficiency.

CHAPTER CLXX.

CONTINUATION OF THE LIFE OF LORD LOUGHBOROUGH DURING THE DISCUSSIONS RESPECTING THE REGENCY.

I AM enabled to let in a flood of new light upon this interesting portion of our history. It has always been notorious that Lord Loughborough was the chief adviser of the Prince of Wales and of the Whigs when the royal authority was suspended; but little has hitherto been known of the measures which he urged. Had they been adopted, they probably would have led to civil war, and it is impossible to defend him from the charge of rashness and recklessness in proposing them. I adhere to the doctrine, that when the two Houses of Parliament, on due inquiry, have found and resolved that the Sovereign is disabled by mental infirmity from exercising the functions of Royalty, the next heir to the Throne is entitled, during the continuance of this disability, to carry on the Executive Government as Regent, with the same authority as if the disabled Sovereign were naturally dead; —instead of admitting that upon such an emergency power is vested in the two Houses of Parliament to elect as Regent whomsoever they please—to confer upon him, or withhold from him, any of the prerogatives of the Crown, and to transfer to another, at their pleasure, any portion of the royal patronage. The view of the question which is consonant to our monarchical constitution would probably have met with general acceptation, but for the circumstance that it suited the interests of an unpopular party, and would have been fatal to an Administration which deservedly stood high in public favor. We shall find that Lord Loughborough, although he did not openly recommend a course different from this, and although he stoutly denied that he had ever done so,—in reality pressed the Prince of Wales to supersede the constitutional jurisdiction of Parliament, and, by his own authority, to place himself upon the throne during his father's lifetime.

His Majesty's indisposition, although it had been coming on for some months, was long anxiously concealed from the public; but in the end of October and beginning of November it was so much aggravated, that rumors of it were spread abroad. Lord Loughborough had heard nothing beyond these, when he received the following note:—

"The Duke of York presents his compliments to Lord Loughborough, and having a commission of the utmost consequence from the Prince of Wales to communicate, desires he will do him the favor to come to Carlton House as soon as he conveniently can.

"Carlton House, 4 o'clock, Thursday, 6th Nov."[1]

Immediately obeying this summons, all the details of the royal malady were disclosed to him, and he was told that to him, in the absence of Mr. Fox, the Prince must look for counsel; that a confidential communication would be made to him daily, upon the state of the King's health; and that he must, as a great constitutional law-

[1] Rossl. MSS.

yer, consider what steps ought to be taken in such an unprecedented emergency.

The person who acted the most important part at this time is as yet not much known to fame,—Mr. J. W. Payne, the Prince's private secretary. This obscure, good-natured, but not very profound or trustworthy individual, had much influence over the mind of his royal Master and was actuated by a keen love of intrigue. Accordingly he opened separate negotiations with the two rivals and enemies,—Lord Loughborough and Lord Thurlow,—holding out to each the certain prospect of favor under the new *régime*, which might be expected speedily to commence. He was stationed at Windsor, where the Prince had established himself to watch over his father's illness.

The following are letters which he wrote to Lord Loughborough :—

"7th Nov.

"MY DEAR LORD,

"In situations of difficulty and moment, one generally looks to those friends, who from presuming are most willing, we know also are most able to administer advice. On this presumption, I shall make no further apology for troubling you.

"I am sorry to tell you, his Majesty is now in a very alarming situation; *so bad*, that I fear his dissolution is almost the best that can be hoped. He has, at present, with a more considerable degree of wandering, a most violent heat, accompanied at the same time with a great chilliness; every moment we fear something dreadful.

"Knowing the friendship and opinion the *best of friends* entertains for you coincides so much with my own, I venture to say to you at a time when he sees nobody, that if anything can suggest itself that can be of use, I shall be happy to be made a vehicle of to his advantage. He has this morning talked to me of rejecting any rule, where somebody was not united to him. I told him, I was persuaded he would be advised to the contrary by his best friends, on the truest principles of public good, if any unfortunate accident should happen. I speak my mind freely to him without much prejudgment, and therefore I only mention this to you as it passed.

"I need not say to you, I beg I may not be understood

to have had any communication with you on this subject, as I have no authority for so doing, and therefore you need not acknowledge any such. Seeing the Prince as much as I do, I am anxious to have the best opinions, and those I know to be most friendly to him, during his great agitation of spirits, in which he displays the most filial and affectionate duty and regard to a very unhappy family.

"I have been up two nights, and a most violent headache will not add to the coherency of saying any more, than that I am,

"Most sincerely and obediently,
"Your Lordship's faithful serv^t
"J. W. PAYNE.

"Friday, 8 o'clock at night.

"If you should have anything to say, direct to me at the Prince's at Windsor; but I hope to be in town the day after to-morrow for a few hours."

"Nov 9th and 10th, 12 o'clock at night.

"MY DEAR LORD,

"I received your first letter this morning in bed, and as the Prince was then asleep, I waited till he was up to communicate the contents of it. I shall best give you his reception of it in his own words:—'Tell Lord Loughborough I am persuaded no less of his attachment than I desire him to be of mine, and shall always receive his advice with the same *great* degree of pleasure I do upon this occasion, and without which I shall not act for any material decision of my present delicate situation.' I can add on my own part, that he expressed the highest respect for all the sentiments contained in it, and which I am convinced will not be lost upon him. As I wrote fully to Sheridan on the subject of his Majesty's situation, I was on the point of addressing myself to you on the subject of your last letter, which I had just received, when I was called away; so I dispatched the messenger with what was finished, that you might have the communication contained in it before you went to bed; since when, matters have gone worse, and continue to increase with the night; but as I do not mean to send this letter till I am up, I will give you the particulars at that time. The Prince has been just applied to, to lay his commands upon all the officers and servants to obey implicitly the directions of the physicians, with respect to the force that might be necessary to use in the course of the night, as their patient was growing much more peremptory; and from what I can understand from the *best* authority, the *last* stroke to this unhappy affair can not be far off. It is what every person in a situation to see, is obliged to wish, as the happiest *possible* termination to the present melancholy scene.

"I took the liberty of mentioning to the Prince the very liberal accommodation of your conduct in promotion of his service. He said, 'Well, if the C. chooses to remain where he is, Lord L. can have the Privy Seal or President for the present, and settle the other arrangement afterwards, if it is more to his mind.' I tell you this only in strict confidence, as I have no authority to say it; but the regard I know *he* bears you assures me *he* would think all precaution of secrecy unnecessary with you. I have not read to *him* the contents of the transcript inclosed in your last, nor the declaration that accompanied it, as he is now very much fatigued; but it shall be the first thing I do in the morning. I have, however, informed him of the receipt of it, and he desires me to thank you for it.

"I need not suggest to your Lordship's better judgment how material it is that there should be no appearance of the *smallest intercourse* between *this place* and town, as it might serve to inflame *some certain people*, who, I have reason to think, are not quite convinced that *a reform* might take place; and all active communication where you are may be well enough accounted for, and expected, without a certain person (who sees nobody) be supposed to be informed, or at least be engaged in it. The person I allude to said to me to-night, 'I hope Lord L. and S. are in close communication together on this occasion,' and I assured him I knew that you were both privy to everything each other did; at which he was much pleased.

"I trust to your Lordship's friendship to myself, no less than your known zeal for H. R. H., for a free communication of your advice on the present occasion, as I can not flatter myself I can be of any essential service to the *person* I am most obliged to, more than in being the medium of conveying more worthy opinions than my own, and

I trust I need not add, that nothing you can say shall not be as sacred as in the repository of your own bosom.

"Half-past ten, Monday morning.

"The King's fever is hardly anything to-day: his pulse is not much above 70. The *other* distemper fixed, and no appearance of the smallest abatement with the amendment of his health. I think something must soon be thought of; for I think all secrecy with regard to his Majesty's situation any longer almost unadvisable. Pray give me your opinion.

"Ever, my dear Lord, yours, &c.,
"J. W. P."

" 10th Nov, Monday night.

"MY DEAR LORD,

"I have just now received the favor of yours, and am sorry I can give no better accounts on the subject of it; the King continuing in the same situation. I am happy to find your Lordship's opinion so strongly corroborate my own. An Act of Regency must necessarily precede the occasion for the exercise of it, as the third state would be wanting to give force to it. No law can be passed before the chasm is filled up, and the succession must be to the uninfringed right of the past inheritor, only subject to a *possible* resumption in case of competency. Some form may perhaps be necessary in requesting the next heir to assume the reins of government; but the first occasion of public business must be the time, and that can not be long postponed. The Prince's task seems to me to be an easy one. He is far from anxious to interfere of his own will, and nothing can possibly proceed without application to him. King William, in a weaker degree, seems to my recollection to be a case in point, if, at least, I am correct in the remembrance of it. Was he not desired to take charge of the government; and when the legislation of the country was thus completed in its three branches, that it proceeded to ratify it by law? I have nobody within reach to borrow the least light from, that I dare speak on the subject, but am happy to find the discussion of it in such good hands. I shall direct the messengers to call on you, and you may rest assured that your letters can by no accident come under the perusal of any other individual than the one you allude to. Before any decided measure is decided on, it is necessary, I think, you should see the Prince, and he says as soon as he has seen S. he will contrive it; but he is extremely jealous of seeing more than one person at a time, and that not by way of *consultation*, but in private friendship. He said to me to-night, he thought it had better be done by your coming to your farm, and thence to Bagshot; but more of this hereafter, of which I will give you the earliest intimation. Take no notice, however, of this communication for the present."

"Tuesday morning.

"His Majesty continues just the same; he has eaten a hearty breakfast, and has no fever; but a *total* deprivation continues. "I am ever, my dear Lord,

"Most faithfully yours,

"J. W. PAYNE." [1]

The next communication which Lord Loughborough received was from Mr. Sheridan:—

"MY DEAR LORD,

"Everything remained late last night at Windsor without the least amendment, and, in consequence of a consultation of the physicians, they are, I believe, ready to give a decided opinion.

"The Prince sends Payne to town this morning. I shall make an attempt at setting his head a little to rights, if possible, for he is growing worse and worse, but a few words from your Lordship will have more weight. Among other things, he tells me he has suggested to the Prince to write directly to the Chancellor, and he tells me that the letter shall be so worded that either he or I may deliver it, so that I suppose his notion is to bring this negotiation into the same train and footing as Lord Sandwich's. It is really intolerable, and I mean to speak very plainly to him. I will endeavor to have the honor of seeing your Lordship this morning; if not, at Lord North's in the evening.

"I have the honor to be,

"With great truth and respect,

"Your Lordship's most sincere and obedient,

"R. B. SHERIDAN.

"Wednesday morning"[2]

The following is Lord Loughborough's answer to Mr. Payne,—to be shown to the Prince of Wales:—[3]

[1] Rossl. MSS.   [2] Ibid.   [3] Ibid.

"My dear Sir,

"I can with truth assure you that my attention has never deviated to any other affair than the subject of our conversation, from the moment I received, last Thursday, an order to turn my thoughts to it. I should feel an equal pride and happiness, if it were in my power to contribute in the smallest degree by any possible exertion of zeal to the ease and tranquillity of H. R. H. in so trying a situation as Providence has prepared for him. I consider that there are but three possible events in immediate expectation; an ambiguous state of the King's disorder; an evidently decided state; or a sudden termination, which can be looked for only in one way; for an entire and speedy recovery seems to be beyond the reach of any reasonable hope. In the two first cases, it is the result of my most deliberate judgment that the administration of government is as directly cast upon the Heir Apparent, as the right to the Crown is in the last case. All are alike the act of God, and the law of England knows no interval in which there can be an interregnum; —but holding, as I do, the principle of right to be as distinct and plain in the extraordinary as it unquestionably is in the ordinary case of a demise, it must be allowed that there would be some material difference in effect. No precedent can be found except one little known, and in times where both the frame of the government and the manners of the age were so little similar to what they now are, that it would be of no authority. In a case, therefore, supposed to be new, men would be, for a moment, uncertain by what rule they were to be guided; and upon a supposition of an ambiguous state of the disorder, great industry would be used to prolong the state of suspense. Every appearance of favorable intervals would be magnified, and the apprehension of a change would be studiously excited to prevent the public opinion from attaching itself to the apparent acting power. To oppose this, great spirit and steadiness would be necessary; but I have no doubt that the only measure would be, to assert that authority which no other person has a right to assume, and which, with an united royal family, no opposition would be able to thwart. Wherever any precedent occurs in which a declaration of the King's pleasure is necessary, that declaration must be made by the only person who can be legally presumed to be authorized to make it. The case of an evidently decided disorder is attended with very little embarrassment. There would be no expectation of change to encourage and rear up an opposition to the full acknowledgment of the right to the administration of government. It would be declared to the nation by Parliament without restriction; for any partition of authority I hold to be totally inconsistent with the frame of our government, which has provided a sufficient control in the Parliament, and admits of no intermediate and secondary control. I doubt not but some wishes might be entertained, for the purposes of private ambition, to create councils and devise restrictions, but they would terminate, as they ought, in the confusion of those who had the presumption to propose them.

"The third case is not new. There are known forms to be observed, which should be carefully inspected and prepared. The most essential is, a declaration to be made and entered at the first meeting of council; the substance of which should be well considered and digested, because it would be taken as an indication of the spirit of the future Government. It should be short, general, and at the same time satisfactory to the public on the great lines of policy. I have not the least apprehension of any mischief, or even inconvenience, that can arise to H. R. H., but from his own virtues. It may sound harsh, and you will with some reason impute it to the coldness of age, when I say that the duties of public life in the highest state of human greatness may often require—not dissimulation, for I hold that unworthy maxim for government to be equally false and foolish,—but a certain reserve and guard upon the frankness of that amiable disposition which is the ornament and delight of society. I should be completely the old man if I should permit myself to run on further. You will excuse, and I am sure not expose, a too forward zeal, from, my *dear* Payne,

"Yours ever,
"LOUGHBOROUGH."[1]

The meditated *coup d'état* is more clearly developed in the paper now lying before me, written in pencil by the hand of Lord Loughborough. Of this I subjoin an exact copy. I have been informed that he himself read it

[1] Copied from draught of the letter in the Rossl. MSS.

to the Prince at a secret interview which they had together at Windsor:—

"Upon the supposition of a state of disorder without prospect of recovery or of a speedy extinction, the principle of the P.'s conduct is perfectly clear. The administration of government devolves to him of right. He is bound by every duty to assume it, and his character would be lessened in the public estimation if he took it on any other ground but right, or on any sort of compromise. The authority of Parliament, as the great council of the nation, would be interposed, not to confer, but to declare, the right. The mode of proceeding which occurs to my mind is, that in a very short time H. R. H. should signify his intention to act by directing a meeting of the Privy Council, where he should declare his intention to take upon himself the care of the State, and should at the same time signify his desire to have the advice of Parliament, and order it by a proclamation to meet early for dispatch of business. That done, he should direct the several Ministers to attend him with the public business of their offices.

It is of vast importance in the outset, that he should appear to act entirely of himself, and, in the conferences he must necessarily have, not to consult, but to listen and direct.

"Though the measure of assembling the Council should not be consulted upon, but decided in his own breast, it ought to be communicated to a few persons who may be trusted, a short time before it takes place; and it will deserve consideration whether it might not be expedient very speedily after this measure, in order to mark distinctly the assumption of government, to direct such persons—at least in one or two instances—to be added to what is called the Cabinet, as he thinks proper. By marking a determination to act of himself, and by cautiously avoiding to raise strong fear or strong hope, but keeping men's minds in expectation of what may arise out of his reserve, and in a persuasion of his general candor, he will find all men equally observant of him."

It would further appear, from another paper, which is likewise in Lord Loughborough's handwriting, that he had at one time contemplated a scheme of supplying the royal authority by a "phantom," somewhat like Thurlow's, which he afterward joined in ridiculing so severely. According to the constitution of this country, the Sovereign may assign any part or the whole of the royal authority to be executed by a deputy or deputies;'¹ and the suggestion was, that a commission should pass the Great Seal in the King's name, although without his consciousness, appointing the Prince of Wales Regent:—" On the supposition of a certain though slow recovery, would it not be the natural course to commit to the Prince, in the name and by the authority of the King, the power of administration, with no other restriction than such as honest advice can suggest, and honorable engagements can secure? Could that fail to be the mode adopted, were the royal family united as it ought to be? And, to accomplish both these ends, it is impossible to establish a confidence between those who fairly mean the public good? On the contrary supposition, that a recovery is not certain, the conclusion would not much vary. In my mind, it would not vary in any respect."

But we are left totally in the dark as to the ingenious contrivance by which Thurlow was to be induced to put the Great Seal to such a commission. The office of Chancellor might have purchased his consent; but this was to be held by the contriver himself.

The following is the "declaration" which was sent by Lord Loughborough to Windsor, and which is alluded to in one of Mr. Payne's letters. I am at a loss to understand whether it was to be read by the Prince in Council as Regent after he had seized the government, or whether it was written in contemplation of the immediate death of George III., which had several times been supposed inevitable,—and so was to be the speech of George IV. reigning in his own right:—

"I feel, more than any other person can, the unspeakable misfortune that the nation and I have sustained by the melancholy occasion upon which you are assembled. The weight of the important duty I am called upon to discharge, by undertaking the government of this great empire, can only be alleviated by the consciousness of the entire affection I bear to my native country, and of the most ardent zeal for promoting its domestic welfare and its just consideration among the other states

¹ Of this we have still instances in giving the royal assent to Bills, and in opening and proroguing Parliament.

of Europe. Animated by such sentiments, I shall not doubt the assistance of every honest man in my unceasing endeavors to maintain and strengthen the religion, laws and liberties of my kingdom. The constitution in church and state which my family was called to defend, shall ever form the rule of my government, and it shall be my constant study to improve the blessings of peace with the protection of the Divine Providence upon my dominions, in the support of public credit and the encouragement of agriculture, manufactures and commerce."

But on the return of Mr. Fox from Italy all these vagaries were swept away. He was confidentially shown Lord Loughborough's suggestions, but he earnestly requested that the noble schemer should not know that he had seen them.

Accordingly, as if things had been quite entire, he opened a negotiation with the Chief Justice by the following note:—

"MY LORD,

"I should be happy, if it is not troublesome, to have half an hour's conversation with your Lordship upon the subject of the measures to be taken by the Houses of Parliament, in case a notification to them should take place, which, according to public rumor, the state of his Majesty's health renders but too likely. It may be proper for me to state previously (though probably your Lordship knows too much of what is passing to make such information necessary), that I wish to speak merely for myself and a few friends, and have no authority from, nor indeed any communication with, any person of higher station. The very circumstance of my applying to your Lordship will also satisfy you that I mean to treat this business as wholly unconnected with general politics, about which I am afraid our sentiments still continue to be widely different. All I wish is a conference, as a member of Parliament with another member, upon a subject of very great importance, upon part of which, at least, our opinions are likely to be similar. I am sure I need not add, that any desire of finding out such of your Lordship's intentions as you may wish to be secret is what I am wholly incapable of. I will call in a few minutes for your answer, in case it should be convenient for you to see me now. If not, I will trouble you to let me know at what time I shall wait upon you—unless you had rather decline the conference altogether—in which case, as I have certainly no right to claim it from you, I beg you will tell me so without ceremony.

"I am, with great regard,
"My Lord,
"Your Lordship's obedient servannt,
"C. J. Fox.
"Thursday,
"I am at Thomas's Hotel, Berkeley Square."[1]

They met; and the notion of superseding the authority of Parliament being declared inadmissible, it was speedily agreed that the constitutional course should be pursued of calling upon the two Houses to declare the King's incapacity, and to address the Heir Apparent, praying that he would take upon himself the exercise of the royal authority as Regent. No opposition by Mr. Pitt to this mode of proceeding was anticipated; and as the King's recovery was then considered impossible, the speedy advent of Whig rule seemed inevitable. In those days it was thought that the personage filling the throne, with the undiminished power and patronage constitutionally belonging to his high office, might easily give an ascendency to any party in the state, and choose his ministers at pleasure. Mr. Fox, regarding himself minister elect, without giving any positive pledge upon the subject, pretty clearly intimated to Lord Loughborough that the Great Seal should be his. It seemed now to this often-disappointed aspirant as if nothing could come "between the cup and the lip;"—he began to calculate how many days would elapse before he must be hailed as Lord Chancellor; he feasted his fancy with an anticipation of Thurlow scowling as he laid down the bauble, and the congratulations which would be showered down upon himself as he carried it away from the Prince's closet; he thought with delight of placing it on the bar of the House of Lords, when he supposed himself to been going thither from the woolsack to receive the messengers of the House of Commons.

It is a curious fact that Mr. Fox had hitherto been kept entirely ignorant of the intrigue that had been going on between Thurlow and Carlton House. This had been

[1] Rossl. MSS.

begun by Payne:—and Sheridan, whether from an old grudge against Wedderburn, or from what other motive, I know not, had warmly entered into it,—so that the Prince had positively engaged that the present Chancellor should be continued under him as Regent, on condition of his supporting the plan of conferring the Regency without any restriction. When the matter was at last mentioned to Fox, the whole truth was not disclosed to him: he was not informed of personal interviews which had taken place between the Prince and the Chancellor at Windsor, and the arrangement was represented to him as generally wished by the party. Having absolutely made up his mind to agree to it, he wrote Sheridan:—" I have swallowed the pill—a most bitter one it was,—and I have written to Loughborough, whose answer, of course, must be *consent*." The following announcement by him to the disappointed party must have been received with amazement and consternation :—

"MY DEAR LORD,

"I am so perfectly ashamed of the letter I am writing that I scarcely know how to begin—but my knowledge of your way of thinking, and the perfect and unreserved freedom with which we have have always conversed together, gives me some courage, and induces me, without any further preface, to state to you the difficulties under which I feel myself.

"When I first came over, I found a very general anxiety among all our friends, and in the Prince still more than others, to have the Chancellor make a part of our new Administration, and (excepting only the D. of Portland) they all seemed to carry their wishes so far as to think his friendship worth buying, even at the expense of the Great Seal. This idea seemed so strange to me, considering the obligations we are all under to you, and so unpleasant to those feelings of personal friendship which I am sure you do not consider as mere professions from me to you, that I took all sorts of means to discourage it, and have actually prevented the Prince, though with some difficulty, from saying anything to Thurlow which might commit him; and, to prevent the possibility of it, I obtained from him the message which I delivered to you, Wednesday night, from his Royal Highness. The difficulties which have arisen within these few days, and which to many seem increasing, have had the effect of increasing the anxiety of our friends for Thurlow's support; and they seem all to be persuaded that the Great Seal would gain him, and nothing else. You know enough of the nature of our party to know how rapidly notions are sometimes propagated among them, and how very difficult it often is for us, who ought to lead, not to be led by them. Under these circumstances, I must own (and I am certain you will approve my freedom in owning it, whatever you may think of my weakness) that I wish to have it in my power to offer Lord Thurlow the Great Seal, not from my own opinion of the advantages like to accrue from such an offer, but from the dread I have, if things turn out in any respect ill, of having the miscarriage imputed to my obstinacy. The invidious point of view in which you would stand yourself in such an event, rather adds to my anxiety; for although they all know the handsome offers you have made, and therefore that the whole blame ought justly to lie on me alone who refused them, yet it is not pleasant to be looked upon as a person whose pretensions, however just, have stood in the way of the success of a party. I have related to you most freely the difficulties of my situation, and I should really take it ill if you answered me but with the most unreserved freedom. If you can call here, it would be the best; but if you can not pray let me have a line, though I know your answer; and the more certain I am of it the more I feel ashamed of this letter. I really feel myself unhinged to a great degree, and till I see you, which I hope will be soon, or hear from you, shall feel very unpleasantly. I feel the part I am acting to be contrary to every principle of conduct I ever laid down for myself, and that I can bring myself to act it at all I strongly suspect to be more owing to my weakness than my judgment.

" I am, with the sincerest friendship,
" My dear Lord,
" Yours ever, "C. J. Fox.
" St. James's Street, Saturday morning." [1]

Loughborough, in the anguish of his soul, wrote to Sheridan the long and resentful letter which I have introduced in the life of Thurlow.[2] But he contented himself with a few formal lines to Fox:—

[1] Rossl. MSS.   [2] Ante, p. 108.

"My dear Sir,

"I will frankly confess to you that the measure appears to me a strong indication of weakness, and I am deceived if it will not be generally so felt as soon as it is known. This affords additional reason why, even on motives of prudence, I should acquiesce in it, which I do, I assure you, without the smallest interruption of those sentiments of friendship and confidence with respect to you or the Duke of P., which will ever remain in my heart.

"I ever am, my dear Sir, yours,
"LOUGHBOROUGH.

"Guildhall."[1]

Though told that he was excessively ill-used, and taunted by some old Tory friends for his credulity in believing that the Whigs would really do him a kindness, and advised to return to his old colors, he steadily adhered to the cause of the Prince of Wales and Mr. Fox, —and he strenuously defended the constitutional doctrine upon which they rested the hereditary right of the heir apparent.[2]

A rumor having been spread of the arbitrary advice he had given, that the Prince should, by proclamation, assume the government, and issue orders to the Parliament, to the army, and to the magistrates, he thought himself justified in disclaiming it, and he actually supported the motion for the appointment of a committee to inquire into and to report to the House the state of the King's health, by an examination of the physicians who attended him,—contending that this proceeding was altogether constitutional, and according to the usage of Parliament.[3] When the report was presented, and Lord Camden commented upon the strange doctrine said to have been asserted *elsewhere*, "that when his Majesty's incapacity was ascertained and declared, the heir apparent, being of age, had a claim to take upon himself the ad-

---

[1] Rossl MSS.
[2] The world has now a whimsical instance of the manner in which the opinions or professed principles of contending factions are influenced by interest. The heir apparent being with the Whigs, they advocated the doctrine of hereditary right, representing it as almost indefeasible; while the Tories, perceiving that they were in great danger of being driven from office if the Regent were appointed by address with unlimited powers, entirely sacrificed the doctrine of hereditary right, and, in substance, made the crown elective.
[3] 27 Parl. Hist. 658.

ministration of the government as a matter of right, while his Majesty labored under the disorder which rendered him unable to discharge the regal functions," Lord Loughborough rose and said,—

"I understand, my Lords, it has been asserted elsewhere, *that the Prince of Wales, the heir apparent to the throne, has no more claim to exercise the government during the continuance of the unhappy malady which incapacitates his Majesty, than any other individual subject.* If the regency be elective, my Lords, such is the consequence; and the regency is elective, if the doctrine which the noble and learned earl so keenly controverts is not a part of our constitution. The question simply is, whether upon the personal incapacity of the Sovereign, the regency is elective? No one, I believe, denies that, by the common law of this realm, and by various statutes, the crown is hereditary. Indeed, any person who, by advised speaking or writing, shall aver the contrary, is liable to be prosecuted, and incurs the penalties of a *præmunire*. How is this compatible with *election*, where there exists a competent heir apparent? There are, indeed, two supposable cases when *ex necessitate* the two Houses must fill the vacant throne, there being no heir apparent *in rerum naturâ*—the one where there is a total subversion of the government, by a breach of the original contract between the King and the people, as at the Revolution; and the other, where the royal line should have become extinct,—a King, on his decease, leaving no heir. Where there is an acknowledged heir apparent, who must succeed on the King's natural death, may the two Houses elect another as Regent, and invest him with all the powers of royalty? He might then give the royal assent, in the name of an incapacitated King, to an Act for changing the succession to the Crown and making himself the head of a new dynasty. It is more probable that the two Houses would set up a mock Regent, and assume the government themselves. A Regent so elected must necessarily be the slave of his electors. The single instance of an elected Regent is that which occurred in the reign of Henry VI, and led on to the wars of York and Lancaster. Then this House, by its own authority, without the concurrence of the Commons, appointed the Duke of York— Regent or Protector. Are your Lordships prepared to follow that precedent, and will its authority be conceded by the other branch of the legislature? Both Houses together now could not make a Turnpike Act, and yet we are told that they may elect a Regent. Then, I suppose, they may elect a plurality of Regents, and give ours the form of a Mahratta government; or put an end to the kingly office, and entirely change the constitution. What, in the mean time, becomes of your connection with Ireland, where the two independent Houses may choose one Regent, while you choose another—in which case the two kingdoms would be as completely severed as Portugal is from Spain? But it is said that the Prince of Wales is only a subject, and that while his father breathes he has no more right to govern than any other subject. No more right! Is the Prince of Wales a common subject? Does not the law describe him to be one and the same with the King? Lord Coke expressly declares this to be so. Is it not as much high treason to imagine or compass the death of the Prince as of the King? Is it high treason to imagine or compass the death of any other individual subject? It so happens that in this case the two Houses are duly summoned by the King's writs, and, in consequence, are legally assembled; but if, upon such an emergency, there had been no Parliament in existence, will any man say that it would not have been warrantable for the Prince of Wales, as heir apparent, to have issued writs, and called Parliament together? What becomes, then, of your assertion, that in his father's lifetime he has no more right to interfere with the government than any other subject? I maintain that by the constitution of England the regency is not elective, but depends on hereditary right; and the heir apparent is entitled, during the interruption of the personal exercise of the royal authority by his Majesty's illness, to assume the reins of government. When I make this observation, *I am very far from meaning to intimate that the Prince of Wales can violently do so without the privity of the two Houses of Parliament;* but I do solemnly maintain, that, upon the authentic notification to him, by the two Houses of Parliament, of the King's unfortunate incapacity, he is of right to be invested with the exercise of the royal authority."

Nevertheless, it was voted by both Houses, "that it

was their right and duty to provide the means of supplying the defect of the personal exercise of the royal authority, arising from his Majesty's indisposition, in such manner as the exigency of the case may appear to them to require."[1]

While these discussions were going on, the three following notes were sent by Mr. Fox to Lord Loughborough; but I am not able to ascertain their dates or the particular occasions when they were written :—

"MY LORD,

"After considering what your Lordship said, and mentioning it to Ld. F. and one other person, I think I had rather decline meeting the persons we mentioned—not so much from any objection to the meeting itself as from an apprehension of the construction that might be put upon it.[2] I am, with great regard, my Lord, your Lordship's obedient servant, "C. J. FOX.

"Thomas Hotel, Friday night.

"P. S.—I beg leave to add that I feel myself much obliged to you for the open manner in which you have spoken to me upon the subjects in question."[3]

"MY DEAR LORD,

"I can not say that I agree with you in your opinion, though I own I am inclined to think it the next best to that which I prefer of fighting in the H. of C'. upon the subject of the establishment. We have a great force in town, and if the leaders will behave stoutly, I have little doubt but the troops will do so, too. Can you come here to-night, or early in the morning? At all events, I can not let slip this opportunity of expressing to you my sense of the very handsome manner in which you have acted throughout, and particularly in regard to what passed this morning.

"I am, very truly, my dear Lord,
"Yours ever, "C. J. FOX.

"Downing Street, Tuesday night.

---

[1] 27 Parl. Hist. 853, 882.
[2] The imprudence with which the Whigs conducted their deliberations at this time, may be surmise 1 from the following extract of a letter from Lord Carlisle to Lord Loughborough:—" Our open councils and our generous confidence in the secrecy and discretion of the whole Club at Brookes's—not excluding the waiters—has, I fear, the small inconvenience of flinging difficulty in the way of negotiations upon which the great affairs of the world turn."—*Rossl. MSS.* [3] Rossl. MSS

"I have not seen H. R. H., but expect him here every minute."[1]

"MY DEAR LORD,

"If this does not find you in town, I hope it will bring you to town as soon as possible. There never was a situation that called for wise advice so much as ours, and we are driven to decision almost before we have time to deliberate. I know you have as much inclination as ability to counsel us, and everything must depend upon what we do before we go down to Parliament this day.

"Yours very sincerely, "C. J. FOX.
"Downing Street, 9 o'clock, Tuesday.

"I shall be here or at home all morning."[2]

Meanwhile, Lord Loughborough's zeal was sharpened by the dazzling prospect again opening to him of being at last able to grasp the Great Seal. Thurlow having obtained secret intelligence from Dr. Addington of an improvement in the King's health, was drawing off from the Prince's party, and was looking out for an opportunity to imprecate curses on his own head when he should forget his Sovereign. Mr. Fox, rejoicing that he was freed from the promise given without his knowledge, and that it was now in his power to realize the hope which he himself had held out respecting the Chancellorship under the Regency, made this communication to Lord Loughborough:—

"MY DEAR LORD,

"I could not collect from the conversation yesterday much of what is like to be the course of Thurlow's argument. He seemed to think it a more confused and difficult case than it has ever appeared to me; and therefore, if I were to guess at all, I should suspect that he will choose rather to answer the arguments of others than produce many of his own. My general conclusion from this part of our conversation, as well as that relative to restrictions, was, that he had thought less upon the subject than I should have supposed possible.

"The negotiation is off, with an express desire on his part that no more may be said to him on the subject till the Regency is settled, and *advice* to the Prince to make his arrangements without any view to him. It was much the pleasantest conversation I have had with him for

[1] Rossl. MSS. [2] Ibid.

many years. Upon the business of our interview, he was perfectly open and explicit, and dismissed the subject as soon as possible with perfect good-humor, in order to talk upon general ones in our old manner of conversing. He was in a talkative humor; and France, Spain, Hastings, Demosthenes, and Cicero were all talked over as if between two friends who had neither political connection nor enmity. In short, I think the negotiation is fairly at an end; and if, when the Regency is settled, the Prince wishes to revive it, it must be considered as a proposition entirely new, and treated on that footing.

"I am very sorry to hear that nothing has been done about a protest, nor do I know whom to employ, as I am going out of town, without an intention to return till Monday My opinion is that it should be very strong in its expressions; and the danger of putting the unlimited power of legislation into the hands of the two Houses of Parliament explained at large.

"I am, my dear Lord, yours ever,
"C J. Fox.

"St. James's Street, 26th Dec.

"If I were to tell you the advantage my health and spirits have received from our conversation yesterday, you would perhaps think either that I exaggerated, or that I am weaker than a man ought to be."[1]

When the resolution came to be debated against the Regent being allowed to make Peers, Lord Loughborough was particularly severe on the suggestion of Lord Camden, that if there was an urgent necessity for a new peerage it might be created by Act of Parliament. He showed the mischief of encouraging any such idea to obtain ground, and urged the danger of its being considered sanctioned even by the opinion of any one individual Peer of Parliament in debate:—

"Let me remind your Lordships," said he, "that although a Peerage Bill may originate in a message from the Regent, the Commons would immediately be let into their share of creating a Peer; the honor of the Peerage would be put to the vote, and thence a most unparliamentary interference of the other House with the constitution of your Lordships' House would be established— a doctrine too monstrous to be endured for a single

[1] Rossl. MSS.

moment! The public good requires that the entire free and unrestrained power of creating peers should remain with the Executive Government, and your Lordships should recollect the ancient mythological fable representing the Temple of Honor as placed behind the Temple of Virtue, indicating to us that a peerage should be conferred for great public services, and not for practicing the arts of a demagogue."[1]

With a view to make the Regency Bill and its author as odious as possible to the Prince, Loughborough pointed out the insulting nature of the restriction against alienating the King's private property, and felicitously quoted a legal decision, in which it was held by the Judges to be a libel for one man to send to another the commandment out of the Decalogue, "THOU SHALT NOT STEAL," as it implied that the person to whom it was sent was a thief.[2]

Having in vain attempted to resist the very unfair proceeding of putting the question jointly on the two resolutions, "That the Queen should have the custody of the King's person—and should likewise have the appointment of all officers of the household"—acknowledging the fitness of the former, he proceeded to combat the latter with great boldness and vigor:—

"In discussing this subject," said he, "it is very material to bear in mind that the object for which the monarchy is established is the good of the people, and that our constitution is framed upon the principle of vesting in the Monarch only that portion of power and influence which is necessary for carrying on the Executive Government. But from party motives, or a mockery of adulation to the afflicted Sovereign (who, if he were conscious of your proceedings, could not decently be supposed, from jealousy of his son, to approve them), having curtailed the salutary prerogative of the Crown, you are now going to deprive it of its patronage. You are establishing two Courts—one of the Regent—another of the Queen,—and there may very likely be a rivalry between them. You may take a lesson from a country which, in all matters of constitutional learning, you affect to despise. Louis XIV. conceived a dislike to his nephew the Duke of Orleans, and, wishing to aggrandize his own natural son the Duke

[1] 27 Parl. Hist. 1067. [2] Ibid. 1082.

de Maine, by his will left the administration of public affairs to the Duke of Orleans, as Regent, and the control of the household, with the custody of the person of the infant King, to the Duke de Maine. The will was duly registered in the Parliament of Paris; and the Duke of Orleans was told by the royal testator that he was to enjoy everything to which his high birth entitled him. But when Louis XIV. died, the Regent, now heir presumptive to Louis XV., by the renunciation of the Duke of Anjou, then King of Spain, claimed all the powers and privileges which properly belonged to the Regency. The Parliament felt itself in an awkward dilemma. It saw the danger of yielding to the claim of the heir presumptive; but it likewise saw the absurdity of placing the Regent at the head of the Government, and placing in the hands of another the means by which the government was to be carried on. Wisely weighing all the difficulties of the case, and preferring the lesser evil to the greater, the Parliament set aside the late King's will, and invested the Regent with all the authorities of the Crown. It is said her Majesty is to be assisted by a council—which will only make matters worse, by rendering her section of the government more conspicuous, more efficient and more mischievous. Around her all will rally who are dissatisfied with the Regent, because he has so little to bestow, and foreign ministers will intrigue with her councillors when they can not carry a point they are pressing on the responsible Ministers of the Crown. We have such idle reasoning in defense of putting the patronage of the household in the hands of the Queen—as that the King would feel his mind disturbed when awakened from his trance, if he found that his lords and grooms in waiting had been removed from about his person. Suppose that his Majesty's trance had taken place some years ago, would it have been any consolation to him if his Ministers, on their first audience after his awakening from it, had thus addressed him: 'Your Majesty has lost thirteen colonies, but—your palace stands where it did! Millions of national debt have been accumulated, but—your lords with white staves stand where you left them! Much of the best blood of your subjects has been spilt, but—not a page of the back stairs has been removed! Many calamities have happened in consequence of your son and representative being deprived of the constitutional power which your Majesty enjoyed, but—be not concerned, the same beef-eaters, holding the same halberds, still surround you! Weep not for national disgrace and universal suffering, for peruse the Red Book, and you will find it as you left it!!!' When his Majesty is restored to reason, he will feel insulted by those who impute to him such paltry and childish considerations, instead of the enlightened patriotism which belongs to the father of his people." [1]

But the resolution was negatived by a majority of 94 to 68.[2]

When the Prince of Wales received the proposal from Mr. Pitt, that he should accept the office of Regent under the mortifying restrictions to be laid upon him, he immediately wrote the following note to Lord Loughborough:—

"MY DEAR LORD,

"I have just received a letter from the Minister, with such restrictions as no Dictator c^d possibly, I think ever have been barefaced enough to have brought forward. Pray come to Charles's as soon as you possibly can, to take these matters into consideration.

"I am my dear Lord,
"Most truly y^{rs}
"G. P."

Lord Loughborough attended the meeting and concurred in the prudent advice that his Royal Highness—protesting against the course which was followed—should still, for the public good, conform to the wishes expressed by a majority of the two Houses.

He took no part in the subsequent debates as to the opening of Parliament by the "phantom" of the Great Seal under the supposed authority of the insane Sovereign, or as to the provisions of the Regency Bill, which, however objectionable, he considered irrevocably settled by the Resolutions previously adopted. He was now de-

---

[1] This prophecy was by no means fulfilled; for George III. looked with absolute abhorrence upon all who he was told had opposed the limitations on the Regent, or the transference of the household to the Queen. He was actuated by a belief that they had entered, with his son, into a conspiracy to prevent him from ever remounting the throne; and in his best subsequent days he never could be convinced of his error.

[2] 27 Parl Hist. 1088–1093.

sirous of seeing the Regency established as soon as possible. The Prince of Wales, having with such reluctance agreed to accept the office with mutilated powers, expressed deep resentment against the present Ministers, who, he conceived had treated him so unhandsomely, and professed himself more than ever a devoted partisan of the Whigs. The intrigue which had induced him to promise that there should be no change in the custody of the Great Seal had actually terminated in Thurlow taking a decided part against him, and weeping in the House of Lords at the thought of deserting the afflicted King. No doubt was entertained, therefore, that as soon as the Regency Bill had received the royal assent by the agency of the "phantom," there would be a Whig Administration, and the Regent would have a new Chancellor. The Chief Justice of the Common Pleas had an express promise, not only from Mr. Fox, but from the Prince himself, that he should be the man.

But while the Chancellor-elect was considering whom he should appoint his Secretary and his purse-bearer, and while applications were pouring in upon him, from all quarters, for commissionerships of bankrupts and livings in the Church, his hopes were again blasted. Rumors of the King's recovery, at first discredited, became stronger and stronger; and on the 19th of February, Lord Chancellor Thurlow, in the House of Lords, as soon as prayers were over, left the woolsack, and announced that his Majesty was convalescent. He therefore suggested the propriety of suspending further proceedings on the Regency Bill; and—casting a malicious glance at the Chief Justice of the Common Pleas—he added, "I congratulate your Lordships on the prospect of his Majesty's complete and speedy recovery, to which I am sure the wishes and prayers of *all* his Majesty's subjects are directed." In a few days George III. resumed the personal exercise of the royal authority, with the deep-seated determination, which he was at no pains to conceal, of showing implacable resentment against all who, during his illness, had taken part with the Prince of Wales. Nor could they entertain any hope that he would be frustrated in his purpose; for the nation rejoiced on this occasion in being rescued from the Whigs; the King's popularity was unbounded, and his power, for a season, was greater than

that of any Plantagenet, Tudor, or Stuart, who ever filled the throne of England.'
Lord Loughborough, although banished from St. James's, continued in high favor with the Heir Apparent, and was for some time his chief counselor. A few days after the notification of the King's recovery, he was summoned to a conference, by the following note from his Royal Highness:—

"MY DEAR LORD,
"I have received a letter from the Queen, which requires some consideration. I wish much to have your advice. Pray call upon me at five o'clock, if you can.
"Ever sincerely yours,
"G. P.
"Carlton House, half-past one o'clock,
Feb 21st, 1789."[2]

Any attempt which he made to bring about a reconciliation between the members of the royal family entirely failed; and both the Prince of Wales, and the Duke of York, who had taken part with him, were treated by their parents with great harshness. In the Rosslyn MSS. I find, in Lord Loughborough's handwriting, the draught of a letter from the Prince to the King, which must have been written during the following summer:—

"Sir,
"Thinking it probable that I should have been honored with your commands to attend your Majesty on Wednesday last, I have unfortunately lost the opportunity of paying my duty to your Majesty before your departure from Weymouth.

"The accounts I have received of your Majesty's health have given me the greatest satisfaction; and should it be be your Majesty's intention to return to Weymouth, I trust, Sir, there will be no impropriety in my then entreating your Majesty's gracious attention to a point of the greatest moment to the peace of my own mind, and one in which I am convinced your Majesty's feelings are equally interested.

"Your Majesty's letter to my brother the Duke of

---

[1] I have heard a high legal dignitary, now no more, say, "It is a remarkable circumstance that George III., at the commencement of his reign, when in the full possession of his faculties, was abused, ridiculed, thwarted, and almost driven into exile, but when he was deprived of reason,—the nation, falling prostrate before him, called out, 'A God! a God!'"   [2] Rossl. MSS.

Clarence in May last, was the first direct intimation I have ever received that my conduct, and that of my brother the Duke of York, during your Majesty's late lamented illness, had brought on us the heavy misfortune of your Majesty's displeasure.

"I should have been wholly unworthy the return of your Majesty's confidence and good opinion, which will ever be the first objects of my life, if I could have read the passage I refer to in that letter without the deepest sorrow and regret for the effect produced upon your Majesty's mind, though at the same time I felt the firmest persuasion that your Majesty's generosity and goodness would never permit that effect to remain without affording us an opportunity of knowing what had been urged against us, of replying to our accusers, and of justifying ourselves, if the means of justification were in our power.

"Great, however, as my impatience and anxiety were on the subject, I felt it a superior consideration not to intrude any unpleasing or agitating discussions upon your Majesty's attention during an excursion devoted to the ease and amusement necessary for the re-establishment of your Majesty's health.

"I determined, therefore, to sacrifice my own feelings, and to wait with resignation till the fortunate opportunity should arrive, when your Majesty's own paternal goodness would, I was convinced, lead you even to invite your sons to that fair hearing, which your justice would not deny to the meanest individual of your subjects.

"In this painful interval I have employed myself in drawing up a full statement and account of my conduct during the period alluded to, and of the motives and circumstances which influenced me. When this shall be humbly submitted to your Majesty's consideration, I may possibly be found to have erred in judgment, and to have acted on mistaken principles, but I have the most assured conviction that I shall not be found to have been deficient in that duteous affection to your Majesty which nothing shall ever diminish. Anxious for everything that may contribute to the comfort and satisfaction of your Majesty's mind, I can not omit this opportunity of lamenting those appearances of a less gracious disposition in the Queen towards my brothers and myself than we were accustomed to experience, and to assure your Majesty that if, by your affectionate interposition, those most unpleasant sensations should be happily removed, it would be an event not less grateful to our minds than satisfactory to your Majesty's own benign disposition.

"I will not longer, &c. &c. &c.
"G. P."

I conclude this long, but I hope not, uninteresting chapter with a letter from the Prince of Wales to Lord Loughborough, showing his Royal Highness in a very amiable point of view—and leading to the charitable belief that, with much native goodness of heart, he was betrayed into his subsequent errors by the perils of his high station, and by adverse circumstances over which he had little control:—

"MY DEAR LORD,

"The excessive goodness and friendship I ever have experienced from you, makes me trespass, I assure you much against my wishes, once more upon you, hoping that you will forgive my absence this evening from a party, which I am certain, from everything I have hitherto witnessed, must afford the greatest pleasure and delight to all whose minds are perfectly at ease, and who have nothing to occupy them but the hospitable and pleasing reception you give all your friends. But, to tell you the truth, my dear Lord, I am very unfit for anything either so gay or so agreeable. The anxiety I have undergone the whole of this day has worried me to death, and though, thank God, the physicians assure me that my brother is as well as can be, considering the violence of his complaint, yet I should feel miserable to leave him. Could I have the pleasure of seeing you in Bedford Square this night, I should wear the same countenance of pleasure, which I am sensible that all those who have not a sick-bed to attend naturally must do at your house. I am sure, from what I know of you, that you will feel for me, and, *for once, forgive me for the disappointment I occasion myself.*

"I remain, my dear Lord,
"Ever most sincerely your friend,
"GEORGE P.

"York House, half past 12 o'clock, P M.,
July 2nd, 1789"[1]

[1] Rossl MSS.

CHAPTER CLXXI.

CONTINUATION OF THE LIFE OF LORD LOUGHBOROUGH TILL HE WAS MADE LORD CHANCELLOR.

ALTHOUGH the Whig party was now in a very low and seemingly hopeless condition, Lord Loughborough adhered to it for several years, and continued on the most friendly and familiar footing with Fox, Sheridan, and Burke. Nevertheless, he attended little in Parliament, and from the King's recovery till the middle of the session of 1791, only one speech by him is to be found in the printed Reports; that was on the malt tax, the increase of which he strenuously resisted; but so slender was the attendance of Opposition peers, that he could not venture to divide the House, lest, being appointed teller, he should be under the difficulty of grammatically reporting to the House that there was only one NOT CONTENT.[1]

While Lord Loughborough continued a leader of the Whigs, he took an active part in all the measures and maneuvers of that party—even to the arrangement of seats in the House of Commons. I will copy one curious letter to him on this subject from William Adam, afterwards Lord Chief Commissioner for jury trial in Scotland—as it gives a curious picture of the old "nomination system:"—

"MY DEAR LORD,

"The following lines are written in consequence of a conversation I had yesterday with the Prince of Wales, when I had the honor to be with his Royal Highness, and in which he expressed himself with the utmost anxiety, and at the same time under difficulty about the mode of obtaining what H. R. H. has so much at heart. At the same time that I am executing the commands of H. R. H., I need not inform your Lordship how much those

---

[1] 28 Parl. Hist. 1202. I have heard a teller in the House of Commons say "the noes were one." He defended himself by observing, that he could not have said the NOES *was* one." *Q.* What ought he to have said,—adhering to the established form?

commands coincide with the wishes of the Duke of Portland and all our friends.

"It is understood that Lord Lonsdale has two seats yet to fill up—one for Haslemere and one for Appleby, and that he has not fixed upon the persons who are to fill those places. H. R. H. is extremely anxious that Sir William Cunnyngham should be recommended to Lord Lonsdale. But under the circumstances in which H. R. H. says he stands with Lord Lonsdale, he thinks it can not flow directly from him. What he has desired me to do, therefore, is to request of your Lordship to open this matter to Lord Lonsdale, to assure him of Sir William Cunnyngham's attachment to H. R. H., and *of his being ready at any time to vacate his seat, if Lord Lonsdale should signify to him his disapprobation of his politics;* and that if the Prince is referred to by Lord Lonsdale, his Lordship will find his Royal Highness most anxiously zealous for Sir William's success.

"Ever, my dear Lord,
"Yours most faithfully,
"WILLIAM ADAM."[1]

After a long silence, Lord Loughborough took courage again to engage in parliamentary conflict, when Mr. Pitt had got into some difficulty and discredit by his negotiation with the Empress Catherine, and by the unpopular "Russian Armament." In the debate which followed the King's message upon this subject, he strongly inveighed against the foreign policy of the Government. "It is matter of serious consideration," said he, "by what fatality it happens that year after year we are thus to be involved in disputes in every quarter of the world. If we are to travel on in this course of blind and irrational confidence, yielding abject assent to every scheme of Ministers, what must be the result? His Majesty has sent a mandate to the Court of Petersburgh which the Empress has not thought fit to obey. Is the mandate to be enforced by arms? It is fortunate that we are still on the brink of the precipice: before we plunge into the abyss below, let us pause and look around us. It is with astonishment and horror that I see the King's Ministers taking a general sweep of all kingdoms and states—meddling, irritating and insulting. To please

[1] Rossl. MSS

them we are now to be involved in a war with Russia, without any provocation and without any object! A tax has lately been imposed which deprives the laboring man of his most wholesome beverage, to defray the expenses of this wanton aggression. Do your Lordships flatter yourselves that this can continue?—that by such resources you are to maintain a system of outrage, of conquest and of depredation? I do not wish to enter into any general eulogium of the National Assembly of France; but surely their unanimous and truly politic declaration that they will forever avoid wars on speculative and theoretical points, ought to have suggested to us a wiser course. The revolution in France presents to us the means of reducing our establishments, of easing the public burdens, and of securing to us for a length of years the blessing of peace."—Afterwards he stongly supported Lord Porchester's motion for a vote of censure on Mr Pitt, for the armament against Russia, saying, "I rejoice that the negotiation has terminated amicably; but it now becomes necessary to inquire whether arming the country was necessary, and what good end it has answered? I admit that this country has an interest in the affairs of the Continent, and in the conduct of Russia towards the Porte; but when you had armed, you receded. It is impolitic to drum to arms, and to be afraid to strike a blow. In my humble opinion an armament and the intention to use it ought never to be disjoined. It appears that Ministers had resolved to abandon their object before the armament was nearly completed, and yet they continued to arm as if the safety of the State had been in peril." Mr. Pitt's conduct was so strongly blamed out of doors, that the Opposition in the Lords, by Lord Loughborough's advice, now ventured to divide; but they could only muster 19 to 98.[1]

Lord Chancellor Thurlow, with the view of rescuing Warren Hastings from his troubles, having contended very obstinately that an impeachment by the House of

[1] 29 Parl. Hist 48, 96. Mr. Pitt's policy at this juncture the nation now regard with much more favor, after seeing the dangerous ascendency which Russia was permitted to acquire, and the war into which we were forced in the middle of the following century to save the Turkish empire from dismemberment, and to preserve the independence of Europe Mr. Fox and the Whigs seem to have been under a strange infatuation in favoring the conquests of Catherine.—*Note to 4th Editt. n, 1856.*

Commons abates on a dissolution of parliament, our Chief Justice not only gained a great victory in argument, but, being supported by the opinions of Lord Camden and Lord Mansfield, actually carried the question by a majority of 66 to 18;[1] so that the impeachment dragged its slow length along, till he himself was actually on the woolsack

The Attorney General of Lord North was now, under the auspices of Mr Fox, the warm supporter of all liberal measures, and was running a similar cycle to that which had astonished mankind, when, after leaving Lord Bute and Toryism, he had gained the loud applause of Lord Chatham by standing up so boldly for " Wilkes and Liberty."

He spoke strongly in favor of the Roman Catholic Relief Bill,[2] although it is now certain that, when he became the keeper of the King's conscience, he poisoned the royal mind by scruples about the coronation oath, and that he obstructed the policy which he at this time supported.

To another measure, which fortunately was then actually passed, he gave very effective aid—without which it must have been defeated—Mr. Fox's famous bill for declaring the right of juries to decide the question of "libel or no libel?" Although Mr. Pitt, still a liberal and constitutional Minister, was favorable to it, his wayward Chancellor most furiously opposed it,—and, sad to relate! he was backed by the whole body of the Judges. In all the stages of the bill during two sessions, Lord Loughborough gallantly defended it by the side of the venerable Camden, to whose consistent and pure love of liberty— ever to be held in reverence—this constitutional triumph is mainly to be ascribed. These were the most striking observations of the occasional patriot :

"The monstrous doctrine of the noble and learned Lord on the Woolsack, though meant to restrain the Press, is highly favorable to libelers. In the struggle between the judge and the jury, the guilt or innocence of the defendant is little thought of, and the jury heedlessly acquit him to show their power. But they must be allowed to consider the intention of the publication,—otherwise the free and fair discussion of political subjects, and even texts of

---

[1] 29 Parl. Hist. 523, 532, 543.   [2] Ibid. 682.

Scripture, may be construed into a libel. For my own part, I have deemed it my duty to state the law as it bore on the facts, and to refer the combined consideration to the jury. Are the judges to say to the jury, '*Find the defendant guilty now, as he is proved to have published the writing complained of, and when he comes before us for sentence, we will tell you whether or not it is a libel.*' It is the admitted maxim of law—'ad quæstionem juris respondeant judices,—ad quæstionem facti juratores;' but when the law and the fact are blended, it is necessarily and undoubtedly the right of the jury to decide. You say that jurymen are incapable of comprehending the character of a publication charged to be criminal, and that this must be referred to enlightened judges. At the Old Bailey, an alderman of London is a co-ordinate judge with the Chief Justice of England. Nay, indictments for libel may be tried at Quarter-Sessions, and fox-hunting squires, being the judges, are exclusively to decide upon the literary production set forth as a libel. One absurdity follows another; it is well known that special jurors whom you disqualify are generally magistrates,—and you would deprive them of all power when impanneled in the jury box,—while sitting on the bench you would make them decide the guilt and award the punishment."[1]

But immediately after the passing of the Libel Bill, events happened which materially influenced the opinions and actions of Loughborough. Thurlow was dismissed from the office of Chancellor, and the Great Seal was put into the hands of Eyre, Ashurst, and Wilson, as commissioners—obscure men, none of whom could aspire to the Woolsack. Sir Archibald Macdonald, the Attorney General, having been promoted by mere family interest, looked no higher than the office of Chief Baron, then considered little better than a sinecure. Sir John Scott was Solicitor General, but he could not be put over the head of his superior officer. The Chief Justice of the Common Pleas saw that if by any means he could be reconciled to the existing Administration, the golden prize might after all be his own.

The times were propitious for such an overture. Mr. Pitt's reputation as a statesman had been a little tarnished

[1] 29 Parl. Hist. 1294, 1299, 1428, 1535.

by the "Russian Armament;"—and the Whig Aristocracy, always powerful in talent and in family connection, had been recovering their popularity,—so that if they remained united, they might be expected soon to be formidable rivals for office. Unhappily, they were divided upon the view to be taken of the French Revolution. The majority of the party, headed by Fox, regarded it as a great regeneration in France, and likely to produce a salutary influence in other countries, by illustrating the beneficial consequences of a constitutional Monarchy, based upon the principles of popular representation and equal rights;—while a considerable section of them concurred with Mr. Burke in thinking it a conspiracy of spoliators and atheists, which, unless it were crushed, would first desolate the land where it broke out, and then throw into confusion the whole civilized world. Lord Loughborough, as we have seen,[1] had hitherto expressed nothing but approbation and hope when he discussed the proceedings of the National Assembly,—but he was now filled with apprehension and alarm; he declared, in all companies, that in such a crisis—without regard to party considerations—the hands of Government should be strengthened, for the purpose of guarding the nation against the imminent peril with which it was threatened; and he openly applauded, in his place in Parliament, the proclamation issued in the King's name against seditious publications.

A negotiation was accordingly opened—one of the most important in our party annals, for, upon the result of it depended, not merely the disposal of the Great Seal, but whether Fox or Pitt was to be Minister, and whether there was to be peace or war between this country and the new Republic of France. We have a very graphic account of it in the Diary of the Earl of Malmesbury, showing that it was chiefly conducted between Loughborough and Henry Dundas; that the Great Seal was the bait by which the wily Chief Justice, leading on the alarmist Whigs, was to be lured; that he himself was eager to join the Government as soon as possible, but that the other side were not willing to receive him till he could bring a large number of converts in his train; and that serious difficulties arose from a lingering

[1] Ante, p. 406.

regard for Mr. Fox, entertained by those who were inclined to follow him, and particularly by the Duke of Portland: [1]

"*June* 14.—Dundas first wrote, and then spoke, to Lord Loughborough, expressing his wish that this temporary union would become a permanent one. He held out four vacant places—the Chancellor (his own), the Secretary of State for Home Affairs, the President of the Council and Privy Seal—besides two or three Privy Councillors' places in the House of Commons, and the Lord Lieutenancy of Ireland. Lord Lough[h] took all this *ad referendum*, and was now come to talk it over with the Duke of Portland." "*June* 15.—The Duke of Portland related to me that Lord Lough[h] had the night before met Pitt at Dundas's; that he spoke with great openness and appearance of sincerity; that on Lord Lough.'s asking him whether the King knew it, Pitt said he did not come with the King's command to propose a coalition, but that he would be responsible it would please the King and Queen, and that the only difficulty likely to arise was about Fox, and that difficulty entirely owing to Fox's conduct in Parliament during the last four months. That *everything else* was entirely forgotten, and that he himself did not recollect, that in all their parliamentary altercations a single word had ever dropped from either of them to prevent their acting together without any fair reproach being made of a disavowal of principles, or an inconsistency of character," &c. "*June* 16.—Dinner at Lord Lough.'s with Fox. While Lord Lough. was engaged with his company, I talked with Fox, and afterwards carried him to Burlington House. He had not heard of the last meeting with Pitt, and did not make himself (as he generally does) practicable. He doubted Pitt's sincerity, and suspected he had no other view than to weaken their party, and strengthen his own; that to divide the Opposition was his great object; he doubted also the King's having con-

---

[1] While these negotiations were going on, Harry Dundas said to an old friend, "Wedderburn would now give all he has in the world not to have framed the York Resolutions [while he was a patriot] he knows that the King will never forgive him for that." Lord Loughborough's present Anti-Jacobin zeal made him well received at court, but George III could not forget his conduct on the Regency which made him more obnoxious even than the York Resolutions, or his inflammatory speech at the Thatched House, when he was toasted as "Steward of the Chiltern Hundreds."

sented accordingly to dismiss the Chancellor, and seemed to think it *possible* that a new administration might be formed through him, from which Pitt was to be excluded." "*June* 17.—Lord Lough. called on me; he related very accurately all that passed between him, Pitt, and Dundas on the Thursday evening. Pitt, he said, wore every appearance of sincerity and frankness." "*June* 19.—Lord Lough. with me. He said he really thought it unreasonable to expect that Pitt should quit the Treasury;—that he could not, and *would not*, make such a proposal." "*June* 22.—Burke wished to see me, aud I went to breakfast with him. He said there was no doing without Fox or with him; that he wished it to be declared by the heads of the great Whig party, that all systematic opposition was at an end; that for the better security, and in order to give a strong and convincing mark of it, Ld. Lough. should, by being made Chancellor, represent the party in the Cabinet, and be the link between them (the Whig party, he meant, and the Government), in order that, if on some future day the difficulties now arising from Fox's character and conduct should decrease, or the distresses of the country increase, a junction might be accomplished in a more easy and natural manner than even by the beginning the whole afresh." "*July* 5.—Lord Lough related to me a long conversation he had a few days before with Fox, in which he said Fox appeared more harsh, impracticable, and opinionative than he could have supposed him to be; that he saw no chance of anything being done while Fox remained in his present temper of mind. He appeared hurt by Fox's behavior and manners towards him." "*July* 27.—The Duke of Portland told me this day that the Garter had been offered to him, through Lord Lough., which he had refused." "*Dec.* 18.—Lord Lough. called on me; he was greatly hurt at the Duke of Portland's inaction and Fox's violence. He urged the necessity of his talking to the Duke of Portland, and going to him in a body, to compel him to declare himself either decidedly for, or decidedly against, Fox." "*Dec.* 20.—At Lord Lough.'s particular request, Sir Gilbert Elliot went to the Duke of Portland, to know what was his opinion as to Lord Lough.'s taking the Seals. The Duke was decidedly against it, and said he would never consent to it."

Loughborough was now in a rage at finding himself thus baffled, and determined to act a very decisive part for his own advantage. Parliament had been suddenly called together by proclamation, and the first anti-Gallican measure was the Alien Bill,—to prevent the importation of republican principles. By this, contrary to the common law, the vexatious and useless system of passports was established for all aliens; the Secretary of State was authorized to expel all aliens from the kingdom; and regulations for the discovery of all aliens were imposed on the keepers of inns and lodging-houses, to be enforced by the punishment of transportation. The second reading of the bill being violently opposed by the Earl of Lauderdale and the Marquis of Lansdowne, it was gallantly defended by the aspirant Chancellor:—

"My Lords," said he, "my regard for the laws of the country and the obligations of religion, and the allegiance I owe to the Crown for the protection I receive from it, demand my support to the Government upon this occasion. The bill is indeed an extraordinary measure; but is not the situation in which we stand extraordinary? The period most resembling the present is the reign of Elizabeth, when the overgrown power of Philip agitated and alarmed every surrounding nation. Actuated not only by ambition, but by religious fanaticism, his greatest efforts were excited against this island. Money, forces, seditious writings, emissaries, were employed to excite plots in England, insurrections in Ireland, and an invasion from Scotland, against the Queen; but they were employed in vain,—owing to the wise regulations adopted by that Princess and her Parliament. At present a great and powerful people, actuated by a new fanaticism of infidelity, are endeavoring to propagate over Europe principles as inconsistent with all established government as they are with the happiness of mankind. However extravagant the new doctrines may be, they have undoubtedly made some proselytes in this country, and though in numbers they are as yet comparatively insignificant, they are stirring and active in their mischievous purposes, in hopes of domestic insurrection and confident of foreign aid. During the temporary success of the combined Sovereigns their voice became more faint, but the

moment that the tide of war turned in favor of France
they resumed their courage ; sedition broke out with increased violence, and clubs and societies for propagating
their baleful opinions were formed all over the kingdom.
Embassies were sent to France to congratulate the National Assembly on their victories, and even to promise
the assistance of numbers here who would rise up in their
cause, and who, in return, expected fraternal help to overturn the Constitution of England. In France anarchy
and confusion triumph. They had long vilified the
Christian religion ; but now, incredible as it may seem,
public professions of Atheism have been made in full convention, and received, with unbounded applause. It has
been solemnly proclaimed that there is no God, and the
basis of their new institutions is Atheism. The sanctity
of the seventh day was very soon abolished by them, and
they have at last destroyed the relation of parent and
child. Their false prophet has taught that no honor is
due to the parent, who in his turn may abandon the
child. Robbery, murder, and licentiousness not only go
unpunished, but are encouraged as meritorious acts.
False testimony is a proof of patriotism ; and so entirely
are all ideas of property subverted, that it has lately been
announced from authority that the farmer has only possession of the corn he has reaped as a trustee, but that
the beneficial property is in the public, who have a right at
their discretion to take it from him without recompense.
It has been said that the fears of Ministers are affected,
and that there is no foundation for the alarms which they
have circulated. Ministers are tauntingly called upon for
their proofs. Parliamentary scepticism may be allowed;
but if any man out of House were to hold such language,
he would be laughed at. A proper sense of danger per-
vades all ranks of men, and all but the disaffected are
ready to come forward in the common cause. Although
the disaffected be few, they must not be despised. Your
Lordships should recollect that the massacres of Paris in
September were perpetrated by not more than 200 persons, in the midst of a city containing 600,000 inhabitants, with 30,000 men under arms. Let us not think
lightly of what may be achieved by a small band, armed
with daggers, under the cry of '*No King!*' We might
already have been in a worse situation than when the

metropolis was blazing and the mob were triumphant in 1780, had not Ministers wisely preserved the public tranquillity by calling out the militia, and making the military preparations that now resound in all quarters. The noble Earl has complained of royal associations,—which are not legal, but meritorious, as tending to strengthen the hands of Government, and preserve civil and religious liberty. By the Constitution of this country, all are bound actively to assist in putting the law in force. I will tell the noble Earl what associations are illegal and punishable; associations to publish resolutions condemning the conduct of judges and juries, and vilifying the free institutions under which we and our fathers have lived and been happy. We ought to give Ministers all the powers they ask, and the confidence which accompanied the decree of the free city of Rome in times of public danger: *Quod caveant Consules ne quid detrimenti capiat respublica!* I have no difficulty in saying that the present situation of this country would have justified a stronger measure than this bill for the regulation of aliens. I hope the people will now rush forward to assist the Executive Government in its paternal purposes,—burying all past differences and disputes in oblivion."

This speech was received with loud cheers by the Ministerialists, and Loughborough flattered himself he had made such an impression upon his own friends, that the Duke of Portland, as the leader of the alarmist party, would immediately have arisen and declared that they approved of all he had said,—in which case the transfer of the Great Seal would have taken place next morning. But the Duke, though repeatedly urged, remained profoundly silent; a suspicion existed that he and those more immediately under his influence still adhered to Fox, and the Chancellorship was too high a price for one solitary desertion. The continuation of Lord Malmesbury's Diary brings the intrigue to its consummation much more strikingly than any labored narrative:—

"*Dec. 22,*—3 o'clock. Lords Loughborough and Porchester, Burke, Sir G. Elliot, Anstruther, Dr. Lawrence, and Elliot of Wells, met at my house. Lord Loughborough said he had been with the Duke of Portland—that he had had a very long and explicit interview with him—that the Duke had entered fairly into the subject—

that he had declared himself as averse as he himself was to Fox's principles and motions—but that he was of opinion it was not yet time to break with him,—and that it would be better to try for every possible means of reconciliation. He was convinced that Fox had lost himself by what Baldwin had told him, and that he himself was a partaker of his unpopularity,—yet that still he wished to keep on terms with him. Lord Loughborough then stated to us how such a conduct, inasmuch as we were considered as belonging to the Portland party, involved us in all the unpopularity and disgrace attending Fox's principles;—that therefore it was become necessary to decide what was to be done, and how the Duke of Portland could be obliged to declare his sentiments to be contrary to those of Fox. Burke, with his usual eloquence, talked for an hour. We sat till it was time to go to the House, without coming to any other conclusion than that we would meet again in greater numbers, and the next day was fixed for that purpose.—At the House of Lords I saw Lord Carlisle; he was for Lord Loughborough's accepting the Seals as a pledge for the good intentions of the party."—"*Dec.* 26. The Alien Bill passed, opposed by Lord Guilford, and Lords Lansdowne and Lauderdale. These two made violent and mischievous speeches. Lord Loughborough answered them in one of the finest speeches possible. But the Duke of Portland, to the great concern and grief of his friends, did not say a word. I urged him repeatedly to get up, but he said he really could not, he felt it impossible; that Lord Loughborough had said all that could be said, and that it was impossible to speak after so fine a speech. I pressed him to say those very words, and nothing more, but without effect."—"*Dec.* 27. I received a letter very early from Lord Loughborough, lamenting and complaining of the Duke of Portland's silence,—lamenting it from public reasons,—complaining of it from the injury it did his numerous body of friends who wish to hold high the honor of his name:—

"'MY DEAR LORD,—Though I am sensible that I spoke with some effect to-night, I am not young enough to feel on that account any satisfaction that can make up for the Duke of Portland's silence. The few words in which he expressed to me his approbation, pronounced upon his legs, would have had more effect on the House and on the public than ten speeches. The House had waited for his declaration ; the course of the debate called for it—particularly in the latter part, between Lord Lansdowne and me, and still he left it in doubt which of us spoke his sentiments,—knowing, too, that Lord Lansdowne's party make no scruple to use his name against his intentions, and will not fail to quote his silence against my speech ; and this at a moment when the connection with Lord Lansdowne was so plainly marked. The Duke of Portland hesitates whether he shall withdraw his countenance from a party formed of Lord Lansdowne, Fox, and Grey, under the auspices of *Chauvelin.* What a position that is for his character, and those numerous friends who, not only from personal attachment, but as a great public point for the country, wish to hold high the honor of his name! I do not think I shall compose myself to-morrow into a fit temper to go to Burlington House, and present my remonstrance to him ; but I dare to say Lord Lauderdale will not fail to be there. I wish Sir Gilbert Elliot and you would consider what is to be done, for I can not devise any measure to retrieve the mischief of this day to the Duke of Portland. The House of Commons will not make up for it. The only thing that could be effectual would be a positive declaration to the party that has left him—that he holds them as entirely detached, and not less in opposition to him than to Government. But that I despair of. I could not help writing this to you, tired as I am, but yet more vexed than tired.'

" *Dec.* 27. At 3 o'clock I went to Lord Loughborough's, in Bedford Square. He had, lying on his table, when I came in (he returned at the same moment, from a ride), a letter from the Duke of Portland. He read it, and on giving it to me to read, said, ' *This is worse and worse.'* The letter was to explain the motives of his silence [out of regard to Fox]. Lord Loughborough was violent ; he said he was betrayed ; and it was with some difficulty I prevented him from going immediately to Burlington House."—" *January* 1, 1793. Lord Loughborough with me early ; he, eager for a further *éclaircissement* with the Duke, and for laying the whole before the public ; I still for waiting, if possible, to the end of the recess. Lord

Loughborough from me went to see the Prince of Wales in the evening."—" *January* 4. Lord Loughborough, at Lady Payne's, showed me a letter from Dundas, pressing him to decide as to taking the Great Seal, saying that he and Pitt had abstained renewing the subject for some time past, under the plea that there were still hopes of having the Duke of Portland; that this was now considered to be at an end. Lord Loughborough answered that he still had some hopes that a letter he intended to write would produce some effect; and it was of such importance to be joined by so respectable a character as the Duke of Portland, he still wished to wait."—" *January* 14. I wrote a letter to the Duke of Portland, explicit of my opinions and intentions. Dined at Batt's; Lord Loughborough there. No answer from the Duke. He had seen Dundas, and stated to him fairly that the consequences of his taking the Great Seal would be, that forty or fifty members *only* would join the Government. That as many more, now with the Government, would probably return to Opposition; that it was for Ministers to consider whether it was for their interest to take him on those conditions."—" *January* 18. I saw Lord Bute in the morning; he a little warped Strongly against Lord Loughborough taking the Seals; said it would make all who followed him, unpopular to a certain degree. I dined with Lord Loughborough, with only Anstruther. He declared his determination of taking the Seals; only doubted as to the time. I advised him to see the Duke of Portland first; and, above all, to fix Windham to engage him to approve it, on his legs, in the House of Commons."—" *January* 20. Called on Lord Loughborough. He returned with me, and went from my house to meet Pitt, by appointment. He stayed with him about an hour and a half, and then came back to me. He told me war was a *decided measure;* that Pitt saw it was inevitable, and that the sooner it was begun, the better—that we might possess ourselves of the French Islands;[1] that the nation now was disposed for war, which might not be the case six weeks hence."—" *January* 21. News of the sentence of death being pronounced on the King of France. Called at Burlington House twice.

[1] This discloses the erroneous principle on which the war was afterwards conducted.

Duke of Portland not at home."—"*January* 22. Wrote a letter to Pitt, at Lord Loughborough's. Dined with Pitt and Dundas, at Wimbledon. I was two hours with the Duke of Portland. He lamented Fox's conduct, and particularly blamed it, if it were true (which he did not think) that he had given Sheridan authority to speak for him, at the meeting held at the 'Crown and Anchor,' on the liberty of the press."—"*January* 23. Lord Loughborough called upon me, on his return from Westminster Hall. He said Pitt had again repeated to him what he had said before about me. I repeated to him what had passed at Burlington House. We concluded it was a favorable moment for him to see the Duke; he therefore read me a letter, stating his intention of taking the Seals; and his reasons, which he rested on the duty of every man now doing his utmost to serve his country, and the cause in which it was going to engage. This letter he asked me to carry; but, on reflection, it was determined that it had better go through Baldwin, of whose understanding the Duke of Portland had a high opinion, and who he thought was attached to him. Baldwin, therefore, was to go to Burlington House in the evening"

In a few days Lord Loughborough was enabled to announce to Mr. Pitt the full adhesion of the Duke of Portland, and thereupon the bargain was closed.

In the Rosslyn MSS. I have found a vast number of letters, written during this negotiation to Lord Loughborough, by Mr. Burke, the Earl of Carlisle, Mr. Ralph Payne (afterwards Lord Lavington) and Mr Pitt, which present a very lively picture of the state of parties during this crisis, and which will be of much use to the historian of the reign of George III.[1]

Lord Loughborough had met with such disappointments when he had thought the Great Seal within his grasp, that he is said to have been very nervous on the day fixed for his receiving it,—feeling a sort of superstitious dread that a spell had been cast upon him, and that by some mysterious decree it had been ordained, that, however often or closely he might approach the object of his pursuit, he should never reach it.

However, no political embarrassment—no visitation

[1] Some of the most interesting of them will be found in the Appendix to Ch. CLXXV.—*3rd Edition.*

from Heaven—now frustrated his hopes,—and on the 28th day of January, 1793, at Buckingham Palace, the Great Seal was actually delivered into his hand by George III.' Carrying it home in his coach, he exultingly showed it to Lady Loughborough, though he afterwards declared he was still a little afraid that he might awake and find that he had once more been deluded by a pleasant dream. He never acknowledged to others the further truth that a few days' possession showed to him the utter worthlessness of the object for which he had made such exertions and such sacrifices.

CHAPTER CLXXII.

CONTINUATION OF THE LIFE OF LORD LOUGHBOROUGH TILL THE CONCLUSION OF HASTINGS'S TRIAL.

THE new Chancellor was most cruelly assailed by the Opposition press as a renegade. The quotation was often repeated—

" Thou hast it now:
 ....and I fear
Thou play'd'st most foully for 't."

His own saying was revived with respect to curing " the bite of the tarantula of Opposition by the music of the Court."² In the midst of much coarse vituperation, which he must have despised, he was probably more stung by the following playful *jeu d'esprit* of Matthias, which was repeated and laughed at in Burlington House, as well as in all other fashionable societies:—

¹ "Jan. 29, 1793.—The Lords Commissioners for the custody of the Great Seal of Great Britain, having delivered the said Great Seal to the King at the Queen's House, on Monday, the 28th day of January, 1793, his Majesty the same day delivered it to Alexander, Lord Loughborough, Chief Justice of the Court of Common Pleas, with the title of Lord High Chancellor of Great Britain, who was then sworn into the said office before his Majesty in Council; and the next morning came into the Court of Chancery in Westminster Hall, attended by several Peers, &c., and in open Court took the oaths of allegiance and supremacy, and the oath of Chancellor of Great Britain, the same being administered by the Deputy Clerk of the Crown, the Master of the Rolls (covered) holding the book, which being done, Mr Attorney General moved that it might be recorded by the Clerk of the Crown in Chancery, which the Court ordered accordingly."—*Minute Book*, No. 2, fol. 42.   ² Ante, p. 279.

"The Serenata of ACIS AND GALATEA has been performed in Downing street, to a private company. The part of *Acis* by Mr. Pitt, *Polypheme* by Lord Thurlow and *Galatea* by Lord Loughborough. The barytone of Lord Thurlow was quite *Polyphemeish*, and fully sustained; but it was impossible to do justice sufficiently to Lord Loughborough's *diminuendo*, when he *died away in the arms of Acis.*"

The object of these pleasantries, however, by no means incurred now the same obloquy as when in 1771 he left his party, without a companion, to be made Solicitor General. If *he* counterfeited what he did not feel,—the dread of revolution professed by the "alarmist Whigs" was sincere; and although they at first discouraged the the notion of his taking office, the Duke of Portland, Lord Spencer and Mr. Windham soon followed his example. We may fairly gather the sentiments of that party from a letter of Sir Gilbert Elliot to Lord Malmesbury, written from Minto, the very day before the transfer of the Great Seal actually took place. After expressing his own determination not to accept office, he says,—

"With regard to Lord Loughborough, I think the question stands on different grounds. His acceptance of the Seals I believe sincerely to be eminently necessary for the public service. His conduct has been highly honorable, and everything like personal claim or even party claim on him by the Duke of Portland is certainly at least canceled, if not converted into a direct *provocation*, by what has passed since the commencement of this session. But the public good, in my opinion, *requires* his services; and for that reason they are *due* from him. I shall certainly not only approve but applaud his acceptance of the Seals. It is for every man to consider whether the public has the same claim on him. I can not feel that my services *in office* are of the smallest moment to the country; but the circumstances of the country may become such as to require all our aid, in every way in which it is called for."

Some who had narrowly watched the career of the "wary Wedderburn" declared that he would have supported a revolutionary movement, and held the Great Seal under the directors of the "Anglican Republic," if this had appeared the better course for gratifying his ambition ; but in the Anti-Jacobin frenzy now prevailing he was very generally applauded for magnanimously leaving his party when it had become infected with the bad principles which he had so boldly denounced, and for the dexterity with which he had carried so many partisans along with him to rally round our time-honored institutions. Thus was he congratulated by Burke:—

"MY DEAR LORD,

"Since I saw you last, the catastrophe of the tragedy of France has been completed.[1] It was the necessary result of all the preceding parts of that monstrous drama.

"Though I looked for something of that kind as inevitable from the day when the Rights of Man were declared, yet when the fatal and final event itself arrived, I was as much leveled and thrown to the ground, in the general consternation, as if it were a thing I had never dreamed of.

"I felt and I feel deeply ; but I have recovered myself. I have now only to think of the part which you, and those who have got enough of spirit, energy, and abilities to come forward in the service of your country, are obliged to take in this awful crisis of the world.

"I hear that your Lordship is to take the Great Seal next Tuesday. I think we are all much obliged to his Majesty for this arrangement. The King has acted wisely in his choice. You have done your duty in your acceptance. I should have thought you criminal, in your circumstances, if you had declined to do a service to the public, which you alone can do.

"The time requires exertions of uncommon vigor and compass. It is therefore proper to add all possible strength to an Administration which has for its object effectually to defend the Constitution of this kingdom, and the liberties of Europe, against French principles and French power. This never can be done by those who have declared their concurrence with the one, and their good wishes in favor of the other. There is a confraternity between the two divisions of the French factions on the other side of the water and on this. They are both guilty, and equally guilty, of the late acts which have wounded to the quick all the moral feelings of mankind. If you had no other reason for going into the great trust

[1] The murder of Louis XVI.

you have accepted than as a mode of expressing your perfect detestation of the English branch of that internal faction, and your total alienation from any connection whatsoever with any of its leaders, I should think that motive alone would be sufficient to recommend the step you have taken to every honest mind. I shall not think that the honor of your high situation is complete until I find you abundantly censured and libeled by them.

"My dear Lord, I regret that you do not carry in along with you those whom I shall ever love, value, and lament. But their error is not your fault. I prognosticate good things to the morals, virtue, and religion of the world from this appointment. Let me not find myself mistaken. You have undertaken a task of great public responsibility. I know the purity of your motives,—but the public will judge of them by your future conduct, and the effect of your services. I am sure you have my most sincere good wishes. "I am, with a very affectionate attachment,
"My dear Lord,
"Your Lordship's faithful and affectionate humble servant.
"EDM. BURKE.
"Duke Street, Jan 27, 1793"[1]

As soon as the intelligence reached Switzerland, it called forth the following effusion from the Historian of the Decline and Fall of the Roman Empire,—now become, from dread of *Sans Culottes*, a convert to Church establishments, and a defender of the Inquisition:—

"MY LORD,

"I do not merely congratulate your Lordship's promotion to the first civil office in the kingdom—an office which your abilities have long deserved. My satisfaction does not arise from an assurance of the wisdom and vigor which administration will derive from the support of so respectable an ally. But as a friend to government in general, I most sincerely rejoice that you are now armed in the common cause against the most dangerous fanatics that have ever invaded the peace of Europe—against the new Barbarians who labor to confound the order and happiness of society, and who, in the opinion of thinking men, are not less the enemies of subjects than of kings. The hopes of the wise and good are now fixed on the success of England, and I am persuaded that my personal

[1] Rossl. MSS.

attachment to your Lordship will be amply gratified by the important share which your counsels will assume in that success.

"I could wish that some of your former associates possessed sufficient strength of mind to extricate themselves from the toils of prejudice and party: but I grieve that a man whom it is impossible for me not to love and admire should refuse to obey the voice of his country, and I begin to fear that the powerful genius of Mr. Fox instead of being useful, will be adverse, to the public service. At this momentous crisis we should enlist our whole force of virtue, ability, and spirit,—and, without any view to his private advantage, I could wish that our active friend Lord Sheffield might be properly stationed in some part of the line.

"Mr. Necker, at whose house I am now residing, on a visit of some days, wishes me to express the sentiments of esteem and consideration which he entertains for your Lordship's character. As a friend of the interest of mankind he is warmly attached to the welfare of Great Britain, which he has long revered as the first, and perhaps as the last, asylum of genuine liberty. His late eloquent work, '*Du Pouvoir Exécutif*,' which your Lordship has assuredly read, is a valuable testimony of his esteem for our Constitution; and the testimony of a sagacious and impartial stranger may have taught some of our countrymen to value the political blessings which they had been tempted to despise.

"I cherish a lively hope of being in England, and of paying my respects to your Lordship, before the end of the summer. But the events of this year are so uncertain, and the sea and land are encompassed with so many difficulties and dangers, that I am doubtful whether it will be practicable for me to execute my purpose.

"I am, my Lord, most respectfully, and (your Lordship will permit me to add) most affectionately,

"Your most obedient and faithful humble servant,

"E. GIBSON.

"Rolle, Feb. 23rd, 1793"[1]

---

[1] Rossl. MSS. In the year 1796, when Lord Sheffield was publishing Gibbon's Miscellaneous Works, he asked Lord Loughborough's permission to include this letter in the collection, but was refused. He then made a second

"On Monday, the 4th of February, the Chancellor came into the Court of Common Pleas to take the oaths on his new appointment, and sat for a short time as Chief Justice. Before he retired, his Lordship took leave of the Bench and the bar in a very elegant address, expressiv: of his gratitude for the uniform attention and respect which he had received during the time he had presided there."[1]

We are now to view him as the chief Equity Judge, and presiding over the general administration of justice in this country. As far as *representation* went, no one ever acted the part with more applause. In the first place, his style of living was most splendid. Ever indifferent about money, instead of showing mean contrivances to save a shilling he spent the whole of his official income in official splendor. Thoughh imself very temperate, his banquets were princely; he entertained an immense retinue of servants, and, not dreaming that his successor would walk through the mud to Westminster, sending the Great Seal thither in a hackney coach, he never stirred abroad without his two splendid carriages, exactly alike, drawn by the most beautiful horses,—one for himself, and another for his attendants. Though of low stature, and slender frame, his features were well chiseled, his countenance was marked by strong lines of intelligence, his eyes were piercing, his appearance was dignified, and his manners were noble. To the Bar he was impartially courteous, never favoring, or being afraid of, any man who practiced before him. While sitting on the bench, he devoted his whole attention to the arguments addressed to him, unless when it was necessary to give a hint of "wandering" or "repetition;"— and from his quick perception of facts, and capacity of being made to understand nice legal questions with which he was little familiar, he was praised by Chancery

application, in a letter which lies before me, and thus begins: "My dear Lord,—Pelham and Sergeant were with me when I received your Lordship's answer on the subject of publishing Gibbon's letter of congratulation They wondered, as well as myself, that you should object. There is nothing fulsome, nor more said than is perfectly natural and proper; but as the letter is happily expressed in regard to the times of Mr Necker, it is a pity it should be lost, and by erasing your name, and the name of your office, your objections perhaps may be removed." Lord Loughborough was very sensitive upon the subject of his coalition with Mr. Pitt, and he remained inflexible.

[1] 2 Hen. Black 132.

practitioners rather beyond his merits, as an Equity Judge. They had no jealousy of him as a common lawyer, for he had been bred in their school, and he certainly knew as much of equity as of law. Unfortunately, he would not now submit to the labor and drudgery necessary for acquiring permanent reputation as a magistrate. When out of court, instead of dedicating his time to the consideration of the cases pending before him, or in reviving and extending his juridical knowledge, he was absorbed in politics, or he mixed in fashionable society, or he frequented the theater. The *beau idéal* of a perfect Chancellor does not present to us a mere slave to judicial duties, neglecting all that is elegant and liberal; but such a man, regularly trained in his profession, and possessing a good understanding and upright intentions, would distribute justice more satisfactorily to the suitors, than another who, without these qualifications, may aim at uniting in his own person the reputation of a Bacon, a Somers, and a Shaftesbury. However, Lord Loughborough's dazzling accomplishments, joined with his characteristic discretion, covered his defects; and, although he lived in very factious times, I do not find incompetence for his office, or remissness in the discharge of it, ever gravely imputed to him. According to Butler, who had often heard him, and was well qualified to compare him with his predecessors, "His judicial oratory was exquisite. The greatest detractors from his merit acknowledged the perspicuity, the luminous order, and chaste elegance of his arguments. Like Lord Camden, he frequently and successfully introduced law phrases into them." Yet the panegyrist is obliged to acknowledge that he betrayed 'a want of real taste for legal learning." The lenient view taken of him while in office, by contemporary lawyers, was partly to be accounted for by their pride in having at their head a gentleman and a scholar—a man "wholly above any sordid feelings of avarice or parsimony, and only valuing his high station for the power which it conferred, and the dignity with which it was compassed round about."[1] But when we come calmly to review his judgments, we can not much commend them, and we are astonished to find with what a small modicum of juridical acquirement a

[1] Lord Brougham's Sketches, i. 85.

man may reputably fill the most exalted judicial office. They are recorded in the 2nd, 3rd, 4th, and 5th volumes of Vesey, Jr.[1] Going through them, with a view to select some of importance and interest, I am a good deal disappointed,—although my expectations were not very high. Considering that Lord Loughborough presided in the Court of Chancery above eight years, it is wonderful how little he added to our equitable code. By far the best judgments given in the Court of Chancery during this period were by Pepper Arden, Master of the Rolls, afterwards Lord Alvanley.

Yet a few cases decided by our Chancellor may be stated, with the hope of instructng or amusing the reader. In *Graham* v. *Johnstone*, in which he held that the personal property of an intestate, wheresoever situate, must be distributed according to the law of the country in which he was domiciled, his acquaintance with the civil law enabled him to deliver an able dissertation on the law of domicile. The suit arose out of a disputed claim to certain personal property in Scotland which had belonged to the last Marquis of Annandale, who had long been a lunatic :—

Lord Loughborough.—" First, I must look to see what was his domicile when he became lunatic, for it could not be changed afterwards by any change of residence. Though of Scottish origin, according to the will of his maternal grandfather, his expectations of fortune, settlement, and establishment were in England, and here he chiefly passed his days. He visited Scotland, but without any purpose of remaining there. Having once gained a domicile in England, there it must remain till it changed by the execution of a purpose permanently to abide elsewhere. The actual place where a man is, *primâ facie*, is his domicile; but his home may be shown to be elsewhere. You encounter the presumption by showing that the resi-

---

[1] He was unlucky in his reporter. I knew this gentleman well When near eighty, he was still called "VESEY, *Jr.*," to distinguish him from his father, " Vesey, Sr," the historiographer of Lord Hardwicke. He was a very good-natured fellow, and very honest and painstaking, but very dull He wrote his notes in short hand, which never will produce good reporting. He has succeeded much better with Sir William Grant, whose judgments, when delivered, were perfect in thought and expression; but he was quite unequal to the task of abridging, arranging, and giving the spirit of any discourse which he heard.

dence is involuntary or transitory. In this case everything tends to the conclusion, that the place where Lord Annandale was found, was the place in which he had resolved to spend the remainder of his life. If the point were new and open, it appeared to me to be susceptible of a great deal of argument, whether, in the case of a person dying intestate, having personal property in different places, and subject to different laws, the law of each place should not obtain in the distribution of the property situate there? Many foreign writers have held the affirmative, and there was a time when the Courts of Scotland concurred in that opinion; but now I am obliged to consider that personal property has no locality except the domicile of the owner." [1]

In *Fells* v. *Read*,[2] Lord Loughborough confirmed the doctrine, that where a man wrongfully withholds the possession of a chattel, the value of which can not be estimated and compensated by payment of damages, equity will compel him to deliver it up specifically. A club had subsisted from very ancient times, called " The Past Overseers of St. Margaret's, Westminster," consisting of persons who had served the office of overseer of the poor of that parish. They had a silver tobacco-box, inclosed in two silver cases, all of which were adorned with engravings of public transactions and heads of distinguished persons. The box and the cases were always kept by the senior overseer for the time being, who, on coming into office, received them with a charge to produce them at all meetings of the club, and deliver them up on going out office to his successor. The defendant, who had so received them, refused to deliver them up, unless certain illegal items in his accounts were allowed by the vestry:—

Lord Loughborough. — " I always regret when I see litigation and expense occasioned by peevishness and obstinacy. But this cause being here, I must decide it upon established principles. A pecuniary estimate can not be put upon this box with its cases, and therefore the remedy of the righful owners shall not be confined to an action of trover or detinue. The 'Pusey hord' and

---

[1] 3 Vesey, Jr, 200. See *Somerville* v *Somerville*, 5 Vesey, Jr, 749, in which the law upon this most important subject was finally settled by the admirable judgment of Sir Pepper Arden.   [2] 3 Vesey, 70.

the 'patera' of the Duke of Somerset were decreed to be delivered up; a jury might not have given two-pence beyond their weight as bullion. We can not refer the owners of such curiosities, to which they are affectionately attached, and which might fetch a great price at an antiquarian's sale, to the estimate of farmers and mechanics. In some such cases, no damages would be a compensation, and the jurisprudence of the country would be strangely defective if the spoliator might, by sacrificing a sum of money, set the rightful owner at defiance. This case calls peculiarly for the interposition of a Court of Equity, as the defendant received the box and cases on condition that he would return them at the end of the year, and he is a trustee for the club."[1]

Lord Loughborough showed a mind well imbued with judicial principle in deciding the case of *Comte de Perigord* v. *Boulanger*. The famous Prince Talleyrand, when the profligate Bishop of Autun, borrowed 70,000 livres from the defendant, a usurer in France. For this sum, he and the plaintiff, as his surety, became bound by an obligation, which, according to the French law, did not subject them to arrest either on mesne process or in execution. At the breaking out of the French revolution, both the plaintiff and the defendant emigrated to this country; afterwards, the plaintiff, being about to sail on an expedition to the coast of Brittany, was arrested by the defendant for this debt, and, to procure his release, paid him £100 in cash, gave him two bills of exchange for £100 each, at two and four months, and executed a bond for the remainder of the debt, payable at the end of six months after a peace should be concluded between England and France—with interest in the meantime. The plaintiff paid the first bill of exchange, but, refusing to make any further payments, and being again arrested, filed this bill for an injunction, and to set aside the securities:

Lord Loughborough.—"I think the proceeding on the part of the defendant has been extremely oppressive and immoral. I am not prepared to say how far the Court will finally grant redress, but I will not allow the defendant to avail himself of an advantage got by duress, which is the sole cause of the new engagement. If it

---
[1] See the authorities collected, 3 Vesey, Jr., 73 *n*.

stood upon the original obligation, it would be contrary to all the rules which guide the Courts of one country in deciding on contracts made in another, to give a greater effect to this contract than it would have by the law of the country where it was made. It is against all conscience, that these parties being driven to our shores by a common calamity, the one should permitted to take advantage of that calamity and to immure the other in a jail." *The injunction was continued.*[1]

The only case of a political aspect which came before Lord Loughborough was *Wallis and Troward* v. *Duke of Portland*.[2] George Tierney, in 1789, before the split in the Whig party, had been started as a candidate for Colchester, under the auspices of the Duke of Portland, and being beaten at the poll, presented a petition complaining of a false return. The bill alleged that Mr Tierney employed the plaintiffs on behalf of the Duke to conduct the petition before the election committee; that they did so, disbursing between three and four thousand pounds; and neither Mr. Tierney nor the Duke would pay them, and that they had no legal evidence against the Duke; they therefore prayed a discovery against him, and particularly that he should answer, whether he had not authorized Mr. Tierney to retain them? There was a demurrer to the bill, on the ground that the transaction relied upon was illegal.

Lord Loughborough.—" The case disclosed is of this nature: an undertaking, supposed to have been entered into between the plaintiffs and the defendant, stipulated that he would defray the expense of a petition against the return of a member of parliament. This is an agreement between two parties to the oppression of a third; in short, it is 'maintenance.' 'Maintenance' is not confined to suits at law, and although there are statutes inflicting penalties for particular sorts of 'maintenance,' it is laid down as a fundamental rule that 'maintenance' is *malum in se*—not merely *malum prohibitum*. Strangers are forbidden to aid the prosecution of suits in which they have no interest—that justice may be equally administered to all. To speak to a counsel or an attorney for the purpose of encouraging a suit in which the speaker has no interest, has been adjudged 'maintenance.' I do not go into the

[1] 3 Vesey, Jr., 449. [2] Ibid. 494.

argument which was very properly urged in support of the demurrer upon considerations of *public policy*, as I think that the discovery would be of a *specific offense*, well known to the law. I am therefore of opinion, that a Court of Equity ought not to permit the suit to proceed further."

Upon appeal to the House of Lords, the order allowing the demurrer was affirmed, without hearing the counsel for the respondent.[1]

The case with which Lord Loughborough seems to have taken most pains, as it attracted a great deal of public attention, was *Myddleton* v. *Lord Kenyon*.[2] The plaintiff, the representative of the ancient family of the Myddletons, of Chirk Castle in Wales, having been very extravagant in his youth—when turned of sixty joined in an arrangement with his son, whereby certain large estates of which he was seized in fee, and others of which he was tenant for life, with remainder to his son in tail, were conveyed to trustees, who were to pay his debts, to allow him such a sum as they should think fit for his support,—and at his death to make over the estates to his son. At this time, having been twice married, he had no thoughts of again entering the state of matrimony, but caught by the charms of a pretty young girl, he married her, much against his son's wishes, and having no means of settling a jointure on her, or providing for the issue expected from this marriage, he filed a bill to have the trust deeds set aside—merely on general charges of fraud and misrepresentation. His counsel chiefly relied upon the improvidence of the father in executing such a settlement, and the equity that he should be relieved from it, after his third marriage. "I admit," said one of them (Mr. Hargrave), " that there is entwisted into the transaction which the plaintiff seeks to invalidate an aggregate of the most unimpeachable integrity; the first of the trustees, Lord Kenyon, is of so peculiar a description, that to suppose him to be privy to a fraud would be to suppose justice itself transmuted—would be to suppose what we must all presume, and I heartily believe, to be a moral impossibility."

Lord Loughborough.—" I lay no stress upon the charac-

[1] 1 Vesey, Jr, 503. *n.*
[2] The judgment extends over fifteen pages of Vesey, Jr., vol. ii. 401–416.

ter of the trustees. It is very fit that, in a court of justice the name of the party should not avail him. But, if instead of names towards which I bear a personal respect, the names of the defendants had been totally unknown to me, or, to put a stronger case, supposing them to be men of whom, from former prejudices, I had entertained a bad opinion, my decree would unhesitatingly have been in their favor. The plaintiff, at an advanced age, repenting too late his past extravagance, found himself possessed of large estates, but without either money or credit. He had long supplied his necessities by granting annuities upon the very worst terms—much worse than those of the most unfortunate dissipated young heir who has fallen into the worst nest of hornets with which this town is infested. The settlement which was made to free him from his difficulties might, in some respects, have been more considerately framed; but, being free from fraud, I have no control over it. The act of the son, in joining to convey the entailed estates to the trustees, is consideration enough flowing from him to support it. Each of the parties is *rei suæ arbiter et moderator*. This Court can not interfere in this case without making itself *arbiter et moderator* of the private affairs of all the families of England. There being no extrinsic fraud charged, none appears on the face of the deeds. Mr. Myddleton complains bitterly of being left dependent on his trustees; but it would have been folly in the extreme for him to have taken to himself a certain income. I ask if there ever was an instance in which, under similar circumstances, a man in this state of debauch, by granting annuities (for it is like dram-drinking —it irritates, and inflames, and deadens), was ever left with a certain income? The purpose would be totally defeated. The old habit would return. If there be a secure fund to be pledged, the facility of raising money offers a temptation known to be irresistible. Then it is objected that no provision is made for a third marriage. I suppose that a third marriage was not in the contemplation of any of the parties. It has taken place. I have no right to blame it, but it was not provided for; and I can no more relieve here than in the not uncommon case of a first marriage early in life, and a settlement without any provision for the jointure of a second wife. An unfortunate situation arises if the first wife dies young; but it would be a strange argument that the settlement should be set aside to the prejudice of those entitled under it, because an event has happened which had not been contemplated by the parties. The last objection is, that the remainder is given to the son. It is sufficient for me that I am satisfied Mr. Myddleton understood what he was about; that he was not deceived as to the extent of this settlement. No person cheated him. They were his own attorneys, friends, and trustees who had the preparation of everything; and when I find a settlement so made, am I to say—he has been over-liberal to his son? Be it so! *Sic voluit.* But I do not know that he could have done a wiser thing than, after he had put his son on a short allowance for a considerable time, in order to clear the estate, thinking it right to give it to him entirely. We are told that the settlement must either have proceeded from misapprehension or misrepresentation; but I cannot presume either. The plaintiff knew that he was tenant in fee-simple of an estate of £7,000 a-year, and no man would have dared to tell him that he could not sell that estate to pay his debts without the consent of his son. But it is true that his son's consent was necessary for the purposes he had in view—purposes of the heart, not of sordid selfishness—purposes that it would be the pride of an honorable man at his time of life to have accomplished—so that he might say, 'I have so arranged that, all my debts being paid, my son will be owner of a great estate, maintaining hospitality in his magnificent castle, and enjoying the station and the respect which have long distinguished our ancient line.' Such feelings, according to the evidence, must have actuated his bosom. An eye-witness gives us a touching representation of the scene, when the son, with duty and affection, threw himself into his father's arms, and desired to be guided in everything by the law advisers whom his father had appointed, and with whom he himself was unacquainted—solicitous only for the honor of the family and his father's happiness. Trustees were named on the part of the father. In this story everything is reversed. There have been cases where an extravagant son, for a temporary accommodation, has been imposed upon by the father in resettling the estate. Here we have extravagant old age and frugal youth. The father complains that, in making provision for the payment of his own debts, he has been overreached by the son. But he suggested everything, he conducted everything, and he named trustees whose very names are allowed to be a guarantee against fraud. Finally, Mr. Hargrave emphatically pressed that I should suspend my judgment, as this matter might be privately arranged better than in a court of justice, and that should interpose by way of accommodation. Sitting here, I must decide when the case is ripe for judgment, and I can not recommend where I have no power to decree. It must be the wish of every honorable mind that harmony may be restored between the father and the son; and it is the particular advantage of such a trust as this, that it vests in the trustees a species of jurisdiction upon nice matters of feeling which the public interest will not permit to reside in a judge. Meanwhile the bill must be dismissed with costs."

Lord Loughborough had the glory of putting an end to the litigation which had been going on half a century respecting the foundation of Downing College, Cambridge,—deciding that the heir at law had no right to the rents and profits of the estates before the devise was carried into effect—and disposing of all the other points in this suit. But he prudently directed that his decree should be confirmed by an Act of Parliament.[1]

In another academical case, he showed that a man educated at a northern university, though perhaps deficient in the niceties of meter, may be as familiarly acquainted with the beauties of the Classics as those who have studied them on the banks of the Isis or the Cam. Mr. Francis Wrangham, afterwards Archdeacon of Chester, and highly distinguished in literature, being a scholar of Trinity Hall, Cambridge, was candidate for a vacant fellowship, contending that he had a *right* to be appointed, as he was the only "scholar" who was a candidate; that by the statutes, upon such a vacancy, it was provided "quod in loco socii Collegii subrogetur scholaris idoneus *moribus et ingenio*," and that no objection could be made to his *morals* or his *talents*. The Master and Fellows, however, expressing a dislike to his *manners*, passed him over, and elected the Reverend John Vickars, A. M., of Queen's

[1] 3 Vescy, Jr, 714, 5 **Vesey, Jr.**, 300.

College. Mr. Wrangham presented a petition to the Lord Chancellor as visitor of Trinity Hall, on failure of the heirs of the founder, praying that this election should be set aside—and the great question debated was, whether he was to be considered "scholaris idoneus moribus et ingenio," which turned chiefly upon the true translation here of the word "moribus," whether it means "morals" or "manners."

The counsel for the petitioner insisted that whenever the word is used by classical writers as descriptive of an individual character, it is particularly confined to *morals*, although when it is appropriated to the description of a nation it becomes a more general term, and includes the whole *manners* of the people—illustrating their distinction with the following examples: In the dialogue between Pamphilus and Davus, in the Andria of Terence— "uxorem his *moribus* dabit nemo." In Quintilian de Philosophia—"*mores* ante omnia oratori studiis sunt excolendi, atque omnis honesti justique disciplina pertractanda." Both senses are found in Horace, according to the rule laid down:

"Quid leges sine *moribus*
Vanæ proficiunt?" *Carm.* 24, lib. iii.
" Utcunque defecere *mores*,
Dedecorant bene nata culpæ." *Carm.* 4, lib. iv.
" Rursus, quid virtus et quid sapientia possit
Utile proposuit nobis exemplar Ulyssem ;
Qui domitor Trojæ multorum providus urbes
Et mores hominum inspexit · latumque per æquor
Dum sibi dum sociis reditum parat, aspera multa
Pertulit, adversis rerum immersabilis undis." *Ep.* 2, lib. 1.
" Ætatis cujusque notandi sunt tibi *mores*." *Ars Poet.*

Virgil says,

——— " Moresque viris et mœnia ponet." *Æn.* i.

Tacitus observes the distinction. Speaking of persons put over the city, he says, "magis alii homines quam alii *mores*;" but describing the manners of a nation, DE MORIBUS GERMANORUM, he says, "plusque ibi boni *mores* valent quam alibi bonæ leges." So Juvenal:

———' de *moribus* ultima fiat
Quæstio.
Et linguam et *mores*." *Sat.* 3.

There he means the *manners* of a city. So Martial, speaking of a picture :—

> " Ars utinam *mores* animumque effingere possit."   *Ep.* 32, lib x.
> " Ardu res hæc est opibus non tradere *mores*."   *Ep* 6 lib. ii
> " Templa Deis *mores* populus dedit."   *Ep.* 104 lib, ix.

The counsel for the College confined themselves to one quotation, with which they had been supplied by the Fellows, and which they declared to be decisive to prove that "moribus," applied to an individual, means *manners*. Ovid, in describing two of his mistresses, for whose *morals* nothing could be said, observes:

> " Hæc specie melior, *moribus* illa, fuit."

Lord Loughborough.—" The petitioner's counsel have with great critical acuteness, and a classical collection of well-arranged instances, contended that in the best Latin writers the word ' mores,' when applied to an individual, is always used to signify *morals,* and when clearly used with respect to a large body it includes all that larger circle which, for want of a more precise and distinct term, we call *manners.* I doubt a little if that distinction is quite correct; and rather apprehend that the term, whether applied to an individual or a nation, may be used indifferently in the more restrained or larger sense. One instance occurs to me in which, being applied to an individual, it signifies both. It is the beginning of Horace's address to Augustus:

> " Quum tot sustineas et tanta negotia solus,
> Res Italas armis tutelis, *moribus* ornes.'

"He does not exclude the virtues, and certainly he meant to include all the ornaments, of the character, I recollect another passage which I wish to quote, because the word appears twice in it, and it has a great analogy to the present case:—says Cicero in his De Officiis,[1] ' Sed omnium societatum nulla præstantior est nulla firmior, quam cum viri boni *moribus* similes, sunt familiaritate conjuncti. Illud enim honestum (quod sæpe dicimus) etiam si in alio cornimus, tamen nos movet; atque illi in quo id inesse vid dur amicos facit. Et quanquam omnis virtus nos ad se alliciat, faciatque ut eos diligamus, in quibus ipsa inesse videatur, tamen justitia et liberalitas id maxime efficit. Nihil autem est amabilius nec copulatius quam *morum* similitudo bonorum. In quibus enim eadem studia sunt eædemque voluntates—in his fit, ut æque

[1] Lib. i.

quisque altero delectetur ac seipso; efficiaturque id, quod Pythagoras ultimum in amicitia putavit, ut unus fiat ex pluribus.' In my conception, considering the manner in which these statutes are framed, the mode of election, and the society the founder has established, he meant to give the electors a full judgment—a taste—a feeling of the qualities of the person they were to subrogate in case of a vacancy—knowing that in such a society, consisting of a small number of persons, to be united under the roof of the same College for the purpose of education, jarring tempers, discordant dispositions, *dissimilitudo morum*, would mar the purpose of the foundation, so different, from larger corporations, instituted for more public purposes, and more mixed with the business of the world. I can not think the founder meant to tie them down to the test of little more than common honesty—without which, a man is unfit to be elected into any society. He rather intended to leave the choice as ample as possible, that the fellows might be in all respects fit for each other. Then have I to inquire further than what they have with great concurrence stated to me, 'that the petitioner is not fit (non idoneus) to be a member of that society?' I can not, therefore, compel them to elect the petitioner, nor order him to be admitted without an election. It would have been unfortunate, if a college consisting of so few members had been in the predicament, that there were means of forcibly introducing among them a gentleman whom, *however fit for greater and better situations*, they have unanimously declared not fit to be elected as their associate. I must therefore dismiss the petition."

The last observation thrown in to soothe the feelings of the petitioner, who probably was excluded for his superior learning and capacity, shows that gentlemanly turn of mind which always distinguished Lord Loughborough, and covered many of his faults.

I ought to mention one other case which he decided, because it not only was perhaps the greatest in point of value that ever came before an English judge, but raised a question of law of much public importance; although it turned on such technical reasoning that I

---

[1] 2 Vesey, Jr. 609–625.

can not enter into the arguments on either side. I mean *Thelluson* v. *Woodford*.[1] Peter Thelluson, by his will, left his immense real and personal property to trustees, that the rents and profits might accumulate during the lives of all his sons, and of all his grandchildren that should be living at his death, and of any grandchild that should be born within the usual time of gestation after his death—to be laid out in landed estates, which were to be finally divided between the representatives of his three sons—and failing his descendants, to go to pay the national debt. His family disputed the validity of the will, on the ground that although the *corpus* of the property might have been rendered inalienable for a period thus limited, the rents and profits could not be so disposed of; and that it was contrary to public policy to allow such an accumulation, which might render the individual in whom the whole might center, dangerous to public liberty, and too powerful for a subject. The suit coming on for a hearing, Lord Loughborough called in the assistance of the Master of the Rolls, and of Mr. Justice Buller and Mr. Justice Lawrence. After arguments which lasted many days, they gave their opinions at great length in favor of the validity of the will, and he very politely and prudently said:—

"I am extremely obliged to his Honor and to my Lords the Judges, not only for the very able assistance which they have given me in forming my own opinion upon this case, which concurs in the result, as in almost the whole of the argument; but also, because they have relieved me from the duty of entering particularly into the discussion of the several points of the case, and the grounds upon which the arguments urged for the family have failed to produce conviction on my mind. I could not go over the case without the necessity of repeating what has been much better stated already. The great amount of the property is a sufficient reason for the family to seek to establish what would have been their natural right if no disposition had intervened to deprive them of it. I have no difficulty in saying that this disposition is so unkind and illiberal, that I think it no breach of duty in them to seek to set it aside if they can. The amount of the property, however, can in no possible shape enter

[1] 4 Vesey, Jr., 227–343.

into the judgment. The same rule must prevail whether it be estimated at £100 or a million. Nor can the piety or prudence of the disposition be considered. I am bound to give effect to the intentions of the testator, if they do not contravene any rule of law." [He then briefly showed that there was nothing, as the law then stood, to prevent a direction to accumulate during any number of lives in being, together with the additional period of gestation—and thus concluded:] "I should do myself no credit, and should convey no sort of information to the Bar, if I were to go further than to express my full assent to what has been so well stated by his Honor and the Judges, and again to return them warm thanks for their able assistance."

The decree supporting the will was affirmed on an appeal to the House of Lords; but an Act of Parliament, introduced by Lord Chancellor Loughborough, was passed (39 & 40 Geo. 3, c. 98), forbidding such accumulations in future for a longer period than twenty-one years All apprehensions of the Thelluson property swelling to a magnitude dangerous to the Crown or to public liberty, were effectually allayed by the Court of Chancery conveniently eating up almost the whole of the annual rents and profits;—and finally the possession of the property was given by Act of Parliament to the family, on their securing to the trust the very moderate sum which would have remained to accumulate after all law expenses were defrayed.

Although hardly any of Lord Loughborough's judgments were reversed, it must be confessed that their authority has not been considered very high among lawyers. When Lord Ellenborough was dining at a puisne Judge's, —having been long engaged in a discussion with him in the drawing-room, the lady of the house stepped up, and said, "Come, my Lord; do give *us* some of your conversation—you have been talking law long enough." "Madam," said the Lord Chief Justice, "I beg your pardon, we have not been talking law, or anything like law; we have been talking of one of the decisions of Lord Loughborough!"

Before taking leave of him as a Judge, I ought to mention that while he held the Great Seal, he disposed satisfactorily of the Appeal business in the House of Lords.

For several years he was assisted in this department by Lord Thurlow; and afterwards, single-handed, he showed how easy is the task of reviewing the judgments of others, to a man of good discretion, who is so far imbued with the general principles of jurisprudence as to be able, *pro re nata*, to understand any question of law well argued before him. He was generally inclined to *affirm*, perhaps unconsciously influenced by the practice which still prevailed, that upon affirmance, no reasons were to be given; but occasionally he found that the Judges of the Court of Session in Scotland were palpably wrong,—when he very unsparingly exposed their blunders—ever retaining a grudge against a tribunal which had done so little justice to his own merits. It is a curious fact, that, although there were now published regular periodical reports of the cases determined in all the Courts of Westminster Hall, the decisions of the Court of *dernier resort* were still neglected; and it is wonderful to observe how little they have contributed to the formation of our Civil Code, whereas in most other countries the decisions of the Courts from which an appeal lies are rarely cited as authority.

We must now view Lord Loughborough presiding as Speaker of the Upper House. Here he appeared to advantage. From his courtesy and high bearing he was respected by the Peers of all parties; and, without arrogating to himself any special control, he had great influence on all questions of order; so that the deliberations of this most irregular assembly proceeded with a tolerable observance of decorum under his auspices. He never gave the signal from the woolsack for Ministerial cheers.

Nevertheless he was a uniform and zealous supporter of the Government, and whatever differences he might have in council with his colleagues, he did not imitate Thurlow's example by displaying a public conflict between the Chancellor and the Prime Minister.

On the accession of the Whig alarmists, whom he had been so instrumental in bringing over, he possessed considerable influence in the measures taken at the commencement of the war. His favorite scheme of subsidizing the Continental sovereigns was adopted, contrary to the opinion of Mr. Pitt and Lord Grenville[1]—and he suc-

[1] "Nov. 14, 1793. Dined with the Chancellor; no one there but Parnell,

ceeded in pressing the appointment of his friend, Lord Malmesbury, as the diplomatist to carry it into effect.¹ But his influence in the Cabinet soon declined, and some of the most important secrets respecting the negotiations with the French Republic were not communicated to him. He strongly took part with Burke in disapproving of Mr. Pitt's policy as a war minister.

His first speech in the House of Lords as Chancellor, was in the debate upon an address to the King for an augmentation of the forces, in consequence of late events in France, and particularly the tragical end of the French King. He immediately followed the Marquis of Lansdowne, who, deploring this event, still expressed an opinion that there was no sufficient ground for quarreling with the new Republic, and insisted that Ministers were going to war only in support of metaphysical distinctions between different forms of government. *Lord Loughborough*: "The catastrophe which has lately happened at Paris has not only changed the garb of this nation, but has impressed every individual in it with sorrow, as on the death of a beloved relative. There would have been a great indecency in excluding all reference to it in the address to the Crown; for it has a material bearing upon our public relations. The noble Marquis has said, that this is to be a war of *metaphysics*, but who are the *metaphysicians* we are to encounter? They are 120,000 French soldiers; their cannon and their bayonets are the arguments which they use. Lessons have been thus taught by them in Nice, Frankfort, Geneva, and the Low Countries. As things now stand, it would not even be sufficient to require France to return within her ancient limits, for she would still leave behind her the contamination of her doctrines, and the poison of her example." He then animadverted upon a profession which Lord Lauderdale had made of a friendship for Brissot: "Friendship and affection," said he, "are matters of

---

Chancellor of the Exchequer in Ireland When he went, I staid some time with the Chancellor Much substantial talk;—*he*, for giving a large subsidy to the King of Prussia, but Pitt and Grenville think otherwise."—*Lord Malmesbury's Diary*, iii 6.

¹ "I received an express dispatched at the desire of the Lord Chancellor, who wrote me a letter saying, 'he had received a note from Lord Grenville. and that both Lord Grenville and Pitt entreated me to accept a commission on the Continent, of great consequence.'"—*Diary*, ii. 5

taste. I possess none of the innovating taste myself, and so am unable to account for it in others; but the prevailing taste of some men is for revolutions, massacre, war, confusion and the killing of Kings. I do not envy the congenial taste which forms friendship with the propagator of principles leading to such enormities."[1] He poured out much more of such invective, which was then very popular;—and an amendment to the address was negatived without a division. I think there is ground to lament the tone of indiscriminate vituperation against all concerned in the French Revolution, which was now assumed in England; for it aggravated the excesses committed in France, it actually endangered the existence of freedom in this country, and it rendered more humiliating to us the victories obtained on the Continent by the republican arms.

Our Chancellor's next appearance was in the character of a jester, which was not natural to him, and which he rarely assumed; but on this occasion he seems to have been much applauded by the Lords spiritual as well as temporal. Miss Pulteney, the heiress of the rival of Sir Robert Walpole, had been created Baroness Bath, there being a Marquis of Bath of another family existing. Lord Radnor made a motion in the House of Lords against this patent,—contending that it was unconstitutional and illegal to create two peers with the same title, and that great inconvenience would arise from it, as in their Lordships' proceedings "BATH" might often appear opposed to "BATH." *Lord Loughborough:* "My Lords, there have sat in this House, at the same time, Lords Grey, Lords Percy, and Lords Howard, without end. Besides, in this case, there is a sure way of preventing the future antagonism which haunts the imagination of the noble Earl, for the heir apparent of the Marquis being a bachelor, he may marry the young and beautiful Baroness—and then 'BATH' will be merged in 'BATH!'"[2] Lord Radnor had only one peer to divide with him.

Much more serious subjects were soon to occupy the public mind. Now began that system of policy, for the repression of French principles, which has caused the period in which it prevailed to be designated, in the language of exaggeration, "the Reign of Terror." I think

[1] 30 Parl. Hist. 331.   [2] Ibid. 57.

the system was unwise, and that Lord Loughborough is chiefly answerable for it. I am afraid that, if he did not originate, he actively encouraged it, and that he, as the organ of the alarmist party, forced it upon the reluctant Prime Minister. Pitt had not only come forward in public life on the popular side, but I believe that his propensities continued liberal, and that if he could have fulfilled his wishes he would have emancipated the Catholics,—he would have abolished slavery,—he would have established free trade,—and he would have reformed the House of Commons. His regard for the liberty of the press he had evinced by carrying Fox's Libel Bill by the influence of Government, notwithstanding the furious opposition of Lord Chancellor Thurlow. He was likewise particularly adverse to any stringent measures against reformers, being aware that having himself very recently belonged to that body, he would appear rather in an invidious light as the persecutor of his former associates. But he found that he could not adhere to constitutional laws and constitutional practices, without the disruption of his Administration. Burke's indignation was now diverted from Warren Hastings and directed against all who did not agree in condemning everything that had been done in France since the calling of the States General, and in defending all the ancient abuses of the French monarchy. Lord Loughborough, as his organ in the Cabinet, pressed for measures of coercion and intimidation.

It must be acknowledged that the crisis was perplexing. There were unprincipled individuals in this country, who were willing to engage in a revolutionary movement, in the hope of at once rising to power and wealth; and there were enthusiasts who were, without any dishonest motive, desirous of making the experiment of a republic. The often-resounded dread of French *emissaries* was most chimerical; for Englishmen will never be influenced by a foreigner who can not address them in their mother tongue. But there was no saying distinctly how far the political frenzy might run. The question arose, what was the most effectual method of checking it? We, from our experience, should say,—" by adhering to the ancient frame of the Constitution, by correcting abuses, and by making the laws more loved and respected." A very different conservative view was taken by Lord Loughborough and his friends in the year 1793. Any reform of any enormity they denounced as a dangerous innovation leading to reolution; they were determined to vest in the Executive Government extraordinary and unconstitutional powers, and they vowed vengeance, by the terrors of criminal law, against all whom they denounced as disaffected. Happily, English juries and the returning sober sense of the English people at last saved public liberty from the great peril to which it was then exposed.

The first measure prompted by Lord Loughborough, after coming into the Cabinet, was called the " Traitorous Correspondence Bill," by which, in addition to the law of Edward III. against adhering to the King's enemies, which had been found sufficient for many ages, it was made high treason, to be punished by hanging, beheading, quartering, forfeiture, and corruption of blood, to hold any correspondence with the French, or to enter into any agreement to supply them with any commodities. This was strongly opposed by Lord Lansdowne and Lord Lauderdale, but, on account of a temporary success of the allies on the Continent, was defended by the Chancellor in a very vaunting and arrogant tone. " Is it quite clear," he asked, " if the policy recommended by noble Lords opposite had been pursued, that the internal peace of the country would have been maintained? Is it certain that deputations of fraternity to the French Convention would have ceased? that the same general spirit of loyalty we now witness would have been called forth? that those clubs to which some of the opposers of this bill belonged would have shrunk from their purpose, and disappeared? that the projected conquest of Holland would have been abandoned? and that a stop would have been put to a systematic attack on the government, the religion, and the morals of the country? The noble Lords opposite have sneered at the small force landed on the Continent under the command of an illustrious Prince: but to the sending out of those troops, and to the promptitude with which the measure was carried into effect, in my opinion, is to be ascribed that Holland is saved; that the French are everywhere defeated and driven back; that all Europe, from Naples to St. Petersburgh, is delivered from the plunder, the confiscation, the rapine, the murder, the destruction of order, morality, and religion, with which it was threatened by the prevalence of French arms and French principles." Seven peers and no more, divided against the bill.¹ Alas! in a few weeks the Duke of York was forced to fly from Dunkirk, Holland became a province of France, and the Republican legions, bearing the tricolor, were crossing the Rhine and the Alps.

In the following year Lord Loughborough supported a bill for the suspension of the *habeas corpus*, on the ground that the societies professing to be founded for parliamentary reform were aiming at revolution. "Parliamentary reform," said he (not very courteously to Mr. Pitt), "was tried, settled, and extinguished in 1781 and 1782, and it can now only be used as a cover for deeper designs. The phrase of *parliamentary reform* no more legalizes seditious meetings than GOD SAVE THE KING written at the bottom of an insurrectionary proclamation would make it innocent. Much is said of the low rank of the members of most of these societies, and their little power to do mischief; but it is easy to treat as imaginary all dangers that are checked in the bud. One of the finest poets has said,—

'Treasons are never own'd but when descried;
Successful crimes alone are justified.'"²

In the debate on the Report of a Secret Committee on Seditious Practices, Lord Lauderdale having alluded to political meetings in former times at the Thatched House, and particularly to the dinner given there on the occasion of Mr. Wedderburn, Steward of the Chiltern Hundreds, vacating his seat in the House of Commons, that he might stand up for Wilkes and Liberty,³ the Lord Chancellor said, "Had the Thatched House meetings of the present day, like their predecessors, confined themselves to foolish speeches, no notice would have been taken of them; but, as they resort to overt acts of treason, they must be put down with a strong hand."⁴

During the recess of Parliament which soon followed, there was a great danger of the Government being dissolved by a quarrel between the old Tories and their new Whig allies. Mr. Burke, notwithstanding his deep afflic-

¹ 30 Parl. Hist. 738.   ² 31 Parl. Hist. 602.
³ See ante, p. 266   ⁴ 31 Parl. Hist. 915.

tion from the loss of his son, being asked by Lord
Loughborough to step in as a mediator, wrote him the
ollowing letter:—

"MY DEAR LORD,

"Nothing can be in itself so disagreeable to me as to
go to London, or to show to the world the face of
a man marked by the hand of God. At first, therefore, I doubted whether I ought to go. I am even now
apprehensive of intruding myself into an affair into which I
am not called by the parties. I know by abundant experience, under what suspicious circumstances all advice
comes that is not required, and how little weight it is
likely to have. But since your Lordship thinks that
heats begin a little to subside, that a way is made for removing difficulties, so that a small matter, even from a
very inconsiderable person, may have its effect in setting
things to rights, I will come to town in order to receive
and to obey your instructions. I propose to be there on
Tuesday. There is nothing in my power which I would
not most willingly do towards clearing up this dreadful
misunderstanding. I really consider the fate of the King
and the country, and perhaps, at no very remote distance,
of mankind itself, may depend upon the good agreement
of those now in place. You certainly have done your
part, and have done it well, and I shall be ready to act
under you as you shall direct. There are none of the
parties to whom I have not great obligations. Since it
has pleased the Great Disposer, contrary to the general
order of nature, to keep me here, and without any effort
of my own to make provision for my existence, He
certainly meant, that as I have neither the aptitude nor
the disposition to enjoy any satisfaction, I have some
duty in suffering or acting to fulfill. As to the latter
part, as I have quitted what is called active life, to which
I have been led by reason, inclination, and the sad necessity imposed upon me by sorrow, age, and infirmity, I do
not know in what way I can be serviceable but by
giving, when asked, such an opinion as I have formed,
impartially, on the long and melancholy experience
in affairs which I have had. I am a pensioner of the
Crown, and I eat the bread of the public, which
has a full right to demand all that in the retreat
provided for me it is possible for me to perform. God

give you success; and believe me ever, with the most sincere sentiments of respect and affection,
"My dear Lord,
"Your Lordship's most faithful and obliged
"humble servant,
"EDM. BURKE.
"Beaconsfield, Nov. 2, 1794"[1]

Mr. Burke, in another letter to Lord Loughborough, gives an account of his vain efforts as a peace-maker:—
"MY DEAR LORD,
"I have written to Mr. Dundas thanking him for his obliging permission to wait upon him, but as he expresses himself with so little hope of any reconciliation, I shall forbear to trouble him till things wear a better aspect than they do at present. What you mention of the conversation at Court, confirms me more strongly in the idea of not seeing him until he desires it. He knows that I am ready to attend him,—and, if he really wishes that we may confer on the matter, he will tell me so. If, notwithstanding the conversation with the D. of P. with which Pitt seemed so fully satisfied, his jealousies and apprehensions are, from some representation or other, grown more violent than ever, what can I say to remove them? I am so far from having any authority from the parties to disclaim any such intentions as are attributed to them, that I have never spoken with the D. of P., nor very lately with Lord F.; so that if Pitt gives credit to his informant, I know not what to say. For my part, I don't believe a syllable of the matter, but that the whole is an absolute invention of somebody to render this misunderstanding incurable. Why, in the name of God, don't they meet together, and know what their mutual intentions are? When I can say or do anything with authority, I shall certainly do it. In the meantime I shall see your Lordship at your desire, and am ever, my dear Lord,
"Yrs. most truly,
"EDM. BURKE.
"Nov. 8, one o'clock, A.M.."[2]

In spite of these inauspicious appearances, the breach between the opposite parties was adjusted for the present, and at the commencement of the new session "the necessity for a vigorous prosecution of the war" was at

[1] Rossl. MSS.   [2] Ib.

the suggestion of the Chancellor, announced in the King's Speech, in such terms as fully satisfied Mr. Burke and his followers.

The next coercive measure brought forward was a "Bill to put down Seditious Practices." When it was in committee the Duke of Leeds having moved an amendment, that after the words "to overturn the established Constitution," there should be added, "consisting of King, Lords and Commons," the Chancellor said, "the amendment would legalize all libels on the Constitution which affected to preserve a King, a House of Lords, and a House of Commons. For instance, a person might write thus: 'The Constitution of England consists of King, Lords and Commons. But I do not like an hereditary monarchy, for it is an absurdity. I think an hereditary House of Lords still worse; and the House of Commons, as at present chosen, is a nuisance. I would have an elective monarchy, a peerage for life or for a session of parliament, and a House of Commons returned by universal suffrage.' Here you have a man admitting a constitution, consisting of 'King, Lords and Commons,' and proposing a Revolutionary Government."[1] The enactments of the bill were so arbitrary, that Lord Thurlow thought this a good opportunity of displaying his patriotism by opposing it; but it passed by great majorities.

The finish was given to the new penal political code by the "Seditious Meetings Bill,"—which forbade the King's subjects to meet together in public for any purpose without the license of a magistrate. Lord Thurlow having furiously opposed it as entirely inconsistent with a free government and unsuitable to our national character, it was defended by Lord Loughborough, who did not venture to taunt his antagonist with inconsistency, but said,—

"The noble and learned lord has contended that the genius and character of the two nations are dissimilar, and that it is absurd to suppose they can both be governed by the same laws. Upon that principle he has refused to take a salutary warning by the dreadful scenes which have passed among our neighbors. Is man so different from man, on the opposite sides of a narrow strait, that

[1] 32 Parl Hist. 255.

similar associations in each—assuming the same forms and affecting the same tone—are not likely to be attended with similar effects? Will the Protestant divines of England declare that they apprehend nothing from the avowed atheism and scandalous profaneness now disgracing France? Do prudent politicians see no danger in the general confusion which must necessarily result from the propagation of doctrines and systems of government destructive of all order, all subordination, all property, all security and all happiness? Will the noble and learned lord venture to assert that we ought to remain supine in the midst of inflammatory and seditious harangues, and libelous and treasonable pamphlets and newspapers? It has ever been the practice of wise governments to anticipate by preventive regulations, in order to ward off impending evil. The libels circulated by the Corresponding Society represent our Monarchy as despotic; the House of Lords as useless; and the Commons corrupt. When the demagogues are asked what they mean by *reform*, and are called upon to produce their plans, they talk of 'universal suffrage, and indefeasible elective rights, which can not be bartered away.' In order to reform, they say, 'you must destroy boroughs and corporations, and divide the whole kingdom into sections.' Does not all this involve us in the miserable state of France? The existing laws are insufficient, and all that we propose, necessity demands."[1]

Worse proceedings were going on than loading the statute books with such enactments,—which might have remained *brutum fulmen* till swept away in better times. Spies and informers employed by the Government not only pretended to give information respecting political associations, but invaded the sacred privacy of domestic life. In consequence, "State trials" took place, both in Scotland and in England, upon which we now look back with shame.

The prosecution of Muir, for sedition, before the Court of Justiciary in Edinburgh, was probably suggested, and was certainly vindicated, by Lord Loughborough and the Government. This "martyr" was a young advocate at the Scotch Bar, of good family, of high literary attain-

[1] The Reform Bill, which was passed in 1832, would have appeared to Lord Loughborough hardly less unconstitutional and pernicious.

ments, of promising talents, and of unblemished honor. The witnesses called against him by the Crown admitted that he was attached to our monarchical form of government, and that he always inculcated obedience to the laws. But he was (as Mr. Pitt had been) a warm friend to parliamentary reform; and he continued to *agitate* for it at a time when, in the eyes of some of its former supporters, it had become as odious as rebellion. He took the lead in proposing resolutions and petitions in favor of the measure in clubs and at public meetings—using language which in the years 1831 and 1832 would have been considered tame and conservative. The charge that he had distributed seditious writings was supported by evidence that a copy of Paine's Rights of Man was found in his great-coat pocket. The presiding Judge (according to the power then vested in him) selected a jury, all of whom belonged to an association that had pronounced a strong opinion against parliamentary reform, and one of whom voluntarily declared his unfitness to serve, as he held an office under Government. I must do the Lord Advocate of that day (Dundas) the justice to observe, that he seems to have been most heartily ashamed of the task imposed upon him; and, in his short and feeble speech, he hardly ventured to contend that a case had been made out for a conviction. Mr. Muir defended himself with force, eloquence, and decency, thus concluding:

"What, then, has been my crime?—having dared to be, according to the measure of my feeble abilities, a strenuous advocate for an equal representation of the people in the House of the people—having dared to attempt to accomplish by legal means a measure which I conscientiously think will diminish the weight of their taxation, and put an end to the effusion of their blood. From my infancy to this moment, I have devoted myself to the cause of the people. It is a good cause, and it will ultimately triumph. If I am to be found guilty, say then that you condemn me only for my attachment to this cause, and not for those vain and wretched pretexts stated in the indictment, intended merely to color and disguise the real motives which have led to my accusation. I may be doomed to languish in the recesses of a dungeon—I may be doomed to ascend the scaffold;—but nothing can deprive me of the recollection of the past—

nothing can destroy my inward peace of mind arising from the consciousness of having done my duty."

The Lord Justice Clerk Braxfield summed up violently against him, and hardly attempted to conceal that the *corpus delicti* was the advocacy of parliamentary reform. Censuring the getting up of a petition on the subject to the Lords and Commons, he said, " Mr. Muir might have known that no attention would be paid to such a rabble. What right have they to representation? He might have told them that the Parliament would never listen to their petition. How could they think of it? A government in every country should be just like a corporation; and in this country it is made up of the landed interest, which alone has a right to be represented. As for the rabble, who have nothing but personal property, what hold has the nation of them? What security for the payment of their taxes? They may pack up all their property on their backs, and leave the country in the twinkling of an eye; but landed property can not be removed." The jury (as had been anticipated when they were sworn) unanimously found the defendant guilty, and the Court sentenced him to be transported beyond the seas for fourteen years,—taking great credit for their humanity in not having pronounced sentence that he should be hanged, or exposed to wild beasts—punishments which, for such an offense, they claimed the power to inflict,—saying, " By the Roman law, which is held to be our common law, where there is no statute, the punishment was various, and transportation was among the mildest mentioned. Paulus, 38 Dig., ' de Pœnis,' writes, ' Actores seditionis et tumultus populo concitato, pro qualitate dignitatis, *aut in furcum tolluntur aut bestiis objiciuntur.*' We have chosen the mildest of these punishments. Baldus writes, ' Provocans tumultum et clamorem in populo, *debet mori* pœnâ seditionis.' "[1]

The case created a deep sensation in England, and was immediately brought before the House of Lords by Earl Stanhope, who pointed out the enormity of the whole proceeding, and moved an address to the Crown, praying that the execution of the sentence might be postponed:

Lord Loughborough.—" Granting that there has been a mistrial—that the verdict of the jury is not justified by

[1] 23 St. Tr. 118–258.

the evidence—that the conduct of the judges has been founded in misapprehension—that there has been a misapplication of the law—in short, if there has been any irregularity in the trial or the sentence, there is a remedy provided by an application to the Crown to bring the whole matter into a revision. But who ever heard of an application to this House to pray his Majesty to postpone the execution of a sentence? If ever your Lordships should think fit to entertain an inquiry into the case, I pledge myself that you will find the conduct of the Judges in Scotland to have been altogether such as your Lordships would desire to find in men intrusted with functions so important."

Such an impression was produced by these observations, that, when the division came, Lord Stanhope went below the bar all alone.[1] Accordingly Mr. Muir, along with the Rev. Thomas Fyshe Palmer, a clergyman of the Church of England, sentenced to transportation by the Court of Justiciary in Scotland, under circumstances hardly less atrocious, having been shipped off for Botany Bay among burglars and persons guilty of the most horrible crimes,—the Earl of Lauerdale, after a very able speech, explaining the mockery of justice which had been exhibited on their trials, moved that there should be laid before the House of Lords copies of the indictments against them, with the minutes of the Court respecting the challenge of jurors, and the subsequent proceedings till the final sentence. But Lord Loughborough boldly defended all that had been done; and, not satisfied with negativing Lord Lauderdale's motion,—carried, without a division, a counter resolution of his own, "That there is no ground for interfering in the practice of the established Courts of Criminal Justice, as administered under the Constitution, by which the rights, liberties, and properties of all ranks of subjects are protected."[2]

Meanwhile there were political prosecutions going on

[1] Content, 1; Non-contents 49. 30 Parl. Hist. 1302.
[2] 31 Parl Hist. 284 There has been a strange attempt lately to defend these atrocious proceedings. But the following is the testimony of an eye-witness who ever remained true to liberty: "The administration of justice in Edinburgh is, I think, detestable I am not surprised that you have been shocked at the account you have read of Muir's trial. You would have been much more shocked if you had been present as I was." Romilly to Dumont, Memoirs, vol 1 p. 23 —*Note to 4th Edition.*

in England still more alarming to liberty, although they were conducted with greater respect for the forms of law. Mr. John Frost, an attorney of eminence, under the influence of wine, and provoked by impertinent questions put to him after dinner in a coffee-house, having foolishly said, "I am for equality, and no King," was, with the entire approbation of the Lord Chancellor, prosecuted by the Attorney General, and sentenced to be imprisoned six months in Newgate, to stand one hour in the pillory at Charing Cross, and to be struck off the roll of attorneys,—whereby he was ruined for life.[1]

The country magistrates naturally followed such a precedent, and similar prosecutions were multiplied at Quarter Sessions. A complaint was made to the Chancellor of a sentence in Kent of a twelvemonth's imprisonment on a loyal yeoman who, in his drink, being rudely assaulted by a constable as drunk as himself, and ordered by him to keep the peace in the King's name, stammered out, "D——n you and the King too;"—but his Lordship said, that "to save the country from revolution, the authority of all tribunals, high and low, must be upheld;" and he refused to interfere. The violence of the times is more thoroughly illustrated by the consideration that he was by nature a mild man,—and that at no former period of his life had he shown the slightest inclination to overstrain the criminal law.

But having begun in this course, and finding, from the revolutionary panic which had seized men's minds, that for the time it was rather popular, and strengthened the Government, he boldly advanced in it, and soon nothing less would satisfy him than having the heads of John Horne Tooke and the leading Reformers stuck on Temple Bar.

I must reserve for the Life of Erskine a full account of the famous Treason Trials which took place in the end of the year 1794,—covering him with glory, and the prosecutors with disgrace,—and I can now only briefly notice the circumstance that Lord Loughborough was a principal adviser of them. He had surrendered himself to the wildest apprehensions of Burke; he feared that any encouragement of parliamentary reform was tantamount to revolution; and he believed that general

[1] 22 St. Tr. 471–522. See a statement of this case in the Life of Erskine

bloodshed would be saved by the sacrifice of a few individuals. The reflection rejoiced him, that on this occasion *he* was not liable to the taunt of being a renegade, for during *his* patriotic days he had only to inveigh against the injustice done to the electors of Middlesex,— and the plan of reforming the representation of the people had not been seriously brought forward. Perhaps he was not sorry to think that the Prime Minister must wince while his own withers were unwrung; for there was an increasing alienation between the *original* and the *conscript* members of the Cabinet,—Pitt confining his confidence more and more to Henry Dundas and Lord Grenville; and the disciples of Burke condemning his conduct of the war, lamenting his want of spirit, and talking among themselves of another Chief. When the plan was first proposed of arresting the members of the Corresponding Society, and proceeding capitally against them, it is said that Pitt, who had studied the law, expressed some disapprobation of the notion of "constructive treason," but he did not like to rely upon the objection that the Duke of Richmond and himself had supported similar doctrines, and no doubt in his heart he believed that under the pretense of parliamentary reform deeper designs were now carried on. The Attorney and Solicitor General, being consulted by the Chancellor, gave an opinion that the imputed conspiracy to change the form of government was a compassing of the King's death within the meaning of the statute of Edward III.,— and the King himself, upon this opinion, was eager for the prosecutions. So in an evil hour an order was made that they should be instituted, and warrants were signed for the arrest of the supposed traitors.

The result is well known. To the credit of George III., when the whole subject was understood by him, he rejoiced in the acquittals, and, laying all the blame on the Chancellor, he said, "You have got us into the wrong box, my Lord, you have got us into the wrong box. Constructive treason won't do, my Lord, constructive treason won't do."

The long-pending trial of Warren Hastings at last approached its conclusion, under the presidency of Lord Loughborough, who, notwithstanding his belief in the truth of most of the charges, conducted himself with impartiality as well as dignity. The interest of the proceeding had greatly declined, and the public sympathy was all with with the accused. Mr. Burke, however, was still unrelenting, and, when the evidence and the speeches had closed, in the fervor of his zeal he wrote the following letter to the Chancellor,—overlooking the impropriety of a prosecutor privately seeking to influence a judge:—

"MY DEAR LORD,

"It would be shameful, after the long toil of both Houses, and the enormous expense of the public, that the trial of Indian peculation and oppression should have an unjust, or a lame and impotent, conclusion. Sequestered as I am from the public, I should be infinitely concerned that such a thing should fall out at any time, but particularly at a time when you presided in the House of Peers. I should be equally sorry to have my poor remains of life employed in justifying the last fourteen years of it by preparing a stable record of their proceeding in every part of Europe, necessarily concluding to the perpetual infamy of a body which, God knows, I wish to be held in perpetual honor, I mean the House of Lords. This affair, in my opinion, ought to be adjourned over until some person can be found to state the several prominent parts—namely, the leading facts, and then the criminal inferences, and lastly, the matters of aggravation or extenuation as they appear in the evidence. This thing cannot be left to the known partisans of the delinquent—amongst the most desperate of whom I must reckon (between ourselves) your clerk, Mr. Cowper. He is likely to make the worst *rapporteur* that can be found. We are preparing a syllabus, which will be printed for the use of such Lords as wish to know what case we would be thought to have made out. Excuse this trouble from one of your sincere well-wishers.

"I am ever, with the most sincere respect and regard,
"My dear Lord,'
"Your Lordship's most faithful and obliged humble serv^t,
"EDM. BURKE.

"Beaconsfield, Jan. 10, 1795."

I am not aware what answer was returned, but I presume it must have been a mild refusal to listen to the proposal, as the Chancellor was bound to take no part in the proceedings except judically.

During the long-continued discussions among the Peers themselves on the merits of the case, he was engaged in several sharp contests with Thurlow, who still eagerly advocated the cause of the defendant. When the verdict was to be given, the Chancellor said "Guilty" on all the sixteen charges except three; but of the Peers who voted—reduced by casualties since the commencement of the prosecution to twenty-nine—there being on every charge a large majority who said "Not Guilty," he had the task, which he performed very courteously, of announcing to Mr. Hastings that he was acquitted of the crimes and misdemeanors whereof he had been impeached.

He afterwards received the following very interesting letter from Mr. Burke, beginning with an allusion to the attack on the writer by the Duke of Bedford, which led to one of the finest effusions of genius,—and concluding with a bitter protest against the proposal, that all the expenses of the prosecution on both sides should be paid by the public:—

"MY DEAR LORD,

"I am, now the thing is over, to thank you for the handsome part you took in the first attack on me. It may appear odd, but the fact is that until the speech was sent to me, under a cover, by post that came in on Saturday, I had never seen an account of the kind things you were pleased to say of me. It will appear odd, but it is true, that I never read the attacks made on me by the D. of Bedford and Lord Lauderdale, but had them merely from a verbal, but I think a faithful and an exact, relator, who told me of them, and of Lord Grenville's defense of me. I trust I am not disposed to be ungrateful, and I should certainly have paid your Lordship the share of the compliment I owed you, if I had known how much I was indebted to you for what I have ever thought, and shall think, a great honor and consolation to me—your acknowledging your long-continued partial opinion of me. The newspapers, and all the matter they contain, have been long hateful to me. I pass months without looking into one of them, and I faithfully assure you, that until Clairfait's victories, I was a long time indeed without casting my eyes on a paper. I only knew what was going on by conversation, from which I could not disengage myself.

"The regard I set on your opinion will not permit me to let you imagine for a moment that I am insensible to the blow which is attempted at my reputation, and at a reputation of infinitely more moment than mine, Mr. Hastings is publicly rewarded for the crimes which your Lordship knows have been *proved* against him at the bar of the House of Lords. The House of Commons, for the first time that this infamy has happened to them, are condemned in costs and damages. It is the first time that any *public* prosecutor has been so condemned. Robbery so rewarded by new robbery. Oh no! It shall never be said, never, never, that the cause of the people of India, taken up for twenty years in Parliament, has been compromised by pensions to the accused and the accursed. The blood of that people shall not be on my head. The example of such a desertion of a cause, and prevarication in justice, is a dreadful example. I shall, I hope, by the end of the week, petition the House of Commons. Excuse this trouble. Your goodness to me entitles you to a communication of every material step I take in life. I confess I never expected this blow. As to the acquittal, that it was total I was surprised at—that it should be so in a good measure, I expected from the incredible corruption of the time.[1]

"I have the honor to be, with the most respectful affection,   "My dear Lord,
"Your most faithful and obliged humble servant,
"Beaconsfield, March 7, 1796."[2]   "EDM. BURKE.

[1] So earnest was Mr Burke on this subject that he likewise sent the following letter to the Duke of Portland.—

"My dear Lord,

"I little expected that, under an Administration in which your Grace had a part, the House of Commons should be condemned in damages to an immense amount to Mr. Hastings. We charged him with a robbery of the people of India—we reward him by a robbery of the same people. Your poor old friend does not choose to be actively or passively a party in this nefarious act of peculation; I therefore propose, as my dying act, and I should have no objection to perish in that act at the bar of the House of Commons, to petition against this robbery of India, and treachery to those employed to prosecute. I only think it right to give your Grace this notice. This poor scroll requires no answer.

"I have the honor to be, with the highest respect and affection,
"My dear Lord,
"Your Grace's most faithful and obedient humble servant,
[2] Rossl. MSS.   "EDM. BURKE."*

* Rossl MSS.

But, notwithstanding Burke's dying efforts, the resolution respecting costs, of which he complained so bitterly, remained unaltered; and he is now generally supposed to have displayed a want of sound judgment and good feeling in the whole course of that prosecution, on which he chiefly relied for a great reputation with posterity.

CHAPTER CLXXIII.

CONTINUATION OF THE LIFE OF LORD LOUGHBOROUGH TILL THE COMMENCEMENT OF THE INTRIGUES WHICH ENDED IN HIS RESIGNATION AND THE DISSOLUTION OF MR. PITT'S ADMINISTRATION.

MR HASTINGS'S acquittal was soon forgotten by the public amidst the stirring events of the war, which raged with such violence. There being an alarm of invasion, a proposal was made to arm the people in mass; but this was strongly opposed by the Chancellor, who contended that arms should never be permitted to any, except under the direction of men of property; and that the conduct of the " National Guard " in France should be a warning to us to intrust our defense exclusively to the King's regular army.[1]

The Opposition in the Upper House was now almost entirely confined to Lord Stanhope;—and, to silence him, the Lord Chancellor put his resolutions from the woolsack without reading them, and, when they were negatived, had them expunged from the Journals.[2]

The Whigs made a rally to support the Duke of Bedford's motion for peace with France; but the Chancellor said that " it was not fit to be put on the Journals;" and a counter-resolution, moved by Lord Grenville, for a vigorous prosecution of the war, was carried, by a majority of 88 to 15.

There was at this time a great coolness between Lord Loughborough and the Prince of Wales. His Royal Highness had been, for a short time, an "*alarmist*," but he ever hated Pitt, and he again associated familiarly with

[1] 31 Parl. Hist. 135.   [2] Ib. 149.

Fox and Sheridan,—regarding him who was to have been his Chancellor under the Regency as little better than an apostate—a character for which, till he actually was Regent, he expressed bitter contempt. The wary Scot was uneasy at this state of affairs; for there were from time to time symptoms indicating that the Regency question might be speedily renewed; and, at any rate, he disliked the notion of encountering the frowns of the Sovereign in a new reign. He was therefore anxious to soothe the Heir Apparent, and he thought he had an opportunity of doing so in supporting the bill for granting an annuity to his Royal Highness, and for preventing him from *assigning* or *charging* it. In this courtly strain did he answer certain objections of Thurlow, who had become a special favorite at Carlton House, and was by no means without hope of resuming the Great Seal:—

"The restrictions complained of by the noble and learned Lord, so far from being insulting to his Royal Highness, testify the profoundest respect for his feelings, as well as his dignity. The reason for the extraordinary circumspection complained of, is because a deeper interest is taken in the conduct of princes than of private individuals. If they out-run their fortune, their ruin is seen by the public with cold indifference; but all sympathize with the imprudence of a prince. He is constantly tempted to expense without habits of economy. Even s virtues here are against him. His taste, his love of the arts, his liberality, his munificence—all lead to expense. In fact, he is educated to expense in every possible shape, and is often reduced to the option of acting with imprudence and extravagance, or appearing mean and narrow-minded. The latter imputation the nation would never wish to see cast upon an English prince. They neither expect nor desire that he should count over pounds, shillings, and pence with the minuteness of a petty tradesman. The restrictions are intended not to wound the honor of the Prince of Wales, but to shield him in future from the perils to which men of his exalted rank are exposed. They are, properly speaking, restrictions not on his Royal Highness, but on those about him—to restrain the hand of extravagance, and to guard against profusion."

Lord Loughborough, finding that the Prince of Wales

was not in any degree appeased by this flattery, never afterwards attempted a reconciliation with him, but leaving him under the undisputed sway of Thurlow, during all the subsequent disputes which disturbed the Royal family, he in a very decided manner took the opposite side. Ever striving to gain the personal favor of George III., he openly enlisted himself in the band of the "King's friends"—which still subsisted, though much diminished in influence by the lofty ascendency of Pitt.

It is curious to observe, from the following note, the terms of distant civility on which he now was with the chief under whose banner he had some years gallantly fought:—

"Mr. Fox presents his compliments to the Lord Chancellor, and as a meeting of his constituents is to assemble to-morrow in Westminster Hall, for the purpose of petitioning Parliament, takes the liberty of submitting to his Lordship that it would be a great accommodation to the meeting, and a civility for which the gentlemen who mean to attend it would be much obliged to his Lordship, if the Court of Chancery could, without injury to public business or inconvenience to his Lordship, be adjourned at an early hour.

"South Street, 15th Nov. 1795."[1]

In fulfilment of a promise made to Lord Loughborough when he led over the "alarmists" to Mr. Pitt, he received a re-grant of his barony of Loughborough, with a remainder to his nephew, Sir James St. Clair Erskine. On this occasion, he had, for some reason that I am not aware of, consulted the Earl of Moira, and he received from him the following congratulation:—

"MY DEAR LORD,   "Donington, Oct. 7th, 1795.

'The letter with which you have honored me claims acknowledgments that, as I trust you will believe, are not merely matter of from. The delicacy of your hesitation respecting the extension of your present title, so very different from the fashionable tone of the day, is a particular and most kind compliment to me. You will feel that, esteeming it such, I could not repay it otherwise than by meeting it with entire frankness; so that you

---

[1] The inconvenience of such political meetings while the Courts were sitting was found to be so great, that afterwards an act was very properly passed forbidding the holding of them in the vicinity of Westminster Hall.

will give full trust to my answer. With the interest which I must take in the credit of the title of Loughborough, I should grieve that you transmitted any other to your family. The further destination of your honors is an event that in itself gives me unfeigned gratification. But I assure you I shall have additional satisfaction if the continuance of the title of Loughborough may be supposed to imply any reciprocation of regard between us. The respect which my uncle bore to you was inherited by me, and has never been shaken by any diversity of public opinion. I always flattered myself that I possessed your friendship. I feel it very sensibly in the present instance, and I only wish that my acquiescence, in a case where certainly you were perfect master to make the decision without reference to me, could have any pretension to being considered as a testimony of esteem.

"The matter shall not be mentioned by me. But in the mean time I beg you to accept my sincerest congratulations on a circumstance which must justly afford you peculiar pleasure.

"I have the honor to be, my dear Lord, with high esteem, your Lordship's very faithful and obedient servant,
"Lord Loughborough, &c. &c. &c."[1]   "MOIRA.'

[1] The following are letters written by the Duke of Portland to Lord Loughborough respecting the new grant of his peerage:
"Tuesday evening, 6th Oct. 1795.
"My dear Lord,—I have great pleasure in assuring you that I am not aware of any circumstance which should retard the manifestation of the King's sense of your services, and that I shall be very happy in receiving his commands to carry his intentions into effect. I did not receive your letter, (though dated on Friday) till yesterday. Had it reached me in its due course I must have disobeyed your orders, for I could not have deferred till Wednesday my thanks for your attention to my assurances of the part I take in an event which must so naturally and so justly contribute to your satisfaction. I am very sincerely,   "My dear Lord,
"Your most faithful and obedient, &c.   "PORTLAND."
"Oct. 14, 1795.
"My dear Lord,—After what you have heard from the King upon the subject of your patent, it would be very unnecessary to inform you of the very gracious manner in which he not only assented to but approved of the insertion of Mr. Erskine's name. ..... His wish was, that it should be made in the manner most agreeable to yourself. ......I was not at the levée, but I was for half an hour in the closet ; and have the satisfaction of informing you that I perceived little, if any, of that agitation which was so striking on this day se'nnight; and this opinion was fully confirmed by Lord Spencer.
"I am, &c.   "PORTLAND"
—*Rossl MSS.* There are many other letters from the Duke of Portland to Lord Loughborough from 1782 downwards, but, generally speaking, they are jejune, confused, and almost unintelligible.   [2] Rossl. MSS.

The Chancellor seldom spoke in the House of Lords, and the brilliant reputation he enjoyed as a debater in the House of Commons had much faded. Some imputed this change to a decline of mental or of physical energy, and others to the coolness between him and the Prime Minister. He took a prominent part, however, in the discussion upon the rupture of the negotiation at Paris, in the end of 1796, between Lord Malmesbury and the Directors of the French Republic. Most strenuously had he always resisted the proposals to treat with them. Like his friend, Lord Auckland, he said that "they ought to be put under the sword of the law," and he declared that it was indecent to send an ambassador to address them in the words of Antony to the assassins of Cæsar--

"Let each man render me his bloody hand."

He therefore greatly rejoiced that the country had escaped the perils of a "regicide peace,"—and an address to the Crown being moved on the occasion, he expressed much indignation against the Earl of Guilford's amendment, which threw blame upon the Ministers for the terms they had demanded, and prayed that his Majesty should make fresh overtures to the Republican Government. "Such an amendment," said "was never before proposed in an English parliament. Can any gloomy imagination suppose that it will be adopted? What effect would it produce in this country and thoughout Europe? The inference would be, that Great Britain is willing to submit to whatever conditions the enemy chooses to impose. It tends to humble the nation before the Executive Directory, and to call upon them to put their feet upon our prostrate necks." He then went over the circumstances of the negotiation, to show the bad faith of the French negotiators,—introduced some important statistics from the Court of Chancery to prove a decrease of bankruptcies,—and an increase of investments for the benefit of the suitors. and asked "whether, after the French had barred and double barred the door of negotiation against us, and our resources were still unexhausted, the House was prepared to send up this groveling amendment to the Throne, in preference to declaring, by the address orginally moved, that they would not submit to a faithless and arrogant enemy? The amendment was negatived by a majority of 86 to 8.[1]

It is curious to consider that at this time the advocate of the Government was very imperfectly acquainted with the real merits of his case. It appears, among other astounding disclosures in the lately published Memoirs of Lord Malmesbury, that all the Cabinet, except Pitt, Dundas and Lord Grenville, were kept in ignorance of that ambassador's most important despatches, and that he was obliged to write one set for the whole Cabinet, and another for the triumvirs. He adds, " The Chancellor, Lord Loughborough, walked home with me from Pitt's;—he not in the whole secret, and, as usual, questioning and apparently sanguine."

Soon afterwards, a crisis arose in which Lord Loughborough displayed the firmness and decision which in times of peril he always brought to the aid of the State. Mr. Pitt, having disregarded several previous warnings, was informed on a Saturday evening, that, from foreign subsidies and unfavorable mercantile operations, such was the low state of bullion and specie at the Bank of England, and so enormously had the market price of gold risen above the Mint price, that they could pay in cash no longer. On Sunday morning the King was sent for from Windsor, and a council was called, at which he presided. Mr. Pitt proposed an order by his Majesty in Council forbidding the Bank of England to make any farther payments in cash; but grave doubts were entertained how far such an order would be constitutional, as since the Revolution of 1688 there had been no instance of the Executive Government avowedly superseding Acts of Parliament and violating the law, unless where the subsistence of the people was concerned, as in prohibiting the exportation of corn or suspending the duty upon the importation of corn during the recess of Parliament,—whereas Parliament was now sitting, and the proposed order affected innumerable private contracts between man and man. Nevertheless the Chancellor, being appealed to, gave a clear opinion that for the safety of the state the Executive should, upon the responsibility of Ministers and in expectation of an indemnity, do any act which the Legislature, if it had the opportunity, would

[1] 32 Parl. Hist. 1505.

sanction; and that, as in this case, if the Executive Government did not interfere, the opinion of Parliament could not be taken till irremediable evils would be brought upon the nation, the Executive Government was bound to interfere,—so that the proposed order, although contrary to law, would be in accordance with the Constitution. The order was accordingly issued, and on Monday morning no payments were made in Threadneedle street except in bank notes, the directors quieting the public with a statement of their affluence and their readiness to continue all their dealings as usual,—substituting paper for gold. The same day a message from the King was brought down to both Houses, announcing what had been done, and calling for the advice of Parliament. Lord Loughborough's doctrine I hold to be sound, and he could not be answerable for the necessity which required the order, nor for its consequences. He was guilty of a little deception, however, when the matter came to be discussed in the House of Lords, in saying that "it had never entered the comtemplation of Ministers to substitute paper for gold by any forcible means, and that they had never thought it would be just or prudent to make bank notes a legal tender."[1] Bank notes were not technically made a legal tender, but if there had been a tender in bank notes, the person of the debtor was protected from legal process; and, till the resumption of cash payments in the year 1819, a paper currency was practically established in the country—by which joint operations hundreds of thousands of individuals were ruined, and hundreds of millions were added to the national debt.

Lord Lougborough deserves credit for the prudence he displayed during the alarming mutiny in the fleet. He found that the seamen had real grievances to complain of, and he strongly supported the policy of concession. When the bill for increasing their pay was pending in the House of Lords, and was likely to be obstructed by long speeches, he said boldly, "Those who would enter into discussion at the present moment partake of the criminality of the mutineers. I entreat your Lordships to consider that the delay occasioned by agitating topics which may as well be postponed to a future day, may put in peril the lives of the best and bravest men in the country

---

[1] 32 Parl. Hist. 1568.

This is like stopping when a conflagration is blazing, to inquire how it originated, instead of employing the engines to extinguish it. I ask a flag of truce for one night Let the bill be passed forthwith, and sent to Portsmouth, and the country may be saved." The bill was passed forthwith, *nemine dissentiente*.[1]

The Chancellor still highly disapproved of the manner in which the war was conducted, and from time to time wrote long letters to Mr. Dundas, who was considered the war minister, as to the inexpediency of surrendering Toulon, and neglecting all concert in acting with the allies whom we subsidized. One of these he concludes by observing, " The *desideratum* is a person who, like the Duke of Marlborough in the time of the Grand Alliance, could settle at the Hague, Berlin, and Vienna, and all the lesser Courts (having an inspection also over the negotiations with St. Petersburgh), the plan of a campaign. What substitute can be found for an agency of equal force, I certainly can not tell ; but without it I fear much our efforts will be very defective."[2]

The Duke of Bedford having moved an address to his Majesty, to dismiss his Ministers for misconduct, Lord Loughborough spoke, but did not attempt any general defense of Mr. Pitt's war policy. He confined himself to reprobating the measure of parliamentary reform, and particularly the disfranchisement of the rotten boroughs, which had been recommended as the means of reconciling the people to the Constitution. " The noble Duke's plan," said he, " is wilder than universal suffrage ; he would despoil corporations of their privileges, and assist the House of Commons in uncreating their creators; he would overwhelm freeholders by ' pot-boilers ;' he would cut up by the roots whatever belongs to franchise, property, or privilege, and introduce in its stead the principle of an agrarian law. The noble Duke says, ' the existing voters will not be injured by an extension of the franchise, because they will still be allowed to vote ;' but will he be contented to see hundreds of ' pot-boilers' called in to share his estate, if he is still allowed rations for the subsistence of himself and his family? I would advise the noble Duke to remember, that in France, those who were first in revolutionizing the country were the earliest vic-

[1] 33 Parl. Hist. 491.   [2] Rossl. MSS.

tims of the fatal doctrines which they propagated."[1] On this occasion the Opposition mustered 12 to 91.[2]

So greatly was the Chancellor elated by the prostrate condition of his opponents, that he treated them at times with contumely,—designating a motion of Lord Guilford as "the thing which he held in his hand, too contemptible to put ;" and lamenting a speech, in which the eccentric Earl Stanhope had called himself "Citizen Stanhope," as "an awful visitation of God."

However, he appeared to great advantage in returning thanks to the winner of the battle of Camperdown, whom he thus addressed :—

"Lord Viscount Duncan,—I am commanded by the Lords to give your Lordship the thanks of this House for your able and gallant conduct in the brilliant and decisive victory obtained over the Dutch fleet on the 11th day of October last; as well as for the zeal, courage, and perseverance which you have uniformly manifested during the arduous period in which you have commanded his Majesty's fleet in the North Sea.

"At the same time that this vote passed unanimously, their Lordships were pleased to order, that all the Peers should be summoned to attend the House on the occasion ; a distinction unprecedented, but called for by the general admiration your conduct has inspired, and strongly expressive of that peculiar satisfaction which the Peers must feel upon your Lordship's promotion to a distinguished seat in this House.

"Splendid in all its circumstances as the victory obtained by his Majesty's fleet under your command has been, important as it must prove in its consequences to the security of all his Majesty's dominions, under the Divine blessing, to the favorable issue of the arduous contest in which they are engaged ; the magnitude and luster of these considerations have not so occupied the observation of the Lords as to make them unmindful of the constant vigilance with which your Lordship had, in the whole course of your command for three successive seasons, watched and frustrated every design of the enemy, nor the manly

---

[1] 33 Parl. Hist. 764.
[2] If one hackney coach would not have contained all the Whig Peers at this time, an omnibus would have been quite sufficient.—Sée Mr. Byng's account of the House of Commons, ante, p. 138.

fortitude with which you had sustained the temporary defection of the greater part of your force; nor, above all, that undaunted resolution with which, at so momentous a crisis, you proceeded to check and to control the presumptuous hopes of the enemy.

"These are merits in which fortune can claim no share; they spring from that energy of mind and that ardent love of your country which have directed your own conduct, and animated the officers and men under your command, to those exertions which are entitled to every testimony of public gratitude and applause." [1]

In the spring of this year the Chancellor had a very serious illness, which caused much anxiety to his friends. Soon after his recovery he received the following letter from Mr. Burke, which has a melancholy interest, as the last which was written to him by this great man, who had been so long, by turns, his foe and his friend:—

"Bath, 1st May, 1797.

"MY DEAR LORD,

"Though not much concerned, nor likely to be long concerned, about anything on this side the grave, I felt a sincere pleasure on your Lordship's recovery; and do trust and hope, from the energy of your Lordship's character, that you will act your part in a total change of the plan of passive defense, so ruinous in point of charge, and not only so inefficient, but in every point of view so highly dangerous to all things except our enemies abroad and at home. I know it will require the greatest resolution and perseverance to make the necessary change in this unfortunate plan; but if it be not done you are all ruined, and all of us along with you. Pardon this friendly liberty at the time when others take so many liberties that are far from friendly. This, though infinitely of greater importance, is not the subject on which I wish just now to trouble your Lordship. It is relative to a little affair that I mentioned to you about five months ago, and which it is no wonder your serious illness and important occupations have put out of your head. I mean that of two worthy persons that are as nearly as possible at the point of dying from actual famine; the first is that character, not so respectable for his rank and family, which are amongst the

[1] 33 Parl. Hist. 978.

highest, as for perfect piety and unbounded charity, the Archbishop of Paris: the other is not inferior to him, in my humble opinion, in virtue and religion, nor in charity neither, according to his more limited means, which, to my knowledge, he particularly extended to distressed English residents at Amiens. The revenue of his bishopric was £2,400 sterling a year, of which he received but £400 to support himself and his dignity in the Church, and he contributed every penny of the rest in charity. He is now in Germany, in a state of the greatest indigence. His name is Machault, son of Machault formerly Minister of the Marine, and who, I believe, is now living in an extreme old age, and thoroughly pillaged by this glorious revolution. Now I ask nothing but that these two should be each put on such allowance as French bishops here receive, and that it should be a quarter antedated for their present necessities. If your Lordship will permit my friend Dr. King, whose hand supplies the infirmity of mine, to manage this affair, he will do it to your Lordship's and Mr. Pitt's satisfaction, and with all possible attention to the fallen dignity of the eminent persons to be relieved; and it is for this reason that I wish the affair to be managed by him only.

"You will not think a solicitation so worthy of humanity to be unworthy of you. God direct you at this arduous moment. Believe me, my dear Lord, with sincere respect and affection, your friend of thirty-five years' standing, and always your most obedient and obliged humble servant, "EDM. BURKE."[1]

Lord Loughborough immediately represented the cases to the Government, and in the meantime, with his usual liberality, ministered to the necessities of these meritorious individuals from his own funds.

In the year 1797 much of his time was occupied with the differences between the Prince and Princess of Wales; and he carried on a long negotiation on the subject with Lord Thurlow, Lord Cholmondeley, and Lord Moira. A sentence in a letter to him from the last-mentioned nobleman may convey a notion of the task imposed upon them; "I am persuaded the Princess is flattered with the prospect of living apart from the Prince, and having the free disposal of a large income.

[1] Rossl. MSS.

She thence, evidently to me, wishes to avoid reconciliation, if she can do it without betraying her view. The Prince, on his part, would give his right hand for a decent excuse to force matters to a separation. Judge of the toil of endeavoring to bring two persons together with such sentiments. It must be tried, however." I have before me a lengthened correspondence between the negotiators;[1] but the subject is not at all instructive, and its interest has passed away.

Lord Loughborough had about the same time a difficult negotiation to conduct between Prince Edward, about to be created Duke of Kent, and Mr. Pitt, who seems to have been disposed to treat him with great rigor in the formation of his establishment. His Royal Highness thus acknowledges the good offices of the Chancellor:—

"St. James's Street, 13th Feb. 1799.

"MY LORD,

"I had intended doing myself the pleasure of calling upon your Lordship this morning to thank you for the very friendly and polite manner in which you were so good as to speak of me to the Duke of Clarence, as also for the extreme readiness you showed in undertaking to speak to Mr. Pitt on some subjects relative to myself, which, I understand from my brother, he mentioned to you."

[His Royal Highness then enters very minutely into all his affairs, and thus very gracefully concludes:]

"Having now laid all these matters candidly before your Lordship in the manner I feel them, I have only to solicit the continuance of your good offices and friendship, so far as you may think I have a right to those comforts and indulgences which I am solicitous to obtain. I trust my conduct throughout life will never disgrace the good opinion you have so kindly formed of me, and that you will never have reason to repent having befriended him who has the honor to subscribe himself, with sentiments of the highest regard, "My Lord,

"Your Lordship's most devoted and
"obedient humble servant, "EDWARD."[2]

[1] Rossl. MSS.
[2] This letter and the others from his Royal Highness to Lord Loughborough are in the most beautiful handwriting I ever saw, bearing a striking resemblance to that of his illustrious daughter, who now fills the throne.

Our Lord Chancellor now received a distressing alarm by the announcement of a publication which was to treat of rather a tender subject—his coalition with Mr. Pitt. Dr. French Lawrence, to whom all Mr. Burke's papers were bequeathed, wrote to him to say he was about to print a letter from Mr. Burke to Lord Fitzwilliam, giving an account of the manner in which the "alarmists" had offered to support the Government, and of a dinner at Lord Loughborough's, in November, 1792, where they had assembled and laid down their plan of operations—inclosing a copy of the passages of the letter in which Lord Loughborough was mentioned, and asking if he had any objection to it. I have not found his remonstrance at full length, but the tenor of it may be gathered from the very interesting reply of Dr. Lawrence, which lies before me:—

"On the letter to Lord Fitzwilliam, of which I sent an extract, your Lordship has said much more than would have been sufficient to satisfy my mind. You and Mr. Anstruther, it seems, differ very essentially from Mr. Burke in your impression of the conversation that passed at your house. That was enough immediately to determine me against the publication of the letter. . . . Permit me, however, my dear Lord, to trespass a little on your patience with regard to the principles which on this occasion you have laid down. They interest me deeply. They relate to the conscientious discharge of the sacred trust which I have undertaken—not the care of Mr. Burke's reputation (he will leave to posterity to enjoy that most glorious inheritance)—but the task of holding out to imitation the purest example of all public virtue. Ill would that great end be promoted if I should do anything even of dubious morality. It has always been my endeavor, to the best of my abilities, such as God has given me, to understand my moral duties. I have meditated still more upon them since I became a public man, to the extent that I am such, and more so I do not wish to be in the present awful crisis of the country, in which, if even the grand impending danger should pass away, I see almost every symptom that has usually forerun the downfall of great states, under free constitutions. . . . In one sense, I accord with the rule which your Lordship has laid down, 'That nothing should be given to the public by representatives which it would have been improper for the person they represent to have committed to the press.' If it be meant *morally* improper, I see no exception to the rule. But there are a thousand little personal considerations of delicacy, and even of prudence, which naturally end with the life of the man. Your Lordship thinks it contrary to morality, that ' any letters should appear which relate to intimate and familiar conversations, where, in mutual confidence, the parties concerned express to each other their sentiments and opinions on men and things.' This, my dear Lord, is a nice question, as I view it, and on the very confines of opposite duties. If it were to be taken in the full latitude which you seem to give it, I am afraid it would go to the annihilation of all history worth reading. I have never seen or heard the morality of Atticus impeached for publishing the valuable series of Cicero's letters, which could only have come directly or indirectly from him, and which, there is reason to think, must have been published while many of the persons very freely mentioned in them were still alive. Posterity has uniformly applauded the act. Perhaps those letters, for real instruction, are worth all ancient history put together. On the other hand, if we were too literally, and without any limitation, to apply to all, what Mr. Burke, in one of his letters, nobly says of himself, ' that he had no secrets with regard to the public,' much mischief would undoubtedly ensue to private society. . . . Long and formal letters, in the nature of protests, containing deliberate opinions, or relating the substance of consultations, had among public men for the systematic guidance of their public conduct—it should seem to me, under the correction of your Lordship's better judgment, have nothing in their own nature which should make it improper to give them to the public, *if the situation of things to which they refer has actually passed away*. . . . . The letters of which Mr. Burke kept copies, and which he spared when he burned a great number of papers, I always understood him to have preserved as a sort of historical documents. . . . . . . Mr. Burke was of opinion, that nothing was done at the meeting in question, that is, nothing towards bringing any number of his and your friends to act together with decision on those good principles which they actually then all held in common. Your Lordship draws a different inference, and considers it as supported by the sequel. I confess, my dear Lord, that I have ever regarded the sequel as making for him. I have ever understood (you will be so good to forgive and instruct me better if I have been wrong) that your Lordship's principal motive for consenting to take office alone, after you had twice refused it, was the impossibility of finding any steady support in doing your duty to your country out of power. My approbation, I am sensible, is of little value; but on these grounds it is that I have ever approved your acceptance of the Seals, under all the circumstances of that day, as a virtuous and manly act."

Dr. Lawrence, having thus abandoned his preliminary publication, employed himself steadily in writing a regular "Life of Burke," in which he intended to have introduced the correspondence fit to be published of that illustrious statesman, orator and philosopher—but, to the unspeakable loss of English literature, his career was prematurely cut short before he had made much progress in this grand design.

In the ensuing year Lord Loughborough was involved in a very disagreeable controversy between the King and the Prince of Wales respecting the profits of the Duchy of Cornwall during his Royal Highness's minority;—the former contending that they belonged to him as guardian in chivalry, without account, or at any rate that he had a right to set off against them the expense of the heir's education and maintenance, which would be more than the amount demanded;—the latter, that he was entitled to the whole without deduction — his education and maintenance being provided for by the public. The following letters were written by the Prince to the Chancellor on this subject:—

"MY LORD,

"Your Lordship will excuse me for troubling you again upon the subject of the Petition of Right I presented to you on the 14th day of February, 1796. The petition not having been delivered to his Majesty, and your Lordship having expressed some doubts whether it fell within your Lordship's province to present Petitions of Right to his Majesty, I find myself under the necessity of requesting your Lordship to be so good as to come to a determination on the subject, and if it shall be finally your Lordship's opinion that such petitions ought not to be presented by the Lord Chancellor, that you will please to communicate that opinion to me, and to return me the petition, that I may be enabled to present it in such manner as shall appear most proper to those whom I must consult in the business.

"I am, my Lord,
"Very sincerely yours,
"GEORGE P.

"Critchill, April 19th, 1799"

"MY DEAR LORD,

"I have been this morning honored by a letter from the King, accompanied by one from your Lordship; the King refers me to you for intelligence respecting his pleasure upon the present occasion. I trust you will not however, give yourself the trouble of coming over here as I shall be in town again in a very few days, when I will make it my business to immediately apprise you, my good Lord, of my arrival.

"I am, with great truth,
"Very sincerely yours,
"GEORGE P.

"Harbledown, near Canterbury, August 30th, 1799."

"MY DEAR LORD,

"I am most extremely concerned that you should have had the trouble of traveling so far, and after all not to have found me at home. I hope you are well persuaded that, could I have expected you, I should have taken care to have been in the way. I have been dining at Sir Charles Grey's, and am only this instant returned, when I found your note, and I shall be most happy to receive you between ten and eleven to-morrow. This day's post carried a letter from me to you, acquainting you that had been honored by a letter from the King, and referring me to you for his intentions and pleasure in the present business, but at the same time I requested you not to hurry yourself, as I should be again in town in the course of a day or two, when I would instantly apprise you of my arrival.

"I am, my dear Lord, ever, with great truth,
"Very sincerely yours,
"GEORGE P.

"Harbledown, Friday night, 11 o'clock, P M., August 30th, 17"

"My dear Lord,

"I arrived late last night here, and am very desirous, now that I have paid my respects to their Majesties, to have half an hour's conversation with you. Will you do me the favor of calling upon me a little before two o'clock this day, or shall I call upon you? I assure you it is a matter of no choice to me; but if you are in the least apprehensive of the badness of the weather, I shall, with the greatest readiness and pleasure, wait upon you.

"I am, my dear Lord,
"Very sincerely yours, "GEORGE P.
"Weymouth, Sept. 17th, 1799,
half-past 12 P M." [1]

The controversy was never brought to a conclusion, and I am not aware that Lord Loughborough gave any opinion upon it beyond the wary saying recorded in the following extract of a letter to him from Lord Thurlow:—
"The Prince expressed himself much gratified with your Lordship's opinion of him, ' *That he could have no wish upon a question of law, but to know what the law is.*' " [2]

The Chancellor was likewise much occupied this year with negotiations in the royal family, arising out of the marriage of the Duke of Sussex with Lady Augusta Murray, and his papers contain an immense mass of correspondence on the subject. In justice to the Prince of Wales, of whom I can not always speak so favorably, I am bound to say that he behaved on this occasion with kindness and generosity. I copy one short letter, which is creditable to both brothers.

"Berlin, Sept. 16, 1799.
"MY DEAR PRINCE OF WALES,

"Having now fixed the day for Augusta's departure, I take the earliest opportunity to inform you of it. She will set out from here on the 19th of the month. I flatter myself, my dear Prince of Wales, you will protect us. Our child will be here to-morrow, and is to return back with Augusta. Being excessively unwell, I can not at present write a long letter. Wherefore I conclude with subscribing myself,

"My dear Prince of Wales,
"Your affectionate and grateful brother,
"AUGUSTUS FREDERICK."

[1] Rossl. MSS. [2] Ibid. [3] Ibid

I am now to relate an affair which reflects much honor on Lord Loughborough, and (I am grieved to say) very little on a learned body to which I belong. Sir James Mackintosh, struck with the defective state of legal education in England, and particularly with the gross ignorance displayed by his brethren at the Bar of the principles of general jurisprudence, proposed to give a course of lectures on "the Law of Nature and Nations," and asked the Benchers of Lincoln's Inn that he might have the use of their hall as a lecture-room. These venerable men, who had reached their present dignity without being required to do more than to eat a certain number of dinners in public, and whose principal occupation now was to order, for their own table, all the choice delicacies of the season, under the name of "exceedings,"[1] were greatly shocked by this proposed innovation, and, being almost all blindly furious Antijacobins, trembled at the idea of the minds of the rising generation being poisoned by the author of the "Vindiciæ Gallicæ." While they were deliberating, there appeared, as a *prospectus*, the Preliminary Discourse, of which Thomas Campbell truly and beautifully said, "If Mackintosh had published nothing else than this 'Discourse,' he would have left a perfect monument of his intellectual strength and symmetry; and even supposing that that essay had been recovered only imperfect and mutilated—if but a score of its consecutive sentences could be shown, they would bear a testimony to his genius as decided as the bust of Theseus bears to Grecian art among the Elgin marbles." But if the Benchers of Lincoln's Inn read it through, they remained untouched even by the concluding sentence: "To discover one new link of that eternal chain by which the Author of the universe has bound together the happiness and the duty of his creatures, and indissolubly

---

[1] At the Benchers' table there is supposed to be the same dinner as at the Students', and the same "commons" are actually put before them, but with the addition of any other dishes that any bencher may fancy. A lean student having complained to a fat old bencher of the starved condition of those who dined in the lower part of the hall, received this answer.—"I assure you, sir, we all fare alike: we have the same commons with yourselves." The student replying,—"I can only say, we see pass by us very savory dishes on their way to your table, of which we enjoy nothing but the smell,"—"Oh!" exclaimed the bencher, "I suppose you mean the '*exceedings*,' but of these the law takes no cognizance."

fastened their interests to each other, would fill my heart with more pleasure than all the fame with which the most ingenious paradox ever crowned the most ingenious sophist." The use of Lincoln's Inn Hall as the place where the eternal chain, with its new link, might be exhibited, was still refused.[1]

Lord Loughborough, ashamed of his order, deemed it his duty to interfere. He had no direct jurisdiction on the subject, but as head of the law, and himself a member of the Society, he thought that his advice would be listened to. In a letter circulated among the benchers, after highly praising the "Preliminary Discourse," he said, "A lecture in the spirit of that Discourse would at all times be of great utility and of much ornament to our profession. In times like the present, it is capable of rendering great service to the cause of religion, morality, and civil policy." He then went on, in soothing and respectful terms, to express a hope that the resolution against the author, which had probably been adopted without a due knowledge of his intention, might be reconsidered.[2]

This appeal was successful; and the lectures being given, it was hoped that the name of Mackintosh would be connected with a new æra in the history of juridical study in England. "The novelty of the undertaking, the acknowledged abilities of the author, and his early fame acquired by the powerful support of opinions which it was known that the course of public events had induced him to modify, threw an interest over the execution of the design, that daily filled Lincoln's Inn Hall with an auditory such as never before was seen on a similar occasion. All classes were there represented;—lawyers, members of Parliament, men of letters, and country gentlemen, crowded to hear him."[3]

[1] An eminent King's counsel being asked "whether he did not admire Mackintosh's character of Grotius?"—certainly one of the finest pieces of composition in our language,—answered by another question, "Who was Grotius?"

[2] Mr. Pitt, always liberally inclined, at the same time wrote a private letter to Mackintosh, in which he said,—"I can not refuse myself the satisfaction of assuring you, that the plan you have marked out appears to me to promise more useful instruction and just reasoning on the principles of government than I have ever met with in any treatise on that subject."

[3] Life of Mackintosh, by his Son, vol. 1. 107. Mackintosh delivered two courses of lectures; but when he withdrew, the plan of reforming legal education was abandoned, and "we still have the sea to drink."

Lord Loughborough expressed deep regret that the discharge of his numerous public duties did not permit him to be of the number of the listeners, but he had full accounts brought to him of the lectures, and he was loud in their praise.

Although the Chancellor had been some time accustomed to mix little in the debates in the House of Lords, when the income tax was brought forward with a view to raise a large portion of the supplies within the year, he made a speech in support of it,—chiefly remarkable for showing with what admiration Mr. Pitt's delusive scheme for paying off the national debt was still regarded. "It ought to be recollected," said he, "that the present Chancellor of the Exchequer, who has proposed this bill, is the very person who proposed and effectually supported the plan of annually setting aside a portion of the supplies to be applied in reduction of the national debt—a plan from which advantages so important have been derived, that the country can never forget the gratitude it owes to the man whose genius prompted him to carry into execution a design so noble and so useful."[1] Lord Grenville cheered these sentiments,—but he afterwards demonstrated that the national debt was much greater, and much less likely to be redeemed, than if the sinking fund had never been established.

CHAPTER CLXXIV.

CONTINUATION OF THE LIFE OF LORD LOUGHBOROUGH TILL HE RESIGNED THE GREAT SEAL.

NOTWITHSTANDING a display of outward courtesy, there was less and less cordiality between the Chancellor and the Prime Minister. Loughborough, a great observer of public decorum, would not, like his predecessor, leave the woolsack to speak against a Government bill; but, feeling that the confidence to which he thought himself entitled was withdrawn from him, he generally satisfied himself with putting the question as Speaker, and on a division saying to the

[1] 34 Parl. Hist. 207.

tellers,— content" or "not content,"[1] never giving an opposition vote. By degrees he began privately to speculate—not upon a change of the Administration, but of its Chief. The Whig Opposition had been nearly annihilated, and Mr. Pitt had overwhelming majorities in both Houses to support whatever measures he brought forward, and to protect him from censure, whatever faults he might commit. But his situation had become very embarrassing. Elated with the success which had attended the arms of the Allies on the Continent while Napoleon was absent in Egypt and Syria, he had refused to treat with him when the successful General had become First Consul—insolently telling him to abdicate his power and to restore the Bourbons. Not long after, he received intelligence of the battle of Marengo,—and, as in the last scene of a tragedy, messenger after messenger announced some new calamity, till at last the great Powers of Europe having succumbed, England had no Allies except three feeble States, which required her aid, instead of adding to her means of resistance,—Naples, Portugal and the Ottoman Porte. Pitt's proud spirit could not brook the notion of proposing humiliating terms of peace to him whom he had insulted; yet he himself was conscious, and those about him began to whisper, that an attempt at accommodation was necessary, and that the nation could only be induced vigorously to carry on the war by finding that peace was unattainable.

The situation of Ireland gave fresh anxiety to the Minister, particularly from his knowledge that the true cure for the evils of that country was most odious to the prejudiced and obstinate King. A dangerous rebellion followed the sudden recall of Lord Fitzwilliam, and the disappointment of the hopes which he had excited. When this had been suppressed, all wise men saw that some new system for governing Ireland must be adopted, or that the empire must be dismembered. Two independent co-ordinate parliaments, upon the footing established in 1782, could not go on long without a fatal collision ; and the Catholic body in Ireland, comprehending about seven-eights of the population, and growing daily in wealth

[1] According to the usages of the Lords, the "contents" always go below the bar, the non-contents remaining in the body of the House; but the Lord Chancellor is allowed to announce his vote sitting on the woolsack.

and intelligence, could not quietly submit to the penalties and disabilities by which they were aggrieved and degraded. Under these circumstances Mr. Pitt formed the splendid project of a Legislative Union between the two islands, and of forcing the King to consent to Catholic emancipation, by producing a state of things in in which a constitutional sovereign would find it necessary to sacrifice his individual wishes, and to adopt the wholesome advice of his Ministers. Happy would it have been for us if this great man had fully succeeded in his intentions!

After many difficulties the Irish Union was carried; but all the corruption resorted to would have been unavailing, if there had not been a distinct intimation to the Catholics, that—although they must be excluded from all political privileges while Ireland remained a separate kingdom—under a united Legislature they safely might be, and they certainly should be, treated in all respects on an equal footing with their Protestant fellow-subjects. Mr. Adolphus, well informed as to what was passing at Court during this period, says (and I believe him) that " the assurance was given to the Irish Catholics without the King's privity, and with a full knowledge of his sentiments upon the subject, in the hope that his Majesty, after the Union had taken place, seeing that Catholic emancipation was indispensable, would agree, however reluctantly, to that measure."[1] Lord Grenville, Lord Spencer and Mr. Dundas[2] were in the secret; but Lord Loughborough (I presume from being notoriously a " King's friend ") was not informed of the liberal policy by which the Union was to be followed up and made effectual;—and the apprehension that he might betray them increased the estrangement between him and the more influential section of the Cabinet.

All went on with apparent smoothness till the Union had been carried,—so far the King and all his Ministers

[1] Hist. vol. vi.
[2] This gentleman was particularly blamed for the part he took, being so well acquainted with the King's private sentiments. In a conversation some time previously, the King having stated the coronation oath as an insuperable objection to any further concession to the Catholics, Harry had tried to argue the King into the belief that this was binding upon him in his executive, not in his legislative capacity, but his Majesty cut him short by exclaiming, ' No Scotch metaphysics, Mr. Dundas, none of your Scotch metaphysics!"

concurring. When the bill was in the House of Lords, Lord Loughborough heartily lent his aid in defending it. The clause allowing Irish peers to sit in the House of Commons, on renouncing the privileges of the peerage, being strongly censured by Lord Mulgrave as derogatory to the dignity of their order, he said,—

"I am a good deal surprised at what has fallen from the noble Lord, whose whole discourse seemed better suited to an assembly of French or German *noblesse* than to a British House of Peers. Did any of your Lordships ever estimate so highly your nobility of blood as to think it vitiated by your mixing as legislators with the gentry of England? The noble says, 'it would be degrading to see an Irish peer of the first rank come to your bar decorated with ribbons, while the youngest English baron may be sitting among your Lordships.' It has fallen to my lot, when junior baron of this House, to walk down to the bar to receive messages from the Commons delivered by the eldest son of the premier Duke of England, and by Irish peers of higher rank than myself—and I never felt any embarrassment in such encounters. Why may not Irish peers sit in the House of Commons after the Union as they have hitherto done,—finding themselves by the side of the eldest sons of the highest English nobility, and training themselves in a popular assembly, to be useful here if they should be chosen representative peers, or if they should be added to the peerage of the United Kingdom?"[1]

The Bill at last received the royal assent; and the King, at the conclusion of the session (probably not being aware of the full import of the speech made for him), was induced to say, "This great measure, on which my wishes have been long earnestly bent, I shall ever consider as the happiest event of my reign, *being persuaded that nothing could so effectually contribute to extend to my Irish subjects the full participation of the blessings derived from the British Constitution.*"[2]

On the 1st of January, 1801, the day on which the Incorporate Union between Great Britain and Ireland took effect, Lord Loughborough attended at a Grand Council held at St. James's, bearing the seal that for some purposes had become the seal of the whole United Kingdom.

[1] 35 Parl. Hist. 160. [2] Ibid. 494.

The ceremony of his resigning it and receiving it back was considered unnecessary; but the Heir Apparent, the Dukes of York, Clarence, and Kent, all the King's Ministers, and the most eminent dignitaries of the Church and Law attending, they were sworn in as Imperial Privy Councillors, and orders were issued for making the necessary alterations in the style of the Sovereign, the national arms,¹ and the Book of Common Prayer.

A great crisis was at hand. Mr. Pitt's Administration, which had lasted near twenty years, and seemed stronger than ever, was speedily to be dissolved. From the new materials with which I have been furnished, I am enabled to give a much fuller and more authentic statement of the circumstances which led to this event, than has yet been laid before the public.

How far the suspicion is well founded, that Mr. Pitt was desirous of a plausible pretext for surrendering office, so that another Minister might conclude a peace with France, must for ever remain a mystery. His conduct has, in some degree, the aspect of his having been actuated by such a motive: he probably felt deeply that without an interval of repose, the contest could not be carried on, and that there were peculiar difficulties in his way, were *he* now to attempt to open a negotiation with the First Consul. But if he did precipitate his resignation with such a view, I believe that he never explained his plan to any human being, and that he hardly owned it to himself. According to all the most private and confidential documents which I have seen, connected with the subject, he was proceeding earnestly and sincerely to emancipate the Irish Roman Catholics,—when, against his will, he quarreled with the King, and was dismissed from office. This result was mainly brought about by the intrigues of Lord Loughborough.

To lay open these properly, I must go back to the year

---

¹ Lord Loughborough was much abused for the order by which the lillies were struck out of the King's shield, and he ceased to be called "King of France." We now read with amazement of the keen objections made to the dropping of these fooleries. George III. was "rightful and lawful King of these realms," by Act of Parliament and the will of the nation, but he would have found it difficult to make himself out heir to Edward III., even supposing that King to have had a title (which he had not) to the French Crown. There was no loss of dignity in voluntarily waiving what might justly be offensive to our neighbors.

1795, when Earl Fitzwilliam was sent as Lord Lieutenant to Ireland, and a bill was proposed in the Irish Parliament to relieve Roman Catholics from their civil disabilities. The King entertaining conscientious doubts how far his consent to such a measure would be consistent with his coronation oath, consulted Lord Kenyon and Sir John Scott, the Attorney General, upon the point, and they then advised him that this oath was not binding upon him so as to prevent him from consenting, in his legislative capacity, to a relaxation of penal laws in favor of any class of his subjects; but Lord Loughborough, by whom it was not supposed that such scruples could have been countenanced (for the purpose, I fear, of gaining favor with the King by flattering his prejudices), wrote him the following paper, which, in the handwriting of George III., is thus entitled:—

"Thoughts on the Emancipation of the Roman Catholics of Ireland, and Dangers arising from granting them.
March 5th, 1795."

"As[1] the object petitioned for by the Roman Catholics of Ireland is the total abolition of all distinctions in religion, it requires consideration how far that object could be effected consistently with the Constitution.

"The only laws which now affect Papists in Ireland, are the Acts of Supremacy and Uniformity, the Test Act, and the Bill of Rights. The question deserves serious investigation how far the King can give his assent to a repeal of any one of these Acts without a breach of his Coronation Oath, and the Articles of Union with Scotland. The construction put upon the Coronation Oath by Parliament at the Revolution, seems strongly marked in the Journals of the House of Commons. A clause was proposed by way of rider to the bill establishing the Coronation Oath, declaring that nothing contained in it should be construed to bind down the King and Queen, their heirs and successors, not to give the royal assent to any bill for qualifying the Act of Uniformity, so far as to render it palatable to Protestant Dissenters; and the clause was negatived upon a division. This leads to the implication that the Coronation Oath was understood at the Revolution to bind the Crown not to assent to a repeal of any of the existing laws at the Revolution, or which were then enacted for

[1] The rest is in the handwriting of Lord Loughborough himself,

the maintenance and defense of the Protestant religion as by law established.[1] If the oath was understood to bind the Crown not to assent to a repeal of the Act of Uniformity in favor of Protestant Dissenters, it would seem to bind the Crown full as strongly not to assent to the repeal of the Act of Supremacy, or the Test Act, in favor of Papists. Another question arises by the provisions of the Act limiting the succession to the Crown, by which a forfeiture of the Crown is expressly enacted, if the King upon the throne should hold communion with, or be reconciled to, the Church of Rome. May or may not a repeal of the Act of Supremacy, and the establishing the Popish religion in any of the hereditary dominions, be invidiously construed as amounting to a reconciliation with the Church of Rome? The Chancellor of England would, perhaps, incur some risk in affixing the English Seal to a bill for giving the Pope a concurrent ecclesiastical jurisdiction with the King.

"It is likewise apprehended, that by the Articles of Union with Scotland it is declared to be an essential and fundamental article that the King of Great Britain shall maintain the Church of England as by law established, in England, Ireland, and Berwick upon Tweed.

"The bargain made by Ireland in 1782 by Yelverton's Act should be referred to, and the question will occur, whether a repeal of any of the English statutes adopted by this Act in this country would not be a direct violation of the compact then made by the Parliament of Ireland with Great-Britain.

"These queries are humbly submitted with a view only to a due investigation of so important a measure.

"March, 1795."

George III., fortified by such authority, drew up the following observations, which he sent to Mr. Pitt:—

"Having yesterday, after the drawing-room, seen the Duke of Portland, who mentioned the receipt of letters from the Lord Lieutenant of Ireland, which to my greatest astonishment propose the total change of the principles of government which have been followed by every Administration in that kingdom since the abdication of

---

[1] The clause may have been very properly rejected as unnecessary, and raising a doubt as to the power of the Crown to give the royal assent to other acts in *pari materia*.

King James II., and consequently overturning the fabric that the wisdom of our forefathers esteemed necessary, and which the laws of this country have directed ; and this after no longer stay than three weeks in Ireland, venturing to condemn the labors of ages ; and wants an immediate adoption of ideas[1] that every man of property in Ireland, and every friend to the Protestant religion, must feel diametrically contrary to those he has imbibed from his earliest youth.

" Undoubtedly the D. of Portland made this communication to sound my sentiments previous to the Cabinet meeting to be held to-morrow on this weighty subject. I expressed my surprise at the idea of admitting the Roman Catholics to vote in Parliament; but I chose to avoid entering further into the subject, and only heard the substance of the propositions, without giving my sentiments. But the more I reflect on this subject, the more I feel the danger of the proposition, and therefore should not think myself free from blame if I did not put my thoughts on paper, even in the present coarse shape, the moment being so pressing, and not sufficient time to arrange them in a more digested state previous to the D. of Portland's laying the subject before the Cabinet.

" The above proposal is contrary to the conduct of every European Government, and, I believe, to that of every State on the globe. In the States, the Lutheran, Calvinist, and Roman Catholic religions are universally permitted, yet each respective state has but one church establishment, to which the states of the country and those holding any civil employment must be conformists ; court offices and military commissions may be held also by persons of either of the other persuasions, but the number of such is very small. The Dutch provinces admit Lutherans and Roman Catholics in some subsidized regiments ; but in civil employments the Calvinists are alone capable of holding them.

" Ireland varies from most other countries by property residing almost entirely in the hands of the Protestants, while the lower classes of the people are chiefly Roman Catholics ; the change proposed, therefore, must disoblige the greater number to benefit a few,—the inferior orders not being of rank to gain favorably by the change. That

[1] Sic.

they may also be gainers, it is proposed that an army be kept constantly in Ireland, and a kind of yeomanry, which in reality would be Roman Catholic police corps, established, which would keep the Protestant interest under awe.

"It is but fair to confess that the whole of this plan is the strongest justification of the old servants of the Crown in Ireland for having objected to the former indulgences that have been granted, as it is now pretended those have availed nothing, unless this total change of political principles be admitted.

"English Government ought well to consider before it gives any encouragement to a proposition which can not fail, sooner or later, to separate the two kingdoms, or, by way of establishing a similar line of conduct in this kingdom, adopt measures to prevent which my family was invited to mount the throne of this kingdom in preference to the House of Savoy.

"One might suppose the authors of this scheme had not viewed the tendency or extent of the question, but are actuated alone by the feverish inclination of humiliating the old friends of English government in Ireland, or from the desire of paying implicit obedience to the heated imagination of Mr. Burke.

"Besides the discontent and charges which must be occasioned by the dereliction of all the principles that have been held as wise by our ancestors, it is impossible to foresee how far it may alienate the minds of this kingdom; for, though I fear religion is but little attended to by persons of rank, and that the word *toleration*, or rather *indifference* to that sacred subject, has been too much admitted by them, yet the bulk of the nation has not been spoiled by foreign travels and manners, and still feels the blessing of having a fixed principle from whence the source of every tie to society and government must trace its origin.

"I can not conclude without expressing that the subject is beyond the decision of any Cabinet of Ministers—that, could they form an opinion in favor of such a measure, it would be highly dangerous without previous [word illegible] with the leading men of every order in the state, to send any encouragement to the Lord Lieutenant on this subject; and if received with the same suspicion I do, I am certain it would be safer even to change the new Administration in Ireland, if its continuance depends on the success of this proposal, than to prolong its existence on grounds that must sooner or later ruin one if not both kingdoms." [1]

'Mr. Pitt yielded,—Earl Fitzwilliam was recalled, and the Irish rebellion in due time followed. But the King believed he had done his duty, and considered Lord Loughborough's reasoning as a sufficient justification for his following the same course in all time to come.

The Catholic question was not again mentioned till after the Irish Union—with the exception of the assurances given privately by Mr. Pitt to the Irish Catholics, that if this measure were carried, their relief could not be longer withheld.

I must now shift the scene to Weymouth, where, in the autumn of the year 1800, the Chancellor was in attendance upon the King. Till the end of September they were both kept in ignorance that any measure was in contemplation respecting the civil disabilities of any class of religionists in the empire,—the deliberations, in which all the members of the Cabinet participated, being confined to the suppression of riots at home on account of the high price of provisions, and to the negotiation of a naval armistice which had been proposed by the Government of France. The two following letters on these subjects were written by Mr. Pitt to Lord Loughborough from Downing Street:—

("Private.") "Sept. 5th, [1800]"

" MY DEAR LORD,

"The King will undoubtedly communicate to you the papers which Lord Grenville is now dispatching, which contain a reply from Otto to our note on the proposal

---

[1] There is a copy of this paper in the Rossl MSS, with the following memorandum upon it in the handwriting of George III.:—" Paper drawn up on the Earl Fitzwilliam pressing a further emancipation of the Irish Papists, and transmitted to Mr Pitt; who, having approved of it then, ought not on the 31st of January to have made a similar proposal, and seemed surprised I would not follow him in changing my opinion. His ground of *expediency* certainly was futile, and the more, as every Irish Protestant felt the ruin of the measure if adopted. And I, certainly feeling the duty I owe to my coronation oath, could not have given my assent to any bill that had but the shadow of putting Papists and Presbyterians in a state of equality with the Church of England.

" 12th April, 1801." " GEORGE R."

for an armistice, and the French *projet* for that purpose, as well as the *contre-projet* which we have thought it right to propose as fit to be adopted. The question is certainly a delicate one, as any naval armistice is now, and the benefits (as far as they go) are all on the side of France. But the absolute refusal of such a measure would, as I conceive, clearly produce the immediate renewal of hostilities between France and Austria, and probably drive the latter, after some fresh disaster, or from the apprehension of it, to an immediate separate peace on the worst terms. We should thereby not only lose the benefit of a joint negotiation (at which we have so long been aiming), but should also give up the present opportunity of negotiating for ourselves in a manner much more creditable and satisfactory than would result from any direct and separate overture which might make at a later period. On the other hand, if the joint negotiation is admitted, its natural course may probably carry us to such a period of the year that it must either terinate in a treaty on terms satisfactory to us and Austria, or be broken off when the season will no longer admit of the French army making any decisive progress in Germany, and when Austria will consequently have the interval till the spring for an additional preparation. In addition to these considerations, it seems to me to be of the *utmost* importance, with the men to support both in Parliament and the country, that we should not reject the proposal in any manner which enemies either abroad or at home may make use of against us. For these reasons I am strongly convinced that it is right to show a readiness to agree to the armistice, with such modifications as may prevent the principal mischief to be apprepended from it, and as are in fact conformable to the model (of the armistice with Austria) which France professes to follow, though the substance of their *projet* widely departs from it. In the shape which we have given to the measure, France will be put, in the essential point of supply of naval stores for her ports, on the same footing (as nearly as the measure of the thing will admit) which she prescribed for the Austrian fortresses blockaded. She will also be restrained from making during the armistice any new disposition of her naval force; and our allies, particularly Portugal, will be secure from annoyance

The season of the year itself (independent of the articles of the convention, as we propose them, and of the right of search which we retain) will render it impossible for them to procure any material supply of naval stores before the end of the year, and will therefore prevent their deriving that advantage which we should have most to apprehend. On the whole, I am persuaded that the inconvenience of the armistice, thus modified, would be much less than that of Austria being driven at the moment either to separate peace or the renewal of hostilities; and that if the modifications are rejected by France, we shall at least have shown that we have done all that in fairness was possible towards general peace, shall stand completely justified to Austria, and shall carry the opinion and spirit of our own country with us in any measures which the continuance of the war on this ground (if such should be the result) may require. I wish W. could have had time to have given notice to yourself and such of our colleagues as are at a distance; but the business has pressed so much to a day as to make it impossible. It will give me great satisfaction if the grounds on which we have acted meet your concurrence. I imagine it will not be long before you return to the neighborhood of town. If the negotiation takes place, we shall very soon have to settle the instructions for Mr. Grenville. The issue of our transactions with Denmark is very satisfactory and opportune. It may perhaps render the tone of M. Talleyrand less offensive than it is in his last note, and may even incline the Consul to close with our proposal; though on the whole I rather expect that our negotiation will be broken off, and that all we can do is to stand ourselves on good ground.

"Ever, my dear Lord,
"Sincerely yours,
"W. PITT.

"A full power will probably be necessary for concluding the Convention, which Lord Grenville, I believe, will prepare and send to-morrow."

"Sept. 16th, [1800].

"MY DEAR LORD,

"In consequence of the tumultuous proceedings in so many parts of the kingdom, on account of the price of corn, it has occurred to myself, and to as many of our colleagues as are in town, to be very desirable to take some public step on the part of Government, which may at least show that its attention is drawn to the subject, and may possibly have a good effect in pointing out to the magistrates the line of conduct which ought to be pursued. The tendency to riot which appeared yesterday in London (though suppressed without difficulty) seems to furnish an additional reason for such a measure. On these grounds we have thought it right to prepare the draft of a proclamation, to be submitted to his Majesty; and if you concur with us in the general opinion, you will, I hope, have the goodness to make such corrections as you think proper in the draft. Mr. Faukener leaves town to-day, and will reach Weymouth in the course of to-morrow or very early on Friday, for the purpose of attending as Clerk of the Council. I imagine you will find no difficulty in procuring the attendance of a sufficient number of Privy Councillors, and it will probably be most convenient to take the opportunity of fixing the prorogation of Parliament to any day which may be thought proper. Probably the middle of November would be as natural a time as any other, though I hope there will be no occasion for really meeting before the commencement of the Union. It seems doubtful whether there is any necessity for prolonging the period for the free importation of grain, as the prices will, of course, keep the ports open for some time. But it may, perhaps, be as well to pass an order for this purpose, receiving the King's permission to make use of it or not, as shall be found expedient.

"After writing thus far I have seen the Duke of Portland, who, I find, means to go himself to Weymouth to attend the Council, which makes it hardly necessary for me to give you the trouble of reading this letter. We shall probably, in the course of the evening, be enabled to send you the answer which has, we know, reached Otto, and probably by this time is transmitted to Lord Grenville.

"Ever, my dear Lord,
"Yours sincerely,
"W. PITT."

The proposed measure was highly disagreeable to the King, who abhorred the idea of entering into any terms with the French regicides; but Lord Loughborough seems with sincerity to have tried to soothe his indignation, and wrote the following letter upon the subject to the War Minister :—

("Private").   "Weymouth, Wednesday, September 17th, 1800

"DEAR DUNDAS,

"You could not have been more surprised than I was with the first communication of a project for a naval armistice. The royal mail had brought a dispatch in the morning, with which the King seemed very much satisfied. He gave it to me upon his landing at Portland Island, and, as Windham and I rode with him, told us that it contained the French project for a naval armistice, which appeared, by Lord Grenville's letter, to be thought *totally inadmissible*. There was no opportunity of reading the dispatch in the course of the morning, but I had run my eye over it very hastily when the carriages were at the door after dinner, and told Windham that the latter did not seem quite so strong as H. M. had taken it to be. Upon our return to the Lodge, we learned that a messenger had arrived: the King called us in, and made me read the dispatch, with which he was very much agitated. The letter did not contain much reasoning upon the subject; but stated the unanimous opinion of those present to transmit the counter-project on our part. It seemed to me, at that moment, that a discussion of the measure itself was useless, and that nothing remained but to fix the limits of concession, that it should go no further. The King's answer was to that effect. When I got home I found a letter from Mr. Pitt, which I ought to have received before I had seen the King, as it contained a much better justification of the measure than Ld. G.'s letter, and made a strong impression not only on my mind, but on Windham's. The consideration which I felt the most strongly was, the influence of the measure at home. There are many men, certainly, who may feel it to be a dangerous concession to admit the possibility of a naval armistice, but among those of that opinion you will find a very considerable proportion who are disinclined to all continental engagements. With only such support it would be a very difficult task to maintain the contest in which we are engaged. Another class of men, from whom no good is ever to be derived, consists of those who, from weakness or malevolence, cry out for peace. To guard against the mischief they may do, it is necessary to risk, to a certain degree, the danger of concession in any approach to negotiation. We have hitherto gained by an appearance of a disposition to treat, and I have great faith in Mr. Pitt's knowledge and judgment of the public mind. For the rest, I concur in a very great degree with your reasoning, except that I do not think it quite so easy to detach ourselves entirely from Austria especially at a moment when, after great efforts, that power is suffering under the adverse fortune of war.

"The King is very much pleased with your dissent, and I showed him your letter to me. It is not impossible that I might have joined in that dissent at Cheltenham; but at Weymouth it was a very different case. After all, however, I have a strong confidence that the answer from Paris will leave no difference of opinion among us, though I feel a little uneasy at the delay, which seems to indicate some hesitation on the part of the Consul, whether to accept or reject our proposal.

"*Thursday*, 18th.—I could not finish my letter yesterday in time for the messenger, and the mail of this morning has made the greater part of it unnecessary. I should hardly have troubled you with it if the King, who is perfectly satisfied with the present state of things, had not directed me to tell you that he agrees entirely with the reasoning of your letter to me,'and that he thinks you had not seen his short note in answer to L⁴. G.'s dispatch on the counter-project. The answer of this day alludes to it. We are now, fortunately, restored to our proper situation, and Otto's note affords a complete justification of our refusal to yield what the enemy acknowledges would have given them the means of retrieving their own losses, and restoring their naval power.

"I must close here for the present, lest I lose the messenger again, who will set off immediately after the council. I have not yet had any conversation with the ·D. of Portland, who is arrived, and waits for me.

"I ever am, dear Dundas, yours most entirely,
"LOUGHBOROUGH." [1]

The terms required by the French being wholly inadmissible, the negotiation for the proposed armistice was

[1] Melville MSS.

at an end, to the mutual satisfaction of the King and his Ministers; and it seemed as if no other subject of difference was likely to arise between them. But Mr. Pitt, who, in concert with Lord Grenville, Mr. Dundas, and Lord Castlereagh, had been laying a plan for the emancipation of the Irish Catholics,—intending that the King should not be made aware of it till it was matured,—on the 25th of September he wrote the following letter to Lord Loughborough:

(" Private).

" MY DEAR LORD

" There are two or three very important questions relative to Ireland, on which it is very material that Lord Castlereagh should be furnished with at least the outline of the sentiments of the Cabinet. As he is desirous not to delay his return much longer, we have fixed next Tuesday for the Cabinet on this subject: and, though I am very sorry to propose anything to shorten your stay at Weymouth, I cannot help being very anxious that we should have the benefit of your presence. The chief points besides the great question on the general state of the Catholics, relate to some arrangement about tithes, and a provision for the Catholics and Dissenting Clergy. Lord Castlereagh has drawn up several papers on this subject and which are at present in Lord Grenville's posession and which you will probably receive from him by the post

" Ever, my dear Lord, yours very sincerely,

" W. PITT."

I am much afraid that Lord Loughborough behaved disingenuously on the receipt of this letter. Sincerely believing that Mr. Pitt was ill qualified for conducting the contest with France, he might patriotically wish that another minister should be substituted for him,[2] but nothing can justify the arts to which he seems to have had recourse for effecting this object. It has been said that, as soon as he gained information of Mr. Pitt's intentions respecting the Roman Catholics, he treacherously made a communication on the subject to the Archbishop of Canterbury, and prevailed upon him

[1] If we may believe Lord Malmesbury's Diary, the King at this time summoned Mr. Windham and the noble Diarist to Weymouth, with the intention of making the former Prime Minister, and the latter Foreign Secretary. He adds,—" I have no doubt it transpired somehow or other through the Chancellor, who has been acting various parts lately."—Vol. iv. p. 23.

and other prelates to make a strong representation to the King that "the Church was in danger." I do not find any sufficient evidence of this fact, but there seems to be no doubt that, in breach of good faith, he showed Mr. Pitt's last letter to the King,—disclosed to him the contents of the papers therein alluded to, which were forwarded by Lord Grenville,—incensed the King against such of his Ministers as were proceeding in this important affair without his Majesty's privity, and advised him to part with those Ministers rather than submit to such an outrage on his dignity, and to such a violation of his coronation oath. We shall by and by see how far these charges are refuted or corroborated, by a paper afterwards drawn up by Lord Loughborough himself, to prove that his colleagues had no reason to complain of him.

He came to London and attended the Cabinet on the 30th of September, when Mr. Pitt explained his simple, comprehensive, and effectual measure to get rid of civil disabilities on account of religious belief,—which was, to abolish the oaths of supremacy and abjuration, and all such oaths and declarations, and to require only the old common-law oath of allegiance, which might be taken by persons of all creeds, and which for many centuries had been found a sufficient recognition of the duties of the subject to the sovereign. Lord Loughborough declared loudly against this plan, or any modification of it, or any relaxation of the penal laws against the Roman Catholics, and declared that nothing could be done to affect the ecclesiastical condition of Ireland except a commutation of tithes. He added, that he had paid much attention to this last subject, and, with the assistance of one of the Judges, he was preparing a Bill to carry his views into effect. He was desired to mature the measure; and—in ignorance of his secret communings on Catholic emancipation with the King—his colleagues were in hopes that, before Parliament met, his objections to Mr. Pitt's plan might be removed, and it might be submitted to the King with the recommendation of all his Ministers.

But the Chancellor set secretly to work, and composed a most elaborate and artful paper, showing forth the dangers likely to arise from Mr. Pitt's plan, in a manner admirably calculated to make an impression on the royal mind.¹ I give, as a specimen, his defense of the Test Act, which was to be repealed. After referring to the statutes passed to insure Protestant ascendency, he says:—

"These are the safeguards of the Protestant Episcopal religion, which the Government in all its departments is bound to support and maintain. The frame of the law, and every part of our civil policy, is adapted to this object. The Test Act alone has been the subject of some cavil among Protestants. It would be well, however, for those objectors to consider whether without such a guard the kingdom would not either have relapsed into popery or fallen into a chaos of independency, irreligion, and anarchy.² To all these acts every Papist must object, not only as inconvenient and hard, but as a violation of what he deems just and legal rights, the effects of a pernicious heresy which he regards as a national calamity. Can a person holding these sentiments,—rendering habitually an account of the movements of his mind, and submitting the direction of his conscience to a priest whose functions oblige him to enforce such opinions,—be a fit member of the deliberative or executive councils of a Protestant community? The exclusion of Papists from Parliament and office, was coeval with the Reformation."

This paper, remarkable for ingenuity rather than observance of logical rules, or a regard for historical accuracy, Lord Loughborough sent to the King, at Windsor, in the beginning of December, and thereby fully fortified him against the forthcoming plan for placing all his subjects on an equal footing as to their civil rights.³

The pro-Catholic section of the Cabinet, remaining ignorant of this correspondence, still tried to make a con-

---

¹ See it at full length in the appendix to the first volume of Dean Pellew's Life of Lord Sidmouth, where it occupies thirteen closely printed octavo pages.
² This defense was particularly unbecoming in a Scotchman to whose country the Test Act was so insulting. If rigidly inforced, no member of the Church of Scotland could have held any office, civil or military, under the Crown. The Presbyterians originally acquiesced in it, that it might be executed against the Roman Catholics,—hoping to be connived at themselves
³ The original was found among Lord Sidmouth's papers, inclosed in an envelope bearing the following words in the handwriting of the King himself.—" The Lord Chancellor's reflections on the proposal from Ireland of emancipating the Roman Catholics, received December 13th, 1800." Underneath the King's writing Mr. Addington has added—" From the King; given to me in February, 1801."

vert of Lord Loughborough. With this view, Mr. Dundas wrote to him a most admirable letter;[1] but all its statesmanlike reasoning was thrown away upon a man actuated by interest—not by conscientious conviction.

Mr. Pitt persevered, and took a course not quite consistent with the respect due to the Sovereign, nor well calculated for success if Catholic emancipation really was his chief object. Lord Malmesbury says, "If Pitt had been provident enough to prepare the King's mind gradually, and to prove to him that the test proposed was as binding as the present oath, no difficulty *could* have arisen. Instead of this, he reckons on his own power, never mentions the idea at St. James's, and gives time for Lord Loughborough directly, and for Lord Auckland indirectly, through the Archbishop of Canterbury and Bishop of London, to raise an alarm in the King's mind, and to indispose and exasperate him against the framers of this measure."[2]

The Premier made no communication whatever to the King upon the removal of Catholic disabilities, till, Parliament having actually assembled, the House of Commons had elected a Speaker,[3]—and then wrote a long letter to him explaining the proposed measure, and pressing that his Majesty should recommend it in his speech from the throne as necessary for the purpose of consolidating the Union, and giving contentment to all classes of his Majesty's subjects. Lord Loughborough thereupon wrote the following letter to the King, which he thought insured to himself long tenure of office with increased power:—

"The Chancellor, after the most anxious deliberation on the very important crisis to which your Majesty's Government is now exposed, feels it to be his duty to expose to your Majesty, in the most unreserved manner, all the ideas he has been able to collect and digest upon a situation so totally unexpected.

"Your Majesty's opinion upon a question of the utmost magnitude, brought into discussion at the present moment

---

[1] The original was communicated to me by the second Viscount Melville his son. See Appendix to Ch. CLXXV., 3rd Edition.   [2] Diary, vol iv
[3] Parliament met Jan. 22, 1801. The speech from the throne was not delivered till the 2nd of February, the interval being filled up with choosing the Speaker and swearing in the members.—*35 Parl. Hist. 858.*

(when no immediate pressure seemed to call for that discussion), had, without doubt, been long known to every one of your confidential servants—at least from the year 1795, at which period you had been pleased not only to express your decision upon the subject then in discussion, but, by an express requisition to the Chancellor, to manifest the grounds upon which that opinion was formed.

"The Chancellor at that period thought it his duty to communicate to his colleagues that opinion, and the very serious grounds on which it was founded, and which seemed to him unalterable, though they were not (as your Majesty knows) so obligatory, according to the opinion he had frankly expressed, as your Majesty had felt them to be.

"In the discussion of the business of the Union, no consideration occurred, according to my recollection, which could call for a review of the opinions known to prevail in 1795, nor, as I believe, any assurance pledged of a change of opinion upon the state of religion, as an inducement for acquiescence or support in that measure.

"The question was (to me most unexpectedly) raised in October last. I opposed the proposition in its extent from its outset, and thought myself not singular in that opposition. I stated the grounds of my opposition in writing, and committed them to a fair circulation among all my colleagues in your Majesty's service. You were pleased, knowing of the discussion that was then going on, to express a desire to know my opinion on the various parts of the deliberation. As it was my duty to do, I sent to your Majesty in an official box those papers which for some weeks had been in circulation, and which you could have commanded to be sent to you from the office, and which were sent through the office.

"Among the strange misconceptions of the times, it is suggested, I understand, that my private communication with your Majesty had excited an indisposition to hear any other representation on the subject. I have ever thought it my duty to express to your Majesty my own opinion on any subject when you pleased to require it, and I trust that I never have disclosed the opinion of any other person; on this occasion particularly I am confident that I told your Majesty that no person except myself seemed to have formed a decided opinion."

It has been said that Lord Loughborough not only, in personal intercourse with the King, advised him to resist the proposal and to dismiss his minister, but actually wrote the answer in which the dismissal is contained. This last statement, however, is without proof, and is very improbable in itself. The King was pleased with the advice he had received from the Chancellor, but by no means placed entire confidence in him. The true "Keeper of the Royal Conscience" now was John, Lord Eldon, whose genuine, uniform, and zealous bigotry (with a slight aberration in 1795) had endeared him to his royal master. The actual holder of the Great Seal not only came from a Presbyterian country, and had spoken as a Ruling Elder in the General Assembly of the Kirk of Scotland against persecuting David Hume, but since he arrived in England had on several occasions notoriously uttered the latitudinarian sentiment, "that political rights should not depend upon religious creed,"—although recently he had professed himself a convert to the doctrine, "that none ought to be permitted to hold office who did not belong to the Anglican Church;" and, further, had pronounced its head to be infallible. The King's answer, likewise, contains internal evidence that it was not dictated nor revised by Lord Loughborough, who always wrote like a man of education, and could not have been privy to the composition of such a production as this:—

"A sense of religious as well as political duty has made me, from the moment I mounted the throne, consider the oath that the wisdom of our ancestors has enjoined the kings of this realm to take at their coronation, and enforced by the obligation of instantly following it, in the course of the ceremony, with taking the Sacrament, as a binding religious obligation on me to maintain the fundamental maxims on which our Constitution is placed, namely, that the Church of England is the established one; and that those who hold employments in the State must be members of it, and consequently obliged not only to take oaths against Popery, but to receive the holy Communion agreeably to the rites of the Church of England. This principle of duty must, therefore, prevent me from discussing any proposition tending to destroy the groundwork of our happy Constitution; and much more so that now mentioned by Mr. Pitt, which is no less than the complete overthrow of the whole fabric. . . . I had flattered myself, that on the strong assurance I gave Mr. Pitt of keeping perfectly silent on the subject whereon we entirely differ, provided, on his part, he kept off from any disquisition on it for the present, we both understood our present line of conduct; but as I unfortunately find Mr. Pitt does not draw the same conclusion, I must come to the unpleasant decision, as it will deprive me of his political service, of acquainting him that, rather than forego what I look on as my duty, I will, without unnecessary delay, attempt to make the most creditable arrangement, and such as Mr. Pitt will think most to the advantage of my service, as well as to the security of the public."[1]

The same day that this letter was written there happened to be a Levee at St. James's, and the King made a declaration, intended to be circulated, " that he should consider any person who voted for the measure proposed by his Minister as personally indisposed towards himself."

Upon these manifestations of the royal will, Mr. Pitt communicated to the whole Cabinet that his Administration was at an end; but as the first United Parliament of Great Britain and Ireland had assembled, and Mr. Addington had been re-elected Speaker, and the session was to be opened next day, it was necessary to frame a Speech for the King which should make no allusion to this unhappy difference, and that the change of Ministry should not be announced till after the Address had been voted by both Houses.

Accordingly, the Speech in vague terms described the Union with Ireland as "a measure calculated to augment the resources of the empire, and to cement more closely the interests and affections of his Majesty's subjects."

While the question of Catholic Emancipation was not alluded to in the debate on the Address in the House of Lords, in the House of Commons regret was expressed that the Speech from the throne held out no hope of

---

[1] Adolphus, vol. vii. 449, 450. There are two letters from the King to Mr. Addington, dated 5th and 6th Feb. 1801, which clearly prove that at the time when Mr. Pitt was dismissed, and Mr. Addington was called in, no communication was going on between the King and Lord Loughborough (Life of Sidmouth, vol. i. p. 294–5).

strengthening the empire in this season of difficulty by communicating equal rights to all classes of the community. Ministers contented themselves with defending their foreign policy. As soon as the Address was carried, Mr. Pitt and Mr. Dundas ceased to attend in the House, and the fact became known that they were virtually out of office.

What was the astonishment of the public when they were informed that Mr. Addington had been sent for to construct the new Cabinet! And what was the consternation of Lord Loughborough when he certainly knew that Lord Eldon was to be Chancellor![1] Never was there such a striking example of the engineer "hoist with his own petard." There had been rumors afloat that Lord Eldon, when made Chief Justice of the Common Pleas, had engaged, at the King's urgent request, to accept the Great Seal as soon as a vacancy could be made for him; but these Lord Loughborough had entirely disbelieved, confiding in the King's courteous behavior to him,—the credit he had gained in quelling the riots in 1780,- his services in bringing over the Whigs in 1792,— the strong Anti-Jacobin zeal he had since displayed,— and, above all, the vigor with which he had opposed Mr. Pitt's measure in favor of the Catholics. But, instead of continuing to hold his high office, and becoming, as he hoped, the most influential member in the new Cabinet, he suddenly found that he was to be reduced to insignificance, and exposed to ridicule.[2]

When the change of Government was announced in the House of Lords by Lord Grenville, he did not mention the name of Lord Loughborough; saying only, that "some time ago, Earl Spencer, the Earl Chatham, and himself, with several of his Majesty's servants in the other House, thinking it expedient that the benefits of the Union should be rendered as extensive as possible, by the removal of certain disabilities from a great portion of the people of Ireland, and that the measure could only be

[1] From a letter of Lord Eldon to Lord Kenyon it appears that even so late as the 14th of February he with coyness talked doubtfully of his appointment, but it had been finally fixed more than a week before.

[2] "Lords Loughborough and Auckland appear to have bungled the business, and not to have resolution or firmness of character to act openly on what they have combined (I apprehend) secretly. The consequence is that the Chancellor will resign against his will."—*Lord Malmesbury's Diary*, iv 5.

effectual by coming from the Executive Government, had proposed it; that it was not deemed eligible ; that not being able to prevail, and their policy remaining unaltered, they considered themselves bound to retire, and that they only held their offices till their successors were appointed." [1] Lord Loughborough remained silent ; and many supposed that he would be included in the arrangement.

While things were in this unsettled state, the confusion was unspeakably aggravated by the King having a sharp attack—not to be concealed—of his former illness. He was for a short time made to sign papers laid before him ; but becoming incapable of this act, the state of his mind was made known by daily bulletins, and, by order of the Privy Council, public prayers were offered up for his recovery. Speculations for a Regency were renewed ; and, the retiring Ministers still holding the seals of office, it was supposed that they would be forced back into power, till by the old "phantom" a Regent should be appointed —probably the Prince of Wales, who was then entirely under the influence of Lord Thurlow, Mr. Fox, Mr. Sheridan, and Mr. Erskine. No contingency now offered any hope to Lord Loughborough; and he watched the progress of the royal malady with feelings very different from those which he had exhibited twelve years before, on a similar occasion. All that he could expect was to continue to hold the Great Seal while the forms were gone through of examining the King's physicians, of appointing secret committees, of providing for the custody of the King's person, of debating the restrictions to be put on the Regent, and by a "forged process" giving the royal assent to the Regency Bill.

Lord Loughborough did make an effort to be reconciled to the Prince of Wales, and had two interviews with him under color of communicating to him the state of the King's health ; but his Royal Highness was inexorable, and he openly expressed his impatience to assume the Regency that he might throw himself into the arms of the Whig Opposition.[2] To mortify him, Lord Loughborough resolved that this consummation should be delayed as long as possible, and set a dangerous precedent, which his successor repeatedly acted upon, by making

[1] Adolphus, vii. 451.   [2] Diary, iv. 17

the King appear personally to exercise the most important prerogative of the Crown when in a state of mental alienation. On the 25th of February, while his Majesty was under the care of Dr. Willis, he was made to sign a Commission for giving his royal assent to an Act of Parliament. Lord Loughborough declaied that "when he carried the King the *Brown Bread Act* to pass by Commission, his Majesty was in the perfect possession of his understanding." [1] But Lord Malmesbury justly considers such a declaration as an aggravation of the offense which was committed.

On this occasion a letter which might have caused some alarm, was addressed to Lord Loughborough by a foimer political associate:—

"MY LORD,

"Upon the distant terms on which we have lately lived, I admit you have a right to consider the following advertisement as a seizure of an opportunity of conveying something petulant and vindictive.

"Probing my own heart, I feel I may cast aside such dirty motives.

"It is believed that you, the Chancellor, was not present in the room when the King's hand was put to the first Commission. It remains with you to choose whether you will force an inquiry from the attendant physician to this important point, or whether you will obviate it by taking a bill of indemnity.

"The hint is not from an enemy, but a friend.

"I shall be happy to find I am mistaken in all my facts, and that the testimony of Dr. Willis will do away this suspicion.

"I am with great respect,
"CARLISLE." [2]

The speculations about a Regency were almost miraculously put an end to by a "prescription" of the new Prime Minister—in a literal, not a figurative, sense. Being the son of a medical man, he had heard from his

[1] Diary, iv. 17. Yet Lord Malmesbury himself seems to have become less scrupulous. He says, under date 7th March,—"Idea of a Council at Buckingham House on Tuesday, but it is hoped not, and that the Chancellor *by himself* will caiiy the Loan Bill to sign"

[2] Rossl MSS The letter is without date; but there is the following indoisement upon it in the handwriting of Lord Loughborough.—"E. of Carlisle, 19th March, 1801."

father that such irritations as now disturbed the nerves of his Majesty might be allayed by the patient's head reposing on a pillow of hops. The recipe was accordingly tried,—sleep was induced,—next morning his Majesty was better, and in a few days, with proper precautions, he could be produced in public.[1]

When his recollection returned to him, he inquired of the Duke of York "what had passed—if any resignation had taken place?" The Duke said, "None could without his Majesty's leave." "Has the Chancellor resigned?" asked the King. "No, Sir," said the Duke: "he never will give the Seals into any hands but yours." This pleased the King, who ordered Dr. Willis to go to Lord Lougborough to say "he was recovered."

After making up his mind to submit to fate, the poor Chancellor was again doomed to feel the cruel pangs of suspense before he was consigned to the gloomy calm of despair. The King, in directing Dr. Willis to speak or write to Mr. Pitt, said, "Tell him I am now *quite* well, quite recovered from my illness; but what has *he* not to answer for, who is the cause of my being ill at all?" Mr. Pitt professed to be much affected, and as he had been deeply blamed by several of his associates for the manner in which he had wantonly broken up a strong Government, and he himself felt some repugnance to the loss of power, he actually offered to give up Catholic emancipation.

In consequence, a negotiation was opened for restoring all the outgoing Ministers to the offices which they had held. Loughborough again believed that the Great Seal was his own, and flattered himself that Pitt, after this humiliation, would be more meek and conciliatory. With these feelings he wrote the following letter to the King:

"Upon a most anxious consideration of the papers your Majesty was pleased to intrust to the Chancellor's perusal, he can not abandon the hope that it is still possible to avert the incalculable mischief which would ensue from Mr. Pitt's withdrawing from your Majesty's service.

"That hope arises from the terms of Mr. Pitt's first communication to your Majesty, proposing to lay aside

[1] It was this cure which fixed upon Mr. Addington the nickname of "the Doctor," and gave rise to Canning's jest against him as being one of the Medici."

for the present the discussion of that important question which never has been brought forward without mischief. An apprehension that an Administration known to be divided on any essential point would appear to have less stability than the exigence of the times requires, seems to have occasioned the second note. There is much force in that consideration. But the remedy is easy, though the generosity of Mr. Pitt's mind would not allow him to suggest it.

"It is far from his intention to intimate the possibility of any relaxation of that opinion which your Majesty most conscientiously has adopted; but, as the discussion of the question at present is in no respect necessary, and in every respect dangerous in the present very arduous and difficult crisis of public affairs, he can not think it impossible, on a view of the correspondence your Majesty has been pleased to intrust to him, to avert the incalculable mischief which would ensue upon Mr. Pitt's withdrawing at this time from your Majesty's service.

"The difficulty which Mr. Pitt seems in his last note most to apprehend from his continuance in office for any time after a difference on what he deems an essential measure, which could not be concealed, is the want of confidence in the permanence of his Administration, which would ensue if he continued to act with a divided Cabinet. That opinion appears to me well founded. An essential difference of opinion among your Majesty's confidential servants, weakens Government, even when it is not known to which side your Majesty inclines. Until this unfortunate occasion, I have never differed with Mr. Pitt. If I could not accommodate the opinion which I had frankly declared to what at last appeared to be his, I had determined to request your Majesty's permission to retire. Had I felt any reason to suppose, at the last communication in Cabinet on the 28th of January, or at a private conversation the day preceding, that his mind had been so made up on the subject as to admit no further discussion on the proposition itself, or on the modifications of which it was said to be susceptible, I should have apprised him of my intention to remove any obstruction which my remaining in office could create to his making the experiment, by requesting your Majesty's permission to withdraw from a situation in the law that gave me more consequence than my single vote and opinion could claim.

"I have new humbly to beseech your Majesty so to dispose of me—which would be a sufficient indication that there exists no opposition in your Majesty's councils to prevent the trial of the public opinion on the question, whenever it shall be brought forward, which I hope and trust will be postponed to a less agitated period than the present. In this and whatever other alterations Mr. Pitt should think expedient to countervail the rumors of the day, I most humbly, but most earnestly, entreat your Majesty to acquiesce, for the vast object of maintaining the external consequence and internal tranquillity of your dominions and, in truth, of the whole habitable world."

But Addington, who had just tasted the importance of the Premiership, was by no means disposed to give it up: and Pitt and Dundas still thought there would be a great advantage in some one else submitting to the disgrace of making a peace;—after which they might displace him at pleasure.[1] So the attempt at restoration proved abortive, and Lord Loughborough was again disappointed. Mr. Addington had intended, on the formation of the new Government, to offer him the office of President of the Council.[2] The reason why this arrangement did not take place has not been fully explained—but probably it was the secret dislike of him still cherished by the King, who, we shall see, would not even permit him to have a seat in the Cabinet. Some have said that Lord Loughborough, stung with resentment at the loss of the Great Seal, spurned from him an office of inferior dignity. I believe that if such an offer had been made, it would have been readily accepted. As ex-Chancellor, he could not

---

[1] "Dundas pretended to be eager for returning to office, and for throwing Addington overboard, if he would not be satisfied with a subordinate place; 'but,' he said, very unadvisedly, probably unintentionally, 'if these new ministers stay in and make peace, it will only smooth matters the more for us afterwards' This betrayed a good deal ...The impression the whole of this taken together leaves at this moment is either that Pitt is inclined to let this ministry remain in office long enough to make peace, and then turn them out, or that he &c. mean and wish to keep the government of the country in their own hands. That, if they can, they will try to be *entreated* by the King to do so, and if this does not succeed, they will gratify their pride another way, by vaporing on the sacrifices they are ready to make for the good of the public The whole is a very sad story."—*Lord Malmesbury's Diary*, iv 39 40, 43.   [2] Life of Sidmouth, vol. i.

look forward to the melancholy pleasures of opposition, the Whigs seeming for ever annihilated, and strong personal objections existing to his rejoining their body. Indeed, he had contracted so great a passion for being connected with the Court, that I am not sure whether he would have refused to walk backwards in the presence of the King, carrying a white wand, as a lord of the bedchamber. It would appear that, upon due deliberation, Mr. Addington, Lord Eldon and the King entertained no confidence in the sincerity of the intolerant principles which he now professed, and were resolved entirely to get rid of him. They behaved to him, however, with courtesy, and, as a *solatium* for the loss of office, they conferred upon him an earldom, descendible to his nephew, and a pension of £4,000 a year.[1]

It is a mysterious fact, that, although the Government was changed on the 10th of March, Mr. Pitt and his other outgoing colleagues giving up their seals on that day, and their successors immediately kissing hands,—the transfer of the Great Seal did not take place till the 14th of April following. I can only conjecture that, from the King having several fresh paroxysms of his disorder, the prudent Eldon had still misgivings as to his Majesty's recovery; for when he had actually received the bauble into his keeping, he declined giving up the office of Chief Justice of the Common Pleas during several weeks following, for the avowed reason that if the royal malady returned in an aggravated degree, he might " fall between two stools."[2]

[1] This was the first pension granted under the Act giving retired allowances to ex-Chancellors. Till then they relied on tellerships, or other sinecures and reversions.

[2] Twiss's Life of Eldon, ch. xvi.—Lord Malmesbury, impartially and indignantly reviewing the conduct of the two sections of the Tory party at this time (the one led by Mr Pitt, and the other by Lord Loughborough), says . "Among each there is little doubt that many acted from principle and conscientiously; but it is also I fear, not without some degree of truth, that others are to be found who had their own private interests in view, or who acted in order to gratify their private resentments, or promote their ambitious views; and these men, let them be who they will, may be considered as the most consummate political villains that ever existed. They ought to be held in execration by the country, and their names handed down to posterity with infamy, for they will have been the first cause of the destruction of the intellects or life of a Sovereign, to whose kingly virtues, and to whose manly and uniform steady exertion of them during a reign of forty years, this country and every subject in it owes the preservation of its liberties, and everything that is valuable to him."—*Diary*, vol iv. 15 However much we may lament

Lord Loughborough presided as Chancellor on the woolsack two months after he was virtually out office. During this interval one very important debate took place, on Lord Darnley's motion for a committee on "the state of the nation;" and he then made his last great speech in Parliament. We are told that on this occasion he summoned up all his ancient energy, and had considerable success; but the printed report of what he said is exceedingly defective. He seems to have taken a masterly view of our contest with France, and of the position in which the nation then stood, and to have been particularly happy in defining and supporting the belligerent right to search neutral vessels,—on which he declared that all our naval greatness depended. The Whigs remained equally prostrate as when Pitt was minister,—dividing only 28 against 115.[1]

On a subsequent day Lord Loughborough left the woolsack, and spoke on the question which then keenly divided public opinion,—" whether, where a wife is divorced for adultery, marriage should be permitted between her and her paramour?" Against all the arguments arising from compassion to the woman, and the fitness of punishing the man by the understood obligation that he must repair, as far as possible, the honor of her whom he has seduced from the path of duty, the Chancellor sternly maintained that such marriages were contrary to religion and morality, and ought to be forbidden in England, as they are in Scotland and most other Protestant countries.—On his suggestion a standing order was made, which is still in force, that no divorce bill shall be introduced into the House of Lords without a clause forbidding such a marriage;—but the clause has always been struck out by the House of Commons, and the Lords have acquiesced in the amendment.

Meanwhile, there being rumors afloat that Lord Loughborough had been acting unfairly in the late crisis,—had

---

the King's resistance to the liberal policy of his Minister, it is impossible not to admire his constancy, and to sympathize with his sufferings on this occasion. At the commencement of his illness, he read his coronation oath to his family—asked them whether they understood it—and added, " If I violate it, I am no longer legal Sovereign of this country, but the crown falls to the House of Savoy." Recovering his recollection, partially, after one of his paroxysms, he said, " I am better now, *but I will remain true to the Church.*"

[1] 35 Parl. Hist. 1199–1203.

abused the King's ear,—and had betrayed his colleagues, —he wrote and circulated among his friends the following explanation of his conduct:—

"The only period in which, from the time of my entering into office, I had been absent from the correspondence among the persons principally concerned in the public business, was in the course of the autumn of 1800. Obliged by the duty of my own office to a constant residence in town, except in autumn, I had during that season never removed further than Tunbridge Wells, or the coast of Kent, each of which brought me nearer to Mr. P. and D., who lived together, than if I had remained at Hampstead, and of course placed me in the way of knowing all that was passing, as well regarding the external as internal business of the State.

"I was not conscious of any reserve towards me; believed the communication to be perfectly frank; and, being naturally indifferent to penetrate into any details of business, had not the least suspicion that there could be any reserve observed towards me on any great measure.
. . . . In the autumn of 1800 I went early, and without any particular occasion to require my presence, to Weymouth, where for two or three years successively I had been obliged to go on public business, and had stayed for a few days each time. It was not my intention to have remained here long; but the King seeming to desire that I should remain some time, and having the goodness to remark that the air and the bathing agreed with me, and his Court being so small that even the addition of my niece and of Mr. N., who was ready to join our party, was not indifferent, I decided to remain there during H. M.'s residence.

"Mr. Windham and Mr. W. were there on my arrival, who also prolonged their stay on the same grounds.

"Soon afterwards it became necessary to hold a Council at W. for the meeting of Parl!, and the presence of W. and myself was a convenient circumstance.

"The D. of P. came down for that occasion, and returned immediately. In a few days after his return, a messenger arrived with a minute of the Cabinet (of which there were very few men in town), the purport of which was not very agreeable to the K.'s ideas, and still less so to W.

"This dispatch was followed the next day by a private letter from Mr. P. to me, explaining the grounds of the former dispatch. I had had the good fortune to check the first emotion of disapprobation that the minute had produced, and to obtain the return of a moderate answer; that which was first written being, not destroyed, but withheld. The sequel of that business made it unnecessary to send it, as the state of affairs had changed.

"On this occasion my presence had been of some use to the easier conduct of public business, on a point which, had all the King's servants been in a situation to have consulted together, seemed very likely to have produced a rupture; for D., who was at Ch., wrote to me a very warm letter, much irritated against the measure that had been taken, and in a degree reproaching me for the assent he supposed I had given to it. My answer explained to him the grounds on which I had not assented, but acquiesced, and prevented an absolute dissent; which must have led to an absolute separation of at least one servant. He, however, had felt so strongly the objection, that he thought it necessary to enter a formal protest against it, after the subject was in effect gone past.

"There happened about the same time one other incident, neither object nor detail of which I distinctly recollect, in which my immediate intercourse prevented a like incident of quick disapprobation.

"In the last days of September, about the 27th as I recollect, I read a letter from Mr. P., who had kept up a correspondence with me, desiring me to return to town for a meeting on the 2nd of October, with L. C., who wished, before his return to Ireland, to be instructed what language he should be authorized to hold with respect to the Catholics. This letter accompanied a box of papers containing L. C.'s exposition of the point in question.

"Not having prepared to leave W. so abruptly, it was impossible for me, especially as the box and letter had been delivered to me by the messenger in the view of the King, not to inform H. M. of the occasion of my sudden departure, and I thought the best way was to show him the letter, in which there was nothing to be kept back.

"The knowledge that a subject of this nature was in discussion, I was aware would occasion some anxiety in H. M.'s mind, and I therefore determined not to open the papers for the short time I should stay at W.—H. M., as I expected, did not fail to talk to me earnestly on the subject, which he supposed might be treated at the appointed meeting. I evaded the discussion by the excuse of not being able to enter upon the perusal of the papers, and confined myself to say that I was persuaded nothing of material importance could be settled at such a meeting, nor without consulting L. C., who was soon expected in this country, and that for my own part I must think that a subject of so much extent as the general description of it in the letter indicated could not be brought in many meetings to any certain conclusion.

"H. M. continued evidently anxious during the time I remained (which he retarded for a whole day) upon this subject, but he permitted me to retain the same reserve.

"I arrived in town the day of the meeting, 30th September; but having had in my journey ample time to consider the papers, and digest my opinion on them, I felt myself sufficiently prepared with my own opinion.

"Except Lord L., Mr. D. and Lord W., all, I think, were present. Lord C. there also. The business was slowly opened, and for some time loosely discussed. I then stated shortly but earnestly, my own opinion decidedly against the general question; proposing a measure as to tithes which had been thought of in this country, and not objecting to the idea of a pecuniary aid to the clergy, Catholic or Dissenting, but much more limited in its extent than the plan proposed, referring to a paper I had formerly given, before the Union was in view, to Mr. P. on that particular point.

"I rested much on the different state of the questions to be discussed since the Union, and before that event,— that now, the churches of both clergies being consolidated, no point could be made in one that would not of necessity affect either as to tithe, or any other part of the ecclesiastical establishment; and the security of the Church of England was necessarily involved in that of Ireland, and the interest of the State was the same in both; that a change here would be most pernicious, and could not be attempted without the utmost hazard, especially as no one could be ignorant how totally adverse it must be to the K.'s opinion, founded on a high sense of religious obligation. The topics I urged did not seem to be new to any one, nor were they much combated by any except Lord G. I rather judged that they were strongly felt by Mr. P.

"The plan I opened with regard to tithe met with very general concurrence, and I undertook to deliver it in writing. The result of the meeting was pointed and express, that Lord C. should be authorized to say, that some regulation with regard to tithe which might be adapted to the peculiar circumstances of Ireland was in contemplation, that there was also a disposition to give some pecuniary aid to the clergy, as well of Catholic persuasion as of Dissenters, the extent and mode of which required more ample information to be gained from themselves. And as to the question of further indulgence to the Catholics, it was a subject of so deep and serious consideration that no assurance on that subject could be held out to them, the Administration not having formed any opinion for or against their expectations.

"From a letter of Lord C., after his return to Ireland, which came afterwards into circulation, there is reason to think that he had understood and followed his instructions.

"It was particularly my part to deliver in the plan with respect to tithe, which consisted in a bill drawn by Mr. J. Heath, which two or three years before I had communicated to some of the Bishops and left with the Archbishop, who all seemed to approve the idea, but thought the time unfavorable for the proposal.

"I sent the next day to Mr. J. Heath for a copy of it, and about two days afterwards transmitted it, with an explanation, to the Secretary of State's office for circulation.

"I then, pursuing the other parts of the subject, drew up a minute of my opinion upon them at considerable length; one copy I sent to Mr. Pitt, the other to the D. of P.; and though I have no note of the date, I think this must have been about the 20th of October, perhaps later, for it took up some time, and prevented my going to Bath.

"The D. of P. at first took it to be a private communication, and desired to take a copy of it. I informed him that I meant it to be official and to be put in circulation, wishing also that the circulation might be extended to Lord Clare, who was then expected in England.

"About the opening of the session of Parliament, the King asked me, one day, in the course of my attendance on him, what had been the result of the council for which I had been called to town. I said, nothing more than to encourage an idea I had formed in conversation with Mr. J. Heath in regard to tithes, and to hold out some hope of pensions to the Catholic and Dissenting clergy, neither of which were at all settled. He observed, these were were not dangerous measures in themselves, and might be good or bad according as they should be adjusted. But had nothing been settled as to the Catholic question? I assured him nothing had been settled on that question, though it had undergone some discussion. He seemed desirous to know how it had been treated; and I said, so loosely, that I could not pretend to know any one's opinions but my own, which I had stated in writing and put in circulation. He then expressed a desire to see both that and my project with respect to tithes; in consequence of which I sent a copy of each to the office of his Majesty. At the next levee he was pleased to tell me that I had not convinced him; that he had always been of the same opinion with regard to the Catholic question, but he though I had reasoned it fairly, and as to the other subject he should have no objection if the Bishops had none.

"This is all the intercourse I had with H. M. on this subject since the year 1795, when, by his express command, I delivered my written answers to some questions he was pleased to put to me upon this subject, which answers fell so short of the high sense of the obligation H. M. felt felt to be imposed upon him, that they were rather displeasing to him."[1]

I abstain from the invidious task of commenting on the document.

At last the inevitable hour arrived to Lord Loughborough when, giving up the Great Seal, he was to be *civiliter mortuus*. This sad catastrophe happened at St. James's Palace, on the 14th of April. George III. affected to treat him very courteously, and thanked him for his very valuable services; but then there was an alacrity in his

[1] Rossl. MSS.

Majesty's manner, and a twinkle in his eye, which, in spite of all attemps at concealment, betrayed his Majesty's high satisfaction at throwing off a man whom he never trusted, and getting a Chancellor whose sentiments he knew to be sincerely and steadily in accordance with his own.

CHAPTER CLXXV.

CONCLUSION OF THE LIFE OF LORD LOUGHBOROUGH.

OUR ex-Chancellor, to the unspeakable surprise of the new Premier, retained his key of the Cabinet of boxes, and continued, unsummoned, actually to attend the meetings of the Cabinet. He was treated on these occasions with respect; but he at last received the following formal dismissal;—

"Downing Street, April 25, 1801.

" MY DEAR LORD,

" A misconception appears to have taken place, in consequence of which I am led to trouble your Lordship from various considerations, and particularly from a sense of duty to the King. I have reason to believe that his Majesty considered your Lordship's attendance at the Cabinet as having naturally ceased upon the resignation of the Seals, and supposed it to be so understood by your Lordship. Much as I should feel personally gratified in having the benefit of your Lordship's counsel and assistance, I will fairly acknowledge to you, that I did not offer to his Majesty any suggestion to the contrary; and, indeed, I must have felt myself precluded from doing so by having previously in more instances than one expressed and acted upon the opinion, that the number of the Cabinet should not exceed that of the persons whose responsible situations in office require their being members of it. Under these circumstances, I feel that I have perhaps given way to a mistaken delicacy, in not having sooner made the communication to your Lordship; but I am persuaded you will see that I should be wanting in duty to the King, and what is due to yourself, if I delayed it beyond the time when a minute of Cabinet with the names of the persons present must be prepared in order to be submitted to his Majesty.

"I hope your Lordship will give me full credit for the motives by which I can alone be actuated upon this occasion, as well as for the sincere sentiments of esteem and regard with which I am, my dear Lord,

"Your Lordship's most obedient and faithful servant,

"HENRY ADDINGTON."[1]

It would have been well for the dignity of Lord Loughborough's character if he had died on the day of his resignation. The world would then have said, that if his life had been prolonged,—after he was freed from the toils and cares of office, he would have devoted his splendid abilities to the task of reforming and improving the laws of his country; and that, the literary ardor which had burned so bright in his bosom when he was the associate of David Hume and Adam Smith being rekindled, he would have rivalled Clarendon in handing down to posterity a valuable history of the times in which he lived. Unfortunately he survived; and thus his real destiny is recorded:—"A still more crafty successor obtained both the place he had just quitted in the King's service, and the place he had hoped to fill in the King's favor; he was made an Earl; he was laid on the shelf; and, as his last move, he retired to a villa remarkable for its want of all beauty and all comforts, but recommended by its near neighborhood to Windsor Castle, where the former Chancellor was seen dancing a ridiculous attendance upon Royalty, unnoticed by the object of his suit, and marked only by the jeering and motley crowd that frequented the terrace.[2] For three years he lived in this state of public neglect, without the virtue to employ his remaining faculties in his country's service by Parliamentary attendance, or the manliness to use them for his own protection and aggrandizement."[3]—There is some the-

[1] Rossl. MSS.
[2] I have been informed by my friend and former colleague, Sir William Horne, who occupied this villa with his family during a long vacation, that although it is not remarkable for picturesque beauty, it is very spacious and commodious, and according to the testimony of Miss Cotes and others, George III., without any real regard for the ex-Chancellor, always behaved to him with courtesy and seeming kindness.
[3] Lord Brougham's Statesmen, 1. 86.

torical exaggeration in this statement; but it is substantially correct. By a reference to the Lord's Journals, we find that the ex-Chancellor was tolerably regular in attending the House during the remainder of the session of 1801,¹ and during the sessions of 1802, 1803, and 1804, although he took very little part in its proceedings. He did not at all assist in judicial business, as, without any open quarrel, there was no cordiality between him and his successor; and he merely, like the great bulk of our hereditary legislators, came to lounge in the House a short time before dinner, that he might inquire after news,—when he had not any more lively occupation. He now and then spoke a few sentences in a conversational tone, but never aimed at an oration. Having once or twice heard him on these occasions, I remember being rather at a loss to conceive how he could have been the formidable opponent of Dunning and Thurlow, of Fox and Burke,—although it might be discovered that he had become unnerved by listlessness, and that, if excited, he might still have been capable of great things.

He first opened his mouth as an ex-Chancellor to express his approbation of Lord Thurlow's doctrine, that a divorce should be granted, on the petition of the wife, for the adultery of the husband with the wife's sister.² When the bill was brought in to indemnify those who should be sued for anything done under the "*Habeas Corpus* Suspension Act," he took merit to the late Administration for having saved the State, and boldly justified their habit of employing spies and informers.³ He supported, against Thurlow, the bill introduced when the Reverend John Horne Tooke was returned to Parliament,—to prevent a priest in orders from ever again sitting in the House of Commons,—and, with some historical research he showed that this regulation was according to ancient usage.⁴ The articles of the Peace of Amiens coming on

---

¹ Having resigned the Great Seal on the 14th of April, he was present on the 18th, 20th, 21st, 22nd, 23rd, and 27th, as " D⁹. Loughborough." On the 28th he was introduced as "Earl of Rosslyn," and he appears in the roll as "C⁹. Rosslyn" about as often as any Earl not in office. In 1804 he was present ten times in March, five times in April, four times in May, once in June, and eleven times in July—the last of these being the day of the prorogation, and I do not find his name afterwards in the Journals, so that I presume he never again appeared in Parliament

² 35 Parl. Hist. 1433.   ³ Ib. 1540.   ⁴ Ib. 1549.

to be debated, he censured them, but chiefly confined his objection to the omission of an article to recognize the honor to which the British flag was entitled in the narrow seas—"an important right, which implied our dominion of the sea, and the maintenance of which warmed the heart of every British seaman."[1] When hostilities were recommenced, he supported the Government, saying that Buonaparte's rudeness to Lord Whitworth was a sufficient cause of war, and that his whole conduct since he signed the treaty, had been a uniform system of arrogance, insult, and injury.[2] In 1804, he made a few unimportant observations on the proceedings against Judge Fox,[3] on the mode of maintaining the London clergy,[4]—and on the Insolvent Debtors' Bill.[5] He never again spoke in the House. Such is the inglorious termination of his Parliamentary career!

He appears to have been treated with neglect by all parties—which is not much to be wondered at, considering the little pains he took to preserve his importance as a public man. The Duke of Portland, the President of the Council, having heard of his complaints of the slights he experienced from the Government, and of his saying that "he now knew nothing except what he read in the newspapers," became alarmed lest he might actually join the Opposition, and thus wrote to Lord Chancellor Eldon: "The most perfect means should be taken to put an end to the sort of language which is held by Lord Rosslyn—to remove from him all cause of complaint upon the ground of want of attention, or shyness, on the part of those who compose the Administration. With permission, I can not help thinking that the station you hold gives you a particular title to commiserate and consult with him; and excuse me for adding, that I am very anxious that the suggestion I have ventured to throw out respecting Lord Rosslyn, may be approved and adopted by you."

But it is not wonderful to see him so fallen as to be a fit object for the commiseration of his former friends, when we find that his prime object of ambition now was the personal notice of the Sovereign. We have observed that as he became alienated from Mr. Pitt, he enlisted

[1] 35 Parl. Hist. 723. [2] Ib. 1511. [3] Parl. Debates, vol. xi. 925.
[4] Ib. 1109. [5] Ib. 1130.

himself in the band of "King's friends." His Majesty, who, notwithstanding his apparent bluntness, had considerable powers of dissimulation, thenceforth treated him with such seeming confidence as to lead the wary Scotsman into the delusion that he was a darling favorite. Even when superseded by Eldon, the King induced him still to believe that this was only for political reasons, and that personally his Majesty was affectionately attached to him—having taken an opportunity to tell him that "the Queen, likewise, found much pleasure in his society, and that they both desired to see him as much as possible at Court." This conversation, which he took *au pied de la lettre*, was the cause of his hiring the ugly villa of Baylis, near Slough, that he might be near Windsor,[1] and he did frequently throw himself in the way of the Royal Family while they were resident there. He likewise followed them to Weymouth, where they spent a considerable part of every summer; and he was intensely delighted to be noticed by them on the Esplanade, or to be invited to join their excursions on the water. In August, 1801, from Weymouth, he writes a letter to Lord Auckland, which, after touching on some private matters, and showing that he was on very familiar terms with the Queen and Princesses, thus proceeds: "I can with perfect satisfaction confirm to you all that you may have heard of their Majesties' perfect health. The King, I think, has at no time when I have had the means of seeing him every day, and often all the day, appeared to be in so steady a state of health. He might at times appear, to those who have always seen him in high spirits, to be rather low; but the case really is, that his manner is much

[1] He likewise had a *farm* at Baylis, which he seems to have bargained for with great deliberation. I find the following memorandum in his handwriting:—
"1. What should be a fair rent?
"2. How far, at a rent of 40s., parts might be underlet?
"3. What number of horses would be necessary for the farm? Expense of their keep?
"4. What number of men? Whether two to each team sufficient for all the work, as plowing, &c.?
"5. What the allowance to bailiff?
"6. What ought to be the produce to cover rent, taxes, tithes, and the charge of management?"
Among his papers are very minute accounts of the farm, the number of laborers employed, and the operations of each day throughout the year.— *Rossl. MSS.*

more composed, and he is always ready to enter into conversation when it is going on, though he does not always start it. He is become also more moderate in his exercise, and admits that it is possible to be fatigued.—Public events seem at present to give no occasion for uneasiness, and I trust they will continue in such a state as not to ruffle his mind, the composure of which is the great point on which the fate of our country depends. The weather here is delightful for sailing, but rather warm for any other exercise." [1]

I do not find that our ex-Chancellor took any part in the ministerial crisis which was terminated by the resignation of Mr. Addington. After Mr. Pitt's return to power, he neither actively opposed nor supported that minister, but continued more sedulously than ever to cling to the Court. Whether he thought that, in party vicissitudes, which were likely to arise, the King's favor might restore him to office, or he considered the King's favor his supreme and ultimate good, I know not; but thus he continued to trifle away his existence;—when the Royal Family were in London, residing at a villa which he had near Hampstead,—fixing himself at Baylis when the Court was at Windsor,—and following in their suite when they removed to the sea-side.[2] In the autumn of 1804, after

---

[1] In a letter from Weymouth, dated Sept. 1800, he gives an interesting picture of the Court of George III. there. Having discussed the question on which his opinion had been asked, "Whether, after a divorce obtained collusively in Scotland, a marriage of one of the parties would be valid?" he says, "The course of life at this place has agreed so well with me that I wish to prolong my stay, if I should not feel it a necessary duty to return to London, where I am afraid the Lord Mayor is proceeding like his predecessor in 1780, and will produce similar excesses. I was the only person at sea this evening without a great-coat, and without a wish to have had one The great advantage of the attendance here is the constant movement in the open air, and the short meals. When I arrived here I was horribly fatigued by the pedestrian exercise; but I am become a very stout walker.—A continental peace would be very desirable; but in truth, no peace which could be expected in the present state of things would amount to more than an armistice."

[2] I have received an amiable and interesting explanation respecting Lord Loughborough's retreat, in a letter from his niece, Miss Cotes.—"19th Nov. 1846.—I am sorry to say that my aunt, Lady Rosslyn, being in the constant habit of burning all letters, I have no written documents to produce that would throw any light upon Lord Rosslyn's life However, I will state my own impression, as derived from my recollection, of what passed at the period to which you refer. From all I saw and heard, I believe that George III. was at all times most gracious and kind to Lord Rosslyn, and particularly so at the time of his resigning the Seals, and during the remainder of his life.

his return from Weymouth, where, as usual, he had been gratified by walking with his Majesty on the Esplanade, and accompanying him in little trips to sea in the royal yacht, he was seized with a severe fit of illness in London, but he soon rallied, and by the advice of his medical attendants he went to Baylis, where the air is supposed to be very salubrious. Here, his recovery being soon completed, he continued his usual mode of life,—frequently paying his duty at the Castle, kindly receiving his relations under his roof, keeping up a friendly intercourse with several agreeable families in the neighborhood, and amusing himself with all the new works of any merit which issued from the press. His constitution, although not robust, seemed unbroken, and his friends hoped that he might reach extreme old age.

A statement has been made which would be very curious if it might be relied upon; "that his Scotticisms and his vernacular tones returned as his vigor was impaired in the decline of life; showing that it was all the while an effort which could not continue when the attention was relaxed and its powers enfeebled."[1] But his niece, an Englishwoman, who lived with him under his roof during his retirement till the hour of his death, says:

Lord Rosslyn was sincerely attached to George III.; and this feeling was probably one great inducement to him, after his retirement from office, to exchange his villa at Hampstead for the place he took near Windsor, from whence he had frequent opportunities of paying his duty to his Sovereign, by whom, as well as by all the royal family, he was always received in the most gracious manner. To a man naturally of a sociable and cheerful disposition, there might also be some inducement to this change in the pleasure which the intercourse with the principal families in the neighborhood afforded; for they courted his society, and respected and esteemed his character, and he was happy to co-operate with them whenever his health permitted. His kindness to his relations was invariable, and his house was at all times open to them, and to friends of all ages, who were welcomed with cheerfulness; and no one could be in his society without deriving some information from his superior mind, the powers of which were never weakened to the last day of his life, though, from severe bodily illness, he was in a great measure removed from public life.

"In the autumn of 1804 Lord Rosslyn was for some weeks at Weymouth, when he was continually in the society of the royal family, and attended his Majesty in his almost daily sailing excursions, as well as at the parties on the shore, in which all his family were included. Their Majesties were so gracious as to admit me to the sailing parties, and in so confined a sphere I had more favorable opportunities of witnessing his Majesty's manner than I could otherwise have had, and his behavior was at all times such as to give me the impression that he had a great regard and esteem for Lord Rosslyn."

[1] Lord Brougham.

"The statement by Lord Brougham as to Lord Rosslyn's *Scotticisms and vernacular tones*, I can safely affirm to be incorrect; and I believe any one who conversed with Lord Rosslyn in his latter years (of whom some few are still alive) would bear testimony both to his intellects being perfectly clear, and his language so purely English, that no one would have perceived him to be a Scotchman."[1]

He was now to receive a sudden summons from the Angel of Death. On the last day of the year he was at a party given by their Majesties at Frogmore,—where, meeting with a gracious reception, and being consequently in high spirits, he stayed till a late hour. Next day, being New Year's day, 1805, while sitting at table, seemingly in his usual health, his head dropped on one side, he fell from his chair, and it was found that he was struck by an attack of gout in the stomach. He never spoke again, and he expired in a few hours, to the inexpressible grief of his family.

I should have been glad if I could have omitted or contradicted the following anecdote, but it has been too widely circulated to be suppressed, and it seems to rest on undoubted authority: Intelligence being carried to George III. early next morning of the sudden death of his "friend," the Monarch, with characteristic circumspection, interrogated the messenger as to whether this might not be a false report, as he had seen the Earl of Rosslyn himself so recently in perfect health; and the messenger having declared that the Earl had certainly died during the night of gout in the stomach, his Majesty was graciously pleased to exclaim, "Then he has not left a greater knave behind him in my dominions."[2]

[1] Letter from Miss Cotes.
[2] It is related that when Thurlow was told this remark of the King, he vented his spleen against both parties by observing with an oath, "I perceive that his Majesty is quite sane at present."

The whole story is utterly denied by Miss Cotes, who thus feelingly expresses herself —" I think it quite incredible that George III., whose benevolence of heart and kind feeling are admitted even by his enemies, could have made such a speech as that recorded at the end of Lord Brougham's Life, on being told of the sudden death of an old and faithful friend, whom he had seen in his house not twenty-four hours before; or that so open and warmhearted a man as his nephew, Henry Wrottesley, could have refrained from naming it at the time, had such a speech reached his ears, or that he should never at any future time have expressed to any of his own family how much he was shocked at hearing a man, to whom he was most strongly attached, spoken of in such a manner. The extreme improbability of the story is all

His remains having been removed to his house in London, were deposited in St. Paul's Cathedral, close to those of Sir Joshua Reynolds. Some of his biographers have stated that a monument has been there erected to his memory, with an epitaph to record his virtues, but " the only memorial which St. Paul's contains of this high legal functionary is a flat stone laid over his grave in the crypt, with the following inscription, on which no human eye ever looks, and which is fast becoming illegible:

" ALEXANDER WEDDERBURN
EARL OF ROSSLYN,
BARON LOUGHBOROUGH.
Born 13th February, 1733.
Died 2nd January, 1805."[1]

At the top of a circle inclosing the inscription are his armorial bearings, with the motto—

" Illæso lumine solem."

Such is the information afforded respecting him to those who visit the secluded vaults of our Metropolitan Minster, and this is now with difficulty deciphered.— I must try to supply the deficiency,—exercising a more impartial judgment than could be expected in a kinsman or a friend.

This memoir, I am afraid, may appear to have been already extended to a disproportionate length, and I hasten to conclude it ;—but the reader must bear in mind that while the greater part of those who have held the

that I can argue upon, as Mr. Henry Wrottesley was probably the only person who could really know the truth. I own to me it appears absolutely impossible." Although Miss Cotes's belief is so sincere and so strong we must recollect that she is not supposed to have been present when the words were spoken, and that they might have been concealed from her on account of her pious respect for the memory of her uncle. I am informed that they were often mentioned to others by Mr. Henry Wrottesley, to whose testimony she refers The improbability of the anecdote is lessened by the consideration that George III had always looked on Lord Loughborough with a considerable degree of suspicion ; first, on account of his country, and, secondly, on account of his inconsistent conduct So early as when he was a law officer of the Crown, his Majesty, in a confidential letter to Lord North, said, " Is Mr. A. G really running right ? I doubt all Scots, and he has been getting everything he could."

[1] Letter from a Canon Residentiary of St Paul's, who kindly made the necessary inquiry for me on this subject ; and who adds,—" Of our forty-five monuments within the cathedral, twenty-one are erected to military, and sixteen to naval heroes The only Judge similarly honored is one whose ashes are not with us—SIR WILLIAM JONES."

office of Chancellor have either emerged from obscurity at a mature age or have been consigned to an early tomb, Lord Loughborough was conspicuous on the stage of public life above half a century, mixing with all the most eminent men of two generations,—that he lived to relish the writings of Wordsworth and of Walter Scott, after many years of personal intimacy with Robertson and Hume,—that having exulted in the glories of the first Administration of Pitt the father, he mourned over the calamities of the last Administration of Pitt the son,—and that he long continued to fill a great space in the eyes of his contemporaries on both sides of the Atlantic. From his origin he might have been expected to aim no higher than being an "Advocate-depute" or the "Sherra" of a Scotch county; but, striking out a path to fortune unknown to his countrymen, he raised himself to be Lord Chancellor of Great Britain, and an Earl,—I may still be allowed to take a rapid glance at the merits and the faults of a person so distinguished.

He received from nature talents of the first order, and, with a longing after the seemingly unattainable, an extraordinary determination of purpose, which enabled him to overcome all the difficulties which obstructed his rise. He achieved greatness, and he might have commanded the respect of mankind. But of public principle he was wholly destitute. Repeatedly going over from the Whigs to the Tories, and from the Tories to the Whigs, he has been not inaptly compared to a ship at single anchor in a river, that changes the direction of her prow every time the tide ebbs and flows. Some palliation of his misconduct may be discovered in the political profligacy of the times in which he lived; but, in aggravation, it must be remembered that he had before him in his own profession the example of the virtuous Camden,—amidst temptations and tergiversations, ever consistent and true.

To render Lord Loughborough's worldly prosperity less demoralizing, I would observe, that I believe his frequent interested transfers of himself were impolitic as well as unprincipled. With his endowments, had he adhered steadily to either party, he probably would have filled the same offices, and with more power as well as more credit. If, in 1771, he had resisted the allurements held out to him by Lord North, he probably would have received the Great Seal from the Whigs in 1782,—and if he had afterwards remained a stanch Tory instead of becoming a Foxite, it would probably have been soon delivered to him by Pitt, when taken from the wayward Thurlow. At all events, what was this bauble, accompanied with reproaches of treachery, and the suspicions and mistrust and equivocal looks of his new friends, compared to the esteem of good men and the self-respect which he sacrificed to obtain it?

I must likewise censure him for not making himself better acquainted with English jurisprudence. He had a very fine legal understanding, and with proper application he was capable of comprehending and expounding the most abstruse questions debated in our courts; but he was contented with the superficial knowledge of his profession, which enabled him, by means of a cursory examination of authorities and a cautious concealment of his ignorance of all beyond what he had got up for the occasion, decently to get through the business of the day. As a Judge he was of spotless integrity, and he could deal well with the facts of every case; but he was often obliged to resort to others for those maxims on which depended the most important rights of the suitors who came before him for justice. Thurlow used to say,—"That d——d Scotchman has the gift of the gab, but he is no lawyer; in the House of Lords I get Taffy Kenyon, or some one else who does my dirty work, to start some law doctrine in such a way that the fellow must get up to answer it, and then I leave the Woolsack and give him such a thump in the bread-basket that he can not recover his wind." Yet Loughborough, by his "gift of the gab," sometimes seems to have had the best of it. Lord Eldon used to relate that on one occasion when the Chief Justice of the Common Pleas was speaking with considerable effect on a law point which Thurlow had not sufficiently studied, the latter, as he sat on the Woolsack, was heard to mutter, "If I were not as lazy as a toad at the bottom of a well, I could kick that fellow Loughborough heels over head any day in the week." [1]

[1] Thurlow, retaining the recollection of the wounds he had received in conflicts with this formidable antagonist, when told by Lord Lauderdale of his intention to make an attack on Lord Loughborough, then Chancellor,

Still deeper blame is to be imputed to Lord Loughborough for omitting to do any thing material, during the forty years he sat in Parliament, to improve our laws, and for opposing the efforts which began to be made by others for this great object. Having effected nothing by "Orders" to reform the abuses of the Court of Chancery, the only law reform which he ever introduced, besides that already mentioned, to prevent the dangerous accumulation of property by means of fantastical wills, was the bill requiring, under the pain of nullity, all annuities to be registered, unless secured on freehold estates. The purpose was to check the ruinous practice of expectant heirs borrowing money on extravagant terms by granting annuities, and thus evading the statutes against usury; but the measure was ill-framed, and has fallen into desuetude.¹ When a bill for altering the criminal law, which had been drawn up by Mr. Wilberforce, came to the House of Lords, Lord Loughborough threw it out, saying, "I can not help lamenting that men not conversant

said to him, "You had better not, sir; he will come over you with his *cold tongue.*"
¹ He likewise caused to be brought in the Act by which a pension of £4,000 a year was provided for a retired Chancellor. Mr. Pitt, by the following letter, proposed that he should take a sinecure like his predecessors.
"Holwood, Sunday, March 2nd, 1794.
"MY DEAR LORD,
"I wish to submit to your Lordship the idea of an arrangement on which I shall be happy to know your sentiments. If it strikes you as it does me, it will be a great satisfaction to me to see it carried into execution. An opportunity occurs of opening the office of Chief Justice in Eyre, now held by Mr. Villiers, the salary of which, as it stands (but subject to some possible deduction), is about £1,900 per annum. The office appears to me to be of a description which might very properly be held with your Lordship's present situation, and there is nothing to prevent an additional pension being granted out of the Civil List, dependent on the event of your ceasing to hold the Great Seal, which might make the amount, in that case, about equal to the salary of a tellership, which has been so frequently the provision for your predecessors. If your Lordship approves of this mode, it appears to be liable to no difficulty, and it would render any idea of an application to Parliament unnecessary. You will, perhaps, have an opportunity of turning this in your mind, so as to let me know your opinion when I have the pleasure of meeting you to-morrow. "Ever, my dear Lord, sincerely yours,
"W. PITT"*
But he very properly objected to the jobbing to which such bargains were apt to give rise; and Mr. Pitt at last agreed in the propriety of a fixed retired allowance for the Chancellor, which has since been extended to all the Judges.—Stat 39 Geo. 3, c. 110.

* Rossl. MSS.

with law now-a-days turn law projectors, and in fits of vivacity come forward with raw, jejune, ill-advised and impracticable schemes for alteration of the mode of distributing and carrying into execution the criminal justice of the country. As Attorney General, I always thought it my duty to check the introduction of every such project. I remember that an offender sentenced to stand in the pillory having lost his life from the fury of the mob, a humane gentleman (Mr. Burke) brought in a bill to make the offense capital, with a view to do away with the punishment of the pillory altogether; but I acted upon the opinion that the Judges were the proper persons with whom alterations in the penal code ought to originate."— He opposed the bill for repealing 25 Geo. 2, which, in cases of murder, subjects the body of the criminal to dissection. "According to my experience," said he, "prisoners hardened in vice, and practiced in villainy, have stood with a firm countenance during trial, and have even heard sentence of death passed upon them without emotion; but when the Judge informed them that they were to undergo a public dissection, their countenances changed, they grew suddenly pale, trembled, and exhibited a visible appearance of the extremest horror. This sort of exhibition has always made a forcible impression on the minds of the bystanders, and, I have not the smallest doubt, is attended with the most salutary consequences in repressing crime."—He even went so far as to reject a bill to change to *hanging* the punishment of *burning*, to which women were liable for "*coining*," then treated as "*high treason*." " I see no great necessity," said he coolly, " for the alteration, because, although the punishment, as a spectacle, is rather attended with circumstances of horror, it is likely to make a more lasting impression on the beholders than mere hanging; and, in fact, no greater degree of personal pain is thus inflicted, the criminal being always strangled before the flames are suffered to approach her body." But such sentiments reflect discredit on the times rather than the individual. When Loughborough was Chancellor, our penal code, having reached its utmost degree of atrocity, was generally defended and approved. All that can be said against him personally is, that on such subjects he was not in advance of his age. Dr. Parr relates the following anecdote in proof of his humanity: "Lord Rosslyn, disregarding the difference of our political sentiments, at my request gave the fullest effect to my exertions for saving an unfortunate person who had committed the crime for which he was on the point of suffering death, but was guiltless of some aggravations hastily imputed to him, and who, by the diligence, sobriety, and honesty which he has uniformly manifested for the space of twenty-five years from the time of his deliverance, has amply repaid to society the mercy shown to him by the Executive Government."

So enthusiastic was the worthy divine, that he adds, "In genius and magnanimity Lord Rosslyn towered above his colleagues."

It is in oratory that Wedderburn is most to be admired; and I am inclined to think that, while in the House of Commons, he was the greatest debater, for a lawyer, that ever sat in that assembly. More sarcastic than Murray, more forcible than Pratt, more polished than Dunning, more conciliating than Thurlow, he combined in himself the great physical and intellectual requisites for swaying a gentlemanlike mob. His manner was rather too precise, from the pains he had taken with it under Sheridan and Macklin, and from his dread of Scotch phrases or accents; but his voice was powerful and sweet, his eye was full of fire, and, without standing on tiptoe (a vain attempt I have witnessed to add a cubit to the stature of a little man), the movements of his body were so energetic, appropriate, and graceful, that, like Garrick, he seemed "six feet high." Another circumstance which gave him weight in the House of Commons was, that he always remained true to the colors under which he served,—not seeking by display to gain separate objects, or to gratify personal vanity; but, under just subordination to his leader, he seemed only to consider the interests of the party to which, for the time, he belonged. Upon the approach of an important debate he took enormous pains to be master of the subject; he prepared in writing some fine sentences, to be opportunely thrown in when replying; and the story went that he even practiced before a looking-glass his starts of surprise at ironical cheers, and his looks of complacency when he expected to be favored with the sympathy of his hearers. Whatever arts he employed, he was always heard with attention and delight;—controlling the sympathies of his hearers, they for a time forgot his political lubricity. Fox, Burke, and Dunning in turn entered the lists against him without gaining any decisive advantage, he could almost make our quarrel with America appear just, and the war to subdue her well conducted. Perhaps the most striking proof of his great rhetorical powers is the position which he maintained in society notwithstanding what might be stated to his discredit. Though much abused behind his back, all were civil to him in his presence—even his opponents, who were influenced by the hope of a compliment from him in debate, or dreaded the keen edge of his sarcasm.

From his articles in the original Edinburgh Review, when a very young man, it might have been expected that he would have gained distinction as an author; but he had not imbibed his friend David Hume's passion for literary fame, and he preferred office, titles, and riches. Lord Commissioner Adam, indeed, says in the Diary which I have before quoted, "He had produced an historical work which never met the light, although he had taken great pains to correct it—a Dissertation on the Reign of Henry II. of England;"—and there is reason to think that he printed anonymously several political pamphlets; but the only publication ever avowed by him was a little treatise which came out in the year 1793, soon after he received the Great Seal, entitled "Observations on English Prisons, by the Right Honorable Alexander Lord Loughborough, Lord Chancellor of Great Britain." It had probably been written when he was Chief Justice of the Common Pleas, and it contains the result of his inquiries and observations as a Criminal Judge. Certainly it does him very considerable credit.

A charge has been brought against him, which, while it would deeply wound his honor, would place him in the first class of English writers. The astounding notion that he actually was the assailant in the "Daily Advertiser" of the Duke of Grafton, Sir W. Draper, the Duke of Bedford, Lord Mansfield, Sir W. Blackstone, and George III, receives countenace from Chalmers;[1]—and thus writes Sir Nathaniel Wraxall: "During many years of his life I nourished a strong belief, approaching to conviction, that the late Chancellor,

---
[1] Biographical Dictionary—"LOUGHBOROUGH."

then Mr. Wedderburn, was the author of Junius. Some persons of credit have recognized the handwriting of the letters to be that of Mrs. Wedderburn, his first wife." The supposed similitude of handwriting in this case amounts to nothing, and the only other circumstance I am aware of to support this strange supposition is, that Junius is uniformly partial to George Grenville, who was Wedderburn's patron. But although an anonymous libeler in the newspapers might, by way of blind, have mentioned his own name with some discourtesy, could he have thus disclosed his selfish system of political warfare,—" The wary Wedderburn never threw away the scabbard, nor ever went upon a forlorn hope "?—or could he have passed sentence of perpetual infamy upon himself in such stinging epigrammatic language as this, to be fixed in every man's memory,—" As for Mr. Wedderburn, there is something about him which even treachery can not trust "?—or could he have tried to mitigate the odium to be cast upon the individual by thus reflecting on his country: " I speak tenderly of this gentleman, for when treachery is in question, I think we should make allowances for a Scotchman "? Although Junius loves to dabble in law, and with the assistance he received could treat a legal question plausibly for the uninitiated, it is quite clear, from the mistakes into which he falls, that he was not a professional lawyer.¹ Thus, in his Address to the English Nation, speaking of the House of Commons, he says, " They are only *trustees*, the *fee* is in us." Now those who are of the craft all know that the fee is in the trustee, not in the " cestui que trust," or person beneficially interested. Besides, there is a case against Francis as the real Junius, which would convict him before any fair and intelligent jury. One would that the writer was of higher rank than a clerk in the War Office, and that he had been instigated to his calumnies against the renowned statesmen of the day by personal rivalry, personal wrongs, and personal resentments; but there is overwhelming evidence to

---

¹ There is strong internal evidence from Shakespeare's plays to support the statement that he had been bred up in an attorney's office. He frequently makes use of law terms, and always with the most exact propriety—from his "fines and recoveries" to his "action of battery." I do not yet despair of writing an Essay on this *lego-literary* subject.

prove that Sir Philip delivered the MS. to Woodfall, and though the letters are certainly superior to any of his acknowledged compositions, there is a family likeness to be discovered among them all; and after his departure for the East Indies, when Junius disappeared, he never again wrote under such excitement, and with such occasions for giving unrestrained vent to his malevolence. No weight can be attached to his denial, supposing it to have been ever so peremptory, instead of being faint or equivocal; for, independently of the personal risk which would have arisen to him, even late in life, from an avowal of his slanders, no man of right feeling, or with any regard to his estimation in society, would submit to the moral disgrace of being considered the author of these letters, for all the literary glory they would confer upon his name.[1]

[1] See "Junius Identified," by JOHN TAYLOR, Esq I can still further refute the supposition that Wedderburn was Junius, and prove that Sir Philip Francis was the man, by the following letter from Lady Francis, his very amiable and intelligent widow, which she was good enough to write for my information, and which I have her permission to publish. After unmerited compliments to "the high character of Lord Campbell's work," she thus proceeds —"Sometimes I have doubted whether I had a right to betray what Sir Philip never would have confessed, and which I could only have obtained the conviction of from his confidence in my discretion, which made him lay aside with me that guard over himself and that strict watch over every word which he felt necessary, but which was often irksome to him *auprès du monde*. I believe *that* was the secret of his attachment and marriage so late in life— like the wife of Midas, he wanted some one to whisper the secret to, and I was his reed, as all dutiful consorts ought to be to their lords; yet though his manner and conversation on that mysterious subject were such as to leave me not a shadow of doubt on the fact of his being the author, telling me circumstances that none but Junius could know, he never avowed himself more than saying he knew what my opinion was, and never contradicting it. Indeed, I made no secret of it to him, though not in a way that called for any declaration either way, but I am certain he would not have allowed me to continue in error, if it had been one, knowing my convictions. His first gift after our marriage was an edition of Junius, which he bid me take to my room, and not let it be seen, or speak on the subject, and his posthumous present which his son found in his bureau was 'Junius Identified,' sealed up and directed to me. Sir Philip never did anything unadvisedly Edmund Burke observed of him, ' He does nothing without a reason , there is thought and motive in all he does, however trifling.' You know Burke and he were inseparables till the former left the Whigs; but their mutual regard, I believe, always continued Sir Philip told me that Burke was convinced he was Junius, yet before he was himself suspected, that is, before the 'Identification' came out, some people, discussing the question before him, asked him if he thought Burke was the writer, as was generally believed at the time,— 'Faith, very likely,' answered Sir Philip, 'for I heard him, and I considered it an ingenious evasion, like his answer to Sir Richard Philips, which he took the trouble to explain to me was no denial, and said, "only fools could take it for

During the discussions in the House of Lords, on the Regency, the Duke of Richmond strongly intimated that Lord Loughborough had been writing abusive articles in one."' He was very anxious to avoid assent or denial, lest he might implicate truth or honor—both of which he was very jealous of committing. He affronted poor Sam Rogers, whom he liked much, to avoid an ensnaring question On the 'Identified' appearing, he withdrew his name from Brooke's, when almost the father of the club, and petted and privileged by all They entreated him not to desert them, and several wrote to beg my intercession, but all in vain, he retired and made no sign On consideration, I found the cause. A club is neutral ground; it was not like the Select Society, and protection of his own or his friends' houses, and he might have been liable to meet with indiscreet or embarrassing questions Junius could never have preserved his incognito for so many years, from the time all London was on his traces, though what I am convinced was *his* detection, being most wished by the enemy, and for near thirty years after, and still have left the world in doubt, had he not, like a skilful chess-player, seen many moves before him, and I firmly believe, such was his skill, that through the whole he was never reduced to a falsehood in terms. In all this I recognize Sir Philip Francis, as if I had looked into his heart all the time. But you will say, 'Why all this fear of discovery so many years after, when the passions he excited and the hearts they inflamed had long been cold in the grave?' I will tell you, in answer, what I collected from what he allowed me to discover,—for so long as I asked no questions, he would give me much curious information, as of a third person,—from which I select the following for Lord Campbell's satisfaction or amusement; prefacing that my inferences were known and uncontradicted by Sir P. You know that he and Philip Rosenhagen were declared by Dr. Thicknesse, the master of St Paul's school, to be the cleverest boys he ever educated; at twelve and thirteen years old he used to associate with men at a table d'hote at Slaughter's Coffeehouse, when his father dined with the great; at seventeen he was Latin Secretary to Lord Chatham, then to an Embassy, then to General Bligh, then clerk in the War Office, where he thought himself ill treated He was at the Court of France in Louis the Fifteenth's time, when the Jesuits were driven away for offending Madame Pompadour; yet people say, at twenty-nine years old to thirty-two he was too young, and could not have gained the lofty tone to be the writer of these Letters, which bear all the stamp of what he must have been at that age, or even younger; but the fire and energy of youth lasted in him even when mature in experience and knowledge, and this union of youth and age not tempered by each other, but both in their extreme, is equally characteristic of Francis and Junius. The former passed his first years with his grandfather, the Dean of Leighlin, John Francis, who was a man highly considered in Ireland. Philip was an only and idolized son; he took the lead of his competitors at school, gaining the gold medal there He was early accustomed to the lofty language and high thoughts of Lord Chatham, who he told me always treated him with consideration, discerning, no doubt, a spirit within him worthy of an appearance greatly in his favor Nor were the discussions his patron often carried on with his colleague thrown away, when he was present, on the young Secretary. So brought forward in the world, besides an innate loftiness of character, and a touch of Hotspur in him that would 'pluck bright honor from the pale-faced moon, or dive into the bosom of the deep' for it, when, therefore he felt himself treated as a mere clerk in an office, deprived of the promotion he expected, and even neglected by Lord Chatham, he wanted no stronger stimulus, but well aware of all the errors of Government which he had been

the newspapers against the Queen, and seems to have alluded to the notion then current that he was the author of the Letters of Junius. Thus he answered the charge: trying to reform or stigmatize * under different signatures for some time, his energy was roused, and vented itself in the first letter of Junius And here let me remark, that a writer who fears discovery should not write too much under one signature. He becomes at length an individual—a character—a living person,—and adds so much to the danger of detection, that nothing but presence of mind, courage, and forethought, like Sir Philip's could parry it This first letter, which was a kind of general attack and challenge, was intended and succeeded in bringing out a champion: the shield was struck and the combat commenced! Sir W. D gallantly wore no vizor, but Junius could not imitate him; this was an advantage to him; but it was an embarassment that Sir W. knew his father well, and himself slightly This made him wish to close the controversy; and when his talents had been fully apparent in the castigation the K B. had received, a new and powerful ally came to his assistance Whether he knew that Junius was Francis I can not say, nor whether he did more than slightly supply some facts that he could not have obtained without such aid: that some of the letters were submitted to him before they appeared, I have no doubt. Perhaps I have no right to mention that person's name, for Sir Philip was so anxious to guard it, that I had no doubt he had given his honor that the discovery should never come from him; nor did it, but he was not bound to volunteer an untruth if another found it out. When Junius says, ' I am the sole depositary of my own secret, and it shall die with me,' I have no doubt he meant something that was like his reply to Sir R P. It might be a necessary evasion. Silence, sometimes, is consent. From the year 1805 to the end of 1818, I was either in constant correspondence with Sir P or was his wife. Most of these beautiful letters were destroyed, as he would have *his* returned at the end of each year; but some few were spared at my earnest request If these ever appear, they will make the world do him more justice. The situation he had in India, given by Government, of course involved a condition that he should never be known The King certainly told General Désarguestiers —' We know who Junius is; he will write no more.' I believe it was hoped he would see home no more; two out of the three colleagues never did, and his return was all but a miracle. Had Hastings and Francis been the same height the ball must have gone through the heart of the latter Do not think it too severe to say, that Hastings, who was an excellent shot, did not intend to make that common mistake of measuring the heart of another by his own. Remember what one of Mr. H's friend said in the House of Lords, and another in the House of Commons —the false account Hastings gives of the nature of the wound looks very like conscience. The determination Mr. H. showed to make Francis challenge him, or lose his honor,—submitting to such an insult as no Irish or English gentleman ever did—shows, in so crafty a man, that he had prepared for his own security in every way. He was sure that Francis did not wish that his antagonist should fall by his hand; as, while Impey was chief criminal Judge in Bengal, F. was certain, in that case, to have soon followed Nundcomar No one that had any observation could be a member of Sir P.'s family, without seeing that there was the 'volto, sciolto, petto stretto' in perfection—not in his character, but produced by habit and necessity Many men have many secrets, but they are by nature cautious, —sometimes timid Sir Philip was daring and open on

---

* " The nation pays all these officers, not the King: *he* is paid himself, and all have duties to-perform to the paymaster before all others."

"I do assure the noble duke that I have never contaminated my hands with any connection with a newspaper. I disdain to taint my character with any such connection. Formerly newspapers contained effusions of wit, candid remarks on public affairs, and compositions which ingenious minds might delight in ; but of late the common contents of newspapers have been dull, uninteresting narrative, or violent personal abuse—dark and malignant insinuations, and foul calumny and aspersion. The reason obviously is the impunity with which such liberties are suffered to be taken with the character of individuals, and the gross and vulgar appetite of the public for scandal."[1] I believe his disclaimer. Newspapers were then in the lowest state of degradation. In a former age their credit had been supported by the lucubrations of Steele and Addison, of Bolingbroke and Pulteney ; and now, in

every other subject; but if the slightest thread of his web were touched, he was instantly on guard; not to *me*, certainly; yet he even kept within the compact that must have passed between the man who, he says, in a character of Fox, was the best tempered public man he ever knew. Some circumstances he always regretted. One was losing the fame of being known; and, even if discovered, it might be said he had sold his power of guarding the liberties and rights of his country. Old people have told me that we have no idea of the sensation Junius created at the time in remote little towns. The postman would call out, as he rode through the streets, 'A letter from Junius to-day!' and all who took in the *D. A.* were besieged with requests. I must do Sir P the justice to believe that he was driven into the measure of giving up the character, that is, the name, of Junius ; but, though the conditions were both honorable and lucrative, he had to give up no principles or friends. he had not to approve the men and measures he once denounced ; the most honorable of all offices was given to him; and his colleagues, perhaps, think the lights I have given you, sufficient to justify my belief. Had any circumstance contradicted it, I would have candidly stated it. Had Sir P. once said to me, 'I am not the writer of Junius's Letters,' I should have given up the belief immediately He would no more have volunteered a falsehood to me than he would have had the meanness of even leaving me in doubt , since it would be stealing more than the purse (that, indeed, is trash compared to fame) were he not Junius; and when the 'Junius Identified' came out, without mischief to the assumed Junius, the *real one might* have appeared ; and then his whole conduct to me must have appeared a studied deceit. He went once so far as to tell me that the truth will be known some time , and you remember the lines which I believe soothed him when he felt he had given up the purest of ambitions. Please to use what evidence you think would tell on a subject I can have no doubts on."

[1] 27 Parl. Hist. 1092. In this speech he says, that, having been calumniated, "he had acted in an open, manly way, and resorted to the laws of his country for redress;" but I can not find any account of the proceeding he refers to, and I do not know even whether it was by action or criminal prosecution. I should be exceedingly obliged to any courteous reader who would furnish me with any information respecting it.

England, as in France, newspapers are conducted by men of education and honor, and no one would deem it any imputation on his character to be supposed to have contributed to them; but in Lord Loughborough's time, pamphlets were considered almost the only medium for reputable political discussion, and the periodical press seems to have been nearly abandoned to men who violated the sanctity of private life, and subsisted by the propagation of scandal and calumny. The evil once begun was continued in an aggravated shape, as long as it was considered that anyone "contaminated his hands by a connection with a newspaper."

I can find no "sayings" of Lord Loughborough worth repeating. He did not seek, like Thurlow, to gain distinction by a display of his colloquial powers; and, thinking of the superior *éclat* to be obtained by a brilliant speech in *Parliament*, he was contented with being rather obscure in the *salon*. According to some accounts, he submitted to this necessity after having found by experience that his genius did not fit him for talk. Boswell, having told us that Johnson, in allusion to Lord Mansfield, had said, "It is wonderful, Sir, with how little real superiority of mind men can make an eminent figure in public life," thus proceeds: "He expressed himself to the same purpose concerning another law lord,[1] who it seems once took a fancy to associate with the wits of London; but with so little success that Foote said, 'What can he mean by coming among us? He is not only dull himself, but the cause of dullness in others.' Trying him by the test of his colloquial powers, Johnson had found him very defective. He once said to Sir Joshua Reynolds, 'This man has been ten years now about town, and has made nothing of it;' meaning, as a companion. He said to me, 'I never heard anything from him in company that was at all striking; and depend upon it, Sir, it is when you come close to a man in conversation that you discover what his real abilities are: to make a speech in a public assembly is a knack.'" The Biographer observes in a note, which, as well as the above criticism, must have been read by the subject of it and made him wince;—"Knowing as well as I do what precision and elegance of oratory his Lordship can display

[1] Evidently Loughborough, though not named.

I can not but suspect that his unfavorable appearance in a social circle, which drew such animadversions upon him, must be owing to a cold affectation of consequence from being reserved and stiff."

He seems hardly ever to have attempted wit or humor,—for which, indeed, some thought he was utterly disqualified by his country. He had grievously offended Miss Burney, by objecting to the Brangtons in her Evelina, as being "too low and vulgar;" but she forgave him "in consideration of his being a Scot, and, therefore, like a blind man criticizing colors."

One "*mot*" by him is to be found in the "Memoirs of a Sexagenarian," and it does not much heighten our regret that it has not a *pendant*. "Beloe was once reading to him from Park's book of Travels in Africa the following adventure:—'My guide, who was a little way before me, wheeled his horse around in a moment, and calling out something in the Foulah language which I did not understand, I inquired in Mandingo what he meant. "*Wara, belli, belli,*—a very large lion," said he, and made signs for me to ride away. But my horse was too much fatigued; so we rode slowly past the bush from which the animal had given us the alarm. Not seeing anything myself, however, I thought my guide had been mistaken, when the Foulah suddenly put his hand to his mouth, exclaiming, "*Soubalı an allahı!*—God preserve us!" and, to my great surprise, I then perceived a large RED LION at a short distance from the bush, with his head crouched between his forepaws.' On hearing the last part of the sentence, Lord Rosslyn laughed heartily, and exclaimed with good humor, 'I suppose it was THE RED LION OF BRENTFORD.'"

He was more felicitous in mimicking the self-laudatory style of Erskine. "The egotism of that pleader," says Miss Burney, "is proverbial, and so happily was his manner hit, rather than caricatured, by the Chancellor, that the audience deemed his inventive faculty a mere exercise of memory. Giving an account of a supposed public meeting, Erskine, he said, opened to this effect:—'As to me, gentlemen, I trust I have some right to give my opinion freely. Would you know whence my title is derived? I challenge any man among you to inquire! If he ask my birth—its genealogy may dispute with kings! If my wealth—it is all for which I have time to hold out my hand! If my talents—no! of these, gentlemen, I leave you to judge for yourselves!'"[1]

If not highly appreciated by Johnson, Foote and others, who devoted the energies of their minds to conversation, he continued through life to be the chosen companion of men of the highest intellectual eminence. There was much private intimacy between him and Fox and Sheridan while they were associated in politics, and the third great historian who arose in the reign of George III. honored him not less than the other two. Gibbon in his autobiography, long after his gratitude for having obtained a seat at the Board of Trade through Loughborough's interest was moderated, mentions him in terms of the highest personal regard; and when driven back to England from Lausanne by the armies of France, a few weeks before his death, he thus wrote to Lord Sheffield to excuse the imprudence of which he had been guilty, in going into society while in a weak state of health:— "The man tempted me, and I did eat; and that man is no less than the Chancellor. He recalls me (the third time this week) to a dinner to-morrow, with Burke and Windham, which I did not possess sufficient fortitude to resist."

Although so early stigmatized by the well-remembered lines of Churchill,—in the latter part of his life, I find few poetical notices of him for good or for evil. Having been a stanch Whig while the contributors to the "Rolliad" were amusing the town, he is neither celebrated in the text of that exquisite Epic, nor introduced as the author of a Probationary Ode. He had the good luck likewise to be on the same side in politics as the "Anti-Jacobin," so that he escaped the cutting jests of Canning, Ellis, and Frere.

He was not the patron of men of genius, like Somers and Talbot, but the Great Seal had not yet been disassociated from all that is elegant and liberal. If a time should hereafter come when the holder of it shall never think of anything beyond his paper of causes,—however well he may dispose of that for the benefit of the suitors,—a heavy blow will be given not only to the dignity, but

[1] This seems to have been the origin of the egotistic speech ascribed to Erskine in the "Anti-Jacobin."

to the permanent usefulness of our "order;" and the profession of the law, hitherto affording scope for noble ambition and generous rivalry, will, like any mechanical trade, be a scramble for employment and for money. Lord Loughborough made the acquaintance of all the distinguished men of letters who appeared in his time—invited them to his table, and was ready to do them a good turn. He advised Maurice, the author of "Indian Antiquities," to dedicate his book to Mr. Pitt, who, amid many high qualities, was lamentably deficient in the encouragement of literature; and, finding that this homage to power produced nothing beyond a coldly civil speech, he himself solaced the disappointed dedicator with a handsome gratuity and a comfortable post for life in the British Museum.[1] He very freely assisted with his purse, Fearne, Hargrave, and other lawyers of profound learning and slender practice; but, what I consider still more meritorious, he was always eager to serve those who were not "mere lawyers," but could combine with jurisprudence a taste for *belles lettres*, for metaphysics, or for political science.

The munificent homage which he was ready to pay to genius, was most honorable to him. He offered to contribute to relieve the embarrassment of Mr. Burke's affairs before the pension was granted to that extraordinary man for his writings against the French Revolution. Dr. Lawrence, in a letter to Lord Loughborough, from Beaconsfield, announcing this grant, says:—"Knowing the confidence which throughout this business he has placed in your Lordship's kind offices, I thought it just to inform him how nobly you had answered that confidence by the intimation which you gave me, and had before given Dr. W. King, of your readiness to be privately of service to his affairs, had it been necessary."

He was not very lucky in the Judges whom he made; but he might be without blame, for they had enjoyed some eminence at the bar, and no one can certainly foretell how the most distinguished advocate will conduct himself on the Bench.[2]

[1] It is said that Mr Maurice, attending in Downing Street to present a copy of his book, with thanks for the honor of being permitted to dedicate it to so great a man, Pitt replied, " The honor, sir, was to me," and bowed him out.

[2] I do not think that he, like his successor, Lord Eldon, could excuse any

He is lauded for the distribution of his ecclesiastical patronage, being desirous of giving away preferment so that the parishioners might be satisfied—perhaps remembering the force given in his own country to a "call" when he was a Ruling Elder of the Church of Scotland. Yielding to the applications of friendless men of merit, he would say to them, "Go to my secretary, and desire him to prepare the presentation for my *fiat* immediately, —or I shall be pestered by some Duke or official man whom I shall not be able to refuse." He used to observe—what, from my own experience on a more limited scale, I can easily believe to have been true—" that his large livings gave him little comparative trouble, their designation being either anticipated or easily determined; but that for his small livings he had always a multitude of applications, and seldom or never one without at least seven small children to back it."

The father of Lord Nelson, a venerable clergyman, wished to resign, in favor of his youngest son, a living, the patronage of which belonged to the Chancellor; and the gallant Admiral thus at once fired a shot at him:—

"141 Bond Street, October 12, 1797.

"MY LORD,

"In addressing a letter to you, some persons may think me wrong, and that I ought to have chosen the interference of a friend; but feeling a conviction that, if what I have to ask is proper for your Lordship to grant, I require, on the present occasion, no interest but your own opinion of my endeavors to serve the state. I therefore inclose my request, which, if your Lordship has the

nominations to high judicial offices by the solicitations of the Royal family; although it would appear from the following warm letter of thanks to him, that he had made a Commissioner of Bankrupts at the request of the then Duchess of Gloucester.—

"Gloucester House, Feb 25, 1801.

" The highest gratification a good mind can receive must be the reflection of having diffused happiness. Such must be your Lordship's present sensation; for you have by your late noble appointment of George Roots, rendered *that* family perfectly happy, and, I really believe, as perfectly grateful The father trotted to town as soon as he heard it, and his overflowing eyes were the best expressions of gratitude he could show.

" For suffering me to have some share in promoting the felicity of these good people, you must, my dear Lord, permit me to subscribe myself

" Your Lordship's most sincerely obliged

" and unalterable and grateful friend, MARIA"

goodness to comply with, will be a small provision for the youngest son of my venerable father, and a lasting obligation conferred upon

"Your most obedient servant,
"HORATIO NELSON."

The following was the becoming answer:—
"SIR,
"You have judged perfectly right in the mode of your application to me; any interference would have much diminished the satisfaction I feel in acknowledging the perfect propriety of your request, and the just title your great services have gained to every mark of attention which, in the exercise of public duty, it is in my power to express.
"Yours, &c.
"LOUGHBOROUGH."

In spite of his services to the Church, it has been asserted that he was without religion, and that shortly before his death he was converted to Christianity by reading Burgh on the "Divinity of our Lord,"—which might have been a good cure for heterodoxy, but could not have been prescribed for infidelity. We are further told, that he must have been sceptically inclined from his early intimacy with David Hume. But there is not the smallest reason to doubt that Robertson, and other distinguished literary characters in Scotland, deploring the ingenious errors of the author of the "Essay on Miracles," were themselves steady believers in the truths of revelation. Lord Loughborough never gave offense to the most pious by anything he said or did, or omitted to do; and notwithstanding a gossiping letter from the Reverend Mr. Gisborne to Mr. Wilberforce, the writer of which must have misunderstood the gentleman on whose information he spoke,[1] I see no ground for doubting that he was from his youth upwards a sincere Christian, although he might not believe that there is no salvation for any who have not received the sacraments from a priest episcopally ordained—a favorite doctrine of his detractors.

His morals were certainly unimpeachable; and, both in his own family and in his intercourse with society, he displayed not only courtesy of manner and evenness of temper, but kindness of heart. Foolish stories were

[1] Townsend's Eminent Lawyers, vol i. 236.

circulated about his being given to play, his being threatened with executions, and his being obliged to pawn his state-coach; but, although he was fond of expense, he never exceeded his income, and although he did not accumulate money to purchase large estates for his heir, he left an ample provision for all those who were dependent upon him.

His portraits represent him with regular features, a fine aquiline nose, and a mouth bespeaking much intelligence. I myself can testify that in his old age he had a handsome as well as dignified presence. Yet at a former period, when he was much subject to obloquy, not only was there said to be "famine in his face," but he was, among other things, reproached for *ugliness;* and, to give point to this charge, the assertion was loudly made that he took delight in admiring himself in the looking-glass. Mrs. Piozzi tells us that, having mentioned in the presence of Dr. Johnson this ridiculous propensity which distinguished Lord Loughborough and Mr. Caton, the great timber merchant,—likewise very ill-favored,—he defended them, and thus moralized the subject in a manner truly Johnsonian: "They see reflected in that glass, men who have risen from almost the lowest situations in life,—one to enormous riches,—the other to everything this world can give,—rank, fame, and fortune. They see likewise men who have merited their advancement, by the exertion and improvement of those talents which God has given them, and I see not why they should avoid the mirror."

Lord Loughborough, although twice married, had no issue by either marriage; and his honors, according to the limitation I have referred to, devolved at his death on his nephew, General Sir James St. Clair Erskine, who filled several high offices in the state in the reigns of George IV. and William IV. The Chancellor is now worthily represented by James Alexander, third Earl of Rosslyn, the gallant Colonel of the 9th regiment of Dragoons, and late Master of her Majesty's Buck-hounds.

I could not with propriety conclude this memoir without giving the reader an opportunity of correcting my balanced estimate of the character it portrays, by the severer strictures of others. "Lord Rosslyn," says Sir Egerton Brydges, "appeared to be a man of subtle and plausible rather than of solid talents. His ambition was great, and his desire of office unlimited. He could argue with great ingenuity on either side ; so that it was difficult to anticipate his future by his past opinions."

He is still more roughly handled by one of his successors—most highly qualified, no doubt, to observe and to delineate his faults as well as his virtues:—" It is the imperative duty of the historian," says Lord Brougham, " to dwell upon the fate, while he discloses with impartial fullness, and marks with just reprobation, the acts of such men ; to the end that their great success, as it is called, may not mislead others, and conceal behind the glitter of worldly prosperity the baser material with which the structure of their fortune is built up. This wholesome lesson, and, indeed, needful warning, is, above all, required when we are called upon to contemplate a professional and political life so eminently prosperous as the one which we have been contemplating, which rolled on in an uninterrupted tide of worldly gains and worldly honors, but was advanced only by shining and superficial talents, supported by no fixed principles, illustrated by no sacrifices to public virtue, embellished by no feats of patriotism, nor made memorable by any monuments of national utility, and which, being at length closed in the disappointment of mean, unworthy desires, ended amidst universal neglect, and left behind it no claim to the respect or gratitude of mankind, though it may have excited the admiration or envy of the contemporary vulgar." [1]

Much of this censure is well deserved; but I think it may be mitigated by considering that Lord Loughborough was distinguished by lofty aspirations, as well as amiable sentiments ; and that he was free from faults and follies which have made other occupiers of the "marble chair" odious or ridiculous.

[1] Historical Sketches, i. 87.

www.ingramcontent.com/pod-product-compliance
Lightning Source LLC
Chambersburg PA
CBHW020727160426
43192CB00006B/135